HTML Quick Reference

STRUCTURE TAGS

`<!--...-->`	Creates a comment
`<html>...</html>`	Encloses the entire HTML document
`<head>...</head>`	Encloses the head of the HTML document
`<meta />`	Provides general information about the document
`<style>...</style>`	Style information
`<script>...</script>`	Scripting language
`<noscript>...</noscript>`	Alternative content when scripting is not supported
`<title>...</title>`	The title of the document
`<body>...</body>`	Encloses the body (text and tags) of the HTML document

HEADINGS

`<h1>...</h1>`	Heading level 1
`<h2>...</h2>`	Heading level 2
`<h3>...</h3>`	Heading level 3
`<h4>...</h4>`	Heading level 4
`<h5>...</h5>`	Heading level 5
`<h6>...</h6>`	Heading level 6

PARAGRAPHS

`<p>...</p>`	A plain paragraph

LINKS

`<a>...</a>`	Creates a link or anchor; includes common attributes
`href="..."`	The URL of the document to be linked to this one
`name="..."`	The name of the anchor
`target="..."`	Identifies the window or location in which to open the link
`rel="..."`	Defines forward link types
`rev="..."`	Defines reverse link types
`accesskey="..."`	Assigns a hotkey to this element
`shape="..."`	Is for use with object shapes
`coords="..."`	Is for use with object shapes
`tabindex="..."`	Determines the tabbing order
`onClick`	is a JavaScript event
`onMouseOver`	is a JavaScript event
`onMouseOut`	is a JavaScript event

LISTS

`<ol>...</ol>`	list
`<ul>...</ul>`	) list
`<menu>...</menu>`	A menu list of items
`<dir>...</dir>`	A directory listing
`<ol>...</ol>`	An ordered (numbered) list
`<li>...</li>`	A list item
`<dl>...</dl>`	A definition or glossary list
`<dt>...</dt>`	A definition term
`<dd>...</dd>`	The corresponding definition to a definition term

CHARACTER FORMATTING

`<em>...</em>`	Emphasis (usually italic)
`<strong>...</strong>`	Stronger emphasis (usually bold)
`<code>...</code>`	Code sample
`<kbd>...</kbd>`	Text to be typed
`<var>...</var>`	A variable of placeholder for some other value
`<samp>...</samp>`	Sample text
`<dfn>...</dfn>`	A definition of a term
`<cite>...</cite>`	A citation
`<b>...</b>`	Boldfaced text
`<i>...</i>`	Italic text
`<tt>...</tt>`	Typewriter font
`<u>...</u>`	Underlined text
`<pre>...</pre>`	Preformatted text

OTHER ELEMENTS

`<hr />`	A horizontal rule
` `	A line break
`<blockquote>...</blockquote>`	Used for long quotes or citations
`<address>...</address>`	Signatures or general information about a document's author
`<font>...</font>`	Change the size, color, and typeface of the font
`size="..."`	The size of the font from 1 to 7
`color="..."`	The font color
`face="..."`	The font type
`<basefont />`	Sets the default size of the font for the current page
`size="..."`	The default size of the font from 1 to 7

HTML Quick Reference

IMAGES

`<img />`		Inserts an inline image into the document; includes common attributes
	`usemap="..."`	A client-side imagemap
	`src="..."`	The URL of the image
	`alt="..."`	A text string that will be displayed in browsers that cannot support images
	`align="..."`	Determines the alignment of the given image
	`height="..."`	Is the suggested height in pixels
	`width="..."`	Is the suggested width in pixels
	`vspace="..."`	The space between the image and the text above and below it
	`hspace="..."`	The space between the image and the text to its left and right

FRAMES

`<frameset>...</frameset>`		Defines a frameset
	`rows="..."`	Number of rows in frame
	`cols="..."`	Number of columns in frame
	`onLoad`	Is an intrinsic event
	`onUnload`	Is an intrinsic event
`<frame>...</frame>`		Defines a frameset
	`name="..."`	Is the name of target frame
	`src="..."`	Calls the frame content source
	`frameborder="..."`	Determines the frame border
	`marginwidth="..."`	Defines margin widths
	`marginheight="..."`	Defines margin heights
	`noresize="..."`	Determines ability to resize frames
	`scrolling="..."`	Determines ability to scroll within frames
`<iframe>...</iframe>`		Defines an inline frame
`<noframes>...</noframes>`		Alternate content when frames not supported

TABLES

`<table>...</table>`		Creates a table
	`background="..."`	Background image for the table
	`bgcolor="..."`	Background color of the table
	`border="..."`	Width of the border in pixels
	`cols="..."`	Number of columns
	`cellspacing="..."`	Spacing between cells
	`cellpadding="..."`	Spacing in cells
	`width="..."`	Table width
`<caption>...</caption>`		The caption for the table
`<tr>...</tr>`		A table row
	`align="..."`	The horizontal alignment of the contents of the cells within this row; possible values are `left`, `right`, `center`, `justify`, and `char`
	`bgcolor="..."`	Background color for the row
	`valign="..."`	The vertical alignment of the contents of the cells within this row; possible values are `top`, `middle`, `bottom`, and `baseline`
`<th>...</th>`		A table heading cell
	`align="..."`	The horizontal alignment of the contents of the cell
	`valign="..."`	The vertical alignment of the contents of the cell
	`bgcolor="..."`	Background color for the cell
	`rowspan="..."`	The number of rows this cell will span
	`colspan="..."`	The number of columns this cell will span
	`nowrap="..."`	Turns off text wrapping in a cell
`<td>...</td>`		Defines a table data cell
	`align="..."`	The horizontal alignment of the contents of the cell
	`valign="..."`	The vertical alignment of the contents of the cell
	`bgcolor="..."`	Background color for the cell
	`rowspan="..."`	The number of rows this cell will span
	`colspan="..."`	The number of columns this cell will span
	`nowrap="..."`	Turns off text wrapping in a cell

Laura Lemay

with revisions by Rafe Colburn
and Denise Tyler

Tea

with

H   ML

SAMS

201 West 103rd St., Indianapolis, Indiana, 46290 U

Sams Teach Yourself Web Publishing with HTML and XHTML in 21 Days, Third Edition

Copyright © 2001 by Sams Publishing

International Standard Book Number: 0-672-32077-0

Library of Congress Catalog Card Number: 00-109552

Printed in the United States of America

First Printing: March 2001

03 02 01   4 3 2 1

Trademarks

Warning and Disclaimer

ACQUISITIONS EDITOR
Betsy Brown

DEVELOPMENT EDITOR
Jonathan Steever

MANAGING EDITOR
Charlotte Clapp

PROJECT EDITOR
Dawn Pearson

COPY EDITOR
Sean Medlock

INDEXER
Sandy Henselmeier

PROOFREADER
Daniel Ponder

TECHNICAL EDITOR
Sunil Hazari

TEAM COORDINATOR
Amy Patton

SOFTWARE DEVELOPMENT SPECIALIST
Matt Bates

INTERIOR DESIGN
Gary Adair

COVER DESIGN
Aren Howell

PRODUCTION
Ayanna Lacey
Heather Hiatt Miller
Stacey Richwine-DeRome

Contents at a Glance

Contents

About the Authors

LAURA LEMAY is a technical writer, author, Web addict, and motorcycle enthusiast. One of the world's most popular authors on Web development topics, she is the author of *Sams Teach Yourself Web Publishing with HTML, Sams Teach Yourself Java in 21 Days*, and *Sams Teach Yourself Perl in 21 Days*. You can visit her home page at `http://www.lne.com/lemay/`.

RAFE COLBURN is a Web application developer and author living in North Carolina. His previous books include *Sams Teach Yourself CGI in 24 Hours* and *Special Edition Using SQL*. If you'd like to read more of his writings, check out his home page at `http://rc3.org/`.

DENISE TYLER is a freelance author, graphic artist, animator, and Web designer who resides in Madison, Wisconsin. She is the author of *Sams Teach Yourself Microsoft FrontPage 2000 in 21 Days*, and co-author of *How to Use Macromedia Flash 5*.

Dedication

For Patricia, who has enough patience and resolve for two.

Acknowledgments

To Sams Publishing, for letting me write the kind of HTML book I wanted to see.

To the Coca-Cola Company, for creating Diet Coke and selling so much of it to me.

To all the folks on the `comp.infosystems.www` newsgroups, the `www-talk` mailing list, and the Web conference on the WELL, for answering questions and putting up with my late-night rants.

To innumerable people who helped me with the writing of this book, including Lance Norskog, Ken Tidwell, Steve Krause, Tony Barreca, CJ Silverio, Peter Harrison, Bill Whedon, Jim Graham, Jim Race, Mark Meadows, and many others I'm sure I've forgotten.

Finally, to Eric Murray, the other half of lne.com, for moral support when I was convinced I couldn't possibly finish writing any of this book on time, for setting up all my UNIX and networking equipment and keeping it running, and for writing a whole lot of Perl code on very short notice.

—Laura Lemay

One of the toughest parts of a book to write is the acknowledgements because deserving people always get left out, and the printed words are rarely enough to properly express the author's gratitude.

I really want to thank the excellent people at Sams Publishing who gave me the opportunity to work on this book, and who supported me as I worked on it. Betsy Brown, Mark Taber, Dawn Pearson, and particularly Jon Steever are all deserving of praise.

—Rafe Colburn

Tell Us What You Think!

As the reader of this book, *you* are our most important critic and commentator. We value your opinion and want to know what we're doing right, what we could do better, what areas you'd like to see us publish in, and any other words of wisdom you're willing to pass our way.

You can e-mail or write me directly to let me know what you did or didn't like about this book—as well as what we can do to make our books stronger.

Please note that I cannot help you with technical problems related to the topic of this book, and that due to the high volume of mail I receive, I might not be able to reply to every message.

When you write, please be sure to include this book's title and author as well as your name and phone number or e-mail address. I will carefully review your comments and share them with the author and editors who worked on the book.

E-mail: webdev@samspublishing.com

Mail: Mark Taber
          Associate Publisher
          Sams Publishing
          201 West 103rd Street
          Indianapolis, IN 46290 USA

Introduction

Over the past few years, the Web has become completely integrated into the fabric of society. Most businesses have Web sites, and it's rare to see a commercial on television that doesn't display a URL. The simple fact that most people now know what a URL is speaks volumes. People who didn't know what the Internet was several years ago are now sending me invitations to parties using Web-based invitation services.

Perhaps the greatest thing about the Web is that you don't have to be a big company to publish things on it. The only things you need to create your own Web site are a computer with access to the Internet and the willingness to learn. Obviously, the reason you're reading this is that you have an interest in Web publishing. Perhaps you need to learn about it for work, or you're looking for a new means of self-expression, or you want to post baby pictures on the Web so that your relatives all over the country can stay up to date. The question is, how do you get started?

There's more than enough information on the Web about how to publish Web sites like a seasoned professional. There are tutorials, reference sites, tons of examples, and free tools to make it easier to publish on the Web. However, the advantage of reading this book instead is that all of the information you need to build Web sites is organized in one place and presented in an orderly fashion. It has everything you need to master HTML, publish sites to a server on the Web, create graphics for use on the Web, and keep your sites running smoothly.

But wait, there's more. Other books on how to create Web pages just teach you the basic technical details, such as how to produce a boldface word. In this book, you'll also learn why you should be producing a particular effect and when you should use it. In addition, this book provides hints, suggestions, and examples of how to structure your overall Web site, not just the words on each page. This book won't just teach you how to create a Web site—it'll teach you how to create a *good* Web site. It will also teach you how to take advantage of the latest web authoring techniques, such as building structured documents using XHTML.

Also, unlike many other books on this subject, this book doesn't focus on any one platform. Regardless of whether you're using a PC running Windows, a Macintosh, some flavor of UNIX, or any other computer system, many of the concepts in this book will be valuable to you. And you'll be able to apply them to your Web pages regardless of your platform of choice.

Who Should Read This Book

Is this book for you? That depends:

- If you've seen what's out on the Web and you want to contribute your own content, this book is for you.
- If you work for a company that wants to create a Web site and you're not sure where to start, this book is for you.
- If you're an information developer, such as a technical writer, and you want to learn how the Web can help you present your information online, this book is for you.
- If you're just curious about how the Web works, some parts of this book are for you, although you might be able to find what you need on the Web itself.
- If you've created Web pages before with text, images, and links, and you've played with a table or two and set up a few simple forms, you may be able to skim the first half of the book. The second half should still offer you a lot of helpful information.

If you've never seen the Web before but you've heard that it's really nifty, this book isn't for you. You'll need a more general book about the Web before you can produce Web sites yourself.

What This Book Contains

This book is intended to be read and absorbed over the course of 21 days (although it depends on how much you can absorb in a day). On each day you'll read one chapter on one area of Web site design. The chapters are arranged in a logical order, taking you from the simplest tasks to more advanced techniques.

Part 1: Getting Started

In Part 1, you'll get a general overview of the World Wide Web and what you can do with it, and then you'll come up with a plan for your Web presentation. You'll also write your first (very basic) Web page.

Part 2: Creating Simple Web Pages

In Part 2, you'll learn how to write simple documents in the HTML language and link them together using hypertext links. You'll also learn how to format your Web pages.

Part 3: Web Graphics

In Part 3, you'll learn how to use images and color in your Web pages. You'll also learn how to compile and create animated graphics, and how to create and use clickable imagemaps to link to other pages on your Web site.

Part 4: Doing More with HTML

In Part 4, you'll learn how to format Web pages by using Cascading Style Sheets (CSS), and how HTML and CSS work together to enhance the appearance of your Web pages. You'll also learn how to create and format tables, and how to design Web sites that use frames to display multiple pages in a single browser window. Finally, you'll learn how to make your pages compliant with the latest HTML standard—XHTML.

Part 5: Multimedia, Forms, and Dynamic HTML

In Part 5, you'll learn how to enhance your Web pages with multimedia, sound, video, and other advanced presentation methods. You'll also learn how to embed Java applets in your pages, create interactive forms, and use Dynamic HTML to enhance your sites.

Part 6: Designing Effective Web Pages

Part 6 will give you some hints for creating a well-constructed Web site, and you'll explore some sample Web sites to get an idea of what sort of work you can do. You'll also learn how to design pages that will reach the types of real-world users you want to reach.

Part 7: Going Live on the Web

In Part 7, you'll learn how to put your presentation up on the Web, including how to advertise the work you've done. Finally, you'll learn how to test and maintain your Web site.

Appendices In the appendices you'll find reference information about HTML, Cascading Style Sheets, the HTML color palette, and common file types on the Web. You'll also find a list of useful Web sites that complement the information in the book.

What You Need Before You Start

There are seemingly hundreds of books on the market about how to get connected to the Internet, and lots of books about how to use the World Wide Web. This book isn't one of them. I'm assuming that if you're reading this book, you already have a working connection to the Internet, you have a Web browser such as Netscape Navigator or Microsoft Internet Explorer, and you've used it at least a couple of times. You should also have at least a passing acquaintance with some other elements of the Internet, such as electronic mail and Usenet news, because I refer to them in general terms in this book.

In other words, you need to have used the Web in order to provide content for the Web. If you meet this one simple qualification, read on!

Note

To really take advantage of all the concepts and examples in this book, you should consider using a recent version of Microsoft Internet Explorer (version 4.0 or later) or Netscape Navigator (version 4.0 or later).

Conventions Used in This Book

This book uses special typefaces and other graphical elements to highlight different types of information.

Special Elements

Four types of "boxed" elements present pertinent information that relates to the topic being discussed: Note, Tip, Caution, and New Term. Each item has a special icon associated with it, as described here.

Note

Notes highlight special details about the current topic.

Tip

It's a good idea to read the tips because they present shortcuts or trouble-saving ideas for performing specific tasks.

Caution

Don't skip the cautions. They help you avoid making decisions or performing actions that can cause you trouble.

Whenever I introduce a new term, I'll set it off with an icon and define it for you. I'll use italic for new terms.

 A *browser* is used to view and navigate Web pages and other information on the World Wide Web.

HTML Input and Output Examples

Throughout the book, I'll present exercises and examples of HTML input and output.

`INPUT` An input icon identifies HTML code that you can type in yourself.

`OUTPUT` An output icon indicates the results of the HTML input in a Web browser such as Microsoft Internet Explorer.

Special Fonts

Several items are presented in a monospace font, which can be plain or italic. Here's what each one means:

`plain mono`   Applied to commands, filenames, file extensions, directory names, Internet addresses, URLs, and HTML input. For example, HTML tags such as `<TABLE>` and `<P>` appear in this font.

`mono italic`   Applied to placeholders. A placeholder is a generic item that replaces something specific as part of a command or computer output. For instance, the term represented by `filename` would be the real name of the file, such as `myfile.txt`.

What's on the Web Site?

To help you get the most out of this book, there's a corresponding Web site at `http://www.tywebpub.com/`. This site contains the source code and graphics for the examples used in this book, plus updated information about where to find tools and hints to help you further develop and expand your Web presentations. Check it out!

PART 1

Getting Started

PART 1

DAY 1

The World of the World Wide Web

A journey of a thousand miles begins with a single step, and here you are at Day 1 of a journey that will show you how to write, design, and publish pages on the World Wide Web. Before beginning the actual journey, however, you should start simple, with the basics. You'll learn the following:

- What the World Wide Web is, and why it's really cool
- Web browsers: what they do, and a couple of popular ones from which to choose
- What a Web server is, and why you need one
- Some information about uniform resource locators (URLs)

If you've spent even a small amount of time exploring the Web, most, if not all, of today's information will seem like old news. If so, feel free to skim it and skip ahead to Day 2, "Get Organized," where you'll find an overview of points to think about when you design and organize your own Web documents.

What Is the World Wide Web?

I have a friend who likes to describe things using many meaningful words strung together in a chain so that it takes several minutes to sort out what he's just said.

If I were he, I'd describe the World Wide Web as a global, interactive, dynamic, cross-platform, distributed, graphical hypertext information system that runs over the Internet. Whew! Unless you understand each of these words and how they fit together, this description isn't going to make much sense. (My friend often doesn't make much sense, either.)

So let's look at all these words and see what they mean in the context of how you'll be using the Web as a publishing medium.

The Web Is a Hypertext Information System

If you've used any sort of basic online help system, you're already familiar with the primary concept behind the World Wide Web: *hypertext*.

The idea behind hypertext is that instead of reading text in a rigid, linear structure (such as a book), you can skip easily from one point to another. You can get more information, go back, jump to other topics, and navigate through the text based on what interests you at the time.

NEW TERM   *Hypertext* enables you to read and navigate text and visual information in a nonlinear way, based on what you want to know next.

Online help systems, such as Windows Help on PCs or Apple Help on the Macintosh, use hypertext to present information. To get more information on a topic, you just click that topic. The topic might be a link that takes you to a new screen (or window or dialog box) that contains the new information. Perhaps you'll find links on words or phrases that take you to still other screens, and links on those screens that take you even farther away from your original topic. Figure 1.1 shows a simple diagram of how this kind of system works.

FIGURE 1.1

A simple online help system.

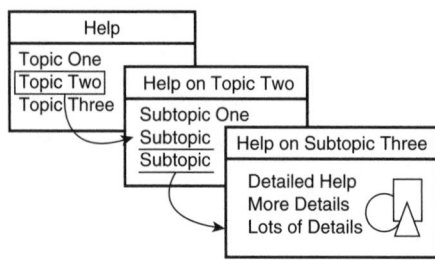

Imagine that your online help system is linked to another online help system on another application related to yours; for example, your drawing program's help is linked to your word processor's help. Your word processor's help is then linked to an encyclopedia, where you can look up any other concepts that you don't understand. The encyclopedia is hooked into a global index of magazine articles that enables you to get the most recent information on the topics the encyclopedia covers. The article index also then is linked to information about the writers of those articles and some pictures of their children (see Figure 1.2).

FIGURE 1.2

A more complex online help system.

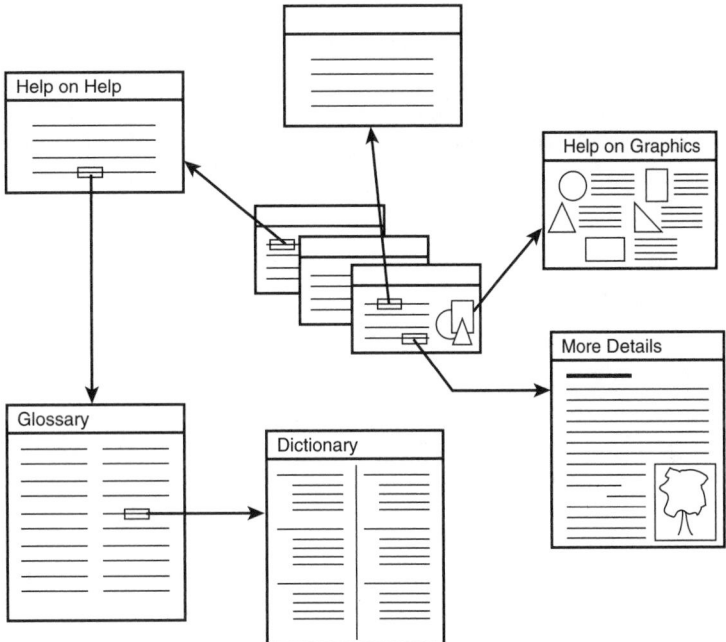

If you had all these interlinked help systems available with every program you bought, you would rapidly run out of disk space. You also might question whether you needed all this information when all you wanted to know was how to do one simple task. All this information could be expensive, too.

However, if the information didn't take up much disk space, it were freely available, and you could get it reasonably quickly any time you wanted, the system would be more interesting. In fact, the information system might very well end up being more interesting than the software you bought in the first place.

That's just what the World Wide Web is: more information than you could ever digest in a lifetime, linked together in various ways, out there on the net, available for you to browse whenever you want. It's big and deep and easy to get lost in, but it's also an immense amount of fun.

 Note
> Because Web technology is so good at organizing and presenting informa-tion, the business world has taken notice. Nearly all large corporations and medium-sized businesses and organizations are using Web technology to manage projects, order materials, and distribute company information in a paperless environment. By locating their documents on a private, secure Web server called an *intranet*, they take advantage of the technologies the World Wide Web has to offer, while keeping the information contained within the company.

The Web Is Graphical and Easy to Navigate

In the early days, using the Internet involved simple text-only connections. You had to navigate the Internet's various services using typed commands and arcane tools. Although plenty of really exciting information was available on the net, it wasn't neces-sarily pretty to look at.

Then along came the first graphical Web *browser*—Mosaic—that paved the way for the Web to display both text and graphics in full color on the same page. This is one of the best parts of the Web, and arguably the reason it has become so popular. Now, Web browsers provide capabilities for graphics, sound, and video to be incorporated with the text, as well as even more for multimedia and embedded applications.

NEW TERM A *browser* is used to view and navigate Web pages and other information on the World Wide Web. Currently, the most popular browsers are Microsoft Internet Explorer and Netscape, and nearly every new computer sold comes with a browser installed on it.

More importantly, you can easily navigate the interface to all these capabilities—just jump from link to link, from page to page, across sites and servers.

 Note
> If the Web incorporates so much more than text, why do I keep calling the Web a hypertext system? Well, if you're going to be absolutely technically correct about it, the Web is not a hypertext system—it's a hyper*media* sys-tem. But, on the other hand, you might argue that the Web began as a text-only system, and much of the content is still text-heavy, with extra bits of media added in as emphasis. Many very educated people are arguing these very points at this moment and presenting their arguments in papers and discursive rants as educated people like to do. Whatever. I prefer the term *hypertext*, and it's my book, so I'm going to use it. You know what I mean.

1

The Web Is Cross-Platform

If you can access the Internet, you can access the World Wide Web, regardless of whether you're working on a low-end PC or a fancy expensive graphics workstation. You can use a simple text-only modem connection, a small 14-inch black-and-white monitor, or a 21-inch full-color super gamma-corrected graphics accelerated display system. And more recently, people are accessing the Internet through their television sets, portable hand-held PCs, and personal information managers. If you think Windows menus buttons look better than Macintosh menus and buttons, or vice versa (or if you think both Macintosh and Windows people are weenies), it doesn't matter. The World Wide Web is not limited to any one kind of machine or developed by any one company. The Web is entirely cross-platform.

NEW TERM   *Cross-platform* means that you can access Web information equally well from any computer hardware running any operating system using any display.

Note

The whole idea that the Web is—and should be—cross-platform is strongly held to by purists. The reality, however, is somewhat different. With the introduction over the years of numerous special features, technologies, and media types, the Web has lost some of its capability to be truly cross-platform. As Web authors choose to use these nonstandard features, they willingly limit the potential audience for the content of their sites. For example, a site centered around a Java program essentially is unusable for someone using a browser that doesn't support Java, or for a user who might have turned off Java in his browser for quicker downloads. Similarly, some programs that extend the capabilities of a browser (known as *plug-ins*) are available only for one platform (either Windows, Macintosh, or UNIX). Choosing to use one of these plug-ins makes that portion of your site unavailable to users who either are on the wrong platform, or who don't want to bother to download and install the plug-in.

The Web Is Distributed

Information takes up a great deal of space, particularly when you include images and multimedia capabilities. To store all the information, graphics, and multimedia that the Web provides, you would need an untold amount of disk space, and managing it would be almost impossible. Imagine that you were interested in finding out more information about alpacas (a Peruvian mammal known for its wool), but when you selected a link in your online encyclopedia, your computer prompted you to insert CD-ROM #456 ALP through ALR. You could be there for a long time just looking for the right CD-ROM!

The Web is successful in providing so much information because that information is distributed globally across thousands of Web sites, each of which contributes the space for the information it publishes. These sites reside on one or more computers, referred to as Web servers. A Web server is just a computer that listens for requests from Web browsers and responds to that request. You, as a consumer of that information, request a resource from the server to view the information. When you're done, you go somewhere else, and your system reclaims the disk space. You don't have to install it, change disks, or do anything other than point your browser at that site.

 A *Web site* is a location on the Web that publishes some kind of information. When you view a Web page, your browser connects to that Web site to get that information.

Each Web site, and each page or bit of information on that site, has a unique address. This address is called a *uniform resource locator*, or *URL*. When people tell you to visit a site at `http://www.coolsite.com/`, they've just given you a URL. You can use your browser (with the Open command, sometimes called Open Page or Go) to enter in the URL (or just copy and paste it).

Note

> URLs are alternatively pronounced as if spelled out "You are Ells" or as an actual word ("earls"). Although I prefer the former pronunciation, I've heard the latter used equally as often.

You'll learn more about URLs later today in "Uniform Resource Locators (URLs)."

The Web Is Dynamic

If you want a permanent copy of some information that's stored on the Web, you have to save it locally because the publisher (or anyone else with appropriate access to that server) can go back and change any of that information whenever they want.

If you're browsing that information, you don't have to install a new version of the help system, buy another book, or call technical support to get updated information. Just launch your browser and check out what's there.

If you're publishing on the Web, you can make sure that your information is up-to-date all the time. You don't have to spend a lot of time re-releasing updated documents. There is no cost of materials. You don't have to get bids on numbers of copies or quality of output. Color is free. And you won't get calls from hapless customers who have a version of the book that was obsolete four years ago.

Consider a book published and distributed entirely online, such as *Thinking in Java* by Bruce Eckel (which you can find at www.bruceeckel.com/). He can correct any mistakes in the book and simply upload the revised text to his Web site, making it instantly available to his readers. He can document new features of Java and include them in the latest version of the book on his site. The Web site for the book appears in Figure 1.3.

FIGURE 1.3

The Web site for Thinking in Java.

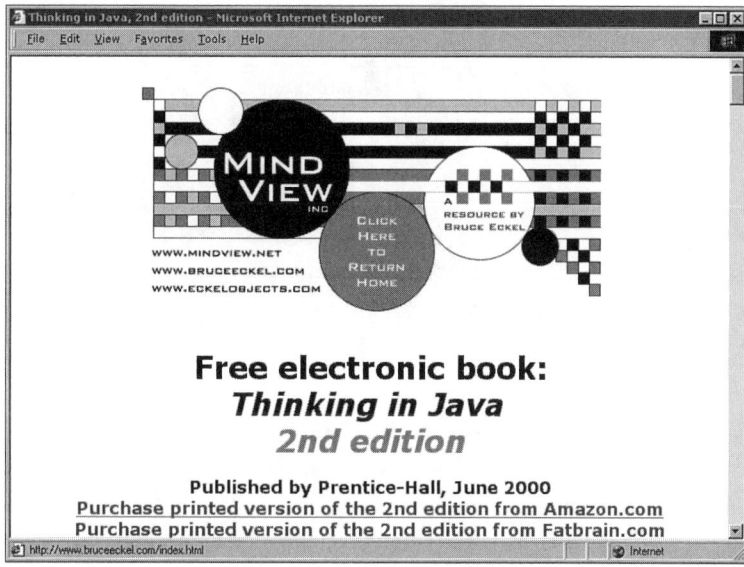

> **Note**
>
> The pictures throughout this book usually are taken from a Windows browser (Microsoft Internet Explorer, most often). The only reason for this use is that I'm writing this book primarily on a Windows PC. If you're using a Macintosh or UNIX system, don't feel left out. As I noted earlier, the glory of the Web is that you see the same information regardless of the platform you're using. So ignore the buttons and window borders, and focus on what's inside the window.

For some sites, the capability to update the site on-the-fly, at any moment, is precisely why the site exists. Figure 1.4 shows the home page for The Nando Times, an online newspaper that is updated 24 hours a day to reflect up-to-the-minute news as it happens. Because the site is up and available all the time, it has an immediacy that neither hard-copy newspapers or most television news programs can match. Visit The Nando Times at http://www.nandotimes.com.

FIGURE **1.4**

The Nando Times.

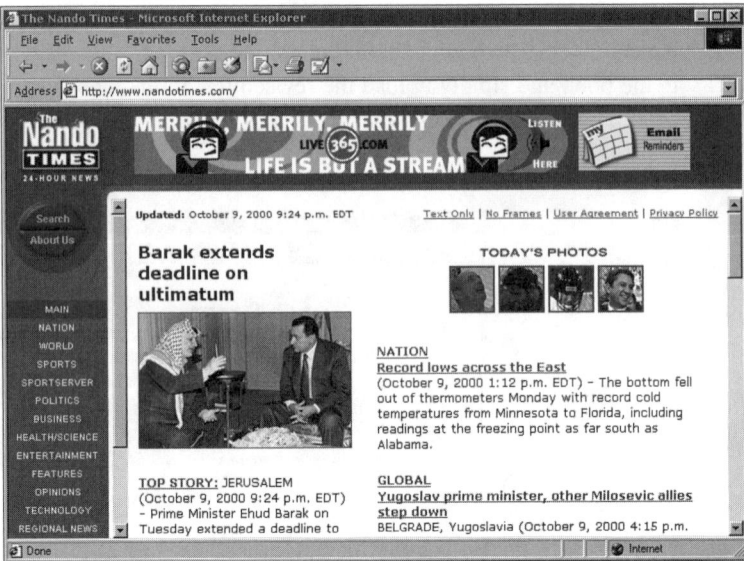

The Web Is Interactive

Interactivity is the capability to "talk back" to the Web server. More traditional media, such as television, isn't interactive at all; all you do is sit and watch as shows are played at you. Other than changing the channel, you don't have much control over what you see. Add WebTV capability to it, however, and television becomes a new experience.

The Web is inherently interactive; the act of selecting a link and jumping to another Web page to go somewhere else on the Web is a form of interactivity. In addition to this simple interactivity, however, the Web also enables you to communicate with the publisher of the pages you're reading and with other readers of those pages.

For example, pages can be designed to contain interactive forms that readers can fill out. Forms can contain text-entry areas, radio buttons, or simple menus of items. When the form is "submitted," the information readers type is sent back to the server from which the pages originated. Figure 1.5 shows an example of an online form for a rather ridiculous census.

As a publisher of information on the Web, you can use forms for many different purposes, such as the following:

- To get feedback about your pages.
- To get information from your readers (survey, voting, demographic, or any other kind of data). You then can collect statistics on that data, store it in a database, or do anything you want with it.

FIGURE 1.5

The Surrealist Census form.

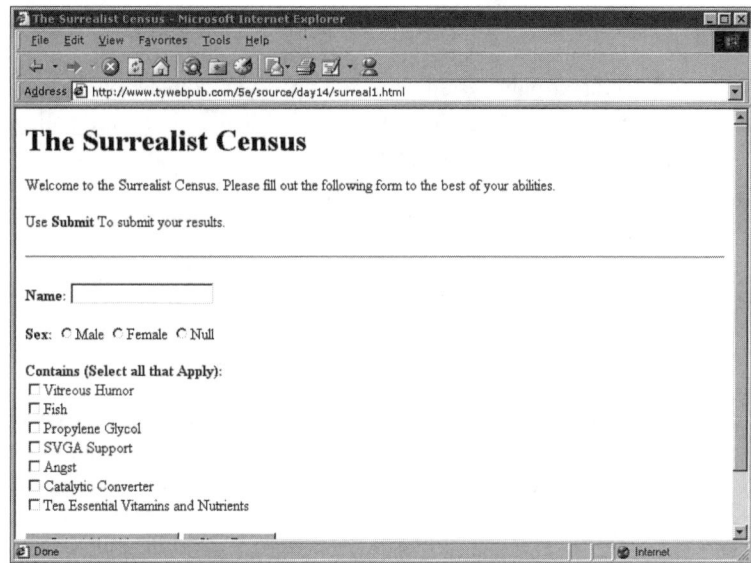

- To provide online order forms for products or services available on the Web.
- To create "guestbooks" and conferencing systems that enable your readers to post their own information on your pages. These kinds of systems enable your readers to communicate not only with you, but also with other readers of your pages.

In addition to forms, which provide some of the most popular forms of interactivity on the Web, advanced features of Web technologies provide even more interactivity. Flash, JavaScript, Java, and Shockwave, for example, enable you to include entire programs and games inside Web pages. Software can run on the Web to enable real-time chat sessions between your readers. Developments in 3D worlds also enable your readers to browse the Web as if they were wandering through real three-dimensional rooms and meeting other people. As time goes on, the Web becomes less of a medium for people passively sitting and digesting information (and becoming "Net potatoes") and more of a medium for reaching and communicating with other people all over the world.

Web Browsers

A Web browser, as mentioned earlier, is the program you use to view pages and navigate the World Wide Web. Web browsers sometimes are called Web *clients* or other fancy names (Internet navigation tools), but *Web browser* is the most common term.

A wide array of Web browsers is available for just about every platform you can imagine, including graphical-user-interface–based systems (Macintosh and Windows, for example), and text-only systems for dial-up UNIX connections. Most browsers are freeware or shareware (try before you buy) or have a lenient licensing policy. Both Netscape Navigator and Microsoft Internet Explorer, for example, are available for free to both individuals and organizations. These days, nearly every computer comes with a Web browser installed. In fact, Microsoft Internet Explorer is now considered to be part of the Windows operating system. Even if your computer didn't come with a Web browser installed, your Internet service provider most likely provided one as part of the software package you got for signing up. Failing that, you can download a browser for free from Microsoft or Netscape.

Currently, the most popular browsers for the World Wide Web are Microsoft Internet Explorer (sometimes called just Internet Explorer or IE) and Netscape. Despite the fact that these browsers have the lion's share of the market, however, they are not the only browsers on the Web. This point will become important later, when you learn how to design Web pages and learn about the diverse capabilities of different browsers. Assuming that Internet Explorer and Netscape are the only browsers in use on the Web and designing your pages accordingly will limit the audience you can reach with the information you want to present.

Note

Choosing to develop for a specific browser, such as Netscape Navigator or Internet Explorer, is suitable when you know a limited audience using the targeted browser software will view your Web site. Developing this way is a common practice in corporations implementing intranets. In these situations, it is a fair assumption that all users in the organization will implement the browser supplied to them and, accordingly, it is possible to design the Web component of the intranet to use the specific capabilities of the browser in question.

What the Browser Does

Any Web browser's job is twofold. Given a pointer to a piece of information on the net (a URL), the browser has to be able to access that information or operate in some way based on the contents of that pointer. For hypertext Web documents, the browser must be able to communicate with the Web server. Because the Web also can manage information contained on FTP and Gopher servers, in Usenet news postings, in email, and so on, browsers often can communicate with those servers or protocols as well.

1

What the browser does most often, however, is deal with formatting and displaying Web documents. Each Web page is a file written in a language called *Hypertext Markup Language* (HTML) that includes the text of the page, its structure, and links to other documents, images, or other media. (You'll learn much more about HTML on Days 3 through 6 because you need to know it so that you can write your own Web pages.) The browser takes the information it gets from the Web server and formats and displays it for your system. Different browsers might format and display the same file in diverse ways, depending on the capabilities of that system and the default layout options for the browser itself.

Retrieving documents from the Web and formatting them for your system are the two tasks that make up the core of a browser's functionality. Depending on the browser you use and the features it includes, however, you also might be able to play multimedia files, view and interact with Java applets, read your mail, or use other advanced features that a particular browser offers.

An Overview of Two Popular Browsers

This section describes the two most popular browsers currently on the Web. They are in no way the only browsers available, and if the browser you're using isn't listed here, don't feel that you have to use one of these. Whichever browser you have is fine as long as it works for you.

You can use the browsers in this section only if you have a direct Internet connection or a dial-up Internet connection. Getting your machine connected to the Internet is beyond the scope of this book, but you can find plenty of books to help you do so.

Finally, if the only connection you have to the Internet is through a dial-up, text-only UNIX (or other) account, you are limited to using text-only browsers such as Lynx. You cannot view documents in color or view graphics online (although you usually can download them to your system and view them there).

Microsoft Internet Explorer

Microsoft's browser, Microsoft Internet Explorer, runs on Windows 3.1, Windows 95/98, Windows NT, Macintosh, and UNIX, and it is free for downloading from Microsoft's Web site (http://www.microsoft.com/windows/ie/). No further license fee is required. In fact, Internet Explorer is built into all the current versions of Microsoft Windows. You can still install and use Netscape Navigator if you want, but if all you want to use is Internet Explorer, you don't need to do anything more.

Note

> If you're serious about Web design, you should install all of the popular browsers on your system and use them to view your pages once you've published them. That way, you can make sure everything is working properly. Even if you don't use a particular browser on a day-to-day basis, your site will be visited by people who do.

Microsoft Internet Explorer has become the most popular Web browser currently in use, in large part due to the fact that it has been tightly integrated with the latest versions of Windows. Microsoft releases new versions of its browser more often than Netscape, and in addition to partial support for most standard Web technologies, Internet Explorer also includes a number of unique features that were developed by Microsoft.

Figure 1.6 shows Internet Explorer running under Windows 98.

FIGURE 1.6

Microsoft Internet Explorer (Windows 98).

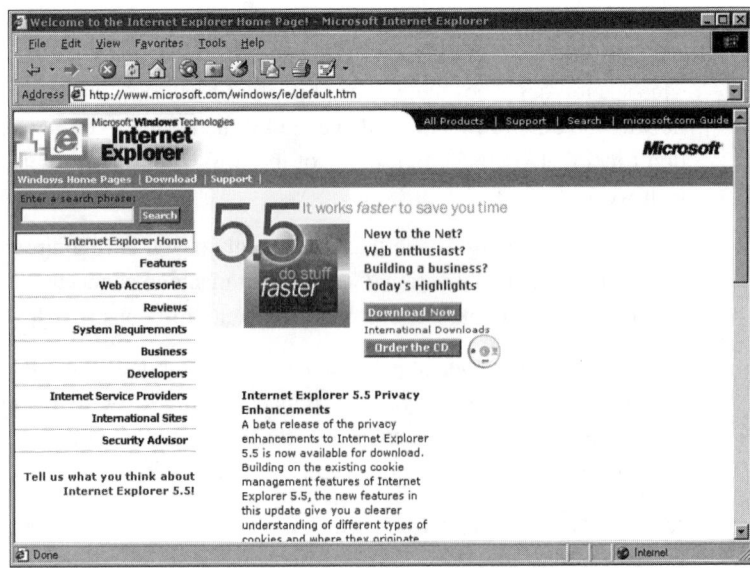

The current version of Internet Explorer for Windows is version 5.5, and the current version for the Mac OS is version 5.0.

> **Note**
>
> With each release of their browsers, Microsoft and Netscape have tried to introduce more new, fancy features. The current releases are no exception. As you will see in Day 12, "XHTML and Style Sheets," these new features include style sheets for providing fine control over the appearance of documents. In Day 15, "Using Dynamic HTML," you'll learn more about Dynamic HTML, which encompasses everything from precise layout control to improved scripting of HTML pages.

Netscape Navigator

Another widely used browser on the Web today is Netscape Navigator, from Netscape Communications Corporation.

The most common way to obtain Netscape Navigator is as part of a suite of Internet tools called *Netscape Communicator*. In addition to Web browsing, this suite includes components for email and newsgroup reading (Netscape Messenger), Web page editing (Netscape Composer) and online collaboration (Netscape Conference). It's available for Windows, Macintosh, and for many different versions of UNIX running the X Window System. Figure 1.7 shows the Windows 95/98 version.

FIGURE 1.7

Netscape (for Windows 95/98).

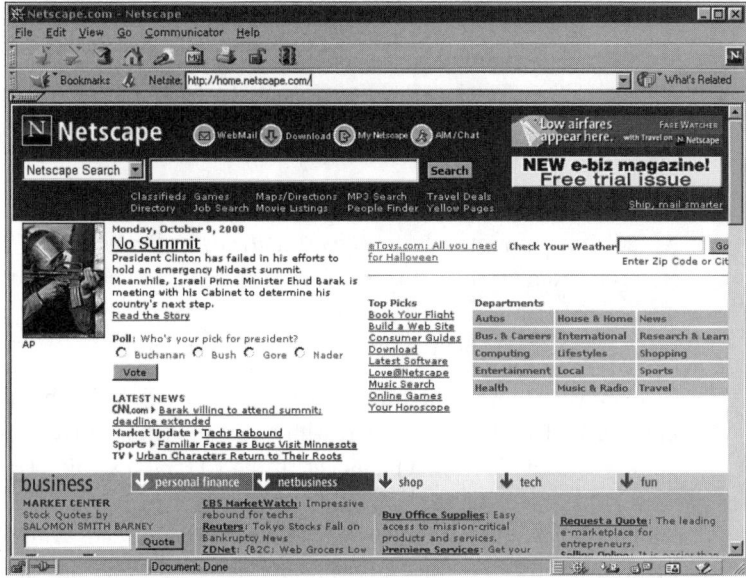

The good news is that you can download and use Netscape Communicator Standard Edition for free. The most widely used version of Netscape is 4.7, which is available for downloading at Netscape's site at `http://home.netscape.com/`. The most recent version is Netscape 6. It will probably have more users than Netscape 4.7 at some point, but it's not used widely yet.

In early 1998, Netscape released the source code for their browser and created the Mozilla project (`http://www.mozilla.org`) to handle further development of the browser. Subsequently, the Mozilla project tossed out all of the Netscape 4.7 source code and started from scratch, and Netscape merged with AOL. The work of the Mozilla project has resulted in Netscape 6, the latest Netscape-branded browser. You can find out more about Netscape 6 at `http://home.netscape.com/browsers/6/`.

Netscape 6 is very powerful, but it's also very different from all of the Web browsers that preceded it. It provides broad support for Web standards and has a fast, flexible rendering engine. It was written in such a way that much of the same code could be compiled and used on many computing platforms in order to reduce development time. This allowed the Mozilla project to create a Web browser that would run and work almost identically under Windows, the Mac OS, and Unix. Unfortunately, the cost of this cross-platform support is that the browser doesn't support many features that people expect. This has hampered adoption of Netscape 6.

Using the Browser to Access Other Services

Internet veterans know that there are dozens of different ways to get information: FTP, Gopher, Usenet news, WAIS databases, Telnet, and email. Before the Web became as popular as it is now, you had to use a different tool for each of these, all of which used different commands. Although all these choices made for a great market for *How to Use the Internet* books, they weren't very easy to use.

Web browsers changed that. Although the Web itself is its own information system with its own Internet protocol (the *Hypertext Transfer Protocol* or *HTTP*), Web browsers can read files from other Internet services also. And even better, you can create links to information on those systems just as you would create links to Web pages. This process is seamless and available through a single application.

To point your browser to different kinds of information on the Internet, you use different kinds of URLs. Most URLs start with `http:`, which indicates a file at an actual Web site. To download a file from a public site using FTP, you would use a URL like `ftp://name_of_site/directory/filename`. You can also view the contents of a directory on a publicly accessible FTP site using an `ftp:` URL that ends with a directory name. Figure 1.8 shows a listing of files from Microsoft's Web site, at `ftp://ftp.microsoft.com/`.

FIGURE 1.8

A listing of files and directories available at Microsoft's FTP site.

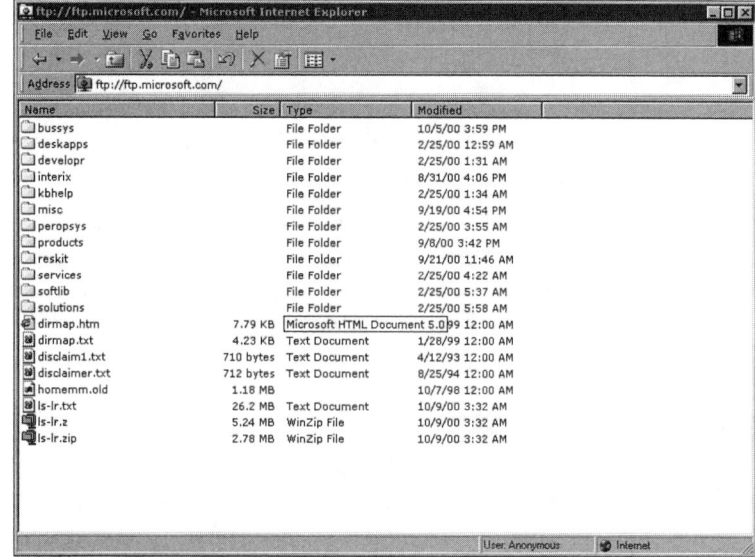

To access a Usenet newsgroup through your Web browser (thereby launching an external news reading program), you can simply enter a `news:` URL, such as `news:alt.usage.english`.

You'll learn more about different kinds of URLs on Day 5, "All About Links."

Web Servers

To view and browse pages on the Web, all you need is a Web browser. To publish pages on the Web, you'll need a Web server.

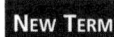 A *Web server* is the program that runs a computer and is responsible for replying to Web browser requests for files. You need a Web server to publish documents on the Web. One point of confusion is that the computer on which a server program runs is also referred to as a server. So when someone uses the term *Web server*, she could be referring to a program used to distribute Web pages or the computer on which that program runs.

When you use a browser to request a page on a Web site, that browser makes a Web connection to a server (using the HTTP protocol). The server accepts the connection, sends the contents of the requested files, and then closes the connection. The browser then formats the information it got from the server.

On the server side, many different browsers can connect to the same server to get the same information. The Web server is responsible for handling all these requests.

Web servers do more than just deposit files. They also are responsible for managing form input and for linking forms and browsers with programs such as databases running on the server.

Just as with browsers, many different servers are available for many different platforms, each with many different features and ranging in cost from free to very expensive. For now, all you need to know is what the server is there for; you'll learn more about Web servers on Day 19, "Putting Your Site Online."

Uniform Resource Locators (URLs)

As you learned earlier, a URL is a pointer to some bit of data on the Web, be it a Web document, a file on FTP or Gopher, a posting on Usenet, or an email address. The URL provides a universal, consistent method for finding and accessing information, not necessarily for you, but mostly for your Web browser. (If URLs were for you, they would be in an easy-to-remember format.)

In addition to typing URLs directly into your browser to go to a particular page, you also use URLs when you create a hypertext link within a document to another document. So, any way you look at it, URLs are important to how you and your browser get around on the Web.

URLs contain information about the following:

- How to get to the information (which protocol to use—FTP, Gopher, HTTP)
- The Internet hostname of the computer where the content is stored (www.ncsa.uiuc.edu, ftp.apple.com, netcom16.netcom.com, and so on)
- The directory or other location on that site where the content is located

You also can use special URLs for tasks such as sending mail to people (called Mailto URLs) and for using the Telnet program.

You'll learn all about URLs and what each part means in Day 5.

Summary

To publish on the Web, you have to understand the basic concepts that make up the parts of the Web. Today, you learned three major concepts. First, you learned about a few of the more useful features of the Web for publishing information. Second, you learned about Web browsers and servers and how they interact to deliver Web pages. Third, you learned about what a URL is and why it's important to Web browsing and publishing.

Workshop

Each day in this book contains a workshop to help you review the topics you learned. The first section of this workshop lists some common questions about the Web. Next, you'll answer some questions that I'll ask you about the Web. The answers to the quiz appear in the next section. At the end of each day, you'll find some exercises that will help you retain the information you learned about the Web.

Q&A

Q Who runs the Web? Who controls all these protocols? Who's in charge of all this?

A No single entity "owns" or controls the World Wide Web. Given the enormous number of independent sites that supply information to the Web, for any single organization to set rules or guidelines would be impossible. Two groups of organizations, however, have a great influence over the look and feel and direction of the Web itself.

The first is the World Wide Web Consortium (W3C), based at Massachusetts Institute of Technology (MIT) in the United States and INRIA in Europe. The W3C is made up of individuals and organizations interested in supporting and defining the languages and protocols that make up the Web (HTTP, HTML, and so on). It also provides products (browsers, servers, and so on) that are freely available to anyone who wants to use them. The W3 Consortium is the closest anyone gets to setting the standards for and enforcing rules about the World Wide Web. You can visit the Consortium's home page at http://www.w3.org/.

The second group of organizations that influences the Web is the browser developers themselves, most notably Microsoft and Netscape Communications Corporation. The competition to be the most popular and technically advanced browser on the Web can be fierce. Although both organizations claim to support and adhere to the guidelines proposed by the W3C, both also include their own new features in new versions of their software—features that often conflict with each other and with the work the W3C is doing.

Sometimes trying to keep track of all the new and rapidly changing developments feels like being in the middle of a war zone, with the W3C trying to mediate and prevent global thermonuclear war. As a Web designer, you're stuck in the middle, and you'll have to make choices about which browsers to support, and how to deal with the rapid changes. But that's what the rest of this book is for!

Q **I've heard that the Web changes so fast that it's almost impossible to stay current. Is this book doomed to be out of date the day it's published?**

A While it's true that things change fast on the Web, the vast majority of the information in this book will serve you well far into the future. New enhancements to HTML and other Web technologies are introduced all the time, but browser makers are generally good about supporting preexisting standards.

Quiz

1. What makes a hypertext information system so cool?

2. Do you need a special type of computer to access the Internet?

3. Besides a connection to the Internet, what else is required to view and navigate Web pages and other information on the World Wide Web? Why is it necessary?

4. What is a URL?

5. What is required to publish documents on the Web?

Quiz Answers

1. A hypertext information system allows you to connect information within a document or a group of documents. Rather than presenting information in a linear fashion, you can organize information so that users can view it in a more flexible manner.

2. You don't need a special computer. You can access the Internet with any computer, from low-end PC to expensive UNIX workstation, using any operating system and any display. The Web is entirely cross-platform. The only thing that's required is a connection to the Internet, usually through an Internet service provider over a modem or a hard-wired link at work or school.

3. You must have a browser to view and navigate Web pages on the Web. In addition to retrieving Web documents, the most important function of the browser is to format and display Web documents and make them readable on your system.

4. A URL, or uniform resource locator, is an *address* that points to a specific document or bit of information on the Internet.

5. Most of the time, you need access to a Web server. Web servers, which are programs that run a Web site, reply to Web browser requests for files and send the requested pages to many different types of browsers. They also manage form input and handle database integration.

Exercises

1. Try navigating to each of the different types of URLs mentioned today (`http:`, `ftp:`, and `news:`). Some links you might want to try are `http://www.tywebpub.com`, `ftp://ftp.cdrom.com`, and `news:comp.infosystems.www`.

2. To become a bit more aware of the vast number of browsers that are available, visit `http://www.browsers.com`, a part of the CNET Web site. Another site that provides lots of up-to-date information on browsers is BrowserWatch at `http://www.browserwatch.com`. Initially, you might find this information quite overwhelming—but the main point of this exercise is to show you that there are far more than two browsers out there, and they support a wide variety of features. You'll want to keep this URL handy as you learn more about HTML. Here, you will keep informed of the latest versions of all available browsers and the features they support.

DAY 2

Get Organized

When you write a book, a paper, an article, or even a memo, you usually don't just jump right in with the first sentence and then write it through to the end. The same goes with the visual arts—you don't normally start from the top left corner of the canvas or page and work your way down to the bottom right.

A better way to write, draw, or design a work is to do some planning beforehand—to know what you're going to do and what you're trying to accomplish, and to have a general idea or rough sketch of the structure of the piece before you jump in and work on it.

Just as with more traditional modes of communication, the process of writing and designing Web pages takes some planning and thought before you start flinging text and graphics around and linking them wildly to each other. It's perhaps even more important to plan ahead with Web pages because trying to apply the rules of traditional writing or design to online hypertext often results in documents that are either difficult to understand and navigate online or that simply don't take advantage of the features that hypertext provides. Poorly organized Web pages also are difficult to revise or to expand.

In this chapter, I describe some of the things you should think about before you begin developing your Web pages. Specifically, you need to do the following:

- Learn the differences between a Web server, a Web site, a Web page, and a home page.
- Think about the sort of information (content) you want to put on the Web.
- Set the goals for the Web site.
- Organize your content into the main topics.
- Come up with a general structure for pages and topics.
- Use storyboarding to plan your Web site.

After you have an overall idea of how you're going to construct your Web pages, you'll be ready to actually start writing and designing those pages in Day 4, "Begin with the Basics." If you're eager to get started, be patient! You will have more than enough HTML to learn over the next three days.

Anatomy of a Web Site

First, here's a look at some simple terminology I'll be using throughout this book. You need to know what the following terms mean and how they apply to the body of work you're developing for the Web:

- Web site—A collection of one or more Web pages linked together in a meaningful way that, as a whole, describes a body of information or creates an overall effect (see Figure 2.1).
- Web server—A computer on the Internet or an intranet that stores one or more Web sites.
- Web pages—A single element of a Web site, usually consisting of an HTML document and any items that are displayed within that document, such as inline images.
- Home page—The "entry" page for a Web site, which can link to additional pages on the same Web site or pages on other sites.

Each Web site is stored on a Web server. Throughout the first week or so of this book, you'll learn how to develop well thought out and well-designed Web sites. Later, you'll learn how to publish your site on an actual Web server.

A *Web page* is an individual element of a Web site in the same way that a page is a single element of a book or a newspaper (although, unlike paper pages, Web pages can be of any length). Web pages sometimes are called *Web documents*. Both terms refer to the same thing. A Web page consists of an HTML document and all of the other components that are included on the page, such as images or other media.

FIGURE 2.1

Web sites and pages.

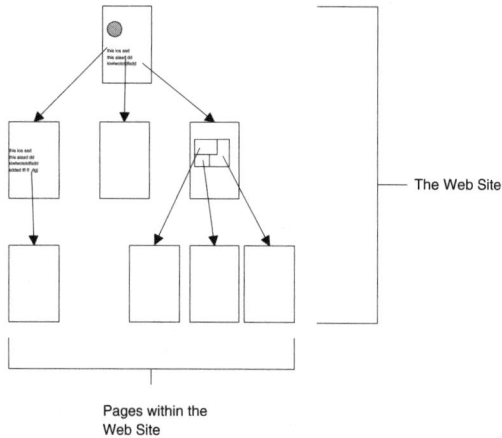

The Web Site

Pages within the
Web Site

One problem with the term *home page* is that it means different things in different contexts. If you're browsing the Web, you usually can think of the home page as the Web page that loads when you start up your browser or when you click the Home button. Each browser has its own default home page, which generally leads to the Web site of the browser's creator. (For example, the Netscape home page is at Netscape's Web site and the Internet Explorer home page is at Microsoft's Web site.)

Within your browser, you can change that default home page to point to any page you want. Many users create a personalized page linking to sites they use often and set that as their browser's home page.

If you're publishing pages on the Web, however, the term *home page* has an entirely different meaning. The home page is the first or topmost page on your Web site. It's the intended entry point that provides access to the rest of the pages you've created (see Figure 2.2).

 **Caution** Most of your users will access your site through your home page, but some will enter your site through other pages. The nature of the Web is that people can link to any page on your site. If you have interesting information on a page other than your home page, people will link directly to that page. On the other pages of your site, you shouldn't assume that the visitor has seen your home page.

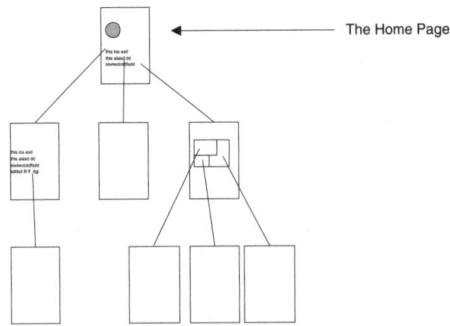

The Home Page

A home page usually contains an overview of the content of the Web site, available from that starting point—for example, in the form of a table of contents or a set of icons. If your content is small enough, you might include everything on that single home page— making your home page and your Web site the same thing.

What Do You Want to Do on the Web?

This question might seem silly. You wouldn't have bought this book if you didn't already have some idea of what you want to put online. But maybe you don't really know what you want to put on the Web, or you have a vague idea but nothing concrete. Maybe it has suddenly become your job to put a page for your company on the Web, and someone handed you this book and said, "Here, this will help." Maybe you just want to do something similar to some other Web page you've seen and thought was particularly cool.

What you want to put on the Web is what I'll refer to throughout this book as your content. *Content* is a general term that can refer to text, graphics, media, interactive forms, and so on. If you tell someone what your Web pages are "about," you are describing your content.

NEW TERM   Your *content* is the stuff you're putting on the Web. Information, fiction, images, art, programs, humor, diagrams, games—all this is content.

What sort of content can you put on the Web? Just about anything you want to. Here are some of the types of content that are popular on the Web right now:

- **Personal information**—You can create pages describing everything anyone could ever want to know about you and how incredibly marvelous you are—your hobbies, your resume, your picture, things you've done.

- **Hobbies or special interests**—A Web page can contain information about a particular topic, hobby, or something you're interested in; for example, music, Star Trek, motorcycles, cult movies, hallucinogenic mushrooms, antique ink bottles, or upcoming jazz concerts in your city.

- **Publications**—Newspapers, magazines, and other publications lend themselves particularly well to the Web, and they have the advantage of being more immediate and easier to update than their print counterparts.

- **Company profiles**—You could offer information about what a company does, where it is located, job openings, data sheets, white papers, marketing collateral, product demonstrations, and whom to contact.

- **Online documentation**—The term *online documentation* can refer to everything from quick-reference cards to full reference documentation to interactive tutorials or training modules. Anything task-oriented (changing the oil in your car, making a soufflé, creating landscape portraits in oil, learning HTML) could be described as online documentation.

- **Shopping catalogs**—If your company offers items for sale, making your lists available on the Web is a quick and easy way to let your customers know what you have available as well as your prices. If prices change, you can just update your Web documents to reflect that new information.

- **Online stores**—You also can use the Web to actually sell items to customers through use of a *shopping basket*. Users place into and remove items from their baskets as they browse the catalog. At the end, they can provide a credit card number and shipping information to place the order.

- **Polling and opinion gathering**—Interactivity and forms on the Web enable you to get feedback from your visitors on nearly any topic, including opinion polls, suggestion boxes, comments on your Web pages or your products, and so on.

- **Online education**—The Web's interactivity and low cost of information delivery in many places make it an attractive medium for delivery of distance-learning programs. Already, numerous traditional universities, as well as new online schools and universities, have begun offering distance learning on the Web.

- **Anything else that comes to mind**—Hypertext fiction, online toys, media archives, collaborative art... anything!

The only thing that limits what you can publish on the Web is your own imagination. In fact, if what you want to do with it isn't in this list, or seems especially wild or half-baked, that's an excellent reason to try it. The most interesting Web pages are the ones that stretch the boundaries of what the Web is supposed to be capable of.

If you really have no idea of what to put up on the Web, don't feel that you have to stop here; put this book away, and come up with something before continuing. Maybe by reading through this book, you'll get some ideas (and this book will be useful even if you don't have ideas). I've personally found that the best way to come up with ideas is to spend an afternoon browsing on the Web and exploring what other people have done.

Set Your Goals

What do you want people to be able to accomplish on your Web site? Are your visitors looking for specific information on how to do something? Are they going to read through each page in turn, going on only when they're done with the page they're reading? Are they just going to start at your home page and wander aimlessly around, exploring your "world" until they get bored and go somewhere else?

Suppose that you're creating a Web site that describes the company where you work. Some people visiting that Web site might want to know about job openings. Others might want to know where the company actually is located. Still others might have heard that your company makes technical white papers available over the Net, and they want to download the most recent version of a particular paper. Each of these goals is valid, so you should list each one.

For a shopping catalog Web site, you might have only a few goals: to enable your visitors to browse the items you have for sale by name or price, and to order specific items after they're done browsing.

For a personal or special-interest Web site, you might have only a single goal: to enable your visitors to browse and explore the information you've provided.

The goals do not have to be lofty ("this Web site will bring about world peace") or even make much sense to anyone except you. Still, coming up with goals for your Web documents prepares you to design, organize, and write your Web pages specifically to reach these goals. Goals also help you resist the urge to obscure your content with extra information.

If you're designing Web pages for someone else—for example, if you're creating the Web site for your company or if you've been hired as a consultant—having a set of goals for the site from your employer definitely is one of the most important pieces of information you should have before you create a single page. The ideas you have for the Web site might not be the ideas that other people have for it, and you might end up doing a lot of work that has to be thrown away.

Break Up Your Content into Main Topics

With your goals in mind, now try to organize your content into main topics or sections, chunking related information together under a single topic. Sometimes the goals you came up with in the preceding section and your list of topics will be closely related. For example, if you're putting together a Web page for a bookstore, the goal of being able to order books fits nicely under a topic called, appropriately, "Ordering Books."

You don't have to be exact at this point in development. Your goal here is just to try to come up with an idea of what, specifically, you'll be describing in your Web pages. You can organize the information better later, as you write the actual pages.

Suppose that you're designing a Web site about how to tune up your car. This example is simple because tune-ups consist of a concrete set of steps that fit neatly into topic headings. In this example, your topics might include the following:

- Change the oil and oil filter.
- Check and adjust engine timing.
- Check and adjust valve clearances.
- Check and replace the spark plugs.
- Check fluid levels, belts, and hoses.

Don't worry about the order of the steps or how you're going to get your visitors to go from one section to another. Just list the points you want to describe in your Web site.

How about a less task-oriented example? Suppose that you want to create a set of Web pages about a particular rock band because you're a big fan, and you're sure other fans would benefit from your extensive knowledge. Your topics might be as follows:

- The history of the band
- Biographies of each of the band members
- A "discography"—all the albums and singles the band has released
- Selected lyrics
- Images of album covers
- Information about upcoming shows and future albums

You can come up with as many topics as you want, but try to keep each topic reasonably short. If a single topic seems too large, try to break it up into subtopics. If you have too many small topics, try to group them together into a more general topic heading. For example, if you're creating an online encyclopedia of poisonous plants, having individual topics for each plant would be overkill. You can just as easily group each plant name under a letter of the alphabet (A, B, C, and so on) and use each letter as a topic. That's assuming, of course, that your visitors will be looking up information in your encyclopedia alphabetically. If they want to look up poisonous plants by using some other method, you would have to come up with different topics.

Your goal is to have a set of topics that are roughly the same size and that group together related bits of information you have to present.

Ideas for Organization and Navigation

At this point, you should have a good idea of what you want to talk about as well as a list of topics. The next step is to actually start structuring the information you have into a set of Web pages. Before you do that, however, consider some "standard" structures that have been used in other help systems and online tools. This section describes some of these structures, their various features, and some important considerations, including the following:

- The kinds of information that work well for each structure
- How visitors find their way through the content of each structure type to find what they need
- How to make sure that visitors can figure out where they are within your documents (context) and find their way back to a known position

Think, as you read this section, how your information might fit into one of these structures, or how you could combine these structures to create a new structure for your Web site.

 Note   Many of the ideas I describe in this section were drawn from a book called *Designing and Writing Online Documentation* by William K. Horton (John Wiley & Sons, 1994). Although Horton's book was written primarily for technical writers and developers working specifically with online help systems, it's a great book for ideas on structuring documents and for dealing with hypertext information in general. If you start doing a lot of work with the Web, you might want to pick up this book; it provides a lot of insight beyond what I have to offer.

Hierarchies

Probably the easiest and most logical way to structure your Web documents is in a hierarchical or menu fashion, as illustrated in Figure 2.3. Hierarchies and menus lend themselves especially well to online and hypertext documents. Most online help systems, for example, are hierarchical. You start with a list or menu of major topics; selecting one leads you to a list of subtopics, which then leads you to a discussion about a particular topic. Different help systems have different levels, of course, but most follow this simple structure.

FIGURE 2.3

Hierarchical organization.

Home

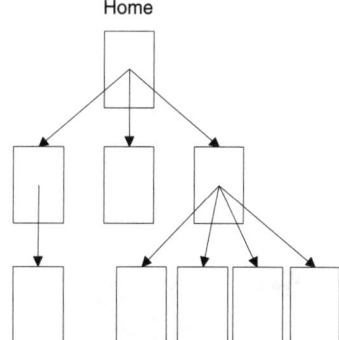

In a hierarchical organization, visitors can easily know their position in the structure. Choices are to move up for more general information or down for more specific information. If you provide a link back to the top level, your visitors can get back to some known position quickly and easily.

In hierarchies, the home page provides the most general overview to the content below it. The home page also defines the main links for the pages further down in the hierarchy.

For example, a Web site about gardening might have a home page with the topics shown in Figure 2.4.

If you select Fruits, you then follow a link "down" to a page about fruits (see Figure 2.5). From there, you can go back to the home page, or you can select another link and go further down into more specific information about particular fruits.

FIGURE 2.4

A Gardening home page with a hierarchical structure.

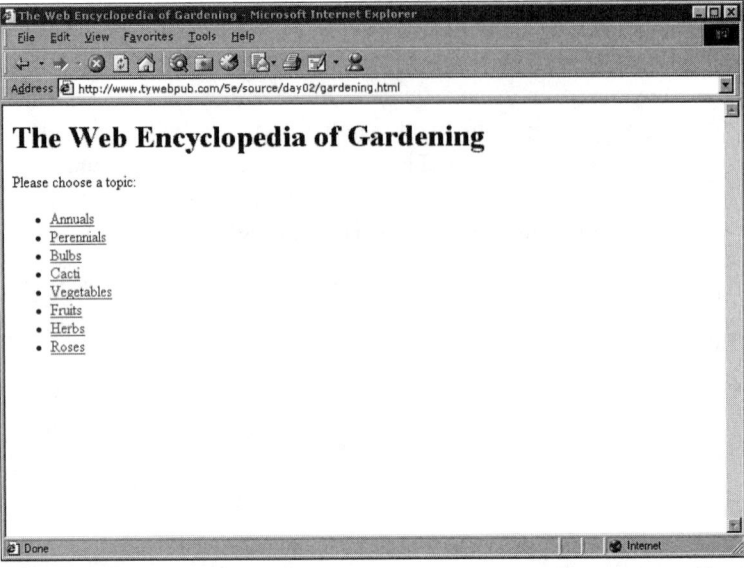

FIGURE 2.5

Your hierarchy takes you to the Fruits page.

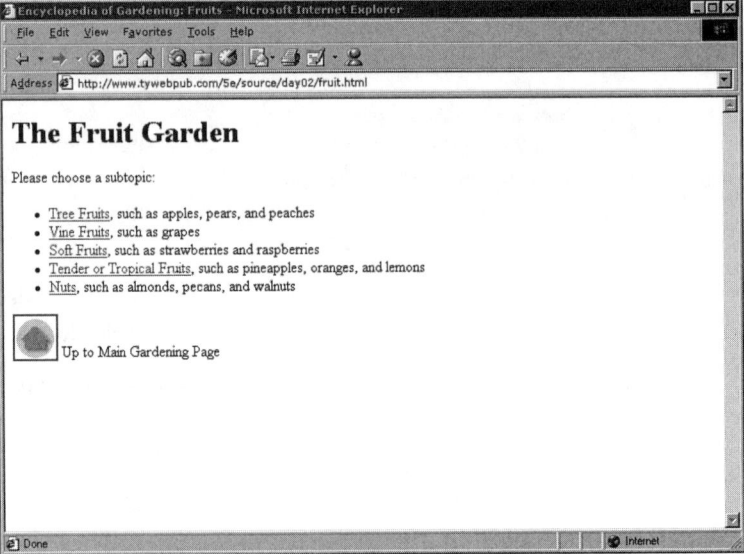

Selecting Soft Fruits takes you to yet another menu-like page, where you have still more categories from which to choose (see Figure 2.6). From there, you can go up to Fruits, back to the home page, or down to one of the choices in this menu.

FIGURE 2.6

From the Fruits page, you can find the Soft Fruits page.

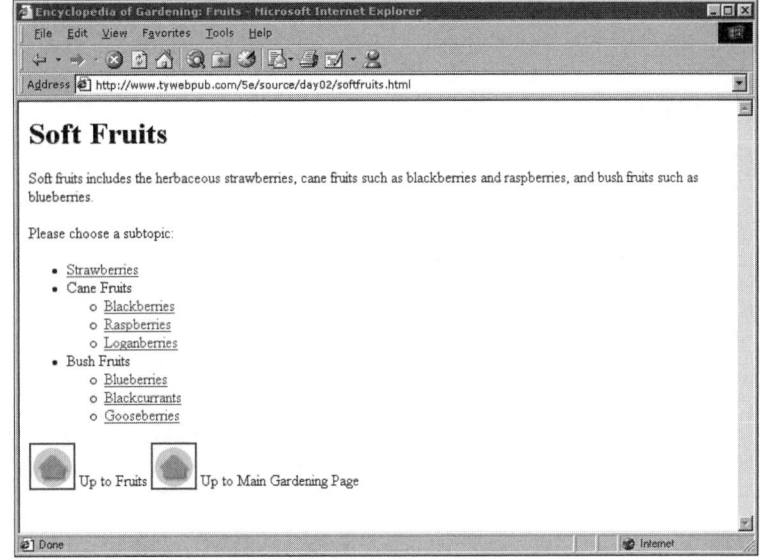

Note that each level has a consistent interface (up, down, back to index), and that each level has a limited set of choices for basic navigation. Hierarchies are structured enough that the chance of getting lost is minimal. (This especially is true if you provide clues about where "Up" is; for example, a link that says "Up to Soft Fruits" as opposed to just "Up.")

Additionally, if you organize each level of the hierarchy and avoid overlap between topics (and the content you have lends itself to a hierarchical organization), using hierarchies can be an easy way to find particular bits of information. If that use is one of your goals for your visitors, using a hierarchy might work particularly well.

Avoid including too many levels and too many choices, however, because you can easily annoy your visitors. Having too many menu pages results in "voice-mail syndrome." After having to choose from too many menus, visitors might forget what they originally wanted, and they're too annoyed to care. Try to keep your hierarchy two to three levels deep, combining information on the pages at the lowest levels (or endpoints) of the hierarchy if necessary.

Linear

Another way to organize your documents is to use a linear or sequential organization, similar to how printed documents are organized. In a linear structure, as illustrated in Figure 2.7, the home page is the title, or introduction, and each page follows sequentially from that structure. In a strict linear structure, links move from one page to another, typically forward and back. You also might want to include a link to "Home" that takes you quickly back to the first page.

FIGURE 2.7

Linear organization.

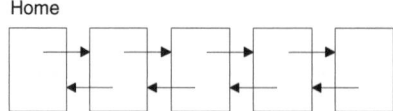

Context generally is easy to figure out in a linear structure simply because there are so few places to go.

A linear organization is very rigid and limits your visitors' freedom to explore and your freedom to present information. Linear structures are good for putting material online when the information also has a very linear structure offline (such as short stories, step-by-step instructions, or computer-based training), or when you explicitly want to prevent your visitors from skipping around.

For example, consider teaching someone how to make cheese by using the Web. Cheese making is a complex process involving several steps that must be followed in a specific order.

Describing this process using Web pages lends itself to a linear structure rather well. When navigating a set of Web pages on this subject, you would start with the home page, which might have a summary or an overview of the steps to follow. Then, by using the link for "forward," move on to the first step, "Choosing the Right Milk"; to the next step, "Setting and Curdling the Milk"; all the way through to the last step, "Curing and Ripening the Cheese." If you need to review at any time, you could use the link for "back." Because the process is so linear, you would have little need for links that branch off from the main stem or links that join together different steps in the process.

Linear with Alternatives

You can soften the rigidity of a linear structure by enabling the visitors to deviate from the main path. You could, for example, have a linear structure with alternatives that branch out from a single point (see Figure 2.8). The off-shoots can then rejoin the main branch at some point further down, or they can continue down their separate tracks until they each come to an "end."

Suppose that you have an installation procedure for a software package that is similar in most ways, regardless of the computer type, except for one step. At that point in the linear installation, you could branch out to cover each system, as shown in Figure 2.9.

FIGURE 2.8

Linear with alternatives.

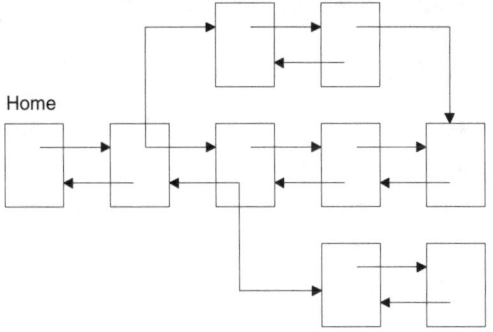

FIGURE 2.9

Different steps for different systems.

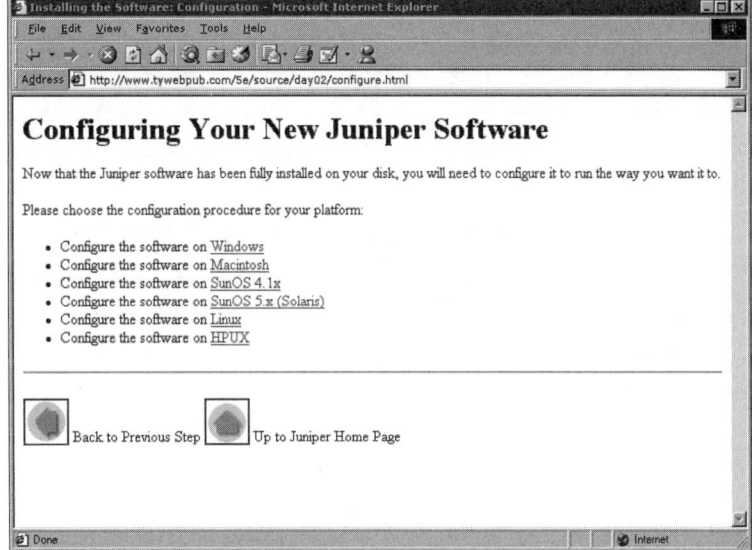

After the system-specific part of the installation, you then could link back to the original branch and continue with the generic installation.

In addition to branching from a linear structure, you also could provide links that enable visitors to skip forward or backward in the chain if they need to review a particular step, or if they already understand some content (see Figure 2.10).

FIGURE 2.10

Skip ahead or back.

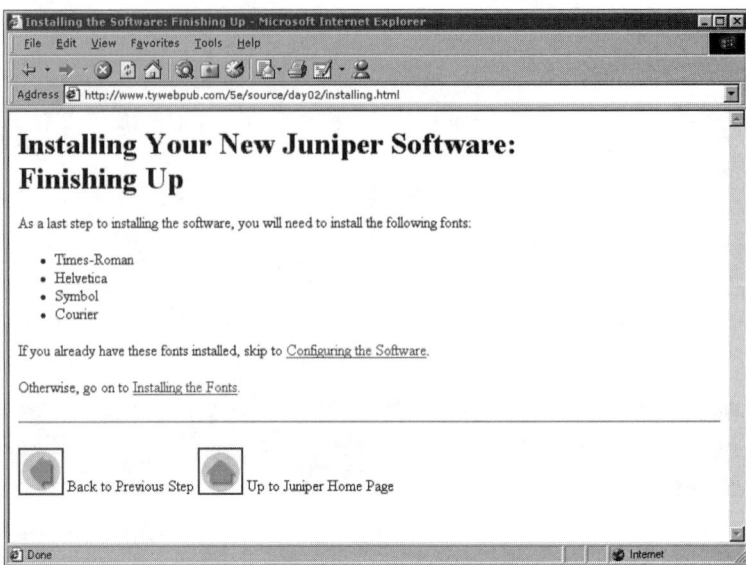

Combination of Linear and Hierarchical

A popular form of document organization on the Web is a combination of a linear structure and a hierarchical one, as shown in Figure 2.11. This structure occurs most often
when very structured but linear documents are put online; the popular Frequently Asked
Questions (FAQ) files use this structure.

FIGURE 2.11

*Combination of linear
and hierarchical orga-
nization.*

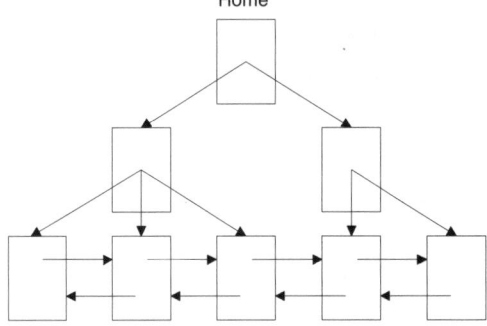

The combination of linear and hierarchical documents works well as long as you have
appropriate clues regarding context. Because the visitors can either move up and down or
forward and backward, they can easily lose their mental positioning in the hierarchy
when crossing hierarchical boundaries by moving forward or backward.

Suppose that you're putting the Shakespearean play *Macbeth* online as a set of Web pages. In addition to the simple linear structure that the play provides, you can create a hierarchical table of contents and summary of each act linked to appropriate places within the text, similar to what is shown in Figure 2.12.

FIGURE 2.12

Macbeth's hierarchy.

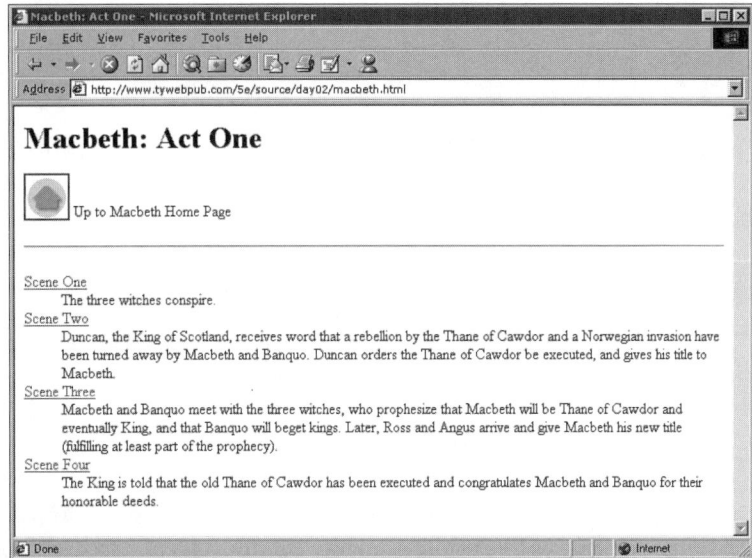

Because this structure is both linear and hierarchical, you provide links to go forward, backward, return to beginning, and up on each page of the script. But what is the context for going up?

If you've just come down into this page from an act summary, the context makes sense. "Up" means go back to the summary from which you just came.

But suppose that you go down from a summary and then go forward, crossing an act boundary (say from Act 1 to Act 2). Now what does "up" mean? The fact that you're moving up to a page you might not have seen before is disorienting given the nature of what you expect from a hierarchy. Up and down are supposed to be consistent.

Consider two possible solutions:

- Do not allow "forward" and "back" links across hierarchical boundaries. In this case, to read from Act 1 to Act 2 in *Macbeth*, you have to move up in the hierarchy and then back down into Act 2.

- Provide more context in the link text. Rather than just "Up" or an icon for the link that moves up in the hierarchy, include a description to where the user is moving.

Web

A Web is a set of documents with little or no actual overall structure; the only thing tying each page together is a link (see Figure 2.13). Visitors drift from document to document, following the links around.

FIGURE 2.13

A Web structure.

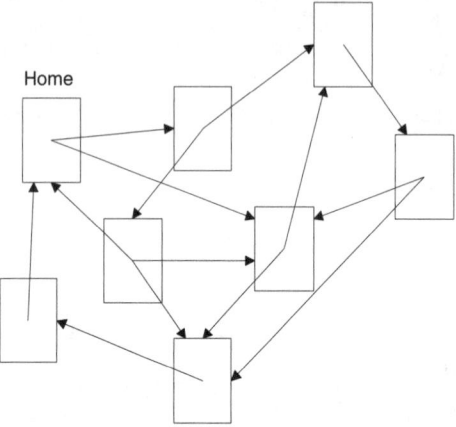

Home

Web structures tend to be free-floating and enable visitors to wander aimlessly through the content. Web structures are excellent for content that is intended to be meandering or unrelated, or when you want to encourage browsing. The World Wide Web itself is, of course, a giant Web structure.

An example of content organized in a Web structure might be a set of virtual "rooms" created by using Web pages. If you've ever played an old text-adventure game like Zork or Dungeon, or if you've used a Multiuser Dungeon (MUD), you are familiar with this type of environment.

In the context of a Web site, the environment is organized so that each page is a specific location (and usually contains a description of that location). From that location, you can "move" in several different directions, exploring the environment much in the way you would move from room to room in a building in the real world (and getting lost just as easily). The initial home page, for example, might look something like the one shown in Figure 2.14.

From that page, you then can explore one of the links, for example, to go into the building, which takes you to the page shown in Figure 2.15.

Each room has a set of links to each "adjacent" room in the environment. By following the links, you can explore the rooms in the environment.

FIGURE 2.14

The home page for a Web-based virtual environment.

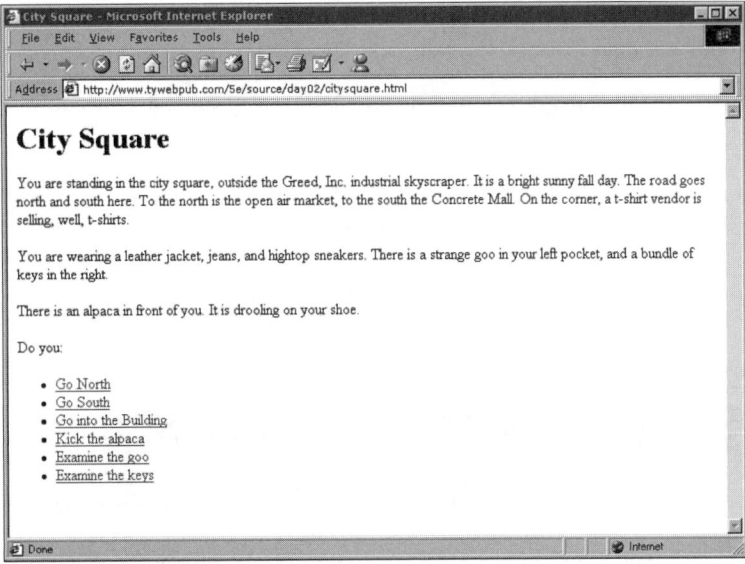

FIGURE 2.15

Another page in the Web environment.

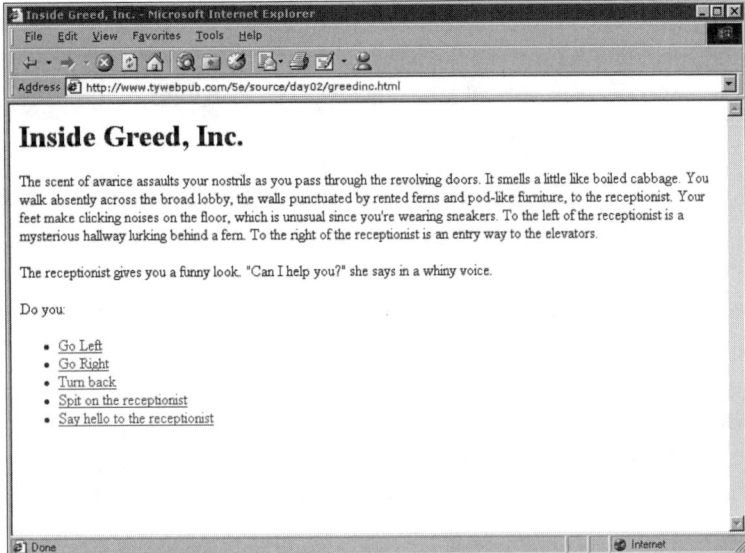

The problem with Web organizations is that you can get lost in them too easily—just as you might in the "world" you're exploring in the example. Without any overall structure to the content, figuring out the relationship between where you are, where you're going, and, often, where you've been is difficult. Context is difficult, and often the only way to find your way back out of a Web structure is to retrace your steps. Web structures can be extremely disorienting and immensely frustrating if you have a specific goal in mind.

To solve the problem of disorientation, you can use clues on each page. Here are two ideas:

- Provide a way out. "Return to Home Page" is an excellent link.
- Include a map of the overall structure on each page, with a "you are here" indication somewhere in the map. It doesn't have to be an actual visual map, but providing some sort of context will go a long way toward preventing your visitors from getting lost.

Storyboarding Your Web Site

The next step in planning your Web site is to figure out what content goes on what page and to come up with some simple links for navigation between those pages.

If you're using one of the structures described in the preceding section, much of the organization might arise from that structure, in which case this section will be easy. If you want to combine different kinds of structures, however, or if you have a lot of content that needs to be linked together in sophisticated ways, sitting down and making a specific plan of what goes where will be incredibly useful later as you develop and link each individual page.

What Is Storyboarding and Why Do I Need It?

Storyboarding a Web site is a concept borrowed from filmmaking in which each scene and each individual camera shot is sketched and roughed out in the order in which it occurs in the movie. Storyboarding provides an overall structure and plan to the film that allows the director and staff to have a distinct idea of where each individual shot fits into the overall movie.

NEW TERM   *Storyboarding* is the process of creating a rough outline and sketch of what your Web site will look like before you actually write any pages. Storyboarding helps you visualize the entire Web site and how it will look when it's complete.

The storyboarding concept works quite well for developing Web pages. The storyboard provides an overall rough outline of what the Web site will look like when it's done, including which topics go on which pages, the primary links, and maybe even some conceptual idea of what sort of graphics you'll be using and where they will go. With that representation in hand, you can develop each page without trying to remember exactly where that page fits into the overall Web site and its often complex relationships to other pages.

In the case of really large sets of documents, a storyboard enables different people to develop various portions of the same Web site. With a clear storyboard, you can minimize duplication of work and reduce the amount of contextual information each person needs to remember.

For smaller or simpler Web sites, or Web sites with a simple logical structure, storyboarding might be unnecessary. For larger and more complex projects, however, the existence of a storyboard can save enormous amounts of time and frustration. If you can't keep all the parts of your content and their relationships in your head, consider creating a storyboard.

So what does a storyboard for a Web site look like? It can be as simple as a couple of sheets of paper. Each sheet can represent a page, with a list of topics each page will describe and some thoughts about the links that page will include. I've seen storyboards for very complex hypertext systems that involved a really large bulletin board, index cards, and string. Each index card had a topic written on it, and the links were represented by string tied on pins from card to card.

The point of a storyboard is that it organizes your Web pages in a way that works for you. If you like index cards and string, work with these tools. If a simple outline on paper or on the computer works better, use that instead.

Hints for Storyboarding

Some things to think about when developing your storyboard are as follows:

- **Which topics will go on each page?**

  A simple rule of thumb is to have each topic represented by a single page. If you have several topics, however, maintaining and linking them can be a daunting task. Consider combining smaller, related topics onto a single page instead. Don't go overboard and put everything on one page, however; your visitors still have to download your document over the net. Having several medium-sized pages (such as the size of two to ten pages in your word processor) is better than having one monolithic page or hundreds of little tiny pages.

- **What are the primary forms of navigation between pages?**

  What links will you need for your visitors to navigate from page to page? They are the main links in your document that enable your visitors to accomplish the goals you defined in the first section. Links for forward, back, up, down, or home all fall under the category of primary navigation.

- **What alternative forms of navigation are you going to provide?**

  In addition to the simple navigation links, some Web sites contain extra information that is parallel to the main Web content, such as a glossary of terms, an alphabetical index of concepts, or a credits page. Consider these extra forms of information when designing your plan, and think about how you're going to link them into the main content.

- **What will you put on your home page?**

  Because the home page is the starting point for the rest of the information in your Web site, consider what sort of information you're going to put on the home page. A general summary of what's to come? A list of links to other topics?

- **What are your goals?**

  As you design the framework for your Web site, keep your goals in mind, and make sure you are not obscuring your goals with extra information or content.

Note   Several utilities and packages can assist you in storyboarding. Foremost among them are site management packages that can help you manage links in a site, view a graphical representation of the relationship of documents in your site, move documents around, and automatically update all relevant links in and to the documents.

Summary

Designing a Web site, like designing a book outline, a building plan, or a painting, can sometimes be a complex and involved process. Having a plan before beginning can help you keep the details straight and help you develop the finished product with fewer false starts. Today, you've learned how to put together a simple plan and structure for creating a set of Web pages, including the following:

- Deciding what sort of content to present
- Coming up with a set of goals for that content
- Deciding on a set of topics
- Organizing and storyboarding the Web site

With that plan in place, you now can move on to the next few days and learn the specifics of how to write individual Web pages, create links between them, and add graphics and media to enhance the Web site for your audience.

Workshop

The first section of the workshop lists some of the common questions people ask while planning a Web site, along with an answer to each. Following that, you'll have an opportunity to answer some quiz questions yourself. If you have problems answering any of the questions in the quiz, go to the next section where you'll find the answers. Today's exercises help you formulate some ideas for your own Web site.

Q&A

Q Getting organized seems like an awful lot of work. All I want to do is make something simple, and you're telling me I have to have goals and topics and storyboards.

A If you're doing something simple, then no, you won't need to do much, if any, of the stuff I recommend today. If you're talking about developing two or three inter-linked pages or more, however, having a plan before you start really helps. If you just dive in, you might discover that keeping everything straight in your head is too difficult. And the result might not be what you expected, making it hard for people to get the information they need out of your Web site as well as making difficult for you to reorganize it so that it makes sense. Having a plan before you start can't hurt, and it might save you time in the long run.

Q You've talked a lot today about organizing topics and pages, but you've said nothing about the design and layout of individual pages.

A I discuss design and layout later in this book, after you've learned more about the sorts of layout HTML (the language used for Web pages) can do, and the stuff that it just can't do. You'll find a whole day and more about page layout and design in Day 16, "Writing and Designing Web Pages: Do's and Don'ts."

Q What if I don't like any of the basic structures you talked about today?

A Then design your own. As long as your visitors can find what they want or do what you want them to do, no rules say you *must* use a hierarchy or a linear structure. I presented these structures only as potential ideas for organizing your Web pages.

Quiz

1. How would you briefly define the meaning of the terms *Web site*, *Web server*, and *Web pages*?

2. In terms of Web publishing, what is the meaning of the term *home page*?

3. After you set a goal or purpose for your Web site, what is the next step to designing your pages?

4. Regardless of the navigation structure you use in your Web site, there is one link that should typically appear on each of your Web pages. What is it?

5. What is the purpose of a storyboard?

Quiz Answers

1. A *Web site* is one or more Web pages linked together in a meaningful way. A *Web server* is the actual computer that stores the Web site. *Web pages* are the individual elements of the Web site, like a page is to a book.

2. A *home page*, in terms of Web publishing, is the entry point to the rest of the pages in your Web site (the first or topmost page).

3. After you set a goal or purpose for your Web site, you should try to organize your content into topics or sections.

4. You should try to include a link to your home page on each of the pages in your Web site. This way, users can always find their way back home if they get lost.

5. A storyboard provides an overall outline of what the Web site will look like when it's done. It helps organize your Web pages in a way that works for you. They are most beneficial for larger Web sites.

Exercises

1. As an exercise, come up with a list of several goals that your visitors might have for your Web pages. The clearer your goals, the better.

2. After you set your goals, visit sites on the Web that cover topics similar to those you want to cover in your own Web site. As you examine the sites, ask yourself whether they are easy to navigate and have good content. Then make a list—what do you like about the sites? How would you make your Web site better?

DAY 3

An Introduction to HTML

After finishing up the discussions about the World Wide Web and getting organized, with a large amount of text to read and concepts to digest, you're probably wondering when you're actually going to get to write a Web page. That is, after all, why you bought the book. Wait no longer! Today, you'll get to create your very first (albeit brief) Web page, learn about HTML (the language for writing Web pages), and learn about the following:

- What HTML is and why you have to use it
- What you can and cannot do when you design HTML pages
- HTML tags: what they are and how to use them

What HTML Is—And What It Isn't

Take note of just one more thing before you dive into actually writing Web pages. You should know what HTML is, what it can do, and most importantly what it can't do.

HTML stands for *Hypertext Markup Language.* HTML is based on the *Standard Generalized Markup Language* (SGML), a much larger document-processing system. To write HTML pages, you won't need to know a whole lot about SGML. However, knowing that one of the main features of SGML is that it describes the general structure of the content inside documents—rather than its actual appearance on the page or onscreen—does help. This concept might be a bit foreign to you if you're used to working with WYSIWYG (What You See Is What You Get) editors, so let's go over the information carefully.

HTML Describes the Structure of a Page

HTML, by virtue of its SGML heritage, is a language for describing the structure of a document, not its actual presentation. The idea here is that most documents have common elements—for example, titles, paragraphs, or lists. Before you start writing, therefore, you can identify and define the set of elements in that document and give them appropriate names (see Figure 3.1).

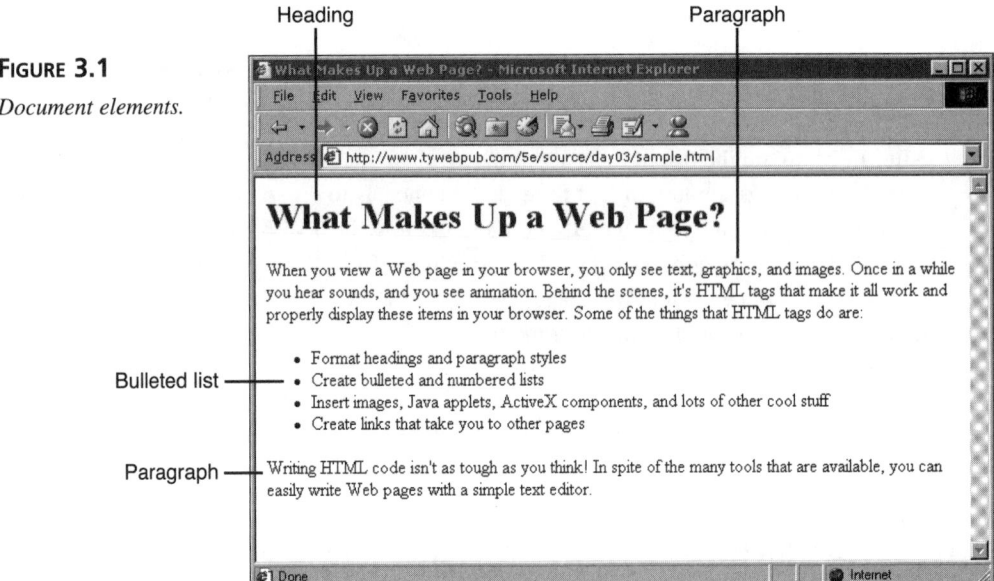

FIGURE 3.1

Document elements.

If you've worked with word processing programs that use style sheets (such as Microsoft Word) or paragraph catalogs (such as FrameMaker), you've done something similar; each section of text conforms to one of a set of styles that are predefined before you start working.

HTML defines a set of common styles for Web pages: headings, paragraphs, lists, and tables. It also defines character styles such as boldface and code examples. Each element has a name and is contained in what's called a *tag*. When you write a Web page in HTML, you label the different elements of your page with these tags that say "this is a heading" or "this is a list item."

HTML Does Not Describe Page Layout

When you're working with a word processor or page layout program, styles are not just named elements of a page—they also include formatting information such as the font size and style, indentation, underlining, and so on. So when you write some text that's supposed to be a heading, you can apply the Heading style to it, and the program automatically formats that paragraph for you in the correct style.

HTML doesn't go this far. For the most part, HTML doesn't say anything about how a page looks when it's viewed. HTML tags just indicate that an element is a heading or a list; they say nothing about how that heading or list is to be formatted. So, as with the magazine example and the layout person who formats your article, the layout person's job is to decide how big the heading should be and what font it should be in. The only thing you have to worry about is marking which section is supposed to be a heading.

3

Note

Although HTML doesn't say much about how a page looks when it's viewed, cascading style sheets (CSS) enable you to apply advanced formatting to HTML tags. Many changes in HTML 4.0 favor the use of CSS tags. After you've learned about the basic HTML tags, you'll begin to learn more about CSS in Day 4, "Begin with the Basics," and Day 12, "XHTML and Style Sheets."

NEW TERM Web browsers, in addition to providing the networking functions to retrieve pages from the Web, double as HTML formatters. When you read an HTML page into a browser such as Netscape or Internet Explorer, the browser interprets, or *parses*, the HTML tags and formats the text and images on the screen. The browser has mappings between the names of page elements and actual styles on the screen; for example, headings might be in a larger font than the text on the rest of the page. The browser also wraps all the text so that it fits into the current width of the window.

Different browsers running on diverse platforms might have various style mappings for each page element. Some browsers might use different font styles than others. For example, a browser on a desktop computer might display italics as italics, whereas a handheld device or mobile phone might use reverse text or underlining on systems that don't have italic fonts. Or it might put a heading in all capital letters instead of a larger font.

What this means to you as a Web page designer is that the pages you create with HTML might look radically different from system to system and from browser to browser. The actual information and links inside those pages will still be there, but the onscreen appearance will change. You can design a Web page so that it looks perfect on your computer system, but when someone else reads it on a different system, it might look entirely different (and it might very well be entirely unreadable.

Why It Works This Way

If you're used to writing and designing documents that will wind up printed on paper, this concept might seem almost perverse. No control over the layout of a page? The whole design can vary depending on where the page is viewed? This is awful! Why on earth would a system work like this?

Remember in Day 1, "The World of the World Wide Web," when I mentioned that one of the cool things about the Web is that it is cross-platform and that Web pages can be viewed on any computer system, on any size screen, with any graphics display? If the final goal of Web publishing is for your pages to be readable by anyone in the world, you can't count on your readers having the same computer systems, the same size screens, the same number of colors, or the same fonts that you have. The Web takes into account all these differences and allows all browsers and all computer systems to be on equal ground.

The Web, as a design medium, is not a new form of paper. The Web is an entirely different medium, with its own constraints and goals that are very different from working with paper. The most important rules of Web page design, as I'll keep harping on throughout this book, are the following:

Do	**DON'T**
Do design your pages so they work in most browsers.	**Don't** design your pages based on what they look like on your computer system and on your browser.
Do focus on clear, well-structured content that is easy to read and understand.	

Throughout this book, I'll show you examples of HTML code and what they look like when displayed. In examples where browsers display code very differently, I'll give you a comparison of how a snippet of code looks in two very different browsers. Through these examples, you'll get an idea for how different the same page can look from browser to browser.

Note

Although this rule of designing by structure and not by appearance is the way to produce good HTML, when you surf the Web, you might be surprised that the vast majority of Web sites seem to have been designed with appearance in mind—usually appearance in a particular browser such as Netscape Navigator or Microsoft Internet Explorer. Don't be swayed by these designs. If you stick to the rules I suggest, in the end, your Web pages and Web sites will be even more successful simply because more people can easily read and use them.

HTML Is a Markup Language

NEW TERM HTML is a *markup language*. Writing in a markup language means that you start with the text of your page and add special tags around words and paragraphs. The tags indicate the different parts of the page and produce different effects in the browser. You'll learn more about tags and how they're used in the next section.

HTML has a defined set of tags you can use. You can't make up your own tags to create new appearances or features. And, just to make sure that things are really confusing, various browsers support different sets of tags. To further explain this, take a brief look at the history of HTML.

A Brief History of HTML Tags

The base set of HTML tags, the lowest common denominator, is referred to as HTML 2.0. HTML 2.0 is the old standard for HTML (a written specification for it is developed and maintained by the W3C) and the set of tags that all browsers must support. In the next few days, you'll primarily learn to use tags that were first introduced in HTML 2.0.

The HTML 3.2 specification was developed in early 1996. Several software vendors, including IBM, Microsoft, Netscape Communications Corporation, Novell, SoftQuad, Spyglass, and Sun Microsystems, joined with the W3C to develop this specification. Some of the primary additions to HTML 3.2 included features such as tables, applets, and text flow around images. HTML 3.2 also provided full backward-compatibility with the existing HTML 2.0 standard.

Note

The enhancements introduced in HTML 3.2 are covered later in this book. You'll learn more about tables in Day 10, "Tables." Day 13, "Multimedia: Adding Sounds, Videos, and More" tells you how to use Java applets.

HTML 4.0, first introduced in 1997, incorporated many new features that gave you greater control than HTML 2.0 and 3.2 in how you designed your pages. Like HTML 2.0 and 3.2, the W3C maintains the HTML 4.0 standard. Although both Internet Explorer 4 and Netscape Navigator 4 support most HTML 4.0 features, users with browsers older than that won't be able to view HTML 4.0 features such as cascading style sheets and dynamic HTML.

Note

Cascading style sheets and dynamic HTML are additional Web technologies that work in conjunction with HTML to give you additional control over the appearance of your Web pages. Style sheets are discussed further in Day 12, "XHTML and Style Sheets." See Day 15, "Using Dynamic HTML" for an introduction to the capabilities of Dynamic HTML.

Framesets (originally introduced in Netscape 2.0) and floating frames (originally introduced in Internet Explorer 3.0) became an official part of the HTML 4.0 specification. Framesets are discussed in more detail in Day 11, "Frames and Linked Windows." We also see additional improvements to table formatting and rendering. By far, however, the most important change in HTML 4.0 was its increased integration with style sheets.

Note

If you're interested in how HTML development is working and just exactly what's going on at the W3C, check out the pages for HTML at the Consortium's site at http://www.w3.org/pub/WWW/MarkUp/.

In addition to the tags defined by the various levels of HTML, individual browser companies also implement browser-specific extensions to HTML. Netscape and Microsoft are particularly guilty of creating extensions, and they offer many new features unique to their browsers.

Confused yet? You're not alone. Even Web designers with years of experience and hundreds of pages under their belts have to struggle with the problem of which set of tags to choose to strike a balance between wide support for a design (using HTML 3.2- and 2.0-level tags) or having more flexibility in layout but less consistency across browsers (HTML 4.0 or specific browser extensions). Keeping track of all this information can be really confusing. Throughout this book, as I introduce each tag, I'll let you know which version of HTML the tag belongs to, how widely supported it is, and how to use it to best effect in a wide variety of browsers.

Preparing for the Future with XHTML 1.0

The Internet is no longer limited to computer hardware and software. WebTV enables you to access the Internet, giving you more reason to become a couch potato. Personal Information Managers and palmtop computers enable you to access the Internet while you're on the road. More and more people are accessing the Internet with mobile phones and other wireless devices. Special interfaces and hardware allow physically challenged individuals to access the Internet. As it has matured, the Internet has become an effective means of communication and education for the masses.

Many of the newer portable technologies, however, pose problems for the old HTML specification. They simply don't have the processing power of a desktop computer, and are not as forgiving of poorly written HTML. The developers of the HTML specification have struggled to accommodate these ongoing changes, and the limitations of HTML have become evident. We are stretching and distorting the HTML specification far beyond its capabilities. As a result, there probably *won't* be an HTML 5.

The future of the Internet demands a markup language that is more extensible and portable than HTML. The direction is heading toward the use of XML (short for *Extensible Markup Language*), a subset of SGML that allows for custom tags to be processed. And here is where XHTML 1.0 comes in to play.

XHTML 1.0 is written in XML, and is the up-and-coming standard that will help Web designers prepare for the future. Documents written in XHTML can be viewed on current browsers, but at the same time they're valid XML documents. The purpose of this book is not only to teach you HTML 4.0, but also to teach you how to format your HTML so that it's compliant with the XHTML 1.0 specification.

Technically, XHTML 1.0 and HTML 4 are *very* similar. The tags and attributes are virtually the same, but a few simple rules have to be followed in order to make sure that a document is compliant with the XHTML 1.0 specification. Throughout this book, I'll explain how to deal with the different HTML tags to make sure that your pages are readable and still look good in all kinds of browsers.

What HTML Files Look Like

Pages written in HTML are plain text files (ASCII), which means that they contain no platform- or program-specific information. Any editor that supports text (which should be just about any editor—more about this subject in "Programs to Help You Write HTML" later in this chapter) can read them. HTML files contain the following:

- The text of the page itself
- HTML tags that indicate page elements, structure, formatting, and hypertext links to other pages or to included media

Most HTML tags look something like the following:

`<thetagname>` affected text `</thetagname>`

The tag name itself (here, thetagname) is enclosed in brackets (< >). HTML tags generally have a beginning and an ending tag surrounding the text they affect. The beginning tag "turns on" a feature (such as headings, bold, and so on), and the ending tag turns it off. Closing tags have the tag name preceded by a slash (/). The opening tag (for example, <p> for paragraphs) and closing tag (for example, </p> for paragraphs) compose what is officially called an *HTML element*.

> **Caution**
>
> Be aware of the difference between the forward slash (/) mentioned with relation to tags, and backslashes (\), which are used by DOS and Windows in directory references on hard drives (as in C:\window or other directory paths). If you accidentally use the backslash in place of a forward slash in HTML, the browser won't recognize the ending tags.

Not all HTML tags have both an opening and closing tag. Some tags are only one-sided, and still other tags are "containers" that hold extra information and text inside the brackets. XHTML 1.0, however, requires that *all* tags be closed. You'll learn the proper way to open and close the tags as the book progresses.

Another difference between HTML 4.0 and XHTML 1.0 relates to usage of lowercase tags and attributes. HTML tags are not case sensitive; that is, you can specify them in uppercase, lowercase, or in any mixture. So, <HTML> is the same as <html>, which is the same as <HtMl>. This is not the case for XHTML 1.0, where all tag and attribute names must be written in lowercase. To get you thinking in this mindset, the examples in this book display tag and attribute names in bold lowercase text.

Exercise 3.1: Creating Your First HTML Page

▼ To Do

Now that you've seen what HTML looks like, it's your turn to create your own Web page. Start with a simple example so that you can get a basic feel for HTML.

To get started writing HTML, you don't need a Web server, a Web provider, or even a connection to the Web itself. All you really need is an application where you can create your HTML files and at least one browser to view them. You can write, link, and test whole suites of Web pages without even touching a network. In fact, that's what you're

▼ going to do for the majority of this book. I'll talk later about publishing everything on the Web so that other people can see your work.

In order to get started, you'll need a text editor. A text editor is a program that saves files in ASCII format. ASCII format is just plain text, with no font formatting or special characters. In Windows, Notepad and Microsoft Wordpad are good basic text editors (and free with your system). Shareware text editors are also available for various operating systems, including DOS, Windows 3.1, Windows 95/98, Windows NT, Macintosh, and Linux. If you point your Web browser to `www.download.com` and enter Text Editors as a search term, you will find many resources available to download.

If you prefer to work in a word processor such as Microsoft Word, don't panic. You can still write pages in word processors just as you would in text editors, although doing so is more complicated. When you use the Save or Save As command, you'll see a menu of formats you can use to save the file. One of them should be Text Only, Text Only with Line Breaks, or DOS Text. All these options will save your file as plain ASCII text, just as if you were using a text editor. For HTML files, if you have a choice between DOS Text and just Text, use DOS Text, and use the Line Breaks option if you have it.

Caution
If you do use a word processor for your HTML development, be very careful. Many recent word processors are including HTML modes or mechanisms for creating HTML or XML code. This feature can produce unusual results or files that simply don't behave as you expect. If you run into trouble with a word processor, try using a text editor and see whether it helps.

What about the plethora of free and commercial HTML editors that claim to help you write HTML more easily? Most of them are text editors that simplify common tasks associated with HTML coding. If you've got one of these editors, go ahead and use it. If you've got a fancier editor that claims to hide all the HTML for you, put it aside for the next couple of days and try using a plain text editor just for a little while. Appendix A, "Sources for Further Information," lists many URLs where you can download free and commercial HTML editors that are available for different platforms. They appear in the section titled "HTML Editors and Converters."

Open your text editor, and type the following code. You don't have to understand what any of it means at this point. You'll learn more about much of this today and tomorrow.
▼ This simple example is just to get you started.

```
<!DOCTYPE html PUBLIC "-//W3C//DTD XHTML 1.0 Transitional//EN"
 "http://www.w3.org/TR/xhtml1/DTD/transitional.dtd">
<html>
<head>
<title>My Sample HTML page</title>
</head>
<body>
<h1>This is an HTML Page</h1>
</body>
</html>
```

Note

Note that the <!DOCTYPE> tag in the previous example doesn't appear in lowercase like the rest of the tags. This tag is an exception to the XHTML rule and should appear in uppercase. This is explained in detail on Day 12.

After you create your HTML file, save it to your hard disk. Remember that if you're using a word processor, choose Save As and make sure you're saving it as text only. When you choose a name for the file, follow these two rules:

- The filename should have an extension of .html (.htm on DOS or Windows systems that have only three-character extensions)—for example, myfile.html, text.html, or index.htm. Most Web software will require your files to have these extensions, so get into the habit of doing it now.

- Use small, simple names. Don't include spaces or special characters (bullets, accented characters)—just letters and numbers are fine.

Exercise 3.2: Viewing the Result

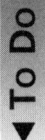

Now that you have an HTML file, start up your Web browser. You don't have to be connected to the network because you're not going to be opening pages at any other site. Your browser or network connection software might complain about the lack of a network connection, but usually it will give up and let you use it anyway.

After your browser is running, look for a menu item or button labeled Open Page, Open File, or maybe just Open. Choosing it will enable you to browse your local disk. The Open command (or its equivalent) opens a document from the Web or from your local disk, parses it, and displays it. By using your browser and the Open command, you can write and test your HTML files on your computer in the privacy of your own home.

If you don't see something similar to what is shown in Figure 3.2 (for example, if parts are missing or if everything looks like a heading), go back into your text editor and compare your file to the example. Make sure that all your tags have closing tags and that all

▼ your < characters are matched by > characters. You don't have to quit your browser to do so; just fix the file and save it again under the same name.

FIGURE 3.2

The sample HTML file.

▲ Next, go back to your browser. Locate and choose a menu item or button called Reload (for Netscape users) or Refresh (for Internet Explorer users). The browser will read the new version of your file, and voilà! You can edit and preview and edit and preview until you get the file right.

If you're getting the actual HTML text repeated in your browser rather than what's shown in Figure 3.2, make sure that your HTML file has an .html or .htm extension. This file extension tells your browser that it is an HTML file. The extension is important.

If things are going really wrong—if you're getting a blank screen or you're getting some really strange characters—something is wrong with your original file. If you've been using a word processor to edit your files, try opening your saved HTML file in a plain text editor (again Notepad or SimpleText will work just fine). If the text editor can't read the file, or if the result is garbled, you haven't saved the original file in the right format. Go back into your original editor, and try saving the file as text only again. Then try viewing the file again in your browser until you get it right.

A Note About Formatting

When an HTML page is parsed by a browser, any formatting you might have done by hand—that is, any extra spaces, tabs, returns, and so on—are all ignored. The only thing that formats an HTML page is an HTML tag. If you spend hours carefully editing a plain text file to have nicely formatted paragraphs and columns of numbers but don't include any tags, when you read the page into an HTML browser, all the text will flow into one paragraph. All your work will have been in vain.

Note

The one exception to this rule is a tag called <pre>. You'll learn about this tag in Day 6, "More Text Formatting with HTML."

3

The advantage of having all whitespace (spaces, tabs, returns) ignored is that you can put your tags wherever you want.

The following examples all produce the same output. Try them!

```
<h1>If music be the food of love, play on.</h1>

<h1>
If music be the food of love, play on.
</h1>

<h1>
If music be the food of love, play on.                </h1>

<h1>    If    music    be    the    food    of    love,
play    on. </h1 >
```

Programs to Help You Write HTML

You might be thinking that all this tag stuff is a real pain, especially if you didn't get that small example right the first time. (Don't fret about it; I didn't get that example right the first time, and I created it.) You have to remember all the tags, and you have to type them in right and close each one. What a hassle!

Many freeware and shareware programs are available for editing HTML files. Most of these programs essentially are text editors with extra menu items or buttons that insert the appropriate HTML tags into your text. HTML-based text editors are particularly nice for two reasons: You don't have to remember all the tags, and you don't have to take the time to type them all.

Many editors on the market purport to be WYSIWYG. As you learned earlier today, there's really no such thing as WYSIWYG when you're dealing with HTML. "What You Get" can vary wildly based on the browser.

With that said, as long as you're aware that the result of working in those editors can vary, using WYSIWYG editors can be a quick way to create simple HTML files. For professional Web development and for using many of the very advanced features, however, WYSIWYG editors usually fall short, and you'll need to go "under the hood" to play with the HTML code anyhow. Even if you intend to use a WYSIWYG editor for the bulk of your HTML work, bear with me for the next couple of days and try these examples in text editors so that you get a feel for what HTML really is before you decide to move on to an editor that hides the tags.

Caution WYSIWYG editors tend to work best with files they've created themselves. If you have some existing HTML files that you need to edit, opening them in a WYSIWYG editor can do more harm than good, particularly if the files were created in a different WYSIWYG editor.

In addition to HTML and WYSIWYG editors, you also can use converters, which take files from many popular word processing programs and convert them to HTML. With a simple set of templates, you can write your pages entirely in your favorite program and then convert the result when you're done.

In many cases, converters can be extremely useful, particularly for putting existing documents on the Web as fast as possible. However, converters suffer from many of the same problems as WYSIWYG editors. The results can vary from browser to browser, and many newer or advanced features aren't available in the converters. Also, most converter programs are fairly limited, not necessarily by their own features, but mostly by the limitations in HTML itself. No amount of fancy converting is going to make HTML do things that it can't do already. If a particular capability doesn't exist in HTML, the converter cannot do anything to solve that problem. (In fact, the converter might end up doing strange things to your HTML files, causing you more work than if you just did all the formatting yourself.)

As previously mentioned, Appendix A lists many of the Web page editors that are currently available. For now, if you have a simple HTML editor, feel free to use it for the examples in this book. If all you have is a text editor, no problem; you'll just have to do a little more typing.

Summary

Today, you learned some basic points about what HTML is, and how you define a text document as a Web page. You learned a bit about the history of HTML and the reasons why the HTML specification has changed several times since the beginning. Using some basic tags that I'll explain tomorrow, you created your first Web page. It wasn't so bad, was it? In tomorrow's lesson, you'll expand on this and will learn more about adding headings, text, and lists to your pages.

Workshop

Now that you've had an introduction to HTML, and a taste of creating your first very simple Web page, here's a workshop that will guide you toward more of what you'll be learning. A couple of questions and answers that relate to HTML formatting are followed by a brief quiz and answers about HTML. Exercises prompt you to examine the code of a more advanced page in your browser.

Q&A

Q Can I do *any* formatting of text in HTML?

A You can do some formatting to strings of characters; for example, making a word or two bold. Tags in HTML 3.2 (the predecessor to HTML 4.0) enabled you to change the font size and color of the text in your Web page (for readers using browsers that support the tags—including Netscape and Microsoft Internet Explorer), but these tags have given way to CSS formatting in HTML 4.0. You'll learn some formatting tricks in Day 6.

Q I'm using Windows. My word processor won't let me save a text file with an extension that's anything except `.txt`. If I type in `index.html`, my word processor saves the file as `index.html.txt`. What can I do?

A You can rename your files after you've saved them so that they have an `html` or `htm` extension, but having to do so can be annoying if you have a large number of files. Consider using a text editor or HTML editor for your Web pages.

Quiz

1. What does HTML stand for?
2. What is the primary function of HTML?
3. Why doesn't HTML control the layout of a page?
4. Which version of HTML provides the lowest common denominator of HTML tags?
5. What is the basic structure of an HTML tag?

Quiz Answers

1. HTML stands for Hypertext Markup Language.
2. HTML defines a set of common styles for Web pages (headings, paragraphs, lists, tables, character styles, and more).

3. HTML doesn't control the layout of a page because it is designed to be cross-platform. It takes the differences of many platforms into account and allows all browsers and all computer systems to be on equal ground.

4. The lowest common denominator for HTML tags is HTML 2.0, the oldest standard for HTML. This is the set of tags that *all* browsers *must* support. HTML 2.0 tags can be used anywhere.

5. Most HTML elements consist of opening and closing tags, and they surround the text that they affect. The tags are enclosed in brackets (<>). The beginning tag turns on a feature, and the ending tag, which is preceded by a forward slash (/), turns it off.

Exercises

1. Before you actually start writing a meatier HTML page, getting a feel for what an HTML page looks like certainly helps. Luckily, you can find plenty of source material to look at. Every page that comes over the wire to your browser is in HTML format. (You almost never see the codes in your browser; all you see is the final result.)

Most Web browsers have a way of letting you see the HTML source of a Web page. If you're using Internet Explorer 5.5, for example, navigate to the Web page that you want to look at. Choose View, Source to display the source code in a text window. In Netscape Navigator/Communicator 4.5, choose View, Page Source.

Tip

In some browsers, you cannot directly view the source of a Web page, but you can save the current page as a file to your local disk. In a dialog box for saving the file, you might find a menu of formats—for example, Text, PostScript, or HTML. You can save the current page as HTML and then open that file in a text editor or word processor to see the HTML source.

Try going to a typical home page and then viewing its source. For example, Figure 3.3 shows the home page for AltaVista, a popular search page at http://www.altavista.com/.

The HTML source code of the AltaVista home page looks something like Figure 3.4.

2. Try viewing the source of your own favorite Web pages. You should start seeing some similarities in the way pages are organized and get a feel for the kinds of tags that HTML uses. You can learn a lot about HTML by comparing the text onscreen with the source for that text.

FIGURE 3.3

AltaVista home page.

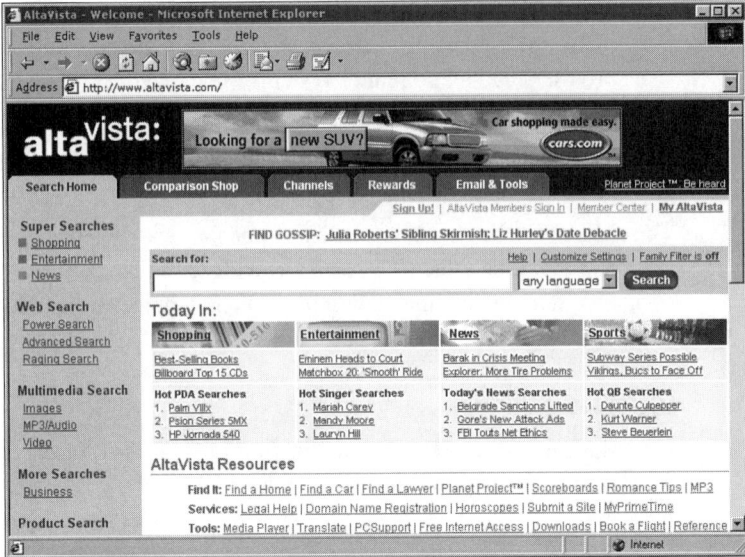

FIGURE 3.4

Some HTML source code.

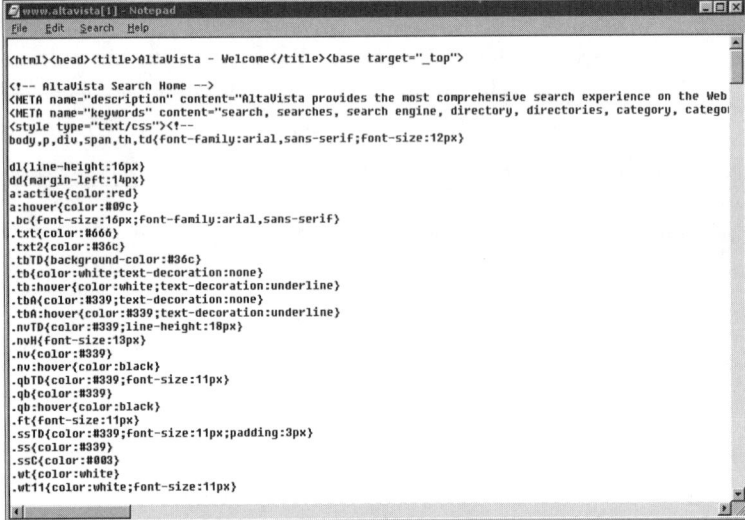

PART 2

Creating Simple Web Pages

DAY 4

Begin with the Basics

Yesterday, you learned about the World Wide Web, how to organize and plan your Web sites, and why you need to use HTML to create a Web page. You even created your first very simple Web page. Today, you'll learn about each of the basic HTML tags in more depth, and begin writing Web pages with headings, paragraphs, and several different types of lists. Today we'll focus on the following topics and HTML tags:

- Tags for overall page structure: `<html>`, `<head>`, and `<body>`
- Tags for titles, headings, and paragraphs: `<title>`, `<h1>` through `<h6>`, and `<p>`
- Tags for comments: `<!--...-->`
- Tags for lists: `<ol>`, `<ul>`, `<li>`, `<dt>`, and `<dd>`

Structuring Your HTML

HTML defines three tags that are used to describe the page's overall structure and provide some simple "header" information. These three tags—`<html>`, `<head>`, and `<body>`—identify your page to browsers or HTML tools. They also provide simple information about the page (such as its title or its author) before loading the entire thing. The page structure tags don't affect what the page looks like when it's displayed; they're only there to help tools that interpret or filter HTML files.

In the strict HTML definition, these tags are optional. If your page does not contain them, browsers usually can read the page anyway. These tags, however, *are* required elements in XHTML 1.0. Tools and browsers that need these tags also will come along. You should get into the habit of including the page structure tags now.

Note

Although it's not a page structure tag, the XHTML 1.0 recommendation includes one additional requirement for your Web pages. The first line of each page must include a DOCTYPE identifier that defines the XHTML 1.0 version to which your page conforms, and the document type definition (DTD) that defines the specification. This is followed by the <html>, <head>, and <body> tags. In the following example, the XHTML 1.0 Strict document type appears before the page structure tags:

```
<!DOCTYPE html PUBLIC "-//W3C//DTD XHTML 1.0 Strict//EN"
    "http://www.w3.org/TR/xhtml11/DTD/strict.dtd">
<html>
<head>
<title>Page Title</title>
</head>
<body>
...your page content...
</body>
</html>
```

Three types of HTML 4.0 document types are specified in the XHTML 1.0 specification: Strict, Transitional, and Frameset. Refer to Day 12, "XHTML and Style Sheets," for more information about the DOCTYPE tag, and Day 18, "Designing for the Real World" for more information about the differences between Strict, Transitional, and Frameset document types.

The <html> Tag

The first page structure tag in every HTML page is the <html> tag. It indicates that the content of this file is in the HTML language. In the XHTML 1.0 recommendation, the <html> tag should follow the DOCTYPE identifier (as mentioned in the previous note) as shown in the following example.

All the text and HTML commands in your HTML page should go within the beginning and ending HTML tags, like the following:

```
<!DOCTYPE html PUBLIC "-//W3C//DTD XHTML 1.0 Transitional//EN"
 "http://www.w3.org/TR/xhtml1/DTD/transitional.dtd">
<html>
...your page...
</html>
```

Before XHTML 1.0, you could play fast and loose with the tags in your documents. In order for your HTML to be valid, you needed to include the <html> tag around all the other tags in your document, but none of the popular browsers cared if you really did. If you left them out, or included the beginning <html> tag but not the closing tag, or whatever, the browser would still display the document without complaining. With XHTML 1.0, your HTML documents must also be valid XML documents, so the rules are much more strict. XML documents require all the elements in a file to be enclosed within a root element. In XHTML 1.0 documents, the root element is the <html> tag.

The <head> Tag

The <head> tag specifies that the lines within the beginning and ending points of the tag are the prologue to the rest of the file. Generally, only a few tags go into the <head> portion of the page (most notably, the page title, described later). You should never put any of the text of your page into the header.

Here's a typical example of how you properly use the <head> tag (you'll learn about <title> later):

```
<!DOCTYPE html PUBLIC "-//W3C//DTD XHTML 1.0 Transitional//EN"
 "http://www.w3.org/TR/xhtml1/DTD/transitional.dtd">
<html>
<head>
<title>This is the Title. It will be explained later on</title>
</head>
...your page...
</html>
```

The <body> Tag

The remainder of your HTML page (represented in the following example as ...your page...) is enclosed within a <body> tag. This includes all the text and other content (links, pictures, and so on). In combination with the <html> and <head> tags, your code resembles the following:

4

```
<!DOCTYPE html PUBLIC "-//W3C//DTD XHTML 1.0 Transitional//EN"
 "http://www.w3.org/TR/xhtml1/DTD/transitional.dtd">
<html>
<head>
<title>This is the Title. It will be explained later on</title>
</head>
<body>
...your page...
</body>
</html>
```

You might notice here that each HTML tag is nested. That is, both <body> and </body> tags go inside both <html> tags; the same with both <head> tags. All HTML tags work this way, forming individual nested sections of text. You should be careful never to overlap tags; that is, to do something like the following:

```
<!DOCTYPE html PUBLIC "-//W3C//DTD XHTML 1.0 Transitional//EN"
 "http://www.w3.org/TR/xhtml1/DTD/transitional.dtd">
<html>
<head>
<body>
</head>
</body>
</html>
```

Whenever you close an HTML tag, make sure that you're closing the most recently opened tag. (You'll learn more about closing tags as you go on.)

**Note**

> In HTML 4.0 and earlier, some tags are optionally closed. In other tags, closing tags are forbidden. In the XHTML 1.0 recommendation, *all* tags *must* be closed. The whys, hows, and wheres of how to close these tags will be discussed in more detail on Day 12. However, in preparation for what you will learn there, the examples shown in this book will display the proper way to close tags so that older browsers will interpret XHTML 1.0 closures correctly.

The Title

Each HTML page needs a title to indicate what the page describes. The title is used by your browser's bookmarks or hotlist program, and also by other programs that catalog Web pages. Use the <title> tag to give a page a title.

The *title* indicates what your Web page is about and is used to refer to that page in bookmark or hotlist entries. Titles also appear in the title bar of graphical browsers such as Netscape Navigator and Microsoft Internet Explorer.

`<title>` tags always go inside the page header (the `<head>` tags) and describe the contents of the page, as follows:

```
<!DOCTYPE html PUBLIC "-//W3C//DTD XHTML 1.0 Transitional//EN"
 "http://www.w3.org/TR/xhtml1/DTD/transitional.dtd">
<html>
<head>
<title>The Lion, The Witch, and the Wardrobe</title>
</head>
<body>
...your page...
</body>
</html>
```

You can have only one title in the page, and that title can contain only plain text; that is, no other tags should appear inside the title.

Try to choose a title that is both short and descriptive of the content. Additionally, your title should be relevant even out of context. If someone browsing on the Web follows a random link and ends up on this page, or if a person finds your title in a friend's browser history list, would he have any idea what this page is about? You might not intend the page to be used independently of the pages you specifically linked to it, but, because anyone can link to any page at any time, be prepared for that consequence and pick a helpful title.

 Note

When search engines index your pages, each page title is captured and listed in the search results. The more descriptive your page title, the more likely it is that someone will choose your page from all of the search results.

Also, because most browsers put the title in the title bar of the window, you might have a limited number of words available. (Although the text within the `<title>` tag can be of any length, it might be cut off by the browser when it's displayed.) The following are some other examples of good titles:

```
<title>Poisonous Plants of North America</title>
<title>Image Editing: A Tutorial</title>
<title>Upcoming Cemetery Tours, Summer 1999</title>
<title>Installing the Software: Opening the CD Case</title>
<title>Laura Lemay's Awesome Home Page</title>
```

Here are some not-so-good titles:

```
<title>Part Two</title>
<title>An Example</title>
<title>Nigel Franklin Hobbes</title>
<title>Minutes of the Second Meeting of the Fourth Conference of the
Committee for the Preservation of English Roses, Day Four, After Lunch</title>
```

Figure 4.1 shows how a title looks in Internet Explorer.

 **INPUT**

```
<title>Poisonous Plants of North America</title>
```

 **OUTPUT**

FIGURE 4.1

*A page containing
only header
elements.*

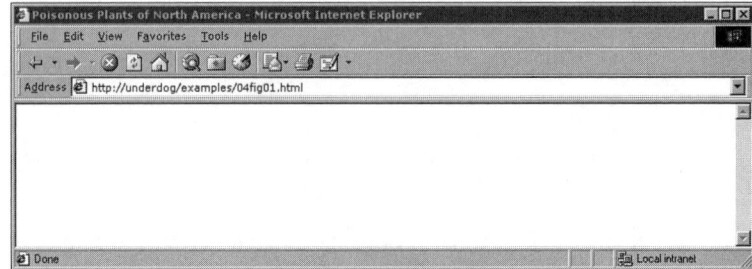

Headings

You use headings to divide sections of text. HTML defines six levels of headings.
Heading tags look like the following:

```
<h1>Installing Your Safetee Lock</h1>
```

The numbers indicate heading levels (h1 through h6). The headings, when they're displayed, are not numbered. They are displayed either in larger or bolder text, are centered
or underlined, or are capitalized—so that they stand out from regular text.

Think of the headings as items in an outline. If the text you're writing has a structure,
use the headings to indicate that structure, as shown in the following code:

```
<h1>Mythology Through the Ages</h1>
    <h2>Common Mythological Themes</h2>
    <h2>Earliest Known Myths</h2>
    <h2>Origins of Mythology</h2>
        <h3>Mesopotamian Mythology</h3>
        <h3>Egyptian Mythology</h3>
            <h4>The Story of Isis and Osiris</h4>
            <h4>Horus and Set: The Battle of Good vs. Evil</h4>
            <h4>The Twelve Hours of the Underworld</h4>
            <h4>The River Styx</h4>
    <h2>History in Myth</h2>
```

(Notice that I've indented the headings in this example to better show the hierarchy. They don't have to be indented in your page; in fact, the indenting will be ignored by the browser.)

Unlike titles, headings can be any length, including many lines of text. (Because headings are emphasized, however, having many lines of emphasized text might be tiring to read.)

A common practice is to use a first-level heading at the top of your page to either duplicate the title (which usually is displayed elsewhere), or to provide a shorter or less contextual form of the title. If you have a page that shows several examples of folding bed sheets—for example, part of a long presentation on how to fold bed sheets—the title might look something like the following:

```
<title>How to Fold Sheets: Some Examples</title>
```

The topmost heading, however, might just be as follows:

```
<h1>Examples</h1>
```

Don't use headings to display text in boldface type or to make certain parts of your page stand out more. Although the result might look cool on your browser, you don't know what it will look like when other people use their browsers to read your page. Other browsers might number headings or format them in a manner that you don't expect. Also, tools to create searchable indexes of Web pages might extract your headings to indicate the important parts of a page. By using headings for something other than an actual heading, you might be foiling those search programs and creating strange results.

Figure 4.2 shows various headings as they appear in Internet Explorer.

INPUT

```
<h1>Mythology Through the Ages</h1>
    <h2>Common Mythological Themes</h2>
    <h2>Earliest Known Myths</h2>
    <h2>Origins of Mythology</h2>
        <h3>Mesopotamian Mythology</h3>
        <h3>Egyptian Mythology</h3>
            <h4>The Story of Isis and Osiris</h4>
            <h4>Horus and Set: The Battle of Good vs. Evil</h4>
            <h4>The Twelve Hours of the Underworld</h4>
            <h4>The River Styx</h4>
    <h2>History in Myth</h2>
```

FIGURE 4.2

HTML heading elements.

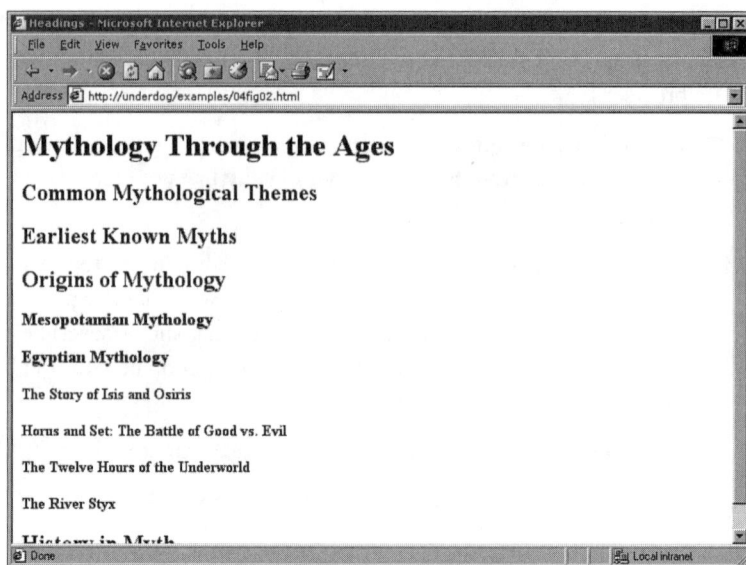

Paragraphs

Now that you have a page title and several headings, you can add some ordinary paragraphs to the page.

The first version of HTML specified the <p> tag as a one-sided tag. There was no corresponding </p>, and the <p> tag was used to indicate the end of a paragraph (a paragraph break), not the beginning. So paragraphs in the first version of HTML looked like the following:

```
Slowly and deliberately, Enigern approached the mighty dragon.
A rustle in the trees of the nearby forest distracted his attention
for a brief moment, a near fatal mistake for the brave knight.<p>
The dragon lunged at him, searing Enigern's armor with a rapid
blast of fiery breath. Enigern fell to the ground as the dragon
hovered over him. He quickly drew his sword and thrust it into the
dragon's chest.<p>
```

Most early browsers assumed that paragraphs would be formatted this way. When they came across a <p> tag, these older browsers started a new line and added some extra vertical space between the line that just ended and the next one.

In the HTML 4.0 specification (as with HTML 3.2 and 2.0), and as supported by most current browsers, the paragraph tag is revised. In these versions of HTML, the paragraph tags are two-sided (<p>...</p>), but <p> indicates the beginning of the paragraph. Also, the closing tag (</p>) is optional. So the Enigern story would look like this in the current versions of HTML:

```
<p>Slowly and deliberately, Enigern approached the mighty dragon.
A rustle in the trees of the nearby forest distracted his attention
for a brief moment, a near fatal mistake for the brave knight.</p>
<p>The dragon lunged at him, searing Enigern's armor with a rapid
blast of fiery breath. Enigern fell to the ground as the dragon
hovered over him. He quickly drew his sword and thrust it into the
dragon's chest.</p>
```

Getting into the habit of using <p> at the start of a paragraph is a good idea; it will become important when you learn how to align text left, right, or centered. Older browsers will accept this form of paragraphs just fine. Although at one time it was optional to use the closing </p> tag, it's required under the XHTML 1.0 recommendation because all tags must be closed. For that reason, I'll use the closing </p> throughout this book.

Some people prefer to use extra <p> tags between paragraphs to spread out the text on the page. Once again, here's the cardinal reminder: Design for content, not for appearance. Someone with a text-based browser or a small screen is not going to care much about the extra space you so carefully put in, and some browsers might even collapse multiple <p> tags into one, erasing all your careful formatting.

Figure 4.3 shows another paragraph about Enigern and the dragon in Internet Explorer.

INPUT

```
<p>The dragon fell to the ground, releasing an anguished cry and
seething in pain. The thrust of Enigern's sword proved fatal as
the dragon breathed its last breath. Now Enigern was free to
release Lady Aelfleada from her imprisonment in the dragon's lair. </p>
```

OUTPUT

FIGURE 4.3

An HTML paragraph.

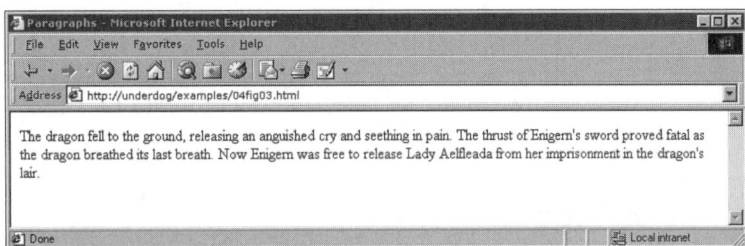

Lists, Lists, and More Lists

In addition to headings and paragraphs, probably the most common HTML element you'll use is the list. After this section, you'll not only know how to create a list in HTML, but also how to create several different types of lists—a list for every occasion!

HTML 4.0 defines these three types of lists:

- Numbered, or ordered lists, typically labeled with numbers
- Bulleted, or unordered lists, typically labeled with bullets or some other symbol
- Glossary lists, in which each item in the list has a term and a definition for that term, arranged so that the term somehow is highlighted or drawn out from the text

Note

You'll also notice a couple of deprecated list types in the HTML 4.0 specification: menu lists (<menu>) and directory lists (<dir>). These two list types are not frequently used, and support for them varies in browsers. Instead, use the <ul> (or bulleted list) tags in place of these deprecated list types.

NEW TERM A *deprecated* tag or attribute is one that is still supported but that has been outdated by newer methods.

Note

Browsers generally continue to support deprecated elements for reasons of backward compatibility. There is still a need to learn about and use the deprecated elements if you expect that a portion of your audience will be using HTML 3.2-level browsers, such as Netscape Navigator 3 or earlier or Microsoft Internet Explorer 3 or earlier. Because deprecated elements might become obsolete in future versions of HTML, however, you should try to use the newer methods when possible.

Note

The majority of tags and attributes that are deprecated in HTML 4.0 are done so in favor of using Cascading Style Sheet (CSS) properties and values, which you will learn more about on Day 12.

List Tags

All the list tags have the following common elements:

- The entire list is surrounded by the appropriate opening and closing tag for the type of list (for example, <ul> and </ul>, or <ol> and </ol>).
- Each list item within the list has its own tag: <dt> and <dd> for the glossary lists, and <li> for all the other lists.

Note

> The closing tags for <dd>, <dt>, and <li> are optional in HTML. To comply with XHTML 1.0, use closing tags of </dd>, </dt>, </li>.

Although the tags and the list items can appear in any arrangement in your HTML code, I prefer to arrange the HTML for producing lists so that the list tags are on their own lines, and each new item starts on a new line. This way, you can easily choose the whole list as well as the individual elements. In other words, I find the following arrangement

```
<p>Dante's Divine Comedy consists of three books:</p>
<ul>
<li>The Inferno</li>
<li>The Purgatorio</li>
<li>The Paradiso</li>
</ul>
```

easier to read than

```
<p>Dante's Divine Comedy consists of three books:</p>
<ul><li>The Inferno</li><li>The Purgatorio</li><li>The Paradiso</li></ul>
```

although both result in the same output in the browser.

4

Numbered Lists

Numbered lists are surrounded by the <ol>...</ol> tags (ol stands for Ordered List), and each item within the list begins with the <li> (List Item) tag.

Note

> In HTML, the <li> tag is one-sided; you do not have to specify the closing tag because it is optional. The existence of the next <li> (or the closing </ol> or </ul> tag) indicates the end of that item in the list. However, to properly form your documents in XHTML 1.0, you must use a closing tag of </li>.

When the browser displays an ordered list, it numbers (and often indents) each of the elements sequentially. You do not have to perform the numbering yourself, and, if you add or delete items, the browser will renumber them the next time the page is loaded.

NEW TERM *Ordered lists* are lists in which each item is numbered.

Use numbered lists only when you want to indicate that the elements are ordered—that is, that they must appear or occur in a specific order. Ordered lists are good for steps to follow or instructions to the readers. If you just want to indicate that something has a number of elements that can appear in any order, use an unordered list instead.

So, the following, for example, is an ordered list of steps that tell you how to install a new operating system, with each list item a step in the set of procedures. The following input and output examples show this list. You can see how it appears in Internet Explorer in Figure 4.4.

INPUT

```
<p>Installing Your New Operating System</p>
<ol>
<li>Insert the CD-ROM into your CD-ROM drive.</li>
<li>Choose RUN.</li>
<li>Enter the drive letter of your CD-ROM (example: D:\),
followed by SETUP.EXE.</li>
<li>Follow the prompts in the setup program.</li>
<li>Reboot your computer after all files are installed.</li>
<li>Cross your fingers. </li>
</ol>
```

OUTPUT

FIGURE 4.4

An ordered list in HTML.

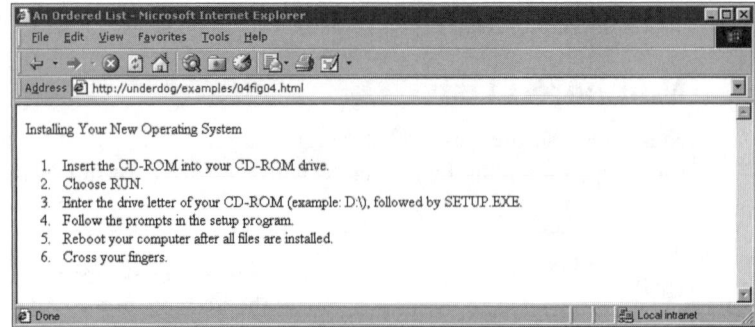

Customizing Ordered Lists with HTML 3.2

HTML 3.2 provided several attributes for ordered lists. They were used to customize how the browser renders the list. These attributes enabled you to control several features of ordered lists including which numbering scheme to use and from which number to start counting (if you don't want to start at 1). In HTML 4.0, the attributes mentioned in this section are deprecated in favor of using style sheet properties and values that accomplish the same task. To support HTML 3.2 browsers, however, you might need to use these attributes on occasion.

NEW TERM *Attributes* are extra parts of HTML tags that contain options or other information about the tag itself.

You can customize ordered lists in two main ways: how they are numbered and the number with which the list starts. HTML 3.2 provides the type attribute that can take one of five values to define which type of numbering to use on the list:

- "1"—Specifies that standard Arabic numerals should be used to number the list (that is, 1, 2, 3, 4, and so on)

- "a"—Specifies that lowercase letters should be used to number the list (that is, a, b, c, d, and so on)

- "A"—Specifies that uppercase letters should be used to number the list (that is, A, B, C, D, and so on)

- "i"—Specifies that lowercase Roman numerals should be used to number the list (that is, i, ii, iii, iv, and so on)

- "I"—Specifies that uppercase Roman numerals should be used to number the list (that is, I, II, III, IV, and so on)

You can specify types of numbering in the <ol> tag, as follows: <ol type="a">. By default, type="1" is assumed.

Note

The nice thing about Web browsers is that they generally ignore attributes they don't understand. If a browser doesn't support the type attribute of the <ol> tag, for example, it will simply ignore it when it is encountered.

4

As an example, consider the following list:

```
<p>The Days of the Week in French:</p>
<ol>
<li>Lundi</li>
<li>Mardi</li>
<li>Mercredi</li>
<li>Jeudi</li>
<li>Vendredi</li>
<li>Samedi</li>
<li>Dimanche</li>
</ol>
```

If you were to add type="I" to the <ol> tag, as follows, it would appear in Internet Explorer as shown in Figure 4.5.

INPUT

```
<p>The Days of the Week in French:</p>
<ol type="I">
<li>Lundi</li>
<li>Mardi</li>
<li>Mercredi</li>
<li>Jeudi</li>
<li>Vendredi</li>
<li>Samedi</li>
<li>Dimanche</li>
</ol>
```

OUTPUT

FIGURE 4.5

An ordered list displayed using an alternate numbering style.

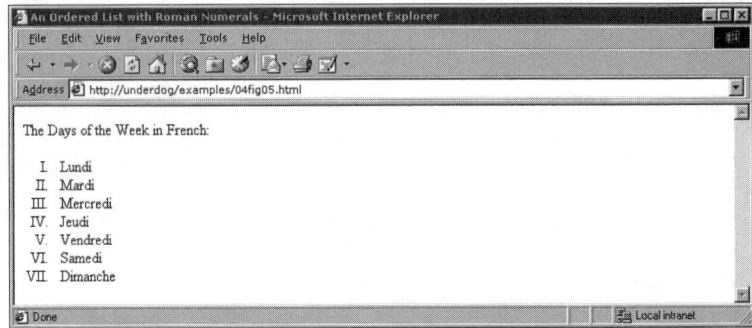

You also can apply the `type` attribute to the `<li>` tag, effectively changing the numbering type in the middle of the list. When the `type` attribute is used in the `<li>` tag, it affects the item in question and all entries following it in the list.

Using the `start` attribute, you can specify the number or letter with which to start your list. The default starting point is 1, of course. You can change this number by using start. `<ol start="4">`, for example, would start the list at number 4, whereas `<ol type="a" start="3">` would start the numbering with c and move through the alphabet from there.

For example, you can list the last six months of the year, and start its numbering with the Roman numeral VII as follows. The results appear in Figure 4.6.

INPUT

```
<p>The Last Six Months of the Year (and the Beginning of the Next
Year):</p>
<ol type="I" start="7">
<li>July</li>
<li>August</li>
<li>September</li>
<li>October</li>
<li>November</li>
<li>December</li>
<li type="1">January</li>
</ol>
```

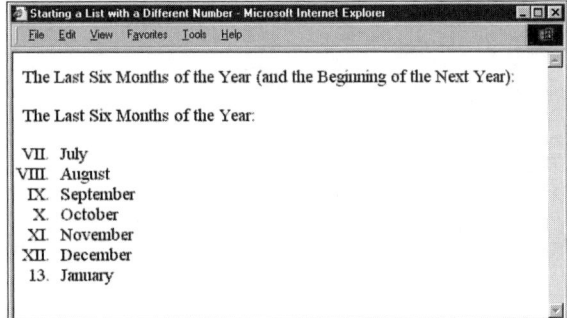

FIGURE 4.6

An ordered list with an alternate numbering style and starting number.

As with the `type` attribute, you can change the value of an entry's number at any point in a list. You do so by using the `value` attribute in the `<li>` tag. Assigning a `value` in an `<li>` tag restarts numbering in the list starting with the affected entry.

Suppose that you wanted the last three items in a list of ingredients to be 10, 11, and 12 rather than 6, 7, and 8. You can reset the numbering at `Eggs` using the `value` attribute, as follows:

```
<p>Cheesecake ingredients:</p>
<ol type="I">
<li>Quark Cheese</li>
<li>Honey</li>
<li>Cocoa</li>
<li>Vanilla Extract</li>
<li>Flour</li>
<li value="10">Eggs</li>
<li>Walnuts</li>
<li>Margarine</li>
</ol>
```

 Note

In this section's examples, all of the attribute values are enclosed in quotation marks. Most Web browsers do not require you to use quotation marks this way, but XHTML 1.0 does.

Unordered Lists

In unordered lists, the elements can appear in any order. An unordered list looks just like an ordered list in HTML except that the list is indicated by using `<ul>...</ul>` tags rather than `ol`. The elements of the list are separated by `<li>`, just as with ordered lists.

Browsers usually format unordered lists by inserting bullets or some other symbolic marker; Lynx, a text browser, inserts an asterisk (*).

The following input and output example shows an unordered list. Figure 4.7 shows the results in Internet Explorer.

 **INPUT**

```
<p>Things I like to do in the morning:</p>
<ul>
<li>Drink a cup of coffee</li>
<li>Watch the sunrise</li>
<li>Listen to the birds sing</li>
<li>Hear the wind rustling through the trees</li>
<li>Curse the construction noises for spoiling the peaceful mood</li>
</ul>
```

OUTPUT

FIGURE 4.7

An unordered list.

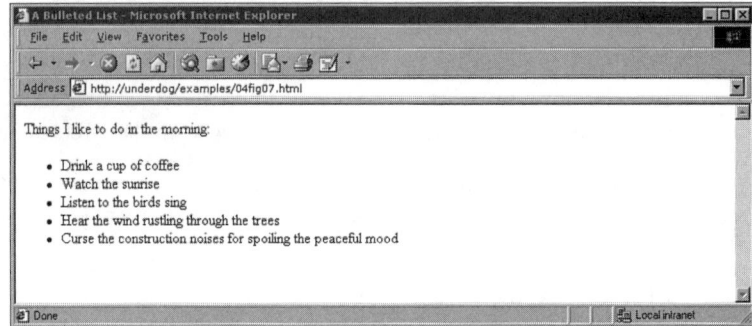

Customizing Unordered Lists in HTML 3.2

As with ordered lists, unordered lists can be customized with HTML 3.2 attributes. (These are also deprecated in HTML 4.0.) By default, most browsers (including Netscape and Internet Explorer) use bullets to delineate entries on unordered lists. Text browsers such as Lynx generally opt for an asterisk.

If you use the `type` attribute in the `<ul>` tag, some browsers can display other types of markers to delineate entries. According to the HTML 3.2 specification, the `type` attribute can take three possible values:

- `"disc"`—A disc or bullet; this style generally is the default.
- `"square"`—Obviously, a square rather than a disc.
- `"circle"`—As compared with the `disc`, which most browsers render as a filled circle, this value should generate an unfilled circle on compliant browsers.

In the following input and output example, you see a comparison of these three types as rendered in Internet Explorer (see Figure 4.8).

INPUT

```
<ul type="disc">
<li>DAT - Digital Audio Tapes</li>
<li>CD - Compact Discs</li>
<li>Cassettes</li>
</ul>
<ul type="square">
<li>DAT - Digital Audio Tapes</li>
<li>CD - Compact Discs</li>
<li>Cassettes</li>
</ul>
<ul type="circle">
<li>DAT - Digital Audio Tapes</li>
<li>CD - Compact Discs</li>
<li>Cassettes</li>
</ul>
```

OUTPUT

FIGURE 4.8

Unordered lists with differing bullet types.

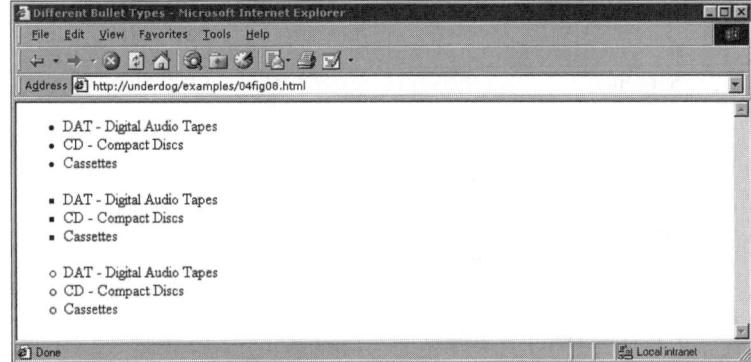

Just as you can change the numbering scheme in the middle of an ordered list, you can change the type of bullet mid-stream in a list by using the `type` attribute in the `<li>` tag. Again, this attribute is deprecated in HTML 4.0.

Glossary Lists

Glossary lists are slightly different from other lists. Each list item in a glossary list has two parts:

- A term
- The term's definition

Each part of the glossary list has its own tag: `<dt>` for the term ("definition term"), and `<dd>` for its definition ("definition definition"). `<dt>` and `<dd>` are both one-sided tags, and they usually occur in pairs, although most browsers can handle single terms or definitions. The entire glossary list is indicated by the tags `<dl>`...`</dl>` ("definition list").

The following is a glossary list example with a set of herbs and descriptions of how they grow:

```
<dl>
<dt>Basil</dt>
<dd>Annual. Can grow four feet high; the scent of its tiny white
flowers is heavenly</dd>
<dt>Oregano</dt>
<dd>Perennial. Sends out underground runners and is difficult
to get rid of once established.</dd>
<dt>Coriander</dt>
<dd>Annual. Also called cilantro, coriander likes cooler
weather of spring and fall.</dd>
</dl>
```

Glossary lists usually are formatted in browsers with the terms and definitions on separate lines, and the left margins of the definitions are indented.

You don't have to use glossary lists for terms and definitions, of course. You can use them anywhere that the same sort of list is needed. Here's an example:

```
<dl>
<dt>Macbeth</dt>
<dd>I'll go no more. I am afraid to think of
what I have done; look on't again I dare not.</dd>
<dt>Lady Macbeth</dt>
<dd>Infirm of purpose! Give me the daggers.
The sleeping and the dead are as but pictures. 'Tis the eye
if childhood that fears a painted devil. If he do bleed, I'll
gild the faces if the grooms withal, for it must seem their
guilt. (Exit. Knocking within)</dd>
<dt>Macbeth</dt>
<dd>Whence is that knocking? How is't wit me when
every noise apalls me? What hands are here? Ha! They pluck out
mine eyes! Will all Neptune's ocean wash this blood clean from
my hand? No. This my hand will rather the multitudinous seas
incarnadine, making the green one red. (Enter Lady Macbeth)</dd>
<dt>Lady Macbeth</dt>
<dd>My hands are of your color, but I shame to
wear a heart so white.</dd>
</dl>
```

The following input and output example shows how a glossary list is formatted in Internet Explorer (see Figure 4.9).

INPUT

```
<dl>
<dt>Basil</dt>
<dd>Annual. Can grow four feet high; the scent
of its tiny white flowers is heavenly.</dd>
<dt>Oregano</dt>
```

```
<dd>Perennial. Sends out underground runners
and is difficult to get rid of once established.</dd>
<dt>Coriander</dt>
<dd>Annual. Also called cilantro, coriander
likes cooler weather of spring and fall.</dd>
</dl>
```

OUTPUT

FIGURE 4.9

A glossary list.

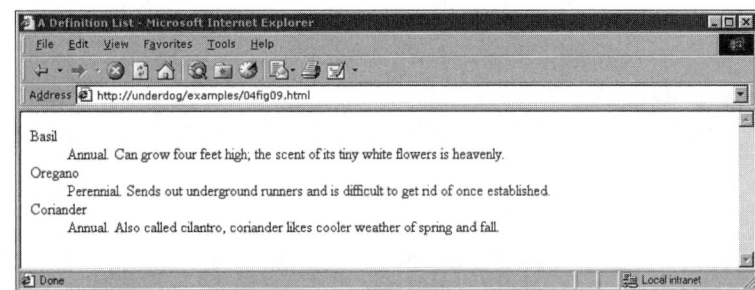

Nesting Lists

What happens if you put a list inside another list? Nesting lists is fine as far as HTML is concerned; just put the entire list structure inside another list as one of its elements. The nested list just becomes another element of the first list, and it is indented from the rest of the list. Lists like this work especially well for menu-like entities in which you want to show hierarchy (for example, in tables of contents) or as outlines.

Indenting nested lists in HTML code itself helps show their relationship to the final layout:

```
<ol>
   <ul>
   <li>WWW</li>
   <li>Organization</li>
   <li>Beginning HTML</li>
   <ul>
      <li>What HTML is</li>
      <li>How to Write HTML</li>
      <li>Doc structure</li>
      <li>Headings</li>
      <li>Paragraphs</li>
      <li>Comments</li>
   </ul>
<li>Links</li>
<li>More HTML</li>
</ol>
```

4

Many browsers format nested ordered lists and nested unordered lists differently from their enclosing lists. They might, for example, use a symbol other than a bullet for a nested list, or number the inner list with letters (a, b, c) rather than numbers. Don't assume that this will be the case, however, and refer back to "section 8, subsection b" in your text because you cannot determine what the exact formatting will be in the final output.

The following input and output example shows a nested list and how it appears in Internet Explorer (see Figure 4.10).

INPUT

```
<h1>Peppers</h1>
<ul>
<li>Bell</li>
<li>Chile</li>
    <ul>
    <li>Serrano</li>
    <li>Jalapeno</li>
    <li>Habanero</li>
    <li>Anaheim</li>
    </ul>
<li>Szechuan</li>
<li>Cayenne </li>
</ul>
```

OUTPUT

FIGURE 4.10

Nested lists.

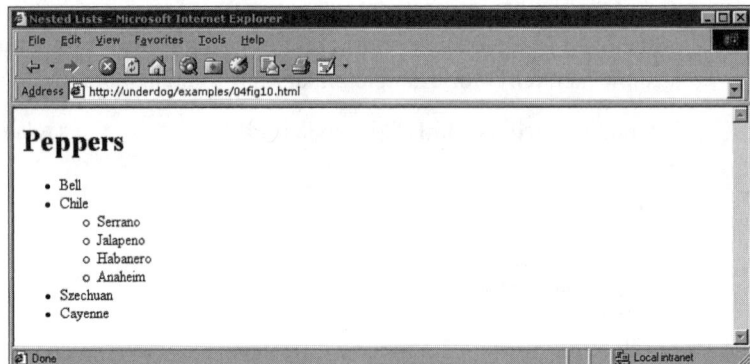

Comments

You can put comments into HTML pages to describe the page itself or to provide some kind of indication of the status of the page. Some source code control programs can put page status into comments, for example. Text in comments is ignored when the HTML file is parsed; comments don't ever show up onscreen—that's why they're comments. Comments look like the following:

```
<!-- This is a comment -->
```

Each line of text should be individually commented. Not including other HTML tags within comments usually is a good idea. (Although this practice isn't strictly illegal, many browsers might get confused when they encounter HTML tags within comments and display them anyway.) As a good rule of thumb, don't include <, >, or -- inside an HTML comment.

Here are some examples:

```
<!-- Rewrite this section with less humor -->
<!-- Neil helped with this section -->
<!-- Go Tigers! -->
```

Exercise 4.1: Creating a real HTML page

At this point, you know enough to get started creating simple HTML pages. You understand what HTML is, you've been introduced to a handful of tags, and you've even tried browsing an HTML file. You haven't created any links yet, but you'll get to that soon enough, in the next chapter.

This exercise shows you how to create an HTML file that uses the tags you've learned about up to this point. It will give you a feel for what the tags look like when they're displayed onscreen and for the sorts of typical mistakes you're going to make. (Everyone makes them, and that's why using an HTML editor that does the typing for you is often helpful. The editor doesn't forget the closing tags, leave off the slash, or misspell the tag itself.)

So, create a simple example in your text editor. Your example doesn't have to say much of anything; in fact, all it needs to include are the structure tags, a title, a couple of headings, and a paragraph or two, Here's an example:

```
<!DOCTYPE html PUBLIC "-//W3C//DTD XHTML 1.0 Transitional//EN"
  "http://www.w3.org/TR/xhtml1/DTD/transitional.dtd">
<html>
<head>
<title>Company Profile, Camembert Incorporated</title>
</head>
<body>
<h1>Camembert Incorporated</h1>
<p>"Many's the long night I dreamed of cheese -- toasted, mostly."
-- Robert Louis Stevenson</p>
<h2>What We Do</h2>
<p>We make cheese. Lots of cheese; more than eight tons of cheese
a year.</p>
<h2>Why We Do It</h2>
<p>We are paid an awful lot of money by people who like cheese.
So we make more.</p>
<h2>Our Favorite Cheeses</h2>
<ul>
```

```
<li>Brie</li>
<li>Havarti</li>
<li>Camembert</li>
<li>Mozzarella</li>
</ul>
</body>
</html>
```

Save the example to an HTML file, open it in your browser, and see how it came out.

If you have access to another browser on your computer or, even better, one on a different computer, I highly recommend opening the same HTML file there so that you can see the differences in appearance between browsers. Sometimes the differences can surprise you; lines that looked fine in one browser might look strange in another browser.

Figure 4.11 shows what the cheesefactory example looks like in Internet Explorer.

FIGURE 4.11

The cheese factory in Internet Explorer.

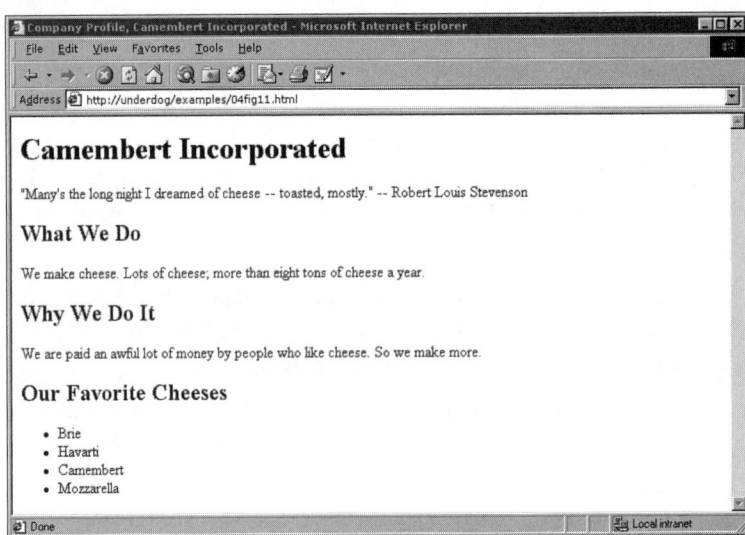

Summary

HTML, a text-only markup language used to describe hypertext pages on the World Wide Web, describes the structure of a page, not its appearance.

Today, you learned what HTML is and how to write and preview simple HTML files. You also learned about the HTML tags shown in Table 4.1.

TABLE 4.1 HTML Tags from Day 4

Tag	Attribute	Use
`<html> ... </html>`		The entire HTML page.
`<head> ... </head>`		The head, or prologue, of the HTML page.
`<body> ... </body>`		All the other content in the HTML page.
`<title> ... </title>`		The title of the page.
`<h1> ... </h1>`		First-level heading.
`<h2> ... </h2>`		Second-level heading.
`<h3> ... </h3>`		Third-level heading.
`<h4> ... </h4>`		Fourth-level heading.
`<h5> ... </h5>`		Fifth-level heading.
`<h6> ... </h6>`		Sixth-level heading.
`<p> ... </p>`		A paragraph.
`<ol>...</ol>`		An ordered (numbered) list. Each of the items in the list begins with `<li>`.
	type	Specify the numbering scheme to use in the list. This attribute is deprecated in HTML 4.0.
	start	Specify at which number to start the list. This attribute is deprecated in HTML 4.0.
`<ul>...</ul>`		An unordered (bulleted or otherwise-marked) list. Each of the items in the list begins with `<li>`.
	type	Specify the bulleting scheme to use in the list. This attribute is deprecated in HTML 4.0.
`<li>...</li>`		Individual list items in ordered, unordered, menu, or directory lists. Closing tag is optional in HTML, but required in XHTML 1.0.
	type	Reset the numbering or bulleting scheme from the current list element. Only applies to `<ul>` and `<ol>` lists. This attribute is deprecated in HTML 4.0.
	value	Reset the numbering in the middle of an ordered (`<ol>`) list. This attribute is deprecated in HTML 4.0.

4

TABLE 4.1 continued

Tag	Attribute	Use
`<dl>...</dl>`		A glossary or definition list. Items in the list consist of pairs of elements: a term and its definition.
`<dt>...</dt>`		The term part of an item in a glossary list. Closing tag is optional in HTML, but required in XHTML 1.0.
`<dd>...</dt>`		The definition part of an item in a glossary list. Closing tag is optional in HTML, but required in XHTML 1.0.
`<!-- ... -->`		A comment.

Workshop

You've learned a lot in this chapter, and the following workshop will help you remember some of the most important points. I've anticipated some of the questions you might have in the first section of the workshop.

Q&A

Q In some Web pages, I've noticed that the page structure tags (`<html>`, `<head>`, `<body>`) aren't used. Do I really need to include them if pages work just fine without them?

A Most browsers will handle plain HTML without the page structure tags. The XHTML 1.0 recommendation requires that these tags appear in your pages. It's a good idea to get into the habit of using them now. Including the tags will allow your pages to be read by more general SGML tools and to take advantage of features of future browsers. And, using these tags is the "correct" thing to do if you want your pages to conform to true HTML format.

Q My glossaries came out formatted really strangely! The terms are indented farther in than the definitions!

A Did you mix up the `<dd>` and `<dt>` tags? The `<dt>` tag is always used first (the definition term), and then the `<dd>` follows (the definition). I mix them up all the time. There are too many d tags in glossary lists.

Q I've seen HTML files that use `<li>` outside a list structure, alone on the page, like this:

```
<li>And then the duck said, "put it on my bill"</li>
```

A Most browsers will at least accept this tag outside a list tag and will format it either as a simple paragraph or as a non-indented bulleted item. According to the true HTML specification, however, using an `<li>` outside a list tag is illegal, so "good" HTML pages shouldn't do this. Enclosing list items within list tags is also required by the XHTML recommendation. Always put your list items inside lists where they belong.

Q You mentioned that some of the list tags and attributes have been deprecated in HTML 4.0. What should I use instead?

A In a way, it depends on your audience. For example, if your Web pages reside on a corporate intranet where you know for sure that everyone is using an HTML 4.0 browser that supports style sheets (CSS), you can use CSS properties and values in place of the deprecated tags. If your Web pages reside on the World Wide Web, however, where people using a wide variety of browsers and PC platforms are accessing your site, it might be to your advantage to continue using the deprecated tags to make your pages presentable in older browsers. You'll learn more about the pros and cons of each approach, and see some examples of how to replace deprecated tags, on Day 18.

Quiz

1. What three HTML tags are used to describe the overall structure of a Web page, and what do each of them define?

2. Where does the `<title>` tag go, and what is it used for?

3. How many different levels of headings does HTML support? What are their tags?

4. Why is it a good idea to use two-sided paragraph tags, even though the closing tag `</p>` is optional in HTML?

5. What two list types have been deprecated? What can you use in place of the deprecated list types?

Quiz Answers

1. The `<html>` tag indicates that the file is in the HTML language. The `<head>` tag specifies that the lines within the beginning and ending points of the tag are the prologue to the rest of the file. The `<body>` tag encloses the remainder of your HTML page (text, links, pictures, and so on).

2. The `<title>` tag is used to indicate the title of a Web page in a browser's book-marks, hotlist program, or other programs that catalog Web pages. This tag always goes inside the `<head>` tags.

3. HTML supports six levels of headings. Their tags are `<h1 ... /h1>` through `<h6 ... /h6>`.

4. The closing `</p>` tag becomes important when aligning text to the left, right, or center of a page (text alignment is discussed on Day 6, "More Text Formatting with HTML"). Closing tags also are required for XHTML 1.0.

5. The `<menu>` and `<dir>` list types have been deprecated in favor of using bulleted, or unordered, lists `<ul>`.

Exercises

1. Using the Camembert Incorporated page as an example, create a page that briefly describes topics that you would like to cover on your own Web site. You'll use this page to learn how to create your own links tomorrow.

2. Create a second page that provides further information about one of the topics you listed in the first exercise. Include a couple of subheadings (such as those shown in Figure 4.2). If you feel really adventurous, complete the page's content and include lists where you think they enhance the page. This exercise also will help prepare you for tomorrow's lesson.

PART 2

DAY 5

All About Links

After finishing yesterday's lesson, you now have a couple of pages that have some headings, text, and lists in them. These pages are all well and good, but rather boring. The real fun starts when you learn how to create hypertext links and link your pages to the Web. Today, you'll learn just that. Specifically, you'll learn about the following:

- All about the HTML link tag (<a>) and its various parts
- How to link to other pages on your local disk by using relative and absolute pathnames
- How to link to other pages on the Web by using URLs
- How to use links and anchors to link to specific places inside pages
- All about URLs: the various parts of the URL and the kinds of URLs you can use

Creating Links

To create a link in HTML, you need two things:

- The name of the file (or the URL of the file) to which you want to link
- The text that will serve as the "hot spot"—that is, the text that will be highlighted in the browser, which your readers can then select to follow the link

Only the text that serves as the "hot spot" is actually visible on your page. When your readers select the text that points to a link, the browser uses the first part as the place to which to "jump."

The Link Tag—`<a>`

To create a link in an HTML page, you use the HTML link tag `<a>...</a>`. The `<a>` tag often is called an anchor tag, as it also can be used to create anchors for links. (You'll learn more about creating anchors later today.) The most common use of the link tag, however, is to create links to other pages.

Unlike the simple tags you learned about in the preceding chapter, the `<a>` tag has some extra features: The opening tag, `<a>`, includes both the name of the tag ("a") and extra information about the link itself. The extra features are called *attributes* of the tag. (You first discovered attributes in Day 4, "Begin with the Basics," when you learned about lists.) So rather than the opening `<a>` tag having just a name inside brackets, it looks something like the following:

```
<a name="Up" href="menu.html" title="The Twelve Caesars">
```

The extra attributes (in this example, `name`, `href`, and `title`) describe the link itself. The attribute you'll probably use most often is the `href` attribute, which is short for "hyper-text reference." You use the `href` attribute to specify the name or URL of the file to which this link points.

Like most HTML tags, the link tag also has a closing tag, `</a>`. All the text between the opening and closing tags will become the actual link on the screen and be highlighted, underlined, or colored blue or red when the Web page is displayed. That's the text you or your readers will click to jump to the place specified by the `href` attribute.

Figure 5.1 shows the parts of a typical link using the `<a>` tag, including the `href`, the text of the link, and the closing tag.

FIGURE 5.1

An HTML link using the <a> tag.

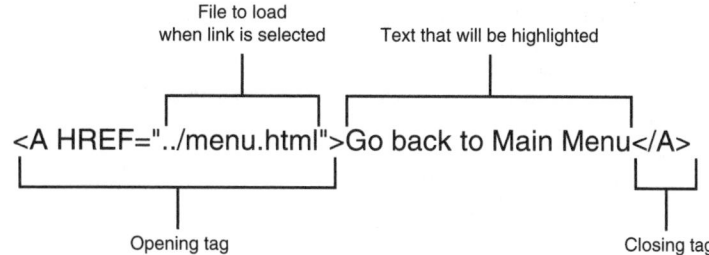

File to load
when link is selected

Text that will be highlighted

<A HREF="../menu.html">Go back to Main Menu</A>

Opening tag

Closing tag

The following example shows a simple link and what it looks like in Internet Explorer (see Figure 5.2).

 INPUT

```
Go back to <a href="menu.html">Main Menu</a>
```

OUTPUT

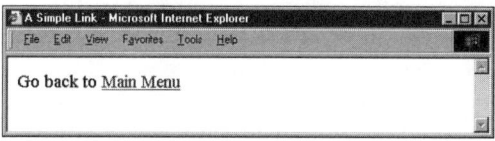

FIGURE 5.2

The output in Internet Explorer.

Exercise 5.1: Linking Two Pages

▲ To Do

Now you can try a simple example, with two HTML pages on your local disk. You'll need your text editor and your Web browser for this exercise. Because both the pages you'll be working with are on your local disk, you don't need to be connected to the network. (Be patient; you'll get to do network stuff in the next section.)

Create two HTML pages and save them in separate files. Here's the code for the two HTML files I created for this section, which I called menu.html and claudius.html. What your two pages look like or what they're called really doesn't matter. However, make sure that you insert your own filenames if you're following along with this example.

The following is the first file, called menu.html:

```
<!DOCTYPE html PUBLIC "-//W3C//DTD XHTML 1.0 Transitional//EN"
 "http://www.w3.org/TR/xhtml1/DTD/transitional.dtd">
<html>
<head>
<title>The Twelve Caesars</title>
</head>
<body>
<h1>"The Twelve Caesars" by Suetonius</h1>
<p>Seutonius (or Gaius Suetonius Tranquillus) was born circa A.D. 70
```

5

▼ and died sometime after A.D. 130. He composed a history of the twelve
Caesars from Julius to Domitian (died A.D. 96). His work was a
significant contribution to the best-selling novel and television
series "I, Claudius." Suetonius' work includes biographies of the
following Roman emperors:`</p>`

```
<ul>
  <li>Julius Caesar</li>
  <li>Augustus</li>
  <li>Tiberius</li>
  <li>Gaius (Caligula)</li>
  <li>Claudius</li>
  <li>Nero</li>
  <li>Galba</li>
  <li>Otho</li>
  <li>Vitellius</li>
  <li>Vespasian</li>
  <li>Titus</li>
  <li>Domitian</li>
</ul>
</body>
</html>
```

The list of menu items (Julius Caesar, Augustus, and so on) will be links to other pages.
For now, just type them as regular text; you'll turn them into links later.

The following is the second file, `claudius.html`:

```
<!DOCTYPE html PUBLIC "-//W3C//DTD XHTML 1.0 Transitional//EN"
 "http://www.w3.org/TR/xhtml1/DTD/transitional.dtd">
<html>
<head>
<title>The Twelve Caesars: Claudius</title>
</head>
<body>
<h2>Claudius Becomes Emperor</h2>
<p>Claudius became Emperor at the age of 50. Fearing the attack of
Caligula's assassins, Claudius hid behind some curtains. After a guardsman
discovered him, Claudius dropped to the floor, and then found himself
declared Emperor.</p>
<h2>Claudius is Poisoned</h2>
<p>Most people think that Claudius was poisoned. Some think his wife
Agrippina poisoned a dish of mushrooms (his favorite food). His death
was revealed after arrangements had been made for her son, Nero, to
succeed as Emperor.</p>
<p>Go back to Main Menu</p>
</body>
</html>
```

Make sure that both of your files are in the same directory or folder. If you haven't called
them `menu.html` and `claudius.html`, make sure that you take note of the names because
▼ you'll need them later.

▼ Create a link from the menu file to the feeding file. Edit the `menu.html` file, and put the cursor at the following line:

`<li>Claudius</li>`

Link tags do not define the format of the text itself, so leave in the list item tags and just add the link inside the item. First, put in the link tags themselves (the `<a>` and `</a>` tags) around the text that you want to use as the link:

`<li><a>Claudius</a></li>`

Now add the name of the file that you want to link to as the `href` part of the opening link tag. Enclose the name of the file in quotation marks (straight quotes [`"`], not curly or typesetter's quotes ["]), with an equal sign between `href` and the name. Filenames in links are case sensitive, so make sure that the filename in the link is identical to the name of the file you created. (`Claudius.html` is not the same file as `claudius.html`; it has to be exactly the same case.) Here I've used `claudius.html`; if you used different files, use those filenames.

`<li><a href="claudius.html">Claudius</a></li>`

Now, start your browser, select Open File (or its equivalent in your browser), and open the `menu.html` file. The paragraph you used as your link should now show up as a link that is in a different color, underlined, or otherwise highlighted. Figure 5.3 shows how it looked when I opened it in Internet Explorer.

FIGURE 5.3

The menu.html file with link.

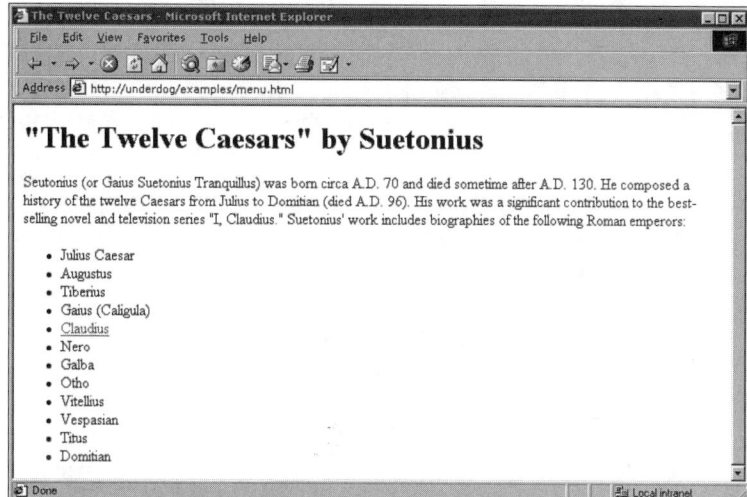

5

▼   Now, when you click the link, your browser should load and display the `claudius.html`
     page, as shown in Figure 5.4.

FIGURE 5.4

*The `claudius.html`
page.*

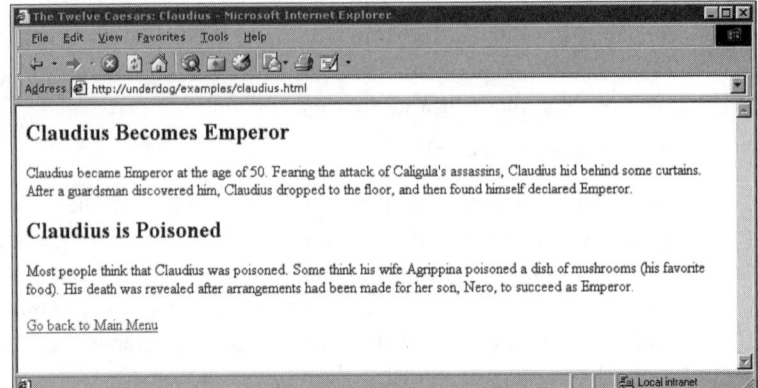

If your browser can't find the file when you click on the link, make sure that the name of
the file in the `href` part of the link tag is the same as the name of the file on the disk,
uppercase and lowercase match, and both files are in the same directory. Remember to
close your link, using the `</a>` tag, at the end of the text that serves as the link. Also,
make sure that you have quotation marks at the end of the filename (sometimes you can
easily forget) and both quotation marks are ordinary straight quotes. All these things can
confuse the browser and prevent it from finding the file or displaying the link properly.

Note
> Don't get confused by this issue of case sensitivity. Tags in HTML are not
> case sensitive (although XHTML 1.0 requires that tags be lowercase).
> However, filenames refer to files on a Web server somewhere, and because
> Web servers often run on operating systems in which filenames are case sen-
> sitive (such as UNIX), you should make sure that the case of letters in your
> links' filenames is correct.

Now you can create a link from the feeding page back to the menu page. A paragraph at
the end of the `claudius.html` page is intended for just this purpose:

`<p>Go back to Main Menu</p>`

Add the link tag with the appropriate `href` to that line, such as the following in which
`menu.html` is the original menu file:

    `<p><a href="menu.html">Go back to Main Menu</a></p>`

▼

Note

> When you include tags inside other tags, make sure that the closing tag closes the tag that you most recently opened. That is, enter
>
> **\<p\> \<a\> ... \</a\> \</p\>**
>
> rather than
>
> **\<p\> \<a\> ... \</p\> \</a\>**
>
> Some browsers can become confused if you overlap tags in this way, so always make sure that you close the most recently opened tag first.

Now when you reload the "Claudius" file, the link will be active, and you can jump

▲ between the menu and the detail page by selecting those links.

Linking Local Pages Using Relative and Absolute Pathnames

The example in the preceding section shows how to link together pages that are contained in the same folder or directory on your local disk (local pages). This section continues that thread, linking pages that are still on the local disk but might be contained in different directories or folders on that disk.

Note

> Folders and directories are the same thing, but they're called different names depending on whether you're on Macintosh, Windows, DOS, or UNIX. I'll simply call them directories from now on to make your life easier.

5

When you specify just the filename of a linked file within quotation marks, as you did earlier, the browser looks for that file in the same directory as the current file. This is true even if both the current file and the file being linked to are on a server somewhere else on the Internet; both files are contained in the same directory on that server. It is the simplest form of a relative pathname.

New Term   *Relative pathnames* point to files based on their locations relative to the current file. They can include directory names, or they can point to the path you would take to navigate to that file if you started at the current directory or folder. A pathname might, for example, include directions to go up two directory levels and then go down two other directories to get to the file.

To specify relative pathnames in links, use UNIX-style pathnames regardless of the system you actually have. You therefore separate directory or folder names with forward slashes (/), and you use two dots to refer generically to the directory above the current one (..).

Table 5.1 shows some examples of relative pathnames and what they mean.

TABLE 5.1   Relative Pathnames

Pathname	Means
`href="file.html""`	`file.html` is located in the current directory.
`href="files/file.html""`	`file.html` is located in the directory (or folder) called `files` (and the `files` directory is located in the current directory).
`href="files/morefiles/file.html""`	`file.html` is located in the `morefiles` directory, which is located in the `files` directory, which is located in the current directory.
`href="../file.html""`	`file.html` is located in the directory one level up from the current directory (the parent directory).
`href="../../files/file.html""`	`file.html` is located two directory levels up, in the directory `files`.

If you're linking files on a personal computer (Macintosh or PC), and you want to link to a file on a different disk, use the name or letter of the disk as just another directory name in the relative path.

When you want to link to a file on a local drive on the Macintosh, the name of the disk is used just as it appears on the disk itself. Assume that you have a disk called `Hard Disk 2`, and your HTML files are contained in a folder called `HTML Files`. If you want to link to a file called `jane.html` in a folder called `Public` on a shared disk called `Jane's Mac`, you can use the following relative pathname:

`href="../../Jane's Mac/Public/jane.html"`

When linking to a file on a local drive on Windows systems, you refer to the drives by letter, just as you would expect. However, rather than using `c:`, `d:`, and so on, substitute a vertical bar (|) for the colon (the colon has a special meaning in link pathnames) and don't forget to use forward slashes as you do with UNIX. So, if the current file is located in `C:\FILES\HTML\`, and you want to link to `D:\FILES.NEW\HTML\MORE\INDEX.HTM`, the relative pathname to that file is as follows:

`href="../../d|/files.new/html/more/index.htm"`

In most instances, you'll never use the name of a disk in relative pathnames, but I've included it here for completeness. Most of the time, you'll link between files that are reasonably close (only one directory or folder away) in the same presentation.

Absolute Pathnames

You can also specify the link to another page on your local system by using an absolute pathname.

NEW TERM *Absolute pathnames* point to files based on their absolute locations on the file system. Whereas relative pathnames point to the page to which you want to link by describing its location relative to the current page, absolute pathnames point to the page by starting at the top level of your directory hierarchy and working downward through all the intervening directories to reach the file.

Absolute pathnames always begin with a slash, which is the way they are differentiated from relative pathnames. Following the slash are all directories in the path from the top level to the file you are linking.

Note

"Top" has different meanings, depending on how you're publishing your HTML files. If you're just linking to files on your local disk, the top is the top of your file system (/ on UNIX, or the disk name on a Macintosh or PC). When you're publishing files using a Web server, the top might or might not be the top of your file system (and generally isn't). You'll learn more about absolute pathnames and Web servers in Day 19, "Putting Your Site Online."

Table 5.2 shows some examples of absolute pathnames and what they mean.

TABLE 5.2 Absolute Pathnames

Pathname	Means
href="/u1/lemay/file.html"	file.html is located in the directory /u1/lemay (typically on UNIX systems).
href="/d|/files/html/file.htm"	file.htm is located on the D: disk in the directories files/html (on DOS systems).
href="/Hard%20Disk%201/HTML Files/file.html"	file.html is located on the disk Hard Disk 1, in the folder HTML Files (typically on Macintosh systems)

Should You Use Relative or Absolute Pathnames?

The answer to this question is: It depends. If you have a set of files that only link to other files within that set, using relative pathnames makes sense. On the other hand, if the links in your files point to files that are not within the same hierarchy, you probably want to use absolute links. Generally, a mix of the two types of links will make the most sense for complex sites.

I can explain this better with an example. Let's say that your site consists of two sections, /stuff and /things. If you want to link from the file index.html in /stuff to history.html in /stuff (or any other file in /stuff), you use a relative link. That way, you can move the /stuff directory around without breaking any of the internal links. On the other hand, if you want to create a link in /stuff/index.html to /things/index.html, an absolute link is probably called for. That way, if you move /stuff to /more/stuff, your link will still work.

The rule of thumb I generally use is that if pages are part of the same collection, I use relative links, and if they're part of different collections, I use absolute links.

Links to Other Documents on the Web

So now you have a whole set of pages on your local disk, all linked to each other. In some places in your pages, however, you want to refer to a page somewhere else on the Internet—for example, to The First Caesars page by Dr. Ellis Knox at Boise State University for more information on the early Roman Emperors. You also can use the link tag to link those other pages on the Internet, which I'll call remote pages.

 *Remote pages* are contained somewhere on the Web other than the system on which you're currently working.

The HTML code you use to link pages on the Web looks exactly the same as the code you use for links between local pages. You still use the <a> tag with an href attribute, and you include some text to serve as the link on your Web page. Rather than a filename or a path in the href, however, you use the URL of that page on the Web, as Figure 5.5 shows.

FIGURE 5.5

Link to remote files.

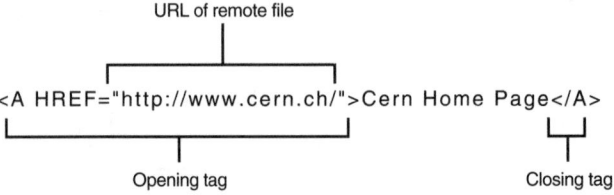

Exercise 5.2: Linking Your Caesar Pages to the Web

▲ To Do

Go back to those two pages you linked together earlier today, the ones about the Caesars. The menu.html file contains several links to other local pages that provide information about 12 Roman Emperors.

Now suppose that you want to add a link to the bottom of the menu file to point to The First Caesars page by Dr. Ellis Knoxat Boise State University, whose URL is http://history.idbsu.edu/westciv/julio-cl/index.html.

First, add the appropriate text for the link to your menu page, as follows:

```
<p><i>The First Caesars</i> page by Dr. Ellis Knox has more information on
these Emperors.</p>
```

What if you don't know the URL of the home page for The First Caesars page (or the page to which you want to link), but you do know how to get to it by following several links on several different people's home pages? Not a problem. Use your browser to find the home page for the page to which you want to link. Figure 5.6 shows what The First Caesars page looks like in your browser.

FIGURE 5.6

The First Caesars page.

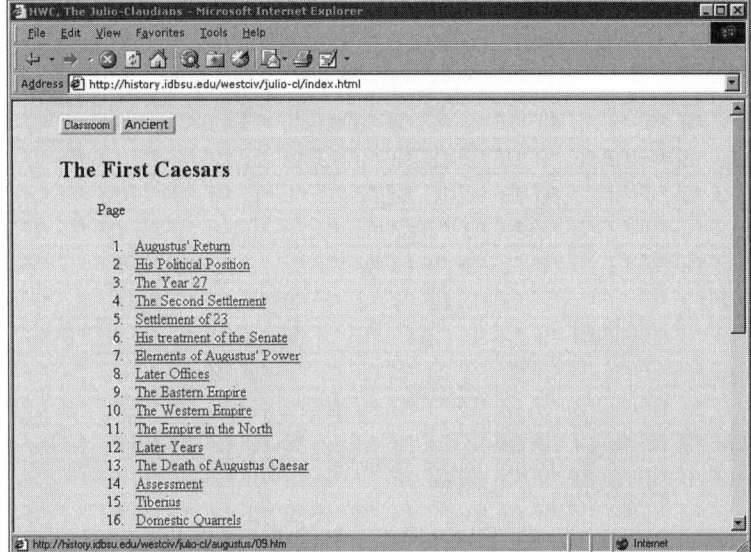

5

Note

If your system isn't connected to the Internet, you may want to connect now so that you can test links to pages stored on the Web.

▼ Most browsers display the URL of the file they're currently looking at in a box somewhere near the top of the page. (In Internet Explorer this box might be hidden; choose
View, Toolbars, Address Bar to see it.) This way, you can easily link to other pages; use
your browser to go to the page to which you want to link, copy the URL from the window, and paste it into the HTML page on which you're working. No typing!

After you have the URL of the page, you can construct a link tag in your menu file and
paste the appropriate URL into the link, like this:

```
<p>"<i><a href="http://history.idbsu.edu/westciv/julio-cl/index.html">The First
Caesars</a></i>"
page by Dr. Ellis Knox has more information on these Emperors.</p>
```

Of course, if you already know the URL of the page to which you want to link, you can
just type it into the href part of the link. Keep in mind, however, that if you make a mistake, your browser won't be able to find the file on the other end. Most URLs are too
complex for humans to be able to remember them; I prefer to copy and paste whenever I
can to cut down on the chances of typing URLs incorrectly.

Figure 5.7 shows how the menu.html file, with the new link in it, looks when it is dis-
▲ played in Internet Explorer.

FIGURE 5.7

The First Caesars link.

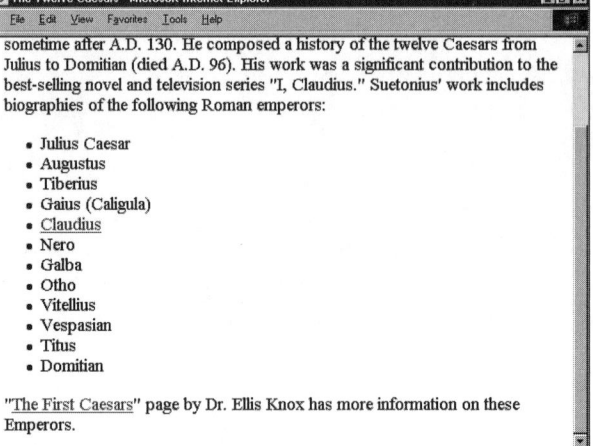

Exercise 5.3: Creating a Link Menu

NEW TERM   Now that you've learned how to create lists and links, you can create a link
menu. Link menus are links on your Web page that are arranged in list form
or in some other short, easy-to-read, and easy-to-understand format. Link menus are ter-
rific for pages that are organized in a hierarchy, for tables of contents, or for navigation
among several pages. Web pages that consist of nothing but links often organize the links
in menu form.

▼ The idea of a link menu is that you use short, descriptive terms as the links, with either no text following the link or with a further description following the link itself. Link menus look best in a bulleted or unordered list format, but you also can use glossary lists or just plain paragraphs. Link menus enable your readers to scan the list of links quickly and easily, a task that might be difficult if you bury your links in body text.

In this exercise, you'll create a Web page for a set of book reviews. This page will serve as the index to the reviews, so the link menu you'll create is essentially a menu of book names.

Start with a simple page framework: a first-level head and some basic explanatory text:

```
<!DOCTYPE html PUBLIC "-//W3C//DTD XHTML 1.0 Transitional//EN"
 "http://www.w3.org/TR/xhtml1/DTD/transitional.dtd">
<html>
<head>
<title>Really Honest Book Reviews</title>
</head>
<body>
<h1>Really Honest Book Reviews</h1>
<p>I read a lot of books about many different subjects. Though I'm not a
book critic, and I don't do this for a living, I enjoy a really good read
every now and then. Here's a list of books that I've read recently:</p>
```

Now add the list that will become the links, without the link tags themselves. It's always easier to start with link text and then attach actual links afterward. For this list, you'll use a tag to create a bulleted list of individual books. The <ol> tag wouldn't be appropriate because the numbers would imply that you were ranking the books in some way. Here's the HTML list of books; Figure 5.8 shows the page in Internet Explorer as it currently looks with the introduction and the list.

```
<ul>
  <li><i>The Rainbow Returns</i> by E. Smith</li>
  <li><i>Seven Steps to Immeasurable Wealth</i> by R. U. Needy</li>
  <li><i>The Food-Lovers Guide to Weight Loss</i> by L. Goode</li>
  <li><i>The Silly Person's Guide to Seriousness</i> by M. Nott</li>
</ul>
</body>
</html>
```

Now, modify each of the list items so that they include link tags. You'll need to keep the <li> tag in there because it indicates where the list items begin. Just add the <a> tags around the text itself. Here you'll link to filenames on the local disk in the same directory as this file, with each individual file containing the review for the particular book:

```
<ul>
  <li><a href="rainbow.html"><i>The Rainbow Returns</i> by E. Smith</a></li>
  <li><a href="wealth.html"><i>Seven Steps to Immeasurable Wealth</i> by R. U.
```
▼

▼
```
Needy</a></li>
<li><a href="food.html"><i>The Food-Lovers Guide to Weight Loss</i> by L.
Goode</a></li>
<li><a href="silly.html"><i>The Silly Person's Guide to Seriousness</i> by M.
Nott</a></li>
</ul>
```

FIGURE 5.8

A list of books.

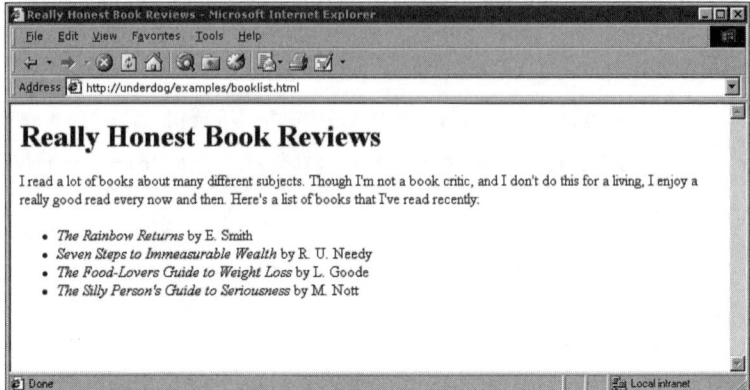

The menu of books looks fine, although it's a little sparse. Your readers don't know anything about each book (although some of the book names indicate the subject matter) or whether the review is good or bad. An improvement would be to add some short explanatory text after the links to provide hints of what is on the other side of the link:

```
<ul>
  <li><a href="rainbow.html"><i>The Rainbow Returns</i> by E. Smith</a>. A
  fantasy story set in biblical times. Slow at times, but interesting.</li>
  <li><a href="wealth.html"><i>Seven Steps to Immeasurable Wealth</i> by R. U.
  Needy</a>. I'm still poor, but I'm happy! And that's the whole point.</li>
  <li><a href="food.html"><i>The Food-Lovers Guide to Weight Loss</i> by L.
Goode
  </a>. At last! A diet book with recipes that taste good!</li>
  <li><a href="silly.html"><i>The Silly Person's Guide to Seriousness</i> by M.
  Nott</a>. Come on ... who wants to be serious?</li>
</ul>
```

The final list looks like Figure 5.9.

▼   You'll use link menus similar to this one throughout this book.

FIGURE 5.9

The final menu listing.

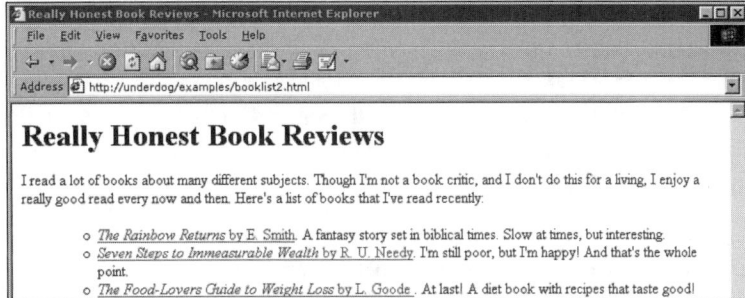

Linking to Specific Places Within Documents

The links you've created so far today have been from one point in a page to another page. But what if, rather than linking to that second page in general, you want to link to a specific place within that page—for example, to the fourth major section down?

You can do so in HTML by creating an anchor within the second page. The anchor creates a special element that you can link to inside the page. The link you create in the first page will contain both the name of the file to which you're linking and the name of that anchor. Then, when you follow the link with your browser, the browser will load the second page and then scroll down to the location of the anchor (Figure 5.10 shows an example).

FIGURE 5.10

Links and anchors.

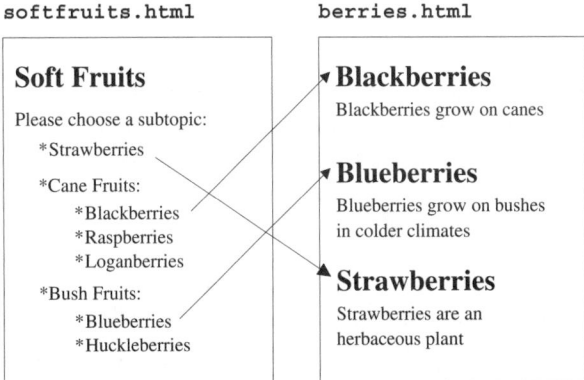

NEW TERM *Anchors* are special places that you can link to inside documents. Links can then jump to those special places inside the page as opposed to jumping just to the top of the page.

You can use links and anchors within the same page so that if you select one of those links, you jump to a different anchor within the page.

Creating Links and Anchors

You create an anchor in nearly the same way that you create a link: by using the <a> tag. If you wondered why the link tag uses an <a> rather than an <l>, now you know: a actually stands for anchor.

When you specify links by using <a>, the link has two parts: the href attribute in the opening <a> tag and the text between the opening and closing tags that serve as a hot spot for the link.

You create anchors in much the same way, but rather than using the href attribute in the <a> tag, you use the name attribute. The name attribute takes a keyword (or words) that will be used to name the anchor. Figure 5.11 shows the parts of the <a> tag when used to indicate an anchor.

FIGURE 5.11

The <a> tag and anchors.

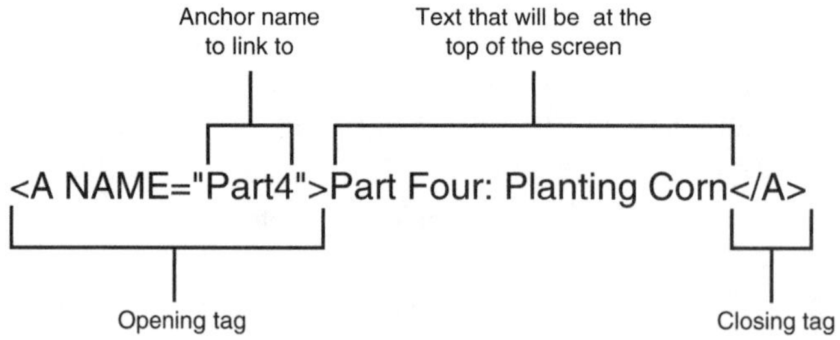

Anchor name to link to

Text that will be at the top of the screen

`<A NAME="Part4">Part Four: Planting Corn</A>`

Opening tag

Closing tag

Anchors also require some amount of text between the opening and closing <a> tags, although they usually point to a single-character location. The text between the <a> tags is used by the browser when a link attached to this anchor is selected. The browser scrolls the page to the text within the anchor so that it is at the top of the screen. Some browsers also might highlight the text inside the <a> tags.

So, for example, to create an anchor at the section of a page labeled Part 4, you might add an anchor called part4 to the heading, similar to the following:

`<h1><a name="part4">Part Four: Grapefruit from Heaven</a></h1>`

Unlike links, anchors do not show up in the final displayed page. Anchors are invisible until you follow a link that points to them.

To point to an anchor in a link, use the same form of link that you would when linking to the whole page, with the filename or URL of the page in the href attribute. After the name of the page, however, include a hash sign (#) and the name of the anchor exactly as it appears in the name attribute of that anchor (including the same uppercase and lowercase characters!), like the following:

```
<a href="mybigdoc.html#part4">Go to Part 4</a>
```

This link tells the browser to load the page mybigdoc.html and then to scroll down to the anchor name part4. The text inside the anchor definition will appear at the top of the screen.

Exercise 5.4: Linking Sections Between Two Pages

Now do an example with two pages. These two pages are part of an online reference to classical music, in which each Web page contains all the references for a particular letter of the alphabet (a.html, b.html, and so on). The reference could have been organized such that each section is its own page. Organizing it that way, however, would have involved several pages to manage, as well as many pages the readers would have to load if they were exploring the reference. Bunching the related sections together under lettered groupings is more efficient in this case. (Day 16, "Writing and Designing Web Pages: Dos and Don'ts," goes into more detail about the trade-offs between short and long pages.)

The first page you'll look at is the one for "M," the first section that looks like the following in HTML:

```
<!DOCTYPE html PUBLIC "-//W3C//DTD XHTML 1.0 Transitional//EN"
  "http://www.w3.org/TR/xhtml1/DTD/transitional.dtd">
<html>
<head>
<title>Classical Music: M</title>
</head>
<body>
<h1>M</h1>
<h2>Madrigals</h2>
<ul>
  <li>William Byrd, <em>This Sweet and Merry Month of May</em></li>
  <li>William Byrd, <em>Though Amaryllis Dance</em></li>
  <li>Orlando Gibbons, <em>The Silver Swan</em></li>
  <li>Claudio Monteverdi, <em>Lamento d'Arianna</em></li>
  <li>Thomas Morley, <em>My Bonny Lass She Smileth</em></li>
  <li>Thomas Weelkes, <em>Thule, the Period of Cosmography</em></li>
  <li>John Wilbye, <em>Sweet Honey-Sucking Bees</em></li>
</ul>
<p>Secular vocal music in four, five and six parts, usually a capella.
15th-16th centuries.</p>
<p><em>See Also</em>
Byrd, Gibbons, Monteverdi, Morley, Weelkes, Wilbye</p>
</body>
</html>
```

▼ To Do

5

▼ Figure 5.12 shows how this section looks when it's displayed.

FIGURE 5.12

Part M of the Online Music Reference.

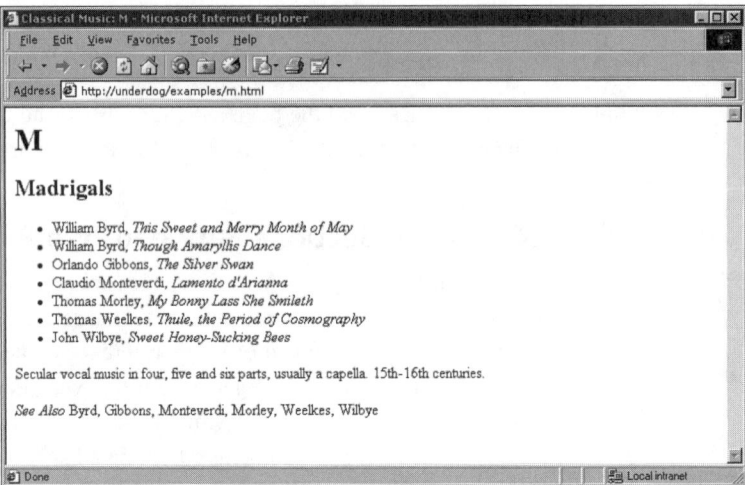

In the last line (the See Also), linking the composer names to their respective sections elsewhere in the reference would be useful. If you use the procedure you learned earlier today, you can create a link here around the word Byrd to the page b.html. When your readers select the link to b.html, the browser drops them at the top of the Bs. These hapless readers then have to scroll down through all the composers whose names start with B (and there are many of them: Bach, Beethoven, Brahms, Bruckner) to get to Byrd—a lot of work for a system that claims to link information so that you can find what you want quickly and easily.

What you want is to be able to link the word Byrd in m.html directly to the section for Byrd in b.html. Here's the relevant part of b.html you want to link. (I've deleted all the Bs before Byrd to make the file shorter for this example. Pretend they're still there.)

Note

In this example you will see the use of the <em> tag. This tag is used to specify text that should be emphasized. The emphasis usually is done by rendering the text italic in Netscape and Internet Explorer.

▼

```
<!DOCTYPE html PUBLIC "-//W3C//DTD XHTML 1.0 Transitional//EN"
"http://www.w3.org/TR/xhtml1/DTD/transitional.dtd">
<html>
<head>
<title>Classical Music: B</title>
</head>
<body>
<h1>B</h1>
<!-- I've deleted all the Bs before Byrd to make things shorter -->
<h2><a name="Byrd">Byrd, William,   1543-1623</a></h2>
<ul>
  <li>Madrigals
    <ul>
       <li><em>This Sweet and Merry Month of May</em></li>
       <li><em>Though Amaryllis Dance</em></li>
       <li><em>Lullabye, My Sweet Little Baby</em></li>
    </ul>
  </li>
  <li>Masses
    <ul>
       <li><em>Mass for Five Voices</em></li>
       <li><em>Mass for Four Voices</em></li>
       <li><em>Mass for Three Voices</em></li>
    </ul>
  </li>
  <li>Motets
    <ul>
       <li><em>Ave verum corpus a 4</em></li>
    </ul>
  </li>
</ul>
<p><em>See Also</em> Madrigals, Masses, Motets</p>
</body>
</html>
```

5

You'll need to create an anchor at the section heading for Byrd. You then can link to that anchor from the See Alsos in the file for M.

As I described earlier today, you need two elements for each anchor: an anchor name and the text inside the link to hold that anchor (which might be highlighted in some browsers). The latter is easy; the section heading itself works well because it's the element to which you're actually linking.

You can choose any name you want for the anchor, but each anchor in the page must be unique. (If you have two or more anchors with the name fred in the same page, how would the browser know which one to choose when a link to that anchor is selected?) A good, unique anchor name for this example is simply byrd because byrd can appear only one place in the file, and this is it.

▼   After you've decided on the two parts, you can create the anchor itself in your HTML file. Add the <a> tag to the William Byrd section heading, but be careful here. If you were working with normal text within a paragraph, you'd just surround the whole line with <a>. But when you're adding an anchor to a big section of text that also is contained within an element—such as a heading or paragraph—always put the anchor inside the element. In other words, enter

```
<h2><a name="byrd">Byrd, William, 1543-1623</a></h2>
```

but do not enter

```
<a name="byrd"><h2>Byrd, William, 1543-1623</h2></a>
```

The second example can confuse your browser. Is it an anchor, formatted just like the text before it, with mysteriously placed heading tags? Or is it a heading that also happens to be an anchor? If you use the right code in your HTML file, with the anchor inside the heading, you avoid the confusion.

You can easily forget about this solution—especially if you're like me and you create text first and then add links and anchors. Just surrounding everything with <a> tags makes sense. Think of the situation this way: If you're linking to just one word, and not to the entire element, you put the <a> tag inside the <h2>. Working with the whole line of text isn't any different. Keep this rule in mind, and you'll get less confused.

Note   If you're still confused, refer to Appendix B, "HTML 4.0 Quick Reference," which has a summary of all the HTML tags and rules for which tags can and cannot go inside each one.

So you've added your anchor to the heading, and its name is "byrd". Now go back to your m.html file, to the line with See Also:

```
<p><em>See Also</em>
 Byrd, Gibbons, Lassus, Monteverdi, Morley, Weelkes, Wilbye</p>
```

You're going to create your link here around the word byrd, just as you would for any other link. But what's the URL? As you learned previously, pathnames to anchors look similar to the following:

page_name#anchor_name

If you're creating a link to the b.html page itself, the href is as follows:

▼   `<a href="b.html">`

 Because you're linking to a section inside that page, add the anchor name to link that section so that it looks like this:

```
<a href="b.html#byrd">
```

Note the small b in byrd. Anchor names and links are case sensitive; if you put #Byrd in your href, the link might not work properly. Make sure that the anchor name you use in the name attribute and the anchor name in the link after the # are identical.

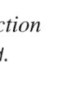 **Caution**

A common mistake is to put a hash sign in both the anchor name and in the link to that anchor. You use the hash sign only to separate the page and the anchor in the link. Anchor names should never have hash signs in them.

So, with the new link to the new section, the See Also line looks like this:

```
<p><em>See Also</em>
 <a href="b.html#byrd">Byrd</a>,
 Gibbons, Lassus, Monteverdi, Morley, Weelkes, Wilbye</p>
```

Of course, you can go ahead and add anchors and links to the other parts of the reference for the remaining composers.

With all your links and anchors in place, test everything. Figure 5.13 shows the Madrigals section with the link to Byrd ready to be selected.

FIGURE 5.13

The Madrigals section with a link to Byrd.

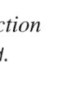

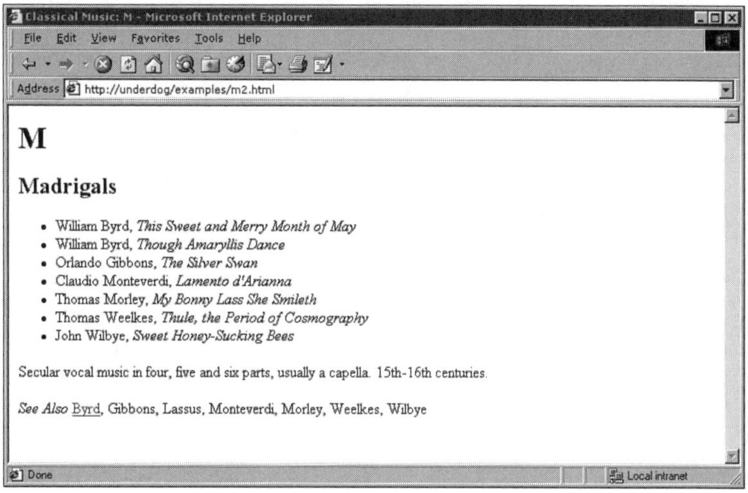

5

▼   Figure 5.14 shows the screen that pops up when you select the Byrd link.

FIGURE 5.14

The byrd section.

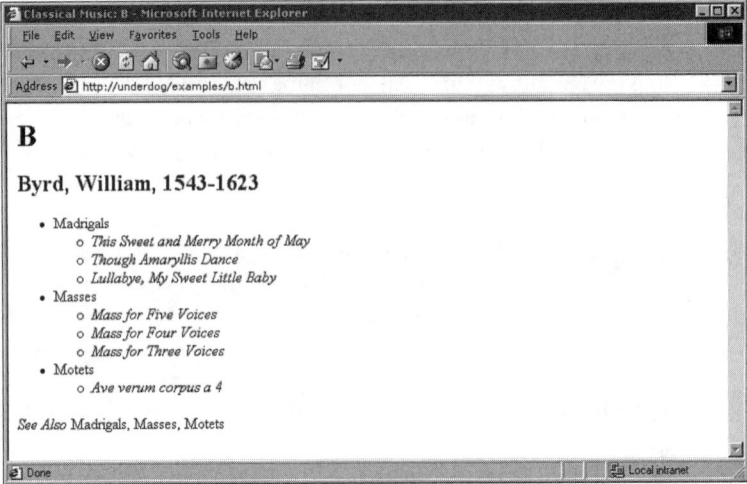

▲

Linking to Anchors in the Same Document

What if you have only one large page, and you want to link to sections within that page? You can use anchors for it, too. For larger pages, using anchors can be an easy way to jump around within sections. To link to sections, you just need to set up your anchors at each section the way you usually do. Then, when you link to those anchors, leave off the name of the page itself, but include the hash sign and the name of the anchor. So, if you're linking to an anchor name called section5 in the same page as the link, the link looks like the following:

```
Go to <a href="#section5">The Fifth Section</a>
```

When you leave off the page name, the browser assumes that you're linking with the current page and scrolls to the appropriate section. You'll get a chance to see this feature in action in Day 6, "More Text Formatting with HTML." There, you'll create a complete Web page that includes a table of contents at the beginning. From this table of contents, the reader can jump to different sections in the same Web page. The table of contents includes links to each section heading. In turn, other links at the end of each section enable the user to jump back to the table of contents or to the top of the page.

Anatomy of a URL

So far in this book, you've encountered URLs twice—in Day 1, "The World of the World Wide Web," as part of the introduction to the Web, and today, when you created links to remote pages. If you've ever done much exploring on the Web, you've encountered URLs as a matter of course. You couldn't start exploring without a URL.

As I mentioned in Day 1, URLs are uniform resource locators. In effect, URLs are street addresses for bits of information on the Internet. Most of the time, you can avoid trying to figure out which URL to put in your links by simply navigating to the bit of information you want with your browser, and then copying and pasting the long string of gobbledygook into your link. But understanding what a URL is all about and why it has to be so long and complex is often useful. Also, when you put your own information up on the Web, knowing something about URLs will be useful so that you can tell people where your Web page is.

In this section, you'll learn what the parts of a URL are, how you can use them to get to information on the Web, and the kinds of URLs you can use (HTTP, FTP, Mailto, and so on).

Parts of URLs

MostURLs contain (roughly) three parts: the protocol, the hostname, and the directory or filename (see Figure 5.15).

FIGURE 5.15

URL parts.

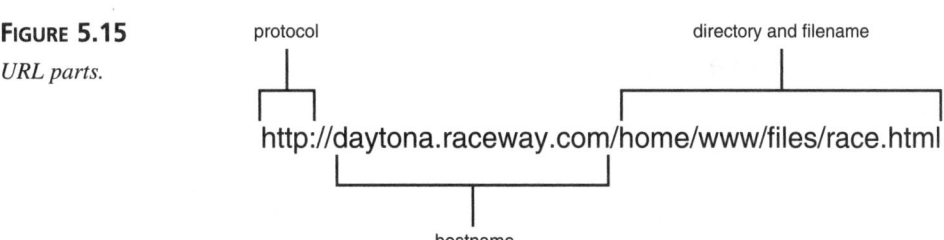

5

The *protocol* is the way in which the page is accessed; that is, the means of communication your browser will use to get the file. If the browser is using HTTP to get to the file, the protocol part is http. If the browser uses FTP, the protocol is ftp. If you're using Gopher, it's gopher, and so on. The protocol matches an information server that must be installed on the system for it to work. You can't use an FTP URL on a machine that does not have an FTP server installed, for example.

The *hostname* is the Internet system on which the information is stored, such as `www.netcom.com`, `ftp.apple.com`, or `www.aol.com`. You can have the same hostname but have different URLs with different protocols, such as the following:

```
http://mysystem.com
ftp://mysystem.com
gopher://mysystem.com
```

It's the same machine with three different information servers, and the browser will use different methods of connecting with each. As long as all three servers are installed and available on that system, you won't have a problem.

The hostname part of the URL might include a port number. The port number tells your browser to open a connection using the appropriate protocol on a specific network port. The only time you'll need a port number in a URL is if the server responding to the request has been explicitly installed on that port. If the server is listening on the default port, you can leave the port number out. (This issue is covered in Day 19.)

If a port number is necessary, it is placed after the hostname but before the directory, as follows:

```
http://my-public-access-unix.com:1550/pub/file
```

Finally, the *directory* is the location of the file or other form of information on the host. The directory can be an actual directory and filename, or it can be another indicator that the protocol uses to refer to the location of that information. (Gopher directories, for example, are not explicit directories.)

Special Characters in URLs

A *special character* in a URL is anything that is not an upper- or lowercase letter, a number (0–9), or the following symbols: dollar sign ($), dash (-), underscore (_), period (.), or plus sign (+). You might need to specify any other characters by using special URL escape codes to keep them from being interpreted as parts of the URL itself.

URL escape codes are indicated by a percent sign (%) and a two-character hexadecimal symbol from the ISO-Latin-1 character set (a superset of standard ASCII). For example, `%20` is a space, `%3f` is a question mark, and `%2f` is a slash.

Suppose that you have a directory named `All My Files`. Your first pass at a URL with this name in it might look like the following:

```
http://myhost.com/harddrive/All My Files/www/file.html
```

If you put this URL in quotation marks in a link tag, it might work (but only if you put it in quotation marks). Because the spaces are considered special characters to the URL, however, some browsers might have problems with them and not recognize the pathname correctly. For full compatibility with all browsers, use %20, as follows:

```
http://myhost.com/harddrive/A||%20My%20Files/www/file.html
```

Most of the time, if you make sure that your file and directory names are short and use only alphanumeric characters, you won't need to include special characters in URLs. Keep this point in mind as you write your own pages.

HTML 4.0 and the <a> tag

HTML 4.0 includes some additional attributes for the <a> tag that are less common. These offer the following:

- tabindex—Support for a tabbing order so that authors can define an order for anchors and links, and then the user can tab between them the way he does in a dialog box in Windows or the MacOS
- Event handlers such as those used in the Netscape JavaScript environment and Microsoft's Active Scripting Model (see onclick, onfocus, and onblur in the list of intrinsic events in section "Common Attributes and Events" of Appendix B)

Kinds of URLs

Many kinds of URLs are defined by the Uniform Resource Locator specification. (See Appendix A, "Sources for Further Information," for a pointer to the most recent version.) This section describes some of the more popular URLs and some situations to look out for when using them.

5

HTTP

HTTP URLs are by far the most common type of URLs, since they point to other documents on the Web. HTTP, which stands for Hypertext Transfer Protocol, is the protocol that World Wide Web servers use to transfer information to browsers.

HTTP URLs follow this basic URL form:

```
http://www.foo.com/home/foo/
```

If the URL ends in a slash, the last part of the URL is considered a directory name. The file that you get using a URL of this type is the default file for that directory as defined by the HTTP server, usually a file called index.html. (If the Web page you're designing is the top-level file for all a directory's files, calling it index.html is a good idea.)

You also can specify the filename directly in the URL. In this case, the file at the end of the URL is the one that is loaded, as in the following examples:

```
http://www.foo.com/home/foo/index.html
http://www.foo.com/home/foo/homepage.html
```

Using HTTP URLs such as the following, where foo is a directory, is also usually acceptable:

```
http://www.foo.com/home/foo
```

In this case, because foo is a directory, this URL should have a slash at the end. Most Web servers can figure out that you meant this to be a directory and "redirect" to the appropriate file. Some older servers, however, might have difficulties resolving this URL, so you should always identify directories and files explicitly and make sure that a default file is available if you're indicating a directory.

Anonymous FTP

FTP URLs are used to point to files located on FTP servers—and usually anonymous FTP servers, that is, the ones that you can log in using anonymous as the login ID and your email address as the password. FTP URLs also follow the standard URL form, as shown in the following examples:

```
ftp://ftp.foo.com/home/foo
ftp://ftp.foo.com/home/foo/homepage.html
```

Because you can retrieve either a file or a directory list with FTP, the restrictions on whether you need a trailing slash at the end of the URL are not the same as with HTTP. The first URL here retrieves a listing of all the files in the foo directory. The second URL retrieves and parses the file homepage.html in the foo directory.

Note

Navigating FTP servers by using a Web browser often can be much slower than navigating them by using FTP itself because the browser does not hold the connection open. Instead, it opens the connection, finds the file or directory listing, displays the listing, and then closes down the FTP connection. If you select a link to open a file or another directory in that listing, the browser will construct a new FTP URL from the items you selected, reopen the FTP connection by using the new URL, get the next directory or file, and close it again. For this reason, FTP URLs are best for when you know exactly which file you want to retrieve rather than for when you want to browse an archive.

Although your browser uses FTP to fetch the file, you still can get an HTML file from that server just as if it were an HTTP server, and it will parse and display just fine. Web browsers don't care how they get a hypertext file. As long as they can recognize the file as HTML, either by the servers telling them it's an HTML file (as with HTTP—you'll learn more about it later), or by the extension to the filename, the browsers will parse and display that file as an HTML file. If they don't recognize it as an HTML file, no big deal. The browsers can either display the file if they know what kind of file it is or just save the file to disk.

Non-Anonymous FTP

All the FTP URLs in the preceding section are used for anonymous FTP servers. You also can specify an FTP URL for named accounts on an FTP server, like the following:

```
ftp://username:password@ftp.foo.com/home/foo/homepage.html
```

In this form of the URL, the `username` part is your login ID on the server, and `password` is that account's password. Note that no attempt is made to hide the password in the URL. Be very careful that no one is watching you when you're using URLs of this form—and don't put them into links that someone else can find!

Furthermore, the URLs that you request may be cached or logged somewhere, either on your local machine or on a proxy server between you and the site you're connecting to. For that reason, it's probably wise to avoid using this type of URL.

Mailto

The Mailto URL is used to send electronic mail. If the browser supports Mailto URLs, when a link that contains one is selected, the browser will prompt you for a subject and the body of the mail message, and send that message to the appropriate address when you're done.

Some browsers do not support Mailto and produce an error if a link with a Mailto URL is selected.

The Mailto URL is different from the standard URL form. It looks like the following:

```
mailto:internet_e-mail_address
```

Here's an example:

```
mailto: lemay@lne.com
```

5

> **Note** If your email address includes a percent sign (%), you'll have to use the escape character %25 instead. Percent signs are special characters to URLs.

Gopher

Gopher URLs use the standard URL file format up to and including the hostname. After that, they use special Gopher protocols to encode the path to the particular file. The directory in Gopher does not indicate a directory pathname as HTTP and FTP URLs do and is too complex for today's lesson.

Most of the time, you'll probably use a Gopher URL just to point to a Gopher server, which is easy. A URL of this sort looks like the following:

```
gopher://gopher.myhost.com/
```

If you really want to point directly to a specific file on a Gopher server, probably the best way to get the appropriate URL is not to try to build it yourself. Instead, navigate to the appropriate file or collection by using your browser, and then copy and paste the appropriate URL into your HTML page.

Usenet Newsgroups

Usenet news URLs have one of two forms:

```
news:name_of_newsgroup
news:message-id
```

The first form is used to read an entire newsgroup, such as `comp.infosystems.www.authoring.html` or `alt.gothic`. If your browser supports Usenet news URLs (either directly or through a newsreader), it will provide you with a list of available articles in that newsgroup.

The second form enables you to retrieve a specific news article. Each news article has a unique ID, called a message ID, which usually looks something like the following:

```
<lemayCt76Jq.CwG@netcom.com>
```

To use a message ID in a URL, remove the angle brackets and include the `news:` part:

```
news:lemayCt76Jq.CwG@netcom.com
```

Be aware that news articles do not exist forever—they expire and are deleted—so a message ID that was valid at one point can become invalid a short time later. If you want a permanent link to a news article, you should just copy the article to your Web presentation and link it as you would any other file.

Both forms of URL assume that you're reading news from an NNTP server, and they can be used only if you have defined an NNTP server somewhere in an environment variable or preferences file for your browser. Therefore, news URLs are most useful simply for reading specific news articles locally, not necessarily for using in links in pages.

Note | News URLs, like Mailto URLs, might not be supported by all browsers.

File

File URLs are intended to reference files contained on the local disk. In other words, they refer to files located on the same system as the browser. For local files, file URLs take one of these two forms: the first with an empty hostname (three slashes rather than two) or with the hostname as `localhost`:

```
file:///dir1/dir2/file
file://localhost/dir1/dir2/file
```

Depending on your browser, one or the other will usually work.

File URLs are very similar to FTP URLs. In fact, if the host part of a file URL is not empty or `localhost`, your browser will try to find the given file by using FTP. Both of the following URLs result in the same file being loaded in the same way:

```
file://somesystem.com/pub/dir/foo/file.html
ftp://somesystem.com/pub/dir/foo/file.html
```

Probably the best use of file URLs is in startup pages for your browser (which are also called *home pages*). In this instance, because you will almost always be referring to a local file, using a file URL makes sense.

The problem with file URLs is that they reference local files, where *local* means on the same system as the browser pointing to the file—not the same system from which the page was retrieved! If you use file URLs as links in your page, and then someone from elsewhere on the Internet encounters your page and tries to follow those links, that person's browser will attempt to find the file on her local disk (and generally will fail). Also, because file URLs use the absolute pathname to the file, if you use file URLs in your page, you cannot move that page elsewhere on the system or to any other system.

If your intention is to refer to files that are on the same file system or directory as the current page, use relative pathnames rather than file URLs. With relative pathnames for local files and other URLs for remote files, you should not need to use a file URL at all.

5

Summary

Today, you learned all about links. Links turn the Web from a collection of unrelated pages into an enormous, interrelated information system. (There are those big words again.)

To create links, you use the <a>...</a> tag, called the link or anchor tag. The anchor tag has several attributes for indicating files to link to (the href attribute) and anchor names (the name attribute).

When linking pages that are all stored on the local disk, you can specify their pathnames in the href attribute as relative or absolute paths. For local links, relative pathnames are preferred because they enable you to move local pages more easily to another directory or to another system. If you use absolute pathnames, your links will break if you change anything in the hard-coded path.

If you want to link to a page on the Web (a remote page), the value of the href attribute is the URL of that page. You can easily copy the URL of the page you want to link. Just go to that page by using your favorite Web browser, and then copy and paste the URL from your browser into the appropriate place in your link tag.

To create links to specific parts of a page, set an anchor at the point you want to link to, use the <a>...</a> tag as you would with a link, but rather than the href attribute, you use the name attribute to name the anchor. You then can link directly to that anchor name by using the name of the page, a hash sign (#), and the anchor name.

Finally, URLs (uniform resource locators) are used to point to pages, files, and other information on the Internet. Depending on the type of information, URLs can contain several parts, but most contain a protocol type and location or address. URLs can be used to point to many kinds of information but are most commonly used to point to Web pages (http), FTP directories or files (ftp), information on Gopher servers (gopher), electronic mail addresses (mailto), or Usenet news (news).

Workshop

Congratulations, you learned a lot today! Now it's time for the workshop. Many questions about links appear here. The quiz focuses on other items that are important for you to remember, followed by the quiz answers. In today's exercises, you'll take the list of items you created yesterday and link them to other pages.

Q&A

Q My links aren't being highlighted in blue or purple at all. They're still just plain text.

A Is the filename in a `name` attribute rather than in an `href`? Did you remember to close the quotation marks around the filename to which you're linking? Both of these errors can prevent links from showing up as links.

Q I put a URL into a link, and it shows up as highlighted in my browser, but when I click it, the browser says "unable to access page." If it can't find the page, why did it highlight the text?

A The browser highlights text within a link tag whether or not the link is valid. In fact, you don't even need to be online for links to show up as highlighted links, although you cannot get to them. The only way you can tell whether a link is valid is to select it and try to view the page to which the link points.

As to why the browser couldn't find the page you linked to—make sure that you're connected to the network and that you entered the URL into the link correctly. Also verify that you have both opening and closing quotation marks around the filename, and that those quotation marks are straight quotes. If your browser prints link destinations in the status bar when you move the mouse cursor over a link, watch that status bar and see whether the URL that appears is actually the URL you want.

Finally, try opening the URL directly in your browser and see whether that solution works. If directly opening the link doesn't work either, there might be several reasons why. The following are two common possibilities:

- The server is overloaded or is not on the Internet.

  Machines go down, as do network connections. If a particular URL doesn't work for you, perhaps something is wrong with the machine or the network. Or maybe the site is popular, and too many people are trying to access it at once. Try again later. If you know the people who run the server, you can try sending them electronic mail or calling them.

- The URL itself is bad.

  Sometimes URLs become invalid. Because a URL is a form of absolute pathname, if the file to which it refers moves around, or if a machine or directory name gets changed, the URL won't be valid anymore. Try contacting the person or site you got the URL from in the first place. See if that person has a more recent link.

5

Q Can I put any URL in a link?

A You bet. If you can get to a URL using your browser, you can put that URL in a link. Note, however, that some browsers support URLs that others don't. For example, Lynx is really good with Mailto URLs (URLs that allow you to send electronic mail to a person's email address). When you select a Mailto URL in Lynx, it prompts you for a subject and the body of the message. When you're done, it sends the mail.

Q Can I use images as links?

A Yup, in more ways than one, actually. You'll learn how to use images as links in Day 7, "Using Images, Color, and Backgrounds," and how to create what are called imagemaps in Day 9, "Creating and Using Imagemaps."

Q You've described only two attributes of the <a> tag: `href` and `name`. Aren't there others?

A Yes. The <a> tag has several attributes including `rel`, `rev`, `shape`, `accesskey`, and `title`. However, most of these attributes can be used only by tools that automatically generate links between pages, or by browsers that can manage links better than most of those now available. Because 99% of the readers of this book won't care about (or ever use) those links or browsers, I'm sticking to `href` and `name` and ignoring the other attributes.

If you're really interested, I've summarized the other attributes in Appendix B, and pointers to the various HTML specifications are listed in Appendix A, as well.

Q My links are not pointing to my anchors. When I follow a link, I'm always dropped at the top of the page rather than at the anchor. What's going on here?

A Are you specifying the anchor name in the link after the hash sign the same way that it appears in the anchor itself, with all the uppercase and lowercase letters identical? Anchors are case sensitive, so if your browser cannot find an anchor name with an exact match, the browser might try to select something else in the page that is closer. This is dependent on browser behavior, of course, but if your links and anchors aren't working, the problem usually is that your anchor names and your anchors do not match. Also, remember that anchor names don't contain hash signs—only the links to them do.

Q It sounds like file URLs aren't overly useful. Is there any reason I'd want to use them?

A I can think of two. The first one is if you have many users on a single system (for example, on a UNIX system), and you want to give those local users (but nobody else) access to files on that system. By using file URLs, you can point to files on the local system, and anyone on that system can get to them. Readers from outside the system won't have direct access to the disk and won't be able to get to those files.

A second good reason for using file URLs is that you actually want to point to a local disk. For example, you could create a CD-ROM full of information in HTML form and then create a link from a page on the Web to a file on the CD-ROM by using a file URL. In this case, because your presentation depends on a disk your readers must have, using a file URL makes sense.

Q Is there any way to indicate a subject in a Mailto URL?

A Not at the moment. According to the current Mailto URL definition, the only thing you can put in a Mailto URL is the address to mail to. If you really need a subject or something in the body of the message, consider using a form instead.

Quiz

1. What two things do you need to create a link in HTML?
2. What is a relative pathname? Why is it advantageous to use them?
3. What is an absolute pathname?
4. What is an anchor, and what is it used for?
5. Besides HTTP (Web page) URLs, what other kinds are there?

Quiz Answers

1. To create a link in HTML, you need the name or URL of the file or page to which you want to link, and the text that your readers can select to follow the link.
2. A relative pathname points to a file, based on the location that is relative to the current file. Relative pathnames are portable, meaning that if you move your files elsewhere on a disk or rename a directory, the links require little or no modification.
3. An absolute pathname points to a page by starting at the top level of a directory hierarchy and working downward through all intervening directories to reach the file.
4. An anchor marks a place that you can link to inside a Web document. A link on the same page or on another page can then jump to that specific location instead of the top of the page.
5. Other types of URLs are FTP URLs (which point to files on FTP servers); File URLs (which point to a file contained on a local disk); Mailto URLs (which are used to send electronic mail); Gopher URLs (which point to files on a Gopher server); and Usenet URLs (which point to newsgroups or specific news articles in a newsgroup).

5

Exercises

1. Remember the list of topics that you created yesterday in the first exercise? Create a link to the page you created in yesterday's second exercise (the page that described one of the topics in more detail).

2. Now, open up the page that you created in yesterday's second exercise, and create a link back to the first page. Also, find some pages on the World Wide Web that discuss the same topic and create links to those pages as well. Good luck!

DAY 6

More Text Formatting with HTML

On Days 4 and 5, you learned the basics of HTML, including several basic page elements and links. With that background, you're now ready to learn more about what HTML can do in terms of text formatting and layout. Today you'll learn about most of the remaining tags in HTML that you'll need to know to construct pages, including tags in standard HTML 2.0 through HTML 4.0, as well as HTML attributes in individual browsers. Today you'll learn how to do the following:

- Specify the appearance of individual characters (bold, italic, underlined)
- Include special characters (characters with accents, copyright marks, and so on)
- Create preformatted text (text with spaces and tabs retained)
- Align text left, right, and centered
- Change the font and font size
- Create other miscellaneous HTML text elements, including line breaks, rule lines, addresses, and quotations

In addition, you'll learn the differences between standard HTML and HTML extensions, and when to choose which tags to use in your pages. Finally, you'll create a complete Web page that uses many of the tags presented today, as well as the information from the preceding four days.

Today you'll cover several tags and options, so you might find it a bit overwhelming. Don't worry about remembering everything now; just get a grasp of what sort of formatting you can do in HTML, and then you can look up the specific tags later.

Character Styles

When you use HTML tags for paragraphs, headings, or lists, those tags affect that block of text as a whole—changing the font, changing the spacing above and below the line, or adding characters (in the case of bulleted lists).

Character styles are tags that affect words or characters within other HTML entities and change the appearance of that text so that it's somehow different from the surrounding text—making it bold or underlined, for example.

To change the appearance of a set of characters within text, you can use one of two kinds of tags: logical styles or physical styles.

Logical Styles

Logical style tags describe the meaning of the text within the tag, not how it should be presented. They're similar to the common element tags for paragraphs or headings. For example, logical style tags might indicate a definition, a snippet of code, or an emphasized word. This can be a bit confusing because there are now ad hoc standards to make the formatting that results from these tags consistent between browsers.

Using logical style tags, the browser determines the actual presentation of the text, whether it's bold, italic, or any other change in appearance. You cannot guarantee that text that's highlighted using these tags will always be bold or italic, so you shouldn't depend on it. These days, browser makers have pretty much agreed on how each of these logical tags are rendered, but it's still important to understand that the logical tags convey more meaning than just the physical styles that they apply.

Note

HTML 4.0 extends HTML's model of physical and logical styles by providing support for style sheets. With style sheets, page authors can define the appearance (including font family, style, and size) of individual elements or entire classes of elements (such as all unordered lists) in a document more precisely. We'll cover style sheets on Days 12, "XHTML and Style Sheets," and 18, "Designing for the Real World."

Each character style tag has both opening and closing sides and affects the text within those two tags. The following are the eight logical style tags in standard HTML:

<em>   This tag indicates that the characters are to be emphasized in some way; that is, they're formatted differently from the rest of the text. In graphical browsers, typically <em> italicizes the text. For example:

              <p>The anteater is the **<em>**strangest**</em>** looking animal,

              isn't it?**</p>**

<strong>   With this tag, the characters are to be more strongly emphasized than with <em>—usually in boldface. Consider the following:

              <p>Take a **<strong>**left turn**</strong>** at **<strong>**Dee's Hop

              Stop**</strong></p>**

<code>   This tag indicates that the text inside is a code sample and displays it in a fixed-width font like Courier. For example:

              <p><code>#include "trans.h"**</code></p>**

<samp>   This tag indicates sample text and generally is presented in a fixed-width font, like <code>. An example of its usage follows:

              <p>The URL for that page is **<samp>**http://www.cern.ch/
              </samp></p>

<kbd>   This tag indicates text that's intended to be typed by a user. It's also presented in a fixed-width font. Consider the following:

              <p>Type the following command: **<kbd>**find . -name "prune"

              -print**</kbd></p>**

<var>   This tag indicates the name of a variable, or some entity to be replaced with an actual value. Often it's displayed as italic or under-line, and is used as follows:

              <p><code>chown **</code><var>**your_name the_file

              </var></p>

<dfn>   This tag indicates a definition. <dfn> is used to highlight a word (usu-ally in italics) that will be defined or has just been defined, as in the following example:

              <p>Styles that are named after how they are actually

6

```
used are called

<dfn>logical styles</dfn></p>
```

`<cite>`   This tag indicates a short quote or citation, as in the following:

```
<p>Eggplant has been known to cause nausea in some

people<cite> (Lemay, 1994)</cite></p>
```

> **Note**   Of the tags in this list, all except <dfn> are part of the official HTML 2.0 specification. <dfn> was added in the HTML 3.2 specification.

HTML 4.0 introduced two additional logical style tags that are most useful for audio browsers. A graphical browser, such as Netscape or Internet Explorer, won't display them any differently. When an audio browser reads content included within one of these tags, however, each letter is spoken individually. For example, FOX is pronounced "F-O-X" rather than "fox."

These tags also use opening and closing sides and affect the text within. The following are new tags:

`<abbr>`   This tag indicates the abbreviation of a word, as in the following:

```
<p>Use the standard two-letter state abbreviation

(such as <abbr>CA</abbr> for California)</p>
```

`<acronym>`   Similar to the <abbr> tag, <acronym> designates a word formed by combining the initial letters of several words, as in the following example:

```
<p>Jonathan learned his great problem-handling skills

from <acronym>STEPS</acronym> (Simply Tackle Each Problem

Seriously)</p>
```

Got all these tags memorized now? Good! There will be a pop quiz at the end of the chapter. The following code snippets demonstrate each of the logical style tags, and Figure 6.1 illustrates how all the tags are displayed in Internet Explorer.

INPUT
```
<p>The anteater is the <em>strangest</em> looking animal, isn't it?</p>
<p>Take a <strong>left turn</strong> at <strong>Dee's Hop Stop
</strong></p>
<p><code>#include "trans.h"</code></p>
<p>The URL for that page is <samp>http://www.cern.ch/</samp></p>
```

```
<p>Type the following command: <kbd>find . -name "prune" -
print</kbd></p>
<p><code>chown </code><var>your_name the_file</var></p>
<p>Styles that are named after how they are used are called <dfn>logical
styles</dfn></p>
<p>Eggplant has been known to cause nausea in some
people<cite> (Lemay, 1994)</cite></p>
<p>Use the standard two-letter state abbreviation (such as
<abbr>CA</abbr> for California)</p>
<p>Jonathan learned his great problem-handling skills from
<acronym>STEPS</acronym> (Simply Tackle Each Problem Seriously)</p>
```

OUTPUT

FIGURE 6.1

Various logical styles displayed in Internet Explorer.

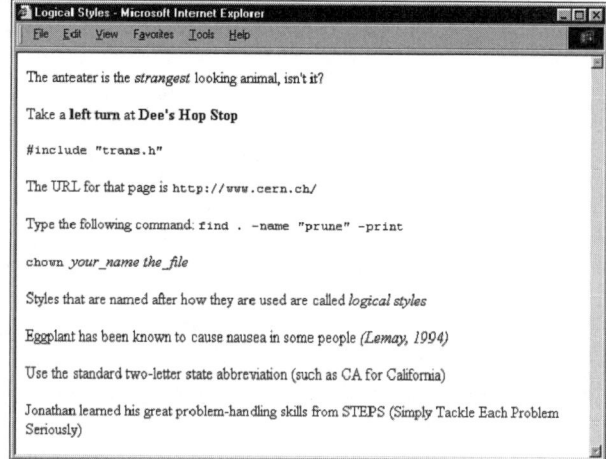

Physical Styles

In addition to these style tags, you can use a set of *physical style tags* to change the actual presentation style of the text—bold, italic, or monospace.

Like the character style tags, each formatting tag has a beginning and ending tag. Standard HTML 2.0 defined three physical style tags:

`<b>`	Bold
`<i>`	Italic
`<tt>`	Monospaced typewriter font

HTML 3.2 defined several additional physical style tags, including the following:

`<u>`	Underline (deprecated in HTML 4.0)
`<s>`	Strikethrough (deprecated in HTML 4.0)

6

`<big>`	Bigger print than the surrounding text
`<small>`	Smaller print
`<sub>`	Subscript
`<sup>`	Superscript

> **Note**
>
> Text-based browsers, like Lynx and those associated with wireless devices, can't render bold, italic, or other styled text. Generally they highlight the text in some way, but the method varies depending on the browser and platform.

You can nest character tags—for example, using both bold and italic for a set of characters—as follows:

```
<b><i>Text that is both bold and italic</i></b>
```

However, the result on the screen is browser-dependent, like all HTML tags. You won't necessarily end up with text that's both bold and italic. You may end up with one style or the other:

INPUT

```
<p>In Dante's <i>Inferno</i>, malaboge was the eighth circle of hell,
and held the malicious and fraudulent.</p>
<p>All entries must be received by <b>September 26, 1999</b>.</p>
<p>Type <tt>lpr -Pbirch myfile.txt</tt> to print that file.</p>
<p>Sign your name in the spot marked <u>Sign Here</u>:</p>
<p>People who wear orange shirts and plaid pants <s>have no taste</s>
are fashion-challenged.</p>
<p>RCP floor mats give you <big>big</big> savings over the
competition!</p>
<p>Then, from the corner of the room, he heard a <small>tiny voice
</small>.</p>
<p>In heavy trading today. Consolidated Orange Trucking
rose <sup>1</sup>/<sub>4</sub>
points on volume of 1,457,900 shares.</p>
```

Figure 6.2 shows some of the physical tags and how they appear in Internet Explorer.

FIGURE 6.2

Logical styles displayed in Internet Explorer.

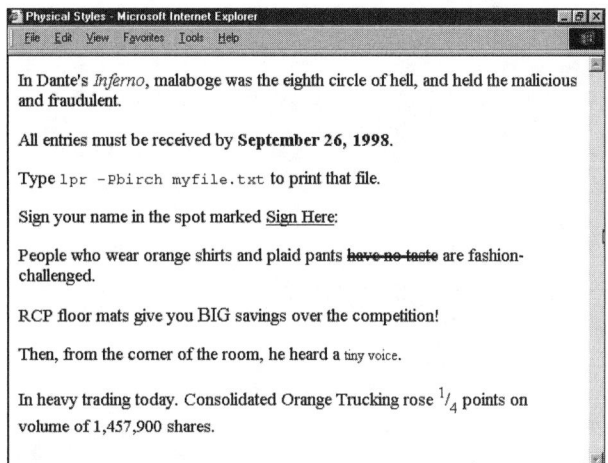

Preformatted Text

Most of the time, text in an HTML file is formatted based on the HTML tags used to mark up that text. As I mentioned on Day 3, "An Introduction to HTML," any extra white space (spaces, tabs, returns) that you put in your text is stripped out by the browser.

The one exception to this rule is the preformatted text tag <pre>. Any white space that you put into text surrounded by the <pre> and </pre> tags is retained in the final output. With these tags, the spacing in the text in the HTML source will be preserved when it's displayed on the page.

The catch is that preformatted text usually is displayed (in graphical displays, at least) in a monospaced font such as Courier. Preformatted text is excellent for displays such as programming code examples, where you want to indent and format lines appropriately. Because you can use the <pre> tag to align text by padding it with spaces, you can use it for simple tables. However, the fact that the tables are presented in a monospaced font may make them less than ideal. (You'll learn how to create real tables on Day 10, "Tables.") The following is an example of a table created with <pre>:

```
<pre>
            Diameter   Distance    Time to    Time to
            (miles)    from Sun     Orbit     Rotate
                       (millions
                        of miles)
-------------------------------------------------------------
-
    Mercury   3100        36       88 days    59 days
    Venus     7700        67       225 days   244 days
    Earth     7920        93       365 days   24 hrs
```

6

```
Mars            4200      141      687 days     24 hrs 24 mins
Jupiter        88640      483      11.9 years   9 hrs 50 mins
Saturn         74500      886      29.5 years   10 hrs 39 mins
Uranus         32000     1782      84 years     23 hrs
Neptune        31000     2793      165 days     15 hrs 48 mins
Pluto           1500     3670      248 years    6 days 7 hrs
</pre>
```

Figure 6.3 shows how it looks in Internet Explorer.

OUTPUT

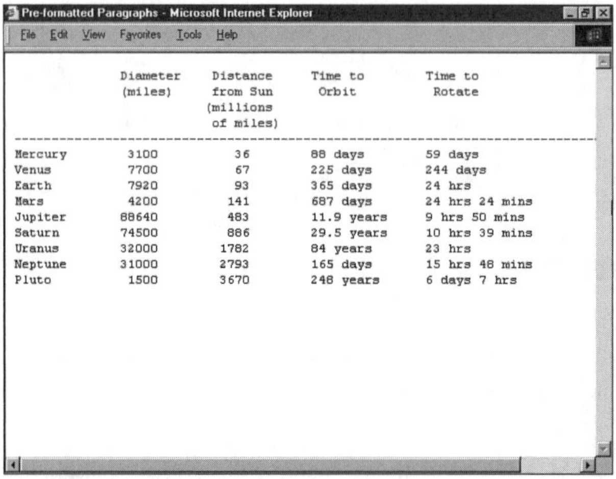

FIGURE 6.3

A table created using <pre>, shown in Internet Explorer.

When you're creating text for the <pre> tag, you can use link tags and character styles, but not element tags such as headings or paragraphs. You should break your lines with hard returns and try to keep your lines to 60 characters or fewer. Some browsers may have limited horizontal space in which to display text. Because browsers usually won't reformat preformatted text to fit that space, you should make sure that you keep your text within the boundaries to prevent your readers from having to scroll from side to side.

Be careful with tabs in preformatted text. The actual number of characters for each tab stop varies from browser to browser. One browser may have tab stops at every fourth character, whereas another may have them at every eighth character. You should convert any tabs in your preformatted text to spaces so your formatting doesn't get messed up if it's viewed with different tab settings than in the program you used to enter the text.

The <pre> tag also is excellent for converting files that originally were in some sort of text-only form, such as mail messages or Usenet news postings, into HTML quickly and easily. Just surround the entire content of the article within <pre> tags and you have instant HTML, as in the following example:

```
<pre>
To: lemay@lne.com
From: jokes@lne.com
Subject: Tales of the Move From Hell, pt. 1

I spent the day on the phone today with the entire household
services division of northern California, turning off services,
turning on services, transferring services and other such fun
things you have to do when you move.

It used to be you just called these people and got put on hold for
and interminable amount of time, maybe with some nice music, and
then you got a customer representative who was surly and hard of
hearing, but with some work you could actually get your phone
turned off.
</pre>
```

One creative use of the <pre> tag is to create ASCII art for your Web pages. The following HTML input and output example shows a simple ASCII-art cow:

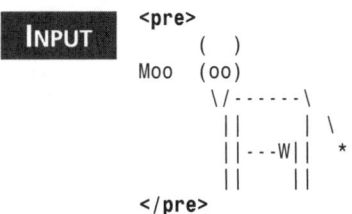

```
<pre>
       ( )
Moo  (oo)
      \/------\
       ||    | \
       ||---W||   *
       ||    ||
</pre>
```

The result in Internet Explorer is displayed in Figure 6.4.

OUTPUT

FIGURE 6.4

A bit of ASCII art that illustrates how preformatted text works.

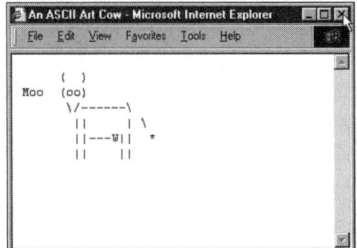

6

Horizontal Rules

The <hr> tag, which has no closing tag in HTML and no text associated with it, creates a horizontal line on the page. Rule lines are excellent for visually separating sections of a Web page—just before headings, for example, or to separate body text from a list of items.

Note

The <hr> tag has no closing tag in HTML. To convert this tag to XHTML and to ensure compatibility with HTML browsers, add a space and a forward slash to the end of the tag:

`<hr />`

If the horizontal line has attributes associated with it, the forward slash still appears at the end of the tag, as shown in the following examples:

`<hr size="2" />`

`<hr width="75%" />`

`<hr align="center" size="4" width="200" />`

The following input and output example shows a rule line and a list as you would write it in XHTML 1.0:

INPUT

```
<hr />
<h2>To Do on Friday</h2>
<ul>
<li>Do laundry</li>
<li>Send FedEx with pictures</li>
<li>Have lunch with Mollie</li>
<li>Read Email</li>
<li>Set up Ethernet</li>
</ul>
<hr />
```

Figure 6.5 shows how they appear in Internet Explorer.

OUTPUT

FIGURE 6.5

An example of an unordered list.

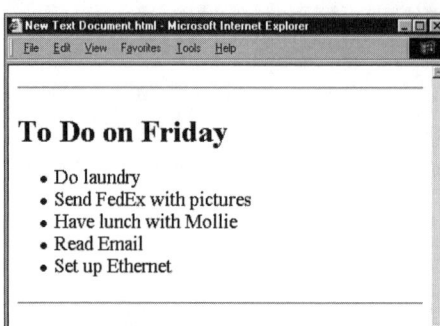

Attributes of the <hr> Tag

In HTML 2.0, the <hr> tag is just as you see it, with no closing tag or attributes. However, HTML 3.2 introduced several attributes to the <hr> tag that give you greater control over the appearance of the line drawn by <hr>. All these attributes have been deprecated in favor of style sheets in the HTML 4.0 specification.

Note

Although presentational attributes such as size, width, and align are still supported in HTML 4.0, style sheets are now the recommended way to control a page's appearance.

The size attribute indicates the thickness, in pixels, of the rule line. The default is 2, and this also is the smallest thickness that you can make the rule line. Figure 6.6 shows the sample rule line thicknesses created with the following code:

INPUT
```
<h2>2 Pixels</h2>
<hr size="2" />
<h2>4 Pixels</h2>
<hr size="4" />
<h2>8 Pixels</h2>
<hr size="8" />
<h2>16 Pixels</h2>
<hr size="16" />
```

OUTPUT

FIGURE 6.6

Examples of rule line thicknesses.

The width attribute indicates the horizontal width of the rule line. You can specify the exact width of the rule in pixels. You can also specify the value as a percentage of the browser width (for example, 30 percent or 50 percent). If you set the width of a horizontal rule to a percentage, the width of the rule will change to conform to the window size if the user resizes the browser window. Figure 6.7 shows the result of the following code, which displays some sample rule line widths:

INPUT
```
<h2>100%</h2>
<hr />
<h2>75%</h2>
<hr width="75%" />
<h2>50%</h2>
<hr width="50%" />
```

6

```
<h2>25%</h2>
<hr width="25%" />
<h2>10%</h2>
<hr width="10%" />
```

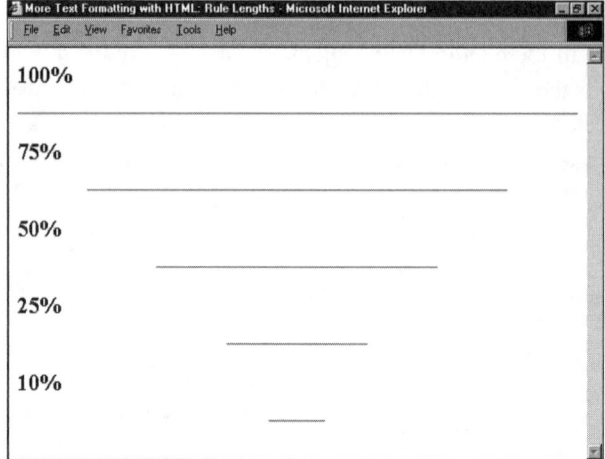

FIGURE 6.7

Examples of rule line widths.

If you specify a width smaller than the actual width of the screen, you also can specify the alignment of that rule line with the align attribute, making it flush left (align="left"), flush right (align="right"), or centered (align="center"). By default, rule lines are centered.

A popular trick used by Web designers who use these attributes is to create patterns with several small rule lines. The following example displays a design created with horizontal rules, and the result is shown in Figure 6.8:

```
<hr align="center" size="4" width="200" />
<hr align="center" size="4" width="300" />
<hr align="center" size="4" width="400" />
<h1 align="center">NorthWestern Video</h1>
<hr align="center" size="4" width="400" />
<hr align="center" size="4" width="300" />
<hr align="center" size="4" width="200" />
<h2 align="center">Presents</h2>
```

FIGURE 6.8

A pattern created with several small rule lines.

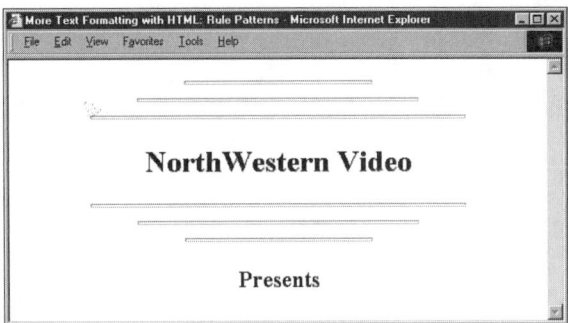

Finally, in most current browsers, the noshade attribute shown in the following example causes the browser to draw the rule line as a plain line without the three-dimensional shading, as shown in Figure 6.9.

Note

In HTML 4.0 and earlier versions, a value isn't required by the noshade attribute. The method you use to apply this attribute appears as follows:

```
<hr align="center" size="4" width="200" noshade>
```

To comply with XHTML 1.0, however, all attributes require a value. The HTML 4.0 specification requires that boolean attributes (like noshade) have only the name of the attribute itself as the value. The following example demonstrates how to apply the noshade attribute to the <hr> tag in compliance with the XHTML 1.0 specification.

INPUT

```
<hr align="center" size="4" width="200" noshade="noshade" />
<hr align="center" size="4" width="300" noshade="noshade" />
<hr align="center" size="4" width="400" noshade="noshade" />
<h1 align="center">NorthWestern Video</h1>
<hr align="center" size="4" width="400" noshade="noshade" />
<hr align="center" size="4" width="300" noshade="noshade" />
<hr align="center" size="4" width="200" noshade="noshade" />
<h2 align="center">Presents</h2>
```

6

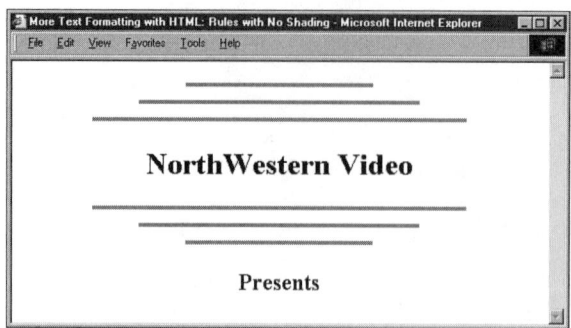

Figure 6.9

Rule lines without shading.

Line Break

The <br> tag breaks a line of text at the point where it appears. When a Web browser encounters a <br> tag, it restarts the text after the tag at the left margin (whatever the current left margin happens to be for the current element). You can use <br> within other elements, such as paragraphs or list items;
 won't add extra space above or below the new line or change the font or style of the current entity. All it does is restart the text at the next line.

> Like the <hr> tag, the <br> tag has no closing tag in HTML. To convert this tag to XHTML and to ensure compatibility with HTML browsers, add a space and forward slash to the end of the tag and its attributes, as shown in the following example:
>
> ```
> And then is heard no more: it is a tale <br />
> Told by an idiot, full of sound and fury, <br />
> Signifying nothing.</p>
> ```

The following example shows a simple paragraph in which each line ends with a <br>:

INPUT

```
<p>Tomorrow, and tomorrow, and tomorrow,<br />
Creeps in this petty pace from day to day,<br />
To the last syllable of recorded time;<br />
And all our yesterdays have lighted fools<br />
The way to dusty death. Out, out, brief candle!<br />
Life's but a walking shadow; a poor player,<br />
That struts and frets his hour upon the stage,<br />
And then is heard no more: it is a tale <br />
Told by an idiot, full of sound and fury, <br />
Signifying nothing.</p>
```

Figure 6.10 shows how it appears in Internet Explorer.

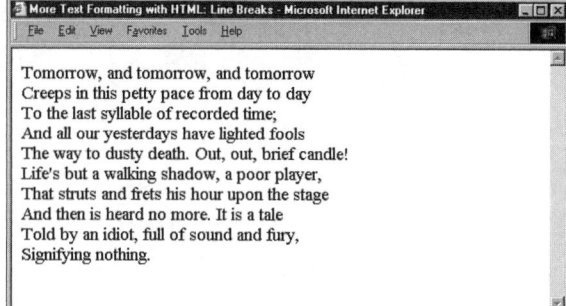

FIGURE 6.10

Line breaks in Internet Explorer.

> **Note**
>
> `clear` is an attribute of the `<br>` tag. It's used with images that have text wrapped alongside them. You'll learn about this attribute on Day 7, "Using Images, Color, and Backgrounds."

Addresses

The address tag `<address>` is used for signature-like entities on Web pages. Address tags usually go at the bottom of each Web page and are used to indicate who wrote the Web page, who to contact for more information, the date, any copyright notices or other warnings, and anything else that seems appropriate. Addresses often are preceded with a rule line (`<hr>`), and the `<br>` tag can be used to separate the lines.

Without an address or some other method of "signing" your Web pages, it's close to impossible to find out who wrote it, or who to contact for more information. Signing each of your Web pages by using the `<address>` tag is an excellent way to make sure that people can get in touch with you. `<address>` is a block level tag that italicizes the text inside it.

The following input shows an address:

```
<hr />
<address>
Laura Lemay lemay@lne.com <br />
A service of Laura Lemay, Incorporated <br />
last revised January 10, 2001 <br />
Copyright Laura Lemay 2001 all rights reserved <br />
Void where prohibited. Keep hands and feet inside the vehicle at all
times.
</address>
```

Figure 6.11 shows it in Internet Explorer.

6

OUTPUT

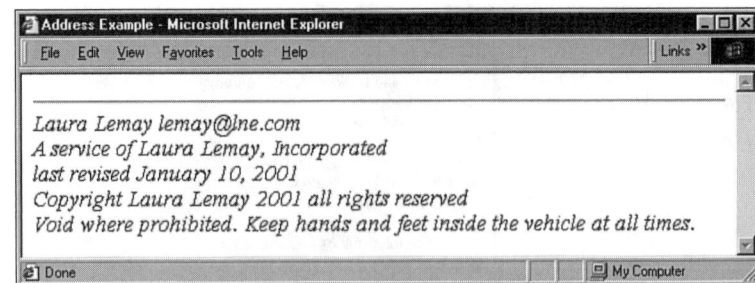

FIGURE 6.11

An address block in Internet Explorer.

Quotations

The <blockquote> tag is used to create a quotation. (Unlike the <cite> tag, which highlights small quotes, <blockquote> is used for longer quotations that shouldn't be nested inside other paragraphs.) Generally, quotations are set off from regular text by indentation or some other method. For example, the *Macbeth* soliloquy I used in the example for line breaks would have worked better as a <blockquote> than as a simple paragraph. Here's an input example:

INPUT

```
<blockquote>
"During the whole of a dull, dark, and soundless day in the autumn
of the year, when the clouds hung oppressively low in the heavens,
I had been passing alone, on horseback, through a singularly dreary
tract of country, and at length found myself, as the shades of evening
grew on, within view of the melancholy House of Usher."--Edgar Allen Poe
</blockquote>
```

As with paragraphs, you can split lines in a <blockquote> using the line break tag, <br>. The following input example shows an example of this use:

INPUT

```
<blockquote>
Guns aren't lawful, <br />
nooses give.<br />
gas smells awful.<br />
You might as well live.<br />
--Dorothy Parker
</blockquote>
```

Figure 6.12 shows how the preceding input example appears in Internet Explorer.

OUTPUT

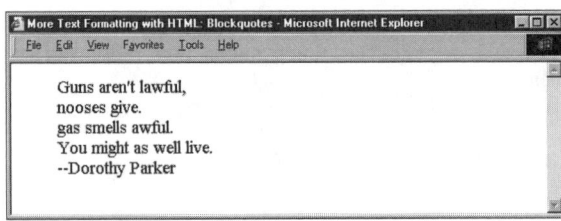

FIGURE 6.12

A quotation in Internet Explorer.

Note

The `<blockquote>` tag often is used not to set off quotations within text, but rather to create margins on both sides of a page in order to make it more readable. This technique works, but strictly speaking, it's a misuse of the tag. These days, you should control margins with Cascading Style Sheets, as explained on Day 12.

Special Characters

As you learned earlier in the week, HTML files are ASCII text and should contain no formatting or fancy characters. In fact, the only characters you should put in your HTML files are the characters that are actually printed on your keyboard. If you have to hold down any key other than Shift, or type an arcane combination of keys to produce a single character, you can't use that character in your HTML file. This includes characters you may use every day, such as em dashes and curly quotes (if your word processor is set up to do automatic curly quotes, you should turn them off when you write your HTML files).

"But wait a minute," you say. "If I can type a character like a bullet or an accented *a* on my keyboard using a special key sequence, and I can include it in an HTML file, and my browser can display it just fine when I look at that file, what's the problem?"

The problem is that the internal encoding your computer does to produce that character (which allows it to show up properly in your HTML file and in your browser's display) probably won't translate to other computers. Someone on the Internet who's reading your HTML file with that funny character in it may end up with some other character, or just plain garbage. Or, depending on how your page is sent over the Internet, the character may be lost before it ever gets to the computer where the file is being viewed.

So what can you do? HTML provides a reasonable solution. It defines a special set of codes, called character entities, that you can include in your HTML files to represent the characters you want to use. When interpreted by a browser, these character entities are displayed as the appropriate special characters for the given platform and font.

Some special characters don't come from the set of extended ASCII characters. For example, quotation marks and ampersands can be presented on a page using character entities even though they're found within the standard ASCII character set. These characters have a special meaning in HTML documents within certain contexts, so they can be represented with character entities in order to avoid confusing the Web browsers. (Modern browsers generally don't have a problem with these characters, but it's not a bad idea to use the entities anyway.)

6

Character Entities for Special Characters

Character entities take one of two forms: named entities and numbered entities.

Named entities begin with an ampersand (&) and end with a semicolon (;). In between is the name of the character (or, more likely, a shorthand version of that name, like agrave for an *a* with a grave accent, or reg for a registered trademark sign). Unlike other HTML tags, the names are case sensitive, so you should make sure to type them in exactly. Named entities look something like the following:

```
&agrave;
&quot;
&laquo;
&copy;
```

The numbered entities also begin with an ampersand and end with a semicolon, but rather than a name, they have a pound sign (#) and a number. The numbers correspond to character positions in the ISO-Latin-1 (ISO 8859-1) character. Every character for which you can type or use a named entity also has a numbered entity. Numbered entities look like the following:

```
&#130;
&#245;
```

You can use either numbers or named entities in your HTML file by including them in the same place that the character they represent would go. So, to place the word *résumé* in your HTML file, you would use either

```
r&eacute;sum&eacute;
```

or

```
r&#233;sum&#233;
```

In Appendix B, "HTML 4.0 Quick Reference," I've included a table that lists the named entities currently supported by HTML. See that table for specific characters.

Character set: ISO-Latin-1 versus Unicode

HTML's use of the ISO-Latin-1 character set allows it to display most accented characters on most platforms, but it has limitations. For example, common characters such as bullets, em dashes, and curly quotes simply aren't available in the ISO-Latin-1 character set. Therefore, you cannot use these characters at all in your HTML files. (If they're absolutely necessary, you can create images representing those characters and use them on your pages. I don't recommend that option, though, because it can interfere with the layout of your page. Also, it can look odd if the user's browser is set to a nonstandard text size.) Also, many ISO-Latin-1 characters may be entirely unavailable in some browsers, depending on whether those characters exist on that platform and in the current font.

HTML 4.0 takes things a huge leap further by proposing that Unicode should be available as a character set for HTML documents. Unicode is a proposed standard character encoding system that, while backward-compatible with our familiar ASCII encoding, offers the capability to encode characters in almost any of the world's languages, including Chinese and Japanese. This means that documents can be created easily in any language, and they also can contain multiple languages. Both Internet Explorer and Netscape support Unicode, and it can render documents in many of the scripts provided by Unicode as long as the necessary fonts are available.

This is an important step because Unicode is emerging as a new *de facto* standard for character encoding. Java uses Unicode as its default character encoding, for example, and Windows 2000 supports Unicode character encoding.

Character Entities for Reserved Characters

For the most part, character entities exist so that you can include special characters that aren't part of the standard ASCII character set. However, there are several exceptions for the few characters that have special meaning in HTML itself. You must use entities for these characters also.

Suppose that you want to include a line of code that looks something like the following in an HTML file:

```
<p><code>if x < 0 do print i</code></p>
```

Doesn't look unusual, does it? Unfortunately, HTML cannot display this line as written. Why? The problem is with the < (less-than) character. To an HTML browser, the less-than character means "this is the start of a tag." Because the less-than character isn't actually the start of a tag in this context, your browser may get confused. You'll have the same problem with the greater-than character (>) because it means the end of a tag in HTML, and with the ampersand (&), meaning the beginning of a character escape. Written correctly for HTML, the preceding line of code would look like the following instead:

```
<p><code>if x &lt; 0 do print i</code></p>
```

HTML provides named escape codes for each of these characters, and one for the double quotation mark as well, as shown in Table 6.1.

TABLE 6.1 Escape Codes for Characters Used by Tags

Entity	Result
&lt;	<
&gt;	>
&amp;	&
&quot;	"

6

The double quotation mark escape is the mysterious one. Technically, if you want to include a double quotation mark in text, you should use the escape sequence and you shouldn't type the quotation mark character. However, I haven't noticed any browsers having problems displaying the double quotation mark character when it's typed literally in an HTML file, nor have I seen many HTML files that use it. For the most part, you're probably safe using plain old quotes (") in your HTML files rather than the escape code.

Text Alignment

Text alignment is the capability to arrange a block of text, such as a heading or a paragraph, so that it's aligned against the left margin (left justification, the default), aligned against the right margin (right justification), or centered. Standard HTML 2.0 has no mechanisms for aligning text; the browser is responsible for determining the alignment of the text (which means most of the time it's left-justified).

HTML 3.2 introduced attributes for text and element alignment, and these attributes have been incorporated into all the major browsers. HTML 4.0 still supports alignment attributes, but the preferred method of controlling text alignment now is with style sheets.

Aligning Individual Elements

To align an individual heading or paragraph, include the `align` attribute in the opening tag. `align` has four values: `left`, `right`, `center`, or `justify`. Consider the following examples in the code snippet that follows.

The following input and output example shows the simple alignment of several headings. Figure 6.13 shows the results in Internet Explorer.

INPUT

```
<h1 align="center">Northridge Paints, Inc.</h1>
<p align="center">We don't just paint the town red.</p>

<h1 align="left">Serendipity Products</h1>
<h2 align="right"><a href="who.html">Who We Are</a></h2>
<h2 align="right"><a href="products.html">What We Do</a></h2>
<h2 align="right"><a href="contacts.html">How To Reach Us</a></h2>
```

OUTPUT

FIGURE 6.13

Headings with varying alignments in Internet Explorer.

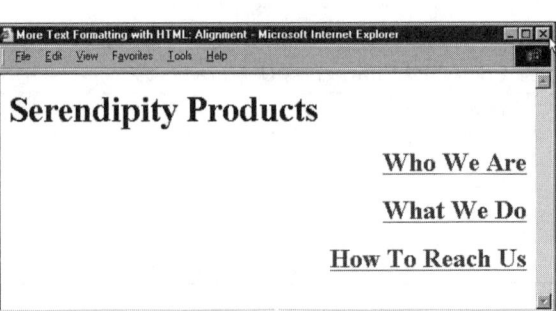

Aligning Blocks of Elements

A slightly more flexible method of aligning text elements is to use the `<div>` (division) tag. `<div>` includes several attributes, which are listed in Appendix B. Among these attributes is `align` (deprecated in HTML 4.0), which aligns elements to the left, right, or center just as it does for headings and paragraphs. Unlike using alignments in individual elements, however, `<div>` is used to surround a block of HTML tags of any kind, and it affects all the tags and text inside the opening and closing tags. Two advantages of `div` over the `align` attribute follow:

- You need to use `div` only once, rather than including `align` repeatedly in several different tags.
- `div` can be used to align anything (headings, paragraphs, quotes, images, tables, and so on); the `align` attribute is available only on a limited number of tags.

To align a block of HTML code, surround it with opening and closing `<div>` tags, and then include the `align` attribute in the opening tag. As in other tags, `align` can have the values `left`, `right`, or `center`:

```
<h1 align="left">Serendipity Products</h1>
<div align="right">
<h2><a href="who.html">Who We Are</a></h2>
<h2><a href="products.html">What We Do</a></h2>
<h2><a href="contacts.html">How To Reach Us</a></h2>
</div>
```

All the HTML between the two `<div>` tags will be aligned according to the value of the `align` attribute. If individual `align` attributes appear in headings or paragraphs inside the `div`, those values will override the global `div` setting.

Note that `<div>` itself isn't a paragraph type; it's just a container. Rather than altering the layout of the text itself, it just allows you to set off a group of text. One function of `<div>` is to change text alignment with the `align` attribute. Normally it's also used with Cascading Style Sheets to apply styles to a specific block of text. This functionality is described on Day 12.

6

In addition to `<div>`, you can use the centering tag `<center>` as well. The HTML 3.2 specification defines it as a short version of `<div align="center">`. The `<center>` tag acts identically to `<div align="center">`, centering all the HTML content inside the opening and closing tags. You put the `<center>` tag before the text you want to center and the `</center>` tag after you're done, as in the following:

```
<center>
<h1>Northridge Paints, Inc.</h2>
<p>We don't just paint the town red.</p>
</center>
```

For consistency's sake, you're probably better off using `<div>` and `align` to center text.

You can also include the align attribute in the `<p>` tag. It's most common to use the `justify` setting for the `align` attribute with the `<p>` and `<div>` tags. When you justify a paragraph, the text is spaced so that it's flush with both the left and right margins of the page.

Fonts and Font Sizes

The `<font>` tag, part of HTML 3.2 but deprecated in HTML 4.0 (again, in favor of style sheets), is used to control the characteristics of a given set of characters not covered by the character styles. Originally, `<font>` was used only to control the font size of the characters it surrounds, but it was then extended to allow you to change the font itself and the color of those characters.

In this section, I'll discuss fonts and font sizes. You'll learn about changing the font color on Day 7.

Changing the Font Size

The most common use of the `<font>` tag is to change the font size of a character, word, phrase, or any range of text. The `<font>...</font>` tags enclose the text, and the `size` attribute indicates the desired font size. The values of `size` are 1 to 7, with 3 being the default size. Consider the following example:

```
<p>Bored with your plain old font?
<font size="5">Change it.</font></p>
```

Figure 6.14 shows the typical font sizes for each value of `size`.

FIGURE 6.14

Font sizes in Internet Explorer.

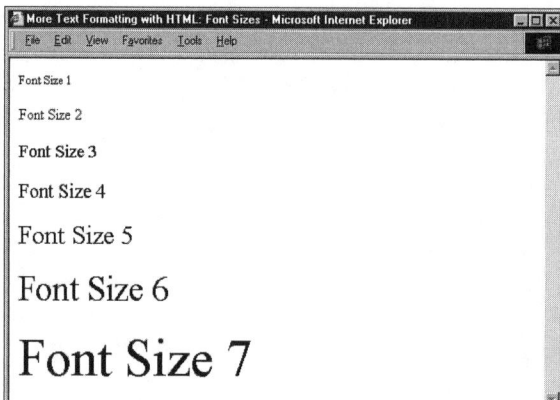

You can also specify the size in the <font> tag as a relative value by using the + or - characters in the value for size. Because the default size is 3, you can change relative font sizes in the range from -3 to +4, as in the following:

```
<p>Change the <font size="+2">Font</font> size again.</p>
```

Here, the word Font (inside the <font> tags) will be two size levels larger than the default font when you view that example in a browser that supports this feature.

Relative font sizes actually are based on a value that you can define by using the <basefont> tag, another tag that is deprecated in the HTML 4.0 specification. The <basefont> tag also has the required attribute size, which can have a value of 1 to 7. All relative font changes in the document after the <basefont> tag will be relative to that value.

Try to avoid using the <font> tag to simulate the larger-font effect of the HTML content-based tags, such as the heading tags (<h1>, <h2>, and so on), or to emphasize a particular word or phrase. If your documents are viewed in browsers that don't support this feature, you'll lose the font sizes and your text will look like any other paragraph. If you stick to the content-based tags, however, a heading is a heading regardless of where you view it. Try to limit your use of the <font> tag to small amounts of special effects.

It's also important to note that the available font sizes—1 through 7—are completely arbitrary. They're not tied in any meaningful way to real point sizes or any other standard metric for font size. Users can choose any font size they like, and all of the sizes available to <font> are applied relative to that size. Various operating systems also display fonts in different sizes on the screen, so there's little consistency from one platform to the other. You can't really count on much consistency when it comes to fonts.

Changing the Font Face

Netscape introduced the <font> tag to HTML with its 1.0 browser. Microsoft's Internet Explorer, playing the same game, extended the <font> tag to include the face attribute. The tag was made a part of HTML 3.2, but with HTML 4.0, the preferred method is to use style sheets to specify the fonts you use.

The face attribute takes as its value a set of font names, surrounded by quotation marks and separated by commas. When a browser that supports face interprets a page with face in it, it will search the system for the given font names one at a time. If it can't find the first one, it'll try the second, and then the third, and so on, until it finds a font that's installed on the system. If the browser cannot find any of the listed fonts, the default font will be used instead. So, for example, the following text would be rendered in Futura. If Futura isn't available, the browser will try Helvetica; it then will fall back on the default if Helvetica isn't available:

6

```
<p><font face="Futura,Helvetica">Sans Serif fonts are fonts without
the small "ticks" on the strokes of the characters. </font></p>
```

Many fonts have different names on different systems; for example, plain old Times is Times on some systems, Times Roman on others, and Times New Roman elsewhere.

Because the names of fonts vary from system to system, and because the list of installed fonts varies on a per-user basis, most browsers enable you to specify font families as well as specific font faces in your lists of fonts. The two families that are usually supported are serif and sans-serif. Usually you tack one of these two families onto your font list in case none of the other fonts you've specified were there. For example, if you want to present a headline in a sans serif font, you might specify a font that's available under the Mac OS, one that's available under X Windows, and one that's available under Microsoft Windows, and follow that up with sans-serif in case the others aren't available:

```
<font face="Geneva,Helvetica,Arial,sans-serif"><h1>Today's news</h1></font>
```

The Dreaded <blink>

You won't find the <blink> tag listed in Netscape's official HTML documentation. Blinking text was originally included in Netscape 2.0 as an Easter egg (hidden, undocumented feature). Still, the tag is used occasionally, and Netscape continues to support it.

The <blink>...</blink> tags cause the text between the opening and closing tags to blink. Depending on the version of Netscape you're using, the text itself can vanish and come back at regular intervals, or an ugly gray or white block may appear and disappear behind the text. Usually, blinking is used to draw attention to a portion of the page.

The problem with blink is that it provides too much emphasis. Because it repeats continually, the blinking draws attention to that one spot on the page and can be so distracting that the other content on the page is ignored. The use of <blink> is greatly discouraged by most Web designers (including myself) because many people find it extremely intrusive, ugly, and annoying. It's the HTML equivalent of fingernails on a blackboard.

If you must use blink, use it sparingly (no more than a few words on a page). Also, be aware that in some versions of Netscape, blinking can be turned off and in Internet Explorer, it doesn't work at all. If you want to emphasize a word or phrase, you should use a more conventional way of doing so in addition to (or in place of) blink, because you cannot guarantee that blink will be available even if your readers are using Netscape to view your pages.

Interestingly, even though support for the <blink> tag is very limited, you can use cascading style sheets to make text blink. Cascading style sheets are discussed on Day 12.

<nobr> and <wbr>

The <nobr>...</nobr> element is the opposite of the <br> tag. The text inside the <nobr> tags always remains on one line, even if it would have wrapped to two more lines without the <nobr>. The <nobr> tag is used for words or phrases that must be kept together on one line, but be careful. Long unbreakable lines can look really strange on your page, and if they're longer than the page width, they might extend beyond the right edge of the screen.

The <wbr> tag (word break) indicates an appropriate breaking point within a line (typically inside a <nobr>...</nobr> sequence). Unlike <br>, which forces a break, <wbr> is used only where it's appropriate to do so. If the line will fit on the screen just fine, the <wbr> is ignored. In XHTML 1.0, add closure to the tag by using the syntax of <wbr />.

Neither <nobr> nor <wbr> are part of HTML 3.2 or HTML 4.0. They're extensions introduced by Netscape, and are currently supported by both Netscape and Internet Explorer.

Exercise 6.1: Creating a Real HTML Page

To Do

Here's your chance to apply what you've learned and create a real Web page. No more disjointed or overly silly examples. The Web page you'll create in this section is a real one, suitable for use in the real world (or the real world of the Web, at least).

Your task for this example is to design and create a home page for a bookstore called The Bookworm, which specializes in old and rare books.

Plan the Page

On Day 2, "Get Organized," I mentioned that planning your Web page before writing it usually makes building and maintaining the elements easier. First, consider the content you want to include on this page. The following are some ideas for topics for this page:

- The address and phone number of the bookstore
- A short description of the bookstore and why it's unique
- Recent titles and authors
- Upcoming events

Now come up with some ideas for the content you're going to link to from this page. Each title in a list of recently acquired books seems like a logical candidate. You also can create links to more information about each book, its author and publisher, its pricing, maybe even its availability.

The Upcoming Events section might suggest a potential series of links, depending on how much you want to say about each event. If you have only a sentence or two about each one, describing them on this page might make more sense than linking them to

6

▼ another page. Why make your readers wait for each new page to load for just a couple of
lines of text?

Other interesting links may arise in the text itself, but for now, starting with the basic link
plan will be enough.

Begin with a Framework

Next, create the framework that all HTML files must include: the document structuring
commands, a title, and some initial headings. Note that the title is descriptive but short;
you can save the longer title for the <h1> element in the body of the text. The four <h2>
subheadings help you define the four main sections you'll have on your Web page:

```
<!DOCTYPE html PUBLIC "-//W3C//DTD XHTML 1.0 Transitional//EN"
  "http://www.w3.org/TR/xhtml1/DTD/transitional.dtd">
<html>
<head>
<title>The Bookworm Bookshop</title>
</head>
<body>
<h1>The Bookworm: A Better Book Store</h1>
<h2>Contents</h2>
<h2>About the Bookworm Bookshop</h2>
<h2>Recent Titles (as of 11-Jan-2001)</h2>
<h2>Upcoming Events</h2>
</body>
</html>
```

Each of the headings you've placed on your page will mark the beginning of a particular
section. You'll create an anchor at each of the topic headings so that you can jump from
section to section with ease. The anchor names are simple: top for the main heading,
contents for the table of contents, and about, recent, and upcoming for the three sub-
sections on the page. The revised code looks like the following with the anchors in place:

```
<!DOCTYPE html PUBLIC "-//W3C//DTD XHTML 1.0 Transitional//EN"
  "http://www.w3.org/TR/xhtml1/DTD/transitional.dtd">
<html>
<head>
<title>The Bookworm Bookshop</title>
</head>
<body>
<a name="top"><h1>The Bookworm: A Better Book Store</h1></a>
<a name="contents"><h2>Contents</h2></a>
<a name="about"><h2>About the Bookworm Bookshop</h2></a>
<a name="recent"><h2>Recent Titles (as of 11-Jan-2001)</h2></a>
<a name="upcoming"><h2>Upcoming Events</h2></a>
</body>
▼ </html>
```

▼ Add Content

Now begin adding the content. Because you're undertaking a literary endeavor, starting
the page with a nice quote about old books would be a nice touch. Since you're adding a
quote, you can use the `<blockquote>` tag to make it stand out as such. Also, the name of
the poem is a citation, so use `<cite>` there, too.

Insert the following code on the line after the level 1 heading:

```
<blockquote>
"Old books are best--how tale and rhyme<br />
Float with us down the stream of time!"<br />
- Clarence Urmy, <cite>Old Songs are Best</cite>
</blockquote>
```

Immediately following the quote, add the address for the bookstore. This is a simple
paragraph with the lines separated by line breaks, like the following:

```
<p>The Bookworm Bookshop<br />
1345 Applewood Dr<br />
Springfield, CA 94325<br />
(415) 555-0034
</p>
```

Adding the Table of Contents

The page you're creating will require a lot of scrolling to get from the top to the bottom.
One nice enhancement is to add a small table of contents at the beginning of the page,
listing the sections in a bulleted list. If a reader clicks one of the links in the table of contents, he'll automatically jump to the section that's of most interest to him. Because
you've created the anchors already, it's easy to see where the links will take you.

You already have the heading for the table of contents. You just need to add the bulleted
list and a horizontal rule, and then create the links to the other sections on the page. The
code looks like the following:

```
<a name="contents"><h2>Contents</h2></a>
<ul>
  <li><a href="#about">About the Bookworm Bookshop</a></li>
  <li><a href ="#recent">Recent Titles</a></li>
  <li><a href ="#upcoming">Upcoming Events</a></li>
</ul>
<hr />
```

6

Figure 6.15 shows an example of the introductory portion of the Bookworm Bookshop
▼ page as it appears in Internet Explorer.

FIGURE 6.15

The top section of the Bookworm Bookshop page.

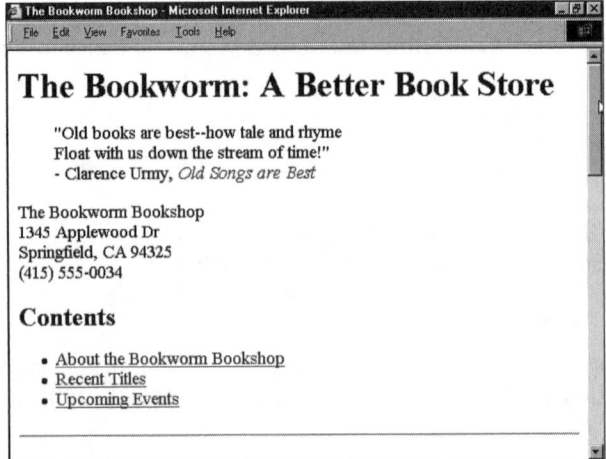

Creating the Description of the Bookstore

Now you come to the first descriptive subheading on the page, which you've added already. This section gives a description of the bookstore. After the heading (shown in the first line of the following example), I've arranged the description to include a list of features to make them stand out from the text better:

```
<a name="about"><h2>About the Bookworm Bookshop</h2></a>
<p>Since 1933, The Bookworm Bookshop has offered
rare and hard-to-find titles for the discerning reader.
The Bookworm offers:</p>
<ul>
<li>Friendly, knowledgeable, and courteous help</li>
<li>Free coffee and juice for our customers</li>
<li>A well-lit reading room so you can "try before you buy"</li>
<li>Four friendly cats: Esmerelda, Catherine, Dulcinea and Beatrice</li>
</ul>
```

Add a note about the hours the store is open, and emphasize the actual numbers:

```
<p>Our hours are <strong>10am to 9pm</strong> weekdays,
<strong>noon to 7</strong> on weekends.</p>
```

Then, end the section with links to the Table of Contents and the top of the page, followed by a horizontal rule to end the section:

```
<p><a href="#contents">Back to Contents</a> | <a href="#top">Back to Top</a></p>
<hr />
```

Figure 6.16 shows you what the About the Bookworm Bookshop section looks like in Internet Explorer.

FIGURE 6.16

The About the Bookworm Bookshop section.

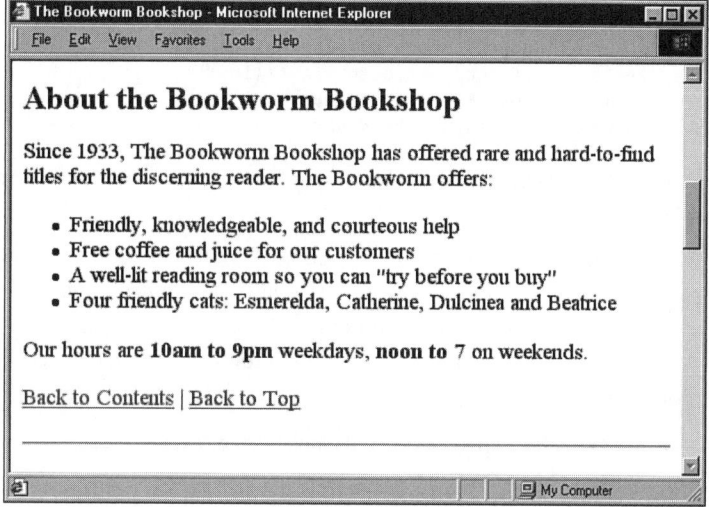

Creating the Recent Titles Section

The Recent Titles section itself is a classic link menu, as I described earlier in this section. Here you can put the list of titles in an unordered list, with the titles themselves as citations, by using the `<cite>` tag. End the section with another horizontal rule.

After the Recent Titles heading (shown in the first line in the following example), enter the following code:

```
<a name="recent"><h2>Recent Titles (as of 11-Jan-2001)</h2></a>
<ul>
<li>Sandra Bellweather, <cite>Belladonna</cite></li>
<li>Jonathan Tin, <cite>20-Minute Meals for One</cite></li>
<li>Maxwell Burgess, <cite>Legion of Thunder</cite></li>
<li>Alison Caine, <cite>Banquo's Ghost</cite></li>
</ul>
<hr />
```

Now add the anchor tags to create the links. How far should the link extend? Should it include the whole line (author and title), or just the title of the book? This decision is a matter of preference, but I like to link only as much as necessary to make sure the link stands out from the text. I prefer this approach to overwhelming the text. Here, I've linked only the titles of the books. At the same time, I've also added links to the Table of Contents and the top of the page:

```
<a name="recent"><h2>Recent Titles (as of 11-Jan-2001)</h2></a>
<ul>
<li>Sandra Bellweather, <a href="belladonna.html">
```

6

▼
```
<cite>Belladonna</cite></a></li>
<li>Johnathan Tin, <a href="20minmeals.html">
<cite>20-Minute Meals for One</cite></a></li>
<li>Maxwell Burgess, <a href="legion.html">
<cite>Legion of Thunder</cite></a></li>
<li>Alison Caine, <a href="banquo.html">
<cite>Banquo's Ghost</cite></a></li>
</ul>
<p><a href="#contents">Back to Contents</a> | <a href="#top">Back to Top</a></p>
<hr />
```

Note that I've put the <cite> tag inside the link tag <a>. I could have just as easily put it outside the anchor tag; character style tags can go just about anywhere. But as I mentioned once before, be careful not to overlap tags. Your browser may not be able to understand what's going on, not to mention that it's invalid XHTML. In other words, don't do the following:

```
<a href="banquo.html"><cite>Banquo's Ghost</a></cite>
```

Take a look at how the Recent Titles section appears in Internet Explorer. An example is shown in Figure 6.17.

FIGURE 6.17

The Recent Titles section.

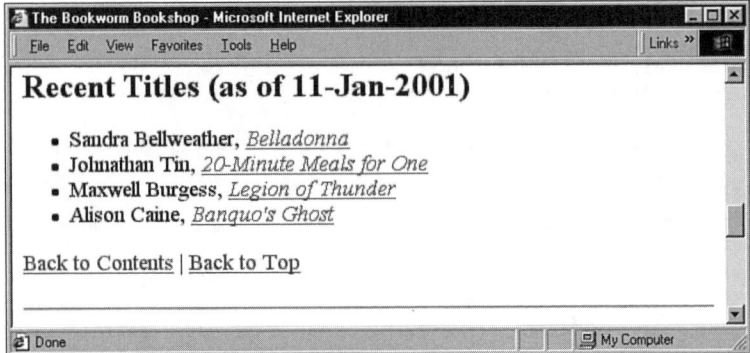

Completing the Upcoming Events Section

Next, move on to the Upcoming Events section. In the planning stages, you weren't sure whether this would be another link menu or whether the content would work better solely on this page. Again, this decision is a matter of preference. Here, because the amount of extra information is minimal, creating links for just a couple of sentences doesn't make
▼   much sense. So for this section, create a menu list (by using the <ul> tag) that results in

▼ short paragraphs (bulleted in some browsers). I've boldfaced a few phrases near the beginning of each paragraph. These phrases emphasize a summary of the event itself so that
each paragraph can be scanned quickly and ignored if the readers aren't interested.

As in the previous sections, you end the section with links to the top and to the contents,
followed by a horizontal rule.

```
<a name="upcoming"><h2>Upcoming Events</h2></a>
<ul>
<li><b>The Wednesday Evening Book Review</b> meets, appropriately, on
Wednesday evenings at 7 pm for coffee and a round-table discussion.
Call the Bookworm for information on joining the group.</li>
<li><b>The Children's Hour</b> happens every Saturday at 1 pm and includes
reading, games, and other activities. Cookies and milk are served.</li>
<li><b>Carole Fenney</b> will be at the Bookworm on Friday, January 19,
to read from her book of poems <cite>Spiders in the Web.</cite></li>
<li><b>The Bookworm will be closed</b> March 1st to remove a family
of bats that has nested in the tower. We like the company, but not
the mess they leave behind!</li>
</ul>
<p><a href="#contents">Back to Contents</a> | <a href="#top">Back to
Top</a></p>
```

Sign the Page

To finish, sign what you have so that your readers know who did the work. Here, I've
separated the signature from the text with a rule line. I've also included the most recent
revision date, my name as the Webmaster, and a basic copyright (with a copyright symbol indicated by the numeric escape ©):

```
<hr />
<address>
Last Updated: 10-Jan-2001<br />
Webmaster: Laura Lemay lemay@bookworm.com<br />
&#169; copyright 2001 the Bookworm<br />
</address>
```

Figure 6.18 shows the bottom portion of the page, which includes the Upcoming Events
▼ section and the page signature as they look in Internet Explorer.

6

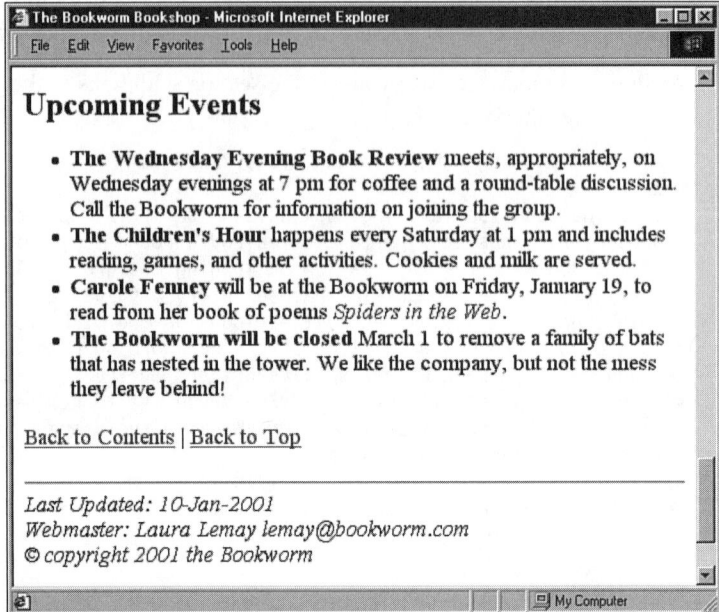

Review What You've Got

Here's the HTML code for the page so far:

```
<!DOCTYPE html PUBLIC "-//W3C//DTD XHTML 1.0 Transitional//EN"
 "http://www.w3.org/TR/xhtml1/DTD/transitional.dtd">
<html>
<head>
<title>The Bookworm Bookshop</title>
</head>
<body>
<a name="top"><h1>The Bookworm: A Better Book Store</h1></a>
<blockquote>
"Old books are best--how tale and rhyme<br />
Float with us down the stream of time!"<br />
- Clarence Urmy, <cite>Old Songs are Best</cite>
</blockquote>
<p>The Bookworm Bookshop<br />
1345 Applewood Dr<br />
Springfield, CA 94325<br />
(415) 555-0034
</p>
<a name="contents"><h2>Contents</h2></a>
<ul>
  <li><a href="#about">About the Bookworm Bookshop</a></li>
```

```
    <li><a href ="#recent">Recent Titles</a></li>
    <li><a href ="#upcoming">Upcoming Events</a></li>
  </ul>
  <hr />
  <a name="about"><h2>About the Bookworm Bookshop</h2></a>
  <p>Since 1933, the Bookworm Bookshop has offered
  rare and hard-to-find titles for the discerning reader.
  The Bookworm offers:</p>
  <ul>
    <li>Friendly, knowledgeable, and courteous help</li>
    <li>Free coffee and juice for our customers</li>
    <li>A well-lit reading room so you can "try before you buy"</li>
    <li>Four friendly cats: Esmerelda, Catherine, Dulcinea and Beatrice</li>
  </ul>
  <p>Our hours are <strong>10am to 9pm</strong> weekdays,
  <strong>noon to 7</strong> on weekends.</p>
  <p><a href="#contents">Back to Contents</a> | <a href="#top">Back to
  Top</a></p>
  <hr />
  <a name="recent"><h2>Recent Titles (as of 11-Jan-2001)</h2></a>
  <ul>
    <li>Sandra Bellweather, <a href="belladonna.html">
      <cite>Belladonna</cite></a></li>
    <li>Johnathan Tin, <a href="20minmeals.html">
      <cite>20-Minute Meals for One</cite></a></li>
    <li>Maxwell Burgess, <a href="legion.html">
      <cite>Legion of Thunder</cite></a></li>
    <li>Alison Caine, <a href="banquo.html">
      <cite>Banquo's Ghost</cite></a></li>
  </ul>
  <p><a href="#contents">Back to Contents</a> | <a href="#top">Back to
  Top</a></p>
  <hr />
  <a name="upcoming"><h2>Upcoming Events</h2></a>
  <ul>
    <li><b>The Wednesday Evening Book Review</b> meets, appropriately, on
      Wednesday evenings at 7 pm for coffee and a round-table discussion.
      Call the Bookworm for information on joining the group.</li>
    <li><b>The Children's Hour</b> happens every Saturday at 1 pm and includes
      reading, games, and other activities. Cookies and milk are served.</li>
    <li><b>Carole Fenney</b> will be at the Bookworm on Friday, January 19,
      to read from her book of poems <cite>Spiders in the Web.</cite></li>
    <li><b>The Bookworm will be closed</b> March 1 to remove a family
      of bats that has nested in the tower. We like the company, but not
      the mess they leave behind!</li>
  </ul>
  <p><a href="#contents">Back to Contents</a> | <a href="#top">Back to
  Top</a></p>
  <hr />
  <address>
```

6

```
Last Updated: 11-Jan-2001<br />
WebMaster: Laura Lemay lemay@bookworm.com<br />
&#169; copyright 2001 the Bookworm<br />
</address>
</body>
</html>
```

Now you have some headings, some text, some topics, and some links, which form the basis for an excellent Web page. With most of the content in place, now you need to consider what other links you might want to create or what other features you might want to add to this page.

For example, the introductory section has a note about the four cats owned by the bookstore. Although you didn't plan for them in the original organization, you could easily create Web pages describing each cat (and showing pictures) and then link them back to this page, one link (and one page) per cat.

Is describing the cats important? As the designer of the page, that's up to you to decide. You could link all kinds of things from this page if you have interesting reasons to link them (and something to link to). Link the bookstore's address to the local Chamber of Commerce. Link the quote to an online encyclopedia of quotes. Link the note about free coffee to the Coffee Home Page.

I'll talk more about good things to link (and how not to get carried away when you link) on Day 16, "Writing and Designing Web Pages: Do's and Don'ts." My reason for bringing up this point here is that after you have some content in place on your Web pages, there may be opportunities for extending the pages and linking to other places that you didn't think of when you created your original plan. So, when you're just about finished with a page, stop and review what you have, both in the plan and in your Web page.

For the purposes of this example, stop here and stick with the links you've got. You're close enough to being done, and I don't want to make this chapter any longer than it already is!

Test the Result

Now that all the code is in place, you can preview the results in a browser. Figures 6.15 through 6.18 show how it looks in Internet Explorer. Actually, these figures show what the page looks like after you fix the spelling errors, the forgotten closing tags, and all the other strange bugs that always seem to creep into an HTML file the first time you create it. These problems always seem to happen no matter how good you get at creating Web pages. If you use an HTML editor or some other help tool, your job will be easier, but

▼ you'll always seem to find mistakes. That's what previewing is for—so you can catch the problems before you actually make the document available to other people.

Get Fancy

Everything I've included on the page up to this point has been plain-vanilla HTML 2.0, so it's readable and will look pretty much the same in all browsers. After you get the page to this point, however, you can add additional formatting tags and attributes that won't change the page for many readers, but might make it look a little fancier in browsers that do support these attributes.

So what attributes do you want to use? I chose two:

- Centering the title of the page, the quote, and the bookstore's address
- Making a slight font size change to the address itself

To center the topmost part of the page, you can use the <div> tag around the heading, the quote, and the bookshop's address, as in the following:

```
<div align="center">
<a name="top"><h1>The Bookworm: A Better Book Store</h1></a>
<blockquote>
"Old books are best--how tale and rhyme<br />
Float with us down the stream of time!"<br />
- Clarence Urmy, <cite>Old Songs are Best</cite>
</blockquote>
<p>The Bookworm Bookshop<br />
1345 Applewood Dr<br />
Springfield, CA 94325<br />
(415) 555-0034
</p>
</div>
```

To change the font size of the address, add a <font> tag around the lines for the address:

```
<p><font size="+1">The Bookworm Bookshop<br />
1345 Applewood Dr<br />
Springfield, CA 94325<br />
(415) 555-0034
</font></p>
```

Figure 6.19 shows the final result, with attributes, in Internet Explorer. Note that neither of these changes affects the readability of the page in browsers that don't support <div>
▼ or <font>; the page still works just fine without them. It just looks different.

6

FIGURE 6.19

The final Bookworm home page, with additional attributes.

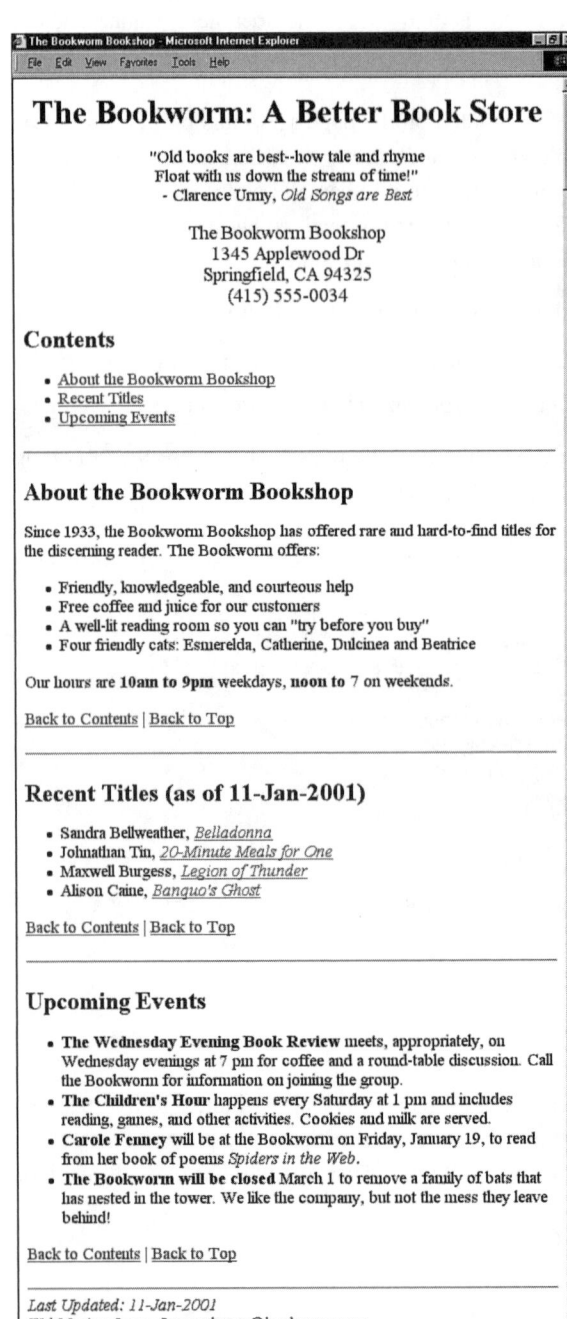

▼ When should you use text-formatting attributes? The general rule that I like to follow is to use these tags only when they won't interfere with other browsers, generally older ones. Similarly, while HTML 4.0 officially encourages Web page authors to use style sheets rather than text formatting tags such as font and attributes such as align, support for style sheets is still not yet universal. So for the time being, if you want to spiff up the appearance of your text, you'll need to continue to use these tags and attributes.

▲ You'll learn more about formatting tags and attributes, as well as how to design well with them, on Day 16.

Summary

Tags, tags, and more tags! Today you learned about most of the remaining tags in the HTML language for presenting text, and quite a few of the tags for additional text formatting and presentation. You also put together a real-life HTML home page. You could stop now and create quite presentable Web pages, but more cool stuff is to come. So don't put down the book yet.

Table 6.2 presents a quick summary of all the tags and attributes you've learned about today that are included in the HTML 4.0 specification.

TABLE 6.2 HTML Tags from Day 6

Tag	Attribute	Use
`<address>...</address>`		A "signature" for each Web page; typically occurs near the bottom of each document and contains contact or copyright information.
`<b>...</b>`		Bold text.
`<big>...</big>`		Text in a larger font than the text around it.
`<blink>...</blink>`		Causes the enclosed text to blink (Netscape only).
`<blockquote>...</blockquote>`		A quotation longer than a few words.
`<cite>...</cite>`		A citation.
`<code>...</code>`		A code sample.
`<dfn>...</dfn>`		A definition, or a term about to be defined.
`<em>...</em>`		Emphasized text.
`<i>...</i>`		Italic text.
`<kbd>...</kbd>`		Text to be typed in by the user.

6

TABLE 6.2   continued

Tag	Attribute	Use
`<pre>...</pre>`		Preformatted text; all spaces, tabs, and returns are retained. Text also is printed in a monospaced font.
`<s>...</s>`		Strikethrough text. (Deprecated in HTML 4.0.)
`<samp>...</samp>`		Sample text.
`<small>...</small>`		Text in a smaller font than the text around it.
`<strong>...</strong>`		Strongly emphasized text.
`<sub>...</sub>`		Subscript text.
`<sup>...</sup>`		Superscript text.
`<tt>...</tt>`		Text in typewriter font (a monospaced font such as Courier).
`<u>...</u>`		Underlined text.
`<var>...</var>`		A variable name.
`<hr>`		A horizontal rule line at the given position in the text. There is no closing tag in HTML for `<hr>`; for XHTML, add a space and forward slash (/) at the end of the tag and its attributes (for example: `<hr size="2" width="75%" />`)
	size	The thickness of the rule, in pixels. (Deprecated in HTML 4.0.)
	width	The width of the rule, either in exact pixels or as a percentage of page width (for example, 50 percent). (Deprecated in HTML 4.0.)
	align	The alignment of the rule on the page. Possible values are left, right, and center. (Deprecated in HTML 4.0.)
	noshade	Displays the rule without three-dimensional shading. (Deprecated in HTML 4.0.)
` `		A line break; starts the next character on the next line, but doesn't create a new paragraph or list item. There is no closing tag in HTML for ` `; for XHTML, add a space and forward slash (/) at the end of the tag and its attributes (for example: `<br clear="left" />`).

TABLE 6.2 continued

Tag	Attribute	Use
`<nobr>...</nobr>`		Doesn't wrap the enclosed text (nonstandard; supported by Netscape and Internet Explorer).
`<wbr>`		Wraps the text at this point only if necessary (nonstandard; supported by Netscape and Internet Explorer). Add a space and forward slash at the end of the tag for XHTML 1.0.
`<p>`, `<h1-6>`	`align="left"`	Left-justifies the text within that paragraph or heading. (Deprecated in HTML 4.0.)
	`align="right"`	Right-justifies the text within that paragraph or heading. (Deprecated in HTML 4.0.)
	`align="center"`	Centers the text within that paragraph or heading. (Deprecated in HTML 4.0.)
`<div>...</div>`	`align="left"`	Left-justifies all the content between the opening and closing tags. (Deprecated in HTML 4.0.)
	`align="right"`	Right-justifies all the content between the opening and closing tags. (Deprecated in HTML 4.0.)
	`align="center"`	Centers all the content between the opening and closing tags. (Deprecated in HTML 4.0.)
`<center>...</center>`		Centers all the content between the opening and closing tags. (Deprecated in HTML 4.0.)
`<font>...</font>`	`size`	The size of the font to change to, either from 1 to 7 (default is 3) or as a relative number using `+N` or `-N`. Relative font sizes are based on the value of `<basefont>`. (Deprecated in HTML 4.0.)
	`face`	The name of the font to change to, as a list of fonts to choose from. (Deprecated in HTML 4.0.)
`<basefont>`	`size`	The default font size on which relative font size changes are based. (Deprecated in HTML 4.0.) There is no closing tag in HTML for `<basefont>`; for XHTML, add a space and forward slash (/) at the end of the tag and its attributes (for example: `<basefont size="-1" />`.

6

Workshop

Here you are at the close of another day (a long one!) and facing yet another workshop. You covered a lot of ground today, so I'll try to keep the questions easy. There are a couple of exercises that focus on building some additional pages for your Web site. Ready?

Q&A

Q If line breaks appear in HTML, can I also do page breaks?

A HTML doesn't have a page break tag. Consider what the term "page" means in a Web document. If each document on the Web is a single page, the only way to produce a page break is to split your HTML document into separate files and link them.

Even within a single document, browsers have no concept of a page; each HTML document simply scrolls by continuously. If you consider a single screen a page, you still cannot have what results in a page break in HTML. The screen size in each browser is different. It's based on not only the browser itself, but also the size of the monitor on which it runs, the number of lines defined, the font currently being used, and other factors that you cannot control from HTML.

When you're designing your Web pages, don't get too hung up on the concept of a page the way it exists in paper documents. Remember, HTML's strength is its flexibility for multiple kinds of systems and formats. Instead, think in terms of creating small chunks of information and how they link together to form a complete presentation.

If page breaks are essential to your document, you might consider saving it in the PDF format and making it available for download.

Q How can I include em dashes or curly quotes (typesetter's quotes) in my HTML files?

A You can't. Neither em dashes nor curly quotes are defined as part of the ISO-Latin-1 character set, and therefore they aren't available in HTML at the moment. HTML 4.0 promises to fix this with its support for Unicode, which provides access to a much richer character set.

Q "`blink` is the HTML equivalent of fingernails on a blackboard"? Isn't that a little harsh?

A I couldn't resist. :)

Many people absolutely detest `blink` and will tell you so at a moment's notice, with a passion usually reserved for politics and religion. Some people might ignore your pages simply because you use `blink`. Why alienate your audience and distract from your content for the sake of a cheesy effect? Besides, most people these days use Internet Explorer, and it doesn't support the `blink` tag at all.

Quiz

1. What are the differences between logical character styles and physical character styles?

2. What are some things that the <pre> (preformatted text) tag can be used for?

3. What is the most common use of the <address> tag?

4. Older versions of HTML provided ways to align and center text on a Web page. What is the recommended way to accomplish these tasks in HTML 4.0?

5. Without looking at Table 6.2, list all eight logical style tags and what they're used for. Explain why you should use the logical tags instead of the physical tags.

Quiz Answers

1. Logical styles indicate how the highlighted text is used (citation, definition, code, and so on). Physical styles indicate how the highlighted text is displayed (bold, italic, or monospaced, for example).

2. Preformatted text can be used for text-based tables, code examples, ASCII art, and any other Web page content that requires extra spaces to align characters.

3. The <address> tag is most commonly used for signature-like entities on a Web page. These include the name of the author of the Web page, contact information, dates, copyright notices, or warnings. Address information usually appears at the bottom of a Web page.

4. Alignment and centering of text can be accomplished with style sheets, which is the recommended approach in HTML 4.0.

5. The eight logical styles are: <em> (for emphasized text), <strong> (for bold text), <code> (for programming code), <samp> (similar to <code>), <kbd> (to indicate user keyboard input), <var> (for variable names), <dfn> (for definitions), and <cite> (for short quotes or citations). Logical tags rely on the browser to format their appearance.

Exercises

1. Now that you've had a taste of building your first really thorough Web page, take a stab at your own home page. What can you include that would entice people to dig deeper into your pages? Don't forget to include links to other pages on your site.

2. Try out your home page in several browsers, and even on multiple platforms if you have access to them. Web developers have to get used to the fact that their designs are at the mercy of their users, and it's best to see right away how different browsers and platforms treat pages.

6

PART 3

Web Graphics

DAY 7

Using Images, Color, and Backgrounds

If you've been struggling to keep up with all the HTML tags I've been flinging at you over the last couple of days, the next few days will be easier. In fact, today you won't be learning very many new HTML tags. Instead, you'll learn about the HTML codes for adding images, color, and backgrounds. In particular, you'll learn the following:

- The kinds of images you can use in Web pages
- How to include images on your Web page, either alone or alongside text
- How to use images as clickable links
- How to use external images as a substitute for, or in addition to, inline images
- How to provide alternatives for browsers that cannot view images
- How to use image dimensions and scaling, and how to provide image previews
- How to change the font and background colors on your Web page
- How to use images for tiled page backgrounds

- How (and when) to use images on your Web pages
- A few tips on image etiquette

After today, you'll know all you need to know about adding images to your Web pages.

Images on the Web

Images for Web pages fall into two general classes: inline images and external images. Inline images appear directly on a Web page, along with the text and links. They're loaded automatically when you load the page itself—assuming, of course, that you have a graphical browser with automatic image loading turned on. External images aren't directly displayed when you load a page. They're downloaded only at the request of your visitors, usually on the other side of a link. You don't need a graphical browser to view external images; you can download an image file just fine using a text-only browser and then view it later with an image editor or viewer.

Whether you're using inline or external images, they must be in a specific format. Inline images should be in one of several formats: GIF, JPEG, or PNG. GIF and JPEG are the popular standards, and they're supported by every graphical browser. PNG is a newer image format that was created in response to some patent issues with the GIF format. It's superior to GIF in almost every respect, but it's only supported by the most recent browsers. Many other image formats are supported by Web browsers, but the problem is that they're not supported by all Web browsers. You should avoid them. You'll learn more about external images and the formats you can use for them later today.

Let's assume that you already have an image you want to put on your Web page. How do you get it into GIF or JPEG format so it can be viewed on your page? Most image editing programs, such as Adobe Photoshop (`http://www.adobe.com/`), Paint Shop Pro (`http://www.jasc.com/`), and CorelDRAW (`http://www.corel.com/`), will convert images to most of the popular formats. You may have to look under the option for Save As or Export in order to find it. There are also freeware and shareware programs for most platforms that do nothing but convert between image formats. Many shareware and demo versions of image editing programs are available at `http://www.download.com` (search for "image editors" using the software platform of your choice).

 Note

You'll learn more about image editing programs on Day 8, "Creating Animated Graphics."

To save files in GIF format, look for an option called CompuServe GIF, GIF87, GIF89, or just plain GIF. Any of them will work. If you're saving your files as JPEG, usually the option will be simply JPEG.

how your HTML files have to have an `.html` or `.htm` extension to work properly? Image files have Remember extensions, too. For GIF files, the extension is `.gif`. For JPEG files, the extension is either `.jpg` or `.jpeg`; either will work fine.

Note
Some image editors will try to save files with extensions in all caps (`.GIF`, `.JPEG`). Although they're the correct extensions, image names are case sensitive, so `.GIF` isn't the same extension as `.gif`. The case of the extension isn't important when you're testing on your local system, but it will be when you move your files to the server. So use lowercase if you can.

Inline Images in HTML: The `<img>` Tag

After you have an image ready to go in GIF or JPEG format, you can include it on your Web page. Inline images are placed in HTML documents using the `<img>` tag. This tag, like the `<hr>` and `<br>` tags, has no closing tag in HTML. For XHTML, you must add an extra space and forward slash to the end of the tag to indicate that it has no closing tag.

The `<img>` tag has many attributes that allow you to control how the image is presented on the page. Many of these attributes are part of HTML 3.2 or HTML 4.0 and may not be understood by some older browsers. Still others have been deprecated in favor of style sheets with the HTML 4.0 and XHTML 1.0 specifications.

The most important attribute of the `<img>` tag is `src`, which is the URL of the image you want to include. Paths to images are derived in the same way as the paths in the `href` attribute of links. So, to point to a GIF file named `image.gif` in the same directory as the HTML document, you can use the following tag:

```
<img src="image.gif" />
```

For an image file one directory up from the current directory, use this tag:

```
<img src="../image.gif" />
```

And so on, using the same rules as for page names in the `href` part of the `<a>` tag. You can also point to images on remote servers from the `src` attribute of an `<img>` tag, just as you can from the `href` attribute of a link. If you wanted to include the image `example.gif` from `www.example.com` on your Web page, you could use the following tag:

```
<img src="http://www.example.com/example.gif" />
```

7

Caution Just because you can use images stored on other servers for your own Web pages doesn't mean that you should. There are a lot of legal, ethical, and technical issues involved with using images on other sites. I'll discuss them later today.

Adding Alternative Text to Images

Images can turn a simple text-only Web page into a glorious visual feast. But what happens if someone is reading your Web page using a text-only browser? What if she has image loading turned off so that all your carefully crafted graphics appear as generic icons? All of a sudden, that visual feast doesn't look quite as glorious.

There's a simple solution to this problem. By using the `alt` attribute of the `<img>` tag, you can substitute something meaningful in place of the image on browsers that cannot display it.

In text-only browsers, such as Lynx, graphics that are specified using the `<img>` tag in the original file usually are displayed as the word "IMAGE" with square brackets around it, like this: `[IMAGE]`. If the image itself is a link to something else, that link is preserved.

The `alt` attribute in the `<img>` tag provides a more meaningful text alternative to the blank `[IMAGE]` for your visitors who are using text-only Web browsers, or who have graphics turned off on their browsers. The `alt` attribute contains a string with the text you want to substitute for the graphic:

```
<img src="myimage.gif" alt="[a picture of a cat]" />
```

Most browsers will interpret the string you include in the `alt` attribute as a literal string. That is, if you include any HTML tags in that string, they will be printed as-is rather than being parsed and displayed as HTML code. Therefore, you can't use whole blocks of HTML code as a replacement for an image—just a few words or phrases.

I bring up image alternatives now for good reason. Alternatives to images are optional in earlier versions of HTML, but they're mandatory in HTML 4.0 Strict and XHTML 1.0 specifications.

Exercise 7.1: Adding Images

▼ To Do

Here's the Web page for a local haunted house that's open every year at Halloween. Using all the excellent advice I've given you in the preceding six days, you should be able to create a page like this one fairly easily. Here's the HTML code for this HTML file, and Figure 7.1 shows how it looks so far:

```
<!DOCTYPE html PUBLIC "-//W3C//DTD XHTML 1.0 Transitional//EN"
"http://www.w3.org/TR/xhtml1/DTD/transitional.dtd">
<html>
<head>
<title>Welcome to the Halloween House of Terror</title>
</head>
<body>
<h1>Welcome to The Halloween House of Terror!!</h1>
<hr />
<p>Voted the most frightening haunted house three years in a row,
the <strong>Halloween House of Terror</strong> provides the
ultimate in Halloween thrills. Over <strong>20 rooms of thrills
and excitement</strong> to make your blood run cold and your hair
stand on end!</p>
<p>The Halloween House of Terror is open from <em>October 20 to
November 1st</em>, with a gala celebration on Halloween night.
Our hours are:</p>
<ul>
<li>Mon-Fri 5PM-midnight</li>
<li>Sat &amp; Sun 5PM-3AM</li>
<li><strong>Halloween Night (31-Oct)</strong>: 3PM-???</li>
</ul>
<p>The Halloween House of Terror is located at:<br />
The Old Waterfall Shopping Center<br />
1020 Mirabella Ave<br />
Springfield, CA 94532</p>
</body>
</html>
```

FIGURE 7.1

The Halloween House home page.

7

▼ So far, so good. Now you can add an image to the page. Suppose that you happen to have an image of a haunted house lying around on your hard drive; it would look excellent at the top of this Web page. The image, called `house.jpg`, is in JPEG format. It's located in the same directory as the `halloween.html` page, so it's ready to go into the Web page.

Now, suppose that you want to put this image on its own line so that the heading appears just below it. To do so, add an `<img>` tag to the file inside its own paragraph, just before the heading:

```
<p><img src="house.jpg" alt="House of Terror" /></p>
<h1>Welcome to The Halloween House of Terror!!</h1>
```

(Images, like links, don't define their own text elements, so the `<img>` tag has to go inside a paragraph or heading element.)

When you reload the `halloween.html` page, your browser should include the haunted house image on the page, as shown in Figure 7.2.

FIGURE 7.2

The Halloween House home page with the haunted house.

If the image doesn't load and your browser displays a funny-looking icon in its place, make sure you've specified its filename properly in the HTML file. Image filenames are case sensitive, so all the uppercase and lowercase letters have to be correct.

If checking the case doesn't work, double-check the image file to make sure that it is indeed a GIF or JPEG image and that it has the proper file extension.

Finally, make sure that you have image loading turned on in your browser. (The option
▼ is called Auto Load Images in Netscape and Show Pictures in Internet Explorer.)

▼ If one image is good, two would be really good, right? Try adding another `<img>` tag next to the first one, as follows, and see what happens:

```
<p><img src="house.jpg" alt="House of Terror" />
<img src="house.jpg" alt="House of Terror" /></p>
<h1>Welcome to The Halloween House of Terror!!</h1>
```

Figure 7.3 shows how the page looks in Internet Explorer. The two images are adjacent to each other, as you would expect.

FIGURE 7.3

Multiple images.

▲ And that's all there is to adding images!

Images and Text

In the preceding exercise, you put an inline image on a page with text below it. You also can include an image inside a line of text. In fact, this is what the phrase "inline image" actually means—it's *in* a *line* of text.

To include images inside a line of text, just add the `<img>` tag inside an element tag (`<h1>`, `<p>`, `<address>`, and so on), as in the following line:

```
<h2><img src="house.jpg" alt="House of Terror" />The Halloween House of
Terror!!</h2>
```

Figure 7.4 shows the difference you can make by putting the image inline with the heading. (I've also shortened the heading itself and changed it to `<h2>` so that it all fits on one line.)

7

FIGURE 7.4

The Halloween House page with an image inside the heading.

The image doesn't have to be large, and it doesn't have to be at the beginning of the text. You can include an image anywhere in a block of text, as in the following:

INPUT

```
<blockquote>
Love, from whom the world
<img src="world.gif" alt="World" />begun,<br />
Hath the secret of the sun.
<img src="sun.gif" alt="Sun" /><br />
Love can tell, and love alone, Whence the million stars
<img src="star.gif" alt="Star" /> were strewn<br />
Why each atom <img src="atom.gif" alt="Atom" />
knows its own.<br />
--Robert Bridges
</blockquote>
```

Figure 7.5 shows how this block looks.

OUTPUT

FIGURE 7.5

Images can go anywhere in text.

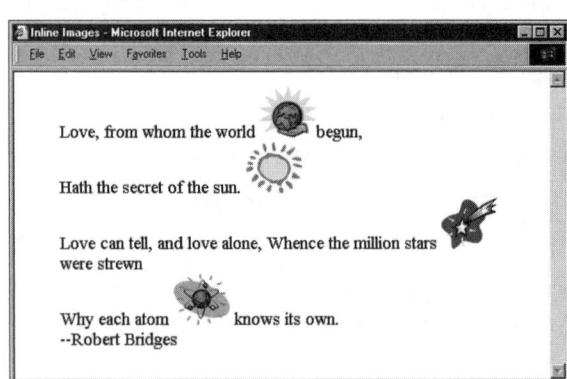

Text and Image Alignment

In these examples, the bottom of the image and the bottom of the text match up. The `<img>` tag also includes the `align` attribute, which enables you to align the top or bottom of the image with the surrounding text or other images in the line.

Note

> The `align` attribute for the `<img>` tag is deprecated in HTML 4.0 in favor of using style sheet attributes. You'll learn more about style sheets on Day 12, "XHTML and Style Sheets."

Standard HTML 2.0 defines three basic values for `align`:

`align="top"`	Aligns the top of the image with the topmost part of the line (which may be the top of the text or the top of another image)
`align="middle"`	Aligns the center of the image with the middle of the line (usually the baseline of the line of text, not the actual middle of the line)
`align="bottom"`	Aligns the bottom of the image with the bottom of the line of text

HTML 3.2 provides two other values: `left` and `right`. These values are discussed in the next section, "Wrapping Text Next to Images."

Figure 7.6 shows the Robert Bridges poem from the previous section with the world image unaligned, the sun image aligned to the top of the line, the star image aligned to the middle, and the atom aligned to the bottom of the text.

INPUT

```
<blockquote>
Love, from whom the world
<img src="world.gif" alt="World" />begun,<br />
Hath the secret of the sun.
<img src="sun.gif" alt="Sun" align="top" /><br />
Love can tell, and love alone, Whence the million stars
<img src="star.gif" alt="Star" align="middle" />
were strewn<br />
Why each atom
<img src="atom.gif" alt="Atom" align="bottom" />
knows its own.<br />
</blockquote>
```

7

FIGURE 7.6

Images unaligned, aligned top, aligned middle, and aligned bottom.

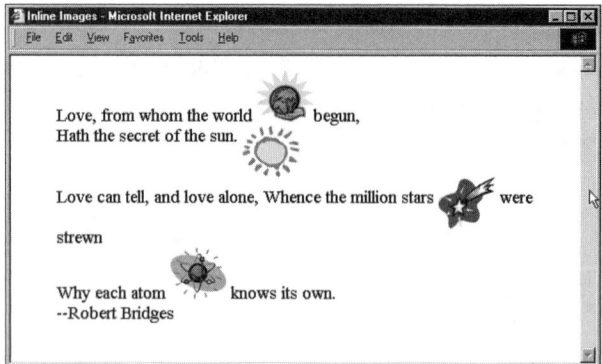

In addition to the preceding values, several other non-standard values for `align` provide greater control over precisely where the image will be aligned within the line. The following values aren't part of HTML 3.2 or 4.0, and are supported unevenly by various browsers. These four attributes aren't approved in the proposed specification for XHTML 1.0, and your page won't be verified as XHTML 1.0-compliant if they're used:

`align="texttop"`	Aligns the top of the image with the top of the tallest text in the line (whereas `align="top"` aligns the image with the topmost item in the line). (Neither Netscape nor Internet Explorer handle this setting properly.)
`align="absmiddle"`	Aligns the middle of the image with the middle of the largest item in the line. (`align="middle"` usually aligns the middle of the image with the baseline of the text, not its actual middle.) (Netscape treats this the same way it does `baseline`.)
`align="baseline"`	Aligns the bottom of the image with the baseline of the text. `align="baseline"` is the same as `align="bottom"`, but `align="baseline"` is a more descriptive name.
`align="absbottom"`	Aligns the bottom of the image with the lowest item in the line (which may be below the baseline of the text). (Netscape treats this the same way it does `baseline`.)

The following code shows these alignment options at work:

```
<h2>Middle of Text and Line aligned, arrow varies:</h2>
<img src="line.gif" alt="Line" />
Align: Top
<img src="uparrow.gif" alt="Up" align="top" />
Align: Text Top
<img src="uparrow.gif" alt="Up" align="texttop" />
```

```
<h2>Top of Text and Line aligned, arrow varies:</h2>
<img src="line.gif" alt="Line" />
Align: Absolute Middle
<img src="forward.gif" alt="Next" align="absmiddle" />
Align: Middle
<img src="forward.gif" alt="Next" align="middle" />
<h2>Top of Text and Line aligned, arrow varies:</h2>
<img src="line.gif" alt="Line" />
Align: Baseline / Bottom
<img src="down.gif" alt="Down" align="baseline" />
Align: Absolute Bottom
<img src="down.gif" alt="Down" align="absbottom" />
```

Figure 7.7 shows examples of all the options as they appear in Netscape Navigator. In each case, the line on the left side and the text are aligned with each other, and the position of the arrow varies.

OUTPUT

FIGURE 7.7

Alignment options in Netscape Navigator.

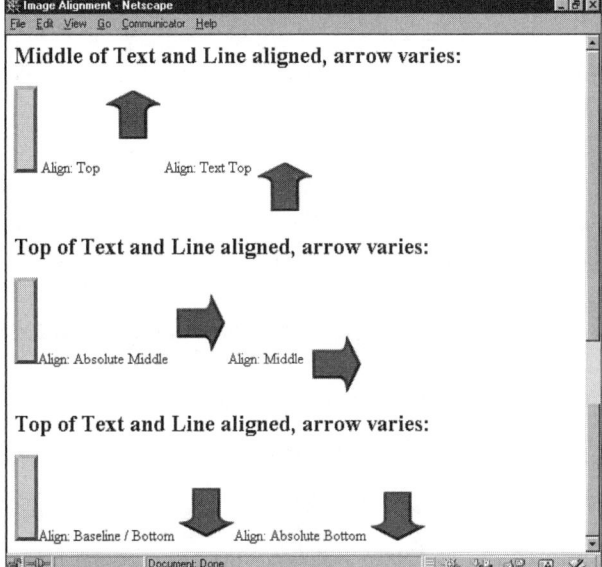

Wrapping Text Next to Images

Including an image inside a line works fine if you have only one line of text. One aspect of inline images that I've sneakily avoided mentioning so far is that in HTML 2.0, this alignment worked only with a single line of text. If you had multiple lines of text and you included an image in the middle of it, all the text around the image (except for the one line) would appear above and below that image.

What if you want to wrap multiple lines of text so it surrounds all sides of an image? Using HTML 2.0, you couldn't. You were restricted to just a single line of text on either side of the image, which limited the kinds of designs you could do.

7

To get around this HTML 2.0 limitation, Netscape defined two new values for the `align` attribute of the `<img>` tag: `left` and `right`. These new values were incorporated into HTML 3.2 and are now supported by   many browsers.

`align="left"` and `align="right"`

`align="left"` aligns an image to the left margin, and `align="right"` aligns an image to the right margin. However, these attributes also cause any text following the image to be displayed in the space to the right or left of that image, depending on the margin alignment:

INPUT

```
<img src="tulips.gif" alt="Tulips" align="left" />
<h1>Mystery Tulip Murderer Strikes</h1>
<p>Someone, or something, is killing the tulips of New South
Haverford, Virginia. Residents of this small town are shocked and
dismayed by the senseless vandalism that has struck their tiny
town.</p>
<p>New South Haverford is known for its extravagant displays of
tulips in the springtime, and a good portion of its tourist trade
relies on the people who come from as far as New Hampshire to see
what has been estimated as up to two hundred thousand tulips that
bloom in April and May.</p>
<p>Or at least the tourists had been flocking to New South
Haverford until last week, when over the course of three days the
flower of each and every tulip in the town was neatly clipped off
while the town slept.</p>
```

Figure 7.8 shows an image with some text aligned next to it.

OUTPUT

FIGURE 7.8

Text and images aligned.

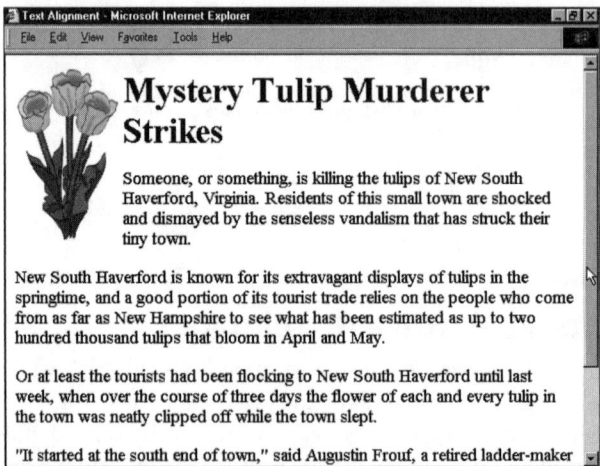

You can put any HTML text (paragraphs, lists, headings, other images) after an aligned image, and the text will be wrapped into the space between the image and the margin. (Or you can have images on both margins and put the text between them.) The browser fills in the space with text to the bottom of the image and then continues filling in the text beneath the image.

Stopping Text Wrapping

What if you want to stop filling in the space and start the next line underneath the image? A normal line break won't do it; it will just break the line to the current margin alongside the image. A new paragraph also will continue wrapping the text alongside the image. To stop wrapping text next to an image, use a line break tag (<br>) with the clear attribute. This lets you break the line so that the next line of text begins after the end of the image (all the way to the margin).

The clear attribute can have one of three values:

left   Break to an empty left margin, for left-aligned images

right   Break to an empty right margin, for right-aligned images

all   Break to a line clear to both margins

Note

> The clear attribute for the <br> tag is deprecated in HTML 4.0, in favor of using style sheet attributes.

For example, the following code snippet shows a picture of a tulip with some text wrapped next to it. A line break with clear="left" breaks the text wrapping after the heading and restarts the text after the image:

INPUT

```
<!DOCTYPE html PUBLIC "-//W3C//DTD XHTML 1.0 Transitional//EN"
"http://www.w3.org/TR/xhtml1/DTD/transitional.dtd">
</head>
<body>
<img src="tulips.gif" alt="Tulips" align="left" />
<h1>Mystery Tulip Murderer Strikes</h1>
<br clear="left" />
<p>Someone, or something, is killing the tulips of New South
Haverford, Virginia. Residents of this small town are shocked and
dismayed by the senseless vandalism that has struck their tiny
town.</p>
<p>New South Haverford is known for its extravagant displays of
tulips in the springtime, and a good portion of its tourist trade
relies on the people who come from as far as New Hampshire to see
what has been estimated as up to two hundred thousand tulips that
bloom in April and May.</p>
<p>Or at least the tourists had been flocking to New South
Haverford until last week, when over the course of three days the
flower of each and every tulip in the town was neatly clipped off
while the town slept.</p>
```

7

Figure 7.9 shows the result in Internet Explorer.

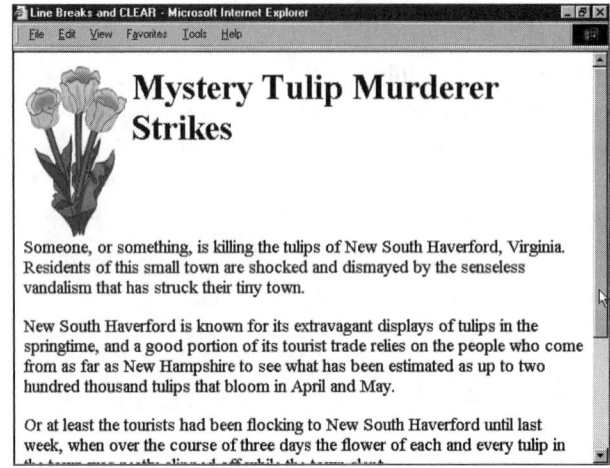

FIGURE 7.9

Line break to a clear margin.

Adjusting the Space Around Images

With the capability to wrap text around an image, you also might want to adjust the amount of space around that image. The vspace and hspace attributes (introduced in HTML 3.2) enable you to make these adjustments. Both take values in pixels; vspace controls the space above and below the image, and hspace controls the space to the left and the right. Note that the amount of space you specify is added on both sides of the image. For example, if you use hspace="10", 10 pixels of space will be added on both the left and right sides of the image.

 Note   The vspace and hspace attributes for the <img> tag are deprecated in HTML 4.0, in favor of using style sheet attributes.

The following HTML code, displayed in Figure 7.10, illustrates two examples. The upper example shows default horizontal and vertical spacing around the image, while the lower example shows the effect produced by the hspace and vspace attributes. Both images use the align="left" attribute so that the text wraps along the left side of the image. However, in the bottom example, the text aligns with the extra space above the top of the image (added with the vspace attribute).

INPUT

```
<img src="eggplant.gif" alt="Eggplant" align="left" />
<p>This is an eggplant. We intend to stay a good ways away from
it, because we really don't like eggplant very much.</p>
<br clear="left" />
<hr />
<img src="eggplant.gif" alt="Eggplant" vspace="50" hspace="50"
align="left" />
<p>This is an eggplant. We intend to stay a good ways away from
it, because we really don't like  eggplant very much.
```

OUTPUT

FIGURE 7.10

The upper example doesn't have image spacing, and the lower example does.

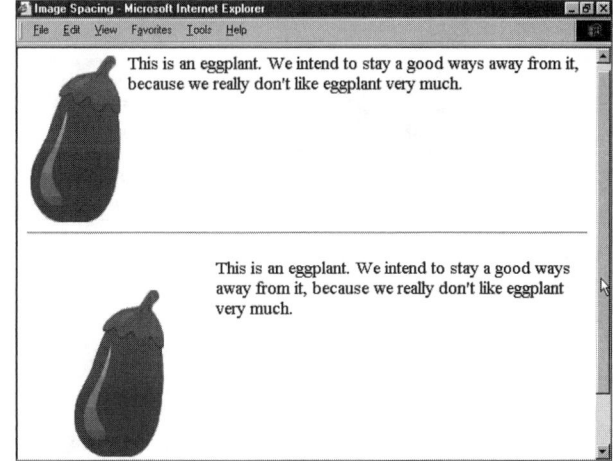

Images and Links

Can an image serve as a link? Sure it can! If you include an <img> tag inside the opening and closing parts of a link tag (<a>), that image serves as a clickable hot spot for the link itself:

```
<a href="index.html"><img src="uparrow.gif" alt="Up" /></a>
```

If you include both an image and text in the anchor, they become hot spots pointing to the same page:

```
<a href="index.html"><img src="uparrow.gif" alt="Up" />Up to Index</a>
```

Tip

One thing to look out for when you're placing images within links, with or without text, is white space between the </a> tag and the <img> tag, or between the text and the image. Some browsers turn the white space into a link, and you get an odd "tail" on your images. To avoid this unsightly problem, don't leave spaces or line feeds between your <img> tags and </a> tags.

7

By default in HTML 2.0, images that also are hot spots for links appear with borders around them to distinguish them from ordinary, non-clickable images. Figure 7.11 shows an example of this. The butterfly image is a non-clickable image, so it doesn't have a border around it. The up arrow, which takes the visitor back to the home page, has a border around it because it's a link.

FIGURE 7.11

Images used as links have a border around them.

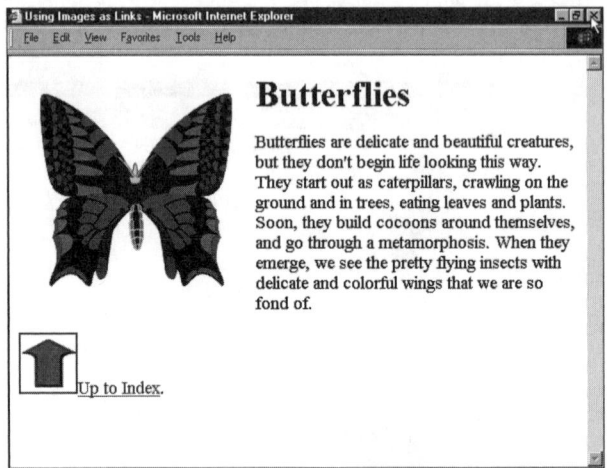

You can change the width of the border around the image by using the border attribute to <img>. The border attribute was a Netscape extension that became part of HTML 3.2, but it has been deprecated in HTML 4.0 in favor of style sheets. This attribute takes a number, which is the width of the border in pixels. border="0" hides the border entirely.

Be careful when you're setting border to 0 (zero) for images with links. The border provides a visual indication that the image also is a link. By removing that border, you make it difficult for visitors to know which are plain images and which are hot spots unless they move the mouse around to find them. If you must use borderless image links, make sure that your design provides some indication that the image is selectable and isn't just a plain image. For example, you might design your images so they actually look like buttons, as shown in Figure 7.12.

FIGURE 7.12

Images that look like buttons.

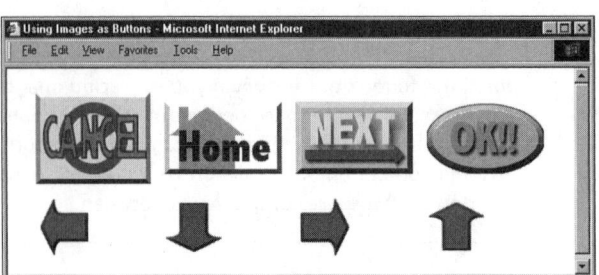

Exercise 7.2: Using Navigation Icons

▲ To Do

Now you can create a simple page that uses images as links. When you have a set of related Web pages in which the navigation takes place in a consistent way (for example, moving forward, back, up, home, and so on), providing a menu of navigation options at the top or bottom of each page tells your visitors exactly how to find their way.

This example shows you how to create a set of icons that are used to navigate through a linear set of pages. You have three icons in GIF format: one for forward, one for back, and a third to enable the visitors to jump to a global index of the entire page structure.

First, you'll write the HTML structure to support the icons. Here, the page itself isn't very important, so you can just include a shell page:

INPUT

```
<!DOCTYPE html PUBLIC "-//W3C//DTD XHTML 1.0 Transitional//EN"
"http://www.w3.org/TR/xhtml1/DTD/transitional.dtd">
<html>
<head>
<title>Motorcycle Maintenance: Removing Spark Plugs</title>
<h1>Removing Spark Plugs</h1>
<p>(include some info about spark plugs here)</p>
<hr />
</body>
</html>
```

Figure 7.13 shows how the page looks at the beginning.

OUTPUT

FIGURE 7.13

The basic page, with no icons.

At the bottom of the page, add your images using `<img>` tags:

INPUT

```
<img src="next.gif" alt="Next" />
<img src="back.gif" alt="Back" />
<img src="uparrow.gif" alt="Up" />
```

▼ Figure 7.14 shows the result.

7

FIGURE 7.14

The basic page with icons.

Now add the anchors to the images to activate them:

```
<a href="replacing.html"><img src="next.gif" alt="Next" /></a>
<a href="ready.html"><img src="back.gif" alt="Back" /></a>
<a href="index.html"><img src="uparrow.gif" alt="Up" /></a>
```

Figure 7.15 shows the result of this addition.

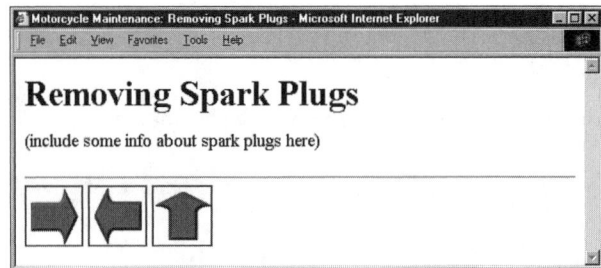

FIGURE 7.15

The basic page with iconic links.

When you click the icons now, the browser jumps to the linked page just as it would have if you had used text links.

Speaking of text, are the icons usable enough as they are? How about adding some text describing exactly what's on the other side of each link? You can add this text inside or outside the anchor, depending on whether you want the text to be a hot spot for the link as well. Here, include it outside the link so that only the icon serves as the hot spot. You also can align the bottoms of the text and the icons using the `align` attribute of the `<img>` tag. Finally, because the extra text causes the icons to move onto two lines, arrange each one on its own line instead:

```
<hr />
<p><a href="replacing.html"><img src="next.gif" alt="Next" /></a>
On to "Gapping the New Plugs"<br />
<a href="ready.html"><img src="back.gif" alt="Back" /></a>
```

▼
```
Back to "When You Should Replace your Spark Plugs"<br />
<a href="index.html"><img src="uparrow.gif" alt="Up" /></a>
Up To Index
</p>
```

See Figure 7.16 for the final menu.

OUTPUT

FIGURE 7.16

The basic page with iconic links and text.

▲

Using External Images

Unlike inline images, external images don't actually appear on your Web page. Instead, they're stored separately from the page and linked from it in much the same way that other HTML pages are.

The reason external images are worth mentioning is that often they can complement inline images. For example:

- Text-only browsers can't display images inline with Web pages, but you can download external images with a text-only browser and view them with an image editing or viewing program.
- You can combine thumbnail images on your Web pages that load quickly with a higher-resolution external image. This way, users can preview your images before deciding whether they want to wait for the larger version to download.

To use an external image, you create the image as you would an inline image and then save it with an appropriate filename. As with other files on the Web, the file extension is important. Depending on the image format, use one of the extensions listed in Table 7.1.

7

TABLE 7.1 Image Formats and Extensions

Format	Extension
GIF	`.gif`
JPEG	`.jpg, .jpeg`
XBM	`.xbm`
TIFF	`.tiff, .tif`
BMP	`.bmp`
PNG	`.png`
PICT	`.pict`
SVG	`.svg`

After you have an external image, all you have to do is create a link to it the same way you would create a link to another HTML page, as in the following:

```
<p>I grew some really huge
<a href="bigtomatoes.jpeg" alt="Tomatoes">tomatoes</a> in
my garden last year</p>
```

For this next exercise, you'll use inline and external images together.

Exercise 7.3: Linking to External GIF and JPEG Files

▼ To Do

It's common practice to provide a small GIF or JPEG image (a "thumbnail") inline on the Web page itself. Then you can link the thumbnail image to its larger external counterpart. Using this approach has two major advantages over including the entire image inline:

- It keeps the size of the Web page small so that it can be downloaded quickly.
- It gives your visitors a taste of the image so they can choose to download it if they want to see more or get a better view.

In this simple example, you'll set up a link between a small image and an larger, external version of that same image. The large image is a rendering of a castle near a river, called `castle.jpg`. It's shown in Figure 7.17.

FIGURE 7.17

The large castle image.

▼

▼ First, create a thumbnail version of the castle image in your favorite image editor. Paint Shop Pro is an image editing application for Windows, while Adobe Photoshop is more or less the standard for professional-level designers on both the Macintosh and Windows PCs. If you're just working on images for the Web, you might also find Macromedia Fireworks to be a good choice. The thumbnail can be a scaled version of the original file, a portion of that file (just the castle rather than the whole scene, for example), or anything else you want to use to indicate the larger image.

Here, I've created a scaled-down version of the larger image to serve as the inline image. (I've called it sm-castle.jpg.) Unlike the large version of the file, which is 24KB, the small picture is only 3KB. By using the <img> tag, you can put your thumbnail image directly on a nearly content-free Web page:

```
<!DOCTYPE html PUBLIC "-//W3C//DTD XHTML 1.0 Transitional//EN"
"http://www.w3.org/TR/xhtml1/DTD/transitional.dtd"><html>
<head>
<title>Castle at Sunrise</title>
</head>
<body>
<h1>Castle at Sunrise</h1>
<img src="sm-castle.jpg" alt="Castle Thumbnail" />
</body>
</html>
```

Now, by using a link tag, you can link the small icon to the bigger picture by enclosing the <img> tag inside an <a> tag:

```
<a href="castle.jpg"><img src="sm-castle.jpg"
alt="Castle Thumbnail" /></a>
```

The final result of the page is shown in Figure 7.18. When you click the small castle image, the larger image will be downloaded and viewed either by the browser itself.

FIGURE 7.18

The Castle at Sunrise home page with link.

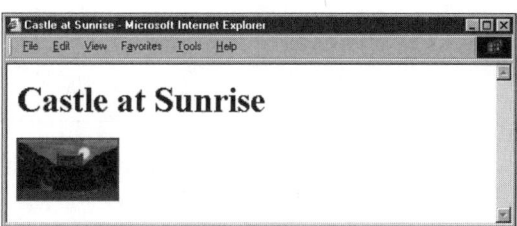

An alternative to linking the small image directly to the larger image is to provide the external image in several different formats and then create plain text links to them. (You might want to take this approach for visitors who have software for one format but not
▼ another.) In this part of the example, you'll link to a TIFF version of that same castle file.

7

▼ To create the version of the castle, you need to use your image editor or converter again to convert the original photograph. Here, I've called it `castle.tiff`.

 Note

> In the real world, you probably wouldn't be converting your thumbnail to a new format. More likely, you'd have the image stored at a higher resolution, probably in a format that doesn't throw away data when it compresses the image. You would link to this higher-resolution version, scale it down, and save it in a compressed format to use as a thumbnail.

To provide both TIFF and JPEG versions of the castle, you'll convert the link on the image into a simple link menu to the JPEG and TIFF files, providing some information about file size:

INPUT

```
<p><img src="sm-castle.jpg" alt="Castle Thumbnail" /></p>
<ul>
<li>Castle at Sunrise (<a href="castle.jpg">25K JPEG
file</a>)</li>
<li>Castle at Sunrise (<a href="castle.tiff">1.5MB TIFF
file</a>)</li>
</ul>
```

The result is shown in Figure 7.19.

OUTPUT

FIGURE 7.19

The Castle at Sunrise link menu.

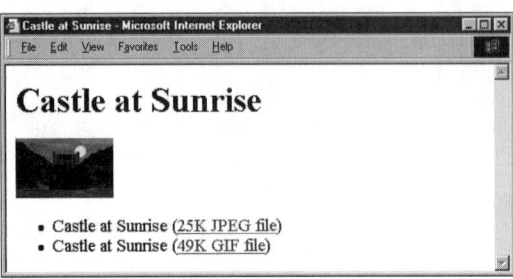

 Note

> Images aren't the only types of files you can store externally. Sound files, video, zip archives—just about anything can be linked as external files. You'll learn more about other alternatives on Day 13, "Multimedia: Adding Sounds, Videos, and More."

▲

Other Neat Tricks with Images

Now that you've learned about inline and external images, images as links, and how to wrap text around images, you know what *most* people do with images on Web pages. But you can play with a few newer tricks as well.

All the attributes in this section were originally Netscape extensions. They were later incorporated into HTML 3.2, but most have been deprecated in its successor, HTML 4.0.

Image Dimensions and Scaling

Two attributes of the `<img>` tag, `height` and `width`, specify the height and width of the image in pixels. Both became part of the HTML 3.2 specification, but they're deprecated in HTML 4.0 in favor of style sheets.

If you use the actual height and width of the image in these values (which you can find out in most image editing programs), in some browsers your Web pages will load and display much faster than if you don't include these values.

Why? In older browsers, when the browser parses the HTML code in your file, it has to load and test each image to get its width and height before proceeding so that it can format the text appropriately. Therefore, the browser loads and formats some of your text, waits for the image to load, formats around the image when it gets the dimensions, and then moves on for the rest of the page. If the width and height are already specified in the HTML code itself, the browser can just make an appropriately sized space for the image and keep formatting all the text around it. This way, your visitors can continue reading the text while the images are loading rather than having to wait. And, because `width` and `height` are ignored in other browsers, there's no reason not to use them for all your images. They neither harm nor affect the images in browsers that don't support them.

> **Tip**
>
> If you test your page with images on it in Netscape Navigator, try choosing View, Document Info. You'll get a window that lists all the images on your page. By selecting each image in turn, you'll get information about that image—including its size, which you can copy into your HTML file.

If the values for `width` and `height` are different from the actual width and height of the image, your browser will automatically scale the image to fit those dimensions. Because smaller images take up less disk space than larger images and therefore take less time to transfer over the network, you can just create a smaller version and then scale it to the dimensions you want on your Web page. Unfortunately, browsers do an awful job of resizing images. If you use the `height` and `width` attributes to change the size of an image, be prepared for it to look pretty bad.

7

Note

> Don't perform *reverse scaling*—creating a large image and then using `width` and `height` to scale it down. Smaller file sizes are better because they take less time to load. If you're just going to display a small image, make it smaller to begin with.

If you want to add a solid block of color to a page, image scaling is an easy way to do so. Just create a one-pixel GIF in the color you want, and then scale it to the size you want using the `height` and `width` attributes. You can also specify image heights and widths as a percentage of the browser window width.

Let's say you wanted to create a red stripe that's 10 pixels high and as wide as the browser window. If the image is called `red_pixel.gif`, you could create such an effect using the following code:

```
<img src="red_pixel.gif" height="10" width="100%" />
```

The resulting image appears in Figure 7.20.

FIGURE 7.20

A single-pixel GIF stretched using the `height` *and* `width` *attributes.*

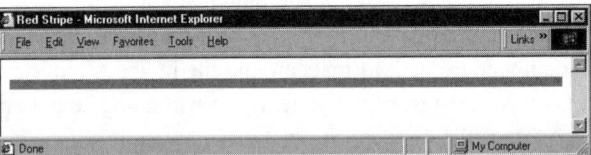

More About Image Borders

You learned about the `border` attribute to the `<img>` tag as part of the section on links, where setting `border` to a number or to 0 determined the width of the image border (or hid it entirely).

Normally, plain images don't have borders; only images that hold links do. However, you can use the `border` attribute to draw a border around a plain image, as in the following:

```
<p><img src="eggplant.gif" alt="Eggplant" align="left" border="5"
width="102" height="178" />
This is an eggplant. We intend to stay a good ways away from it,
because we really don't like eggplant very much.</p>
```

Figure 7.21 shows an image with a border around it.

FIGURE 7.21

An image border.

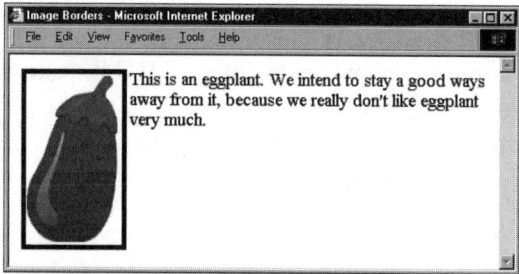

Image Previews

One completely optional HTML extension (supported by both Netscape and Internet Explorer) is the `lowsrc` attribute to `<img>`, which provides a sort of preview for the actual image on the page. You use `lowsrc` just like you use `src`, with a pathname to another image file, as follows:

```
<img src="wall.gif" lowsrc="wallsmall.gif" />
```

When a browser that supports `lowsrc` encounters a `lowsrc` tag, it loads the `lowsrc` image first, in the first pass for the overall page layout. Then, after all the layout and `lowsrc` images are done loading and displaying, the image specified in `src` is loaded and fades in to replace the `lowsrc` image.

Why would you want this type of preview? The image in `lowsrc` usually is a lower-resolution or reduced-color depth preview of the actual image, one that can load very quickly and give the visitors an idea of the overall effect of the page. (Make sure your `lowsrc` image is indeed a smaller file; otherwise, there's no point including it.) Then, after all the layout is done, the visitors can scroll around and read the text while the better images are quietly loaded in the background.

Using `lowsrc` is entirely optional; it's simply ignored in older browsers.

Using Color

As you've seen, one way to add a splash of color to the black and gray and white on your Web pages is to add images. However, several HTML attributes enable you to change the colors of the page itself, including changing the background color, changing the color of the text and links, and adding "spot color" to individual characters.

In this section, you'll learn how to make all these changes in HTML 3.2. However, as is the case with most of the presentational attributes we've covered thus far, color attributes are deprecated in HTML 4.0 in favor of style sheets. You'll learn more about the style sheet approach on Day 12.

7

Naming Colors

Before you can change the color of any part of an HTML page, you have to know what color you're going to change it to. You can specify colors using the color extensions to HTML in two ways:

- Using a hexadecimal number representing that color
- Using one of a set of predefined color names

The most flexible and widely supported method of indicating color involves finding out the numeric value of the color you want to use. Most image editing programs have what's called a *color picker*—some way of choosing a single color from a range of available colors. Most color pickers, in turn, will tell you the value of that color in RGB form, as three numbers (one for red, one for green, and one for blue—that's what RGB stands for). Each number is usually 0 to 255, with `0 0 0` being black and `255 255 255` being white.

If you're forced to use one of these tools on a Web page, you'll have to convert the decimal numbers to hexadecimal. These days, most tools with color pickers also provide the hexadecimal values for red, green, and blue, which is what Web browsers require. In fact, the color picker that's built into the Mac OS includes the hexadecimal values to make things easy on Web publishers.

The final hex number you need is all three numbers put together with a hash sign (#) at the beginning, as in the following:

```
#000000
#de04e4
#ffff00
```

Netscape and Internet Explorer support a much easier way of indicating colors. Rather than using arcane numbering schemes, you just choose a color name such as Black, White, Green, Maroon, Olive, Navy, Purple, Gray, Red, Yellow, Blue, Teal, Lime, Aqua, Fuchsia, or Silver.

Although color names are easier to figure out and remember than the numbers, they offer less choice of colors and aren't as widely supported in browsers. Keep in mind that if you do use color names, you may lose the colors in most other browsers.

After you have a color name or number in hand, you can apply that color to various parts of your HTML page.

There are also a number of Web sites that are designed to help Web designers choose colors. One of the best is Clear Ink's Palette Man application at `www.paletteman.com/`. It allows you to view several colors next to each other to see how they match. The current Palette Man interface appears in Figure 7.22.

FIGURE 7.22

Clear Ink's Palette Man.

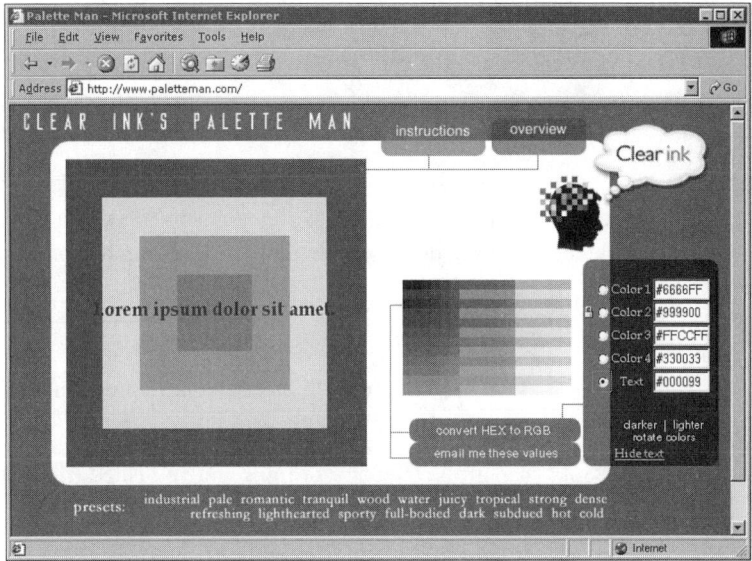

Changing the Background Color

To change the color of a page's background, decide what color you want and then add an attribute called bgcolor to the <body> tag. The <body> tag, in case you've forgotten, is the tag that surrounds all the content of your HTML file. <head> contains the title, and <body> contains almost everything else. bgcolor is an HTML extension introduced by Netscape in the 1.1 version of the browser and incorporated into HTML 3.2.

To use color numbers for backgrounds, you enter the value of the bgcolor attribute of the <body> tag (the hexadecimal number you found in the preceding section) in quotation marks. They look like the following:

```
<body bgcolor="#ffffff">
<body bgcolor="#934ce8">
```

To use color names, simply use the name of the color as the value to bgcolor:

```
<body bgcolor="white">
<body bgcolor="green">
```

Note

Some browsers enable you to indicate color numbers without the leading hash sign (#). Although this method may seem more convenient, because it's incompatible with many other browsers, the inclusion of the one extra character doesn't seem like that much of a hardship.

7

Changing Text Colors

When you can change the background colors, it also makes sense to change the color of the text itself. Other attributes of the <body> tag enable you to change the color of the text globally on your pages.

To change the text and link colors, you'll need your color names or numbers just as you did for changing the backgrounds. With a color in hand, you can add any of the following attributes to the <body> tag with either a color number or color name as their values:

text   Controls the color of all the page's body text that isn't links, including headings, body text, text inside tables, and so on.

link   Controls the color of normal, unfollowed links on the page (the ones that are blue by default).

vlink   Controls the color of links you've visited (the ones that are purple by default).

alink   Controls the color of a link that has had the mouse button clicked on it but not released (an activated link). They're red by default.

Remember the haunted house image that you inserted on a page earlier? The page would be decidedly more spooky with a black background, and orange text would be so much more appropriate for the holiday. To create a page with an orange background, black text, and deep red unfollowed links, you might use the following <body> tag:

```
<body bgcolor="#ff9933" text="#000000" link="#800000">
```

Using the following color names for the background and unfollowed links would produce the same effect:

```
<body bgcolor="orange" text="black" link="#800000">
```

Both these links would produce a page that looks something like the one shown in Figure 7.23.

FIGURE 7.23

Background and text colors.

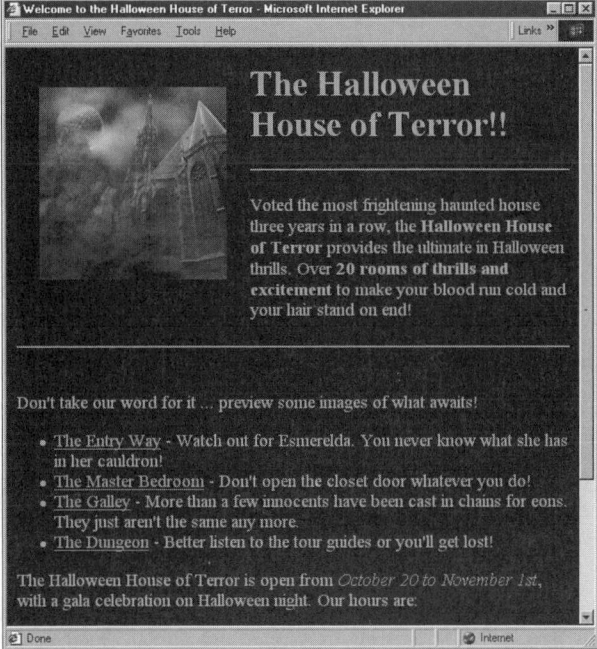

Spot Color

When you change a page's text colors by using attributes to the <body> tag, that change affects all the text on the page. *Spot color* is the capability to change the color of individual characters on your page, which you can use instead of or in addition to a global text color.

Yesterday you learned about using the HTML tag <font> for setting the font size and font name. A third attribute to <font>, color, enables you to change the color of individual words or phrases. The value of color is either a color name or number:

```
<p>When we go out tonight, we're going to paint the town
<font color="#ff0000">RED</font>.
```

Of course, you can use font spot colors in addition to font names and sizes.

Note

> The current recommended method for adding spot color to Web pages is to use Cascading Style Sheets, which are explained on Day 12.

7

Image Backgrounds

The last topic for today is using an image as a background for your pages, rather than simply a solid-colored background. When you use an image for a background, that image is "tiled"; that is, it's repeated in rows to fill the browser window.

To create a tiled background, you'll need an image to serve as the tile. Usually, when you create an image for tiling, you need to make sure that the pattern flows smoothly from one tile to the next. You can do some careful adjusting of the image in your favorite image editing program to make sure the edges line up. The goal is for the edges to meet cleanly so that you don't have a seam between the tiles after you've laid them end to end. (See Figure 7.24 for an example of tiles that don't line up very well.) You also can try clip art packages for wallpaper or tile patterns that are designed specifically to be tiled in this fashion.

FIGURE 7.24

Tiled images with seams.

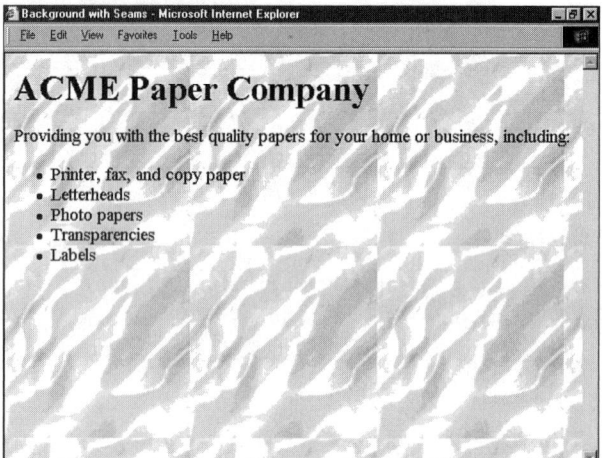

When you have an image that can be tiled cleanly, all you need to create a tiled image background is the background attribute, which is part of the <body> tag. The value of background is a filename or URL that points to your image file, as in the following example:

```
<body background="tiles.gif">
<body background="backgrounds/rosemarble.gif">
```

Figure 7.25 shows the result of a simple tiled background.

FIGURE 7.25

A tiled background in Internet Explorer.

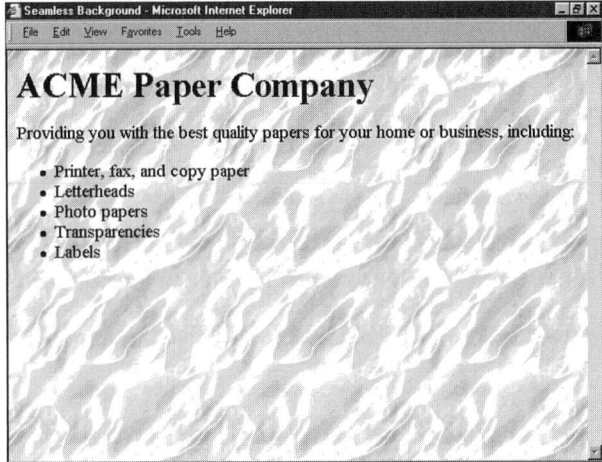

Internet Explorer offers a twist on the tiled background design, a fixed tile pattern called a *watermark*. The idea here is that when you scroll a page, only the page foreground (text and images) scrolls by rather than everything on the page. The tiles in the background stay rooted in one place. To create this effect, use the `bgproperties="fixed"` attribute to the <body> tag, as follows:

```
<body background="backgrounds/rosemarble.gif" bgproperties="fixed">
```

Note

You can also use Cascading Style Sheets to add a fixed background to a Web page. This approach works not only in Internet Explorer, but also in Netscape 4 and higher.

Hints for Better Use of Images

One of the bigger arguments among users and providers of Web pages today is how best to use images. For everyone who wants to design Web pages with bigger and brighter images to take full advantage of the graphical capabilities of the Web, someone on a slow network connection is begging for fewer images so that his browser doesn't take three hours to load a page.

As a designer of Web pages, you should consider both of these points of view. Balance the fun of creating a highly visual Web page with the need to get your information to as many people as possible—and that includes people who may not have access to your images at all.

7

This section explains some compromises you can make in your Web page design so that you can try to make everyone happy.

Do You Really Need This Image?

For each image you put inline on your Web page, consider why you're putting it there. What does the image add to the design? Does it provide information that could be presented in the text instead? Is it just there because you like how it looks?

Try not to clutter your Web page with pretty but otherwise unnecessary images. A simple Web page with only a few iconic images can be more effective than a page that opens with an enormous graphic and continues with flashy 3D buttons, drop-shadow bullets, and psychedelic line separators.

Keep Your Images Small

Smaller images take less time to transfer over the Internet, which makes your Web page load faster and causes less frustration for people with slow connections. What could be easier?

To create small images, you can reduce their actual physical dimensions onscreen. You also can give your images smaller file sizes by reducing the number of colors. Your goal is to reduce the file size of the image so that it transfers faster, but a four-inch by four-inch black-and-white image (two colors) may be smaller in file size than a ½-inch by ½-inch full-color photographic image. With most image-processing programs, you can reduce the number of colors and touch up the result so that it looks good even with fewer colors.

A good rule to follow is to keep your inline images somewhere under 20KB. That size may seem small, but a single 20KB file takes nearly 5 seconds to download over a 56Kbps connection. Multiply that by the number of images on your Web page, and the page may take a substantial amount of time to load even if you're using a browser that can load multiple images at once. The pipe is only so wide. Will people care about what's on your Web page if they have to go off and have lunch while it's loading?

Reuse Images as Often as Possible

In addition to keeping individual images small, try to reuse the same images as often as you can, on single pages and across multiple pages. For example, if you're using images as bullets, use the same image for all of them. Reusing images has two significant advantages over using different images:

- It gives your design a consistency across pages, which is part of creating an overall look for your site.

- Even more importantly, it means that your browser has to download the image only once. After the browser has the image in memory, it can simply draw the image multiple times without having to make more connections back to the server.

To reuse an image, you don't have to do anything special; just make sure you refer to each image with the same URL each time you use it. The browser will take care of the rest.

Provide Alternatives to Images

If you're not using the `alt` attribute in your images, you should be. The `alt` attribute is extremely useful for making your Web page readable by text-only browsers. But what about people who turn off images on their browsers because they have a slow link to the Internet? Most browsers don't use the value of `alt` in this case. And sometimes `alt` isn't enough; because you can specify text only inside an `alt` string, you can't substitute HTML code for the image.

To get around all these problems while still keeping your nifty graphical Web pages, consider creating alternative text-only versions of your pages and putting links to them on the full-graphics versions of those pages, as in the following:

```
<p>A <a href="TextVersion.html">text-only</a>
version of this page is available.</p>
```

The link to the text-only page takes up only one small paragraph on the "real" Web page, but it makes the information much more accessible. Providing this low-bandwidth version is a courtesy that visitors with slow connections will thank you for, and it still enables you to load up your "main" Web page with as many images as you like for those people who have fast connections If you're going to provide such a link on your pages, you should include the `height` and `width` attributes for all of the images so that the pages can be laid out and the user sees the link before all of the actual images are downloaded.

Image Etiquette

There are great images on sites all over the Web: cool icons, great photographs, excellent line art, and plenty of other graphics as well. You might feel the temptation to link directly to these images and include them on your own pages, or to save them to disk and then use them. There are a number of reasons why it's wrong to do so.

First of all, you're stealing bandwidth from that site. Every time someone requests your page, they'll also be issuing a request to the site where the image is posted and downloading the image from there. If you get a lot of traffic, you can cause problems for the remote site.

7

The second reason is actually a problem regardless of how you use images from other sites. If you don't have permission to use an image on your site, you're violating the rights of the image's creator. Copyright law protects creative work from use without permission, and it's granted to every creative work automatically.

The best course of action is to create your own images or look for images that are explicitly offered for free use by their creators. Even if images are made available for your use, you should download them and store them with your Web pages rather than linking to them directly. This will prevent you from abusing the bandwidth of the person providing the images.

Summary

One of the major features that makes the World Wide Web stand out from other elements of the Internet is that Web pages can contain full-color images. Arguably, it was the existence of those images that allowed the Web to catch on so quickly.

Today you learned that to place images on your Web pages. Those images are normally in GIF or JPEG format and should be small enough that they can be downloaded quickly over a slow link. You also learned that the HTML tag <img> enables you to put an image on a Web page either inline with text or on a line by itself. The <img> tag has three primary attributes supported in standard HTML:

src	The location and filename of the image to include.
align	How to position the image vertically with its surrounding text. align can have one of three values: top, middle, or bottom. (Deprecated in HTML 4.0 in favor of style sheets.)
alt	A text string to substitute for the image in text-only browsers.

You can include images inside a link tag (<a>) and make them hot spots for the links.

In addition to the standard attributes, several other attributes to the <img> tag provide greater control over images and layout on Web pages. You learned how to use these HTML 3.2 attributes today, but most of them have been deprecated in HTML 4.0 in favor of style sheets. They include the following:

align="left"	Places the image against the appropriate margin, allowing all of the following text to flow into the space alongside the image.

`align="right"`	
`clear`	A Netscape extension to ` ` that allows you to stop wrapping text alongside an image. `clear` can have three values: `left`, `right`, and `all`.
`align="texttop"`	Allows greater control over the alignment of an inline image and the text surrounding it.
`align="absmiddle"`	
`align="baseline"`	
`align="absbottom"`	
`vspace`	Defines the amount of space between an image and the text surrounding it.
`hspace`	
`border`	Defines the width of the border around an image (with or without a link). `border="0"` hides the border altogether.
`lowsrc`	Defines an alternative, lower-resolution image that's loaded before the image indicated by `src`.

In addition to images, you can add color to the background and the text of a page by using attributes to the `<body>` tag, or to individual characters by using the `color` attribute to `<font>`. Finally, you learned that you can add patterned or tiled backgrounds to images by using the `background` attribute to `<body>` with an image for the tile.

Workshop

Now that you know how to add images and color to your pages, you can really get creative. This workshop will help you remember some of the most important points about using images and color on your pages so that they'll be compatible with HTML 3.2 and HTML 4.0 browsers. If you want to design your pages strictly around the HTML 4.0 specification, you'll need to forego many of the presentation options you learned today in favor of style sheets.

7

Q&A

Q What's the difference between a GIF image and a JPEG image? Is there any rule of thumb that defines when you should use one format over the other?

A As a rule, you should use GIF files when images contain 256 colors or fewer. Some good examples are cartoon art, clip art, black-and-white images, and images with many solid color areas. You'll also need to use GIF files if you want your images to contain transparent areas, or if you want to create an animation that doesn't require a special plug-in or browser helper. Remember to use your image editing software to reduce the number of colors in the image palettes whenever possible, because this also reduces the size of the file.

JPEG images are best for photographic-quality or high-resolution 3D rendered graphics, because they can display true-color images to great effect. Most image editing programs enable you to specify how much to compress a JPEG image. The size of the file decreases the more an image is compressed; however, compression can also deteriorate the quality and appearance of the image if you go overboard. You have to find just the right balance between quality and file size, and this can differ from image to image.

Q How can I create thumbnails of my images so that I can link them to larger external images?

A You'll have to do that with some type of image editing program (such as Adobe Photoshop or Paint Shop Pro); the Web won't do it for you. Just open up the image and scale it down to the right size.

Q What about those images that are partially transparent to display the page background? They look like they sort of float on the page. How do I create those?

A This is another task you can accomplish with an image editing program. These types of images are known as *transparent GIFs*, and you can only achieve this effect with a GIF image. I'll show you how to create a transparent GIF on Day 8.

Q Can I put HTML tags in the string for the `alt` attribute?

A That would be nice, wouldn't it? Unfortunately, you can't. All you can do is put an ordinary string in there. Keep it simple, and you should be fine.

Q You discussed a technique for including `lowsrc` images on a page that are loaded in before regular images are. I've seen an effect where an image seems to load in as a really blurry image and then becomes clearer as time goes on. Is that a `lowsrc` effect?

A No, that's something called an interlaced GIF. There's only one image; it's just displayed differently from regular GIFs as it's loading. Progressive JPEGs provide the same effect for JPEG images. You'll learn more about interlaced GIFs on Day 8.

lowsrc images load just like regular images with no special visual effects.

Q **I've seen some Web pages where you can click different places on an image to link to different places, such as a map of the United States where each state has a different page. How do you do this in HTML?**

A You use something called an imagemap, which is an advanced form of Web page development. I'll explain how to create imagemaps on Day 9, "Creating and Using Imagemaps."

Quiz

1. Describe the two classes of images that are used on Web pages.

2. What's the most important attribute of the <img> tag? What does it do?

3. If you see a funny-looking icon rather than an image when you view your page, the image isn't loading. What are some of the reasons this could happen?

4. As a rule, what distinguishes a clickable image (one that's used as a link) from a non-clickable image?

5. Why is it important to use the alt attribute to display a text alternative to an image? When is it most important to do so?

Quiz Answers

1. Inline images appear directly on a Web page, along with the text and links. External images are downloaded at the request of your visitors, usually as a result of clicking a link.

2. The most important attribute of the <img> tag is the src attribute. It indicates the filename or URL of the image you want to include on your page.

3. There are several things that cause an image not to load. The URL may be incorrect; the filename might not be correct (they're case sensitive); it might have the wrong file extension; it might be the wrong type of file; or image loading might be turned off on your browser.

4. By default, clickable images (those used for links) are surrounded by a border, whereas non-clickable images aren't.

5. It's a good idea to provide text alternatives with images because some people use text-only browsers or have their graphics turned off. It's especially important to provide text alternatives for images used as links.

7

Exercises

1. Create or find some images that you can use as navigation icons or buttons on one or more pages of your Web site. Remember that it's always advantageous to use images more than once. Create a simple navigation bar that you can use on the top or bottom of each page.

2. Create or find some images that you can use to enhance the appearance of your Web pages. Images such as small banners (for page titles), bullets, horizontal rules, and background images are always handy to keep around. After you find some that you like, try to create background, text, and link colors that are compatible with them.

DAY 8

Creating Animated Graphics

You've probably had enough of coding for a while, so today you'll get a break from typing and learn how to move pixels around! Animated graphics add spark and emphasis to Web pages, and they're not as difficult to create as you might think. With the right software tools, you can create your own original animations for your Web pages. Get ready to learn how to do the following:

- When and where to use animation on your Web pages
- How to create a transparent GIF file, and how to choose a transparent color
- Learn about tools for image editing and GIF creation that help you create your own animated GIF files
- Review software features that are very useful in an image editing package
- Learn how to compile and reduce the size of an animated GIF file
- Create your own animation frames from scratch
- Create a rollover effect using JavaScript

What Is an Animation?

Imagine that you have a stack of photographs, one on top of the other. They're arranged in a specific sequence, with each picture slightly different than the one that precedes it. When you flip the pictures, you see the illusion of movement. The speed of the animation varies depending on how fast you flip the pictures.

Basically, any animation file, whether it's an animated GIF, Flash animation, Windows AVI file, QuickTime movie, or MPEG file, is nothing more than a virtual picture flipbook. You arrange several images, usually of the same size, in a specific order with software that in one way or another generates a script. The script is built into the animation file and defines parameters such as how fast the images flip (the speed of the animation), how one image should overlay the next one, and so on. Rather than having to load each individual image one at a time, what you have is a single file consisting of multiple frames that play in a sequence somewhat like a movie.

When and Where to Use Animation

Animation can be captivating and attractive, but at the same time, if it's used improperly, it can be a distraction. So how can you effectively use animation on a Web page?

The general rule of thumb is to use animation to draw attention to something. Too much animation detracts from a page. The reader won't know where to look first, and it might draw him away from the important text on your page. Use animation sparingly and appropriately. Above all, don't pile a whole slew of animations on a single page because it will take forever to load.

The following are some common uses of animation:

- **Banner advertisements**. Some people find these annoying and sometimes avoid them. If your Web site is sponsored by an organization, however, or if you want to draw attention to your own products and capabilities, banner advertisements are a fairly standard way to do it.

- **Animated bullets**. These are nice for lists, but try to keep it brief. If the list contains more than 10 items, a busy animated bullet can be very distracting.

- **Horizontal rules**. Many times, you'll see thin lines of animated gradients that are used as horizontal rules. You can create much more clever rules—a line of piano keys, musical notes playing on a staff, Cupid shooting an arrow, two people hitting a tennis ball back and forth, a shark fin swimming from left to right and back again, or anything else that fits the theme of a Web page. Try to keep the width and height of the animation fairly reasonable, however, or the file size will become too large.

8

- **Animated logos**. An animated logo on a home page can draw attention to your company or product name. If your logo is large, you can split it into several different sections and create an animated graphic in one of the sections. Then you can use borderless tables to fit the sections together so that they appear on your page as one graphic.
- **Icons**. Animations can be quite effective in drawing attention to important information on your page. Place an animated envelope or mailbox near your email address, a flashing "New!" icon near a worthy piece of news, a ringing telephone near your phone number, a burning fire near a hot link, and so on.

Tip

Just because these are common uses of animation doesn't mean that they're appropriate for your audience. A lot of animation is overdone and detracts from the message of a Web site rather than adding to it. You should think carefully about where and how you want to use animation before you start placing animation on your site.

Creating Transparent GIF Files

No doubt you've seen images that appear as if they're floating on the Web page. Rather than appearing as a square or a rectangle, a transparent GIF appears to be irregularly shaped and allows the background to show through.

You can apply transparency to animated GIF files also, if the software you use to create or compile your GIFs allows it. Some GIF animation compilers enable you to define a transparent color when you compile your animation, and others don't. Based on this, you can use one of two different approaches to creating transparent GIF animations:

- If your GIF animation program enables you to choose a transparent color, globally or on a frame-by-frame basis, you can add the transparency before you save the animation.
- If your GIF animation doesn't let you select transparent colors, you'll need to choose a transparent color for each of the still images in your image editing software. Save each individual frame as a transparent GIF and import it into your GIF animation program. It takes a little bit longer to create your animation this way, but it still works.

Choosing a Transparent Color

Here's how a transparent GIF works. Typically you use an image with a solid background color behind the areas that will be visible on your Web page. You designate this solid background color as the transparent color for your image. If you're designing your animation for a page that uses a background image, create or choose GIF files with a background color that's a close match. If your page's background is a black sky with stars, for example, use a solid black background for your transparent GIF. If your background is a soft pastel color, create or choose GIF images on a white or light-colored background.

Why image-editing programs use *antialiasing* to soften the appearance of diagonal or curved lines. Antialiasing basically blends the color of the element on the page with the background color. Because transparency only affects a single hue, all of the blended colors will show up exactly as they did before transparency was applied. So, if you add an antialiased red element to an image with a white background, make the white background transparent, and place the image on a black page, the red element will appear to have a white-ish border around it. So, it's best to start with a background that's similar in color or tone to the page where you're going to put the graphic.

NEW TERM   *Antialiasing* is a process that softens the jagged edges in images containing curved or diagonal lines. It achieves this by blending pixels that are intermediate in color between the element and the background on which it was placed. For example, if you have a black line on a white background, the image editor softens its appearance by inserting shades of gray.

Figure 8.1 shows antialiasing in action. The cartoon in this image was created against a white background. You might notice some strange pixels and *ghosting* around the image on the left side, while the same transparent GIF file looks fine on the right side. This is an extreme example, but it illustrates how antialiasing can affect a transparent GIF file.

FIGURE 8.1

Antialiasing can sometimes cause ghosting around a transparent GIF.

If you're creating your own images for transparent GIFs, be sure not to use the background color in any other portion that you don't want to be transparent. There's a reason for this: Any instance of the color you select as transparent will *be* transparent. If any portions of your image also contain that color, your nice artwork will appear to have holes in it that you don't want.

What do you do if you want to use the same color that you've selected as transparent within your image? Suppose that you're creating a cartoon on a white background, but you want to use white in a character's eyes. The solution is simple: Use pure white (Red 255, Green 255, Blue 255) as the background color, and use an *almost* white color (Red 255, Green 255, Blue 250, for example) for your eyes. The colors look very nearly the same, but to the image editing program, color 255,255,255 is different than color 255,255,250. Your character's eyes will be safe.

Programs to Help You Compile Animated GIFs

Assume that you've selected or created a series of images that you want to turn into an animated GIF. The next step is to compile the individual images into a single animated file. There's a wide variety of utilities that help you create animated GIFs for the Web. Animated GIFs have become so popular that several commercial and shareware graphics programs now include built-in support for creating them. Adobe Photoshop, Jasc Paint Shop Pro, Macromedia Fireworks, and ULead PhotoImpact are all popular image editors for creating Web graphics that also include GIF animation builders. A few of these applications are described in more detail later today in "Tools to Help You Create Your Pictures."

Even presentation programs, such as Microsoft PowerPoint, enable you to create and save presentations as animated GIF files that can be used as banner advertisements.

Although most image editing programs allow you to create GIF files, not all of them enable you to create *animated* GIF files. Conversely, there are programs that help you create animated GIF files but don't create the images themselves. If you have your heart set on a graphics program that doesn't save animated GIFs, have no fear. Here are a couple of standalone programs that help you compile animated GIF files.

GIF Construction Set (Windows Platform)

One of the most popular shareware GIF builders for the Windows platform is GIF Construction Set by Alchemy Mindworks. This reasonably priced shareware utility features an animation wizard that makes constructing animated GIFs a breeze. You build your GIF files through drag-and-drop file selection. The program's slick features enable you to manage your palette, select transparent colors, add effect transitions and timing, convert AVI video clips to animated GIFs, and much, much more.

You can download GIF Construction Set from Alchemy Mindwork's Web site at `http://www.mindworkshop.com/alchemy/gifcon.html`. The site offers many demos and examples as well.

GifBuilder (Macintosh Platform)

One very popular GIF animation program for the Macintosh is GifBuilder by Yves Piquet. GifBuilder is a freeware scriptable utility that enables you to input graphics in several different formats. You can modify existing animated GIFs or import a collection of GIF, TIFF, PICT, or PSD (Photoshop) files. GifBuilder also enables you to input several other animation formats, such as QuickTime movies, PICS files, Adobe Premiere FilmStrip files, or the layers of an RGB or grayscale Adobe Photoshop file. The current version is 1.0, and it features frame icons in the Frames window, filters, transitions, animation cropping, and more.

The home page for GifBuilder is located at `http://homepage.mac.com/piguet/gif.html`.

Creating Animated GIFs

After you have a program that you can use to create an animated GIF, you can actually begin creating one. An animated GIF is basically just a GIF file that comprises several GIF images that are treated as frames in an animation. A delay is specified with each frame in the file, which indicates how long to wait before showing the next frame in the animation. You can also specify whether your animated GIFs loop—if they do, the animation will be played repeatedly as long as the image is displayed on the page.

When you think about GIFs as a stack of individual images, the method for creating GIFs from existing images becomes clear. You import the GIFs into an animation program, put the frames in the correct order for your animation, specify the delays, and export them as an animation. That's really all there is to it. In Exercise 8.1, we'll take a look at creating an animated GIF from a set of 10 files that will serve as the individual frames.

Exercise 8.1: Creating an Animation

To Do

The following exercise creates an animated GIF of a bouncing ball consisting of 10 frames. I'm using Macromedia Fireworks to create my GIF animation.

8

Note   You can download a trial version of Fireworks from the Macromedia Web site at http://www.macromedia.com/software/fireworks/.

To compile a GIF animation from existing files using Macromedia Fireworks, follow these steps:

1. Import the files that will be used as the frames in your animation into your GIF animation program. Select Open from the Fireworks File menu and locate the drive and folder where the images you'll use as frames are stored. Click the last file-name (ball10.gif) and then Shift+click the first filename (ball01.gif) to select all the frames in the proper order. Click the Open as Animation checkbox at the bottom of the window to make them into an animation automatically. Then click Open to create a new animated image with each of the individual images as a frame. The dialog box used to open the files appears in Figure 8.2.

FIGURE 8.2

The Fireworks Open File dialog.

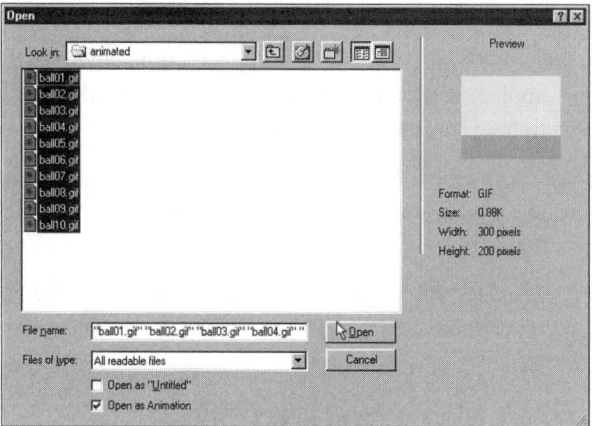

2. Take a look at the Frames window in Fireworks (shown in Figure 8.3). You'll see that each of the 10 images is stored as a separate frame in the animation. The numbers in the column on the right indicate the delay between the current frame and the next one, in hundredths of a second. As you can see, they're set to 7 hundredths of a second by default. To change the delay between two frames, just double-click that column and enter the new delay. The currently selected frame is displayed in the image window.

Tip | If you're unsure that your frames are in order, you can view each frame in the sequence in the Frames window. If they're out of order, you can drag frames up and down the list in the Frames window to correct the order.

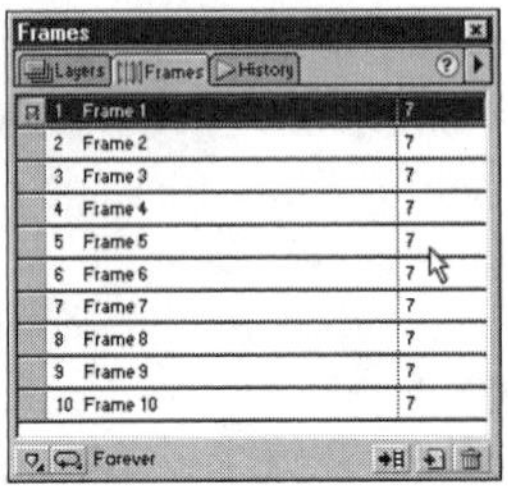

FIGURE 8.3

The Frames window in Fireworks.

> **Frames**
> Layers | Frames | History
> 1 Frame 1   7
> 2 Frame 2   7
> 3 Frame 3   7
> 4 Frame 4   7
> 5 Frame 5   7
> 6 Frame 6   7
> 7 Frame 7   7
> 8 Frame 8   7
> 9 Frame 9   7
> 10 Frame 10   7
> Forever

3. When all your frames are set to the delay you want and are in the correct order, you're ready to export the image as an animated GIF. We'll take a look at that in the next exercise.

Now you know the basic steps for creating an animated GIF file in Fireworks. Other GIF animation compilers have their own additional features that are worth looking into. I'll leave the studying and experimenting up to you.

Before you export your file in Fireworks, I have to explain *optimization* because you'll probably want to make some decisions about file size and quality when you export the file.

Optimization enables you to strike a balance between the size and quality of your animation file so that it looks as good as possible and doesn't take too long to download.

Optimizing Animation Size

When you're creating an animation, you should keep in mind a number of considerations when thinking about graphics size. The first consideration is the size (in pixels) of the file. A 100×100 image will be smaller (in bytes) than a 500×500 image of the same subject, but it might be too small for the person who's viewing it to see what's going on. You should make your images as small as is acceptable to get your point across.

The second consideration is the number of frames to include in the animation. It takes experimentation to decide on a good number. The standard speed of videotape in the U.S. is approximately 30 frames per second; however, this is not at all practical for the Internet because the download times would be horrendous. Ten to fifteen frames per second is a far more reasonable speed, but you can often get away with even less.

8

The bouncing ball animation has the delays set so that it's displayed at about 10 frames per second.

Note
> If you're dropping frames out of an existing animation to reduce its size, it's important to remember to adjust the delays between the frames to make up for the lost frames. For example, if you want to reduce a five-second animation with 150 frames to 50 frames, you need to up the delay between frames from 3.33/100 of a second to 10/100 of a second.

The third way to reduce file size is to look at color reduction. A GIF image can contain up to 256 colors. However, the fewer colors in your GIFs, the smaller the size of your files. Generally, when you export GIFs, you can experiment with the number of colors used and see what effect that has on the image quality and the file size. By playing around with the color settings, you can strike an acceptable balance between file size and quality.

Exercise 8.2: Color Reduction in an Animation

Minimizing the colors in your animated GIF can have a dramatic effect on the file size. In this case, the bouncing ball animation is very simple, so the file sizes will be pretty small in the first place. A more complex image would be much larger. In Table 8.2, look at what the optimization of colors does to the size of a 12-frame 400×400 animation. Check out the differences in the total file sizes when you reduce the number of colors in the palette. The download times shown in the table are based on a 56Kbps modem.

TABLE 8.2   Results of Bouncing Ball Color Palette Reduction

Number of Colors	File Size	Download Time at 56k
256-color palette	33.6k	5 seconds
Reduced to 128 colors	29.7k	5 seconds
Reduced to 64 colors	24.5k	4 seconds
Reduced to 32 colors	19.7k	3 seconds
Reduced to 16 colors	15.9k	2 seconds

A three-second reduction in download time might not seem like much, but when you have several graphics on a page, every little byte counts. Sixteen colors is perfectly acceptable for many images.

Tip

Animations that are photographic-quality and contain many subtle color changes won't look so wonderful if too much color reduction is applied. In these cases, the only options you have to make the file size smaller are to reduce the number of frames or reduce the dimensions of the animation.

To optimize the number of colors in your animation, follow these steps in Fireworks:

1. Select Export Preview from the File menu.

2. By default, Fireworks expects to create a single static GIF of the currently selected Frame. Choose Animated GIF from the Format menu to indicate that you want to create an animated GIF using all the frames in the image. The Export Preview window appears in Figure 8.4. After you have the format set to animated GIF, you can preview the animation by using the buttons below the preview image.

FIGURE 8.4

The Fireworks Export Preview window for an animated GIF.

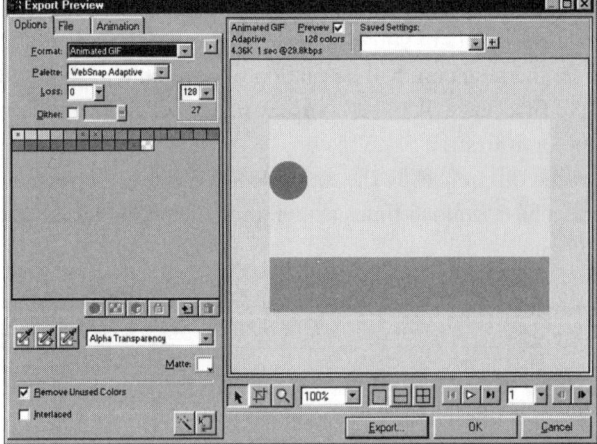

3. By default, Fireworks offers to export your image using 128 colors and the Websnap Adaptive palette. Most of the time, this is a perfectly acceptable choice. It automatically discards any unused colors in the palette, thus saving space.

4. You can see the effect any changes to the image settings have by looking at the information above the preview window. Fireworks shows you how large the file will be and how long the file will take to download with a 28.8kbps modem. After you have the export settings tweaked the way you want them, you can click OK to save those settings for later or click Export to go ahead and create the animated GIF.

▼
▲
   5. When you select Export from the File menu after storing your export settings, or click Export in the Export Preview window, just navigate to the directory where you want to save the file, choose a filename, and you're done.

8

Tools to Help You Create Your Pictures

It's not hard to find examples of the state of the art in computer animation, just check out recent Disney movies such as *Toy Story 2* and *Dinosaur*. Of course, those films involve software that costs tens of thousands of dollars and massively powerful server farms to render the individual frames. The good news is that you don't *really* need expensive software to create animations for your Web pages. Several very respectable image editors are available as reasonably priced shareware. You can download them from the Internet and evaluate their features before you purchase them. If you prefer retail software and the advantages of a nice user manual, there are several retail packages that are powerful and reasonably priced as well.

Earlier, I mentioned that one of the more popular image editing tools for Windows is Paint Shop Pro 7. This powerful retail graphics program also includes an animated GIF compiler called Animation Shop that steps you through the process of creating animated GIF files quite easily. You can download the most current version of Paint Shop Pro (and Animation Shop) from `http://www.jasc.com/`.

ULead PhotoImpact 6 (`http://www.ulead.com/pi/runme.htm`) is a retail graphics editor that also includes many image editing and animation capabilities. Integrated with PhotoImpact is a companion program called GIF Animator. You can download a 15-day trial version of PhotoImpact from ULead's Web site.

Applications commonly used by professionals for creating and optimizing Web graphics include Adobe Photoshop, Adobe Illustrator, and Macromedia Fireworks. Photoshop, currently at version 6, is the industry standard image editor. You can find out more about it at `http://www.adobe.com/products/photoshop/`. Illustrator, currently at version 9, is Adobe's tool for image composition. You can find out more about it at `http://www.adobe.com/products/illustrator/`. Macromedia Fireworks, which I used earlier to create an animated GIF, is also an excellent image creation package. I'll explain in a bit how I used Fireworks to create the images for the bouncing ball animation.

The ClNET Web site is a great resource for product demos and shareware downloads in all different categories. Its Download.com site offers easy access to information on just about every type of software program you can imagine. Some are time-limited or save-disabled demos of retail software, whereas others are shareware applications that you can try fully before you buy. You can easily tell at a glance which programs are the most popular by the number of downloads, but most products also include a comprehensive list of features that you can review before clicking the Download button.

For animation, image editing, or multimedia authoring tools, check out the Multimedia and Design category at Download.com. Just go to `http://download.cnet.com/` and look for your platform of choice.

Alternatively, you can visit CINET's shareware download areas at `http://www.shareware.com/` or the Web Building area at `http://www.builder.com`. Shareware.com enables you to search through more than 250,000 different shareware titles for the shareware of your choice, while the Web Building area focuses on software that is more related to the Web.

Useful Software Features

Not all graphics programs are created equal, and there are so many of them that often it is hard to decide which ones are the best. There are some features that are advantageous, however, especially when you're creating animations for the Web. The following are a few recommendations for what your software should include:

- The capability to open, create, and save images in a wide variety of file formats. Most importantly, you want to be able to create and save GIF and JPEG images for Web pages.
- The capability to reduce the number of colors in a 256-color GIF image. Saving an image that has only three or four colors with a 256-color palette wastes a *lot* of bytes, as you learned earlier today.
- The capability to work with selections, objects, and layers. Selections enable you to work with a portion of an image without affecting the remaining part of the image. Objects "float" in an image, enabling you to easily reposition or resize them as necessary to fit the composition. Layers enable you to place objects in front of or behind each other.
- The ability to work with layers or frames. If you're creating animation effects, the ability to split your image into layers makes things much easier when you want to leave the background unchanged and move items on the foreground around.
- The capability to save an image with transparent regions. This is important if you want to create transparent GIF files that appear as though they're floating on your Web page. It's even better if your GIF animation compiler also has this feature.

After you find an image editor you like, the remaining ingredients are a bit trickier. You need an eye for movement, a reasonable amount of patience, and a lot of creativity.

Exercise 8.3: Creating the Bouncing Ball Animation from Scratch

8

▲ To Do

I've chosen Macromedia Fireworks to create the example in this lesson. If you're using a different graphics program, don't worry. The concepts I'll discuss here are fairly common. Although it might be a bit challenging if the software is new to you, you should be able to muddle your way through a similar example with your own image editor. My intent is to spark ideas and software features you should look for in an image editing package. If your graphics program supports selections and gradient fills, the bouncing ball animation should be fairly easy to reproduce.

1. It's easiest to begin any animation with the portions that remain the same from frame to frame. To start the bouncing ball animation, create a 300×200-pixel image with a light blue background.

2. Then use the Rectangle tool to create a simple "horizon" across the middle of the image, as shown in Figure 8.5. The rectangle will appear in a layer that's called "Layer 1" by default. Double-click the layer in the Layers window, and change its name to "ground." Also, click the "Share Across Frames" checkbox. This will come in handy later.

Rectangle tool

FIGURE 8.5

Add a rectangle to your image to serve as the ground.

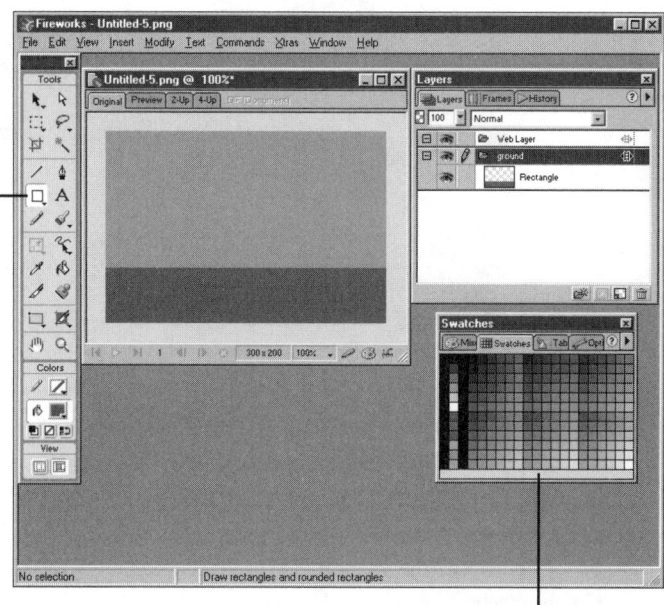

Click to select paint
color from Color Picker

▼

▼   3. Easy enough so far? Now let's create the ball. For this, you'll create a red circle in
       a new layer. First, create the new layer by clicking the New / Duplicate Layer but-
       ton in the Layers window. Change its name to "ball," but don't share it across
       frames. Then create your circle, making sure that the "ball" layer is selected. To do
       that, click and hold down the mouse button on the rectangle tool (the same tool we
       used in step 2) until it allows you to choose another shape—a circle. Then, select a
       shade of red from the Color Picker. To create a circle rather than an oval, hold
       down the Shift key as you place the circle on the page. Create the circle toward the
       upper-left corner of the image as shown in Figure 8.6; you can always move it
       around later.

FIGURE 8.6

*Adding a circle to
a new layer in
the bouncing ball
image.*

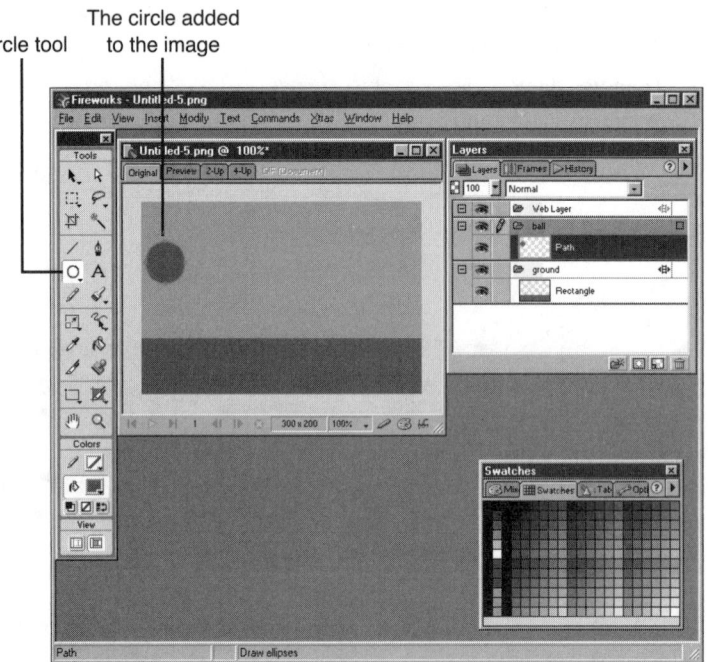

4. Now you have a single frame with the ball in its initial position for the animation.
   The next step is to add frames to the animation. Use the Pointer tool to select the
   circle, and then copy it to the clipboard. We'll use the circle in all the frames of the
   animation. In the Layers window, click the Frames tab. Click the Add button to
   create a new frame. As shown in Figure 8.7, the new layer does not have the ball in
   it, but it does have the ground. This is because the layer "ground" is shared
   between frames, but the "ball" layer is not.

▼

8

FIGURE 8.7

Adding a new frame to your bouncing ball animation.

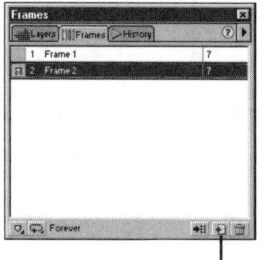

New frame button

5. Paste the circle that you just copied to the clipboard into the frame. It will appear in the same place in this frame that it did in the last one. Drag it over a bit so that it's in the appropriate spot to continue the animation sequence. Continue adding new frames and copying the ball image into the "ball" layer on those frames until you have 10 frames, and the ball looks like it's bouncing all the way across the animation.

6. One problem you might run into is remembering exactly where the ball was placed in the previous frame. Just going on your gut feeling could produce an animation in which the ball follows a rather unnatural looking path.

   Fortunately, Fireworks has a tool called Onion Skinning that can help you out here. Onion Skinning shows the changes from one frame to the next. To turn on Onion Skinning, use the Onion Skinning button on the Frames tab. Figure 8.8 shows the image with Onion Skinning set to show the onion skins for all frames.

FIGURE 8.8

The bouncing ball animation with Onion Skinning turned on for all frames.

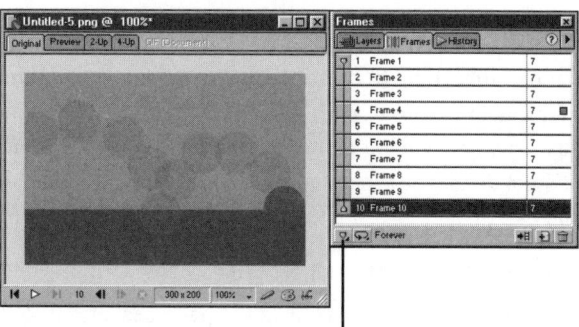

Onion skin button

7. As you can see in Figure 8.8, the ball is not taking a very realistic course across my image. With Onion Skinning turned on, you can move the balls around in any frame without actually changing frames. Go ahead and adjust them to make the ball's flight look a bit better. In Figure 8.9, I've used Onion Skinning to fix the path of the ball.

FIGURE 8.9

The bouncing ball animation with a better flight path.

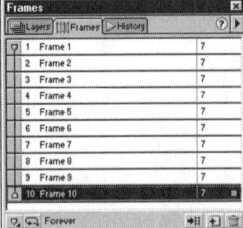

After the flight path for the ball is corrected, I'm finished with my animation. At this point, the only thing I have to do is optimize and export it using the steps explained in Exercise 8.2.

Creating an Image Rollover

Image rollover is one of the most popular JavaScript applications around. It's just an image that is replaced by a different image when someone positions their mouse pointer over it. Rollovers are often used with navigational elements to give viewers visual feedback indicating what will happen if they click on the image. This technique is particularly useful when you have a number of navigational elements positioned close together and you want to make it easier to see which element they'll be clicking on.

Even if you don't bother to learn any other JavaScript, you might still want to learn how to use image rollovers because they're such a commonly used effect on Web sites.

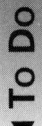

Exercise 8.4: Setting Up a JavaScript Image Rollover

In this example, I'm going to create a page that contains an image that will be swapped out when the cursor is moved over it. Generally, image rollovers are made up of three components: an event handler associated with the image, a preload script to load the image that's not displayed when the page loads, and a function that actually switches between the two images. We'll take a look at each of these components.

Putting the Script on the Page

All the scripts listed here will appear in the page header, inside the `<script>` tag, which I'll discuss on Day 15, "Using Dynamic HTML." The `<script>` tag is used as follows:

```
<script language="JavaScript">
<--
// Code goes in here.

// -->
</script>
```

The language in which the script is written is specified in the `language` attribute of the tag; in this case, I'm using `JavaScript`. You might notice that I include an HTML comment inside the `<script>` tag. This prevents old browsers from displaying the script on the page. The `//` in front of the closing comment causes JavaScript to ignore the closing HTML comment rather than trying to treat it as JavaScript code.

Browser Detection

One big disadvantage of using JavaScript is that it works differently from browser to browser. A feature that exists in Netscape Communicator 4.6 might not exist in Microsoft Internet Explorer 3.0. This problem is compounded by the fact that JavaScript capabilities change with each new version of these browsers. Originally, most people handled this problem by determining which browser made the request and then turning on only those features that worked with that browser. Unfortunately, this was an overly complex way to write JavaScript code. As new versions of browsers were released, all the JavaScript code with browser detection had to be changed.

Fortunately, a better technique is available. Rather than relying on the inexact technique of determining the user's browser, you can detect whether the actual object you want to manipulate exists and then base your functionality on that. In this case, I need to manipulate the images on the page, which can be accessed using an object called `document.images`. It contains information about all of the images used on the page. The browser detection code I use is very simple; it consists of one statement:

```
if (document.images) {
    // manipulate image object here
}
```

When I want to replace one image with another based on a user action, I wrap the code inside this `if` statement. If the browser acknowledges the existence of the `document.images` object, you can manipulate that object.

The Preload Script

When you add an image rollover to a Web page, you should preload the images so that the first time the user moves their mouse over the rollover, the browser won't have to download the image before it can be displayed. Preload scripts load the images into memory so that they can appear instantly when the pointer is positioned over the image they will replace. The preload script creates new objects for all of the images involved in the rollover. This example page contains only one image, so the preload code is very simple:

```
if (document.images) {
    buttonOn = new Image();
    buttonOn.src = "on.gif";
```

```
        buttonOff = new Image();
        buttonOff.src = "off.gif";
}
```

As you can see, the preload code is wrapped within the object detection code. Two new images are created, one containing the "on" image and the other containing the "off" image. When the page loads, both of the image files assigned to the source attributes of the images will be downloaded from the server.

The Rollover Functions

There are two functions associated with an image rollover—one that replaces the "on" image with the "off" image, and another that replaces the "off" image with the "on" image. In this example, the two functions are called `activate` and `deactivate`. Here's the source code:

```
function activate(image_name) {
    if (document.images) {
        document[image_name].src = eval(image_name + "On.src");
    }
}

function deactivate(image_name) {
    if (document.images) {
        document[image_name].src = eval(image_name + "Off.src");
    }
}
```

Again, note that the object detection code is used to protect users whose browsers don't allow the document's images to be manipulated using JavaScript. Both of these functions are generic. Rather than acting on a specific, predefined image, they accept the name of the image to be swapped out. This way, the same function can be used to swap out any named image on the page. Take a look at this line:

```
function activate(image_name) {
```

The function declaration indicates that the function expects to receive the image name as an input argument. This is the most important code in the `activate` function:

```
document[image_name].src = eval(image_name + "On.src");
```

`document[image_name]` just points to the image on the page with the name that's specified when the function was called. The `.src` after it says, "change the `src` attribute of that `image` tag to whatever is on the right of the equal sign." This code basically changes the `image` tag associated with the named image so that it refers to a different image file. Let's look at how it knows what to change it to. The stuff to the right of the equal sign is used to figure out what the new image should be. It sticks together the name that we've been referring to so far, and the value `On.src`. So, if the name that's passed in is `button`, the value it derives is `buttonOn.src`. The `eval()` function tells the script not to set the `src` attribute to the value `buttonOn.src`, but rather to the image that it points to.

This is a bit tricky. `document[image_name].src` points to the `src` attribute of a named image on the actual page. `buttonOn.src` points to the `src` attribute of an image object that exists only in my script—it's not actually displayed anywhere. This code just changes the `src` attribute of the image on the page to be the same as the `src` attribute of the image in the script. In other words, if the two images are different, it swaps out the old one for the new one.

When I put images on the page, I give them a `name` attribute so that they can be referred to by name in my JavaScript. Those names are mirrored in the preload script that I demonstrated earlier. All this makes it possible to use the `activate()` and `deactivate()` functions for swapping out many images on the page. The code in the `deactivate()` function works the same way, except that it assigns the "off" image to the image object on the page.

Calling the Functions

After all the code used to drive the rollover functions is in place, the next step is to place the image tags on the page. To make the rollover work, I create special link tags containing *event handlers*.

 An *event handler* is an attribute added to a tag that runs some JavaScript code whenever a user performs a particular action.

The event handlers are placed within a link tag that surrounds the `<img>` tag for the image that will be swapped out. The two event handlers that will call the rollover functions I wrote previously (`activate()` and `deactivate()`) are `onMouseOver` and `onMouseOut`.

The `onMouseOver` event is triggered when the user moves their mouse over the link in question. The `onMouseOut` event is then triggered when the user moves their mouse from above the link. The `<a>` tag with the event handler and the `<img>` tag are as follows:

```
<a href="rollover.html"
    onMouseOver="activate('button')"
    onMouseOut="deactivate('button')">
<img name="button" border=0 height=100 width=100 src="off.gif"></a>
```

As you can see, the link doesn't point to another page. It's there only so that the event handler can be used to trigger the rollover. The `<img>` tag contains an additional attribute with which you're probably not familiar—`name`. The `name` attribute enables you to refer to the image by name in your JavaScript code. You can still create rollovers without using the `name` attribute, but it's tougher to write your code in a readable fashion.

Putting It All Together

Let's look at the source code for the full page and see how it all looks when you put it together. Because this page contains only the image rollover, there's not a lot of content. Most of the code consists of the scripts used to add the rollover effect. Here's the HTML source for the page:

```
<html>
<head>
    <title>JavaScript Rollover Example</title>
</head>
<script language="JavaScript">
<!--
    // Preload the images for the rollover

    if (document.images) {
        buttonOn = new Image();
        buttonOn.src = "on.gif";
        buttonOff = new Image();
        buttonOff.src = "off.gif";
    }

    // Function to replace the off images with on images.

    function activate(image_name) {
        if (document.images) {
            document[image_name].src = eval(image_name + "On.src");
        }
    }

    // Function to replace the on images with off images

    function deactivate(image_name) {
        if (document.images) {
            document[image_name].src = eval(image_name + "Off.src");
        }
    }

// -->
</script>
<body>

<a href="rollover.html"
    onMouseOver="activate('button')"
    onMouseOut="deactivate('button')">
<img name="button" border=0 height=100 width=100 src="off.gif"></a>

</body>
</html>
```

That's it for the code. As you can see, it's pretty easy to add image rollovers to your pages. One thing you'll want to make sure of is that the images you use in your rollover are both the same size (in pixels). If your initial image is 100 pixels wide and 100 pixels high, the rollover image must also be 100 pixels wide and 100 pixels high. For more details on JavaScript and how all this works, check out Day 15.

Summary

Hopefully, you've had a nice relaxing break while doing the exercises in today's lesson. The simple examples should teach you some very basic concepts that will help you progress further. If you can't create a perfect animation the first time, don't be discouraged—it takes a bit of practice. Just keep at it, and eventually you'll get there. Also, study the features and capabilities of the software you select. Each program has its own bag of tricks that help make graphics and animation creation easy for you.

I also explained how to add image rollover effects to your pages. Unlike the other effects in this lesson, this effect isn't created using an application for producing graphics. Instead, it requires you to add a bit of JavaScript to your site. The good news is that some Web-specific graphics programs, like Macromedia Fireworks, will actually generate rollover code for you. If you provide the images, it will generate the code to swap them out, saving you the work.

Workshop

This workshop covers the most important points in creating animations for the Web, and you also have a couple more exercises that will take you to the next step in animation.

Q&A

Q I'd like my animated GIF file to pause at the end and then start from the beginning again. How do I do this?

A Most animated GIF compilers allow you to adjust the display times of each frame individually. Simply select the last frame in your animation and increase the display time for that frame. To pause it for one second, for example, enter 100 hundredths of a second. The other frames will still play at their original speed, and when you reach the last frame, it's displayed for one second before the animation begins again.

Q Can I create an animated background for my Web page?

A You can, but it's not really a good idea. Although animated clouds or twinkling stars seem like neat ideas for backgrounds, they'll distract people from the information on your page. Remember what's most important on your page and use animation to enhance it where appropriate.

Q How do I create animations in other file formats, such as Video for Windows (AVI), QuickTime, or MPEG?

A The development process is pretty much the same. You'll still need to create each individual frame of your animation, but you'll need to obtain a software program that saves animations in the formats you desire.

Q I was completely mystified by the image rollover example. What should I do?

A The image rollover example rapidly introduced many complex concepts. Fortunately, you should be able to use the code on your pages by simply copying it and making a few small modifications, even if you don't understand it all that well. On Day 15, I go into more detail on JavaScript, but if you really want to understand it, you'll need to research it on the Web or purchase a book on JavaScript. I provide some pointers to more information on JavaScript on Day 15 and in Appendix A, "Sources for Further Information."

Quiz

1. How does an animated GIF differ from a regular GIF file?
2. What's the easiest way to begin an animation?
3. Name three ways that you can reduce the download time of an animation file.
4. Why is it a good idea to save your individual frames with filenames that are numbered sequentially?
5. What's the best use of animation on a Web page?

Quiz Answers

1. An animated GIF file contains multiple images that are compiled into one. They play in sequence to give the illusion of movement.
2. The easiest way to begin an animation is by drawing the portions of the image that will stay the same from frame to frame.
3. You can reduce the size of an animation file by reducing its dimensions, decreasing the number of frames in an animation, or reducing the number of colors in the animation.

8

4. Some animation programs will change the order of frames when you select more than one at a time. By numbering your frames in order, you can tell at a glance if this has happened.

5. Animations are best used to draw attention to an important piece of information on a Web page.

Exercises

1. Now that you've learned how to add some movement, try a slightly more challenging example: creating a simple face. Make the eyes blink, and change the expression from a frown to a smile.

2. Create a text banner. Animate the text by changing color, position, or both from frame to frame.

DAY 9

Creating and Using Imagemaps

An imagemap is a special kind of clickable image. Usually, when you embed an image inside a link, clicking anywhere on that image takes you to a single location. Clicking on different areas of an imagemap, however, takes you to different locations. In this chapter, you'll learn all about imagemaps and how to create them, including the following:

- What an imagemap is
- Creating client-side imagemaps

What Is an Imagemap?

In Chapter 7, "Using Images, Color, and Backgrounds," you learned how to create an image that doubles as a link simply by including the <img> tag inside a link tag (<a>). In this way, the entire image becomes a link. You then can click the image, the background, or the border and get the same effect.

In an imagemap, different parts of the image activate different links. You can create a visual hyperlinked map that links you to pages describing the regions you click, as in Figure 9.1. Or you can create visual metaphors for the information you're presenting, such as a set of books on a shelf or a photograph with each person described individually.

FIGURE 9.1

Imagemaps: different places, different links.

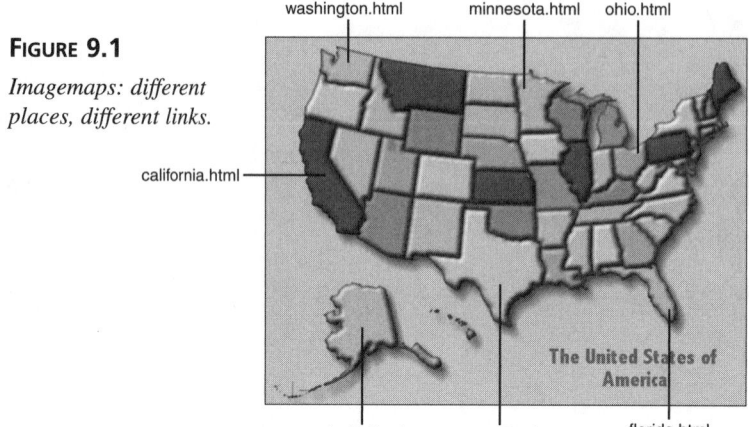

There are two kinds of imagemaps: *server-side* imagemaps and *client-side* imagemaps. Server-side imagemaps were used in the earlier days of the Web, but they posed some problems for Web authors that will be discussed in this chapter. Today, client-side imagemaps, which are handled completely by the browser, are used almost exclusively and offer many advantages over older, server-side imagemaps.

NEW TERM   *Server-side imagemaps* are implemented using an image displayed by the client and a program that runs on the server.

NEW TERM   *Client-side imagemaps* work in the same ways as server-side imagemaps, except no program runs on the server. All the processing of coordinates and pointers to different locations occurs in the browser.

Although server-side imagemaps aren't used as frequently as they used to be, learning about both types of imagemaps can be advantageous. If you want to provide backward-compatibility for imagemaps, you'll need to learn both methods.

Server-Side Imagemaps

When imagemaps first appeared on the Web, they were created with special programs that ran on the server. Such imagemaps are referred to as *server-side* imagemaps.

When a browser activates a link on a server-side imagemap, it calls a special imagemap program stored on a Web server. The browser also sends the program the x,y coordinates of the position on the image where the mouse was clicked. The imagemap program then looks up a special map file that matches regions in the image to URLs, performs some calculations to determine which page to load, and then loads the page.

Server-side imagemaps were among the earliest Web features. They're supported by all modern graphical browsers. There are problems associated with server-side imagemaps, however, as the following list explains:

- Normally, when you move your cursor over a hyperlink, the corresponding URL appears in the Web browser's status bar. However, a Web browser has no idea where the parts of a server-side imagemap point, so all you see is the URL of the imagemap program itself (not very helpful), or that URL and a set of x,y coordinates (still not very helpful).

- You cannot use or test server-side imagemaps with local files. Imagemaps require the use of a Web server to run the imagemap program and process the x,y coordinates.

- Because a special program must be run by the server every time a user clicks a page that contains imagemaps, they're much slower to respond to mouse clicks than normal links or images as links. Consequently, it can seem like imagemaps take forever to respond to requests for a new page.

Client-Side Imagemaps

Although server-side imagemaps were in common use for some time, their weaknesses led Netscape to add support for client-side imagemaps to version 2.0. Because they were vastly superior to server-side imagemaps, soon all the other browser makers added support for them as well. Client-side imagemaps address all of the problems with server-side imagemaps by eliminating the need for a special imagemap program on the server. Instead, they manage all the imagemap processing locally in the Web browser itself (the "client"). Web designers are now using this method instead.

 Note Client-side imagemaps are supported by the latest Web browsers, including Netscape (2.0 and later) and Internet Explorer (3.0 and later). The proposal for client-side imagemaps made its way into the HTML 3.2 specification and also is part of HTML 4.0.

Now you know the basic differences between server-side and client-side imagemaps. Later today, you'll learn how to create client-side imagemaps.

Imagemaps and Text-Only Browsers

Because of the inherently graphical nature of imagemaps, they work well only in graphical browsers. Lynx, the most popular text-based browser, provides limited support for client-side imagemaps. If you load a page in Lynx that contains a client-side imagemap, you can get a list of the links contained in the imagemap.

Creating Client-Side Imagemaps

As mentioned previously, client-side imagemaps offer several improvements over server-side imagemaps. The most significant improvement is that the link doesn't need to be processed on the server. All modern browsers process the imagemap locally on the users' computers. Let's take a look at the steps involved in creating a client-side imagemap.

Getting an Image

To create an imagemap, you'll need an image (of course). This image will be the most useful if it has several discrete visual areas that can be selected individually. For example, use an image with several symbolic elements or that can be easily broken down into polygons. Photographs don't make good imagemaps because their various elements tend to blend together or are of unusual shapes. Figures 9.2 and 9.3 show examples of good and poor images for imagemaps.

FIGURE 9.2

A good image for an imagemap.

FIGURE 9.3

A not-so-good image for an imagemap.

Determining Your Coordinates

When you add a client-side imagemap to a page, it includes tags that define the regions of the image where the user can click and the links associated with those regions. In order to define these tags, you'll need to determine the exact coordinates on your image that define the regions you'll use as links.

You can determine these coordinates either by sketching regions and manually noting the coordinates or by using an imagemap creation program. The latter method is easier because the program automatically generates a map file based on the regions you draw with the mouse.

The Mapedit program for Windows, Linux, and the Mac OS can help you create client-side imagemaps. (See Appendix A, "Sources for Further Information," for a full list of related FTP sites.) In addition, many of the latest WYSIWYG editors for HTML pages and Web graphics allow you to generate imagemaps.

Table 9.1 lists the current tools for generating imagemaps.

TABLE 9.1 Imagemap Creation Software

Name	Platform	URL
Imaptool	Linux/X Window	`http://www.sspitzer.org/imaptool/`
LiveImage	Windows	`http://www.mediatec.com/`
Mapedit	Windows/UNIX/Mac	`http://www.boutell.com/mapedit/`
Poor Person's Image Mapper	X Window	`http://www.pangloss.com/ seidel/ClrHlpr/imagemap.html`

These programs will not only create client-side imagemaps for you, but will also create server-side imagemap files in the two most popular formats. This is less important than it used to be because server-side imagemaps have fallen into disfavor (and for good reason), but it's nice to know that they still support the older standard.

If you must create your imagemaps by hand, here's how. First, make a sketch of the regions that will be active on your image. Figure 9.4 shows the three types of shapes that you can specify in an imagemap: circles, rectangles, and polygons.

FIGURE 9.4

There are three types of shapes available for creating imagemaps.

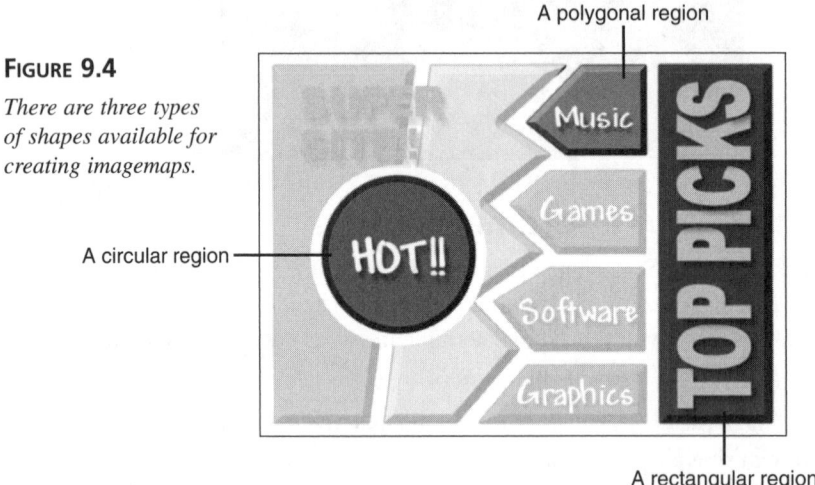

You next need to determine the coordinates for the endpoints of those regions. Most image-editing programs have an option that displays the coordinates of the current mouse position. Use this feature to note the appropriate coordinates. (All the mapping programs mentioned previously will create a map file for you, but for now, following the steps manually will help you better understand the processes involved.)

Defining a Polygon

Figure 9.5 shows the x,y coordinates of a polygon region. These values are based on their positions from the upper-left corner of the image, which is coordinate 0,0. The first number in the coordinate pair indicates the x value and defines the number of pixels from the extreme left of the image. The second number in the pair indicates the y measurement and defines the number of pixels from the top of the image.

Note The 0,0 origin is in the upper-left corner of the image, and positive y is down.

FIGURE 9.5

Getting the coordinates for a polygon.

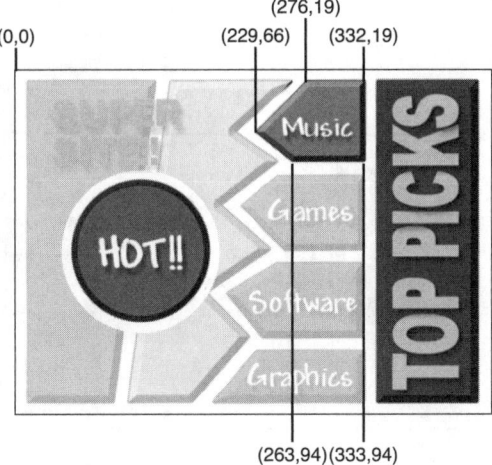

9

Defining a Circle

Figure 9.6 shows how to get the coordinates for circles. Here you note the coordinates for the center point of the circle and the radius, in pixels. The center point of the circle is defined as the x,y coordinate from the upper-left corner of the image.

FIGURE 9.6

Getting the coordinates for a circle.

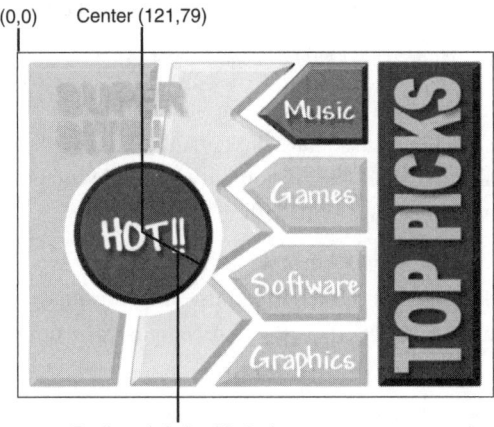

Defining a Rectangle

Figure 9.7 shows how to obtain coordinates for rectangle regions. Note the x,y coordinates for the upper-left and lower-right corners of the rectangle

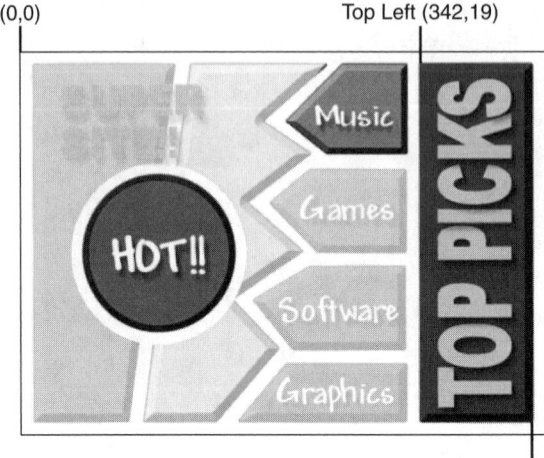

FIGURE 9.7

Getting the coordinates for a rectangle.

The <map> and <area> Tags

If you're creating your imagemap manually and you've written down all of the coordinates for your regions and the URLs they'll point to, you can include this information in the client-side imagemap tags on a Web page. To include a client-side imagemap inside an HTML document, use the <map> tag, which looks like the following:

```
<map name="mapname"> coordinates and links  </map>
```

The value assigned to the name attribute is the name of this map definition. This is the name that will be used later to associate the clickable image with its corresponding coordinates and hyperlink references. So, if you have multiple imagemaps on the same page, you can have multiple <map> tags with different names.

Between the <map> and the </map> tags, enter the coordinates for each area in the imagemap and the destinations of those regions. The coordinates are defined inside yet another new tag: the <area> tag. To define a rectangle, for example, you would write the following:

```
<area shape="rect" coords="41,16,101,32" href="test.html">
```

The type of shape to be used for the region is declared by the shape attribute, which can have the values rect, poly, circle, and default. The coordinates for each shape are noted using the coords attribute. For example, the coords attribute for a poly shape appears as follows:

```
<area shape="poly" coords="x1,y1,x2,y2,x3,y3,...,xN,yN" href="URL">
```

Each x,y combination represents a point on the polygon. For rect shapes, x1,y1 is the upper-left corner of the rectangle, and x2,y2 is the lower-right corner:

```
<area shape="rect" coords="x1,y1,x2,y2" href="URL">
```

For circle shapes, x,y represents the center of a circular region of size radius:

```
<area shape="circle" coords="x,y,radius" href="URL">
```

The default shape is different than the others—it doesn't require any coordinates to be specified. Instead, the link associated with the default shape is followed if the user clicks anywhere on the image that doesn't fall within another defined region.

Another attribute you need to define for each <area> tag is the href attribute. You can assign href any URL you usually would associate with an <a> link, including relative pathnames. In addition, you can assign href a value of "nohref" to define regions of the image that don't contain links to a new page.

Note

> When you're using client-side imagemaps with frames, you can include the target attribute inside an <area> tag to open a new page in a specific window, as in this example:
>
> ```
> <area shape="rect" coords="x1,y1,x2,y2" href="URL" target=
> "window_name">
> ```

You need to include one more attribute in HTML 4.0. In Chapter 7, you learned how to assign alternate text to images. In HTML 4.0, the alt attribute is an additional requirement for the <area> tag that displays a short description of a clickable area on a client-side imagemap when you pass your cursor over it. Using the <area> example that I already cited, the alt attribute appears as shown in the following example:

```
<area shape="rect" coords="41,16,101,32" href="test.html" alt="test link">
```

The usemap Attribute

After you define your client-side imagemap using the <map> tag, you put the image on your Web page. To do this, you use a special form of the <img> tag that includes an attribute called usemap. usemap looks like the following, where *mapname* is the name of a map defined by the <map name="*mapname*"> tag:

```
<img src="image.gif" usemap="#mapname">
```

 Note The value assigned to usemap is a standard URL. This is why *mapname* has a pound symbol (#) in front of it. As with links to anchors inside a Web page, the pound symbol tells the browser to look for *mapname* in the current Web page. If you have a very complex imagemap, however, you can store it in a separate HTML file and reference it using a standard URL.

Exercise 9.1: A Clickable Jukebox

To Do

Let's take a look at how to create a client-side imagemap for a real image. In this example, you'll define clickable regions on an image of a jukebox. The image you'll be using appears in Figure 9.8.

FIGURE 9.8

The jukebox image.

First, define the regions that will be clickable on this image. There are six rectangular buttons with musical categories on them, a center area that looks like a house, and a circle with a question mark inside it. Figure 9.9 shows regions on the image.

FIGURE 9.9

The jukebox with areas defined.

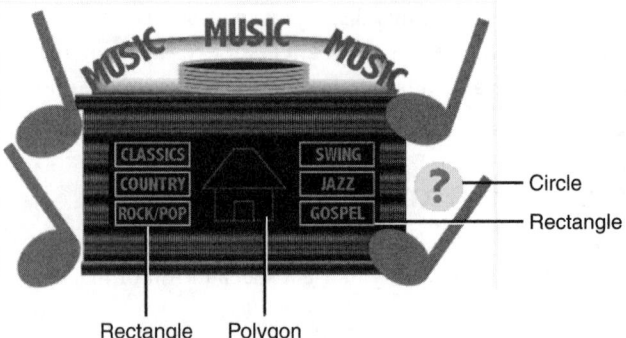

▼ Now that you know where the various regions are, you'll need to find the exact coordinates of the areas as they appear in your image. You can use a mapping program such as Mapedit or WebMap (highly recommended), or you can do it manually. If you try it manually, most image-editing programs display the x and y coordinates of the image when you move the mouse over it.

9

Tip

You don't have an image-editing program? If you use Netscape as your browser, here's a trick: Create an HTML file with the image inside a link pointing to a fake file, and include the `ismap` attribute inside the `<img>` tag. You don't need a real link; anything will do. The HTML code might look something like the following:

`<a href="nothing"><img src="myimage.gif" ismap></a>`

WhenWhen you load this into your browser, the image is displayed as if it were an imagemap. When you move your mouse over it, the x and y coordinates appear in the status line of the browser. Using this trick, you can find the coordinates for the map file of any point on that image.

With regions and a list of coordinates, all you need are the Web pages to jump to when the appropriate area is selected. These can be documents, scripts, or anything else you can call from a browser as a jump destination. For this example, I've created several documents and stored them inside the music directory on my Web server. These are the pages you'll define as the end points when the clickable images are selected. Figure 9.10 identifies each of the eight clickable areas in the imagemap. Table 9.2 shows the coordinates of each and the URL that's called up when it's clicked.

TABLE 9.2   Clickable Areas in the Jukebox Image

Number	Type	URL	Coordinates
1	rect	music/classics.html	101,113,165,134
2	rect	music/country.html	101,139,165,159
3	rect	music/rockpop.html	101,163,165,183
4	poly	music/home.html	175,152,203,118
			220,118,247,152
			237,153,237,181
			186,181,186,153
5	rect	music/swing.html	259,113,323,134
6	rect	music/jazz.html	259,139,323,159
7	rect	music/gospel.html	259,163,323,183
8	circle	music/help.html	379,152,21

▼

FIGURE 9.10

Eight hotspots, numbered as identified in Table 9.2.

For the jukebox image, the <map> tag and its associated <area> tags and attributes look like the following:

```
<map name="jukebox">
<area shape="rect" coords="101,113, 165,134"
   href="/music/classics.html"
   alt="Classical Music and Composers" />
<area shape="rect" coords="101,139, 165,159"
   href="/music/country.html"
   alt="Country and Folk Music" />
<area shape="rect" coords="101,163, 165,183"
   href="/music/rockpop.html"
   alt="Rock and Pop from 50's On" />
<area shape="poly" coords="175,152, 203,118, 220,118, 247,152,
   237,153, 237,181, 186,181, 186,153"
   href="code/music/home.html"
   alt="Home Page for Music Section" />
<area shape="rect" coords="259,113, 323,134"
   href="/music/swing.html"
   alt="Swing and Big Band Music" />
<area shape="rect" coords="259,139, 323,159"
   href="/music/jazz.html"
   alt="Jazz and Free Style" />
<area shape="rect" coords="259,163, 323,183"
   href="/music/gospel.html"
   alt="Gospel and Inspirational Music" />
<area shape="circle" coords="379,152, 21"
   href="/music/help.html"
   alt="Help" />
</map>
```

The <img> tag that refers to the map coordinates uses usemap , as follows:

▼   `<img src="jukebox.gif" usemap="#jukebox">`

▼ Finally, put the whole thing together and test it. Here's a sample HTML file for The
Really Cool Music Page with a client-side imagemap, which contains both the <map> tag
and the image that uses it:

INPUT

```
<!DOCTYPE html PUBLIC "-//W3C//DTD XHTML 1.0 Transitional//EN"
    "http://www.w3.org/TR/xhtml1/DTD/transitional.dtd">
<html>
<head>
<title>The Really Cool Music Page</title>
</head>
<body bgcolor="#ffffff">
<div align="center">
<h1>The Really Cool Music Page</h1>
<p>Select the type of music you want to hear.<br />
 You'll go to a list of songs that you can select from.</p>
<p>
<img src="jukebox.gif" alt="Juke Box" usemap="#jukebox" />
<map name="jukebox">
<area shape="rect" coords="101,113, 165,134"
    href="/music/classics.html"
    alt="Classical Music and Composers" />
<area shape="rect" coords="101,139, 165,159"
    href="/music/country.html"
    alt="Country and Folk Music" />
<area shape="rect" coords="101,163, 165,183"
    href="/music/rockpop.html"
    alt="Rock and Pop from 50's On" />
<area shape="poly" coords="175,152, 203,118, 220,118, 247,152,
    237,153, 237,181, 186,181, 186,153"
    href="code/music/home.html"
    alt="Home Page for Music Section" />
<area shape="rect" coords="259,113, 323,134"
    href="/music/swing.html"
    alt="Swing and Big Band Music" />
<area shape="rect" coords="259,139, 323,159"
    href="/music/jazz.html"
    alt="Jazz and Free Style" />
<area shape="rect" coords="259,163, 323,183"
    href="/music/gospel.html"
    alt="Gospel and Inspirational Music" />
<area shape="circle" coords="379,152, 21"
    href="/music/help.html"
    alt="Help" />
</map></p>
<p>
<a href="code/music/home.html">Home</a> |
<a href="code/music/classics.html">Classics</a> |
<a href="code/music/country.html">Country</a> |
<a href="code/music/rockpop.html">Rock/Pop</a> |
<a href="code/music/swing.html">Swing</a> |
```

▼

▼
```
<a href="code/music/jazz.html">Jazz</a> |
<a href="code/music/gospel.html">Gospel</a> |
<a href="code/music/help.html">Help</a>
</p>
</div>
</body>
</html>
```

OUTPUT   Figure 9.11 shows the imagemap in Internet Explorer.

FIGURE 9.11

*The finished Really
Cool Music Page with
client-side imagemap.*

▲

Summary

In this chapter, you learned how to add client-side imagemaps to your Web pages. Now you know the difference between server-side and client-side imagemaps. You also learned how to find regions and the coordinates that defined them, and how to create map files for client-side imagemaps.

Table 9.2 presents a summary of the tags and attributes you learned about in this chapter.

TABLE 9.2   HTML Tags Presented in This Chapter

Tag	Attribute	Use
`<map>`		Defines a map for a client-side imagemap.
	`name`	Used to define the map's name.
	`usemap`	Used to associate an image with a client-side imagemap specified by `<map name="mapname">`.
`<area>`		The individual regions within a `<map>` element.
	`shape`	Indicates the type of region. Possible values are `rect`, `poly`, and `circle`.
	`coords`	Indicates the point bounding the region.
	`href`	Indicates the URL of the region.
	`nohref`	An attribute of the `<area>` tag that indicates a region that has no action when clicked (or one that has no associated URL).
	`alt`	Displays alternate text for a clickable area. (This is now a requirement for HTML 4.0.)

Workshop

You've covered a lot in this chapter! Here are a few common questions and answers that pertain to imagemaps (server-side and client-side). The quiz questions will help you remember the advantages and disadvantages of each type of imagemap. Finally, a couple of examples are here to help you experiment with imagemaps on your own.

Q&A

Q Do I need a server to create imagemaps? I want to create and test all this offline, in the same way I did with my regular HTML files.

A You can create and test all your client-side imagemaps on your local system. (Assuming, of course, that your map destinations all point to files in your local presentation as well.)

Q My client-side imagemaps aren't working. What's wrong?

A Make sure the pathnames or URLs in your `<area>` tags point to real files. Also, make sure the map name in the `<map>` file matches the name of the map in the `usemap` attribute in the `<img>` tag. Only the latter should have a pound sign in front of it.

Quiz

1. What is an imagemap?

2. What are the two types of imagemaps, and what are the advantages and disadvantages of each?

3. Why is it a good idea to also provide text versions of links that you create on an imagemap?

4. True or false: You can use a relative URL when you specify a URL destination in an imagemap file.

Quiz Answers

1. An imagemap is a special image in which different areas point to different locations on the Web.

2. Server-side imagemaps are supported by more browsers. However, the hotspots are processed by the server, so the browser has no idea where each hotspot points to. Also, they cannot be tested with local files and they're slower to respond to mouse clicks.

   Client-side imagemaps eliminate the need for a special program on the server and are faster because the processing is done in the Web browser. This method is being used by most Web designers.

3. It's a good idea to include text versions of imagemap links in case there are users who visit your page with text-only browsers or with images turned off. This way, they can still follow the links on the Web page and visit other areas of your Web site.

4. False. URLs in a map file must be absolute pathnames from the top of the Web root. The URLs cannot be relative from the map file.

Exercises

1. Create and test a simple client-side imagemap that links to pages that reside in different subdirectories in a Web site, or to other sites on the World Wide Web.

2. Create and test a client-side imagemap for your own home page, or for the entry page in one of the main sections of your Web site. Remember to include alternatives for those who are using older or text-only browsers.

PART 4

Doing More with HTML

Day 10

Tables

So far in this book, you've used plain vanilla HTML to build and position the elements on your pages. Although you can get your point across using paragraphs and lists, there is another way to present content on your pages. Using tables, you can lay out any page content in rows and columns, with or without borders. And, the content you include within your tables isn't restricted to text. Tables provide more control over the appearance of your pages because you can include *any* type of HTML content (images, links, forms, and more).

Tables were officially introduced in HTML 3.2. Since then, they've had an enormous influence on Web page design and construction. HTML 4.0 includes changes that improve the way tables are loaded and displayed in browsers. Authors can specify tables that display incrementally or that are more accessible to users that browse the Web with nonvisual browsers. Additional elements create tables with fixed headers and footers that render larger tables across several pages (such as for printouts).

Today, you'll learn all about tables, including the following:

- The state of table development on the Web
- Defining tables in HTML

- Creating captions, rows, and heading and data cells
- Modifying cell alignment
- Creating cells that span multiple rows or columns
- Adding color to tables
- How tables are used in Web documents

A Note About the Table Definition

When they were first introduced by Netscape in early 1995, tables almost immediately revolutionized Web page design. Not only could they be used for presenting data in a tabular form, but they gave a Web page designer much finer control over page layout and the placement of various HTML elements on a page. For a long time, tables were in a state of flux. Every time a new version of Netscape or Internet Explorer was released, the way tables worked was changed or enhanced in some way. The standard for tables is finalized in HTML 4.01, but there are still some differences between how Netscape and Internet Explorer render tables. You should view your pages in both browsers to make sure everything looks right.

Creating Tables

To create tables in HTML, you define the parts of your table and which bits of HTML go where. You then add HTML table code around those parts. Following that, you refine the appearance of the table with alignments, borders, and colored cells. In this section, you'll learn how to create a basic table with headings, data, and a caption.

One more note, however: Creating tables by hand in HTML is no fun. The code for tables wasn't designed for that, so it can be confusing. You'll need to do a lot of experimenting, testing, and going back and forth between your browser and your code to get a table to work out right. HTML editors can help a great deal with this, as can working in a word processor's table editor or a spreadsheet initially to get an idea of what goes where. But I suggest doing at least your first bunch of tables the hard way so you can get an idea how HTML tables work.

Table Parts

Before getting into the actual HTML code to create a table, let's look at the following terms so we both know what we're talking about:

- The *caption* indicates what the table is about: for example, "Voting Statistics, 1950–1994," or "Toy Distribution Per Room at 1564 Elm St." Captions are optional.

- The *table headings* label the rows, columns, or both. Usually they're in a larger or emphasized font that's different from the rest of the table. They are optional.

- *Table cells* are the individual squares in the table. A cell can contain normal table data or a table heading.

- *Table data* is the values in the table itself. The combination of the table headings and table data makes up the sum of the table.

Figure 10.1 shows a typical table and its parts.

FIGURE 10.1

The elements that make up a table.

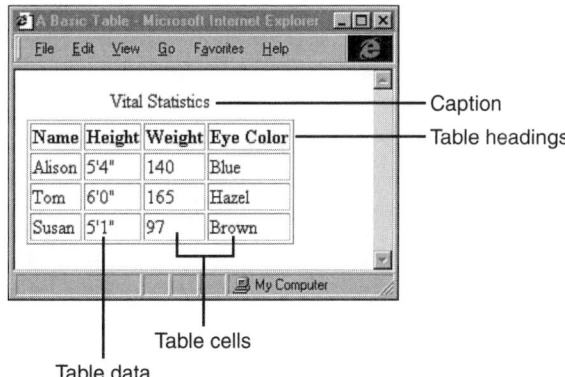

10

The `<table>` Element

To create a table in HTML, you use the `<table>...</table>` element to enclose the code for an optional caption, and then add the contents of the table itself:

```
<table>
...table caption (optional) and contents...
</table>
```

To demonstrate what the HTML code for a complete table looks like, here's an example of the code that created the table shown in Figure 10.1. Don't be concerned if you don't know what this all means right now. For now, notice that the table starts with a `<table>` tag and its attributes, and ends with a `</table>` tag:

```
<table border="1">
<caption>Vital Statistics</caption>
  <tr>
    <th>Name</th>
    <th>Height</th>
    <th>Weight</th>
    <th>Eye Color</th>
  </tr>
  <tr>
    <td>Alison</td>
    <td>5'4"</td>
```

```
      <td>140</td>
      <td>Blue</td>
    </tr>
    <tr>
      <td>Tom</td>
      <td>6'0"</td>
      <td>165</td>
      <td>Hazel</td>
    </tr>
    <tr>
      <td>Susan</td>
      <td>5'1"</td>
      <td>97</td>
      <td>Brown</td>
    </tr>
</table>
```

Rows and Cells

Now that you've been introduced to the `<table>` element, we'll move on to the rows and cells. Inside the `<table>...</table>` element, you define the actual contents of the table. Tables are specified in HTML row by row, and each row definition contains definitions for all the cells in that row. So, to define a table, you start by defining a top row and each cell in turn, left to right. Then you define a second row and its cells, and so on. The number of columns is automatically calculated based on how many cells there are in each row.

Each table row starts with the `<tr>` tag and ends with the appropriate closing `</tr>`. Your table can have as many rows as you want and as many cells in each row as you need for your columns, but you should make sure that each row has the same number of cells so the columns line up.

The cells within each table row are created using one of two elements:

- `<th>...</th>` elements are used for heading cells. Generally, browsers center the contents of a `<th>` cell and render any text in the cell in boldface.

- `<td>...</td>` elements are used for data cells. td stands for table data.

Note

In early definitions of tables, the closing tags `</tr>`, `</th>`, and `</td>` were required for each row and cell. Since then, the table definition has been refined such that each of these closing tags is optional. However, many browsers that support tables still expect the closing tags to be there, and the tables might even break if you don't include them. Closing tags are required for all tags in the XHTML 1.0 standard, so you definitely should include them.

In this table example, the heading cells appear in the top row and are defined with the following code:

```
<tr>
  <th>Name</th>
  <th>Height</th>
  <th>Weight</th>
  <th>Eye Color</th>
</tr>
```

The top row is followed by three rows of data cells, which are coded as follows:

```
<tr>
  <td>Alison</td>
  <td>5'4"</td>
  <td>140</td>
  <td>Blue</td>
</tr>
<tr>
  <td>Tom</td>
  <td>6'0"</td>
  <td>165</td>
  <td>Blue</td>
</tr>
<tr>
  <td>Susan</td>
  <td>5'1"</td>
  <td>97</td>
  <td>Brown</td>
</tr>
```

As you've seen, you can place the headings along the top edge by defining the <th> elements inside the first row. Let's make a slight modification to the table. You'll put the headings along the left edge of the table instead. To accomplish this, put each <th> in the first cell in each row, and follow it with the data that pertains to each heading. The new code looks like the following:

INPUT

```
<tr>
  <th>Name</th>
  <td>Alison</td>
  <td>Tom</td>
  <td>Susan</td>
</tr>
<tr>
  <th>Height</th>
  <td>5'4"</td>
  <td>6'0"</td>
  <td>5'1"</td>
</tr>
<tr>
  <th>Weight</th>
  <td>140</td>
```

```
    <td>165</td>
    <td>97</td>
  </tr>
  <tr>
    <th>Eye Color</th>
    <td>Blue</td>
    <td>Blue</td>
    <td>Brown</td>
  </tr>
```

Figure 10.2 shows how this table is displayed in Internet Explorer.

FIGURE 10.2

An example of a table that includes headings in the leftmost column.

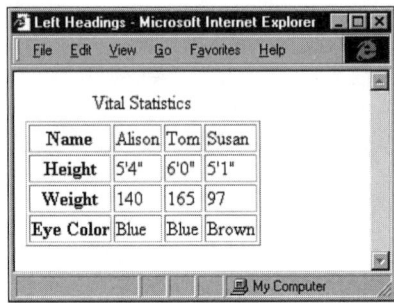

Empty Cells

Both table heading cells and data cells can contain any text, HTML code, or both, including links, lists, forms, images, and other tables. But what if you want a cell with nothing in it? That's easy. Just define a cell with a `<th>` or `<td>` element with nothing inside it:

```
<table border="1">
<tr>
    <td></td>
    <td>10</td>
    <td>20</td>
</tr>
</table>
```

Some browsers display empty cells of this sort as if they don't exist at all. If you want to force a *truly* empty cell, you can add a line break with no other text in that cell by itself:

```
<table border="1">
<tr>
    <td><br /></td>
    <td>10</td>
    <td>20</td>
</tr>
</table>
```

Figure 10.3 shows examples of both types of empty cells: the empty cell, and the really empty cell with the line break added.

FIGURE 10.3

The difference between empty cells and really empty cells.

An empty cell

An empty cell, really empty

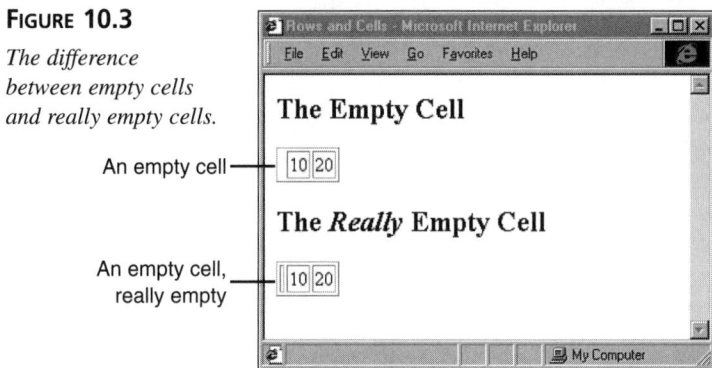

10

Captions

Table captions tell your visitor what the table is for. The <caption> element, created just for this purpose, labels table captions as captions. Although you could use a regular paragraph or a heading as a caption for your table, tools that process HTML files can extract <caption> elements into a separate file, automatically number them, or treat them in special ways simply because they're captions.

If you don't want a caption, they're optional. If you just want a table and don't care about a label, leave the caption off.

The <caption> element goes inside the <table> element just before the table rows, and it contains the title of the table. It closes with the </caption> tag:

```
<table>
<caption>Vital Statistics</caption>
<tr>
```

Exercise 10.1: Create a Simple Table

Now that you know the basics of how to create a table, try a simple example. You'll create a table that indicates the colors you get when you mix the three primary colors together.

Figure 10.4 shows the table you're going to re-create in this example.

▼ To Do

Figure 10.4

A simple color table.

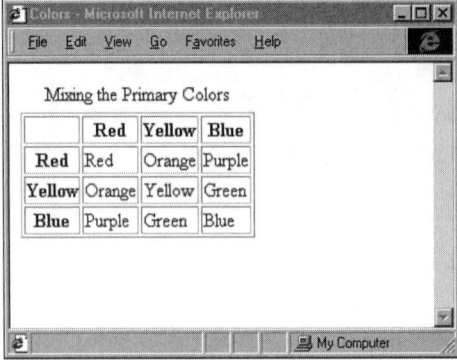

Here's a quick hint for laying out tables: Because HTML defines tables on a row-by-row basis, sometimes it can be difficult to keep track of the columns, particularly with very complex tables. Before you start actually writing HTML code, it's useful to make a sketch of your table so that you know the heads and the values of each cell. You might find that it's easiest to use a word processor with a table editor (such as Microsoft Word) or a spreadsheet to lay out your tables. Then, when you have the layout and the cell values, you can write the HTML code for that table.

Start with a simple HTML framework for the page that contains a table. Like all HTML files, you can create this file in any text editor:

```
<html>
<head>
<title>Colors</title>
</head>
<body>
<table border="1">
...add table rows and cells here...
</table>
</body>
</html>
```

Now start adding table rows inside the opening and closing <table> tags (where the line "add table rows and cells here" was in the framework). The first row is the three headings along the top of the table. The table row is indicated by <tr>, and each cell by a <th> tag:

```
<tr>
    <th>Red</th>
    <th>Yellow</th>
    <th>Blue</th>
</tr>
```

> You can format the HTML code any way you want. As with all HTML, the
> browser ignores most extra spaces and returns. I like to format it like this,
> with the contents of the individual rows indented and the cell elements on
> separate lines, so that I can pick out the rows and columns more easily.

Now add the second row. The first cell in the second row is the Red heading on the left
side of the table, so it will be the first cell in this row, followed by the cells for the table
data:

```
<tr>
    <th>Red</th>
    <td>Red</td>
    <td>Orange</td>
    <td>Purple</td>
</tr>
```

Continue by adding the remaining two rows in the table, with the Yellow and Blue headings. Here's what you have so far for the entire table:

```
<table border="1">
<tr>
    <th>Red</th>
    <th>Yellow</th>
    <th>Blue</th>
</tr>
<tr>
    <th>Red</th>
    <td>Red</td>
    <td>Orange</td>
    <td>Purple</td>
</tr>
<tr>
    <th>Yellow</th>
    <td>Orange</td>
    <td>Yellow</td>
    <td>Green</td>
</tr>
<tr>
    <th>Blue</th>
    <td>Purple</td>
    <td>Green</td>
    <td>Blue</td>
</tr>
</tr>
</table>
```

Finally, add a simple caption. The <caption> element goes just after the <table
border> tag and just before the first <tr> tag:

10

▼
```
<table border="1">
<caption>Mixing the Primary Colors</caption>
<tr>
```

With a first draft of the code in place, test the HTML file in your favorite browser that supports tables. Figure 10.5 shows how it looks in Internet Explorer.

FIGURE **10.5**

The not-quite-perfect color table.

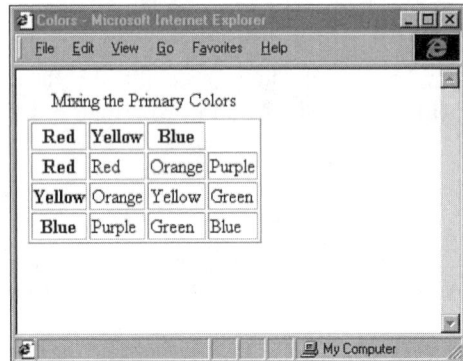

Oops! What happened with that top row? The headings are all messed up. The answer, of course, is that you need an empty cell at the beginning of that first row to space the headings out over the proper columns. HTML isn't smart enough to match it all up for you. (This is exactly the sort of error you're going to find the first time you test your tables.)

Add an empty table heading cell to that first row (here, it's the line <th>
</th>):

```
<tr>
    <th><br /></th>
    <th>Red</th>
    <th>Yellow</th>
    <th>Blue</th>
</tr>
```

Note | I used <th> here, but it could be <td> just as easily. Because there's nothing in the cell, its formatting doesn't matter.

If you try it again, you should get the right result with all the headings over the right
▲ columns, as the original example in Figure 10.4 shows.

Sizing Tables, Borders, and Cells

With the basics out of the way, now you'll look at some of the attributes that can change the overall appearance of your tables. The attributes you'll learn about in this section control the width of your tables and cells, the amount of spacing between cell content and rows and columns, and the width of the borders.

Setting Table Widths

The table in the preceding example relied on the browser itself to decide how wide the table and column widths were going to be. In many cases, this is the best way to make sure your tables are viewable on different browsers with different screen sizes and widths. Simply let the browser decide.

In other cases, however, you might want more control over how wide your tables and columns are, particularly if the defaults the browser comes up with are really strange. In this section, you'll learn a couple of ways to do just this.

The width attribute of the <table> element defines how wide the table will be on the page. width can have a value that is either the exact width of the table (in pixels) or a percentage (such as 50 percent or 75 percent) of the current browser width, which can therefore change if the window is resized. If width is specified, the width of the columns within the table can be compressed or expanded to fit the required width.

To make a table as wide as the browser window, you add the width attribute to the table, as shown in the following line of code:

```
<table border="1" width="100%">
```

The result is shown in Figure 10.6.

FIGURE 10.6

A table set to 100% width.

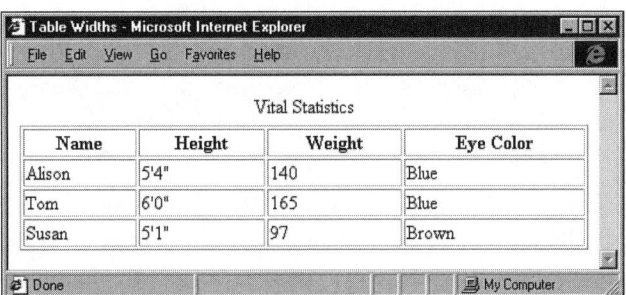

Name	Height	Weight	Eye Color
Alison	5'4"	140	Blue
Tom	6'0"	165	Blue
Susan	5'1"	97	Brown

Vital Statistics

Note | If you make your table too narrow to contain its content, the browser will ignore your settings and make the table as wide as it needs to be to hold the content.

It's always a better idea to specify your table widths as percentages rather than as specific pixel widths. Because you don't know how wide the browser window will be, using percentages allows your table to be reformatted to whatever width the browser is. Using specific pixel widths might cause your table to run off the page. Also, if you make your tables too wide using a pixel width, your pages might not print properly.

Changing Table Borders

The `border` attribute, which appears immediately inside the opening `<table>` tag, is the most common attribute of the `<table>` element. With it, you specify whether border lines are displayed around the table, and if so, how wide the borders should be.

The `border` attribute has undergone some changes since it first appeared in HTML:

- In HTML 2.0, you used `<table border>` to draw a border around the table. The border could be rendered as fancy in a graphical browser or just a series of dashes and pipes (|) in a text-based browser.

- Starting with HTML 3.2 and later, the correct usage of the `border` attribute is a little different: It indicates the width of a border in pixels. `<table border="1">` creates a 1-pixel wide border, `<table border="2">` a 2-pixel wide border, and so on. HTML 3.2 and later browsers are expected to display the old HTML 2.0 form of `<table border>`, with no value, with a 1-pixel border (as if you specified `<table border="1">`.

- To create a border that has no width and is not displayed, you specify `<table border="0">`. Borderless tables are useful when you want to use the table structure for layout purposes, but you don't necessarily want the outline of an actual table on the page. Browsers that support HTML 3.2 and higher are expected not to display a border (the same as `<table border="0">`) if you leave out the `border` attribute entirely.

You can change the width of the border drawn around the table. If `border` has a numeric value, the border around the outside of the table is drawn with that pixel width. The default is `border="1"`. `border="0"` suppresses the border, just as if you had omitted the `border` attribute altogether.

Figure 10.7 shows a table that has a border width of 10 pixels. The table and border definition looks like this:

```
<table border="10" width="100%">
```

FIGURE 10.7

A table with the border width set to 10 pixels.

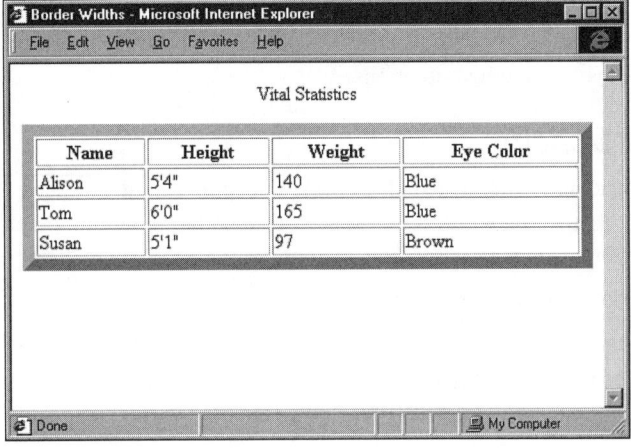

10

Cell Padding

The cell padding attribute defines the amount of space between the edges of the cells and the content inside a cell. By default, many browsers draw tables with a cell padding of 2 pixels. You can add more space by adding the `cellpadding` attribute to the `<table>` element, with a value in pixels for the amount of cell padding you want.

Here's the revised code for your `<table>` element, which increases the cell padding to 10 pixels. The result is shown in Figure 10.8:

```
<table border="10" width="100%" cellpadding="10">
```

FIGURE 10.8

A table with the cell padding set to 10 pixels.

Cell padding increases space
between cell contents and its borders

The `cellpadding` attribute with a value of 0 causes the edges of the cells to touch the edges of the cell's contents. This doesn't look good when you're presenting text, but it can be useful in other situations.

Cell Spacing

Cell spacing is similar to cell padding except that it affects the amount of space between cells—that is, the width of the space between the inner and outer lines that make up the table border. The `cellspacing` attribute in the `<table>` element affects the spacing for the table. Cell spacing is 2 pixels by default.

Cell spacing also includes the outline around the table, which is just inside the table's border (as set by the `border` attribute). Experiment with it, and you can see the difference. For example, Figure 10.9 shows our table with cell spacing of 8 and a border of 4, as shown in the following code:

```
<table border="4" width="100%" cellpadding="10" cellspacing="8">
```

FIGURE 10.9

How increased cell spacing looks.

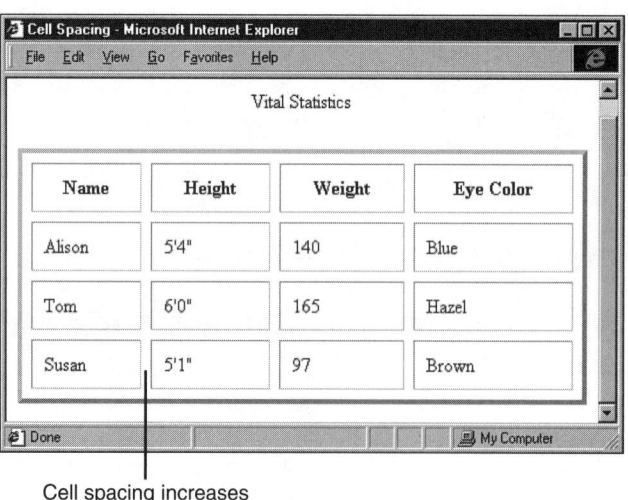

Cell spacing increases
space between cells

> **Note**
>
> If you want to completely eliminate any whitespace separating content in table cells, you must set the table's border, cell padding, and cell spacing to 0. Laying out your tables this way is unusual, but it can be useful if you've sliced up an image and you want to reassemble it properly on a Web page.

Column Widths

You also can apply the `width` attribute to individual cells (`<th>` or `<td>`) to indicate the width of columns in a table. As with table widths, discussed earlier, you can make the `width` attribute in cells an exact pixel width or a percentage (which is taken as a percentage of the full table width). As with table widths, using percentages rather than specific pixel widths is a better idea because it allows your table to be displayed regardless of the window size.

Column widths are useful when you want to have multiple columns of identical widths, regardless of their contents (for example, for some forms of page layout).

Figure 10.10 shows your original table from Figure 10.1. This time, however, the table spans 100 percent of the screen's width. The first column is 40 percent of the table width, and the remaining three columns are 20 percent each.

To accomplish this, the column widths are applied to the heading cells as follows:

```
<table border="1" width="100%">
<caption>Vital Statistics</caption>
<tr>
    <th width="40%">Name</th>
    <th width="20%">Height</th>
    <th width="20%">Weight</th>
    <th width="20%">Eye Color</th>
</tr>
```

FIGURE 10.10

A table with manually set column widths.

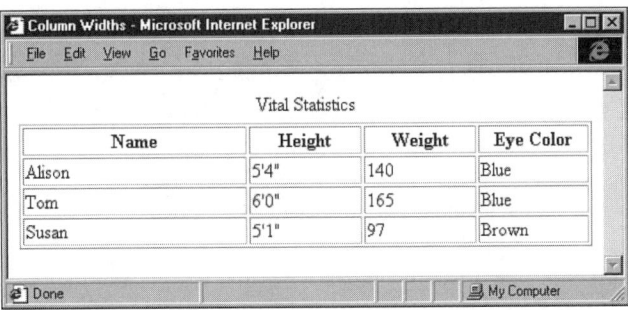

What happens if you have a table that spans 80 percent of the screen, and it includes the same header cells (40 percent, 20 percent, 20 percent, and 20 percent) as in the preceding example? Revise the code slightly, changing the width of the entire table to 80 percent, as shown in the following example. When you open the new table in your browser, you'll see that the table now spans 80 percent of the width of your screen. The four columns still span 40 percent, 20 percent, 20 percent and 20 percent of the *table*. To be more specific, the columns span 32 percent, 16 percent, 16 percent, and 16 percent of the entire screen width:

```
<table border="1" width="80%">
<caption>Vital Statistics</caption>
<tr>
    <th width="40%">Name</th>
    <th width="20%">Height</th>
    <th width="20%">Weight</th>
    <th width="20%">Eye Color</th>
  </tr>
```

Setting Breaks in Text

Often, the easiest way to make small changes to how a table is laid out is by using line breaks (
 elements). Line breaks are particularly useful if you have a table in which most of the cells are small and only one or two cells have longer data. As long as the screen width can handle it, generally the browser just creates really long rows. This looks rather funny in some tables. For example, the last row in the table shown in Figure 10.11 is coded as follows:

```
<tr>
    <td>TC</td>
    <td>7</td>
    <td>Suspicious except when hungry, then friendly</td>
  </tr>
```

FIGURE 10.11

A table with one long row.

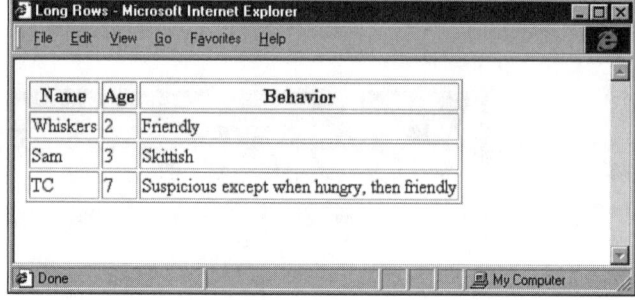

By putting in line breaks, you can wrap that row in a shorter column so that it looks more like the table shown in Figure 10.12. The following shows how the revised code looks for the last row:

```
<tr>
    <td>TC</td>
    <td>7</td>
    <td>Suspicious except<br />
        when hungry, <br />
        then friendly</td>
  </tr>
```

FIGURE 10.12

The long row fixed with <br />.

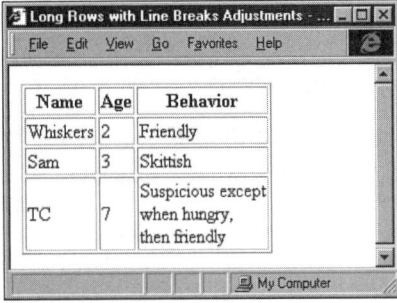

On the other hand, you might have a table in which a cell is being wrapped and you want all the data on one line. (This can be particularly important for things such as form elements within table cells, where you want the label and the input field to stay together.) In this instance, you can add the nowrap attribute to the <th> or <td> elements, and the browser keeps all the data in that cell on one line. Note that you can always add <br /> elements to that same cell by hand and get line breaks exactly where you want them.

 **Note**   The nowrap attribute has been deprecated in HTML 4.0 in favor of using style sheet properties.

Be careful when you hard-code table cells with line breaks and nowrap attributes. Remember, your table might be viewed by users with many different screen widths. Try resizing the window in which your table is being viewed and see whether your table can still hold up under different widths with all your careful formatting in place. For the most part, you should try to let the browser itself format your table and make minor adjustments only when necessary.

Table and Cell Color and Alignment

After you have your basic table layout with rows, headings, and data, you can start refining how that table looks. You can refine tables in a couple of ways. One way is to add color to borders and cells.

Changing Table and Cell Background Colors

To change the background color of a table, a row, or a cell inside a row, use the bgcolor attribute of the <table>, <tr>, <th> or <td> elements. Just like in the <body> tag, the value of bgcolor is a color specified as a hexadecimal triplet or, in many browsers including Internet Explorer and Netscape Navigator, one of the 16 color names: Black,

White, Green, Maroon, Olive, Navy, Purple, Gray, Red, Yellow, Blue, Teal, Lime, Aqua, Fuchsia, or Silver. The `bgcolor` attribute is now part of the HTML 4.0 specification, but it has been deprecated in favor of style sheets.

Each background color overrides the background color of its enclosing element. For example, a table background overrides the page background, a row background overrides the table's, and any cell colors override all other colors. If you nest tables inside cells, that nested table has the background color of the cell that encloses it.

Also, if you change the color of a cell, don't forget to change the color of the text inside it so that you can still read it. If you want your pages to be compatible with browsers older than Internet Explorer 4.0 and Netscape Navigator 4.0, use `<font color...>`. For browsers that support cascading style sheets, such as Internet Explorer 4.0 (or later) or Netscape 4.0 (or later), use the CSS `color` property.

Note

In order for table cells to show up with background colors, they have to have some sort of contents. Simply putting a `<br />` element in empty cells works fine.

Here's an example of changing the background and cell colors in a table. I've created a checkerboard using an HTML table. The table itself is white, with alternating cells in black. The checkers (here, red and black circles) are images.

Note

Speaking of using images in tables, generally it doesn't matter in the final output where white space appears in your original HTML code. In Netscape, however, there's one exception to the rule, and it applies when you're placing images in table cells. Suppose that you've formatted your code with the `<img>` tag on a separate line, like the following:

```
<td>
     <img src="check.gif">
</td>
```

With this code, the return between the `<td>` tag and the `<img>` tag is significant—your image won't be placed properly within the cell (this shows up in centered cells particularly). This quirk of the Netscape browser remains the case even in the latest release of Netscape Navigator. To correct the problem, just put the `<td>` and the `<img>` on the same line like this:

```
<td><img src="check.gif"></td>
```

I've applied the rule mentioned in the previous note in the following example:

INPUT

```
<html>
<head>
<title>Checkerboard</title>
</head>
<body>
<table bgcolor="#ffffff" width="50%">
<tr align="center">
<td bgcolor="#000000" width="33%">
<img src="redcircle.gif" alt="Red Circle" width="75" height="75"></td>
<td width="33%">
<img src="redcircle.gif" alt="Red Circle" width="75" height="75"></td>
<td bgcolor="#000000" width="33%">
<img src="redcircle.gif" alt="Red Circle" width="75" height="75"></td>
</tr>

<tr align="center">
<td><img src="blackcircle.gif" alt="Black Circle" width="75"
height="75"></td>
<td bgcolor="#000000"><br />
</td>
<td><img src="blackcircle.gif" alt="Black Circle" width="75"
height="75"></td>
</tr>

<tr align="center">
<td bgcolor="#000000"><br />
</td>
<td><img src="blackcircle.gif" alt="Black Circle" width="75"
height="75"><br />
</td>
<td bgcolor="#000000"><br />
</td>
</tr>
</table>
</body>
</html>
```

10

The result in Internet Explorer is shown in Figure 10.13.

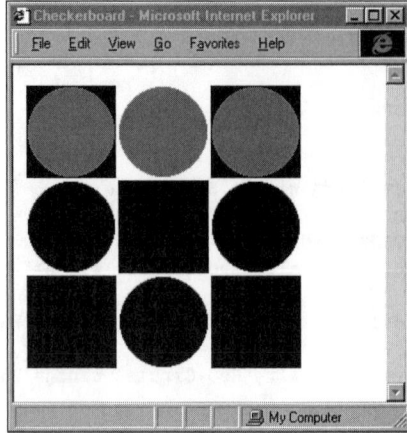

Changing Border Colors

Internet Explorer also enables you to change the colors of the table's border elements by using the bordercolor, bordercolorlight, and bordercolordark attributes. Each of these attributes takes either a color number or name and can be used in <table>, <td>, or <th>. Like background colors, the border colors each override the colors of the enclosing element. All three require the enclosing <table> tag to have the border attribute set.

Currently, these extensions are only supported in Internet Explorer, with the exception of bordercolor, which is supported in Netscape. All of these have been deprecated in favor of style sheets.

- bordercolor sets the color of the border, overriding the 3D look of the default border.
- bordercolordark sets the dark component of 3D-look borders and places the dark color on the right and bottom sides of the table border.
- bordercolorlight sets the light component of 3D-look borders and places the light color on the left and top sides of the table border.

Figure 10.14 shows an example of the table with a border of 10 pixels. To demonstrate the Internet Explorer attributes, bordercolordark and bordercolorlight have been added to give the thicker border a 3D look. The first line of the code has been changed as follows:

```
<table border="10" bordercolorlight="Red" bordercolordark="Black"
bgcolor="#ffffff" width="50%">
```

This line of code is getting a little long, isn't it? You might find it easier to read if you put each attribute on a separate line, as the following example shows. It still works the same. Just remember that the closing bracket (>) must appear only after the final attribute:

```
<table border="10"
   bordercolorlight="Red"
   bordercolordark="Black"
   bgcolor="#ffffff"
   width="50%">
```

FIGURE 10.14

Table border colors.

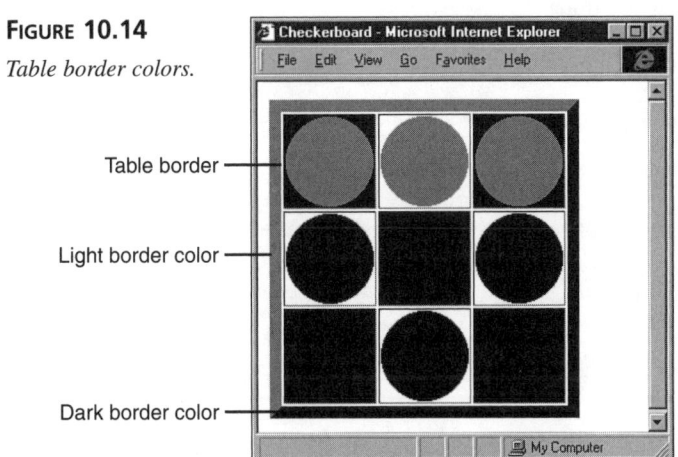

Table border

Light border color

Dark border color

10

Aligning Your Table Content

Another enhancement that you can make to your tables is to adjust the alignment of their content. The `align` attribute aligns content horizontally, while the `valign` attribute aligns content vertically. Both of these attributes were introduced in HTML 3.2, but they have been deprecated in HTML 4.0, in favor of style sheets. The following sections describe how to use these attributes in tables.

Table Alignment

By default, tables are displayed on a line by themselves along the left side of the page, with any text above or below the table. However, you can use the `align` attribute to align tables along the left or right margins and wrap text alongside them the same way you can with images.

`align="left"` aligns the table along the left margin, and all text following that table is wrapped in the space between that table and the right side of the page. `align="right"` does the same thing, with the table aligned to the right side of the page.

In the example shown in Figure 10.15, a table that spans 70 percent of the width of the page is aligned to the left with the following code:

```
<table border="1" align="left" width="70%">
```

FIGURE **10.15**

*A table with text
alongside it.*

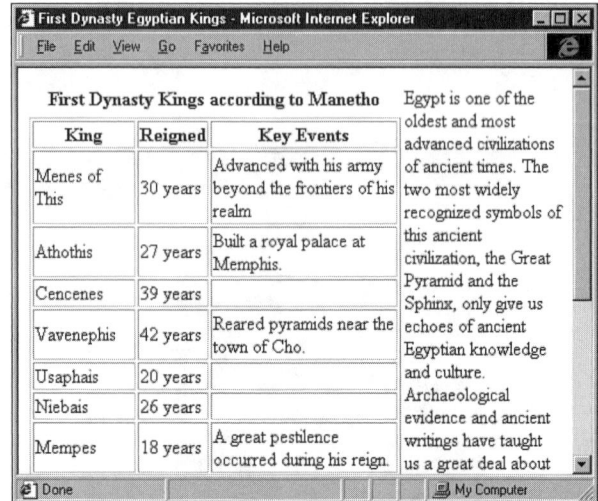

As with images, you can use the line break element with the `clear` attribute to stop wrapping text alongside an image.

Centering tables is slightly more difficult. Recent browsers support the `align="center"` attribute in `table` tags. To ensure backward-compatibility with older browsers, you can use the `<center>` or `<div align="center">` elements (both of which you learned about in Day 6, "More Text Formatting with HTML") to center tables on the page. As with other formatting attributes, however, the align attribute has been deprecated in HTML 4.0 in favor of style sheets.

Cell Alignment

After you have your rows and cells in place inside your table and the table is properly aligned on the page, you can align the data within each cell for the best effect, based on what your table contains. Several options allow you to align the data within your cells both horizontally and vertically. Figure 10.16 shows a table (a real HTML one!) of the various alignment options.

FIGURE **10.16**

Aligning content within cells.

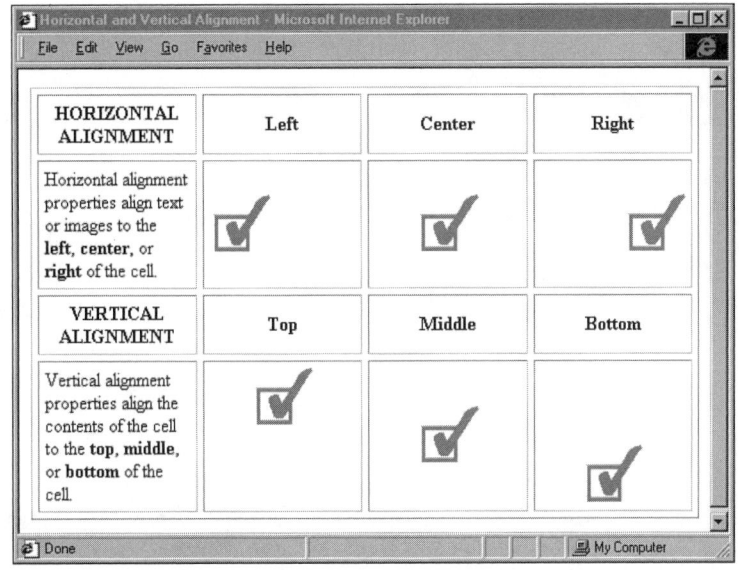

Horizontal alignment (the align attribute) defines whether the data within a cell is aligned with the left cell margin (left), the right cell margin (right), or centered within the two (center).

Vertical alignment (the valign attribute) defines the vertical alignment of the data within the cell: flush with the top of the cell (top), flush with the bottom of the cell (bottom), or vertically centered within the cell (middle). Newer browsers also implement valign="baseline", which is similar to valign="top" except that it aligns the baseline of the first line of text in each cell. (Depending on the contents of the cell, this might or might not produce a different result than align="top".)

By default, heading cells are centered both horizontally and vertically, and data cells are centered vertically but aligned flush left.

You can override the defaults for an entire row by adding the align or valign attributes to the <tr> element, as in the following:

```
<tr align="center" valign="top">
```

You can override the row alignment for individual cells by adding align to the <td> or <th> elements:

```
<tr align="center" valign="top">
    <td>14</td>
    <td>16</td>
    <td align=left>No Data</td>
    <td>15</td>
</tr>
```

10

The following input and output example shows the various cell alignments and how they look in Internet Explorer (see Figure 10.17):

INPUT

```html
<html>
<head>
<title>Cell Alignments</title>
</head>
<body>
<table border="1">
<tr>
<th width="25%"><br /></th>
<th width="25%">Left</th>
<th width="25%">Centered</th>
<th width="25%">Right</th>
</tr>

<tr>
<th>Top</th>
<td align="left" valign="top">
<img src="button.gif" alt="Button" width="15" height="13"></td>
<td align="center" valign="top">
<img src="button.gif" alt="Button" width="15" height="13"></td>
<td align="right" valign="top">
<img src="button.gif" alt="Button" width="15" height="13"></td>
</tr>

<tr>
<th>Centered</th>
<td align="left" valign="middle">
<img src="button.gif" alt="Button" width="15" height="13"></td>
<td align="center" valign="middle">
<img src="button.gif" alt="Button" width="15" height="13"></td>
<td align="right" valign="middle">
<img src="button.gif" alt="Button" width="15" height="13"></td>
</tr>

<tr>
<th>Bottom</th>
<td align="left" valign="bottom">
<img src="button.gif" alt="Button" width="15" height="13"></td>
<td align="center" valign="bottom">
<img src="button.gif" alt="Button" width="15" height="13"></td>
<td align="right" valign="bottom">
<img src="button.gif" alt="Button" width="15" height="13"></td>
</tr>
</table>
</body>
</html>
```

FIGURE **10.17**

*A matrix of cell align-
ment settings.*

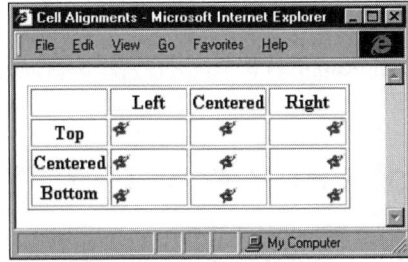

Caption Alignment

The optional `align` attribute of the `<caption>` tag determines the alignment of the caption. Depending on which browser you're using, however, you have different choices for
what `align` means.

In most browsers, `align` can have one of two values: `top` and `bottom`. This is the correct
HTML standardized use of the `align` attribute. By default, the caption is placed at the
top of the table (`align="top"`). You can use the `align="bottom"` attribute to the caption
if you want to put the caption at the bottom of the table, like the following:

```
<table>
<caption align="bottom">Torque Limits for Various Fruits</caption>
```

In Internet Explorer, however, captions are different. You use the `valign` attribute to put
the caption at the top or the bottom, and `align` has three different values: `left`, `right`,
and `center`, which align the caption horizontally.

To achieve similar results in Netscape, use `align="bottom"` or `align="top"`, and then
use the `<div>` element with its `align` attribute to align the caption text to the left, right,
or center. This also works in Internet Explorer.

If you want to place the caption at the bottom of the table in Internet Explorer, aligned to
the right, you can use the following:

```
<caption valign="bottom" align="right">This is a caption</caption>
```

Or you can use the `<div>` element, as in the following, which also works in Netscape
Navigator:

```
<caption align="bottom"><div align="right">This is a caption</div></caption>
```

In general, unless you have a very short table, you should leave the caption in its default
position—centered at the top of the table. That way your visitors will see the caption first
and know what they're about to read, instead of seeing it after they're already done reading the table (at which point they've usually figured out what it's about anyway).

10

Tip

> If your table contains an image, you may prefer putting the caption at the bottom. This will be more familiar to people who are used to print media.

Spanning Multiple Rows or Columns

The tables you've created up to this point all had one value per cell or the occasional empty cell. You also can create cells that span multiple rows or columns within the table. Those spanned cells then can hold headings that have subheadings in the next row or column, or you can create other special effects within the table layout. Figure 10.18 shows a table with spanned columns and rows.

This cell spans two
rows and two columns

FIGURE 10.18

Using span settings to alter table layout.

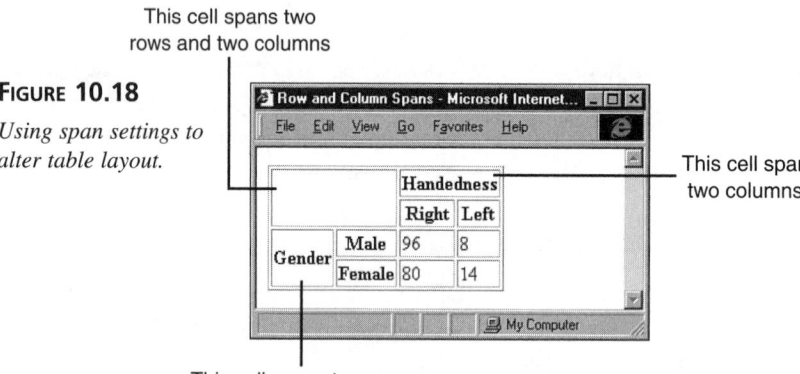

This cell span
two columns

This cell spans two rows

To create a cell that spans multiple rows or columns, you add the rowspan or colspan attribute to the <th> or <td> elements, along with the number of rows or columns you want the cell to span. The data within that cell then fills the entire width or length of the combined cells, as in the following example:

INPUT

```
<html>
<head>
<title>Row and Column Spans</title>
</head>
<body>
<table border="1">
<tr>
<th colspan="2">Gender</th>
</tr>

<tr>
<th>Male</th>
<th>Female</th>
</tr>
```

```
<tr>
<td>15</td>
<td>23</td>
</tr>
</table>
</body>
</html>
```

Figure 10.19 shows how this table might appear when displayed.

FIGURE 10.19

Using span settings to widen a column.

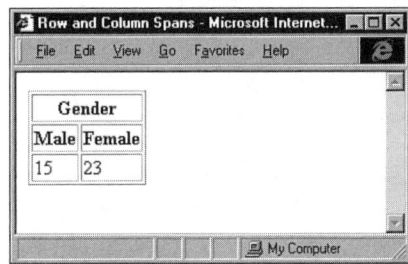

10

Note that if a cell spans multiple rows, you don't have to redefine it as empty in the next row or rows. Just ignore it and move to the next cell in the row. The span will fill in the spot for you.

Cells always span downward and to the right. To create a cell that spans several columns, you add the colspan attribute to the leftmost cell in the span. For cells that span rows, you add rowspan to the topmost cell.

The following input and output example shows a cell that spans multiple rows (the cell with the word "Piston" in it). Figure 10.20 shows the result in Internet Explorer.

INPUT

```
<html>
<head>
<title>Ring Clearance</title>
</head>
<body>
<table border="1">
<tr>
<th colspan="2"> </th>
<th>Ring<br />
 Clearance</th>
</tr>

<tr align="center">
<th rowspan="2">Piston</th>
<th>Upper</th>
<td>3mm</td>
</tr>

<tr align="center">
```

```
<th>Lower</th>
<td>3.2mm</td>
</tr>
</table>
</body>
</html>
```

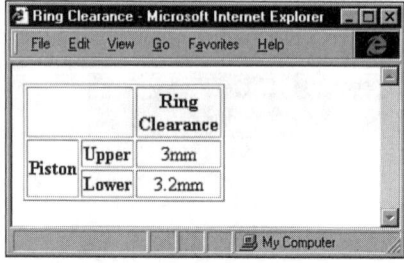

OUTPUT

FIGURE 10.20

Cells that span multiple rows and columns.

Exercise 10.2: A Table of Service Specifications

▲ To Do

Had enough of tables yet? Let's do another example that takes advantage of everything you've learned here: tables that use colors, headings, normal cells, alignments, and column and row spans. This is a very complex table, so we'll go step-by-step, row-by-row, to build it.

Figure 10.21 shows the table, which indicates service and adjustment specifications from the service manual for a car.

FIGURE 10.21

The really complex service specification table.

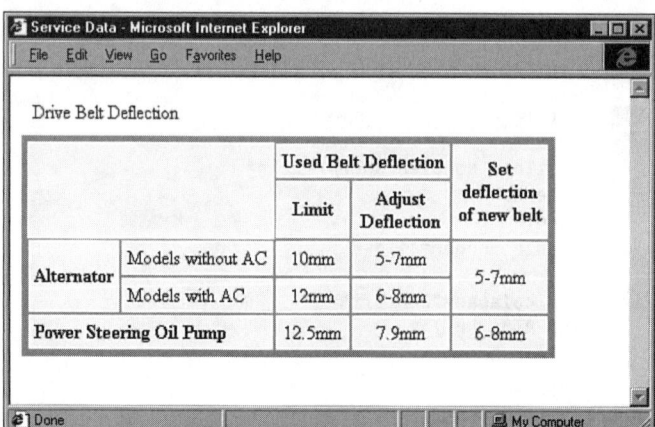

There are actually five rows and columns in this table. Do you see them? Some of them span columns and rows. Figure 10.22 shows the same table with a grid drawn over it so

▼ that you can see where the rows and columns are.

FIGURE 10.22

Five columns, five rows.

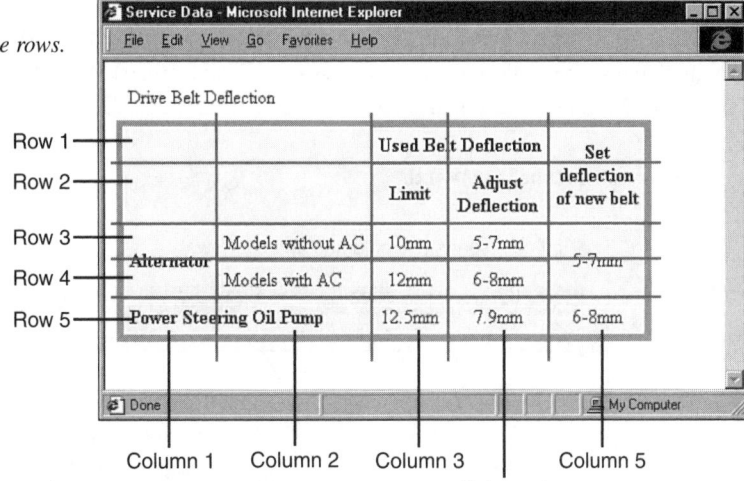

With tables such as this one that use many spans, it's helpful to draw this sort of grid to figure out where the spans are and in which row they belong. Remember, spans start at the topmost row and the leftmost column.

Ready? Start with the framework, just as you have for the other tables today:

```
<html>
<head>
<title>Service Data</title>
</head>
<body>
<table border="1">
<caption>Drive Belt Deflection</caption>
</table>
</body>
</html>
```

To enhance the appearance of the table, you'll make all of the cells light yellow (#ffffcc) by using the bgcolor attribute. The border will be increased in size to 5 pixels, and you'll color it deep gold (#cc9900) by using the bordercolor attribute that is compatible with both Netscape and Internet Explorer. You'll make the rules between cells appear more solid by using a cellspacing setting of 0, and increase the white space between the cell contents and the borders of the cells by specifying a cellpadding setting of 5. The new table definition now looks like the following:

```
<table border="5"
   bgcolor="#ffffcc"
   bordercolor="#cc9900"
```

▼
```
    cellspacing="0"
    cellpadding="5">
```

Now create the first row. With the grid on your picture, you can see that the first cell is empty and spans two rows and two columns (see Figure 10.23). Therefore, the HTML for that cell would be as follows:

```
<tr>
<th rowspan="2" colspan="2"></th>
```

The first cell (spans two columns and two rows)

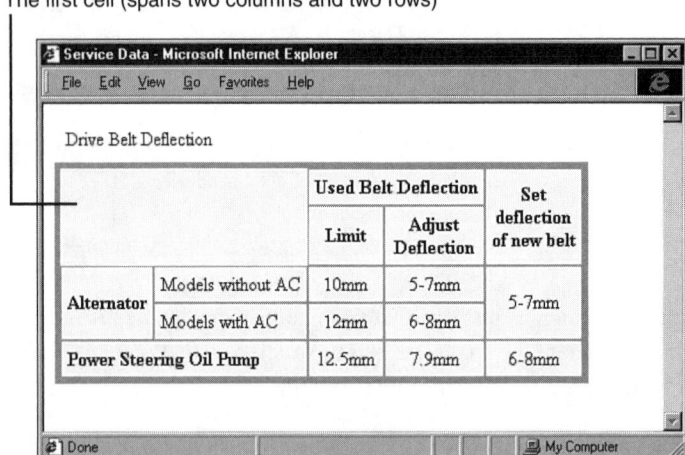

The second cell in the row is the Used Belt Deflection heading cell, which spans two columns (for the two cells beneath it). The code for that cell is as follows:

```
<th colspan="2">Used Belt Deflection</th>
```

Now that you have two cells that span two columns each, there's only the one left in this row. However, this one, like the first one, spans the row beneath it:

```
<th rowspan="2">Set deflection of new belt</th>
</tr>
```

Now go on to the second row. This isn't the one that starts with the Alternator heading. Remember that the first cell in the previous row has a rowspan and a colspan of two, meaning that it bleeds down to this row and takes up two cells. You don't need to redefine it for this row. You just move on to the next cell in the grid. The first cell in this row

▼ is the Limit heading cell, and the second cell is the Adjust Deflection heading cell:

```
<tr>
    <th>Limit</th>
    <th>Adjust Deflection</th>
</tr>
```

What about the last cell? Just like the first cell, the cell in the row above this one had a rowspan of two, which takes up the space in this row. The only values you need for this row are the ones you already defined.

Are you with me so far? Now is a great time to try this out in your browser to make sure that everything is lining up. It will look kind of funny because you haven't really put anything on the left side of the table yet, but it's worth a try. Figure 10.24 shows what you've got so far.

FIGURE 10.24

The table so far.

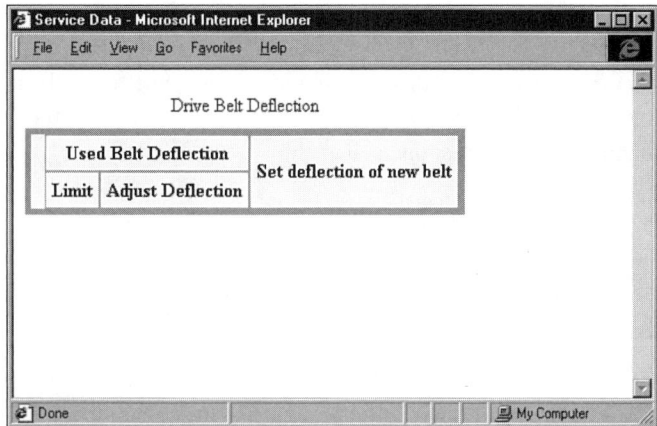

Next row! Check your grid if you need to. Here, the first cell is the heading for Alternator, and it spans this row and the one below it:

```
<tr>
    <th rowspan="2">Alternator</th>
```

Are you getting the hang of this yet?

The next three cells are pretty easy because they don't span anything. Here are their definitions:

```
<td>Models without AC</td>
<td>10mm</td>
<td>5-7mm</td>
```

The last cell in this row is just like the first one:

```
<td rowspan="2">5-7mm</td>
</tr>
```

▼   You're up to row number four. In this one, because of the rowspans from the previous
row, there are only three cells to define: the cell for Models with AC, and the two cells
for the numbers:

```
<tr>
    <td>Models with AC</td>
    <td>12mm</td>
    <td>6-8mm</td>
</tr>
```

 Note   In this table, I've made the Alternator cell a heading cell and the AC cells
plain data. This is mostly an aesthetic decision on my part. I could have
made all three into headings just as easily.

Now for the final row—this one should be easy. The first cell (Power Steering Oil Pump)
spans two columns (the one with Alternator in it and the with/without AC column). The
remaining three are just one cell each:

```
<tr>
    <th colspan="2">Power Steering Oil Pump</th>
    <td>12.5mm</td>
    <td>7.9mm</td>
    <td>6-8mm</td>
</tr>
```

That's it. You're done laying out the rows and columns. That was the hard part. The rest
is just fine-tuning. Try looking at it again to make sure there are no strange errors (see
Figure 10.25).

FIGURE 10.25

*The table with the data
rows included.*

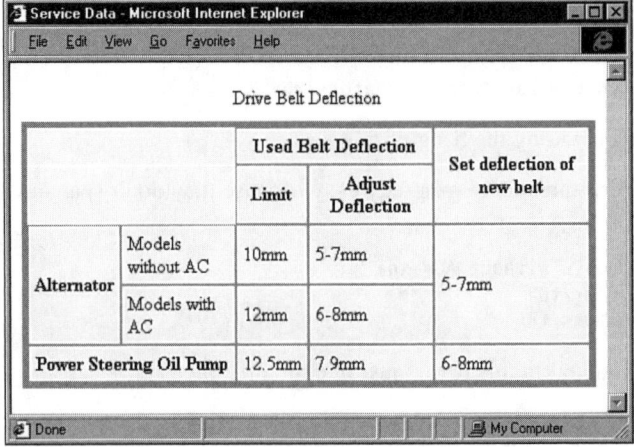

Now that you have all the rows and cells laid out, adjust the alignments within the cells. The numbers should be centered, at least. Because they make up the majority of the table, center the default alignment for each row:

```
<tr align="center">
```

The labels along the left side of the table (Alternator, Models with/without AC, and Power Steering Oil Pump) look funny if they're centered, however, so left-align them using the following code:

```
<th rowspan="2" align="left">Alternator</th>
<td align="left">Models without AC</td>
<td align="left">Models with AC</td>

<th colspan="2" align="left">Power Steering Oil Pump</th>
```

I've put some line breaks in the longer headings so that the columns are a little narrower. Because the text in the headings is pretty short to start with, I don't have to worry too much about the table looking funny if it gets too narrow. Here are the lines I modified:

```
<th rowspan="2">Set<br />deflection<br />of new belt</th>
<th>Adjust<br />Deflection</th>
```

For one final step, you'll align the caption to the left side of the table:

```
<caption align="left">Drive Belt Deflection</caption>
```

Voilà—the final table, with everything properly laid out and aligned! Figure 10.26 shows the final result.

FIGURE 10.26

The final Drive Belt Deflection table.

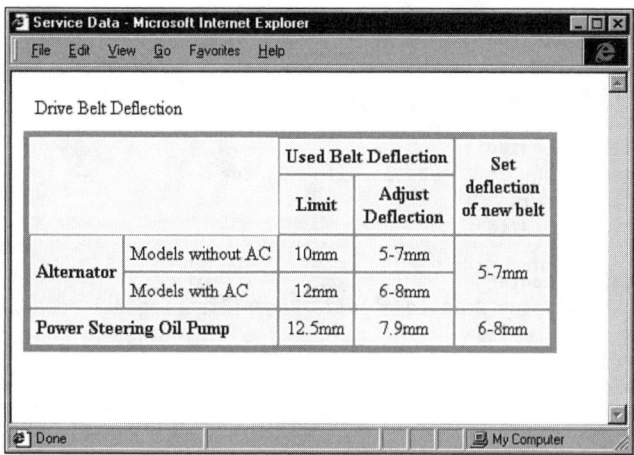

Note   If you got lost at any time, the best thing you can do is pull out your handy text editor and try it yourself, following along tag by tag. After you've done it a couple of times, it becomes easier.

Here's the full text for the table example:

```html
<html>
<head>
<title>Service Data</title>
</head>
<body>
<table border="5"
    bgcolor="#ffffcc"
    bordercolor="#cc9900"
    cellspacing="0"
    cellpadding="5">
<caption align="left">Drive Belt Deflection</caption>
<tr>
    <th rowspan="2" colspan="2"></th>
    <th colspan="2">Used Belt Deflection</th>
    <th rowspan="2">Set<br />deflection<br />of new belt</th>
</tr>
<tr>
    <th>Limit</th>
    <th>Adjust<br />Deflection</th>
</tr>
<tr align="center">
    <th rowspan="2" align="left">Alternator</th>
    <td align="left">Models without AC</td>
    <td>10mm</td>
    <td>5-7mm</td>
    <td rowspan="2">5-7mm</td>
</tr>
<tr align="center">
    <td align="left">Models with AC</td>
    <td>12mm</td>
    <td>6-8mm</td>
</tr>
<tr align="center">
    <th colspan="2" align="left">Power Steering Oil Pump</th>
    <td>12.5mm</td>
    <td>7.9mm</td>
    <td>6-8mm</td>
</tr>
</table>
</body>
</html>
```

More Advanced Table Enhancements

Believe it or not, after all the work you've done, you're *finally* getting to the table elements that were introduced in HTML 4.0. There are many improvements in the way that you define table columns and rows, which I'll cover in the following sections.

Grouping and Aligning Columns

One of the table enhancements offered in HTML 4.0 is the capability to render tables incrementally, rather than having to wait for all of the data in the table to load. This is accomplished, in part, by defining the columns of the table with the `<colgroup>` and `<col>` elements. These elements enable the Web page author to create structural divisions of table columns, which then can be enhanced visually through the use of style sheet properties.

The `<colgroup>`...`</colgroup>` element is used to enclose one or more columns in a group. The closing `</colgroup>` tag is optional in HTML 4.0, but it's required by the XHTML 1.0 standard. This element has two attributes:

- `span` defines the number of columns in the column group. Its value must be an integer greater than `0`. If `span` is not defined, the `<colgroup>` element defaults to a column group that contains one column. If the `<colgroup>` element contains one or more `<col>` elements (described later), however, the `span` attribute is ignored.

- `width` specifies the width of each column in the column group. Widths can be defined in pixels, percentages, and relative values. You also can specify a special width value of "`0*`" (zero followed by an asterisk). This value specifies that the width of the each column in the group should be the minimum amount necessary to hold the contents of each cell in the column. If you specify the "`0*`" value, however, browsers will be unable to render the table incrementally.

Suppose that you have a table that measures 450 pixels in width and contains six columns. You want each of the six columns to be 75 pixels wide. The code looks something like the following:

```
<table border="1" width="450">
<colgroup span="6" width="75">
</colgroup>
```

Now you want to change the columns. Using the same 450-pixel-wide table, you make the first two columns 25 pixels wide, and the last four columns 100 pixels wide. This requires two `<colgroup>` elements, as follows:

```
<table border="1" width="450">
<colgroup span="2" width="25">
</colgroup>
<colgroup span="4" width="100">
</colgroup>
```

10

What if you don't want all of the columns in a column group to be the same width or have the same appearance? This is where the <col> element comes into play. Where <colgroup> defines the structure of table columns, <col> defines their attributes. To use this element, begin the column definition with a <col> tag. The end tag is forbidden in this case. Instead, you should use the XHTML 1.0 construct for tags with no closing tag and write the tag as <col />.

Going back to your 450-pixel-wide table, you now want to make the two columns in the first column group 75 pixels wide. In the second column group, you have columns of 50, 75, 75, and 100 pixels, respectively. Here's how you format the second column group with the <col> tag:

```
<table border="1" width="450">
<colgroup span="2" width="75">
</colgroup>
<colgroup>
   <col span="1" width="50">
   <col span="2" width="75">
   <col span="1" width="100">
</colgroup>
```

Now apply this to some *real* code. The following example shows a table that displays science and mathematics class schedules. Start by defining a table that has a 1-pixel-wide border and spans 100 percent of the browser window width.

Next, you define the column groups in the table. You want the first column group to display the names of the classes. The second column group consists of two columns that display the room number for the class, as well as the time that the class is held. The align and valign attributes you learned about earlier today have not been deprecated in HTML 4.0 for the <col> and <colgroup> elements, so you'll take advantage of them here. The first column group consists of one column of cells that spans 20 percent of the entire width of the table. The contents of the cell are aligned vertically toward the top and centered horizontally. The second column group consists of two columns, each spanning 40 percent of the width of the table. Their contents are vertically aligned to the top of the cells.

Finally, you enter the table data the same way that you normally do. Here's what the complete code looks like for the class schedule, and the results are shown in Figure 10.27 in Internet Explorer:

INPUT

```
<html>
<head>
<title>Grouping Columns</title>
</head>
<body>
<table border="1" width="100%" summary="Grouping Columns">
```

```
<caption><b>Science and Mathematic Class Schedules</b></caption>

<colgroup width="20%" align="center" valign="top"></colgroup>

<colgroup span="2" width="40%" valign="top"></colgroup>

<tr>
<th>Class</th>
<th>Room</th>
<th>Time</th>
</tr>

<tr>
<td>Biology</td>
<td>Science Wing, Room 102</td>
<td>8:00 AM to 9:45 AM</td>
</tr>

<tr>
<td>Science</td>
<td>Science Wing, Room 110</td>
<td>9:50 AM to 11:30 AM</td>
</tr>

<tr>
<td>Physics</td>
<td>Science Wing, Room 107</td>
<td>1:00 PM to 2:45 PM</td>
</tr>

<tr>
<td>Geometry</td>
<td>Mathematics Wing, Room 236</td>
<td>8:00 AM to 9:45 AM</td>
</tr>

<tr>
<td>Algebra</td>
<td>Mathematics Wing, Room 239</td>
<td>9:50 AM to 11:30 AM</td>
</tr>

<tr>
<td>Trigonometry</td>
<td>Mathematics Wing, Room 245</td>
<td>1:00 PM to 2:45 PM</td>
</tr>
</table>
</body>
</html>
```

10

FIGURE 10.27

The class schedule with formatted column groups.

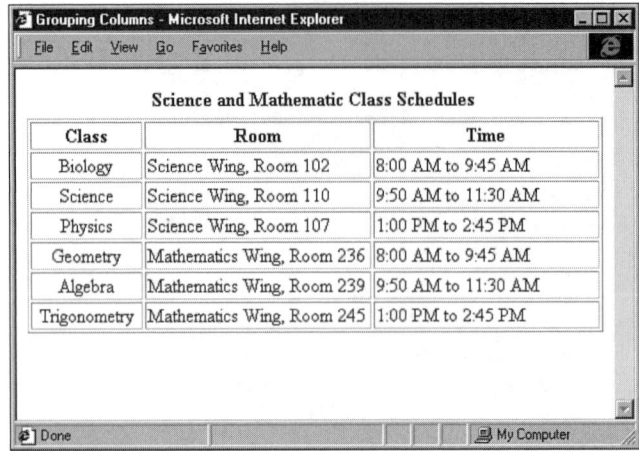

Grouping and Aligning Rows

Now that you know how to group and format columns, let's turn to the rows. You can group the rows of a table into three sections: table heading, table footer, and table body. You can apply cascading style sheet properties to emphasize the table heading and table footer, and give the body of the table a different appearance.

The table header, footer, and body sections are defined by the `<thead>`, `<tfoot>`, and `<tbody>` elements, respectively. Each of these elements must contain the same number of columns.

The `<thead>...</thead>` element defines the heading of the table, which should contain information about the columns in the body of the table. Typically, this is the same type of information that you've been placing within header cells so far today. The starting `<thead>` tag is always required when you want to include a head section in your table, as is the closing `</thead>` tag under XHTML 1.0.

The head of the table appears right after the `<table>` element or after `<colgroup>` elements, as the following example shows, and must include at least one row group defined by the `<tr>` element. It is formatted as follows:

INPUT

```
<table border="1" width="100%">
<caption><b>Science and Mathematic Class Schedules</b></caption>
<colgroup width="20%" align="center" valign="top">
  <colgroup span="2" width="40%" valign="top">
<thead>
  <tr>
    <th>Class</th>
    <th>Room</th>
    <th>Time</th>
  </tr>
</thead>
```

The `<tfoot>...</tfoot>` element defines the footer of the table. The starting `<tfoot>` tag is always required when defining the footer of a table. The closing `<tfoot>` tag was optional in HTML 4.0, but it's required for XHTML 1.0 compliance. The footer of the table appears immediately after the table heading if one is present, or after the `<table>` element if a table heading is not present. It must contain at least one row group, defined by the `<tr>` element. A good example of information that you could place in a table footer is a row that totals columns of numbers in a table.

You must define the footer of the table before the table body because the browser has to render the footer before it receives all the data in the table body. For the purposes of this example, we'll include the same information in the table head and the table footer. The code looks like this:

INPUT
```
<tfoot>
  <tr>
   <th>Class</th>
   <th>Room</th>
   <th>Time</th>
  </tr>
</tfoot>
```

10

After you define the heading and footer for the table, you define the rows in the table body. A table can contain more than one body element, and each body can contain one or more rows of data. This may not seem to make sense, but using multiple body sections enables you to divide up your table into logical sections. I'll show you one example of why this is rather cool in a little bit.

The `<tbody>...</tbody>` element defines a body section within your table. The `<tbody>` start tag is required if at least one of the following is true:

- The table contains head or foot sections
- The table contains more than one table body

The following example contains two table bodies, each consisting of three rows of three cells each. The body appears after the table footer, as follows:

INPUT
```
<tbody>
  <tr>
   <td>Biology</td>
   <td>Science Wing, Room 102</td>
   <td>8:00 AM to 9:45 AM</td>
  </tr>
  <tr>
   <td>Science</td>
   <td>Science Wing, Room 110</td>
   <td>9:50 AM to 11:30 AM</td>
  </tr>
  <tr>
   <td>Physics</td>
```

```
      <td>Science Wing, Room 107</td>
      <td>1:00 PM to 2:45 PM</td>
     </tr>
   </tbody>
   <tbody>
     <tr>
      <td>Geometry</td>
      <td>Mathematics Wing, Room 236</td>
      <td>8:00 AM to 9:45 AM</td>
     </tr>
     <tr>
      <td>Algebra</td>
      <td>Mathematics Wing, Room 239</td>
      <td>9:50 AM to 11:30 AM</td>
     </tr>
     <tr>
      <td>Trigonometry</td>
      <td>Mathematics Wing, Room 245</td>
      <td>1:00 PM to 2:45 PM</td>
     </tr>
   </tbody>
   </table>
```

OUTPUT Put all the preceding together and you get a table that looks like that shown in Figure 10.28.

FIGURE 10.28

The class schedule with a head, two bodies, and a foot.

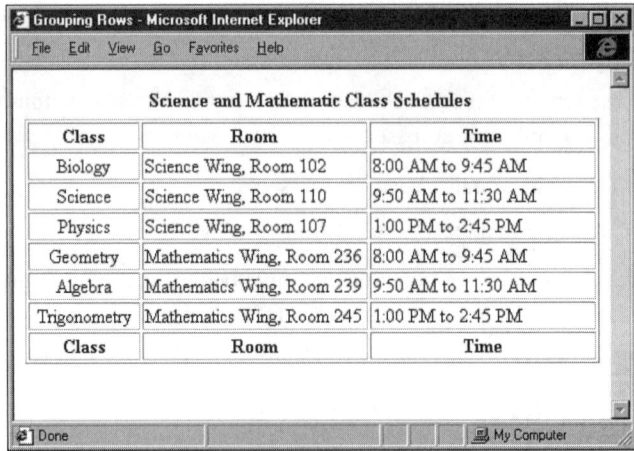

The `frame` and `rules` Attributes

In the preceding example, it's not really clear where the column groups and row groups begin and end. You can use the `frame` and `rules` attributes of the `<table>` element to selectively control table borders.

The `frame` attribute affects how the external border of the table is rendered. You can specify one of several different values to define which sides of the external border are visible:

void	The default value. No sides of the external border are visible.
above	Renders only the top side of the border.
below	Renders only the bottom side of the border.
hsides	Renders the top and bottom sides of the border.
lhs	Renders the left side of the border.
rhs	Renders the right side of the border.
vsides	Renders the right and left sides of the border.
box	Renders all four sides of the border.
border	Renders all four sides of the border.

The `rules` attribute is somewhat similar to the `frame` attribute, except that it defines the rules that appear between the cells within a table. The following values apply to the `rules` attribute:

none	The default value. No rules are drawn around any of the cells.
groups	Rules will appear between row groups as defined by `<thead>`, `<tfoot>` and `<tbody>`, and between column groups as defined by `<colgroup>` and `<col>`.
rows	Rules will appear only between rows.
cols	Rules will appear only between columns.
all	Rules will appear between all rows and columns.

Now let's alter the borders in the table so that your column groups and row groups stand out better. You'll draw a border around the Class Schedule table, but you'll place the border only along the top and bottom of the table by applying `frame="hsides"` to the `<table>` tag.

Inside the table, you'll separate the heading and footer from the two body sections (one table body for the Science subjects and one table body for the Math subjects). You'll also separate the Subject column group and the Room/Time column group. All this is accomplished by using `rules="groups"` with the `<table>` element.

You only need to modify one line in your code to accomplish all of this now. The revised table element appears as follows, and Figure 10.29 shows the results in Internet Explorer:

```
<table border="1" width="100%" frame="hsides" rules="groups">
```

FIGURE 10.29

The class schedule with rules added.

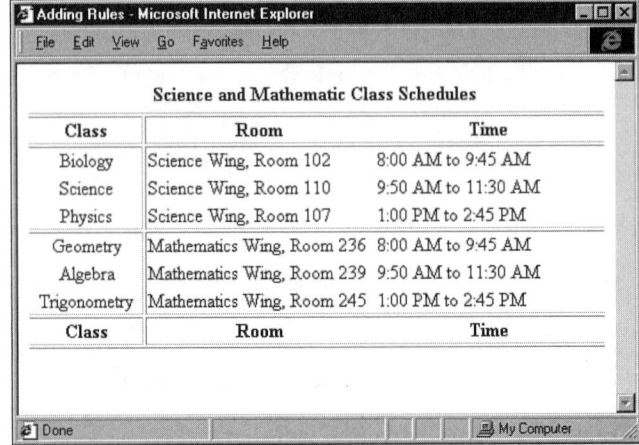

Other Table Elements and Attributes

Table 10.1 presents some of the additional elements and attributes that pertain to tables.

TABLE 10.1   Other Table Elements and Attributes

Attribute	Applied to Element	Use
char	See "Use" Column	Specifies a character to be used as an axis to align the contents of a cell. For example, you can use it to align a decimal point in numerical values. Can be applied to colgroup, col, tbody, thead, tfoot, tr, td and th elements.
charoff	See "Use" Column	Specifies the amount of offset applied to the first occurrence of the alignment character that is specified in the char attribute. Applies to colgroup, col, tbody, thead, tfoot, tr, td, and th elements.
summary	\<table\>	Provides a more detailed description of the contents of the table and is primarily used with nonvisual browsers.

How Tables Are Used

In this chapter, I demonstrated the usage of tables in publishing tabular data. That was the original purpose for HTML tables. However, Netscape 2.0 introduced the option of turning off table borders, and this broadened the manner in which tables are used.

Before style sheets were created and implemented in most browsers, there was only one way to lay out elements on a page other than straight down the middle—tables. Every time you see a page that has navigational links running down one side or elements enclosed in boxes with a background of a different color, someone has laid things out using tables. In fact, tables are such a huge part of Web publishing that it's rare to see a page that doesn't contain any.

The reason tables are used so often is that support for style sheets is still inconsistent, even in the most recent versions of Netscape and Internet Explorer. More than that, many users are still using older versions of these browsers that have even worse support for style sheets, or no support at all. Besides, most Web developers are more familiar with tables than they are with style sheets, so they go with what they know.

Let's look at a page that uses tables for layout—the home page for the Mozilla project. It's a good example because it uses several clearly marked tables with nice, bold borders. The page, rendered in Internet Explorer, appears in Figure 10.30.

FIGURE 10.30

The Mozilla.org home page.

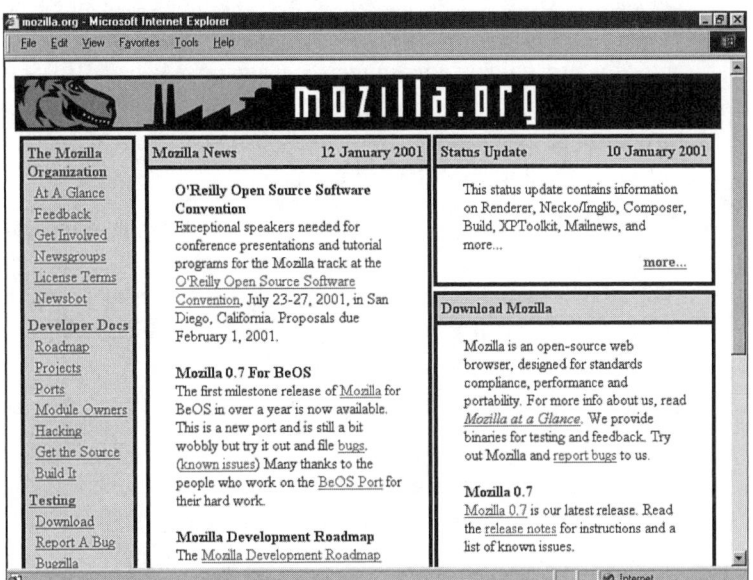

As you can see, the main body of the page is divided into three columns. The entire page is enclosed in a table with a width of 100%, and the table has three columns. The banner across the top of the page is in a cell with a `colspan` of 3.

As you can see, each column contains boxes with thick, black borders. Each of these boxes is a separate table that's placed within the cell that makes up its column. More accurately speaking, it's actually two tables.

The black borders are created by first making a table with a single row and column and a black background. The table with the content in it is placed within that table, and each cell has its own background color. The black background shows through `cellpadding` and `cellspacing` in the inner table to make it look like the inner table has black borders. So what you're looking at on the Mozilla.org home page is, in fact, tables nested three deep in most places.

This type of layout is typical. As you can see from the Mozilla.org page, tables can be used for a very precise layout of the elements on a page. The best way to learn how to create your own pages using these techniques is to view the source code of pages you like. It's unethical to copy someone else's code directly, but there's nothing wrong with using other people's HTML as a source of inspiration or instruction.

Image Slicing

On Day 7, "Using Images, Color, and Backgrounds," I explained how to include images on your Web pages. On Day 9, "Creating and Using Imagemaps," I explained how to embed multiple links in those images using imagemaps. By combining tables and images, you can slice up the images so that they're downloaded separately but appear to be one image once rendered onscreen. Also, you can make each slice of an image a separate link so that it works like an image map.

Because client-side imagemaps are so easy to implement, these days image slicing is rarely used to duplicate the functionality of imagemaps. However, you may still want to slice up images so that they download separately. There's a good chance that you'll run into this technique if you work with pages created by other people, so it's good to know how it works.

The most important thing to understand is that you have to put all of your image slices into a table with the `cellpadding`, `cellspacing`, and `border` attributes set to 0. This leaves absolutely no space between the cells. The second thing you have to remember is to leave no white space between the `<img>` tag and the `</td>` tag. In some browsers, this will put a space in the page layout and mess things up.

Once you understand those simple rules, image slicing is pretty easy. You just load your favorite image editor, cut up the image, and then create a table that mirrors the slicing scheme you used and puts the images in the cells where they belong. For example, let's say you want to slice up an image into three pieces horizontally. You just create a one-column, three-row table and put one slice of the image in each row. That's all there is to it.

Summary

Today, you've learned quite a lot about tables. They enable you to arrange your information in rows and columns so that your visitors can get to the information they need quickly.

While working with tables today, you've learned about headings and data, captions, defining rows and cells, aligning information within cells, and creating cells that span multiple rows or columns. With these features, you can create tables for most purposes.

As you're constructing tables, it's helpful to keep the following steps in mind:

- Sketch your table, indicating where the rows and columns fall. Mark which cells span multiple rows and columns.
- Start with a basic framework and lay out the rows, headings, and data row by row and cell by cell in HTML. Include row and column spans as necessary. Test frequently in a browser to make sure it's all working correctly.
- Modify the alignment in the rows to reflect the alignment of the majority of the cells.
- Modify the alignment for individual cells.
- Adjust line breaks, if necessary.
- Make other refinements such as cell spacing, padding, or color.
- Test your table in multiple browsers. Different browsers may have different approaches to laying out your table, or may be more accepting of errors in your HTML code.

Table 10.2 presents a quick summary of the HTML elements that you've learned about today, and which remain current in HTML 4.0. Attributes that apply to each element are listed in Table 10.3.

TABLE 10.2 Current HTML 4.0 Table Elements

Tag	Use
`<table>...</table>`	Indicates a table.
`<caption>...</caption>`	Creates an optional caption for the table.
`<colgroup>...</colgroup>`	Encloses one or more columns in a group.

TABLE 10.2   continued

Tag	Use
`<col>`	Used to define the attributes of a column in a table.
`<thead>...</thead>`	Creates a row group that defines the heading of the table. A table can contain only one heading.
`<tfoot>...</tfoot>`	Creates a row group that defines the footer of the table. A table can contain only one footer. Must be specified before the body of the table is rendered.
`<tbody>...</tbody>`	Defines one or more row groups to include in the body of the table. Tables can contain more than one body section.
`<tr>...</tr>`	Defines a table row, which can contain heading and data cells.
`<th>...</th>`	Defines a table cell that contains a heading. Heading cells are usually indicated by boldface and centered both horizontally and vertically within the cell.
`<td>...</td>`	Defines a table cell containing data. Table cells are in a regular font, and are left-aligned and vertically centered within the cell.

Because several of the table attributes apply to more than one of the preceding elements, I'm listing them separately. Table 10.3 presents a quick summary of the HTML attributes you learned about today that remain current in HTML 4.0.

TABLE 10.3   Current HTML 4.0 Table Attributes

Attribute	Applied to Element	Use
`align`	`<tr>`	Possible values are `left`, `center`, and `right`, which indicate the horizontal alignment of the cells within that row (overriding the default alignment of heading and table cells).
	`<th>` or `<td>`	Overrides both the row's alignment and any default cell alignment. Possible values are `left`, `center`, and `right`.
	`<thead>`,`<tbody>`,`<tfoot>`	Used to set alignment of the contents in table head, body, or foot cells. Possible values are `left`, `center`, and `right`.
	`<col>`	Used to set alignment of all cells in a column. Possible values are `left`, `center`, and `right`.
	`<colgroup>`	Used to set alignment of all cells in a column group. Possible values are `left`, `center`, and `right`.

TABLE 10.3 continued

Attribute	Applied to Element	Use
	`<table>`	Deprecated in HTML 4.0. Possible values are `left`, `center`, and `right`. `align="center"` and are not supported in HTML 3.2 and older browsers. Determines the alignment of the table and indicates that text following the table will be wrapped alongside it.
	`<caption>`	Deprecated in HTML 4.0. Indicates which side of the table the caption will be placed. The possible values for most browsers are `top` and `bottom`. HTML 4.0 browsers also support `left` and `right`. In Internet Explorer, the possible values are `left`, `right`, and `center`, and they indicate the horizontal alignment of the caption.
`bgcolor`	`All`	(HTML 3.2, deprecated in HTML 4.0) Changes the background color of that table element. Cell colors override row colors, which override table colors. The value can be a hexadecimal color number or a color name.
`border`	`<table>`	Indicates whether the table will be drawn with a border. The default is no border. If `border` has a value, it's the width of the shaded border around the table.
`bordercolor`	`<table>`	(Internet Explorer and Netscape extension) Can be used with any of the table elements to change the color of the border around that elements. The value can be a hexadecimal color number or a color name.
`bordercolorlight`	`<table>`	(Internet Explorer extension) Same as `bordercolor`, except it affects only the light component of a 3D-look border.
`bordercolordark`	`<table>`	(Internet Explorer extension) Same as `bordercolor`, except it affects only the dark component of a 3D-look border.
`cellspacing`	`<table>`	Defines the amount of space between the cells in the table.
`cellpadding`	`<table>`	Defines the amount of space between the edges of the cell and its contents.

10

TABLE 10.3   continued

Attribute	Applied to Element	Use
char		Specifies a character to be used as an axis to align the contents of a cell (for example, a decimal point in numerical values). Can be applied to colgroup, col, tbody, thead, tfoot, tr, td, and th elements.
charoff		Specifies the amount of offset to be applied to the first occurrence of the alignment character specified by the char attribute. Applies to the same elements previously listed in char.
frame	`<table>`	Defines which sides of the frame that surrounds a table are visible. Possible values are void, above, below, hsides, lhs, rhs, vsides, box, and border.
height	`<th>` or `<td>`	Deprecated in HTML 4.0. Indicates the height of the cell in pixel or percentage values.
nowrap	`<th>` or `<td>`	Deprecated in HTML 4.0. Prevents the browser from wrapping the contents of the cell.
rules	`<table>`	Defines which rules (division lines) will appear between cells in a table. Possible values are none, groups, rows, cols, and all.
width	`<table>`	Indicates the width of the table, in exact pixel values or as a percentage of page width (for example, 50 percent).
span	`<colgroup>`	Defines the number of columns in a column group. Must be an integer greater than 0.
	`<col>`	Defines the number of columns which a cell spans. Must be an integer greater than 0.
width	`<colgroup>`	Defines the width of all cells in a column group.
	`<col>`	Defines the width of all cells in one column.
colspan	`<th>` or `<td>`	Indicates the number of cells to the right of this one that this cell will span.
rowspan	`<th>` or `<td>`	Indicates the number of cells below this one that this cell will span.
valign	`<tr>`	Indicates the vertical alignment of the cells within that row (overriding the defaults). Possible values are top, middle, and bottom.

TABLE 10.3 continued

Attribute	Applied to Element	Use
	`<th>` or `<td>`	Overrides both the row's vertical alignment and the default cell alignment. Possible values are `top`, `middle`, and `bottom`.
		In Netscape, `valign` can also have the value `baseline`.
	`<thead>`,`<tfoot>`,`<tbody>`	Defines vertical alignment of cells in the table head, table foot, or table body.
	`<colgroup>`	Defines the vertical alignment of all cells in a column group.
	`<col>`	Defines the vertical alignment of all cells in a single column.
`width`	`<th>` or `<td>`	Deprecated in HTML 4.0. Indicates width of the cell, in exact pixel values or as a percentage of table width (for example, 50 percent).

Workshop

Today's lesson covered one of the more complex subjects in HTML—tables. Before you move on to frames and linked windows, you should work through the following questions and exercises to make sure that you've really got a good grasp of how tables work.

Q&A

Q **Tables are a real hassle to lay out, especially when you get into row and column spans. That last example was awful.**

A You're right. Tables are a tremendous pain to lay out by hand like this. However, if you're using writing editors and tools to generate HTML code, having the table defined like this makes more sense because you can just write out each row in turn programmatically. Sooner or later, we'll all be working in HTML editors anyhow, so you won't have to do this by hand for long.

Q **My tables work fine in Netscape Navigator, but they're all garbled in many other browsers. What did I do wrong?**

A Did you remember to close all your `<tr>`, `<th>`, and `<td>` elements? Make sure you've put in the matching `</tr>`, `</th>`, and `</td>` tags, respectively. The closing tags might be optional, but often other browsers need those tags to understand table layout.

Q Can you nest tables, putting a table inside a single table cell?

A Sure! As I mentioned earlier, you can put any HTML code you want inside a table cell, and that includes other tables.

Q Why does most of the world use `align` for positioning a caption at the top or bottom of a page, but Internet Explorer does something totally different?

A I don't know. And worse, Microsoft claims it got that definition for Internet Explorer from HTML 3.0, but no version of HTML 3.0 or the tables specification in HTML 3.2 has it defined in that way. HTML 4.0 added left and right aligning to this attribute, but Internet Explorer added this alignment before HTML even mentioned the possibility.

Quiz

1. What are the basic parts of a table, and which tags identify them?
2. Which attribute is the most common attribute of the table tag, and what does it do?
3. What attributes define the amount of space between the edges of the cells and their content, and the amount of space between cells?
4. Which attributes are used to create cells that span more than one column or row?
5. Which elements are used to define the head, body, and foot of a table?

Quiz Answers

1. The basic parts of a table (the `<table>` tag) are the border (defined with the `border` attribute), the caption (defined with the `<caption>` tag), header cells (`<th>`), data cells (`<td>`), and table rows (`<tr>`).
2. The `border` attribute is the most common attribute for the table tag. It specifies whether border lines are displayed around the table, and how wide the borders should be.
3. `cellpadding` defines the amount of space between the edges of the cell and their contents. `cellspacing` defines the amount of space between the cells.
4. The `rowspan` attribute creates a cell that spans multiple rows. The `colspan` attribute creates a cell that spans multiple columns.
5. `<thead>`, `<tbody>`, and `<tfoot>` define the head, body, and foot of a table.

Exercises

1. Here's a brain-teaser for you: Create a simple nested table (a table within a table) that contains three rows and four columns. Inside the cell that appears at the second column in the second row, create a second table that contains two rows and two columns.
2. Modify the table shown in Figure 10.28 so that the rules in the table only appear between columns.

DAY 11

Frames and Linked Windows

In the early days of the Web, two significant limitations of Web browsers were that they could only display one document in a browser window at a time and the site couldn't open more browser windows if needed. Frames allow you to divide the browser window into sections, each with a different document, and linked windows allow you to create links that open new browser windows. Used properly, these two techniques can make your Web site easier to navigate. Unfortunately, they can also be misused to make your site confusing, difficult to use, and annoying to your users.

Today, you'll learn all about the following topics:

- What frames are, how they can affect your layout, and who supports them
- How to work with linked windows
- How to work with frames
- How to create complex framesets
- Floating frames

What Are Frames and Who Supports Them?

Today you'll learn about the tags that you can use to create *frames*. Simply put, frames enable you to divide a browser window and load a different document in each section of the window that you define. Due to the nature of these tags, Web pages that use frames simply can't be displayed on old browsers. They were introduced as a new feature with Netscape Navigator 2.0, which is several years old. Frames rapidly became popular, and they were included in the HTML 4.0 standard. Every popular Web browser supports them these days.

With version 3.0 of Internet Explorer, Microsoft introduced floating frames. Instead of dividing the browser window into sections, floating frames enable you to include frames inline in your documents, the same way you would with images. Floating frames were also included in the HTML 4.0 standard, and they're supported by Netscape 6 as well as every version of Internet Explorer since 3.0.

Frames give you an entirely different level of layout control than you've had so far in this book. For example, consider the example shown in Figure 11.1.

FIGURE 11.1

*A sample Web page
with frames.*

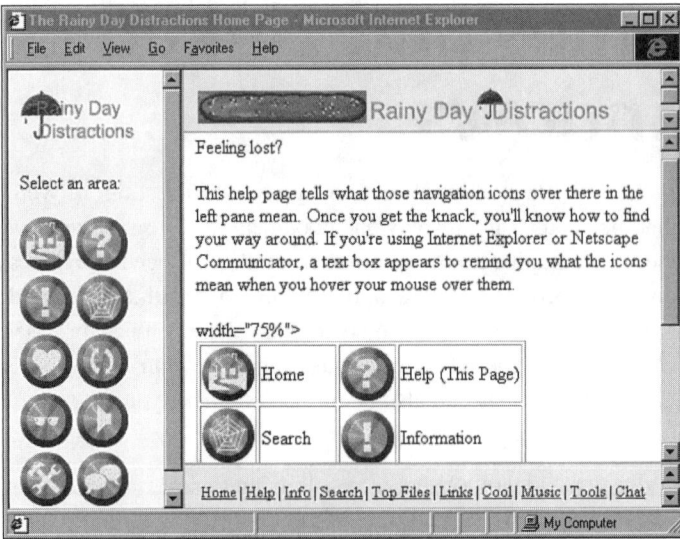

On this screen, you see two documents displayed within one browser window. The left frame contains graphical navigation elements, the lower-right frame contains text navigational links, the upper-right frame contains the page header, and the middle-right frame contains the main content of the site. This screen shot also illustrates one of the disadvantages of using frames. The frame that contains the actual page content actually uses a fairly small section of the browser window; the rest is consumed by the other frames. When you separate your layout using frames, you can detract from the important content on your site.

Because the information displayed on the page is separated into individual frames, the contents of a single frame can be updated without affecting the contents of any other frame. If you click on one of the linked images in the left frame, for example, the contents of the large frame on the right are automatically updated to display the details about the subject you've selected. When this update occurs, the contents of the left frame and the bottom frame aren't affected.

Working with Linked Windows

Before looking at how frames are added to a page, you need to learn about the `target` attribute of the `<a>` tag. This attribute takes the following form:

```
target="window_name"
```

Usually, when you click a hyperlink, the page to which you're linking replaces the current page in the browser window. In a *frameset* environment, however, there's no technical reason why the contents of the new page can't be displayed in a new window, with the contents of the original page still onscreen in its own window.

NEW TERM A *frameset* is a group of frames that's defined within a framed document through the use of the `<frameset>` tags. The `target` attribute tells the Web browser to display the information pointed to by a hyperlink in a window called *window_name*. Basically, you can call the new window anything you want, except that you can't use names that start with an underscore (_). These names are reserved for a set of special `target` values that you'll learn about later in the section "Magic `target` Names."

When you use the `target` attribute inside an `<a>` tag, a frames-compatible browser first checks whether a window with the name *window_name* exists. If it does, the document pointed to by the hyperlink replaces the current contents of *window_name*. On the other hand, if no window called *window_name* currently exists, a new browser window opens with that name. Then the document pointed to by the hyperlink is loaded into the newly created window.

Exercise 11.1: Working with Windows

Framesets rely on the `target` attribute to load pages into specific frames in a frameset. Each of the hyperlinks in the following exercise uses the `target` attribute to open a Web page in a different browser window. The concepts you'll learn here will help you understand later how targeted hyperlinks work in a frameset.

11

▼ To Do

▼ In this exercise, you'll create four separate HTML documents that use hyperlinks, including the `target` attribute. You'll use these hyperlinks to open two new windows called
`yellow_page` and `blue_page`, as shown in Figure 11.2. The top window is the original
Web browser window (the red page), `yellow_page` is at the bottom left, and `blue_page`
is at the bottom right.

FIGURE 11.2

*You can make hyper-
links to open a new
window for each of the
pages to which they
point.*

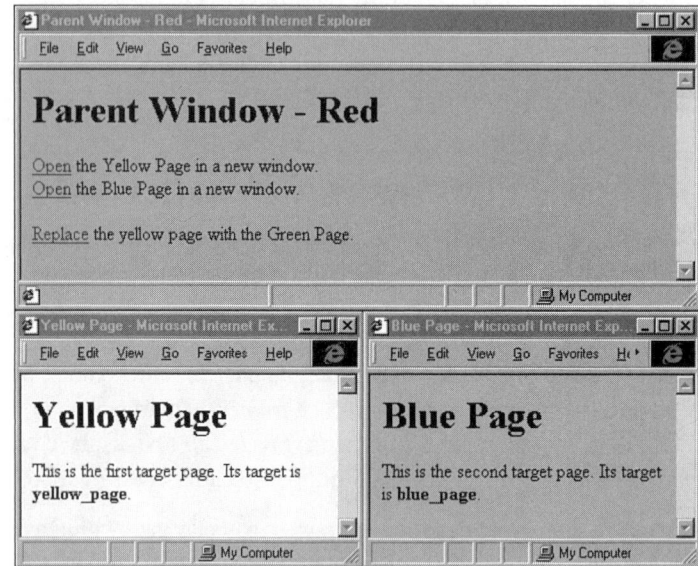

First, create the document to be displayed by the main Web browser window, shown in
Figure 11.3, by opening your text editor of choice and entering the following lines of
code:

INPUT

```
<html>
<head>
<title>Parent Window - Red</title>
</head>
<body bgcolor="#ff9999">
<h1>Parent Window - Red</h1>
<p><a href="yellow.html" target="yellow_page">Open</a> the Yellow Page
in a new window. <br>
   <a href="blue.html" target="blue_page">Open</a> the Blue Page in a new
   window. </p>
<p><a href="green.html" target="yellow_page">Replace</a> the yellow page
```

▼
```
        with the Green Page.</p>
        </body>
        </html>
```

OUTPUT

FIGURE 11.3.

*The parent window
(the red page).*

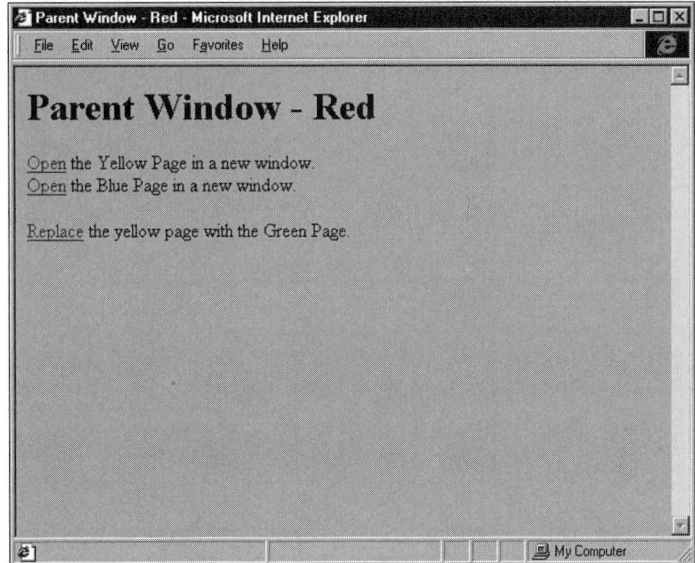

This creates a light-red page that links to the other three pages. Save this HTML source as parent.html.

Next, create a document called yellow.html (see Figure 11.4) by entering the following code:

INPUT
```
<html>
<head>
<title>Yellow Page</title>
</head>
<body bgcolor="#ffffcc">
<h1>Yellow Page</h1>
<p>This is the first target page. Its target is <b>yellow_page</b></p>
</body>
</html>
```
▼

11

OUTPUT

FIGURE **11.4**

*yellow.html displayed
in the Web browser
window named
yellow_page.*

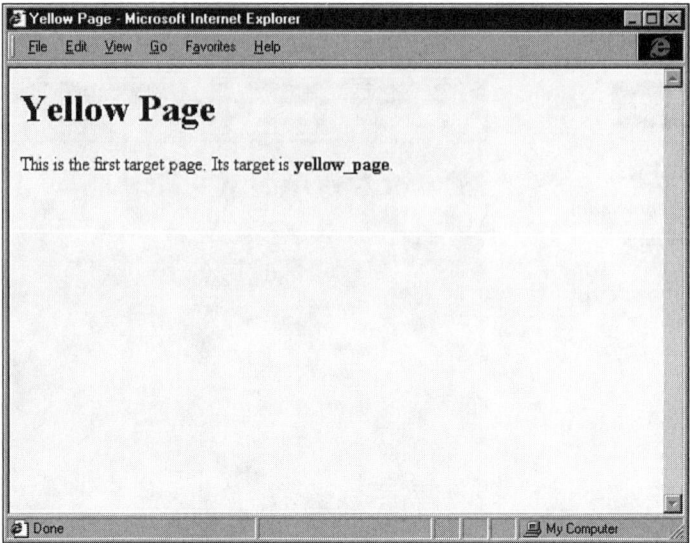

After saving `yellow.html`, create another document called `blue.html` (see Figure 11.5)
by entering the following code:

INPUT

```
<html>
<head>
<title>Blue Page</title>
</head>
<body bgcolor="#99ccff">
<h1>Blue Page</h1>
<p>This is the second target page. Its target is <b>blue_page</b>.</p>
</body>
</html>
```

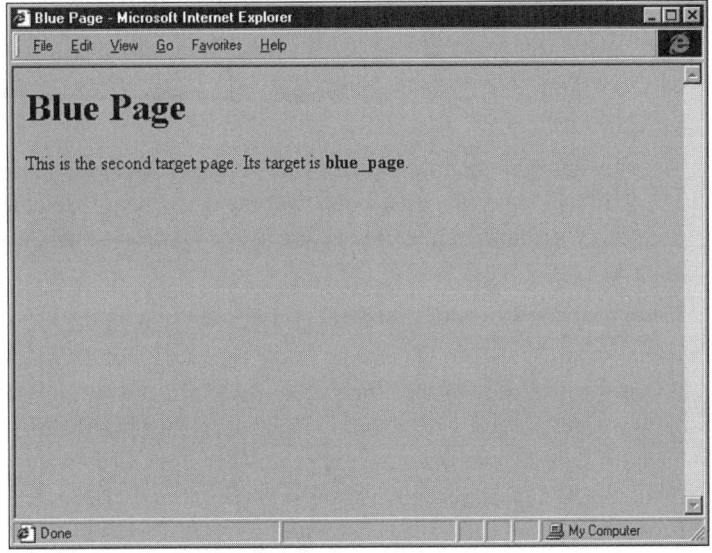

FIGURE 11.5.

blue.html displayed in the Web browser window named blue_window.

Next, create a fourth document called green.html, which looks like the following:

INPUT

```
<html>
<head>
<title>Green Page</title>
</head>
<body bgcolor="#ccffcc">
<h1>Green Page</h1>
<p>This is the third target page. Its target is <b>yellow_page</b>.
It should replace the yellow page in the browser.</p>
</body>
</html>
```

To complete the exercise, load parent.html (the red page) into your Web browser. Click the first hyperlink to open the yellow page in a second browser window. This happens because the first hyperlink contains the attribute target="yellow_page", as the following code from parent.html demonstrates:

```
<p><a href="yellow.html" target="yellow_page">Open</a> the Yellow Page in a
   new window.<br />
```

▼ Now return to the red page and click the second link. The blue page opens in a third
   browser window. Note that the new windows probably won't be laid out like the ones
   shown in Figure 11.2; usually they overlap each other. The following `target="blue_`
   `page"` statement in the `parent.html` page is what causes the new window to open:

```
<a href="blue.html" target="blue_page">Open</a> the Blue Page in a new
    window.</p>
```

The previous two examples opened each of the Web pages in a new browser window.
The third link, however, uses the `target="yellow_page"` statement to open the green
page in the window named `yellow_page`. You accomplish this using the following code
in `parent.html`:

```
<p><a href="green.html" target="yellow_page">Replace</a> the yellow page
    with the Green Page.</p>
```

Because you already opened the `yellow_page` window when you clicked the link for the
yellow page, the green page should replace the page that's already in it. To verify this,
click the third hyperlink on the red page. This replaces the contents of the yellow page
(with the `yellow_page` target name) with the green page (`green.html`), as shown in
Figure 11.6.

OUTPUT

FIGURE 11.6.

*green.html displayed
in the Web browser
window named
yellow_page.*

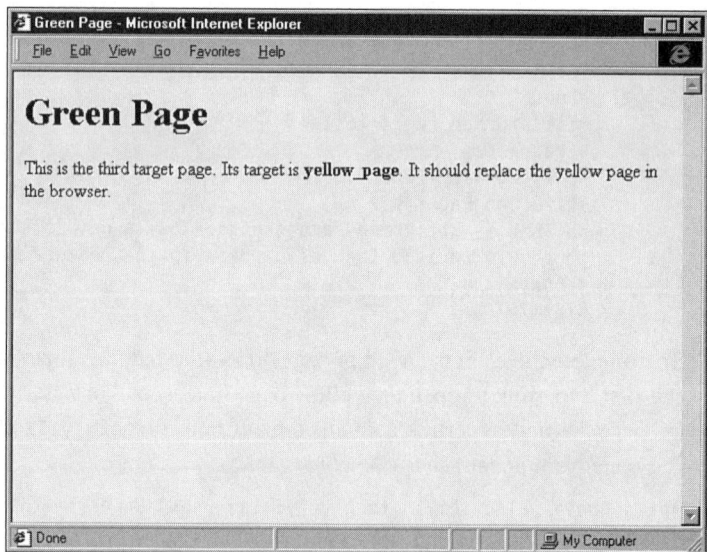

▲

The <base> Tag

When you're using the target attribute with links, sometimes you'll find that all or most of the hyperlinks on a Web page point to the same window. This is especially true when you're using frames, as you'll discover in the following section.

In such cases, rather than including a target attribute for each <a> tag, you can use another tag, <base>, to define a global target for all the links on a Web page. The <base> tag takes the following form:

```
<base target="window_name">
```

If you include the <base> tag in the <head>...</head> block of a document, every <a> tag that doesn't have a corresponding target attribute will display the document it points to in the window specified by <base target="window_name">. For example, if you had included the tag <base target="yellow_page"> in the HTML source for parent.html, the three hyperlinks could have been written the following way:

```
<html>
<head>
<title>Parent Window - Red</title>
<base target="yellow_page">  <!-- add base target="value" here -->
</head>
<body bgcolor="#ff9999">
<h1>Parent Window - Red</h1>
<p>
<a href="yellow.html">Open</a> <!-- no need to include a target -->
  the Yellow Page in a new window.<br />
<a href="blue.html" target="blue_page">Open</a> the Blue Page in a new
  window. </p>
<p><a href="green.html">Replace</a> <!-- no need to include a target -->
the yellow page with the Green Page.</p>
</body>
</html>
```

In this case, yellow.html and green.html load into the default window assigned by the <base> tag (yellow_page); blue.html overrides the default by defining its own target window of blue_page.

You also can override the window assigned with the <base> tag by using one of two special window names. If you use target="_blank" in a hyperlink, it opens a new browser window that doesn't have a name associated with it. Alternatively, if you use target="_self", the current window is used rather than the one defined by the <base> tag.

11

 **Note**   If you don't provide a `target` using the `<base>` tag and you don't indicate a target in a link's `<a>` tag, the link will load the new document in the same frame as the link.

Working with Frames

The introduction of frames in Netscape 2.0 heralded a new era for Web publishers. With frames, you can create Web pages that look and feel entirely different from other pages. You can have tables of contents, banners, footnotes, and sidebars, just to name a few common features.

At the same time, frames change what a "page" means to the browser and to your visitors. Unlike all the preceding examples, which use a single HTML page to display a screen of information, a single screen actually consists of a number of separate HTML documents that interact with each other. Figure 11.7 shows how a minimum of five separate documents is needed to create the screen shown earlier in Figure 11.1.

FIGURE 11.7

You must create a separate HTML document for each frame.

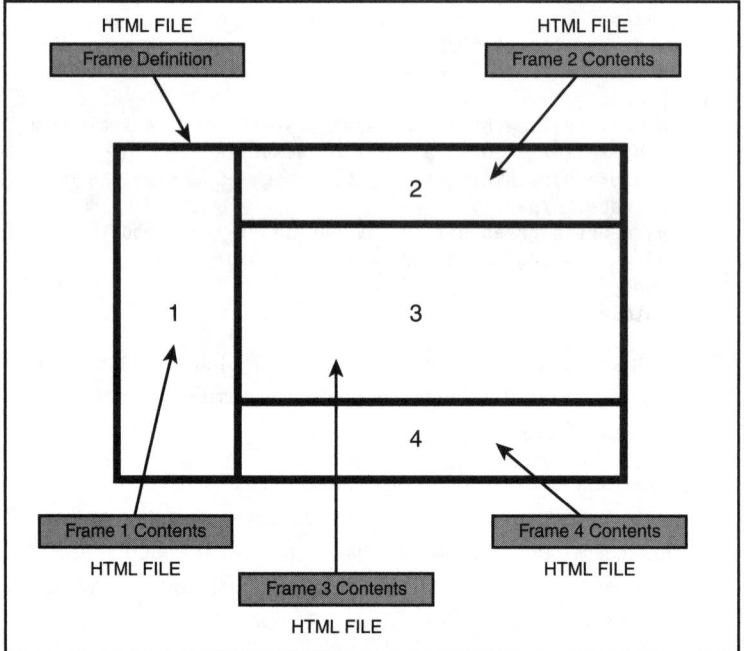

The first HTML document you need to create is called the *frameset document*. In this document, you enter the HTML code that describes the layout of each frame. In the preceding example, the document has three frames.

The *frameset document* also includes the names of the HTML documents that will appear in each of the frames. Each of the three remaining HTML documents (the ones that load in the frames) contains normal HTML tags that define the physical contents of each separate frame area. These documents are referenced by the frameset document.

NEW TERM   The *frameset document* is the page that contains the description of how the frames are laid out and the names of the HTML documents that will fill those frames.

The `<frameset>` Tag

To create a frameset document, you begin with the `<frameset>` tag. When used in an HTML document, the `<frameset>` tag replaces the `<body>` tag, as shown in the following code:

```
<html>
<head>
<title>Page Title</title>
</head>
<frameset>
    ... your frameset goes here ...
</frameset>
</html>
```

It's important that you understand up front how a frameset document differs from a normal HTML document. If you include a `<frameset>` tag in an HTML document, you cannot include a `<body>` tag also. Basically, the two tags are mutually exclusive. In addition, no other formatting tags, hyperlinks, or document text should be included in a frameset document. (The exception to this is the `<noframes>` tag, which you'll learn about later today in the section called, appropriately enough, "The `<noframes>` Tag.") The `<frameset>` tags contain only the definitions for the frames in this document—what's called the page's *frameset*.

The HTML 4.0 specification supports the `<frameset>` tag along with two possible attributes: `cols` and `rows`.

The `cols` Attribute

When you define a `<frameset>` tag, you must include one of two attributes as part of the tag definition. The first of these attributes is the `cols` attribute, which takes the following form:

```
<frameset cols="column width, column width, ...">
```

11

The cols attribute tells the browser to split the screen into a number of vertical frames whose widths are defined by *column width* values separated by commas. You define the width of each frame in one of three ways: explicitly in pixels, as a percentage of the total width of the <frameset>, or with an asterisk (*). When you use the asterisk, the frames-compatible browser uses as much space as possible for the specified frame.

When included in a complete frame definition, the following <frameset> tag creates a screen with three vertical frames, as shown in Figure 11.8. The fifth line in the following code example creates a left frame 100 pixels wide, a middle column that's 50 percent of the width of the screen, and a right column that uses all the remaining space:

INPUT

```
<html>
<head>
<title>Three Columns</title>
</head>
<frameset cols="100,50%,*">
    <frame src="leftcol.html">
    <frame src="midcol.html">
    <frame src="rightcol.html">
</frameset>
</html>
```

OUTPUT

FIGURE 11.8

The cols *attribute defines the number of vertical frames or columns in a frameset.*

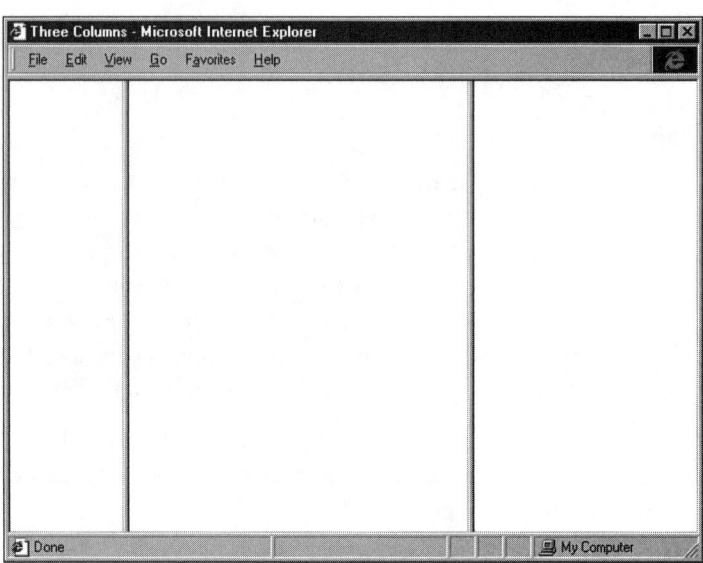

 Note

Because you're designing Web pages for users with various screen sizes, you should use absolute frame sizes sparingly. Whenever you do use an absolute size, ensure that one of the other frames is defined using an * to take up all the remaining screen space.

> **Tip**
>
> To define a frameset with three columns of equal width, use cols="*,*,*". This way, you won't have to mess around with percentages because frames-compatible browsers automatically assign an equal amount of space to each frame assigned a width of *.

The rows Attribute

The rows attribute works the same as the cols attribute, except that it splits the screen into horizontal frames rather than vertical ones. To split the screen into two frames of equal height, as shown in Figure 11.9, you would write the following:

INPUT

```html
<html>
<head>
<title>Two Rows</title>
</head>
<frameset rows="50%,50%">
    <frame src="toprow.html">
    <frame src="botrow.html">
</frameset>
</html>
```

Alternatively, you could use the following line:

INPUT

```html
<frameset rows="*,*">
```

11

FIGURE 11.9

The rows attribute defines the number of horizontal frames or rows in a frameset.

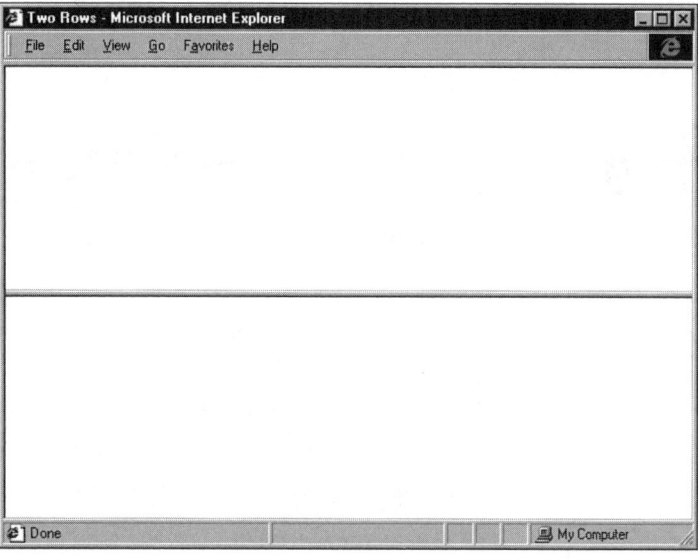

Note

If you try either of the preceding examples for yourself, you'll find that the `<frameset>` tag doesn't appear to work. You get this result because there are no contents defined for the rows or columns in the frameset. To define the contents, you need to use the `<frame>` tag, which is discussed in the next section.

The `<frame>` Tag

After you have your basic frameset laid out, you need to associate an HTML document with each frame by using the `<frame>` tag, which takes the following form:

```
<frame src="document URL">
```

For each frame defined in the `<frameset>` tag, you must include a corresponding `<frame>` tag, as shown in the following:

INPUT

```
<html>
<head>
<title>The frame Tag</title>
</head>
<frameset rows="*,*,*">
    <frame src="document1.html" />
    <frame src="document2.html" />
    <frame src="document3.html" />
</frameset>
</html>
```

This example defines a frameset with three horizontal frames of equal height (see Figure 11.10). The contents of `document1.html` are displayed in the first frame, the contents of `document2.html` in the second frame, and the contents of `document3.html` in the third frame.

OUTPUT

FIGURE 11.10

You use the `<frame>` tag to define the contents of each frame.

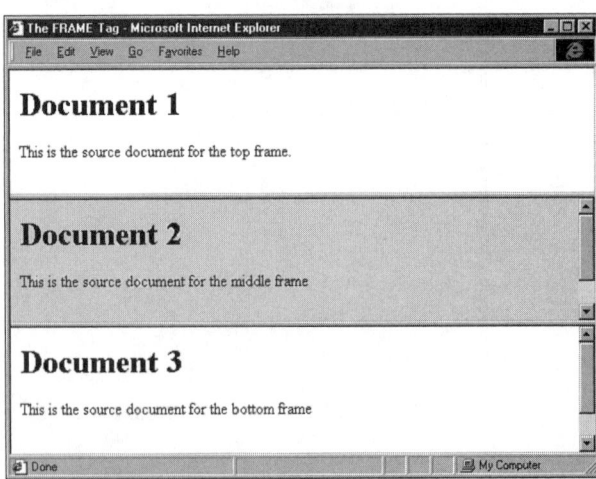

Tip

> When you're creating frameset documents, you might find it helpful to indent the `<frame>` tags so that they're separated from the `<frameset>` tags in your HTML document. This has no effect on the appearance of the resulting Web pages, but it does tend to make the HTML source easier to read.

The `<noframes>` Tag

What happens if a browser that doesn't support frames navigates to a frameset document? Nothing. You get a blank page. Fortunately, there's a way around this problem.

A special tag block called `<noframes>` enables you to include additional HTML code as part of the frameset document. The code you enclose within the `<noframes>` element isn't displayed in frames-compatible browsers, but it is displayed in browsers that don't support frames. The `<noframes>` tag takes the following form:

```
<html>
<head>
<title>Frameset with No Frames Content</title>
</head>
<frameset>
 your frameset goes here.
<noframes>
  Include any text, hyperlinks, and tags you want to here.
</noframes>
</frameset>
</html>
```

Using the frames' content and tags inside `<noframes>`, you can create pages that work well with both kinds of browsers. Later today, you'll add some `<noframes>` content to a frameset.

Note

> The way the `<noframes>` tag works is actually kind of interesting. It works because Web browsers are designed to ignore tags that they don't understand. So browsers that don't support frames ignore the `<frameset>` and `<frame>` tags. They also ignore the `<noframes>` tag and just display whatever is inside it. Browsers that do support frames know to render the frames and ignore the text inside the `<noframes>` tag.

Changing Frame Borders

Notice that all the frames in today's lesson have thick borders separating them. There are a number of attributes that can be set to control the appearance of frame borders, or prevent them from appearing altogether.

11

Start with the `<frame>` tag. By using two attributes, `bordercolor` and `frameborder`, you can turn borders on and off and specify their color. You can assign `bordercolor` any valid color value, either as a name or a hexadecimal triplet. `frameborder` takes two possible values: 1 (to display borders) or 0 (to turn off the display of borders).

> **Note**
>
> If you turn off the border, frames-compatible browsers won't display its default three-dimensional border. However, a space will still be left for the border.

> **Note**
>
> HTML 4.0 currently only lists the `frameborder` attribute. The `bordercolor` attribute qualifies as an extension.

For example, the following code adds a deep red border (defined by #cc3333) around the middle frame in the frameset:

```
<html>
<head>
<title>The frame Tag</title>
</head>
<frameset rows="*,*,*">
   <frame src="document1.html">
   <frame frameborder="1" bordercolor="#cc3333" src="document2.html">
   <frame src="document3.html">
</frameset>
</html>
```

Although HTML 4.0 doesn't provide either of these attributes for the `<frameset>` tag, you can use both of them to define default values for the entire frameset in Netscape and Microsoft Internet Explorer.

Of course, there's room for confusion when colored borders are defined. In the following frameset definition, a conflict arises because the two frames share a single common border, but each frame is defined to have a different border color with the `bordercolor` attribute:

```
<html>
<head>
<title>Conflicting Borders</title>
</head>
<frameset frameborder="0" rows="*,*,*">
   <frame frameborder="1" bordercolor="yellow" src="document1.html">
   <frame bordercolor="#cc3333" src="document2.html">
```

```
    <frame src="document3.html">
</frameset>
</html>
```

In addition, the frameset is defined as having no borders, but the first frame is supposed to have a border. How do you resolve this problem? You can apply three simple rules:

- Attributes in the outermost frameset have the lowest priority.
- Attributes are overridden by attributes in a nested <frameset> tag.
- Any bordercolor attribute in the current frame overrides previous ones in <frameset> tags.

Additional Attributes

Table 11.1 shows a few extra attributes for the <frame> tag. These attributes can give you additional control over how the user interacts with your frames. Other attributes control margins or spacing between frames and whether scrollbars appear when required.

TABLE 11.1 Control Attributes for the *<frame>* Tag

Attribute	Value	Description
frameborder	1	Displays borders around each frame (default).
frameborder	0	Creates borderless frames.
longdesc	*URL*	Specifies a URL that provides a longer description of the contents of the frameset. Primarily used with nonvisual browsers.
marginheight	*pixels*	To adjust the margin that appears above and below a document within a frame, set marginheight to the number indicated by *pixels*.
marginwidth	*pixels*	The marginwidth attribute enables you to adjust the margin on the left and right sides of a frame to the number indicated by *pixels*.
name	*string*	Assigns a name to the frame for targeting purposes.
noresize		By default, the users can move the position of borders around each frame on the current screen by grabbing the borders and moving them with the mouse. To lock the borders of a frame and prevent them from being moved, use the noresize attribute.
scrolling	auto	(Default) If the contents of a frame take up more space than the area available, frames-compatible browsers automatically add scrollbars to either the right side or the bottom of the frame so that the users can scroll through the document.
scrolling	no	Setting the value of scrolling to no disables the use of scrollbars for the current frame. (Note that if you do this but the document contains more text than can fit inside the frame, the users won't be able to scroll the additional text into view.)

11

TABLE 11.1 continued

Attribute	Value	Description
scrolling	yes	If you set `scrolling` to yes, the scrollbars are included in the frame even if they aren't required.
src	URL	Specifies the URL of the initial source document that appears in a frame when the frameset first opens in the browser.

Creating Complex Framesets

The framesets you've learned about so far are the most basic types of frames that can be displayed. In day-to-day use, however, you'll rarely use these basic frame designs. On all but the simplest sites, you'll most likely want to use more complex framesets.

Therefore, to help you understand the possible combinations of frames, links, images, and documents that can be used by a Web site, this section will explore complex framesets.

Exercise 11.2: Creating the Content Pages for Your Frameset

▼ To Do

Most commonly, framesets provide navigation bars that keep navigational elements in view as the user scrolls through the contents of the document. By far, the most common place to present the navigation bars is on the left side of the browser window. Each time the visitor clicks a link in the left navigation frame, the content in the main frame displays the selected page. The (very silly) frameset that you'll create in this exercise demonstrates this technique. Although it's not a really practical example, it's simple and fun and demonstrates the very same techniques you would use for a navigation bar.

Normally, when you design a Web page that uses frames, you design the frameset before you go through all the trouble of designing the content that goes into it. This is because you'll want to know how big your frames are going to be before you start designing graphics and other page content to put into them.

I'm doing things a little backward here, but for good reason. It may help you to better understand how things fit together if you see real content in the frames as you design the frameset. For this reason, I'll have you design the content first.

The following content pages don't include any of the frameset tags discussed so far. There are eight pages in all, but I promise that I'll keep the code for these pages really brief. Ready?

▼

Tip

> When you lay out the basic structure of a frameset, normally you don't want to be bothered with details such as the actual contents of the frames. However, your frameset won't be displayed properly when it's loaded into a frames-compatible browser for testing unless you define `<frame>` tags that include valid documents. If you want to design a frameset before you create the content, you can create a small empty HTML document called `dummy.html` and use it for all your frame testing.

The frameset that you'll create in Exercises 11.3 through 11.7 consists of three frames. The layout of the frameset will be as shown in Figure 11.11. The frameset page loads first and instructs the browser to divide the browser window into three frames. Next, it loads the three pages that appear in the top, left, and main frames. Finally, if a user browses to the frameset without a frames-compatible browser, an alternate page will appear.

FIGURE 11.11

You will create a frameset that consists of three frames: top, left, and main.

11

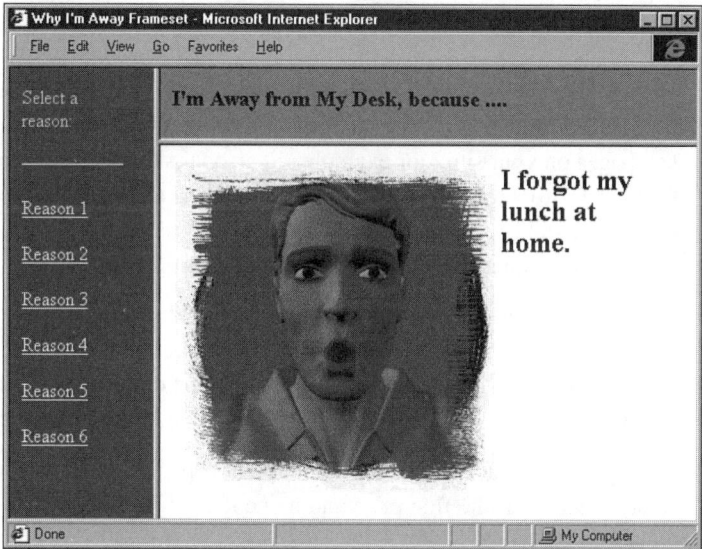

The top frame always displays the same Web page—`away.html`. The `choices.html` page that appears in the frame on the left side contains a list of links to six different pages named `reason1.html` through `reason6.html`. Each of these six pages will load into the main frame on the bottom-right portion of the frameset.

Start with the page displayed in the top frame. This page will always appear in the frame-
▼ set. Here you can include any information you want to display permanently as visitors

▼ browse through your site. Real-world examples for the content of this frame include the name of your Web site, a site logo, a link to your email address, or other similar content. Type in the following code and save it to your hard drive as away.html:

```
<html>
<head>
<title>I'm Away from My Desk Because</title>
</head>
<body bgcolor="#cc6600" text="#000000">
<h3>I'm Away from My Desk, because .... </h3>
</body>
</html>
```

Figure 11.12 shows this page.

OUTPUT

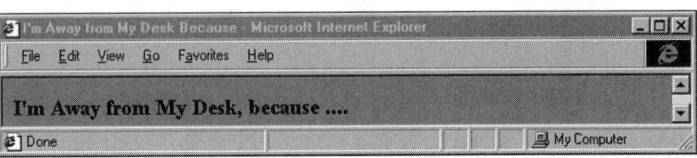

FIGURE 11.12

The top frame in the frameset.

Next, you'll create the left frame in the frameset. On real Web sites, typically this is the frame used for text or image navigation links that take your visitors to several different key pages on your site. For example, a personal site might have a navigation bar that takes its visitors to a home page, a guest book, a links page, and other sections of interest. A corporate or business site could contain links for products, customer support, frequently asked questions, employment opportunities, and so on.

The contents page in the following example works exactly the same way that a real-world navigation bar does. When the appropriate link is selected, it displays one of the six pages in the main frame of the frameset. The contents page contains links to six pages, reason1.html through reason6.html, which you'll create next.

After you enter the following code into a new page, save it to your hard drive in the same directory as the first page and name it choice.html:

INPUT

```
<html>
<head>
<title>Reason I'm Out</title>
</head>
<body bgcolor="#006699" text="#ffcc66" link="#ffffff" vlink="#66ccff"
alink="#ff6666">
<p>Select a reason:</p>
<hr />
▼      <p><a href="reason1.html">Reason 1</a></p>
```

▼
```
      <p><a href="reason2.html">Reason 2</a></p>
      <p><a href="reason3.html">Reason 3</a></p>
      <p><a href="reason4.html">Reason 4</a></p>
      <p><a href="reason5.html">Reason 5</a></p>
      <p><a href="reason6.html">Reason 6</a></p>
      </body>
      </html>
```

Your page should look as shown in Figure 11.13 when you open it in a browser.

OUTPUT

FIGURE 11.13

The left frame in the frameset.

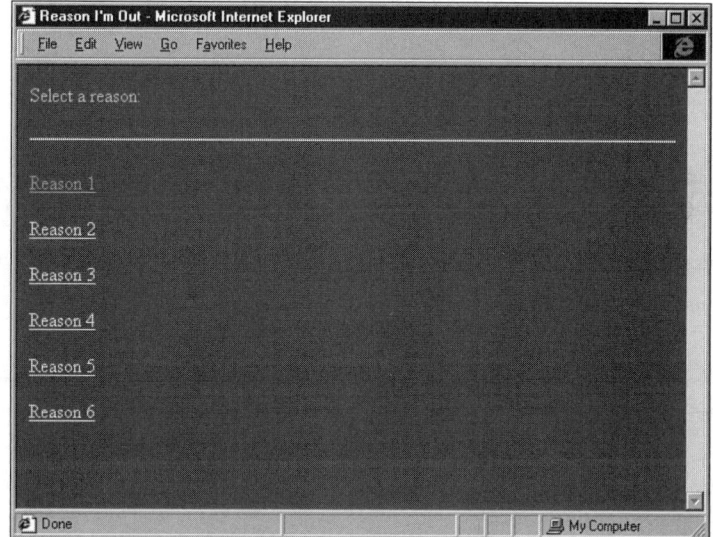

Now you need to create the six pages that will appear in the main frame when the visitor selects one of the links in the contents frame. The main frame is designed to display pages that normally you would display in a full browser window. However, if you're going to display your pages in a frameset that has a left navigation bar, you'll have to account for the reduced size of the frame in your design.

To keep the page examples relatively easy, I've given them all the same basic appearance. This means that the code for all of these pages is pretty much the same. The only items that change from page to page are the following:

- The title of the page.
- The image that appears on each page: uhoh.jpg, flirty.jpg, grumpy.jpg, happy.jpg, scared.jpg, and duh.jpg. All of these images are available on the Web support site for this book at http://www.tywebpub.com/.
▼
- The text that describes what each image means.

▼   To create the first of the six pages that will appear in the main frame, type the following
    code into a new page and save it as reason1.html:

INPUT
```
<html>
<head>
<title>Reason 1 - Forgot My Lunch</title>
</head>
<body bgcolor="#ffffff">
<h2><img src="uhoh.jpg" width="275" height="275" align="left">I forgot
my lunch at home.</h2>
</body>
</html>
```

Figure 11.14 shows what this page should look like in Internet Explorer.

OUTPUT

FIGURE 11.14

*The first of the six
pages that appear in
the main frame.*

You code the remaining five pages for the main frame similarly. Modify the code you
just created to build the second of the six main pages. The only differences from the previous code (reason1.html) are shown with a gray background. Save the new page as
reason2.html. The complete code appears as follows:

```
<html>
<head>
<title>Reason 2 - By the Water Cooler</title>
</head>
<body bgcolor="#ffffff">
<h2><img src="flirty.jpg" width="275" height="275" align="left">I'm flirting by
the water cooler.</h2>
```

▼
```
</body>
</html>
```

For the third page, modify the code again and save it as reason3.html. The complete code appears as follows:

```
<html>
<head>
<title>Reason 3 - Don't Ask!</title>
</head>
<body bgcolor="#ffffff">
<h2><img src="grumpy.jpg" width="275" height="275" align="left">None of
  your business!</h2>
</body>
</html>
```

Here's the fourth page (reason4.html):

```
<head>
<title>Reason 4 - Out to Lunch</title>
</head>
<body bgcolor="#ffffff">
<h2><img src="happy.jpg" width="275" height="275" align="left">I'm out
  to lunch.</h2>
</body>
</html>
```

The fifth page (reason5.html) looks like the following:

```
<head>
<title>Reason 5 - Boss's Office</title>
</head>
<body bgcolor="#ffffff">
<h2><img src="scared.jpg" width="275" height="275" align="left">The boss
  called me into his office.</h2>
</body>
</html>
```

The last main page (reason6.html) appears as follows:

```
<head>
<title>Reason 6 - I Don't Work Here Anymore</title>
</head>
<body bgcolor="#ffffff">
<h2><img src="duh.jpg" width="275" height="275" align="left">I just
  got fired.</h2>
</body>
</html>
```

11

Now you have the six pages that will appear in the main frame of the frameset. You're
▲ finally ready to build the frameset itself.

Exercise 11.3: Combining `rows` and `cols`

To remind you of the basic layout of the frameset that you'll create, Figure 11.15 is another look at the complete page. It provides a simple example of how you can combine framesets to create complex designs.

FIGURE 11.15

The frameset with three frames: top, left, and main.

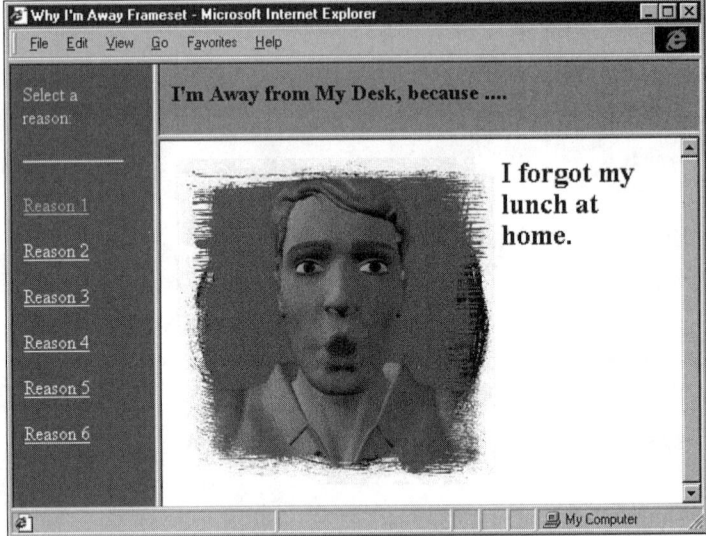

Tip

When you're designing complex frame layouts, a *storyboard* is an invaluable tool. It helps you block out the structure of a frameset, and it can be invaluable when you're adding hyperlinks (as you'll see in Exercise 11.5, "Using Named Frames and Hyperlinks").

In Figure 11.15, the right section of the screen is split into two horizontal frames, and the third frame at the left of the page spans the entire height of the screen. To create a frameset document that describes this layout, open your text editor and enter the following basic HTML structural details:

```
<html>
<head>
<title>Why I'm Away Frameset</title>
</head>
<frameset>
</frameset>
</html>
```

▼ Next, you must decide whether you need to use a `rows` or `cols` attribute in your base `<frameset>`. Look at your storyboard—in this case Figure 11.15—and work out whether any frame areas extend right across the screen or from the top to the bottom. If any frames extend from the top to the bottom, as in this example, you need to start with a `cols` frameset; otherwise, you need to start with a `rows` frameset. On the other hand, if no frames extend completely across the screen either vertically or horizontally, you should start with a `cols` frameset.

To put it more simply, here are three easy-to-remember rules:

- Left to right, use `rows`
- Top to bottom, use `cols`
- Can't decide, use `cols`

Note

> The reasoning behind the use of the "Left to right, use `rows`" rule relates to how frames-compatible browsers create frames. Each separate `<frameset>` definition can split the screen (or a frame) either vertically or horizontally, but not both ways. For this reason, you need to define your framesets in a logical order to ensure that you achieve the layout you want.

11

In Figure 11.15, the left frame extends across the screen from top to bottom. As a result, you need to start with a `cols` frameset by using the rules mentioned previously. To define the base frameset, enter the following:

```
<frameset cols="125,*">
  <frame src="choice.html"> <!-- loads the choices page into the left frame -->
  <frame src="dummy.html"> <!-- this line is only temporary -->
</frameset>
```

Writing this code splits the screen into two sections. The first line defines a small frame at the left of the screen that is 125 pixels wide, and a large frame at the right of the screen that uses the rest of the available space.

As mentioned earlier today, the frameset document itself doesn't describe the contents of each frame. The documents indicated by the `src` attribute of the `<frame>` actually contain the text, images, and tags displayed by the frameset. You can see an example of this tag in the second and third lines of the preceding code. The second line specifies the URL of the Web page in the left frame (the `choice.html` page that you created earlier). The third line would display a Web page named `dummy.html` (if you created one, that is),
▲ but we're just using this as a placeholder for the next exercise.

Exercise 11.4: Nesting Framesets

The next step in the process is to split the right frame area into two horizontal frames. You achieve this effect by placing a second `<frameset>` block inside the base `<frameset>` block. When one `<frameset>` block is nested inside another, the nested block must replace one of the `<frame>` tags in the outside frameset. In this case, you'll replace the line that loads the temporary `dummy.html` page (which doesn't really exist).

To split the right frame into two frame areas, you replace the dummy `<frame>` tag with an embedded `<frameset>` block. This embeds the new frameset inside the area defined for the `<frame>` tag it replaces. Inside the `<frameset>` tag for this new block, you then need to define a `rows` attribute, as shown in the complete code:

```
<html>
<head>
<title>Why I'm Away Frameset</title>
</head>
<frameset cols="125,*">
  <frame src="choice.html" <!-- this loads the choices page
into the left frame -->
  <frameset rows="60,*">        <!-- the frame for column 2 -->
    <frame src="away.html">    <!-- has been replaced -->
    <frame src="reason1.html"> <!-- with an embedded -->
  </frameset>                   <!-- frameset block -->
</frameset>
```

The embedded `rows` frameset defines two rows, the first being 60 percent of the height of the embedded frame area and the second taking up all the remaining space in the embedded frame area. In addition, two `<frame>` tags are embedded inside the `<frameset>` block to define the contents of each column. The top frame loads `away.html`, and the bottom frame loads `reason1.html`.

Note

> When used inside an embedded frameset, any percentage sizes are based on a percentage of the total area of the embedded frame, not on a percentage of the total screen.

Save the finished HTML document to your hard drive as `frameset.html`. Test it using a frames-compliant browser. Also, if you happen to have a copy of a Web browser that isn't frames-compliant, try loading the document into it. You shouldn't see anything onscreen.

Exercise 11.5: Using Named Frames and Hyperlinks

If you were to load your `frameset.html` page into a frames-compatible browser at this stage, you would see a screen similar to the one shown in Figure 11.15. Some of the text sizes and spacing might be slightly different, but the general picture would be the same.

Although it looks right, it doesn't *work* right yet. If you click any of the hyperlinks in the left frame, the frames-compatible browser will attempt to load the contents of the file you select into the left frame. What you really want it to do is to load each document into the larger right frame.

Earlier today, you learned about the `target` attribute, which loads different pages into a different browser window. To make the frameset work the way it should, you need to use a slight variation on the `target` attribute. Rather than the `target` pointing to a new window, you want it to point to one of the frames in the current frameset.

You can achieve this by first giving each frame in your frameset a frame name, or window name. To do so, include a `name` attribute inside the `<frame>` tag, which takes the following form:

```
<frame src="document URL" name="frame name">
```

Therefore, to assign a name to each of the frames in the `frameset.html` document, you add the `name` attribute to each of the `<frame>` tags. Your frameset page now looks like the following, with the additions indicated with the gray background:

```
<html>
<head>
<title>Why I'm Away Frameset</title>
</head>
<frameset cols="125,*">
  <frame src="choice.html" name="left">
  <!-- this loads the choices page into the left frame -->
  <frameset rows="60,*">          <!-- the frame for column 2 -->
    <frame src="away.html" name="top">     <!-- has been replaced -->
    <frame src="reason1.html" name="main"> <!-- with an embedded -->
  </frameset>                       <!-- frameset block -->
</frameset>
```

This source code names the left frame `"left"`, the top-right frame `"top"`, and the bottom-right frame `"main"`. Next, resave the updated `frameset.html` file, and you're just about finished with the example.

To Do

11

Exercise 11.6: Linking Documents to Individual Frames

To Do

Once you've named the frames, you have to fix the links in the choice.html page so that they load the target pages in the main frame rather than the left frame.

You might recall that the target attribute was used with the <a> tag to force a document to load into a specific window. You'll use the same attribute to control into which frame a document is loaded.

In this exercise, you want to load a page in the main (bottom-right) frame whenever you click a hyperlink in the left frame. Because you've already named the bottom-right frame "main", all you need to do is add target="main" to each tag in the choice.html document. The following snippet of HTML source code demonstrates how to make this change:

```
<p><a href="reason1.html" target="main">Reason 1</a></p>
<p><a href="reason2.html" target="main">Reason 2</a></p>
<p><a href="reason3.html" target="main">Reason 3</a></p>
<p><a href="reason4.html" target="main">Reason 4</a></p>
<p><a href="reason5.html" target="main">Reason 5</a></p>
<p><a href="reason6.html" target="main">Reason 6</a></p>
```

Alternatively, you could use the <base target="*value*"> tag because every tag in the choice.html document points to the same frame. In this case, you don't need to include target="main" inside each <a> tag. Instead, place the following inside the <head>...</head> block of the document:

```
<base target="main">
```

With all the changes and new documents created, now you should be able to load frameset.html into your frames-compatible browser and view all your HTML reference documents by selecting from the choices in the left frame.

Tip

After you get all your links working properly, you might need to go back and adjust the size of the rows and columns as defined in the <frameset> tags to get the layout exactly right. Remember, the final appearance of a frameset is still determined by the size of the screen and the visitor's operating system.

Exercise 11.7: Adding Your noframes Content

Although you have a frameset that works perfectly now, there's another feature you need to add to it. Remember, some people who visit your frames page won't be using frames-compatible browsers. The following addition to the frameset page creates some content that they'll see when they open the frameset.

Once again, open the `frameset.html` page. At this point, your code looks like the following:

```
<html>
<head>
<title>Why I'm Away Frameset</title>
</head>
<frameset cols="125,*">
  <frame src="choice.html" name="left">
  <!-- this loads the choices page into the left frame -->
  <frameset rows="60,*">        <!-- the frame for column 2 -->
    <frame src="away.html" name="top">    <!-- has been replaced -->
    <frame src="reason1.html" name="main"> <!-- with an embedded -->
  </frameset>                    <!-- frameset block -->
</frameset>
</html>
```

Immediately after the last `</frameset>` tag and before the final `</html>` tag, insert the following `<noframes>`...`</noframes>` element and content:

```
<noframes>
   <body bgcolor="#ffffff">
<h1>I'm Away from My Desk, because ...</h1>
<ul>
  <li>Reason 1 -
  <a href="reason1.html">I forgot my lunch at home.</a></li>
  <li>Reason 2 -
  <a href="reason2.html">I'm flirting by the water cooler.</a></li>
  <li>Reason 3 - <a href="reason3.html">None of your business.</a></li>
  <li>Reason 4 - <a href="reason4.html">I'm out to lunch.</a></li>
  <li>Reason 5 -
  <a href="reason5.html">The boss just called me in his office.</a></li>
  <li>Reason 6 - <a href="reason6.html">I just got fired.</a></li>
</ul>
</body>
</noframes>
```

When a user who isn't using a frames-compatible browser navigates to the frameset, she'll see the page that's similar to the one shown in Figure 11.16.

▼

11

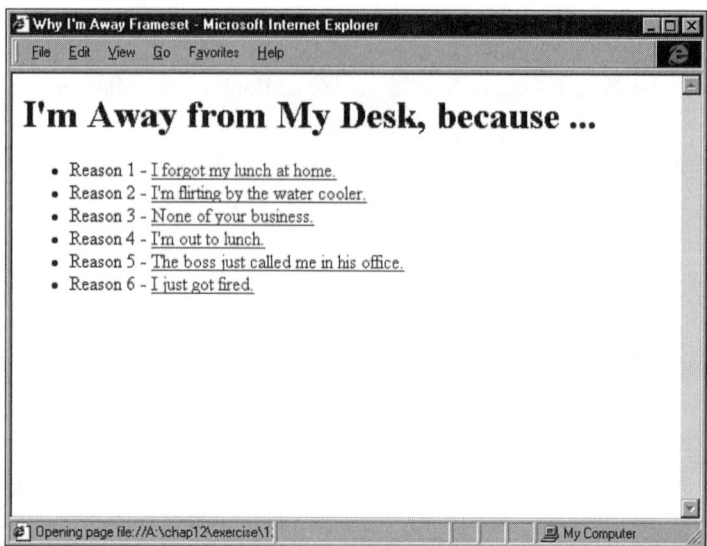

FIGURE 11.16

*This page appears
when users view the
frameset with a
browser that isn't
frames-compatible.*

Magic target Names

Now that you've learned what the `target` attribute does in a frameset, you should know
that there are some special target names you can apply to a frameset.

You can assign four special values to a `target` attribute, two of which (`_blank` and
`_self`) you've already encountered. Netscape calls these values Magic `target` names.
They're case sensitive. If you enter a magic target name in anything other than lowercase, the link will attempt to display the document in a window with that name, creating
a new window if necessary. Table 11.2 lists the Magic `target` names and describes their
use.

TABLE 11.2 Magic *target* Names

target *Name*	*Description*
target="_blank"	Forces the document referenced by the `<a>` tag to be loaded into a new unnamed window.
target="_self"	Causes the document referenced by the `<a>` tag to be loaded into the window or frame that held the `<a>` tag. This can be useful if the `<base>` tag sets the target to another frame but a specific link needs to load in the current frame.
target="_parent"	Forces the link to load into the `<frameset>` parent of the current document. If the current document has no parent, however, `target="_self"` will be used.

TABLE 11.2 continued

target *Name*	*Description*
target="_top"	Forces the link to load into the full Web browser window, replacing the current <frameset> entirely. If the current document is already at the top, however, target="_self" will be used. More often than not, when you create links to other sites on the Web, you don't want them to open within your frameset. Adding target="_top" to the link will prevent this from occurring.

Floating Frames

With Internet Explorer 3.0, Microsoft introduced a novel variation on frames: floating frames. This concept, which is a part of HTML 4.0, is somewhat different from the original frames idea that was introduced in Netscape.

Floating frames have their advantages and disadvantages. One advantage is that you can position a floating frame anywhere on a Web page, just as you can with an image, a table, or any other Web page element. This offers a lot of layout possibilities that you can't get with the standard framesets you've learned about today.

Note

The authors of the HTML 4.0 frames specification have included floating frames, with some hesitation. According to the specification, you can use the <object> tag to achieve the same effect as floating frames, so the inclusion of this type of frame is questionable. Still, the tag is included in the HTML 4.0 specification, and all versions of Internet Explorer since version 3, Netscape 6, and Opera 5 all support it. Learning to use floating frames is worthwhile.

There are precautions you need to follow when using floating frames, however. First, Internet Explorer 3.0 and later releases appear to be the only browsers that support them at the present time.

Before you design pages that include floating frames, you should be aware of another caveat. Standard framesets enable you to specify alternate content that can be viewed when someone without a frames-compatible browser navigates to a frameset. Unfortunately, you don't have this option with the <iframe> element. If you include a floating frame on your Web page and a user navigates to it with a browser that doesn't support them, she'll see absolutely nothing at all in the area where the frame should be. Therefore, you might not want to use floating frames unless you're certain that your entire audience will be using Internet Explorer 3.0 or later.

11

With that warning out of the way, here's a brief runthrough of how to create floating frames. First, you define them by using the `<iframe>` tag. Like images, these frames appear inline in the middle of the body of an HTML document (hence the `i` in `<iframe>`). The `<iframe>` tag enables you to insert an HTML document in a frame anywhere in another HTML document.

Table 11.3 shows how `<iframe>` takes the key attributes—all of which, except for those indicated as Internet Explorer extensions, appear in HTML 4.0.

TABLE 11.3   Key Attributes

Attribute	Description
width	Specifies the width, in pixels, of the floating frame that will hold the HTML document.
height	Specifies the height, in pixels, of the floating frame that will hold the HTML document.
src	Specifies the URL of the HTML document to be displayed in the frame.
name	Specifies the name of the frame for the purpose of linking and targeting.
frameborder	Indicates whether the frame should display a border. A value of 1 indicates the presence of a border, and a value of 0 indicates no border should be displayed.
marginwidth	Specifies the width of the margin, in pixels.
marginheight	Specifies the height, in pixels, of the margin.
noresize	Indicates that the frame should not be resizable by the user (Internet Explorer extension).
scrolling	As with the `<frame>` tag, indicates whether the inline frame should include scrollbars. (This attribute can take the values yes, no, or auto; the default is auto.)
vspace	Specifies the height of the margin (Internet Explorer extension).
hspace	Specifies the width of the margin (Internet Explorer extension).
align	As with the `<img>` tag, specifies the positioning of the frame with respect to the text line in which it occurs. Possible values include left, middle, right, top, and bottom, which is the default value. absbottom, absmiddle, baseline, and texttop are available as Internet Explorer extensions.

Because you know how to use both regular frames and inline images, using the `<iframe>` tag is fairly easy. The following code displays one way to use the Away from My Desk pages in conjunction with a floating frame. In this example, you begin by creating a page with a red background. The links that the user clicks appear on a single line, centered above the floating frame. For clarity, I've placed each of the links on a separate line of code.

Following the links (which target the floating frame named `"reason"`), the code for the floating frame appears within a centered `<div>` element. As the following code shows, the floating frame will be centered on the page and will measure 450 pixels wide by 315 pixels high:

INPUT

```html
<html>
<head>
<title>I'm Away From My Desk</title>
</head>
<body bgcolor="#ffcc99">
<h2>I'm away from my desk because ...</h2>
<p align="center">
    <a href="reason1.html" target="reason">Reason 1</a> |
    <a href="reason2.html" target="reason">Reason 2</a> |
    <a href="reason3.html" target="reason">Reason 3</a> |
    <a href="reason4.html" target="reason">Reason 4</a> |
    <a href="reason5.html" target="reason">Reason 5</a> |
    <a href="reason6.html" target="reason">Reason 6</a> </p>
<div align="center">
<iframe name="reason"
    src="reason1.html"
    width="450"
    height="315">
</div>
</body>
</html>
```

Figure 11.17 shows the result.

11

OUTPUT

FIGURE 11.17

An inline (or floating) frame.

Summary

If your head is hurting after today, you're probably not alone. Although the basic concepts behind the use of frames are relatively straightforward, their implementation is somewhat harder to come to grips with. As a result, the best way to learn about frames is by experimenting with them.

Today, you learned how to link a document to a new or existing window. In addition, you learned how to create framesets and link them together by using the tags listed in Table 11.4.

TABLE 11.4   New Tags Discussed on Day 11

Tag	Attribute	Description
`<base target="window">`		Sets the global link window for a document.
`<frameset>`		Defines the basic structure of a frameset.
	`cols`	Defines the number of frame columns and their width in a frameset.
	`rows`	Defines the number of frame rows and their height in a frameset.
	`frameborder`	Indicates whether the frameset displays borders between frames.
	`bordercolor`	Defines the color of borders in a frameset.
`<frame>`		Defines the contents of a frame within a frameset.
	`src`	Indicates the URL of the document to be displayed inside the frame.
	`marginwidth`	Indicates the size in pixels of the margin on each side of a frame.
	`marginheight`	Indicates the size in pixels of the margin above and below the contents of a frame.
	`scrolling`	Enables or disables the display of scrollbars for a frame. Values are yes, no, and auto.
	`noresize`	Prevents the users from resizing frames.
	`frameborder`	Indicates whether the frameset displays borders between frames.
	`bordercolor`	Defines the color of borders in a frameset.
	`longdesc`	Specifies a URL that provides a longer description of the contents of the frameset. Used with nonvisual browsers.
	`name`	Assigns a name to the frame, for targeting purposes.

TABLE 11.4 continued

Tag	Attribute	Description
`<iframe>`		Defines an inline or floating frame.
	`src`	Indicates the URL of the document to be displayed in the frame.
	`name`	Indicates the name of the frame for the purpose of linking and targeting.
	`width`	Indicates the width of the frame in pixels.
	`height`	Indicates the height of the frame in pixels.
	`marginwidth`	Indicates the width of the margin in pixels.
	`marginheight`	Indicates the height of the margin in pixels.
	`scrolling`	Enables or disables the display of scrollbars in the frame. Values are `yes`, `no`, and `auto`.
	`frameborder`	Enables or disables the display of a border around the frame. Values are `1` or `0`.
	`vspace`	Indicates the height of the margin in pixels.
	`hspace`	Indicates the width of the margin in pixels.
	`align`	Specifies the alignment of the frame relative to the current line of text. Values are `left`, `right`, `middle`, `top`, and `bottom` (also `absbottom`, `absmiddle`, `texttop`, and `baseline` in Internet Explorer).
`<noframes>`		Defines text to be displayed by Web browsers that don't support the use of frames.

11

Workshop

As if you haven't had enough already, here's a refresher course of questions, quizzes, and exercises that will help you remember some of the most important points you learned today.

Q&A

Q Is there any limit to how many levels of `<frameset>` tags I can nest within a single screen?

A No, there isn't a limit. Practically speaking, however, the available window space starts to become too small to be usable when you get below about four levels.

Q What would happen if I included a reference to a frameset document within a `<frame>` tag?

A Netscape handles such a reference correctly, by treating the nested frameset document as a nested `<frameset>`. In fact, this technique is used regularly to reduce the complexity of nested frames.

One limitation does exist, however. You cannot include a reference to the current frameset document in one of its own frames. This situation, called recursion, causes an infinite loop. Netscape Communicator has included built-in protection to guard against this type of referencing.

Quiz

1. What are the differences between a *frameset document*, a *frameset*, a *frame*, and a *page*?

2. When you create links to pages that are supposed to load into a frameset, what attribute makes the pages appear in the right frame? (Hint: it applies to the `<a>` element.)

3. When a Web page includes the `<frameset>` element, what element cannot be used at the beginning of the HTML document?

4. What two attributes of the `<frameset>` tag divide the browser window into multiple sections?

5. What attribute of the `<frame>` tag defines the HTML document that first loads into a frameset?

Quiz Answers

1. A *frameset document* is the HTML document that contains the definition of the frameset. A *frameset* is the portion of the frameset document that is defined by the `<frameset>` tag, which instructs the browser to divide the window into multiple sections. A *frame* is one of the sections, or windows, within a frameset. The *page* is the Web document that loads within a frame.

2. The `target` attribute of the `<a>` tag directs linked pages to load into the appropriate frame.

3. When a Web page includes the `<frameset>` element, it cannot include the `<body>` element at the beginning of the page. They're mutually exclusive.

4. The `cols` and `rows` attributes of the `<frameset>` tag divide the browser window into multiple frames.

5. The `src` attribute of the `<frame>` tag defines the HTML document that first loads into the frameset.

Exercises

1. Create a frameset that divides the browser window into three sections, as follows:

   - The left section of the frameset will be a column that spans the entire height of the browser window and will take up one-third of the width of the browser window. Name this frame `contents`.

   - Divide the right section of the frameset into two rows, each taking half the height of the browser window. Name the top section `top` and the bottom section `bottom`.

2. For the preceding frameset, create a page that you will use for a table of contents in the left frame. Create two links on this page, one that loads a page in the top frame and another that loads a page in the bottom frame.

11

DAY 12

XHTML and Style Sheets

In the last five days, you've seen several references to HTML tags as "deprecated in HTML 4.0 in favor of *style sheets*." Well, it's time to solve this style sheet mystery and show you the current state of the art in Web development. Today, you'll look at the World Wide Web Consortium's approach to formatting and design.

As you learned on Day 3, "An Introduction to HTML," HTML is a markup language that describes the structure of a page, not the layout. It was never intended to describe the way a page looks (specifying fonts, colors, and spacing); it was intended only to describe the elements that make up that page (headings, text, images, and so on). The extensions to the original HTML tags (<font>, <color>, <margin>, and so on) have enabled Web authors to go beyond the original purpose of the language.

To bring back the structure of HTML and still give authors the design control they have been seeking, the World Wide Web Consortium has introduced *Cascading Style Sheets* (or CSS) and XHTML (eXtensible HyperText Markup Language).

Today you'll learn the following:

- The differences between HTML and XHTML
- The concept behind Cascading Style Sheets
- A brief history of style sheets
- How to create and implement external, embedded, and inline styles
- Commonly used style sheet properties and values
- How to control page layout, fonts, and colors with CSS properties

What Is XHTML, and Why Use It?

The World Wide Web Consortium (W3C) calls XHTML "a reformulation of HTML 4.0 as an XML 1.0 application." I call it good news for new Web authors. These days, Web usage goes beyond the world of Web browsers running on desktop computers. There are now cellular phones and handheld organizers that provide Web access, and soon you'll find Web browsers built into an even greater variety of devices. It's no longer sufficient to build Web sites that just work in Netscape and Internet Explorer. The XHTML standard requires documents to adhere to strict structural rules so that applications will be able to read them. This will make life easier for users, who won't have as much badly written markup to deal with, as well as for publishers, who will have one set of documented rules to follow.

The <DOCTYPE> Identifier

You'll remember that all HTML pages must include certain elements—<html>, <head>, <body>—and their ending tags, as in the following example:

```
<html>
<head>
<title>Basic HTML Pages</title></head>
<body>
The simplest HTML pages contain 3 tags.
</body>
</html>
```

XHTML adds one more required element: the <DOCTYPE> identifier. This tag indicates to the XML parser what type of document it's parsing. In the XHTML 1.0 world, it indicates whether the document adheres to the transitional, strict, or frameset DTD.

- Use the transitional version of the <DOCTYPE> tag when your document uses a style sheet to perform most document formatting. However, include some HTML formatting attributes, such as color and size, that enable the document to be viewed by older browsers:

```
<!DOCTYPE html PUBLIC "-//W3C//DTD XHTML 1.0 Transitional//EN"
 "http://www.w3.org/TR/xhtml1/DTD/transitional.dtd">
<html>...</html>
```

- Use the strict version of the <DOCTYPE> tag when your document uses a style sheet to perform all document formatting. Only a browser that supports Cascading Style Sheets, such as Internet Explorer 3 (and up) and Netscape Navigator 4 (and up), will be able to view this type of document

```
<!DOCTYPE html PUBLIC "-//W3C//DTD XHTML 1.0 Strict//EN"
 "http://www.w3.org/TR/xhtml1/DTD/strict.dtd">
<html>...</html>
```

- Use the frameset version of the <DOCTYPE> tag when your document uses a frameset:

```
<!DOCTYPE html PUBLIC "-//W3C//DTD XHTML 1.0 Frameset//EN"
 "http://www.w3.org/TR/xhtml1/DTD/frameset.dtd">
<html>...</html>
```

Note

The examples and exercises in this book comply with the transitional XHTML standard.

XHTML Syntax

HTML is a very forgiving markup language. For example, it knows that although you forgot to close your <li> (list item) tag within an <ol> (ordered, or numbered list), you wanted that tag to close when you added the next one. In HTML, the following three examples are all the same, although only the first one uses the correct syntax:

12

```
<ol>
<li start="3">One ring-y, ding-y</li>
<li>Two ring-y, ding-ys</li>
</ol>

<OL>
<LI START="3">One ring-y, ding-y
<LI>Two ring-y, ding-ys</LI>
</OL>

<ol>
<Li start="3">One ring-y, ding-y</Li>
<LI>Two ring-ys, ding-ys</li>
</Ol>
```

In XHTML, on the other hand, all these examples are different. You must follow these guidelines to create valid XHTML documents:

- **Use lowercase tags and attributes**. In XHTML, `<LI>`, `<li>`, and `<Li>` are all separate tags that should be treated differently. You should write all HTML tags and attributes in lowercase letters to avoid confusing document viewers. This is probably the most significant change from HTML. Many people prefer using uppercase tags, and many HTML authoring tools produce tags in uppercase. XML tags are case sensitive, so when the XHTML 1.0 specification was written, they had to choose upper- or lowercase for all of the tags. They picked lowercase.

- **Place attribute values in quotes**. Make sure that you enclose all of your attribute values in quotes, regardless of the type of value associated with the attribute.

- **Terminate all nonempty elements**. As mentioned earlier, in HTML you could forget to close a tag and the browser would still be able to render your document correctly. XHTML requires you to close *all* tags. So how do you close the `<br>` (line break) and `<hr>` (horizontal rule) tags that don't have a closing tag? Just include the closing slash (/) to the tag, as shown in the following example:

```
<!DOCTYPE html PUBLIC "-//W3C//DTD XHTML 1.0 Strict//EN"
  "http://www.w3.org/TR/xhtml1/DTD/strict.dtd">
<html>
<head>
<title>Line Breaks and Horizontal Rules</title></head>
<body>
<hr />                  <!-- Opens and closes the hr tag -->
The first line<br />    <!-- Opens and closes the br tag -->
The second line
<hr />                  <!-- Opens and closes the hr tag -->
</body>
</html>
```

Note

As you might have noticed, comments in XHTML 1.0 (and in XML) are identical to those in HTML. You don't need to add a slash to close the comment properly like you do with regular tags.

- **Use nested tags and don't overlap**. HTML didn't make a distinction between following the two examples, but XHMTL does. XHTML requires you to close nested tags in the order that you opened them. The first example shows the correct XHTML syntax; the second is incorrect:

```
<b>This text is bold.<i>This is bold and italicized.</i></b><i>This is
just italicized.</i>

<b>This text is bold.<i>This is bold and italicized.</b>This is just
italicized.</i>
```

- **Include values for all attributes.** In HTML, many attributes simply acted as flags and did not require a value to be associated with them. For example, you could use the `noshade` attribute with the `<hr>` tag without any value. XHTML requires that all attributes have values. If the attribute is a flag, you simply supply the name of the attribute as the value. In the case of the `noshade` attribute, you'd specify it as `noshade="noshade"`.

I'd like to talk briefly about what's next in the world of structured markup—XHTML 1.1. Currently it's a W3C working draft and isn't an approved standard yet, but it's likely that it will be adopted with few changes.

As you might guess from the version number, XHTML 1.1 isn't radically different from XHTML 1.0. In fact, nothing new is going to be added to XHTML 1.1. Instead, the W3C is removing all of the deprecated markup elements from the standard that have been superseded by Cascading Style Sheet properties.

So things like the center tag, the align attribute of the heading tags, and the font tag will be gone, once and for all. Unfortunately, actually enforcing this standard in a browser would wreck most of the pages currently on the Web. Even if this working draft is adopted, it's unlikely that the browser makers will support it wholeheartedly. They might add support for files specifically defined as XHTML 1.1-compliant, but they'll have to maintain support for the legacy HTML files forever.

If you're interested in reading more about XHTML 1.1, check out http://www.w3.org/TR/xhtml11/.

12

The Concept of Style Sheets

Now that you know how to write your HTML documents using the proper syntax for XHTML, and you know how to use the `<DOCTYPE>` identifier to describe the type of HTML document you are authoring, understanding style sheets should be simple. First, the author creates a standard Web page using standard HTML tags (the same as in the past). This standard Web page is designed so it can be displayed properly in browsers that don't support style sheets. The following is a simple example:

```
<!DOCTYPE html PUBLIC "-//W3C//DTD XHTML 1.0 Strict//EN"
 "http://www.w3.org/TR/xhtml1/DTD/strict.dtd">
<html>
<head>
<title>Using Style Sheets</title></head>
<body>
<h1> Using Style Sheets </h1>
<p> In this simple example, the heading will be blue, and the
   paragraph will be rendered in a different font. </p>
</body>
</html>
```

The Web page in the preceding example doesn't contain any attributes that define its appearance. As the code suggests, the author wants a blue heading and a different font for the paragraphs. To accomplish this, the author creates *style rules* that format the content on the Web page in the manner that he or she chooses.

Style rules combine HTML tags (such as h1 or p) with properties (such as color: blue) to format each HTML tag. In the case of style sheets, an HTML tag is used as a *selector*. The property and value of the selector are combined into what is called a *declaration*. For example, color: blue specifies the color as the property and blue as the value.

Style rules can define the layout of a tag, as well as other typographic and design properties. The following are some examples of style rules:

```
h1 { color: blue }
p { font-family: Arial, Helvetica, sans-serif; color: black }
```

In the first line of the preceding example, the style rule renders the heading h1 on the page in blue text. In the second line, all paragraph text on the page (p tag) will be rendered in Arial, Helvetica, or another sans-serif font and will be colored black.

Now that the Web author has designed the page content (the standard Web page) and the style rules that define its appearance, the author attaches the style rules to the standard HTML document using one of three methods: an external style sheet, an embedded style sheet (as the following example shows), or an inline style. You'll learn more about these approaches later today in "Approaches to Style Sheets."

The following example shows how our simple HTML example is formatted with an embedded style sheet:

```
<!DOCTYPE html PUBLIC "-//W3C//DTD XHTML 1.0 Strict//EN"
 "http://www.w3.org/TR/xhtml1/DTD/strict.dtd">
<html>
<head>
<title>Using Style Sheets</title>
<style type="text/css">
```

```
<!--
h1 { color: blue }
p { font-family: Arial, Helvetica, sans-serif; color: black }
-->
</style>
</head>
<body>
<h1>Using Style Sheets</h1>
<p> In this simple example, the heading will be blue, and the
    paragraph will be rendered in a different font. </p>
</body>
</html>
```

The preceding example contains an embedded style sheet—the author has separated the styles from the standard HTML document. The code that defines the appearance of the Web page appears within the opening <style> tag and closing </style> tag. Browsers that don't support style sheets can still render the document as a standard HTML document, while those that do support style sheets render the content on the page as defined by the style rules.

Some Background on Style Sheets

The first implementation of Cascading Style Sheets, known as CSS1, enables you to specify everything from typefaces for different HTML elements to font colors, background colors and graphics, margins, spacing, type style, and much more. Browsers that support this type of style sheet, which include Netscape Navigator 4 and later and Internet Explorer 4 and later, apply the style definitions to the final appearance of the document.

The next generation of style sheets, CSS2, became a formal recommendation in May 1998. Many CSS2 tags are supported in the latest versions of both Internet Explorer and Netscape Navigator. In the future, style sheets will enable you to accomplish even more exciting things on the Web. With CSS2, XHTML, and compliant browsers, you'll be able to generate Web pages that target different types of media. For example, you'll be able to design aural style sheets that speak page elements to a user while using spatial audio and surround-sound properties. You'll also be able to split Web pages into multiple pages, much as you do in a word processor or page layout program. You'll be able to control page breaks, widows, orphans... Exciting stuff indeed!

This brings up yet another advantage to style sheet technology. Style sheets will allow Web documents to be viewed in nonstandard ways, such as through audio players for the visually impaired or through other means where standard browser technology is inaccessible. The standard HTML document can still be rendered in a useful way without being affected by the superfluous, and often confusing, HTML extension tags intended to provide the nonstandard layouts in a browser.

12

Just as browsers support HTML differently, cascading Style Sheets meet the same fate. Netscape has created its own alternative version of style sheets. Netscape Navigator has an alternative for layers, which positions objects on a page while still supporting the emerging standard. It also has its own JavaScript style sheets (supported in Netscape 4, but discontinued in Netscape 6) while continuing to support Cascading Style Sheets.

Because this is a new technology, it's a confusing situation. As is the case with all new technologies, however, things will settle down and the "VHS" of style sheets will emerge while the "Betamax" falls to the side. In the meantime, you need to be aware that no two browsers handle CSS technology the same way.

The remainder of this chapter will provide an introduction to style sheets and an overview of some common properties. Note that the properties you'll learn about today are only a sampling of those that are available in CSS1 and CSS2. To adequately cover this topic would double the size of this book. Still, today you'll get a basic understanding of the power of style sheet properties and values. (Further online resources are listed at the end of this day.)

The Bookworm Bookshop Revisited

Rather than continue with a bunch of theory all at once, I'll take you through some CSS properties that you'd probably use when designing a real Web page. On Day 6, "More Text Formatting with HTML," I demonstrated the usage of various tags on a page for The Bookworm Bookshop. Now you'll learn how to apply cascading style sheet properties and values to the page and give it an entirely new appearance.

To refresh your memory, here's a version of The Bookworm Bookshop Web page as it was coded before you added the fancy items at the end of Day 6:

INPUT

```
<!DOCTYPE html PUBLIC "-//W3C//DTD XHTML 1.0 Strict//EN"
  "http://www.w3.org/TR/xhtml1/DTD/strict.dtd">
<html>
<head>
<title>The Bookworm Bookshop</title>
</head>
<body>
<a name="top"><h1>The Bookworm: A Better Book Store</h1></a>
<blockquote>
"Old books are best--how tale and rhyme<br />
Float with us down the stream of time!"<br />
- Clarence Urmy, <cite>Old Songs are Best</cite>
</blockquote>
<p>The Bookworm Bookshop<br />
1345 Applewood Dr<br />
Springfield, CA 94325<br />
(415) 555-0034
</p>
```

```
<a name="contents"><h2>Contents</h2></a>
<ul>
  <li><a href="#about">About the Bookworm Bookshop</a></li>
  <li><a href ="#recent">Recent Titles</a></li>
  <li><a href ="#upcoming">Upcoming Events</a></li>
</ul>
<hr />
<a name="about"><h2>About the Bookworm Bookshop</h2></a>
<p>Since 1933, The Bookworm Bookshop has offered
rare and hard-to-find titles for the discerning reader.
The Bookworm offers:</p>
<ul>
<li>Friendly, knowledgeable, and courteous help
<li>Free coffee and juice for our customers
<li>A well-lit reading room so you can "try before you buy"
<li>Four friendly cats: Esmerelda, Catherine, Dulcinea and Beatrice
</ul>
<p>Our hours are <strong>10am to 9pm</strong> weekdays,
<strong>noon to 7</strong> on weekends.</p>
<p><a href="#contents">Back to Contents</a> |
<a href="#top">Back to Top</a></p>
<hr>
<a name="recent"><h2>Recent Titles (as of 11-Nov-99)</h2></a>
<ul>
<li>Sandra Bellweather, <a href="belladonna.html">
<cite>Belladonna</cite></a>
<li>Johnathan Tin, <a href="20minmeals.html">
<cite>20-Minute Meals for One</cite></a>
<li>Maxwell Burgess, <a href="legion.html">
<cite>Legion of Thunder</cite></a>
<li>Alison Caine, <a href="banquo.html">
<cite>Banquo's Ghost</cite></a>
</ul>
<p><a href="#contents">Back to Contents</a> |
<a href="#top">Back to Top</a></p>
<hr>
<a name="upcoming"><h2>Upcoming Events</h2></a>
<ul>
<li><b>The Wednesday Evening Book Review</b> meets, appropriately, on
Wednesday evenings at 7:00 pm for coffee and a round-table discussion.
Call the Bookworm for information on joining the group and this week's
reading assignment.
<li><b>The Children's Hour</b> happens every Saturday at 1pm and
includes reading, games, and other activities. Cookies and milk are
served.
  <li><b>Carole Fenney</b> will be at the Bookworm on Friday, September
      17, to read from her book of poems <cite>Spiders in the
      Web.</cite>

  <li><b>The Bookworm will be closed</b> October 1 to remove a family
of bats that has nested in the tower. We like the company, but not
the mess they leave behind!
```

12

```
</ul>
<p><a href="#contents">Back to Contents</a> |
<a href="#top">Back to Top</a></p>
<hr>
<address>
Last Updated: 11-Nov-99<br>
WebMaster: Laura Lemay lemay@bookworm.com<br>
&#169; copyright 1999 the Bookworm<br>
</address>
</body>
</html>
```

You'll be formatting this with style sheets in today's exercise. Save the file as
bookwrm.html. Figure 12.1 shows the upper portion of this page, which is fairly repre-
sentative of the types of items that appear throughout the entire page.

OUTPUT

FIGURE 12.1

*The Bookworm
Bookshop as a stand-
alone HTML Web page.*

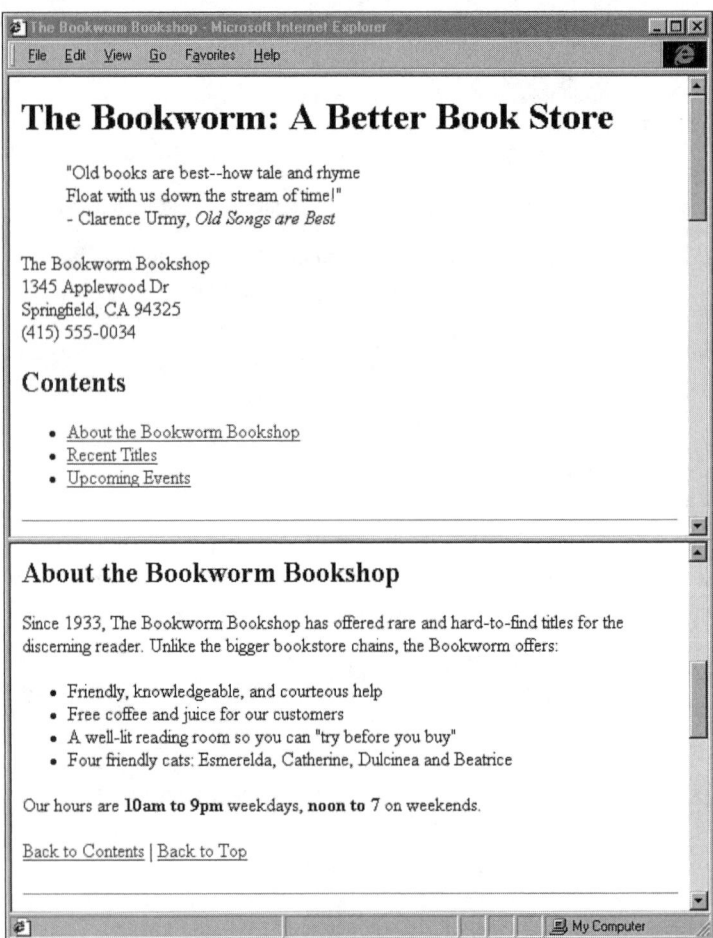

What Figure 12.1 shows is a Web page that will stand on its own in a browser that doesn't support style sheets. Granted, it's not exceptionally fancy. Perhaps we can spice it up with color, different fonts, page margins, and so on. These are the very problems that style sheets were designed to solve.

Approaches to Style Sheets

So how do you apply CSS technology to this standard Web page? There are basically three ways that you can apply CSS rules to HTML elements. The wonder of style sheets is that they're flexible. The HTML tags and attributes used to apply style rules to HTML documents don't tie authors and browser makers to a single type of style sheet.

Instead, the W3C has defined a set of tags and attributes that can be used to apply style definitions (which will be discussed later) to any document or HTML tag. These tags enable you to work with style rules in three ways: external style sheets, embedded style sheets, and inline styles. The following sections cover the first two methods. You'll become more familiar with inline styles later in the day.

External Style Sheets

External style sheets keep the style rules in a separate file, apart from the HTML Web documents. The advantage of external style sheets is that you can use one style file for many pages and then change the appearance of all the pages by making one change to the style file. By defining your styles in a single document and linking them to multiple pages, you only need to edit the style sheet to change the presentation style of all pages linked to it.

Like an HTML document, a style sheet document is nothing more than an ASCII text document with a special extension. Although a Web page is saved with an `.htm` or `.html` extension, an external style sheet is saved with a `.css` extension. It defines all the common style rules that are to be shared between your Web documents. Then, using the `<link>` tag, you can link the external style sheet to each Web page.

I'll get into the particulars of creating the `.css` file in the following exercise. For now, suppose that you have created a style sheet and saved it in the same directory as your Bookworm Bookshop Web page. You use a filename of `mystyle.css`. The following code demonstrates how you attach the external style sheet to the header of the Bookworm Bookshop Web page:

```
<!DOCTYPE html PUBLIC "-//W3C//DTD XHTML 1.0 Strict//EN"
 "http://www.w3.org/TR/xhtml1/DTD/strict.dtd">
<html>
<head>
<title>The Bookworm Bookshop</title>
```

12

```
<link rel="stylesheet" href="mystyle.css">
</head>
<body>
```

The `<link>` tag associates the external style sheet file (`mystyle.css`) with the current HTML document. By applying the same code in each page of the site, the site manager can specify a consistent style and apply it to documents created by any author in an organization.

The `rel` attribute of the `<link>` tag performs an important function. To effectively use the `<link>` tag, you need an understanding of persistent, default, and alternate styles. The following are the basics:

- *Persistent styles* are always applied regardless of users' local selections.
- *Default styles* are applied when a page is loaded, but they can be disabled by the user in favor of an alternate style.
- *Alternate styles* are provided as options for the user to choose (as opposed to the default style).

The `rel` attribute controls some of this process. When you specify `rel="stylesheet"`, as in the previous code example, it forces the use of persistent styles and applies them in your style sheet, regardless of the user's local selections.

By adding a `title` attribute, the style becomes a default style. An example of this follows:

```
<link rel="stylesheet" title="mainstyle" href="mystyle.css">
```

Changing `rel="stylesheet"` to `rel="alternate stylesheet"` creates an alternate style sheet with a different title.

In this way, you can create a persistent style that contains those definitions that have to be applied, regardless of what choices a user makes, as well as provide a default and one or more alternatives that supplement the persistent style. Unfortunately, this information is strictly theoretical at this point. No current browsers allow you to switch between the default style sheet and alternate style sheets. Until browsers do support that functionality, you might as well set up all your style sheets with the `rel` attribute set to `stylesheet`.

Exercise 12.1: Creating and Linking an External Style Sheet

▼ To Do

If you haven't already done so, reopen or create the Bookworm Bookshop Web page from Day 6 and save it as `bookwrm.html`. The original code is shown in "The Bookworm Bookshop Revisited" section earlier today. To attach an external style sheet (which you will create shortly) to the page, enter the following line of code in the document header, immediately following the page title:

▼
```
<link rel="stylesheet" href="mystyle.css">
```

The entire header looks like the following:

```
<!DOCTYPE html PUBLIC "-//W3C//DTD XHTML 1.0 Strict//EN"
 "http://www.w3.org/TR/xhtml1/DTD/strict.dtd">
<html>
<head>
<title>The Bookworm Bookshop</title>
<link rel="stylesheet" href="mystyle.css">
</head>
```

Resave the page with the new header information. Now, you have linked a style sheet to the page, but you need to create the style sheet. Unless you define a few styles in a style sheet, you won't be able to tell whether your style sheet works correctly after it is linked. So in the next part of the exercise, you'll create a second document that contains a few basic styles.

The following example might not make sense to you at this point, but you'll learn what it all means as the day progresses. To explain briefly, here is what the following code accomplishes:

- It creates a style sheet that changes the background color of a Web page to light aqua.
- The body text is rendered in Arial, Helvetica, or another sans-serif font, depending on the fonts the user has.
- The body text color will be very dark aqua.

Link colors also are changed to the following:

- Unvisited links will be magenta.
- Visited links will be deep brown.
- Active links will be red.
- When the mouse hovers over a link, the link text will be bright gold.

Create a new text document and enter the code shown in the following example. The one thing to watch out for when you enter the following code is that the style rules are enclosed in curly braces (`{}`) rather than parentheses. Also, most often you see a single space between the style rules and the opening and closing braces—for example, `h1 { color: blue }`. After you enter the following text, save the page in the same directory as your Bookworm Bookshop page. Use the filename `mystyle.css`, which is the same filename you referenced in the header of the Bookworm Bookshop Web page.

▼ The following is the code to enter:

12

▼
```
body { background-color: #ccffff; font-family: Arial, Helvetica, sans-serif;
color: #330066 }
    a:link { color: #ff00ff }
    a:visited { color: #660000 }
    a:hover { color: #ffcc00 }
    a:active { color: #ff0000 }
```

The first style rule in the preceding example specifies the background color of the Web page (light aqua, or #ccffff in this case). The text on the page will be rendered in Arial, Helvetica, or another sans-serif font that resides on the visitor's hard drive. The color of the text on the page will be deep blue (#330066):

```
body { background-color: #ccffff; font-family: Arial, Helvetica, sans-serif;
color: #330066 }
```

The next four lines of code define four pseudo-classes that format the link colors. Unvisited links (the same as the link= attribute in HTML) are formatted with the a:link pseudo-class. Visited links (HTML's vlink= attribute) are defined with the a:visited pseudo-class. Active links (the alink= attribute in HTML) are defined with a:active. The a:hover pseudo-class (which has no HTML equivalent) defines the color of the link when a pointer hovers over it:

```
a:link { color: #ff00ff }
a:visited { color: #660000 }
a:hover { color: #ffcc00 }
a:active { color: #ff0000 }
```

In just a moment, with only a few lines of code and an external style sheet, you've created a Web page with an entirely different appearance. Open the bookwrm.html page in a Web browser that supports Cascading Style Sheets, such as Internet Explorer 5.5 or Netscape Navigator 6. You should now see something that looks similar to the page in
▼   Figure 12.2.

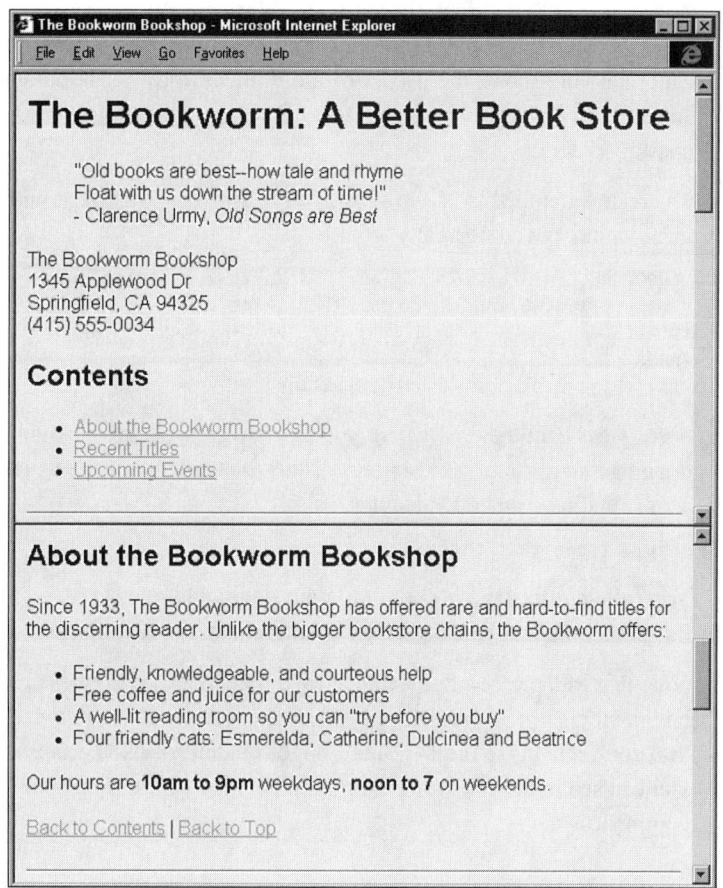

FIGURE 12.2

The Bookworm Book-shop with attached external style sheet.

12

Embedded Style Sheets

Embedded style sheets are standard HTML Web pages that have style rules included within them. Suppose that you want your home page to appear on a black background with really huge, bright text and vivid link colors. The remaining pages in your Web site are more subdued (to make it easier on your visitors' eyes) and have lighter background colors. It doesn't make much sense to make an external style sheet for one home page. (Why create two files when you can create just one?) So, you use an embedded style sheet for the home page and an external style sheet for the others.

"But wait a moment," you say. "Isn't the whole point of style sheets to keep the style rules separate?" In effect, they still are. The style rules appear in the header of the document, before your HTML content begins. The rules are still isolated from the content. The following shows the header of the Bookworm Bookshop home page as it might appear with embedded styles. In this case, you assign colors for body text, background, and link colors.

To create an embedded style sheet, you begin your Web page with the following header information as you normally would:

```
<!DOCTYPE html PUBLIC "-//W3C//DTD XHTML 1.0 Strict//EN"
 "http://www.w3.org/TR/xhtml1/DTD/strict.dtd">
<html>
<head>
<title>The Bookworm Bookshop</title>
```

Next, you begin the area where you insert your style rules, which are enclosed within opening and closing <style> tags. The type attribute of the style tag defines the page as one that uses embedded styles, as follows:

```
<style type="text/css">
```

You follow the opening style tag with your style rules. The example that follows is similar to the one that was used for the external style sheet discussed earlier today.

Note that in the case of embedded style sheets, the style rules are enclosed within comment tags (<!-- and -->). If you don't enclose them in this manner, older browsers that don't recognize the style tag might render your style rules on your Web page. As you can see in the following example, the body of the style sheet is enclosed within a comment:

```
<!--
    body { color: #000000; background-color: #ffffff }
    a:active { color: #666699 }
    a:hover { color: #3366ff }
    a:link { color: #0066ff }
    a:visited { color: #9966cc }
-->
```

You complete the header of the page by closing the style and head tags as follows:

```
</style>
</head>
```

Exercise 12.2: Creating an Embedded Style Sheet

Reopen the Bookworm Bookshop HTML Web page, which you saved as bookwrm.html. Using a different filename, such as bookback.html, save a backup copy of this file before you make the following changes. In this exercise, you'll convert the bookwrm.html into a Web page that uses embedded styles.

▼ You want to identify this Web page as one that includes embedded styles. For this, you need to modify the page header slightly. Remember that embedded style sheet code is enclosed between opening and closing `<style>` tags and that the style definitions are enclosed in curly brackets. First, remove the following line that references the external style sheet from the Web page:

```
<link rel="stylesheet" href="mystyle.css">
```

Next, edit the header so that it includes the code that defines it as using an embedded style sheet. Add the `<style>` and comment tags as shown in the following example. The new header should look like the following:

```
<!DOCTYPE html PUBLIC "-//W3C//DTD XHTML 1.0 Strict//EN"
 "http://www.w3.org/TR/xhtml1/DTD/strict.dtd">
<html>
<head>
<title>The Bookworm Bookshop</title>
<style type="text/css">
<!--
-->
</style>
</head>
```

To illustrate the styles you define in the embedded style sheet, make a slight modification to the styles you defined in the previous example. Rather than a light blue background, make it light green by changing the background color to `#ccffcc`. The text and link properties remain the same.

This time, however, the style rules go *inside* your Bookworm Bookshop HTML Web page, between the `<!--` and `-->` comment tags.

Enter the following style rules between the comment tags in your page header:

```
body { background-color: #ccffcc; font-family: Arial, Helvetica, sans-serif;
color: #330066 }
   a:link { color: #cc9900 }
   a:visited { color: #660000 }
   a:hover { color: #ffcc00 }
   a:active { color: #ff0000 }
```

In total, your page header now looks as shown in the following code example:

```
<!DOCTYPE html PUBLIC "-//W3C//DTD XHTML 1.0 Strict//EN"
 "http://www.w3.org/TR/xhtml1/DTD/strict.dtd">
<html>
<head>
<title>The Bookworm Bookshop</title>
<style type="text/css">
```
▼ `<!--`

12

```
body { background-color: #ccffcc; font-family: Arial, Helvetica,
       sans-serif; color: #330066 }
   a:link { color: #cc9900 }
   a:visited { color: #660000 }
   a:hover { color: #ffcc00 }
   a:active { color: #ff0000 }
-->
</style>
</head>
```

Resave the page as bookwrm.html and open it in your style sheet-compatible browser. The page now has a light green background. Otherwise, it looks quite the same as the external style sheet version shown in Figure 12.2.

For comparison's sake, open the same Web page in a browser that does not support Cascading Style Sheets. In Figure 12.3, you see a portion of the same page as it is rendered in NCSA Mosaic 3.0. As you can see, all the information is still there because the HTML code stands on its own. The colors and fonts that you added in the style sheet aren't rendered in this browser, however.

FIGURE 12.3

The Bookworm Book-shop page displayed in a browser that does not support Cascading Style Sheets.

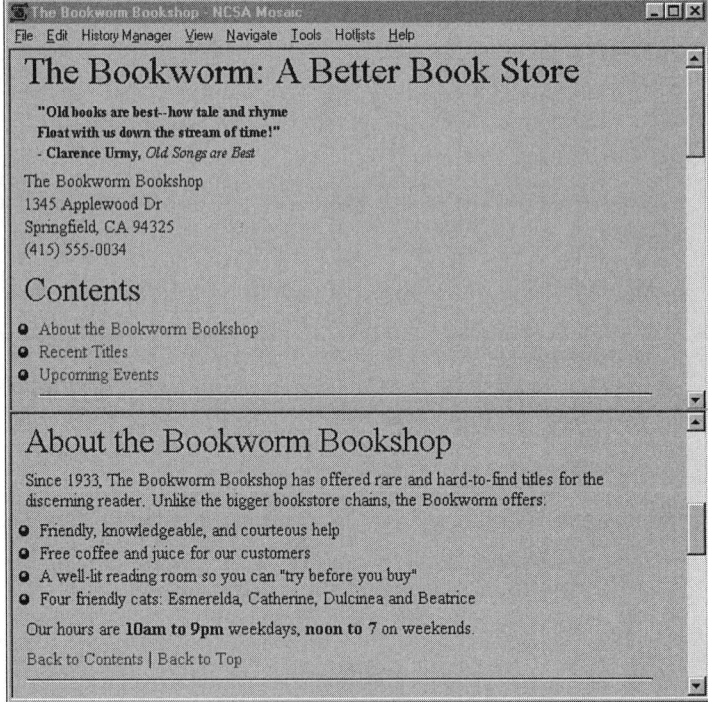

About Cascading

Just what does it mean that this particular brand of style sheets is *cascading*? Clearly, there are no cascading waterfalls involved.

Cascading refers to the capability to combine style information from more than one source. As you've learned already, you can apply style rules to a page in a variety of ways. External style sheets can be linked to one or more pages, applying the same style rules to all. Embedded style sheets apply style rules to a single page. *Inline styles*, which you'll learn about later today, apply style rules to page elements. You can combine all three approaches within a single page, if you want.

The cascading part of the picture comes into play because there is an ordered sequence to the style sheets. The closer a rule is to the HTML element it affects, the higher in precedence it is. Simply defined, here is what happens when external, embedded, and inline styles are applied to the same page:

- The styles defined in an external style sheet are applied to the page first.
- The styles defined in the embedded style sheet are applied second and override the styles in the first, where applicable.
- The inline styles override both the external and embedded style sheets where applicable.

Commonly Used Style Sheet Properties and Values

12

Now you will look at some of the main properties and how to use them. There are far too many to cover in a single section of a single day. If you need more information, you can find the complete specification of Cascading Style Sheets Level 1 (CSS1) on the Web at `http://www.w3.org/TR/REC-CSS1`. This recommendation is dated January 11, 1999.

Recommendations for CSS2 also appear on the Web at `http://www.w3.org/TR/REC-CSS2/`. The most current version of this document is dated May 12, 1998. These documents, although fairly technical, tell you precisely what each property does and what is legal and illegal to code into your pages. Also, they give several examples that help you create pages compatible with old and new browsers.

In the previous examples, you've only scratched the surface at what style rules can accomplish. CSS1 and CSS2 provide many tags that enable you to control the appearance of just about every aspect of a Web page. Unfortunately, support for CSS1 and CSS2 in real browsers lags way behind the standards, and it will probably continue to lag behind for quite some time. You can read the standards and use properties from them on your pages, but you need to test them as widely as possible to make sure that those properties are really supported.

Before I demonstrate how to use some of these properties, be forewarned that you may see some unexpected surprises and variances in each CSS-compatible browser. Always test, test, *test* to make sure you get acceptable results.

Controlling Page Layout CSS Properties

In Exercises 12.1 and 12.2, you added some simple style rules that affected the fonts and colors on your Web page. These were accomplished through the background-color, font-family, and color properties that you applied to the body of the Web page. The colors for the links were applied by first defining four pseudo-classes for the <a> tag: a:link (for the link color), a:visited (for the visited links), a:hover (for the color of the link when the mouse hovers over it), and a:active (for the active link color).

There is much more that you can do to affect how the text appears on the page as well. You can control margins and padding with a style sheet much as you can in a page layout or word processing software package. Table 12.1 highlights some of the most frequently used properties.

TABLE 12.1 Useful Page Layout Properties

Property	Description
margin-top	Sets the top margin of an element. Values are entered in numerical lengths, percentages, or auto.
margin-right	Sets the right margin of an element. Acceptable values are the same as margin-top.
margin-bottom	Sets the bottom margin of an element. Acceptable values are the same as margin-top.
margin-left	Sets the left margin of an element. Acceptable values are the same as margin-top.
margin	A shorthand property that sets margin-top, margin-right, margin-bottom, and margin-left at the same location in the style sheet. Acceptable values are expressed in numerical lengths, percentages, or auto.

TABLE 12.1   continued

Property	Description
padding-top	Sets the space between the top border and the content of an element. Values are entered in numerical lengths, percentages, or auto.
padding-right	Sets the space between the right border and the content of an element. Acceptable values are the same as padding-top.
padding-bottom	Sets the space between the bottom border and the content of an element. Acceptable values are the same as padding-top.
padding-left	Sets the space between the left border and the content of an element. Acceptable values are the same as padding-top.
padding	A shorthand property that sets padding-top, padding-right, padding-bottom, and padding-left in the same location in the style sheet. Acceptable values are expressed as numerical lengths, percentages, or auto.

NEW TERM   Margins and padding are expressed in numerical length followed by a *length unit*, a *percentage value*, or by assigning a value called auto.

Length units are expressed in relative or absolute values. Relative length units include em (the size of the relevant font), ex (the x-height of the relevant font), or px (pixels, relative to the device that the page is being viewed upon). Absolute values include pt (points), in (inches), cm (centimeters), mm (millimeters), and pc (picas).

Percentage values are always relative to another value, such as a length. You specify percentages by an optional + or - sign, immediately followed by a number, immediately followed by a percent sign.

You might notice that Table 12.1 makes mention of the term *shorthand property*. Several properties use many attributes to define their appearance. You can combine several values together with a shorthand property. For example, you can specify top, right, bottom, and left margins in a single property called margin. The same applies to the four individual padding settings in relation to the padding property.

Both margin and padding can accept> from one to four values as follows:

One value	Applies to all sides.
Two values	The first value applies to the top and bottom; and the second applies to the left and right.
Three values	The first value applies to the top; the second value applies to the left and right; and the third applies to the bottom.
Four values	Applies to the top, right, > bottom, and left, respectively.

12

Exercise 12.3: Applying Margins and Padding to a Page

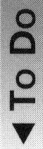

In this exercise, you'll apply some margin and padding settings to the Bookworm Bookshop page. You'll add the following style definitions to the style sheet:

- Twenty-pixel margins at the top and bottom of the page, and 30-pixel margins at the left and right of the page
- Fifteen-pixel padding at the top and bottom of each heading

To add the margin and padding settings to your Web page, add the following code to either the external style sheet (mystyle.css) or to the Web page that has the embedded style sheet properties defined within it (bookwrm.html). If you didn't save a backup copy of the Web page that uses the external style sheet, the embedded version is your only choice, so I'll continue using that page in my examples.

To accomplish this, you can use the margin shorthand property with two values to specify the top/bottom and left/right margin settings for the <body> tag and padding-top and padding-bottom properties to the <h1> and <h2> tags. A revised version of your style definitions looks as follows (I've rearranged the style definitions for the <body> tag in this example, so that you can see each CSS style rule more clearly):

```
<!--
body { background-color: #ccffcc;
       font-family: Arial, Helvetica, sans-serif;
       color: #330066;
       margin: 50px 70px }
   a:link { color: #cc9900 }
   a:visited { color: #660000 }
   a:hover { color: #ffcc00 }
   a:active { color: #ff0000 }
h1 { padding-top: 10px;
     padding-bottom: 5px }
h2 { padding-top: 5px;
     padding-bottom: 3px }
-->
```

After you save the new version of your style sheet, open it in a CSS-compatible browser and view the results. Figure 12.4 shows the new page margins and the additional padding on the upper portion of the Web page.

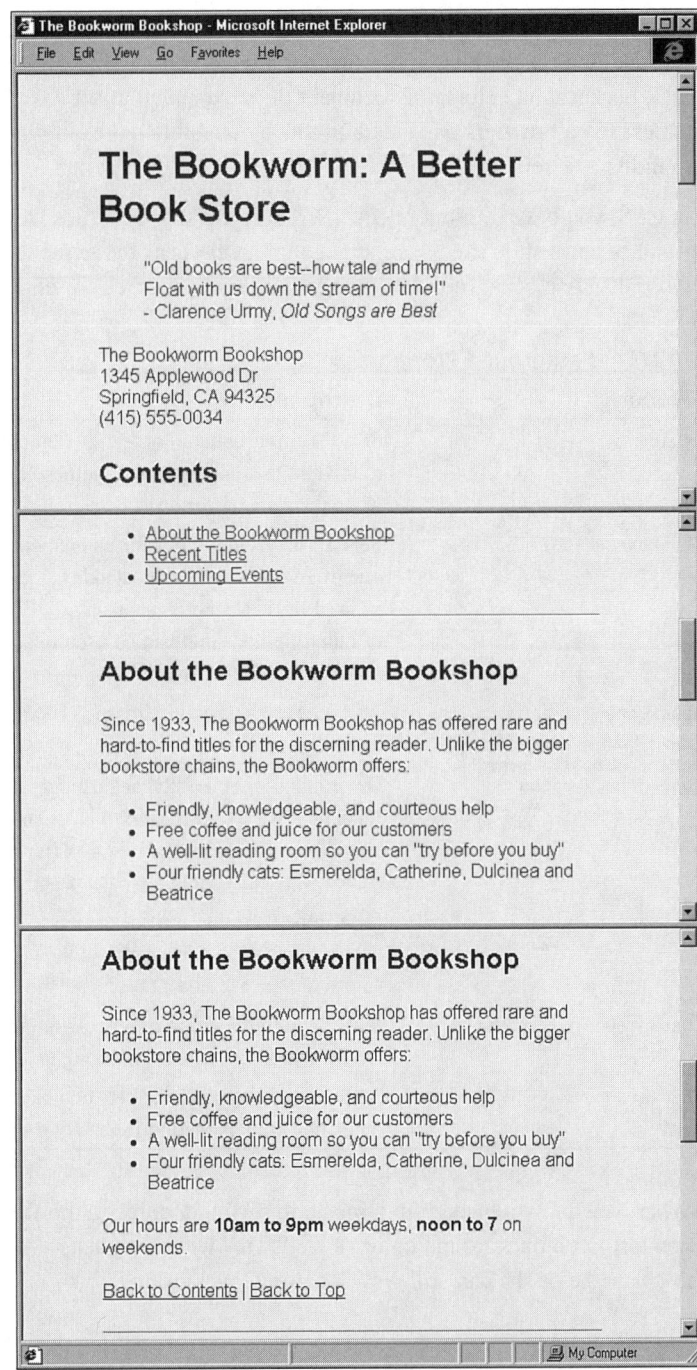

FIGURE 12.4

Margin and padding settings applied to the Bookworm Bookshop page.

12

Backgrounds, Colors, and Images

As you learned on Day 7, "Using Images, Color, and Backgrounds," you have basic control over the background appearance of a document in HTML. You can use bgcolor to set a background color of a document or background to set a background image. With tables, some browsers expanded on this by enabling page authors to apply backgrounds to individual cells in a table.

In CSS, you have even more control. There are six properties for controlling background. Also, because style sheets are applied on an element-by-element basis, you can have more than one background on a page. The six properties are outlined in Table 12.2.

TABLE 12.2   Background Properties in CSS

Property	Description
color	Sets the foreground color for an element (most often, this applies to the text that appears in an element). The color value can be one of 16 color names or one of several variations of an RGB triplet.
background-color	Sets a background color for an element. The color value can be one of 16 color names, a standard hexadecimal color specification as used in HTML, or transparent. (CSS also supports a number of other methods that can be used to specify a color. I'll discuss them in the sidebar that follows this table.)
background-image	Assigns the background image. The value should be the URL of an image or none.
background-repeat	Determines whether the background image is repeated (tiled) and if so, how it's repeated. Possible values are repeat (repeat horizontally and vertically), repeat-x (repeat horizontally), repeat-y (repeat vertically), and no-repeat (no repetition of the image).
background-attachment	Determines whether the background image remains stationary (is attached to the document) or scrolls with the document. Possible values are scroll and fixed.
background-position	Sets the initial position of a background image. Possible values are described in the text following this table.
background	A shorthand property that sets one or more of the preceding properties in a single location in the style sheet.

When you apply a background image to a Web document, the W3C recommends that you also set a background color as well. This way, if a background image is unavailable to a user, he or she can still view a colored background.

Note You can find a list of the color names and RGB triplets that are applicable to style sheets in Appendix C, "Cascading Style Sheet (CSS) Quick Reference."

Alternate Color Specification Methods

There are a number of methods you can use to specify colors in style sheets. If you decide to stick with using the HTML method—specifying hexadecimal values for the red, green, and blue hues in a color—you'll be fine. However, you might see these other methods used as well. Here, I'm going to show you how to express the color #CCFFCC in other ways. Colors can be specified in a hexadecimal format using only three digits, as follows:

```
background-color: #cfc;
```

This assumes a system where only 16 values are available for each hue, rather than 256. You can also specify colors using decimal numbers as follows:

```
background-color: rgb(203,255,203);
```

Finally, you can specify the value in percentage strengths of the hue being used. For example, the color #CCFFCC could be expressed in percentages as follows:

```
background-color: #rgb(80%, 100%, 80%);
```

The background-position property requires further comment, because it's a little complex. This property accepts two values that are separated by a space. They are specified in one of the following ways:

- *By keyword.* The keyword top, center, or bottom identifies the vertical position of the background; the keyword left, center, or right identifies the horizontal position. To position the center of the image at the horizontal and vertical centers of a Web page, for example, you specify the values center center.

- *By length unit.* The values are given in x,y coordinates, with x being the horizontal axis (distance from the left side of the page) and y being the vertical axis (distance from the top of the page). A position of 20 25 positions the upper-left corner of the image 20 pixels to the left and 25 pixels from the top of the page or element.

- *By percentage value.* The default positioning of the background-position property is 0% 0%. This value is equal to the upper-left corner of the element. A value of 100% 100% positions the image at the bottom-right corner.

12

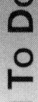

Exercise 12.4: Applying Backgrounds and Colors to Elements with CSS

You've already added some color to the Bookworm Web page through the use of CSS tags, but there's more to come. The following CSS code adds a background image to your Web page. The `background-image` property specifies the URL of the background image and tells the browser to tile the background image.

> **Note**
>
> The `background.gif` file referenced in the following example is available on the Web support site for this book, `http://www.tywebpub.com/`.

The Web page isn't the only thing to which you can apply backgrounds and colors. You also can apply different colors and backgrounds to the elements on the Web page. The following CSS code also adds some different colors to the headings on the page for an interesting effect. You'll change the color of the level 1 and level 2 headings to brown. The level 1 heading will be rendered over a light yellow background (signified by the color `#ffffcc`), and the level 2 headings will be rendered over a light green background color (signified by the color `#ccffcc`).

To clarify the new style rules that you should insert on your page, the next few examples show the new additions with a gray shading. Revise your style definition to include the following lines highlighted in gray:

INPUT

```
<!--
body { background-color: #ccffcc;
        font-family: Arial, Helvetica, sans-serif;
        color: #330066;
        margin: 50px 70px;
        background-image: url(background.gif);
        background-repeat: repeat }
    a:link { color: #cc9900 }
    a:visited { color: #660000 }
    a:hover { color: #ffcc00 }
    a:active { color: #ff0000 }
h1 { color: #996633;
    padding-top: 10px;
    padding-bottom: 5px;
    background-color: #ffffcc }
h2 { color: #996633;
    padding-top: 5px;
    padding-bottom: 3px;
    background-color: #ccffcc }
-->
```

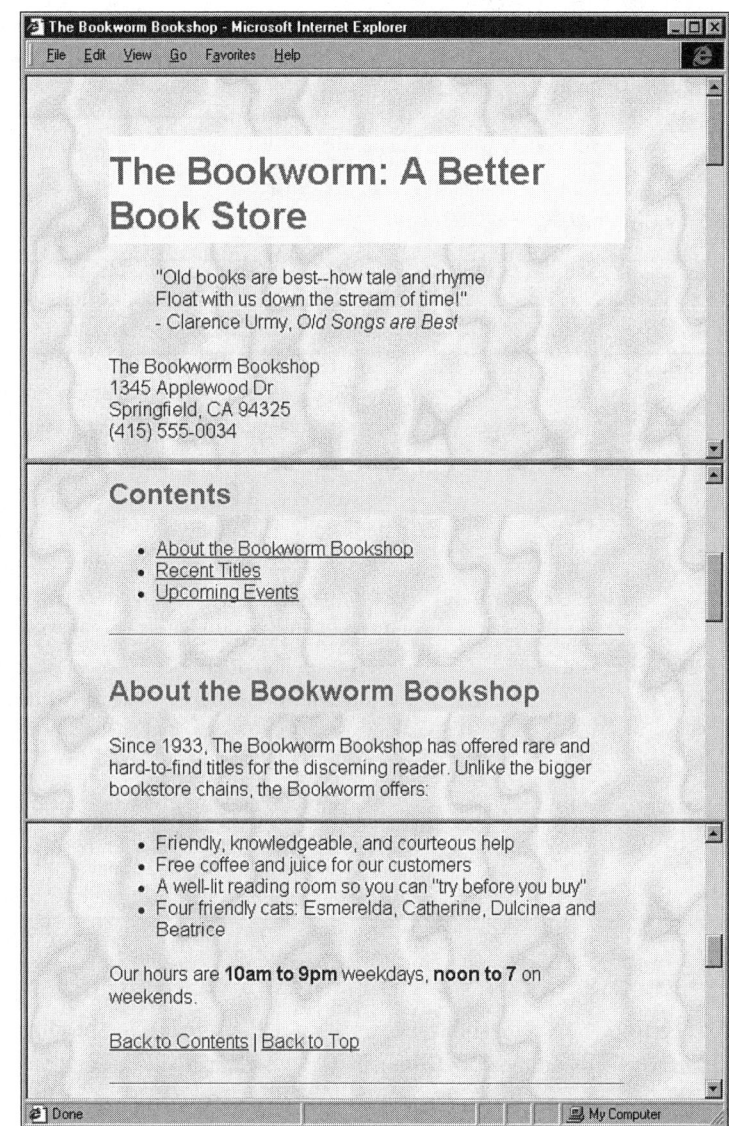

FIGURE 12.5

Background and color property settings applied to the Bookworm Bookshop page.

Setting Border Appearance

Cascading Style Sheets provide numerous properties for controlling the borders of elements in a page. In HTML, you had borders on only a few objects, such as images and table cells, but with CSS, theoretically you can apply a border to any page element.

Table 12.3 displays the properties for controlling border appearance.

TABLE 12.3 Border Properties in CSS

Property	Description
border-style	Sets the style of all four borders of an element. Values are the same as those indicated for border-bottom-style. You can set borders individually with border-bottom-style, border-left-style, border-right-style, or border-top-style. Values are none, dotted, dashed, solid, double, groove, ridge, inset, and outset.
border-color	Sets the color for all four borders of an element. You can set border colors individually set with border-bottom-color, border-left-color, border-right-color, or border-top-color. The color value can be one of 16 color names, one of several variations of an RGB triplet, or transparent.
border-width	Sets the width of all four borders. You can set border widths individually with border-bottom-width, border-left-width, border-right-width, and border-top-width. Values are thin, medium, thick, or a width value.
border	A shorthand property that sets the same width, color, and style on all four borders of an element. You can set width, color, and style for individual borders with border-bottom, border-left, border-right, or border-top.

Exercise 12.5: Applying Borders to Elements with CSS

▼ To Do

The following code shows borders that are applied to the headings on the page. This makes the headings look somewhat like banner images. The border-color, border-style, and border-width properties have been applied to each of the headings. The top and left borders of each heading type will have a different color than the bottom and right borders. You can accomplish this by specifying two values for the border-color property. The borders on the level 1 heading give the appearance that it is facing outward

▼ from the Web page, while the level 2 headings seem to face inward. You can accomplish this by applying the `border-style: outset` and `border style: inset` properties and attributes to the respective tags.

To add the colors to the borders around the headings, add the code highlighted in gray to the CSS section in your Bookworm Bookshop Web page:

INPUT

```
<!--
body { background-color: #ccffcc;
       font-family: Arial, Helvetica, sans-serif;
       color: #330066;
       margin: 50px 70px;
       background-image: url(background.gif);
       background-repeat: repeat }
a:link { color: #cc9900 }
a:visited { color: #660000 }
a:hover { color: #ffcc00 }
a:active { color: #ff0000 }
h1 { color: #996633;
     padding-top: 10px;
     padding-bottom: 5px;
     background-color: #ffffcc;
     border-color: #cccc33 #cc9933;
     border-style: outset;
     border-width: thin }
h2 { color: #996633;
     padding-top: 5px;
     padding-bottom: 3px;
     background-color: #ccffcc;
     border-color: #99cc33 #996633;
     border-style: inset;
     border-width: thin }
-->
```

When you preview your Web page in a CSS-compatible browser, it should look similar to Figure 12.6 in Internet Explorer. Netscape renders the borders and backgrounds a little bit differently. Netscape's borders are thinner and slightly offset from the background ▼ color.

12

OUTPUT

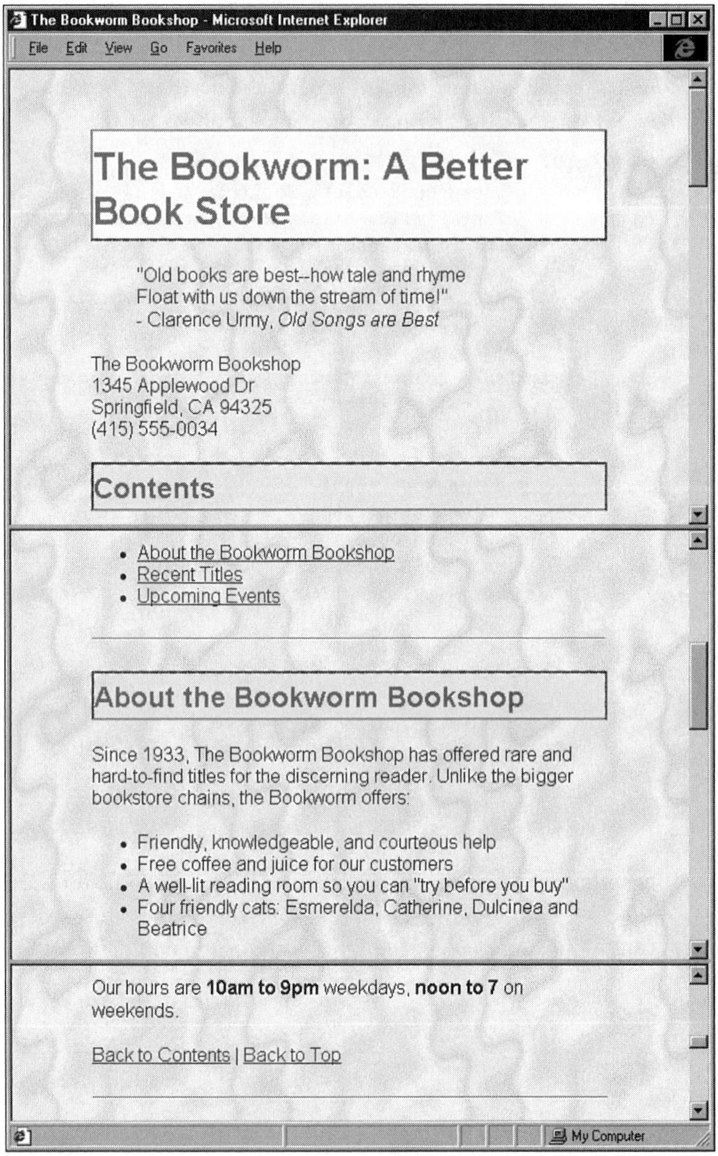

FIGURE 12.6

Border property settings in Internet Explorer.

The Bookworm Bookshop - Microsoft Internet Explorer

File Edit View Go Favorites Help

The Bookworm: A Better Book Store

"Old books are best--how tale and rhyme
Float with us down the stream of time!"
- Clarence Urmy, *Old Songs are Best*

The Bookworm Bookshop
1345 Applewood Dr
Springfield, CA 94325
(415) 555-0034

Contents

- About the Bookworm Bookshop
- Recent Titles
- Upcoming Events

About the Bookworm Bookshop

Since 1933, The Bookworm Bookshop has offered rare and hard-to-find titles for the discerning reader. Unlike the bigger bookstore chains, the Bookworm offers:

- Friendly, knowledgeable, and courteous help
- Free coffee and juice for our customers
- A well-lit reading room so you can "try before you buy"
- Four friendly cats: Esmerelda, Catherine, Dulcinea and Beatrice

Our hours are **10am to 9pm** weekdays, **noon to 7** on weekends.

Back to Contents | Back to Top

My Computer

Font Appearance and Style

Cascading Style Sheets have a strong collection of properties for defining font appearance. In fact, with Cascading Style Sheets, page authors have more control than they had with the simplistic `<font>` tag in HTML.

Table 12.4 outlines the main properties for controlling font appearance.

TABLE 12.4 CSS Font Properties

Property	Description
font-family	Sets font face. Specify a typeface name (such as Arial, Times, or Palatino) or one of five generic font names: serif, sans-serif, cursive, fantasy, or monospace.
font-size	Sets the font size in absolute, relative, or percentage terms.
font-style	Sets the font style as oblique, italic, or normal.
font-weight	Sets the font weight as normal, bold, bolder, or lighter.
font-variant	Sets the font to small-caps or normal.
font	A shorthand property that sets font-weight, font-size, font-style, font-family, and line-height in the same location in the style sheet. The line-height property is explained in "Text Alignment Properties in CSS," which follows this section.

The following are a few things worth noting in this list:

- When you set the font family, using font-family, you can provide a comma-separated list of font names. If the system that the browser is running doesn't have the first specified font, it moves on to the next font on the list. The W3C advises that a generic family name should be the last name in the list. The reason for this is that every browser will have a default font for a given generic family.

- When you're using generic family names, be careful when using cursive or fantasy fonts. The appearance of these two family names is highly dependent on the fonts that the visitor has installed on his or her hard drive. Serif, sans-serif, and mono-space fonts are installed with most operating systems or Web browsers, but cursive and fantasy fonts might not be.

- When you're setting font size using font-size, absolute sizes are defined via a keyword such as xx-small, x-small, small, medium, large, x-large, or xx-large. These values map to specific font sizes in the browser. Relative sizes are relative to the font size of the parent element and can be defined as larger or smaller.

- Font weights are set on a scale of numerical values: 100, 200, 300, 400, 500, 600, 700, 800, and 900. The font-weight property can take either one of the values normal, bold, bolder, or lighter, or one of the numbers. normal maps to 400, and bold maps to 700 on the numerical scale. bolder and lighter set the weight relative to a parent element.

12

The following code example demonstrates some of these font properties:

```
<!DOCTYPE html PUBLIC "-//W3C//DTD XHTML 1.0 Strict//EN"
 "http://www.w3.org/TR/xhtml1/DTD/strict.dtd">
<html>
<head>
<title>CSS Font Properties</title>
<style type="text/css">
<!--
body { background-color: #ffffff }
-->
</style>
<p><span style="font-family: Arial">font-family: Arial</span> <br />
  <span style="font-family: fantasy">font-family: fantasy</span> </p>
<hr />
<span style="font-size: small">font-size: small</span>
<span style="font-size: medium">font-size: medium</span>
<span style="font-size: xx-large"> font-size: xx-large</span>
<hr />
<span style="font-style: italic">font-style: italic</span>
<hr />
<span style="font-weight: 100">font-weight: 100</span>
<br />
<span style="font-weight: 500">font-weight: 500</span>
<br />
<span style="font-weight: 900">font-weight: 900</span>
<hr />
<span style="font-variant: normal">font-variant: normal</span>
<br />
<span style="font-variant: small-caps">font-variant: small-caps</span>
</body>
</html>
```

Figure 12.7 shows the result.

FIGURE 12.7

Various font properties.

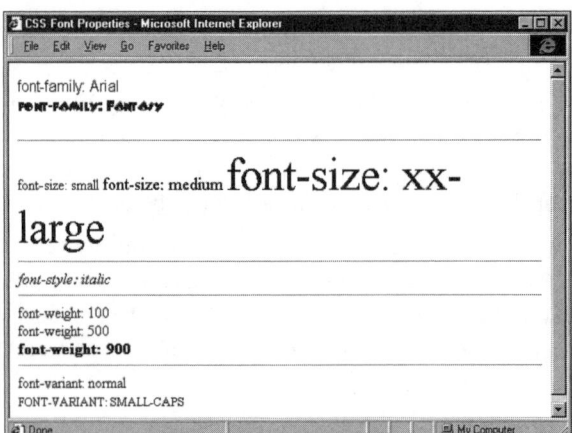

Text Alignment Properties in CSS

In addition to the font properties, CSS includes numerous properties that enable page authors to align text. These properties allow the type of fine typographic control that is achieved in word processors and desktop publishing applications, which were not available on the Web until the development of CSS.

The main text alignment properties are outlined in Table 12.5.

TABLE 12.5 Text Alignment Properties in CSS

Property	Description
word-spacing	Sets space to add to the default space between words. Possible values are an absolute length or normal (the default). Currently not supported in either Internet Explorer 5.5 or Netscape Communicator 4.7 (and Netscape 6).
letter-spacing	Sets space to add to the default space between letters. Possible values are an absolute length or normal (the default). Currently supported in Internet Explorer 5.5 and Netscape 6, but not in Netscape Communicator 4.7.
line-height	Sets the distance between the baseline of two line. A numerical value means the line height is the font size multiplied by the number. For example, line-height: 2 creates line spacing that is twice the size of the font. Absolute lengths can be defined for line height as well. For example, line-height: 15px spaces the lines 15 pixels apart. Percentage values are based on the height of the element. line-height: 200% is the same as specifying a numerical value of line-height: 2. You also can use normal, which sets the height to the default. Currently supported in Internet Explorer 5.5, Netscape Navigator 4.7, and Netscape 6.
vertical-align	Sets the vertical alignment for an element relative to the parent element, the line the element is part of, or the line height of the line the element is contained in. Values of baseline, middle, sub, super, text-top, and text-bottom are relative to the parent element. top and bottom are relative to the line itself. A percentage raises the baseline of the element above the baseline of the parent. Fully supported in Internet Explorer 5.5 and Netscape 6; partially supported in Netscape Communicator 4.7.
text-align	Sets the alignment of text within an element to left, center, right, or justify. The text-align: justify property is currently supported by Internet Explorer 5.5 and Netscape 6, but is not supported in Netscape Communicator 4.7.
text-decoration	Sets the font decoration as underline, overline, line-through, or blink. The first three values are supported in Internet Explorer 5.5, Netscape 6, and Netscape Communicator 4.7, while blink is only supported by Netscape.

12

TABLE 12.5 continued

Property	Description
text-indent	Sets the indentation of the first line of formatted text in an element. The value can either be an absolute length or a percentage of the element width. Percentages are based on the width of the element and work best in most cases. Currently supported by Netscape Navigator 4.7 and Internet Explorer 5.5.
white-space	Indicates how whitespace inside an element should be handled. Possible values are normal (whitespace is collapsed as with standard HTML), pre (just like the <PRE> tag), and nowrap (need to use to wrap). Currently unsupported by Internet Explorer, partially supported by Netscape 4.7, and fully supported by Netscape 6.

As the preceding table shows, these CSS properties are supported differently within Internet Explorer 5.5, Netscape 6, and Netscape Communicator 4.7. Some properties are supported in one browser but not the other, and others are supported in both browsers. So if you're getting confused about what's what, it might not be your coding!

The following example includes many of the text properties and applies them to different text elements. Notice how differently the same code is treated within the two major browsers. Here, you'll see why it's a good idea to check your pages in multiple browsers:

INPUT

```
<!DOCTYPE html PUBLIC "-//W3C//DTD XHTML 1.0 Strict//EN"
  "http://www.w3.org/TR/xhtml1/DTD/strict.dtd">
<html>
<head>
<title>CSS Text Properties</title>
<style type="text/css">
<!--
body { background-color: #ffffff }
-->
</style>
<p><span style="word-spacing: normal"> word-spacing: normal </span>
<br />
  <span style="word-spacing: 25px"> word-spacing: 25px </span>
</p>
<hr />
<span style="letter-spacing: normal">letter-spacing: normal<br />
</span>
<span style="letter-spacing: 10px">letter-spacing: 10px</span>
<hr />
<span style="line-height: normal">line-height: normal</span>
<br />
<span style="line-height: 10px">line-height: 15px</span>
<br />
<span style="line-height: 150%">line-height: 150%</span>
<hr />
<span style="vertical-align: middle">vertical-align: middle</span>
<span style="vertical-align: sub">sub</span>
```

```
<span style="vertical-align: super">super</span>
<hr />
<span style="text-align: left">text-align: left<br />
</span>
<span style="text-align: center">text-align: center<br />
</span>
<span style="text-align: right">text-align: right<br />
</span>
<hr />
<span style="text-decoration: underline">text-decoration:
underline</span><br />
<span style="text-decoration: overline">text-decoration:
overline</span><br />
<span style="text-decoration: line-through">text-decoration:
line-through</span><br />
<span style="text-decoration: blink">text-decoration: blink</span>
<hr />
<span style="text-indent: 20px">text-indent: 20px</span><br />
<span style="text-indent: 40px">text-indent: 40px</span><br />
<span style="text-indent: 60px">text-indent: 60px</span><br />
</body>
</html>
```

Figures 12.8 and 12.9 show how Internet Explorer 5.5 and Netscape 4.6 render these properties differently.

OUTPUT

FIGURE 12.8

Various text properties in Internet Explorer 5.5.

12

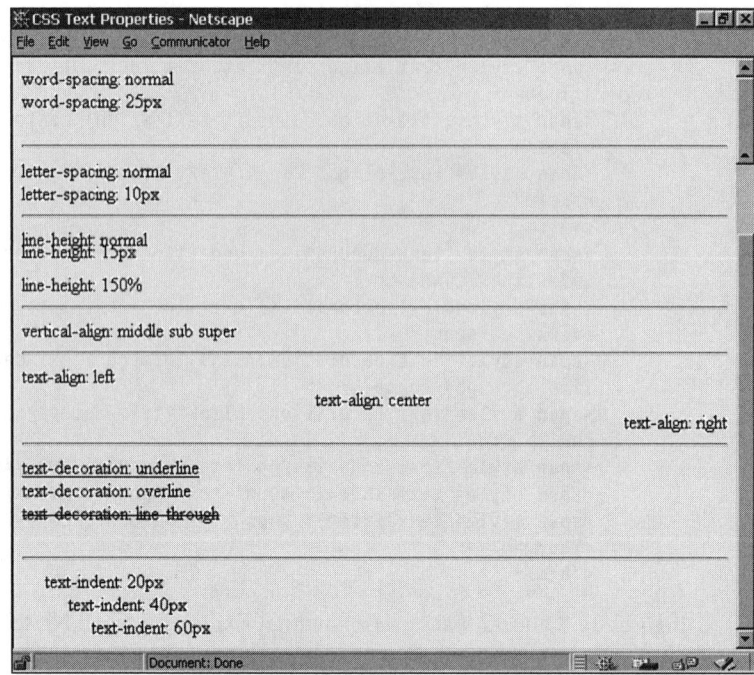

FIGURE 12.9

Various text properties in Netscape 4.6.

Inline Styles

Before you apply font and text properties to the Bookworm Bookshop page, I'll tell you about the third way to apply styles: *inline styles*. This method of application enables you to attach a style rule to a specific element on a page rather than across the entire page. For example, if you have a heading or a paragraph that you want to emphasize with a different color or alignment, and you only want to use that emphasis on one page in one place, that's a case for an inline style.

HTML includes several attributes that enable you to attach style rules to HTML tags. The main attributes that apply are the `style` and `class` attributes. The `<span>` tag is another that also relates to style sheets. All these are discussed next.

The `style` Attribute

In the section "Embedded Style Sheets," you were introduced to the `<style>` *tag*, which attached an external style sheet to a standard HTML Web *page*. The `style` *attribute* enables you to attach a style rule to a single *element* on a Web page.

Whereas external and embedded style sheets keep the style definitions separate from the HTML content, the `style` attribute is applied within the code of the Web document itself.

Note You can assign the `style` attribute to any HTML tag *except* the following: `<base>`, `<basefont>`, `<head>`, `<html>`, `<meta>`, `<param>`, `<script>`, `<style>`, and `<title>`.

Suppose that you want to change the color of a single paragraph on your Web page using a style rule. Normally, the color of the text on your page is black, and the text is not emphasized in any way. You want the paragraph to be rendered in a bold, red font.

The values you specify for the `style` attribute (the color `red` and the `bold` emphasis) are enclosed in quotes. The style rules that define these attributes (`color: red` and `font-weight: bold`) are separated by a semicolon within the quotes.

The following code demonstrates the `style` attribute as it is applied to a paragraph:

```
<p style="color: red; font-weight: bold">I want this paragraph to be bold and
red.</p>
```

The class Attribute

A *class* is a broadly defined style that defines properties for some or all elements in a document. Classes are defined in an external style sheet, or in the header of a standard Web page that uses embedded styles. Then, the `class` attribute assigns the special class to one or more elements on a Web page. The advantage of using this method over using the `style` attribute is that you can apply the same style rule to several elements on a Web page without having to type the rule repeatedly.

 Note You can assign the `class` attribute to any HTML tag *except* the following: `<base>`, `<basefont>`, `<head>`, `<html>`, `<meta>`, `<param>`, `<script>`, `<style>`, and `<title>`.

12

The following CSS code example demonstrates two paragraph style rules. The first rule specifies the properties for the "normal" paragraphs on the page. The second rule defines a special class for some of the paragraphs on the page. This special class is called `p.bigger`, with p being the paragraph tag designation and `bigger` being the class name:

```
<!DOCTYPE html PUBLIC "-//W3C//DTD XHTML 1.0 Strict//EN"
 "http://www.w3.org/TR/xhtml1/DTD/strict.dtd">
<html>
<head>
<title>Need New Glasses</title>
<style type="text/css">
```

```
<!--
p { font-family: Arial, Helvetica, sans-serif; color: black }
p.bigger { font-family: Arial, Helvetica, sans-serif; font-size: larger }
-->
</style>
</head>
```

Now that you've defined the special `bigger` class in your style sheet, you attach the style to the paragraphs in the page that you want to enlarge. To apply the `bigger` class to a specific paragraph, the syntax for the `class` attribute is as follows:

```
<p class="class-name">.
```

To further demonstrate this, the following shows the remaining code on this simple Web page. The first paragraph is normal, and the second paragraph uses the `bigger` style. Figure 12.10 displays the results:

INPUT

```
<p>Are you having a hard time reading the text on these pages? If you
haven't
    had your eyes checked lately, and the following paragraph is still
hard to read,
    you might want to have your eyes checked.</p>
<p class="bigger">You might need new glasses!</p>
</body>
</html>
```

OUTPUT

FIGURE 12.10

Applying the class *property to a page element.*

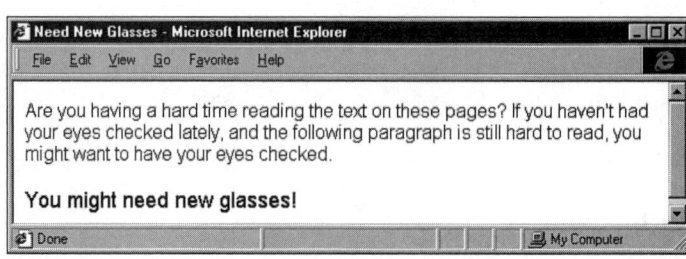

You can also create classes that aren't associated with a particular tag. Let's say that you define the class as follows:

```
.bigger { font-family: Arial, Helvetica, sans-serif; font-size: larger }
```

You can then use `class="bigger"` with nearly any tag and apply those styles to the text within the tag. For example, you could then use the `bigger` class in the following contexts:

```
<ul>
  <li class="bigger">This is bigger.</li>
</ul>
<p class="bigger">This is bigger, too.</p>
```

The `<span>` Tag

The following exercise makes extensive use of the `<span>` property, which allows you to apply a style to a portion of text without a structural role (which, therefore, isn't contained within a specific HTML structural tag). You can even use this property to apply a style to the first letter or word of a document. Because `<span>` itself has no effect on the text, only the style will affect the text's appearance.

Exercise 12.6: Applying Font and Text Properties with CSS

▼ **To Do**

For the final exercise today, you'll apply some font formatting properties to the previous examples. Note that the following examples use the `fantasy` generic family font name. Typically, these types of fonts are installed with page layout or graphics software. If you don't have a fantasy type font on your computer, substitute all instances of `fantasy` in the following code with `fixed`.

The first portion of your `bookwrm.html` page looks like the following example:

```
<!DOCTYPE html PUBLIC "-//W3C//DTD XHTML 1.0 Strict//EN"
 "http://www.w3.org/TR/xhtml1/DTD/strict.dtd">
<html>
<head>
<title>The Bookworm Bookshop</title>
<style type="text/css">
<!--
body { background-color: #ccffcc;
       font-family: Arial, Helvetica, sans-serif;
       color: #330066;
       margin: 50px 70px;
       background-image: url(background.gif);
       background-repeat: repeat }
a:link { color: #cc9900 }
a:visited { color: #660000 }
a:hover { color: #ffcc00 }
a:active { color: #ff0000 }
h1 { color: #996633;
     padding-top: 10px;
     padding-bottom: 5px;
     background-color: #ffffcc;
     border-color: #cccc33 #cc9933;
     border-width: thin;
     border: thin outset;
```

At this point, you want to add a style rule that changes the font for `h1` to `fantasy` (or `fixed`, if you don't have a fantasy font) and align it to the center with the `text-align` property, as in the following example:

```
font-family: "fantasy";
    text-align: center }
```

▼

12

▼ The existing code continues as follows:

```
h2 { color: #996633;
     padding-top: 5px;
     padding-bottom: 3px;
     background-color: #ccffcc;
     border-color: #99cc33 #996633;
     border-width: thin;
     border: thin inset;
```

Apply the fantasy (or fixed) font family name to the second-level heading as well and align it to the center:

```
font-family: "fantasy";
    text-align: center }
```

The code that you presently have in your bookwrm.html file finishes up with a block-quote style rule, which appears as follows:

```
blockquote { font-family: "Book Antiqua";
    line-height: 12pt;
    font-weight: normal;
    font-variant: normal;
    color: #996633;
    word-spacing: 2em;
    text-align: center }
```

After the blockquote section, you add a class called fantasy (or fixed, if you don't have a fantasy font installed on your computer). You use this class to change some of the inline page elements to the fantasy (or fixed) font as well. To create the class, enter the following code, replacing all instances of fantasy with fixed, if necessary:

```
.fantasy { text-align: left;
    font-family: "fantasy";
    font-size: 16pt; color: #996600}
```

And the style section ends with the following:

```
-->
</style>
</head>
```

You're not quite done! You still have to apply the inline styles to the HTML portion of your Web page. There are two parts of the Web page to which you should apply an inline style. The name of the bookstore appears in a couple of locations on the Web page, and you want to change them to the fantasy (or fixed) style. The following two sections of
▼ code demonstrate where the changes should go. Here's the first section:

▼
```
<p><span class="fantasy">The Bookworm Bookshop</span><br />
1345 Applewood Dr<br />
Springfield, CA 94325<br />
(415) 555-0034
</p>
```

And here's the second section:

```
<p>Since 1933, <span class="fantasy">The Bookworm Bookshop</span>
 has offered rare and hard-to-find titles for the discerning
 reader. The Bookworm offers:</p>
```

The following is a complete listing of the final code on the Web page, with Figure 12.11 showing the upper portion of the page in Internet Explorer:

INPUT
```
<!DOCTYPE html PUBLIC "-//W3C//DTD XHTML 1.0 Strict//EN"
  "http://www.w3.org/TR/xhtml1/DTD/strict.dtd">
<html>
<head>
<title>The Bookworm Bookshop</title>
<style type="text/css">
<!--
body { background-color: #ccffcc;
       font-family: Arial, Helvetica, sans-serif;
       color: #330066;
       margin: 50px 70px;
       background-image: url(background.gif);
       background-repeat: repeat }
a:link { color: #cc9900 }
a:visited { color: #660000 }
a:hover { color: #ffcc00 }
a:active { color: #ff0000 }
h1 { color: #996633;
     padding-top: 10px;
     padding-bottom: 5px;
     background-color: #ffffcc;
     border-color: #cccc33 #cc9933;
     border-width: thin;
     border: thin outset;
     font-family: "fantasy";
     text-align: center }
h2 { color: #996633;
     padding-top: 5px;
     padding-bottom: 3px;
     background-color: #ccffcc;
     border-color: #99cc33 #996633;
     border-width: thin;
     border: thin inset;
     font-family: "fantasy";
     text-align: center }
```
▼

12

```
▼          blockquote { font-family: "Book Antiqua";
               line-height: 12pt;
               font-weight: normal;
               font-variant: normal;
               color: #996633;
               word-spacing: 2em;
               text-align: center }
           .fantasy { text-align: left;
               font-family: "fantasy";
               font-size: 16pt; color: #996600}
           -->
           </style>
           </head>
           <body>
           <a name="top"><h1>The Bookworm: A Better Book Store</h1></a>
           <blockquote>
           "Old books are best--how tale and rhyme<br />
           Float with us down the stream of time!"<br />
           - Clarence Urmy, <cite>Old Songs are Best</cite>
           </blockquote>
           <p><span class="fantasy">The Bookworm Bookshop</span><br />
           1345 Applewood Dr<br />
           Springfield, CA 94325<br />
           (415) 555-0034
           </p>
           <a name="contents"><h2>Contents</h2></a>
           <ul>
             <li><a href="#about">About the Bookworm Bookshop</a></li>
             <li><a href ="#recent">Recent Titles</a></li>
             <li><a href ="#upcoming">Upcoming Events</a></li>
           </ul>
           <hr />
           <a name="about"><h2>About the Bookworm Bookshop</h2></a>
           <p>Since 1933, <span class="fantasy">The Bookworm Bookshop</span>
             has offered rare and hard-to-find titles for the discerning
             reader. The Bookworm offers:</p>
           <ul>
           <li>Friendly, knowledgeable, and courteous help</li>
           <li>Free coffee and juice for our customers</li>
           <li>A well-lit reading room so you can "try before you buy"</li>
           <li>Four friendly cats: Esmerelda, Catherine, Dulcinea and Beatrice</li>
           </ul>
           <p>Our hours are <strong>10am to 9pm</strong> weekdays,
           <strong>noon to 7</strong> on weekends.</p>
           <p><a href="#contents">Back to Contents</a> |
▼          <a href="#top">Back to Top</a></p>
```

```
<hr />
<a name="recent"><h2>Recent Titles (as of 11-Nov-99)</h2></a>
<ul>
<li>Sandra Bellweather, <a href="belladonna.html">
<cite>Belladonna</cite></a></li>
<li>Johnathan Tin, <a href="20minmeals.html">
<cite>20-Minute Meals for One</cite></a></li>
<li>Maxwell Burgess, <a href="legion.html">
<cite>Legion of Thunder</cite></a></li>
<li>Alison Caine, <a href="banquo.html">
<cite>Banquo's Ghost</cite></a></li>
</ul>
<p><a href="#contents">Back to Contents</a> |
<a href="#top">Back to Top</a></p>
<hr />
<a name="upcoming"><h2>Upcoming Events</h2></a>
<ul>
<li><b>The Wednesday Evening Book Review</b> meets, appropriately, on
Wednesday evenings at 7:00 pm for coffee and a round-table discussion.
Call the Bookworm for information on joining  the group and this week's
reading assignment. </li>
<li><b>The Children's Hour</b> happens every Saturday at 1pm and
includes reading,
games, and other activities. Cookies and milk are served. </li>
  <li><b>Carole Fenney</b> will be at the Bookworm on Friday,
      September 17, to read from her book of poems <cite>Spiders
      in the Web.</cite></li>
  <li><b>The Bookworm will be closed</b> October 1 to remove a family
of bats that has nested in the tower. We like the company, but not
the mess they leave behind! </li>
</ul>
<p><a href="#contents">Back to Contents</a> |
<a href="#top">Back to Top</a></p>
<hr />
<address>
Last Updated: 11-Nov-99<br />
WebMaster: Laura Lemay lemay@bookworm.com<br />
&#169; copyright 1999 the Bookworm<br />
</address>
</body>
</html>
```

12

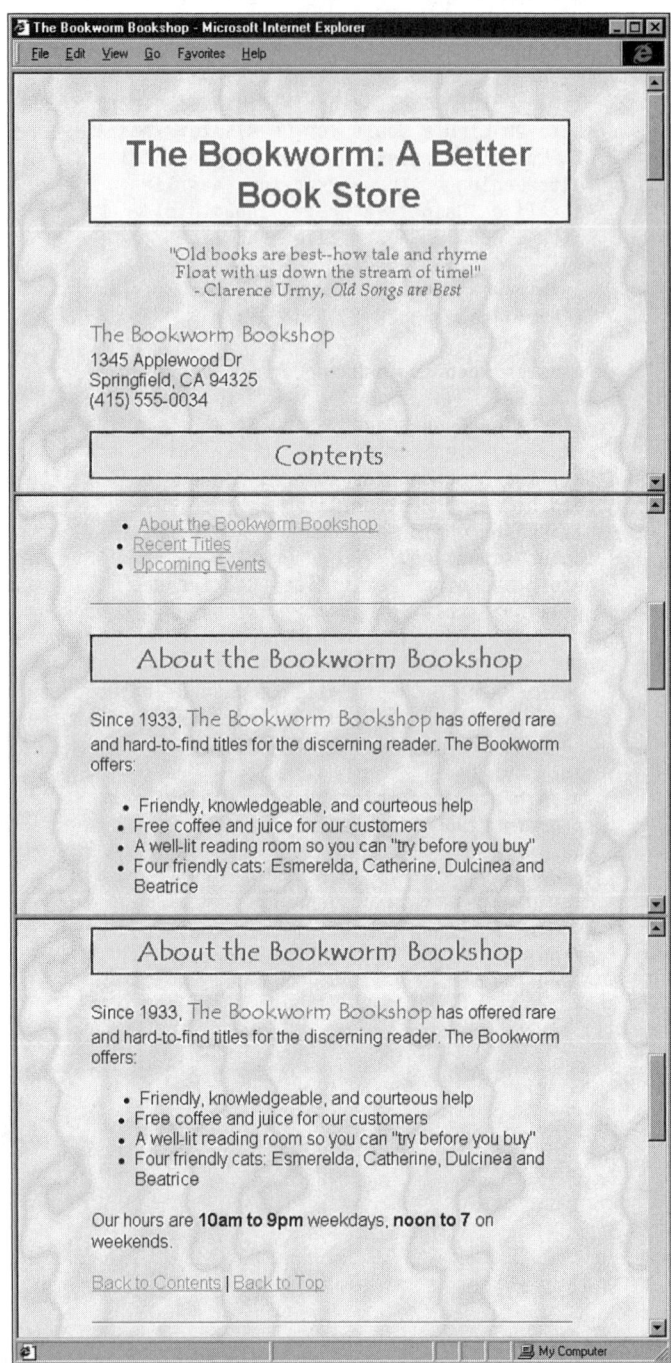

FIGURE 12.11

The Bookworm Bookshop with font and text styles added.

Note | If you viewed this example in Netscape Navigator, you probably noticed that the <span> tag is treated the same as the <br /> tag. It moves any text that follows the tag to the next line. Knowing this, you'll probably want to avoid placing the <span> tag in the middle of a paragraph as we did here.

Sources of Information About Cascading Style Sheets

This section has only touched the surface of CSS, mostly because it's too large of a topic and no browser really implements CSS well enough to dive deep into the possibilities.

If you want more information on Cascading Style Sheets, you can find it at the W3C Web site, which has a specification of CSS. The address for the Cascading Style Sheets page is http://www.w3.org/Style/CSS/.

The following are some other useful sources of information as well:

- *Webreview.com*. Includes a cascading style sheet guide. A useful portion of this guide highlights the various ways that browsers implement CSS tags. http://www.webreview.com/style/index.shtml

- *Cascading Style Sheets*. This thorough reference from the Web Design Group gives great insight and information about the style sheet properties introduced in CSS Level 1. http://www.htmlhelp.com/reference/css/

- *W3C's CSS Home Page*. Start here for an extensive list of links to examples, history, and upcoming trends that relate to style sheets and other Web technologies. http://www.w3.org/Style/

- *W3C CSS1 Test Suite*. The W3C has developed a set of tests to determine how well your browser complies with the CSS1 standard. If you're having problems with style sheets, you might take a look at the tests to make sure that the problems aren't caused by your browser. http://www.w3.org/Style/CSS/Test/

12

Workshop

It's the close of a very long and jam-packed day, and here's another workshop. These questions and quizzes will help you remember some of the important things you've learned about Cascading Style Sheets.

Q&A

Q **It seems like support for style sheets across browsers is very spotty. How will I know whether my style sheets will work in all browsers?**

A The only way to be sure is to test your style sheets in as many browsers as possible. Appendix C will discuss browser support for style sheets in more detail.

Q **I'm confused by these background color and image properties. Why don't I just use tables and apply background images and colors to specific cells?**

A You're absolutely correct that you can achieve some similar results using tables. However, table tags have some problems. First, they aren't strictly structural mark-up tags, so they cannot be rendered correctly in browsers such as Lynx and spoken-word browsers for the blind. This means that the text within the table can come out in the wrong order and will look awful in these browsers. By using style sheets to achieve some of the same results, you can focus on strict structural markup of your document. This ensures that the document is at least clear and useable even on a browser that doesn't support style sheets.

Quiz

1. What's the difference between the strict and transitional HTML document types?

2. What's a CSS style rule?

3. What are the three main ways that you can apply Cascading Style Sheet rules to HTML elements?

4. When you want to apply the same styles to multiple Web pages, which method is best to use? What special file extension is required?

5. True or False: You can use external, embedded, and inline styles on the same Web page.

Quiz Answers

1. The strict HTML document type uses a style sheet to define all the document's formatting, including colors and emphasis. The transitional HTML document uses a style sheet, but also incorporates HTML attributes to enable older browsers to see the document's formatting.

2. A CSS style rule defines a style that is to be applied to an HTML element. It consists of a selector (which can be an HTML tag), followed by a declaration that defines the property and value of the selector.

3. Cascading Style Sheet rules can be applied to HTML elements through the use of external style sheets, embedded style sheets, and inline styles.

4. External style sheets are best to use when you want to apply styles to more than one page. The external style sheet is saved with a `.css` file extension.

5. True. The properties you define in the embedded style sheet take precedence over those in the external style sheet. Likewise, the properties you define in the inline styles take precedence over the external and embedded styles.

Exercises

1. Create a simple Web page and apply some style rules of your own. Create your first example as an external style sheet that you can apply to more than one page.

2. Revise the example you created in Exercise 1 to use an embedded style sheet. If you really feel adventurous, keep the external style sheet linked to the Web page. Add some new styles that override the styles in the external style sheet and see what happens!

12

PART 5

Multimedia, Forms, and Dynamic HTML

DAY 13

Multimedia: Adding Sounds, Videos, and More

Learning how to integrate multimedia into your Web pages is as simple as creating hyperlinks to sound or video files. Presto! You have added multimedia to your Web site. That's not the whole story, of course. Aside from linking to multimedia files, you also can embed them in your Web pages. Unfortunately, embedding them can be a little tricky. Although you only need to learn a few HTML elements, the multimedia-related HTML elements suffer from what seems like schizophrenia. They either are implemented differently in Microsoft Internet Explorer and Netscape Navigator, not supported at all in one or the other of the two browsers, or are a part of the HTML standard to which no one seems to be paying attention. In addition, there are quite a few competing audio and video formats available today. It's almost impossible to learn the ins and outs of each one before more appear with the promise of being the "be all and end all" of multimedia.

Even with recent advances in communications speed (most home modems now support speeds up to 56Kbps, and high-bandwidth services like cable modems and DSL are becoming increasingly common), improved sound and video compression/decompression technologies (MP3 audio files come to mind), and powerful audio and video adapter cards, the Web is not the sound and video showcase that multimedia proponents dream of—not yet anyway.

Part of the problem is the incongruity between what we know today's computers are capable of and what we think the Web should deliver. Pop a CD or DVD into your drive and blammo! 3D graphics, stereo Surround Sound, and full-screen, 30-frames-per-second digital video jump out and assault your auditory and visual senses without letting up until you slump over in a blathering heap from the multimedia overload. Contrast that with most multimedia on the Web, and you can be sorely disappointed. Low-quality sound, small video sizes, and long download times are par for the course.

Things are getting better. Witness the advent of MP3 audio file and Macromedia Flash animations and their increasing popularity. Each offers a low-bandwidth, high-quality multimedia option; however, there is a price to pay for the progress being made. Namely, as Web users, we are being deluged with audio and video formats each requiring special plug-ins or helper applications. As a Web developer, you have to purchase expensive audio/video equipment and software in order to create your own multimedia content.

Having said all this, I will try to strike a balance in this lesson between showing you the techniques you can use immediately and the technologies that require you to devote a significant amount of time and energy in order to apply what you have learned. You will learn to accomplish the following:

- Create links to audio and video files so that visitors can download or play them
- Use the embed and object elements to include sound and video files in Web pages
- Learn how to embed QuickTime, Shockwave, Flash, and RealAudio or RealVideo files into your Web pages
- Use some of the unique multimedia capabilities of Microsoft Internet Explorer
- Recognize the most popular multimedia file types and the plug-ins or helper applications they require

Understanding How to Present Sound and Video

Despite all the complexity surrounding multimedia files and the number of formats available, it all boils down to choosing a method to integrate them into your Web pages. You can choose to create hyperlinks to those files or embed them directly into your Web pages. Linking to files is relatively foolproof, but embedding them can be problematic.

A linked sound or video file, no matter what type of sound or video file it is, has a hyperlink to the source file within the Web page. When you click on a linked sound or video file, one of three possible events occurs. First, you can download the file and save it to your computer. This method enables you to listen or view your file at a later time in whatever application you choose. Second, the file can download and automatically launch a helper application or plug-in to play. This occurs when the file is a recognized type, and a suitable player or plug-in is configured to play the file. Third, if the file is recognized as streaming audio or video, a player is launched as a separate process that will begin to play the file as it downloads.

Support for embedded sound and video is integrated into most Web browsers. Generally, a browser plug-in is used to play the audio or video file, but the file is actually part of the Web page rather than something that loads separately and is viewed in an external application. Without further ado, let's get down to business and add some sound and video to Web pages.

The Old Standby: Linking

The sure-fire way to include multimedia files on your Web site is to provide a hyperlink to them. Simple hyperlinks are supported by all versions of all browsers. People can decide whether they want to download the file and either listen to or view it at their convenience.

A common technique is to link to the file and provide a thumbnail preview of the multimedia clip, a description, and the file size. This is considered a common courtesy so that people can estimate the download time. You also should provide links to any players required so that people can download the appropriate player, should they need it.

If I have a QuickTime video that I want to share, for example, I might fashion the code as follows:

```
<div align="center">
<h1>Apollo 17 Videos</h1>
<p><a href="Apollo_17_Flag.qt">Astronauts placing the flag on the Moon</a><br>
[2.75Mb]</p>
<img src="Apollo_17_Flag.gif" align="texttop" width="160" height="120" />
<p>Apple <a href="http://www.apple.com/quicktime">QuickTime</a> is required
to view this movie.
<a href="http://www.apple.com/quicktime"><img src="getquicktime4.gif" border="0"
align="absmiddle" width="88" height"31" /></a></p>
</div>
```

13

Figure 13.1 shows the resulting Web page.

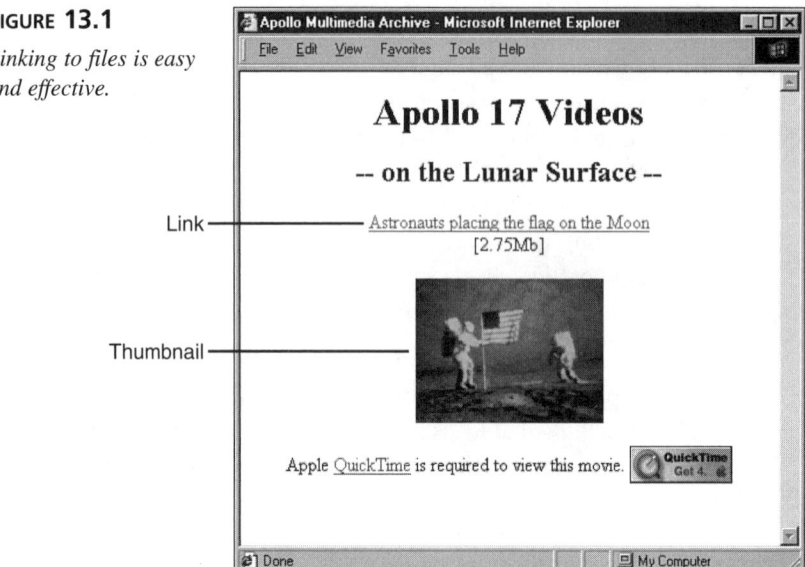

It's also considered good form to provide multiple types of multimedia to download, if your visitors have a preference:

```
<html>
<head><title>Apollo Multimedia Archive</title></head>
<body>
<div align="center">
<h1>Apollo 17 Videos</h1>
<p>Astronauts placing the flag on the Moon</p>
<table border="0">
    <tr>
        <td rowspan="3">
        <img src="Apollo_17_Flag.gif" width="160" height="120" /></td>
        <td><a href="Apollo_17_Flag.qt">QuickTime</a> [2.75Mb]</td>
    </tr>
    <tr>
        <td><a href="Apollo_17_Flag.mpg">MPEG</a> [2.45Mb]</td>
    </tr>
    <tr>
        <td><a href="Apollo_17_Flag.avi">AVI</a> [3.11Mb]</td>
    </tr>
</table>
<br />
<a href="http://www.apple.com/quicktime">
<img src="getquicktime4.gif" width="88" height"31" border="0"
```

```
alt="Get QuickTime" vspace="7" /></a>
<br>
<a href="http://microsoft.com/windows/mediaplayer/download/default.asp">
<img src="getmedia_white.gif" width="65" height="57" border="0"
alt="Get Windows Media Player" vspace="7" /></a>
<br />
</div>
</body>
</html>
```

Figure 13.2 shows the resulting Web page.

FIGURE 13.2

When linking sound and video, provide multiple formats if possible.

Links to player Web pages ⎯

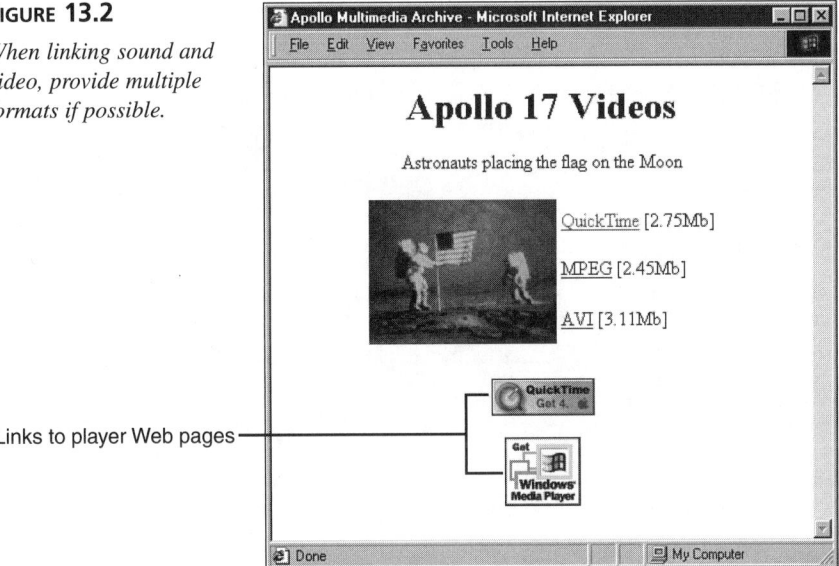

Exercise 13.1: Creating a Family History Multimedia Archive

One of the common types of pages available on the Web is a media archive. A *media archive* is a Web page that serves no purpose other than to provide quick access to images or other multimedia files for viewing and downloading.

Before the Web became popular, multimedia files such as images, sounds, and video were stored in FTP or Gopher archives. The text-only nature of these sorts of archives makes it difficult for people to find what they're looking for, as the filename usually serves as the only description of the contents of the files. Even reasonably descriptive filenames, such as `the-trees-last-fall.gif` or `ave-maria.wav`, aren't very useful when you're talking about images or sounds. Although they might describe the files, the only way people actually can sample them is to go through the process of downloading the entire file and playing it.

13

▼   By using inline images as thumbnails and splitting up sound and video files into small
sample clips with larger files, you can create a multimedia archive on the Web that is far
more usable than any of the text-only archives.

> **Note**
>
> Keep in mind that this sort of archive, with its heavy use of inline graphics
> and large multimedia files, is optimally useful in graphical browsers attached
> to fast networks.

In this exercise, you'll create a simple example of a multimedia archive with several GIF
and JPEG images, WAV sounds, and a mixture of MPEG and AVI video.

By using your favorite image editor, you can create thumbnails of each of your pictures
to serve as the inline icons and then insert `<img>` links in the appropriate spots in your
archive file.

First, start with the framework for the archive, and then add a table for the thumbnail
images, as in the following example:

INPUT
```
<!DOCTYPE html PUBLIC "-//W3C//DTD XHTML 1.0 Transitional//EN"
"http://www.w3.org/TR/xhtml1/DTD/transitional.dtd">

<html>
<head>
<title>My Family History</title>
</head>
<body>
<h1>My Family Media Archive</h1>

<div align="center">
<table border="0">
<tr>
    <td width="80"><h2>Images</h2></td>
    <td><p>Select an image to view it in a larger size</p></td>
</tr>
<tr>
    <td width="80">A bunch of family members in the early 1950s.</td>
    <td><img src="groupoldsmall.gif" height="103" width="150"
        alt="An old group photo" /></td>
</tr>
<tr>

    <td width="80">Aunts Betsy and Phyllis sitting on the porch.</td>
    <td><img src="auntssmall.gif" height="96" width="150"
        alt="Two aunts on a porch" /></td>
</tr>
```

```
    <tr>
        <td width="80">Don when he was a child.</td>
        <td><img src="donoldsmall.gif" height="100" width="61"
            alt="Young Don" /></td>
    </tr>
    </table>
    </div>

    </body>
    </html>
```

Note that I include values for the alt attributes of the <img> tags, which will be substituted for the images in browsers that cannot view these images. Although you might not intend for your Web page to be seen by nongraphical browsers, at least offering a clue to people who stumble onto it is polite. This way, everyone can access the multimedia files you're offering on this page.

Figure 13.3 shows how the page looks so far.

OUTPUT

FIGURE 13.3

The Web page with the image archive almost completed.

13

The next step is to create the hyperlinks to each image that point to the larger file. By clicking them, people can choose either to view these files or download them to their computers.

▼

INPUT

```
...
<tr>
    <td width="80">A bunch of family members in the early 1950s.</td>
    <td><a href="groupoldlarge.jpg">
    <img src="groupoldsmall.gif" height="103" width="150"
     alt="An old group photo"/></a></td>
</tr>
<tr>
    <td width="80">Aunts Betsy and Phyllis sitting on the porch.</td>
    <td><a href="auntslarge.jpg"><img src="auntssmall.gif" height="96"
width="150" alt="Two aunts on a porch"/></a></td>
</tr>
<tr>
    <td width="80">Don when he was a child.</td>
    <td><a href="donoldlarge.jpg"><img src="donoldsmall.gif"
height="100" width="61"
    alt="Young Don" /></a></td>
</tr>
```

Figure 13.4 shows the result.

OUTPUT

FIGURE 13.4

The image now linked to larger images.

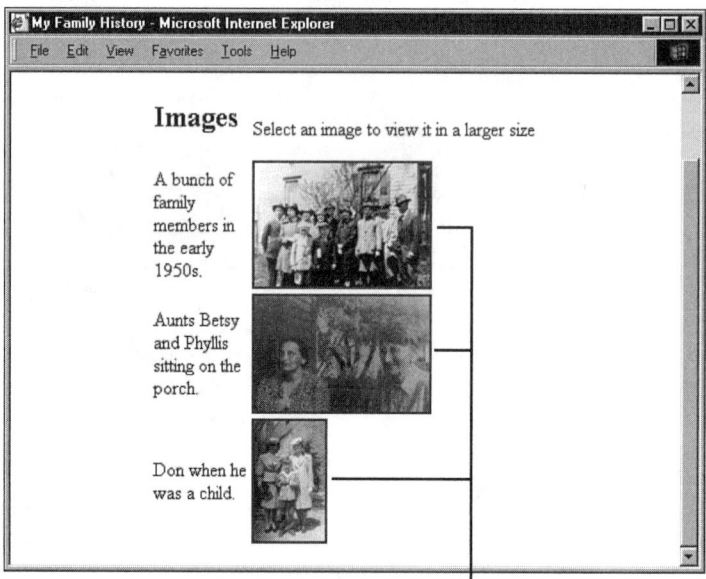

Thumbnail images form links

If I leave the archive like this, it looks nice, but I'm breaking one of my own rules: I haven't noted how large each file is. Here, you have several choices for formatting, but the easiest is to simply add the file size after the description of each picture, as follows:

INPUT

```
<tr>
    <td width="80">A bunch of family members in the early 1950s.
[103k]</td>
    <td><a href="groupoldlarge.jpg"><img src="groupoldsmall.gif"
        height="103" width="150" alt="An old group photo"/></a></td>
</tr>
<tr>
    <td width="80">Aunts Betsy and Phyllis sitting on the porch.
[83k]</td>
    <td><a href="auntslarge.jpg"><img src="auntssmall.gif" height="96"
        width="150" alt="Two aunts on a porch"/></a></td>
</tr>
<tr>
    <td width="80">Don when he was a child. [284k]</td>
    <td><a href="donoldlarge.jpg"><img src="donoldsmall.gif"
height="100" width="61" alt="Young Don" /></a></td>
</tr>
```

Figure 13.5 shows this result.

OUTPUT

FIGURE 13.5

Adding file sizes to the description of each image enables people to determine how long it will take to load the image.

File sizes

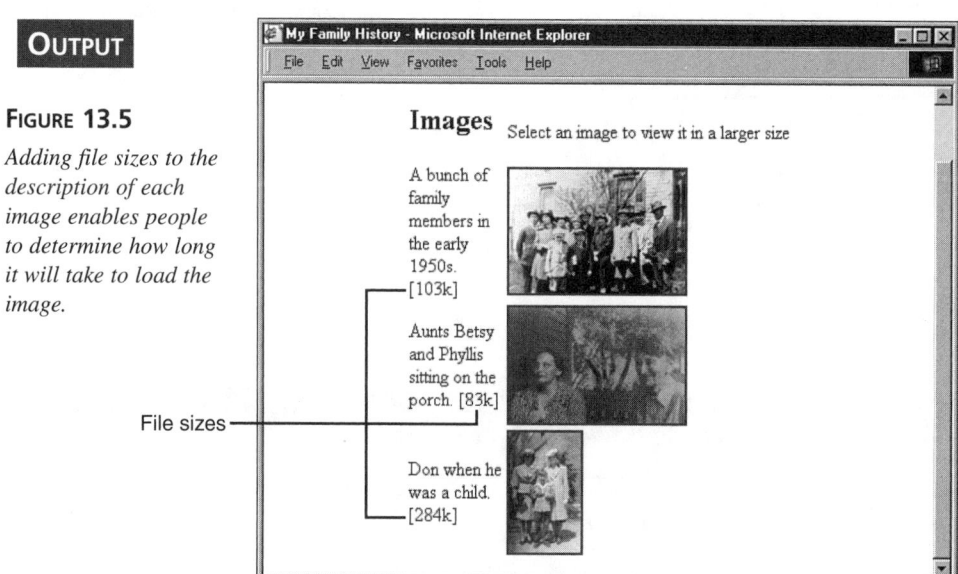

13

Now, let's move on to the sound and video sections. There are two approaches to formatting these sections. You can add the material in the same table that contains the images, or you can create two new tables—either way is fine. For this exercise, you are going to create new tables virtually identical to the table that held the images.

Start by adding three sound and two video files. Because the sound files can't be reduced to a simple thumbnail image, you need to describe them better in the text in the archive; however, you normally can use your video player to copy one frame of the clip and provide that as a thumbnail. I've included icons with the links to the sound files. Following is the code for the sound portion of your archive:

INPUT

```
<div align="center">
<table border="0">
<tr>
    <td width="150"><h2>Sound Bites</h2></td>
    <td><p>Select a sound bite to download or listen to it.</p></td>
</tr>
<tr>
    <td width="150">An oral family history describing
    how we survived the tornado of 1903. [1192k]</td>
    <td><a href="tornado.wav"><img src="soundicon.gif" height="29"
    width="33"></a></td>
</tr>
<tr>

    <td width="150">Don describing his first job. [1004k]</td>
    <td><a href="donjob.wav"><img src="soundicon.gif" height="29"
    width="33"></a></td>
</tr>
<tr>
    <td width="150">Grandma Jo telling how she came to America.
[2459k]</td>
    <td><a href="jo.wav"><img src="soundicon.gif" height="29"
    width="33"></a></td>
</tr>
</table>
</div>
```

Figure 13.6 shows how the linked sounds look on the Web page.

OUTPUT

FIGURE 13.6

Linked sound files in a family history archive.

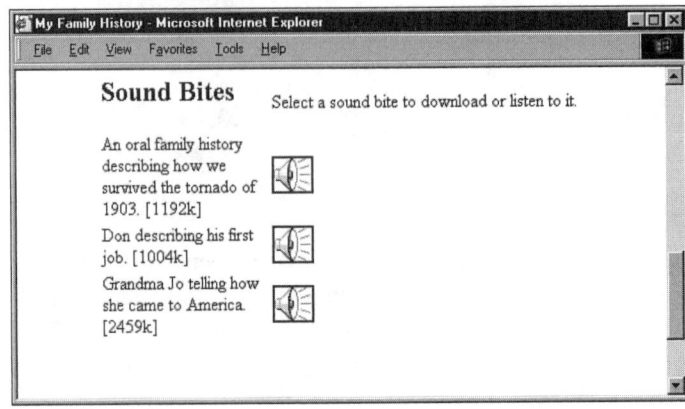

▼ Finally, add the video clip section just as you have for the previous two. It's getting easier!

INPUT

```
<div align="center">
<table border="0">
<tr>
    <td width="100"><h2>Video Clips</h2></td>
    <td><p>Select a video clip to download it.</p></td>
</tr>
<tr>
    <td width="100">A video of a family wedding. [2492k]</td>
    <td><a href="wedding.mpeg"><img src="wedding.gif" height="120"
    width="180"></a></td>
</tr>
<tr>

    <td width="100">Don and Mary talking. [3614k]</td>
    <td><a href="donandmary.mpeg"><img src="donandmary.gif" height="120"
    width="180"></a></td>
</tr>
</table>
</div>
```

Figure 13.7 shows how the linked videos with thumbnails look on the Web page.

OUTPUT

FIGURE 13.7

The video section of our multimedia archive.

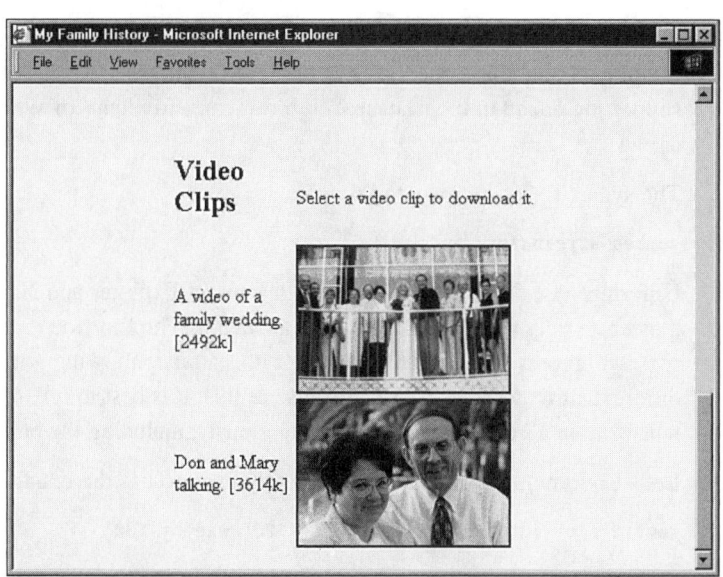

13

Your multimedia archive is finished. Creating one is simple with the combination of inline images and external files. With the use of the alt attribute, you can even use it
▲ reasonably well in text-only browsers.

Embedding Sound and Video

Embedding sound and video is achieved through the embed or object elements. Remember, the principle behind embedding sound or video is to include it in a Web page so that it can be played as part of the page.

The embed element has been around for some time and is supported by both Internet Explorer and Netscape Navigator. It was created so that file types requiring plug-ins (multimedia primarily) could be added to Web pages. Despite this support, embed is not sanctioned by the World Wide Web Consortium (W3C) and can't be found in the official HTML standard. Of course, because both major browsers support the element, you can safely ignore the W3C for the time being.

The competing element, object, is officially sanctioned by the W3C, although browser support (mainly Netscape Communicator 4.7) is somewhat buggy at this time. The object element is supposed to provide a generic solution for embedding in Web pages all sorts of file types, from images to Java Applets to sound and video files. It is hoped that by standardizing a one-size-fits-all element, you will be able to include more types of files as well as have an element ready for any future multimedia types.

Using the embed Element

Despite the fact that embed isn't in the HTML standard, Microsoft and Netscape continue supporting embed in their latest Web browsers, and plenty of Web pages make use of embed.

The syntax for using embed is simple:

```
<embed attributes />
```

Unfortunately, despite the fact that both Internet Explorer and Navigator support embed, they share only a handful of common attributes. The flip side to that coin is that each Web browser ignores the attributes it doesn't understand, allowing you to include as many different attributes as you like. Because of this, it is best to rely on a set of attributes that will work in all cases, and use them religiously, including the others for added value.

Let's explore the attributes you absolutely need to use the embed element.

```
<embed src="a01607av.avi" height="120" width="160" />
```

The src attribute indicates the path and name of the multimedia file you want to embed in the Web page, whereas the height and width attributes set a region of the browser window aside to display the multimedia file.

Internet Explorer and Netscape Navigator handle the height and width a bit differently. In Internet Explorer, the multimedia controls of the appropriate plug-in are always displayed—Netscape 4.7 seems never to want to display them. This causes a huge problem in that setting the `height` and `width` attribute for Internet Explorer includes the space devoted to those controls. Setting the `height` and `width` to the exact size of the video display causes the video to become "crunched" because the controls take up some of this valuable real estate. You would think that increasing the `height` and `width` would solve this problem by increasing the space and allowing the controls and the video to be displayed at their proper sizes. Because of the Netscape Navigator implementation, however, that doesn't work. Netscape Navigator expands the video to the full size of the `height` and `width` attributes and ignores the controls entirely, resulting in a video that is stretched and distorted.

Figures 13.8 and 13.9 demonstrate the problem using this code:

```
<embed src="a01607av.avi" type="video/x-msvideo" height="120" width="180" />
```

FIGURE 13.8

Internet Explorer displays the controls and sizes the overall box accordingly.

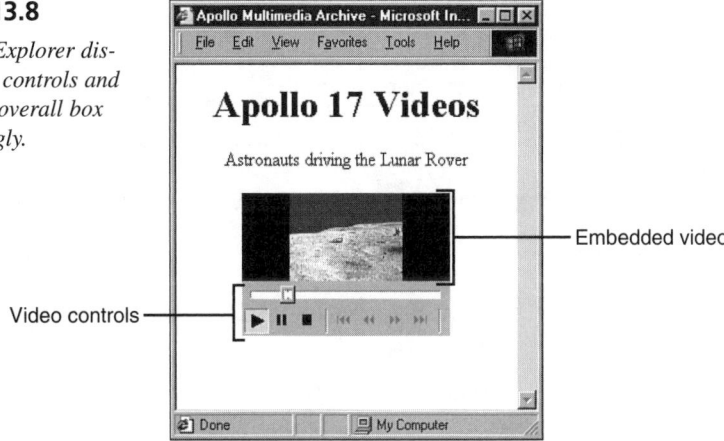

Video controls

Embedded video

FIGURE 13.9

Netscape Navigator ignores the controls and expands the video to fit the box.

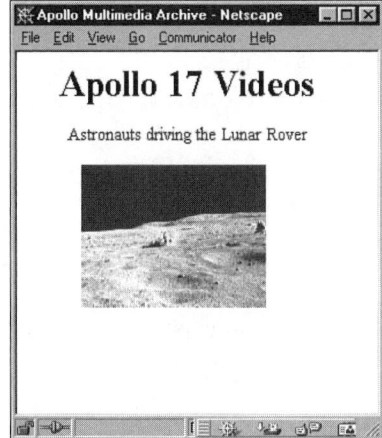

13

Not using the `height` and `width` attributes and allowing the browsers to handle this will work, but only in Internet Explorer. Netscape Navigator displays a small window for the plug-in, cutting off much of the video.

So what's a person to do? Apart from throwing your hands up in complete frustration, writing letters to each company telling them how mad you are, or tossing your computer out the window, if embedding video is important to you, you can do one of the following things:

- Pick your poison and ignore how it looks in the other browser.
- Use scripting to "sniff" for the browser type and base your use of `embed` on the visitor's Web browser.
- Use both the `object` and `embed` elements for certain file types to provide cross-browser support.

Table 13.1 summarizes the `embed` attributes supported by Internet Explorer.

TABLE 13.1   `embed` Attributes Used in Internet Explorer

Attribute	Description
`align`	Aligns the element in relation to the Web page. Allowable values are `absbottom`, `absmiddle`, `baseline`, `bottom`, `left`, `middle`, `right`, `texttop`, and `top`.
`class`	Sets or retrieves the class of the element.
`height`	The height of the element.
`id`	The ID of the element.
`name`	The name of the element.
`pluginspage`	The URL of the page with the plug-in used to view this object.
`src`	The source of the multimedia file.
`style`	Style sheet declaration.
`title`	The title of the element.
`units`	Sets or retrieves the `height` or `width` units. Pixels are the default unit of measurement.
`unselectable`	Specifies that the object cannot be selected. Valid values are `on` and `off` (the default is `off`).
`width`	The width of the element.

Table 13.2 summarizes the `embed` attributes supported by Netscape Navigator.

TABLE 13.2   embed Attributes Used in Netscape Navigator

Attribute	Description
src	The file location.
type	The MIME type of the embedded multimedia.
pluginspage	A URL pointing to a Web page that has instructions for installing the required plug-in.
pluginurl	A URL to a Java Archive (JAR) file.
align	Aligns the element in relation to the Web page. Allowable values are left, right, top, and bottom.
border	The width of a border drawn around the element.
frameborder	Does not draw a border around the element when set to no.
height	The height of the element.
width	The width of the element.
units	The units used to measure the height and width. Pixels are the default unit of measurement.
hidden	Hides the element when set to true and displays it when set to false, which is the default value.
hspace	The horizontal margin around the element.
vspace	The vertical margin around the element.
name	The name of the plug-in required to play the file.
palette	For use in Windows only. foreground makes the plug-in use the foreground palette, whereas background (the default) makes the plug-in use the background palette.

In addition to these attributes, additional attributes might be available for specific plug-ins, such as the Macromedia Flash Player.

Finally, you can include the noembed element to provide support for visitors who do not have a Web browser that can display plug-ins.

```
<noembed>This Web page requires a web browser that can display
objects.</noembed>
<embed src="a01607av.avi" height="120" width="160" />
```

Using the object Element

According to the World Wide Web consortium, you should use the object element when embedding sound and video (among other things) in Web pages. This can be problematic because versions of Netscape before version 6 do not fully support object and Internet Explorer is sometimes quirky about it.

13

To use the `object` element, start with the opening `object` tag and attributes, as follows:

```
<object data="movie.mpeg" type="application/mpeg">
```

The `data` attribute indicates the source file for your sound or video, and `type` is the MIME type of the file.

Next, include any content you want to display, such as a caption, and close the `object` element with the closing tag, as in the following:

```
<object data="movie.mpeg" type="video/mpeg">
My homemade movie.
</object>
```

You also can cascade objects so that if one cannot be displayed, the browser keeps trying down the list.

```
<object data="movie.mpeg" type="video/mpeg">
    <object data="moviesplash.gif" type="image/gif">
    </object>
My homemade movie.
</object>
```

`object` also uses the `param` element to initialize any parameters the embedded file might require. The `param` element is included in the body of the `object` element and has no closing tag, as in the following:

```
<object data="movie.mpeg" type="video/mpeg">
    <param name="height" value="120" valuetype="data" />
    <param name="width" value="160" valuetype="data" />
My homemade movie.
</object>
```

The preceding code sets the height and width of the embedded object to 120×160 pixels. Parameters supplied by the `param` element are dependent on the type of object you are trying to embed. For example, if you use the `object` tag to place a Flash movie on a page, the `param` tags will be used to specify the movie's URL, whether to play the movie when the page loads, and whether to loop through the movie continually or just play it once.

Combining `embed` and `object`

As you will see in the next few sections, you can often use `embed` and `object` simultaneously to provide support for Netscape Navigator and Internet Explorer. To do this, create the `object` element with any required parameters (the `param` element), and include the `embed` element before you enter the closing `object` tag. The following generic code snippet illustrates how:

```
<object classid="value" codebase="value" height="480" width="512" name="myname">
<param name="src" value="source location" />
<embed src="filename" height="480" width="512" name="myname" />
</object>
```

When Internet Explorer loads the Web page, it will read the `object` element and use that to embed the multimedia file in the page, ignoring the `embed` element entirely. Netscape Navigator will use the `embed` element.

Embedding Flash Animations

Macromedia Flash files are painless to publish on your Web site because the Flash authoring program will actually generate the necessary HTML. Figure 13.10 shows the Macromedia Flash interface used to create Flash files.

FIGURE 13.10

Use Macromedia Flash to create your Flash files and save them in Web pages.

Flash produces the code for embedding animations using HTML templates that are configured by setting your publishing preferences within the Flash authoring tool. The following code is the default template:

```
<OBJECT classid="clsid:D27CDB6E-AE6D-11cf-96B8-444553540000"
 codebase="http://active.macromedia.com/flash5/cabs/swflash.cab#version=5,0,0,0"
 ID=$TI WIDTH=$WI HEIGHT=$HE>
 $PO
<EMBED $PE WIDTH=$WI HEIGHT=$HE
 TYPE="application/x-shockwave-flash"
PLUGINSPAGE="http://www.macromedia.com/shockwave/download/
```

13

```
➥index.cgi?P1_Prod_Version=ShockwaveFlash">
</EMBED>
</OBJECT>
```

Notice that Flash uses both the object and embed elements to embed the animation in a Web page. The dollar signs ($) are variables that Flash replaces with your custom preferences when you publish your file. You can modify the HTML settings through a convenient dialog box shown in Figure 13.11.

FIGURE 13.11

Flash enables you to publish your animations using an HTML template that is customizable from this dialog box.

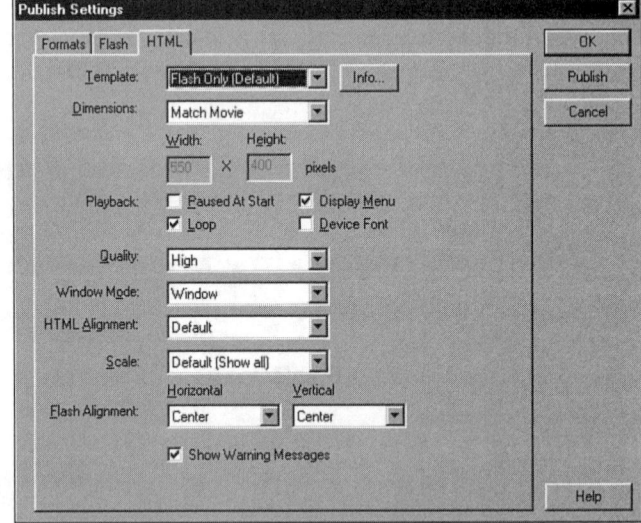

Embedding Shockwave Animations

Unless you are using Macromedia Dreamweaver, which automatically inserts the proper HTML code into your Web page, you will have to input the code manually to embed a Shockwave file (Shockwave files are created in Macromedia Director).

To embed a Shockwave file, use a combination of the object element (for Microsoft support) and the embed element (for Netscape support). You should use both to ensure maximum compatibility.

For most Shockwave applications, you can enter the code as shown and simply substitute your own values for the location and size of the movie. Other embedded objects might require different information. You should always consult any information from the object retailer or developer for the exact parameters.

The source code for embedding Shockwave files takes the following general form:

```
<OBJECT CLASSID="clsid:166B1BCA-3F9C-11CF-8075-44553540000"
CODEBASE="http://download.macromedia.com/pub/shockwave/
```

```
⮫cabs/director/sw.cab#version=8,0,0,0"
" WIDTH="512" HEIGHT="480" NAME="MovieName">
<PARAM NAME="SRC" VALUE="MYMOVIE.DCR">
<EMBED SRC="MYMOVIE.DCR" HEIGHT=480 WIDTH=512 NAME="MovieName">
</OBJECT>
```

Table 13.3 lists the attributes you can use in the `object` element.

TABLE 13.3   *object* Attributes

Attributes	Description
classid	The universal class identifier for the Shockwave ActiveX Control. It must be set to the following value: `clsid:166B1BCA-3F9C-11CF-8075-444553540000`

codebase	Specifies the download location of the Shockwave control, if not currently installed. It must be set to the following value:
	
	`http://download.macromedia.com/pub/shockwave/cabs/`
	`⮫director/sw.cab#version=7,0,0`

width	The width of the Shockwave file (in pixels).
height	The height of the Shockwave file (in pixels).
name	The name of the Shockwave movie (text).
pluginspage	The URL where the Shockwave plug-in can be downloaded.
src	This attribute is used in a `param` element within the `object` element. The `name` should be `src` and the `value` points to the URL of the movie. Following is the code: `<param name="src" value="URL">`
bgcolor	The background color of box that holds the movie before it appears (hexadecimal number).
swmodifyreport	If `true`, it removes the `src` URL from Shockwave statistics collection (`true`).

Table 13.4 lists the `embed` attributes.

TABLE 13.4   *embed* Attributes

Attribute	Description
width	The width of the Shockwave file (in pixels).
height	The height of the Shockwave file (in pixels).
name	The name of the Shockwave movie (text).
src	The location and name of the movie (URL).
pluginspage	Applies to Netscape Navigator only. The URL of the Shockwave Plug-in. The value should be as follows: `http://www.macromedia.com/shockwave`

13

TABLE 13.4 continued

Attribute	Description
bgcolor	The background color of box that holds the movie before it appears (hexadecimal number).
swmodifyreport	If true, it removes the src URL from Shockwave statistics collection (true).

Embedding RealAudio and RealVideo

RealNetwork's RealAudio and RealVideo files also use object and embed. Following is the syntax for including the files:

```
<object id="RVOCX" classid="clsid:CFCDAA03-8BE4-11cf-B84B-0020AFBBCCFA"
width="300" height="134">
Optional parameters
<embed src="source" width="value" height="value" />
<noembed><a href="download page">Play with RealPlayer.</a></noembed>
</object>
```

Table 13.5 lists the available attributes for embed and the parameters (<param name="name" value="value" />) for the object element.

TABLE 13.5 embed Attributes and object Parameters

Attribute/Parameter	Description
autostart	Sets automatic playback (true or false).
backgroundcolor	Sets background color (hexadecimal color value or name).
center	Centers clip in window (true or false).
console	Links multiple controls (yes, name, _master, or _unique).
controls	Adds RealPlayer controls (control name).
height	Sets window or control height (in pixels or percentage).
loop	Loops clips indefinitely (true or false).
maintainaspect	Preserves image aspect ratio (true or false).
nojava	Prevents the Java Virtual Machine from starting (true or false).
nolabels	Suppresses presentation information (true or false).
nologo	Suppresses RealLogo (true or false).
numloop	Loops clip a given number of times (number).
region	Ties clip to SMIL region (SMIL region).
shuffle	Randomizes playback (true or false).
src	Specifies source clip (URL).
width	Sets window or control width (in pixels or percentage).

You also can use the Web Page Wizard in RealProducer Plus to automatically create Web pages with embedded RealMedia.

Multimedia Techniques Using Microsoft Internet Explorer

Microsoft Internet Explorer offers a few unique capabilities worth mentioning: background sounds and inline video. Note, however, that although Netscape Navigator does not support either of these two techniques, you can safely include them in your Web pages. Navigator will ignore background sounds and you can code inline video in such a way that Navigator will display a static image in place of a video.

Including Background Sounds

Internet Explorer supports an element that loads and plays audio files in the background. These sound files load when the page loads, and they play automatically. Because no visual effect is created, there will be no indication that a sound is playing unless the users have a sound card and the volume is turned up. To add an embedded background sound to a page, use the bgsound element:

```
<bgsound src="ElevatorMusic.wav" />
```

Use the loop attribute to repeat the sound multiple tag>times. If the value of loop is a number, the sound is played that number of times. If loop is –1 or infinite, the sound will repeat continually, until the visitor leaves the page.

```
<bgsound src="ElevatorMusic.wav" loop="-1" />
```

Explorer supports three different formats for inline sounds: Sun's popular AU format, Windows WAV files, and MIDI files with a MID extension.

As with the inline video extensions, covered in the following section, the bgsound element is not supported in Netscape's browsers.

Tip

If you include sound on a page, be sure to provide a way for the user to turn it off. If they spend any time at all on your page, the sound might start to irritate them.

13

Inline Video with dynsrc

You can integrate video clips (AVI or MPEG) into Web pages displayed in Microsoft Internet Explorer 4 and above by using the dynsrc attribute in the img element, as in the following simple syntax:

```
<img dynsrc="a01607av.avi" loop="2" start="fileopen" />
```

In the previous line of code, Internet Explorer will play the video clip, indicated by the `dynsrc` attribute, two times after the Web page finishes loading. The `loop` attribute specifies the number of times to play the video clip, with one time being the default value. To play the clip indefinitely, use -1 instead. The `start` attribute defines when the video clip starts playing. You can choose from `fileopen`, which is the default, or `mouseover`, which plays the video when a person moves her mouse over the video.

Because you're using the `img` element, you can use other `img` attributes, such as `alt`, `align`, `border`, `height`, `width`, and so on, to format the video clip.

To make this compatible with Netscape Navigator, you should use the `src` attribute to designate a static `GIF` or `JPG` image that will be displayed in place of the video. The code would resemble the following:

```
<img src="a01607av.gif" dynsrc="a01607av.avi" loop="2" start="fileopen" />
```

Internet Explorer will ignore the value of the `src` attribute as long as the video supplied by `dynsrc` is valid.

Exercise 13.2: Embedding a QuickTime Movie

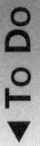

For your second exercise, you'll try your hand at embedding a QuickTime movie in a Web page. QuickTime is a video format created by Apple and is very popular because there are players for both Windows and the Mac OS.

According to Apple, you should use the `embed` element to embed QuickTime movies in your Web pages. This is a good example of a company that sponsors a multimedia file type creating additional attributes for you to use.

For starters, create or open a Web page template similar to the following:

```
<!DOCTYPE html PUBLIC "-//W3C//DTD XHTML 1.0 Transitional//EN"
"http://www.w3.org/TR/xhtml1/DTD/transitional.dtd">

<html>
<head>
<title></title>
</head>
<body>

</body>
</html>
```

From here, title the page and add a `div` element that you will use to center everything on the page.

Next, add a heading that appropriately describes the video and a title for the video.

```
<div align="center">
<h1>Apollo 17 Videos</h1>
```

▼ `<p>`Astronauts placing the flag on the Moon`</p>`

`</div>`

Now it's time to add the video itself. Begin with the `embed` element (place it under the video title), and enter the source and size of the video. Remember, those attributes are required.

```
<embed src="Apollo_17_Flag.qt"
       width="160"
       height="136"
```

For this exercise, you will add an assortment of attributes (described in more detail later). Add them under the `height` of the video. Don't forget to close the `embed` tag at the end of your final attribute.

```
        autoplay="false"
        controller="true"
        kioskmode="true
        dontflattenwhensaving
        pluginspage="http://www.apple.com/quicktime/download/" />
```

Okay, to see whether this works, test the page using your Web browser. When you are satisfied, add a final piece to the page that will show people where to get the QuickTime plug-in, if they need it. Because this is the last element on the page, remember to close the `div` with the end tag.

```
<p>Apple <a href="http://www.apple.com/quicktime">QuickTime</a> is
required to view this movie.
<a href="http://www.apple.com/quicktime"><img src="getquicktime4.gif"
border="0" align="absmiddle" width="88" height="31" /></a></p>
```

When it's all put together, the source code for your Web page resembles the following:

```
<!DOCTYPE html PUBLIC "-//W3C//DTD XHTML 1.0 Transitional//EN"
"http://www.w3.org/TR/xhtml1/DTD/transitional.dtd">

<html>
<head>
<title>Apollo Multimedia Archive</title>
</head>
<body>

<div align="center">
<h1>Apollo 17 Videos</h1>
<p>Astronauts placing the flag on the Moon</p>
<embed src="Apollo_17_Flag.qt"
       width="160"
       height="136"
       autoplay="false"
       controller="true"
▼      kioskmode="true
```

13

▼
```
            dontflattenwhensaving
            pluginspage="http://www.apple.com/quicktime/download/" />

<p>Apple <a href="http://www.apple.com/quicktime">QuickTime</a> is
required to view this movie.
<a href="http://www.apple.com/quicktime"><img src="getquicktime4.gif"
border="0" align="absmiddle" width="88" height="31" /></a></p>
</div>

</body>
</html>
```

Figure 13.12 shows the result in Internet Explorer.

FIGURE 13.12

Embedded QuickTime movies use special attributes created by Apple.

Embedded video —

Player controls —

Links to download QuickTime —

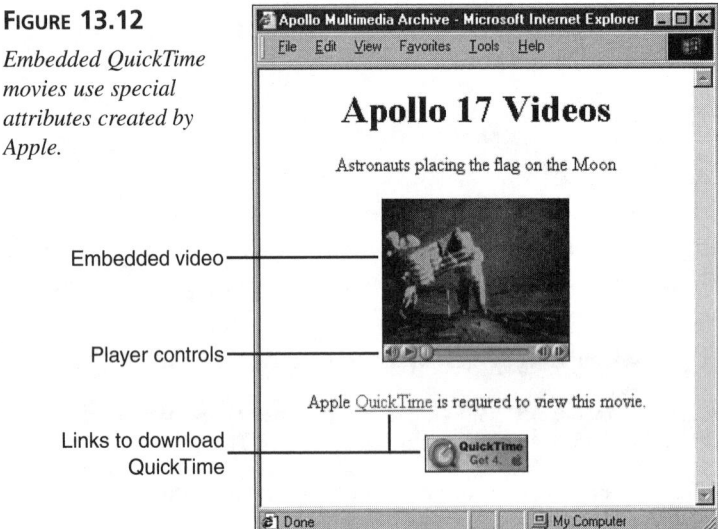

▲   Table 13.6 summarizes the attributes that QuickTime 4 supports.

TABLE 13.6   Attributes Supported by QuickTime 4

Attribute	Description
autoplay	When true, plays the movie when the plug-in estimates the clip can be played without waiting for more data (true or false).
bgcolor	Specifies the background color of any space not taken up by the movie. QuickTime 4 accepts the 16 HTML color names defined by the W3C (hexadecimal color value).
cache	When true, the browser caches movies, resulting in the browser replaying a movie from its cache rather than downloading again. Supported by Netscape Navigator 3 and later only (true or false).

TABLE 13.6 continued

Attribute	Description
controller	When `true`, makes the movie controller visible. Sixteen pixels should be added to the height of the movie when the controller is shown and the `height` attribute is used (`true` or `false`).
correction	Applicable to QuickTime VR only (`none` or `full`).
dontflattenwhensaving	Saves the move without flattening (no value).
enablejavascript	If this is set to true, you'll be able to control the QuickTime plug-in using JavaScript on the page.
endtime	Defines the last frame of the movie (time in hours:minutes:seconds:frames).
fov	The initial field of view angle for QuickTime VR movies (integer between 8 and 64).
height	Required. Defines the height of the region in which to display the movie. If the movie controller is visible, add 16 to the movie height to reach the total height required (in pixels).
hidden	Hides the movie, and really is only useful for background sound (no value).
hotspotn	Enables hotspots in a VR panorama where n is the hotspot ID (URL).
href	Links to another Web page or movie (URL).
kioskmode	When `true`, no pop-up menu is available for the movie and you cannot save it by dragging and dropping it (`true` or `false`).
loop	When `true`, the movie plays in an infinite loop. When set to `palindrome`, the movie will play alternately forward and backward (`true`, `false`, or `palindrome`).
movieid	A numeric ID (integer).
moviename	The movie name (text).
node	Sets the initial node for multinode QuickTime VR movies (integer).
pan	Sets the initial pan angle for QuickTime VR movies (integer from 0 to 360 degrees).
playeveryframe	When set to `true`, audio tracks are turned off and every frame of the movie is required to play, even if that forces a slower frame rate (`true` or `false`).
pluginspage	The URL to the QuickTime download page. You should set this to `http://www.apple.com/quicktime/download/`.
qtnextn	Identifies the URL for a movie to load and play when the current movie finishes. The number n can be an integer from 1 to 255 and defines the index of the URL in the playlist. The number nn is the index of the next qtnext URL to load (URL or `gotonn`).

13

TABLE **13.6**   continued

Attribute	Description
qtsrc	Forces a Web browser to use the QuickTime plug-in. The URL overrides any value in the src attribute (URL).
qtsrcchokespeed	Specifies the data rate of a movie, regardless of the actual connection speed (number).
qtsrcdontusebrowser	Instructs the plug-in to load the movie using its own internal methods rather than using the browser, thus preventing caching.
scale	tofit scales the movie to the dimensions set by the height and width attributes. aspect scales it to fit this box while maintaining the original aspect ratio of the movie. A number scales the movie by that ratio (tofit, aspect, or a number).
src	Sets the URL of the movie (URL).
starttime	Sets the first frame of the movie (time in hours:minutes:seconds:frames).
target	Launches the QuickTime Player to play the movie. The href attribute must be set to the movie in order for this to work (quicktimeplayer).
targetn	Used with hotspot and href. Sets the target for links that use the hotspot or href attribute. The number n corresponds to the hotspot number (name of a valid HTML frame).
targetcache	Caches the movie that is targeted by another movie (true or false).
tilt	Sets the initial tilt angle for QuickTime VR movies (integer).
type	Defines the MIME type of the movie. If the movie is visible and has width and height values, type must be included. This attribute is supported by Netscape Navigator 2 or later only (MIME type).volume Sets the initial audio volume. The default is 100 (integer from 0 to 100).
width	Sets the width of the display area for the movie (in pixels).

Note   QuickTime VR enables the author to create movies with a 360-degree view of an object that the user can pan through using the QuickTime viewer.

Sound and Video File Types

I challenge anyone to come up with a complete list of the audio and video formats currently in use on the Web today! There are so many that it defies a comprehensive inspection of the different multimedia file types, their extensions, and MIME types. So, I'll just cover the most popular ones, or at least the ones you might be inclined to include in your Web pages.

Before I list them, however, it would be useful for you to understand what factors to consider when choosing a multimedia type. By this, I mean sound or video quality, the size of the final file, how many plug-ins or players are compatible with the file type, and how readily availability the file type is.

The quality of sound and video files depends primarily on the original sampling rate, number of bits used per sample, and the number of channels.

The sampling rate is the number of times per second the sound or video is sampled, or measured. This value is represented in thousands of cycles per second, or kilohertz (KHz). Imagine yourself walking through a room and being able to open your eyes only once every five seconds. Do you see how that might be dangerous? Now imagine yourself opening and closing your eyes every second. You get a much better picture of what is around you and a closer approximation of reality. It's the same with sampling rates: The faster the sample, the closer the sound or video will represent the original recording. The only problem with this is that when you increase the number of times you sample per second, the amount of data quickly becomes voluminous.

The number of bits you use determines the fidelity of the sound. An 8-bit sample, for example, can measure 256 discrete values whereas 16-bit samples measure over 65,000 values. The more bits you use, the closer you come to the actual pitch of a sound or the color in a video clip.

The number of channels refers primarily to audio files, where you can have mono (one-channel) recordings, stereo (two-channel), and even more. Having more channels enriches the sound and makes for a more enjoyable experience, but again, at the price of file size.

Five audio file types are in common use on the Web today, each with its own unique advantages and drawbacks.

- *Audio Interchange File Format (AIFF)* files are uncompressed audio files and are most commonly used in the Macintosh community. The file sizes can be very large.

- *Musical Instrument Digital Interface (MIDI)* are synthesized rather than recorded sound. The file sizes are small; however, because you can't play back recorded sound, MIDI plays a niche role.

- µ-law (usually pronounced mu-law, also called Basic Sound) is the oldest form of audio on the Internet; however, its sound quality prevents it from being very attractive today. The good news is that the file sizes are small.

- Moving Picture Experts Group (MPEG) Audio offers three types (or layers) of sound files and is very popular because of MPEG's widespread acceptance as an audio and video format. The most recently successful type is MP3 audio, which offers almost CD-quality sound in a very small file size.

13

- Waveform (WAVE) files originally were created by Microsoft and IBM, and mostly are used on Windows computers.

Table 13.7 summarizes the popular audio formats.

TABLE 13.7 Common Audio File Formats

Name	Extension(s)	MIME Type
AIFF	AIFF, AIF, AIFC	audio/aiff
μ-law	AU, SND	audio/basic
MIDI	MID, RMI	audio/mid
Waveform (WAVE)	WAV	audio/wav
MPEG Audio	MP2, MP3	audio/x-mpeg
RealAudio	RA, RAM	audio/vnd.rn-realaudio

The common video types available are AVI, MPEG, and QuickTime, and are described in the following list:

- AVI, which stands for *Audio/Video Interleaved*, is a very popular Microsoft Windows video format. It is most compatible with Windows computers; however, in the last few years, it has become more accepted in other computing circles.
- MPEG video perhaps is the middleman between AVI and QuickTime and, as such, is very successful.
- QuickTime video is created by Macintosh and, much like AVI, finds the most support in circles that use the operating system of its creator. QuickTime has gained acceptance outside of the Macintosh community, however, so don't be afraid to use it.

Table 13.8 summarizes these video formats.

TABLE 13.8 Common Video File Formats

Name	Extension(s)	MIME Type
Audio/Video Interleaved	AVI	video/x-msvideo
MPEG	MPEG, MPG	video/mpeg
QuickTime	MOV, QT	video/quicktime
RealVideo	RV	video/vnd.m-realvideo

Another factor you might want to consider is whether a particular file type is *streamable*. This means it can be played as it's being downloaded. At one time, RealAudio and

RealVideo were the two main streamable audio and video formats. These days, though, there are players for many file types that allow the files to be streamed. For example, many MP3 players will allow MP3s to be played as they're downloaded, and QuickTime files are also streamed to the player. When you're choosing a multimedia format, you should strongly consider one that supports streaming.

Of Plug-Ins and Players

Of all the advances made recently to support more inline multimedia and animation on the Web, plug-ins, over the longer term, will likely have the most significant effect.

Plug-ins are sort of like built-in helper applications for your browser. Rather than existing entirely separate from the browser, however, they plug-in to your browser (hence, the name) and work internally in conjunction with your browser, adding new capabilities to the browser itself. A video plug-in allows video files to be played directly inline with the browser. Similarly, a spreadsheet plug-in allows editable spreadsheets to be included as elements in a Web page. The plug-ins can enable links back to the browser as well. So, the spreadsheet, for example, could theoretically contain links that could be activated and followed from inside the plug-in.

Netscape introduced the concept of plug-ins with the 2.0 version of its browser, and maintains a current list of them on its site. Several plug-ins are available for many forms of sound and video; in fact, Netscape includes sound and video plug-ins already installed, supporting formats such as AU, AIFF, WAV, MIDI, AVI, and QuickTime.

As you learned earlier today, the problem with plug-ins is that if you use them in your Web pages, all your visitors will need to have browsers that support plug-ins (such as Netscape or Microsoft Internet Explorer). They must also have the correct plug-in installed and available. (Visitors who don't have your plug-in will get empty space or broken icons on your page where the multimedia should be.) To further complicate the matter, some plug-ins are available only for some platforms. For some forms of multimedia, you also might need to configure your server to deliver the new multimedia with the correct type of content.

13

Windows Media Player

The Windows Media Player, available at www.microsoft.com/windows/mediaplayer, is included as part of the Windows operating system and can play many multimedia file types. Version 7.0, shown in Figure 13.13, is currently available. Users of Windows 2000, Windows ME, or Windows 98 can use version 7.0. If you're using Windows NT 4.0 or Windows 95, you must stick with Windows Media Player 6.4.

FIGURE 13.13

*The Windows Media
Player can play AVIs
and other popular
multimedia formats.*

Although version 7.0 is optimized for Microsoft Internet Explorer 4 and above, versions
for previous versions of Internet Explorer and other non-Microsoft browsers are available. In addition, a Macintosh version also is available.

Version 7.0 of the Media Player can play the following file types:

- WMF—Windows Media Format
- MP3—MPEG Layer 3 audio format
- MPG, MPEG—Standard MPEG Layer 1 video and Layer 2 audio formats
- WAV, AU, AIFF—Legacy sound files
- AVI—Audio/Video Interleave video (Microsoft)
- ASF—Active Streaming Format (Microsoft)
- MID—MIDI sound files
- VOD—Voice on Demand
- RMI—Remote method invocation

Macromedia Flash

Developed by Macromedia, the Flash player is a popular plug-in that enables you to
stream low-bandwidth animations (created with Macromedia Flash) into your Web pages.
Flash animations are extremely compact in comparison to traditional bitmap animations.

The Flash player offers the advantage of streaming the animations as your browser receives them rather than having to wait for the entire animation to download.

Flash is becoming a platform for deploying all sorts of Web content. Not only can users create animations, but they can also create application interfaces because Flash is scriptable using JavaScript. You can also stream audio files to the browser through Flash. For further information, visit the Macromedia Flash Web site at `http://www.macromedia.com/flash`.

Macromedia Shockwave

Shockwave is a plug-in that enables Macromedia Director movies to be played as inline multimedia on a Web page. Macromedia Director is an extremely popular tool among professional multimedia developers for creating multimedia presentations, including synchronized sound and video as well as interactivity. (In fact, many of the CD-ROMs you can buy today were developed by using Macromedia Director.) If you're used to working with Director, Shockwave provides an easy way to put Director presentations on the Web. Or, if you're looking to do serious multimedia work on the Web or anywhere else, Director is definitely a tool to check out. You can find additional information on Macromedia Shockwave at `http://www.macromedia.com/shockwave`.

QuickTime 4 by Apple

Apple QuickTime 4 is both a file format and a player. The player, available from Apple at `www.apple.com/quicktime`, plays Apple's QuickTime movies (`QT`, `MOV`) and is available for both Macintosh and Windows platforms (see Figure 13.14).

FIGURE 13.14

Use the QuickTime 4 player to play saved or streaming QuickTime movies.

13

When you install the player, plug-ins for both Internet Explorer and Netscape Navigator are installed.

In addition to playing QuickTime movies, QuickTime VR (for virtual reality) is also supported. These aren't movies per se, but rather interactive images that provide a three-dimensional view of a scene. For example, using QuickTime VR, you can provide an image of a car that allows the user to view it from any angle.

RealNetworks Grab Bag

RealNetworks has two popular players available today for both Windows and Macintosh computers: RealPlayer and RealJukebox (see Figure 13.15).

FIGURE 13.15

Use RealPlayer to check out streaming audio and video.

RealPlayer plays streaming RealAudio and RealVideo files of the following variety:

- RM, RA, RAM—RealAudio/RealVideo streamed content
- RT—Real Text streamed text formats
- RP—RealPix streamed GIF and JPG images
- GIF, JPG—Standalone JPG and GIF images
- MP3—MPEG Layer 3 audio format
- SWF—RealFlash and Shockwave Flash animation
- SMIL, SMI—SMIL-formatted (multiple data type layout) files
- .VIV, .VIVO—Vivo video files
- .MPG, .MPEG—Standard MPEG Layer 1 video and Layer 2 audio formats

- WAV, AU, AIFF—Legacy sound files
- QT, MOV—QuickTime video (uncompressed)
- AVI—Audio/Video Interleave video (Microsoft)
- ASF—Active Streaming Format (Microsoft)
- MID—MIDI sound files

RealNetworks also produces a product called RealJukebox, which is a player that enables you to record and play CDs, download and play music off the Internet, and manage your music collection (see Figure 13.16). File types RealJukebox can encode include RealAudio files as well as MP3, and WAV. RealJukebox can play all the files in the preceding list, as well as Liquid Audio (LQT), A2B, and EMMS files. New formats are scheduled to be added as they become popular.

FIGURE 13.16

RealJukebox playing a downloaded MP3 audio file.

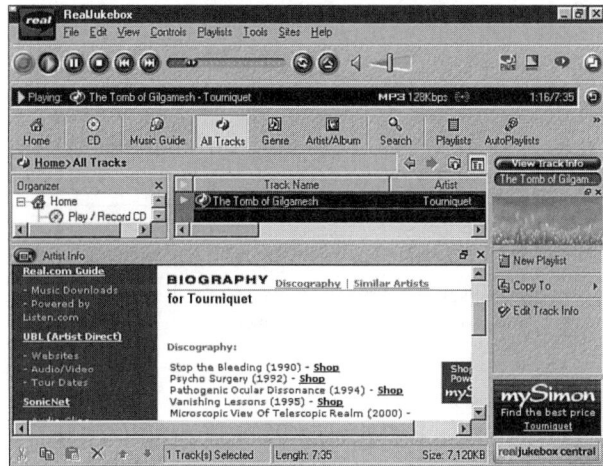

WinAmp

WinAmp is the quintessential MP3 player. It was one of the first popular MP3 players, and it has remained very popular even as nearly every other audio application has added support for MP3 files. Not only can WinAmp play MP3 files that you create yourself or download over the Internet, but it can tune into Internet radio stations that stream MP3 audio and can play other popular audio formats, like WAV. WinAmp appears in Figure 13.17.

13

FIGURE 13.17

WinAmp.

Other Plug-Ins

Although there isn't enough space to completely cover all the available audio and video plug-ins, following is a short list of some other popular plug-ins:

- The Adobe SVG Viewer is a free plug-in that enables you to view Scalable Vector Graphics files, which are an alternative to Flash animations. SVG isn't nearly as widespread as Flash, but it should become more popular in the future because Adobe is behind it and it's a documented W3C standard. You can get the viewer at `http://www.adobe.com/svg/viewer/install/main.html`.

- mBED, by mBED Software (`http://www.mbed.com`), is available as a Netscape plug-in as well as an OCX version for Internet Explorer. This plug-in enables you to display animation, sounds, interactive buttons, and synchronized Real Audio.

- Sizzler, by Totally Hip Software (`http://www.totallyhip.com/Products/Products.html`), enables simultaneous viewing and interaction with Web pages while it streams animation to your browser. You can easily convert popular animations to Sizzler format.

- Crescendo, by LiveUpdate (`http://www.liveupdate.com/crescendo.html`), uses a CD-like control panel with transport controls and a digital counter to stream MIDI music into a Web page.

- Beatnik, by Headspace (`http://www.headspace.com`), plays Rich Music Format (RMF) and other sound file formats (`MIDI`, `MOD`, `WAV`, `AIFF`, and `AU`) within Web browsers. The sound comes through at a fidelity and quality that is comparable to high-end soundcards, and sounds the same across multiple platforms.

Summary

Well, today's lesson was certainly an eye- and earful! You learned that there are only two ways to include audio and video files in your Web pages: linking to them and embedding them.

External multimedia files cannot be read directly by your Web browser. Instead, if you link to an external file, your browser starts up a "helper" application to view or play these files. You also learned how external multimedia works, how to use sound and video files as external multimedia, and some hints for designing by using external multimedia files.

Much of this lesson focuses on examples of embedding multimedia files directly into the Web browser. You can use the embed element, or a combination of embed and object.

Table 13.9 shows a summary of the tags you learned about today.

TABLE 13.9   Tags for Inline Multimedia

Tag	Attribute	Use
`<a>`	`href`	Links to a sound or video file exactly as you link to any other type of file.
`<embed>`		Embeds objects into Web pages.
`<object>...<object>`		Embeds objects into Web pages.
`<param>...</param>`		Specifies parameters to be passed to the embedded object. Used in the `object` element.
`<img>`	`dynsrc`	Includes a sound or video file instead of an image. If the file cannot be found or played, the normal image (in `src`) is shown. Used by Internet Explorer only.
`<bgsound>`		Plays a background sound. Used by Internet Explorer only.

Workshop

The following workshop includes questions you might ask about including sound and video in Web pages, quizzes to test your knowledge, and two quick exercises.

Q&A

Q What's the quickest way to get started adding multimedia to my site?

A Remember that you can use at least one absolutely sure-fire method to include sound and video in your Web pages: link to them. Although that might not be as exciting as embedding them in the Web browser window, you know the Web page will work. Of course, the person visiting your site must still have the appropriate application to play the file, but you can help her out by providing links to any required players or plug-ins.

13

Q Should I be worried about Web browser and HTML compatibility when it comes to audio and video?

A Unfortunately, yes. Most other HTML elements and techniques are standardized to the point in which you can be confident that your code will work across most popular Web browsers. Embedding audio and video is a completely different ballgame. My best advice is for you to study up on the different ways to include sound and video, the differences in how the Web browsers embed these files, and then test your Web pages relentlessly in both Microsoft Internet Explorer and Netscape Navigator.

Q What are the differences between AVI, MPEG, and QuickTime movies?

A The underlying differences are beyond the scope of this lesson, but it has to do with how the audio and video data is encoded, compressed, and stored in the resulting files. Each file type uses different methods that are all unique. The practical difference is that each one might require a different player to be heard/viewed properly.

Q Should I bother using the techniques solely compatible with Internet Explorer, such as `dynrsrc`?

A My advice is not to bother with them because you might be ignoring (and hence alienating) a good portion of your audience. If you are in an environment that is "IE-only," you can feel free to use them. Ultimately, the choice is up to you.

Quiz

1. What are the differences between a helper application (also called a player) and a plug-in?

2. In what ways can you insert multimedia into your Web pages?

3. What are the advantages and disadvantages of using plug-ins?

4. What is streaming multimedia?

Quiz Answers

1. Helper applications run externally to your Web browser and open files that your browser does not support. The browser downloads a file and then passes it on to an external helper application that reads and plays the file. Plug-ins work within the browser to read and play files.

2. You can link to them or embed them.

3. The advantage to using plug-ins is that they enable you to insert many different types of content into your pages. The disadvantage to using them is that you can't guarantee that everyone will have them or will want to take the time to download

them to experience your site. Some people use browsers that don't support them, and not all plug-ins are universally supported across Web browsers and operating systems.

4. Streaming multimedia doesn't wait to be completely downloaded before it can begin playing.

Exercises

1. Tour the Web and visit sites that use multimedia. You might start out at `http://www.adcritic.com` for an example of video, and `http://www.broadcast.com` for streaming audio. Macromedia's Showcase at `http://www.macromedia.com/showcase/` always features sites that create multimedia content. See how others include it in their Web sites. Try visiting the same site using Internet Explorer and Netscape Navigator. Is there a difference? What prompts you to download a plug-in?

2. Explore the plug-ins page at Netscape's site (`http://home.netscape.com/plugins/index.html`) to learn more about the wide range of available plug-ins, and which platforms are supported by each of them.

13

DAY 14

Designing Forms

Up to this point, you have learned almost everything you need to know to create functional, attractive, and somewhat interactive Web pages. If you think about it, however, the pages you've created thus far have a one-way information flow. Your HTML documents, images, sounds, and video have been traveling to Web browsers with no return ticket.

Today's lesson is about creating HTML forms in order to collect information from people visiting your Web site. Forms enable you to gather just about any kind of information for immediate processing by a server-side script or for later analysis using other applications. If you've spent much time browsing the Web, undoubtedly you have run across forms of various flavors. Many forms exist: simple forms that perform searches, forms that log you in to Web sites, forms that enable you to order products online, and so on. They all share one thing in common: accepting input from a Web page visitor.

If you're one to worry about compatibility, you can set your mind at ease. HTML forms have been around since the beginning of the HTML language and are supported by every Web browser in common use. I'll make sure to point out any possible compatibility problems along the way.

Don't be intimidated by forms! Although they may look complex, actually they are very easy to code. The hardest part is formatting them. Today's lesson covers the following topics, which will enable you to create any type of form possible with HTML:

- How HTML forms interact with server-side scripts to provide interactivity
- Creating simple forms to get the hang of it.
- Learning all the types of form controls you can use to create radio buttons, check boxes, and more
- Using more advanced form controls to amaze your friends and co-workers
- Form planning so that your data matches any server-side scripts you use

Understanding Form and Function

Right off the bat, you need to understand a few things about forms. First, a form is part of a Web page that you create using HTML elements. Each form contains a form element that has special controls, such as buttons, text fields, check boxes, submit buttons, and menus. These controls make up the user interface for the form (that is, the pieces of the form users see on the Web page). When people fill out forms, they are interacting with the controls of the forms. In addition, you can use many other HTML elements within forms to create legends, provide additional information, add structure, and so on. These elements are not part of the form itself, but they can enhance your form's look or improve its usability.

When someone fills out an HTML form, she enters information or makes choices using the form controls. The final step is submitting it, at which time several things happen. First, the form identifies the controls within the form that contain data and builds a form data set to contain it. Next, the data set is encoded and sent to the Web server to be processed.

It is very important that you understand the implications of this final step. The data is what you want, after all! This is the reason you've chosen to create a form in the first place. After a user clicks the Submit button, the process ceases to be one of pure HTML and becomes reliant upon scripts (called *Common Gateway Interface*, or *CGI* scripts, most often written in a scripting language called Perl) that are resident on the Web server. In other words, for your form to be successful, you must already have a script on the server that will store or manipulate the data in some manner.

There are a few important exceptions to this rule. First, a form may redirect people to another Web page based on their input, or it may send an email containing the form data to an email address. The second exception is useful and is an easy way for you to test forms. Rather than using a script, you can simply instruct the form to email the contents to you. One final exception is that forms sometimes are used in Dynamic HTML because they trap user events, such as clicking the mouse. A form on a dynamic Web page might not be used to collect data, but to create buttons from which the user can choose to perform some action.

Exercise 14.1: Creating a Simple Form That Accepts a Name and Password

Okay, let's get right to it and create a simple form that illustrates the concepts just presented.

It's a Web page that prompts the user to enter a name and a password to continue.

Start by opening up your favorite HTML editor (mine is Notepad) and creating a Web page template. Enter the standard HTML header information, include the `body` element, and then close the `body` and `html` elements to form a template from which to work. If you have a template similar to this already, just load it into your HTML editor:

```
<!DOCTYPE html PUBLIC "-//W3C//DTD XHTML 1.0 Transitional//EN"
"http://www.w3.org/TR/xhtml1/DTD/transitional.dtd">
<html>
<head>
<title>myTitle</title>
</head>
<body>


</body>
</html>
```

Note

I tend to use Transitional HTML and note it in the `<!doctype>` declaration. This gives me the flexibility of adding deprecated HTML elements if I choose, without having to worry about validation errors.

Next, add your `title` so that people will understand the purpose of the Web page:

```
<title>Enter the Wabbit Hole</title>
```

Within the `body` of the Web page, add a `form` element. I have added both the opening and closing tags, with an empty line between them so that I don't forget to close the `form` when I'm finished:

```
<form action="http://www.example.com/cgi-bin/entrance.cgi" method="post">

</form>
```

14

▼

Before continuing, you need to know more about the `form` element and the attributes you see within the opening tag. Obviously, `form` begins the element and indicates that you are creating an HTML form. The `action` attribute, which is required, specifies the URL to the server-side script (including the filename) that will process the form when it is submitted. It is very important that the script with the name you have entered is present on your Web server at the location the URL specifies.

Note

Prior to "going live" with forms, you should contact your ISP and ask whether you can use their scripts or add your own. You also need to determine the URL that points to the directory on the server that contains the scripts. Some ISPs rigidly control scripts for security purposes and will not allow you to create or add scripts to the server. If that is the case, and you really need to implement forms on your Web pages, you should consider searching for a new ISP.

The next attribute is `method`, which can accept one of two possible values: `post` or `get`. These values define how form data is submitted to your Web server. The `post` method includes the form data in the body of the form and sends it to the Web server. The `get` method appends the data to the URL specified in the `action` attribute and most often is used in searches.

Now add some form controls and information to make it easy for a visitor to understand how to fill out the form. Within the `form` element, begin by adding a helpful description of the data to be entered by the user, and then add a `text` form control. This prompts them to enter their name in a text-entry field. Don't worry about positioning just yet, because later you will put all the form controls into a table:

```
<form action="http://www.example.com/cgi-bin/entrance.cgi"
method="post">
Your wascawy name:<input type="text" name="username" />
</form>
```

Next, add another bit of helpful text and a password control:

```
<form action="http://www.example.com/cgi-bin/entrance.cgi" method="post">
Your wascawy name:<input type="text" name="username" />
Your just as wascawy password:<input type="password"
name="userpassword" />
</form>
```

Notice that both of these form controls are part of the `input` element. The `type` attribute defines which type of control will be created. In this case, you have a text control and a

▼

password control. Each type of control has a distinct appearance, accepts a different type

▼ of user input, and is suitable for different purposes. Each control is also assigned a name that distinguishes it and its data from the other form controls.

Finally, add a submit button so that the user can send the information he or she entered into the form. Add a reset button that clears the form in case the user made a mistake or wants to start over:

```
<form action="http://www.example.com/cgi-bin/entrance.cgi" method="post">
Your wascawy name:<input type="text" name="username" />
Your just as wascawy password:<input type="password"
name="userpassword" />
<input type="submit" value="Enter" />
<input type="reset" value="Oops!" />
</form>
```

The submit and reset buttons represent other types of input element. Notice that I've included the value attribute with each. In this case, the value attribute modifies the text that is shown in the button and displayed in the Web browser. You can choose not to use the value attribute with these buttons. If so, the Web browser will display default text for these two types of buttons.

Note   When you're naming form controls and labeling buttons, you should strive for clarity and meaning. If a form is frustrating or hard to figure out, visitors will leave your site for greener pastures!

Figure 14.1 contains a screen shot of the form with all of the form elements in place.

FIGURE 14.1

The form with all of the input elements in place.

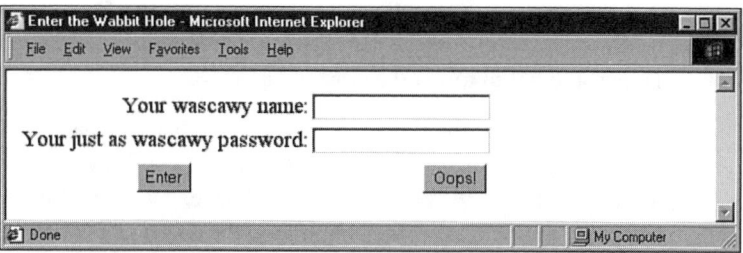

At this point, you've created the form and it's ready to rumble. However, if you load it into your Web browser, you'll see that it doesn't look all that appealing. It's time to add a few graphical elements to make the page look better, and arrange the elements of the
▼ form into a nicely aligned table.

14

▼   I've created three graphics to place at the top of the page and used a `table` to arrange
them:

```
<table border="0">
    <tr>
        <td><img src="sign.gif" width="174" height="200" /></td>
        <td align="center"><img src="arrow.gif" width="85"
        height="100" /><br>
        <img src="hole.gif" width="143" height="58" /></td>
    </tr>
</table>
```

Next, create another `table` and that contains four rows and two columns. You're going to
put your `form` in the table to position all the elements:

```
<table border="0">
<tr>
    <td></td>
    <td></td>
</tr>
<tr>
    <td></td>
    <td></td>
</tr>
<tr>
    <td></td>
    <td></td>
<tr>
    <td></td>
    <td></td>
</tr>
</table>
```

Now, add the form elements by inserting the opening `form` tag after the opening `table`
tag. Insert the form controls into the rows and columns of the table as I have shown,
making sure not to forget the closing `form` tag.

Notice that I've left the third row of the `table` blank—that's because I'm cheating! After
I completed the source code for this example, I wanted a bit more space between the
`password` field and the buttons. After a bit of experimentation, I also aligned the text
prompts to the right, set each column to take up 50 percent of the total width of the table,
and centered the buttons in their respective columns:

```
<table border="0">
    <form action="http://www.example.com/cgi-bin/entrance.cgi"
    method="post">
    <tr>
        <td align="right" width="50%">Your wascawy name:</td>
        <td width="50%"><input type="text" name="username" /></td>
▼       </tr>
```

▼
```
    <tr>
        <td align="right">Your just as wascawy password:</td>
        <td><input type="password" name="userpassword" /></td>
    </tr>
    <tr>
        <td></td>
        <td></td>
    </tr>
    <tr>
        <td align="center"><input type="submit" value="Enter" /></td>
        <td align="center"><input type="reset" value="Oops!" /></td>
    </tr>
    </form>
</table>
```

This looks like it stands a chance of working, so now put all the source code together.

A few final notes are warranted: First, I wrapped everything up in a div element and set the align attribute to center in order to center everything on the page. Note the location of the opening and closing div tags on the page. To add some extra space between the graphics and the form, I also included a line break using the br element:

INPUT

```
<!DOCTYPE html PUBLIC "-//W3C//DTD XHTML 1.0 Transitional//EN"
"http://www.w3.org/TR/xhtml1/DTD/transitional.dtd">
<html>
<head>
<title>Enter the Wabbit Hole</title>
</head>
<body>
<div align="center">
<table border="0">
    <tr>
        <td><img src="sign.gif" width="174" height="200" /></td>
        <td align="center"><img src="arrow.gif" width="85"
        height="100" /><br>
        <img src="hole.gif" width="143" height="58" /></td>
    </tr>
</table>
<br>
<table border="0">
    <form action="http://www.example.com/cgi-bin/entrance.cgi"
    method="post">
    <tr>
        <td align="right" width="50%">Your wascawy name:</td>
        <td width="50%"><input type="text" name="username" /></td>
    </tr>
    <tr>
        <td align="right">Your just as wascawy password:</td>
        <td><input type="password" name="userpassword" /></td>
    </tr>
```
▼

14

▼

```
    <tr>
        <td></td> <!-- Comment: left blank to add space -->
        <td></td> <!-- Comment: left blank to add space -->
    </tr>
    <tr>
        <td align="center"><input type="submit" value="Enter" /></td>
        <td align="center"><input type="reset" value="Oops!" /></td>
    </tr>
    </form>
</table>
</div>
</body>
</html>
```

That took a little work, but I think the final product shown in Figure 14.2 looks good.

OUTPUT

FIGURE 14.2

A simple HTML form with four form controls provides access to the Secret Wabbit Hole.

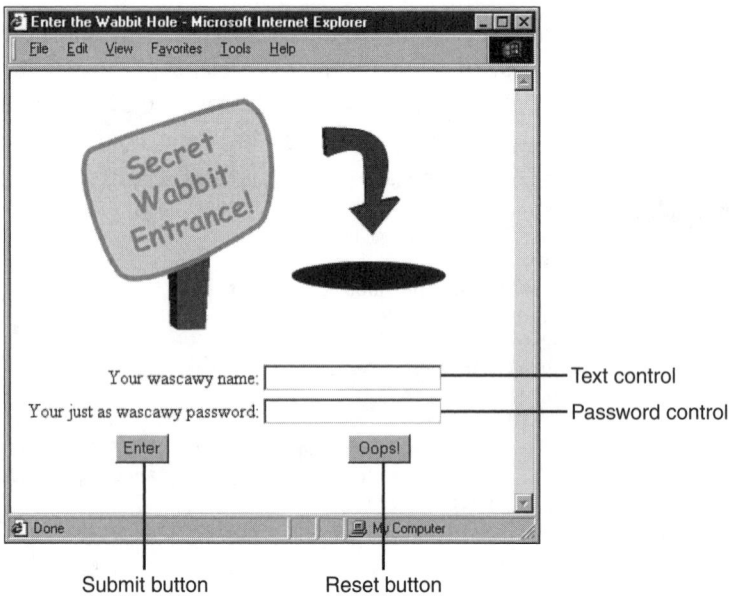

To complete the exercise, I tested the form to see whether it returned the data I wanted. The following is what the data set looks like:

```
username=Elmer&userpassword=hunter
```

It's pretty measly, but you can see that each form element name contains data that I entered into the form and is nicely tied to that data. Using a script, you'll find it easy to

▲ parse this output, manipulate it, and achieve your overall purpose.

Essential Elements of a Form

The first exercise showed you how to use the `form` element, including simple form controls, and the `submit` and `reset` buttons. This section fully explains and expands upon this. The discussion is divided into two major areas: the `form` element, and the controls created by the `input` element. After this discussion, you'll walk through a more complicated exercise.

Using the `form` Element to Create Forms

Because the `form` element is the basis for all forms created in Web pages, it is important that you understand how to use it.

First, forms are considered *block-level elements*. To understand this, you need to know about the other basic HTML content model: *inline elements*. You apply inline elements, such as `<b>` and `<u>`, to text or individual characters to modify their appearance. As such, they contain the text they modify, such as `<b>I Love this game!</b>`, and can contain other nested inline elements. `<b>I <i>Love</i> this game!</b>` is perfectly valid HTML.

Block-level elements are larger organizational structures (such as the `form` and `table` elements). They can include Web page content and inline elements, in addition to other block-level HTML elements. If you display the following HTML in a Web browser, the existence of the nested inline element does not start a new line:

```
<b>Nesting <i>inline</i> elements does not cause a line-break.</b>
```

However, block-level elements such as form start a new line in the Web browser. The upshot of all of this is that if you are concerned about the layout of your page, the opening tag of the `form` element will cause a new line to be created. Consider the following code fragment:

```
<p>Oatmeal <form action="http://www.example.com/cgi-bin/register.cgi"
method="post">
lovers wishing to view our private stock of recipes need to enter
your name and password.</p>
```

Placing the `form` tag in its current location causes a line break to be inserted after `Oatmeal`, resulting in the inappropriate visual effect shown in Figure 14.3.

To sum up thus far, the `form` element causes a new line to be created, and the form can contain content, inline, and other block-level elements. The one exception to this is that you cannot nest forms—only one form at a time, please!

The syntax for creating the `form` element is fairly straightforward. The two most commonly used attributes are `action` and `method`. Both of these attributes are optional. The following example shows the typical usage of the `<form>` tag:

```
<form action="someaction" method="get or post">
```

14

```
content, form controls, and other HTML elements
</form>
```

Line breaks at form tag

FIGURE 14.3

Placing a form *element within an inline element, such as the paragraph <p>, causes a line break.*

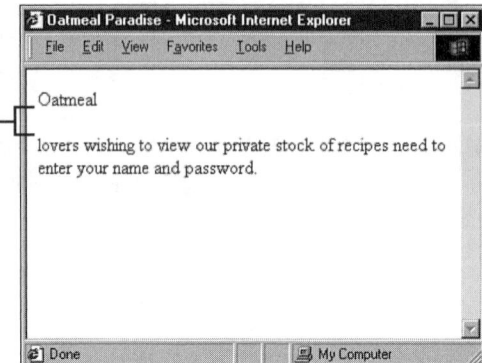

action defines the action taken when the form is submitted, and it generally contains a URL for a CGI script on the Web server. Again, remember that in order for the form to be submitted successfully, the script must be in the exact location you specify and working properly.

If you leave out the action attribute, the form is submitted to the current URL. In other words, if the form appears on the page http://www.example.com/form.html and you leave off the action attribute, the form will be submitted to that URL by default. This probably doesn't seem very useful, but it is if your form is generated by a program instead of residing in an HTML file. Then the form will just be submitted back to that program for processing.

Although most forms send their data to scripts, you also can make the action link to another Web page or a mailto link. The latter is formed as follows:

```
<form action="mailto:somebody@isp.com" method="post">
```

This attaches the form data set to an email, which then is sent to the email address listed in the action attribute.

Tip

To test your forms, I recommend using mailto to send yourself the results of your test form. This enables you to see the data submitted using the form and make sure that it's what you expect. The advantage of this is that you can make sure the form works properly without linking it up with the script that will be used to process the data.

The `method` attribute can be one of two possible values: `get` or `post`. The method indicates how the form data should be packaged in the request that's sent back to the server. The `get` method appends the form data onto the URL in the request. The form data is separated from the URL in the request by a question mark and is referred to as the query string. If I had a text input field named `searchstring` and had entered `Orangutans` in the field, the resulting would look like the following:

```
http://www.example.com/cgi-bin/search?searchstring=Orangutans
```

The `method` attribute is not required; if you leave it out, the `get` method will be used. The other method is `post`. Rather than appending the form data to the URL and sending the combined URL-data string to the server, `post` sends the form data to the location specified by the `action` attribute in the body of the request.

That about does it for the `form` element, but you've really only just begun. The `form` element alone is just a container for the form elements that are actually used to gather data from users. It just indicates where the data should go and how it should be packaged. To actually gather information, you're going to need items called form controls.

Creating Form Controls with the `input` Element

Now it's time to learn how to create the elements that gather information within a form. The `input` element enables you to create many different types of controls.

NEW TERM *Form controls* are special HTML elements used in a `form` that allow you to gather information from visitors to your Web page. The information is collected into a data set that is sent to the location of the `action` attribute when the form is submitted.

The `input` element consists of an opening tag with attributes, no other content, and no closing tag:

```
<input attributes />
```

The key point here is choosing the right attributes that will create the type of form control you need. The most important of these is `type`, which defines the control. For all controls, except submit and reset buttons, the `name` attribute is required. It names the control so that data can be assigned to the form control name when sent to the server. The rest of this section describes the different types of controls you can create using the `input` element.

Creating Text Controls

Text controls enable you to gather information from a user in small quantities. This control type creates a single-line text input field in which users can type information, such as their name or a search term. Unlike other controls, such as radio buttons (which have

14

only two states—on and off) or menu items (which are predefined), text controls give visitors complete freedom to enter any text they desire.

Text controls always are part of an `input` element, which is included in the `form` element. Begin by creating an `input` element and choose `text` as the value for the `type` attribute. Make sure to name your control so that the server script will be able to process the value:

```
<p>Enter the name of your pet: <input type="text" name="petname" /></p>
```

Figure 14.4 shows this text control, which tells the user what to type in.

FIGURE **14.4**

Text controls create a single-line text entry field.

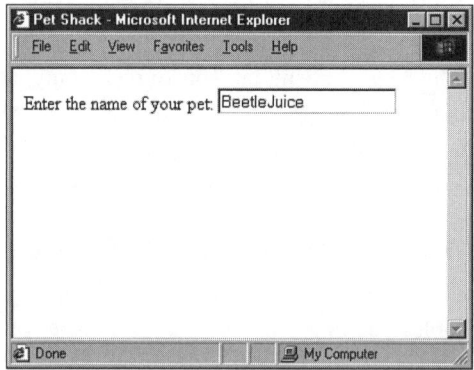

You can modify the appearance of text controls by using the `size` attribute. Entering a number sets the width of the text control in characters, as in the following:

```
<input type="text" name="petname" size="15" />
```

To limit the number of characters a user can enter, add the `maxlength` attribute to the text control. This does not affect the display of the field; it just prevents the user from entering more characters than specified by this attribute. If users attempt to enter more text, their Web browsers will stop accepting input for that particular control.

```
<input type="text" name="petname" size="15" maxlength="15" />
```

To display text in the text control before the user enters any information, use the `value` attribute. It can act as a prompt or reminder to the user to enter data, as in the following:

```
<input type="text" name="petname" size="15" maxlength="15" value="Enter Pet
Name" />
```

In this case, "Enter Pet Name" appears in the control when the form is drawn in the Web browser. It remains there until the user modifies it.

When you're using the `value` attribute, using a value that is larger than the size of the text control can confuse the user because the text will appear to be cut off. Try to use only enough information to make your point. Ensure that any `value` is less than or equal to the number of characters you specified in `maxlength`.

To make text controls read-only, include the `readonly` attribute, as in the following:

```
<input type="text" name="year" value="1999" readonly="readonly" />
```

This prevents users from entering text in the text control. You might want to use this if the form is prepopulated when it appears and you want the users to be able to see the value without actually changing it.

Creating Password Controls

The password control is very similar to the text control because users enter only a small amount of text in the form. The difference is that it masks the user's input with asterisks.

You don't have to limit your use of the `password` control to just passwords. You can use it for any sensitive material that you feel needs to be hidden when the user enters it into the form.

To create a `password` control, create an `input` element and assign `password` to the `type` attribute. To limit the size of the password control and the maximum number of characters a user can enter, you can use the `size` and `maxlength` attributes, as in the following code:

```
<p>Enter your password: <input type="password" name="userpassword"
size="8" maxlength="8" /></p>
```

Figure 14.5 shows a password control with some helpful text that tells the user the purpose of the control.

Note that you do not need to include the `value` attribute because the value you enter is masked when drawn into the user's Web browser.

14

FIGURE 14.5

Create masked text input fields with password controls.

 **Caution**   When data entered in a `password` field is sent to the server, it is not encrypted in any way. Therefore, this is not a secure means of transmitting sensitive information. Although the users can't read what they are typing, the `password` control provides no other security measures.

Creating Submit Buttons

You use the submit button to transmit form data for processing by a server-side script or other program. Entering `submit` as the `type` of control creates a submit button with the default label of Submit Query. To change the button text, use the `value` attribute and enter your own description, as follows:

```
<input type="submit" value="Send Form Data" />
```

  Note   Your forms can contain more than one submit button.

If you specify a `name` attribute for a `submit` field, the `value` that you assign to the field will be sent to the server as well if the user clicks on that submit button. This allows you to take different actions based on which submit button the user clicks on, if you have more than one. For example, you could create two submit buttons, both with the `name` attribute set to `"action"`. The first might have a value of `"edit"` and the second a value of `"delete"`. In your script, you could test the value associated with that field to determine what the user wanted to do when she submitted the form.

Creating Reset Buttons

You use reset buttons to clear the contents of the form and set all the form controls to their initial default values. In most cases, this is the value you specify using the `value` attribute when you create each control. As with the `submit` button, you can change the default caption of `reset` to one of your own choosing by using the `value` attribute, as in the following:

```
<input type="reset" value="Clear Form" />
```

 **Caution**

> Reset buttons can be a source of some confusion for users. Unless you have a really good reason to include them on your forms, you should probably just avoid using them. If your form is large and the user hits the reset button when she meant to hit the submit button, she's not going to be very pleased with having to go back and reenter all of her data.

Creating Check Box Controls

Check boxes enable you to create a control that can be toggled between checked and unchecked, reflecting an on or off state (see Figure 14.6). To create a check box, use the `input` element and enter `checkbox` as the type of control. Be sure to include the `name` attribute so that the script will know to which control the data is assigned, as in the following example:

```
<p>Check to receive SPAM e-mail <input type="checkbox" name="spam" /></p>
```

FIGURE 14.6

Check box controls create boxes for users to check.

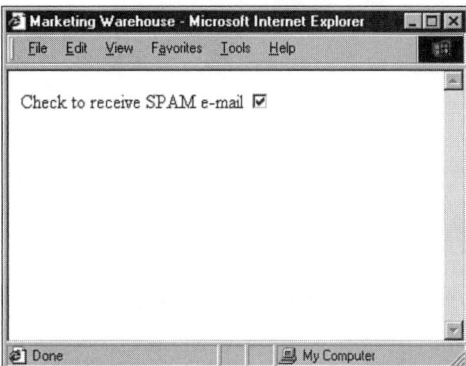

14

To display the check box as checked, include the `checked` attribute, as in the following:

```
<input type="checkbox" name="year" checked="checked" />
```

You can group check boxes together and assign them the same control name. This allows multiple values to be chosen and applied to one property:

```
<p>Check all symptoms that you are experiencing:<br />
Nausea <input type="checkbox" name="symptoms" value="nausea" /><br />
Light-headedness <input type="checkbox" name="symptoms"
value="lightheadedness" /><br />
Fever <input type="checkbox" name="symptoms" value="fever" /><br />
Headache <input type="checkbox" name="symptoms" value="headache" /><br />
</p>
```

When this form is submitted to a script for processing, each check box that is checked returns a value associated with the name of the check box.

Creating Radio Buttons

Radio buttons are almost identical to check boxes, but they appear differently in the Web browser. Rather than a box that can be checked or unchecked, a small circular button is drawn and filled when the user selects it (see Figure 14.7). You create radio buttons in an `input` element by entering `radio` as the type of control. The `value` attribute, which is mandatory, assigns data to the radio button. When the `form` is submitted, the `value` is sent to the server if the radio button is selected.

```
<p>Do you agree? <input type="radio" name="agree" value="Yes" /></p>
```

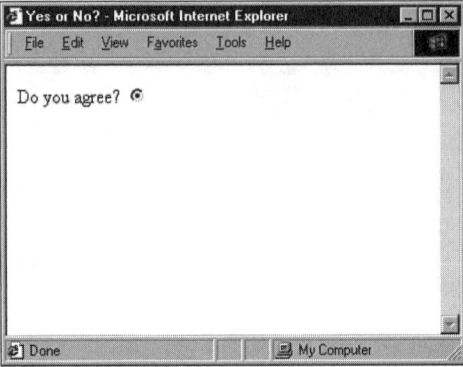

FIGURE 14.7

Radio buttons are useful for yes or no questions or choosing one item from a list.

When two or more radio buttons share the same control name, they form a mutually exclusive data set. In other words, only one radio button can be selected. In the following code snippet, both radio buttons have a `name` of `sex`, which means that the user can select only one. If a user selected Male, realized it was a mistake, and then selected Female, the Male radio button would then be unselected automatically:

```
<input type="radio" name="sex" value="Male" />
<input type="radio" name="sex" value="Female" />
```

As with check boxes, if you want a radio button to be selected by default when the form is displayed, the checked attribute is used. One point of confusion is that even though browsers prevent users from selecting more than one member of a check box group at a time, they won't prevent you from setting more than one member of a group as checked. You should avoid doing so yourself.

Creating Graphical Buttons

Using image as the type of input control creates a submit button represented by the image at the location you specify in the src, as in the following:

```
<input type="image" src="submit.gif" name="submitformbtn" />
```

Figure 14.8 shows a custom button created with an image.

FIGURE 14.8

Create custom buttons with type="image".

Custom button —

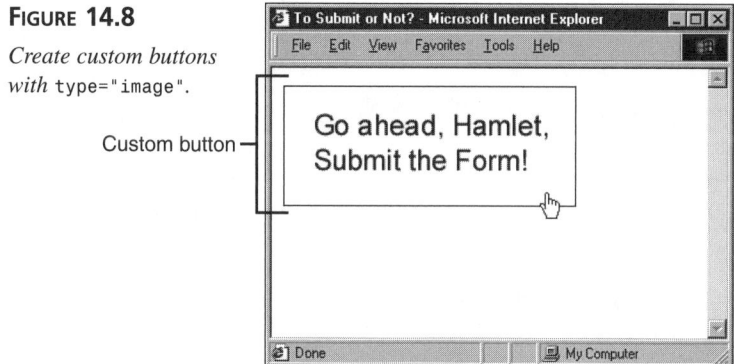

In addition to submitting the form data, the x and y coordinates of the point the user clicked are transmitted to the server. The data is submitted as *name*.x = *x coord* and *name*.y = *y coord*, where *name* is the name of the control. Using the preceding code, the result might look like the following:

```
submitoformbtn.x=150&submitformbtn.y=200
```

You can omit the name if you choose. If you do so, the coordinates returned would just be x = and y =. Form controls with the type image support all of the attributes of the <img> tag. You can remove the border from the image using border="0", or add a

14

horizontal buffer around it using `hspace="10"`. To refresh your memory on the attributes supported by the `<img>` tag, go back to Day 7, "Using Images, Color, and Backgrounds."

Creating Push Buttons

In addition to creating submit, reset, and image buttons, you also can create push buttons that cause client-side scripts to execute when they are enabled. Figure 14.9 shows a button that takes a client-side script when it is pressed. Use the following code to create a push button:

```
<input type="button" name="verify" value="verify" onclick="verifydata()" />
```

FIGURE 14.9

Push buttons can be tied to client-side scripts.

This example creates a button that runs a script function called `verifydata` when it's clicked. You provide the label that appears on the button with the `value` attribute of `Verify Data`.

Buttons created using this method are more limited than those created by using the `submit` element. Don't confuse the two!

Hiding Controls with `hidden`

Hidden are special controls that are hidden from, and cannot be modified by, the user. When the user submits the form, the value assigned to the hidden control is sent along with the other data:

```
<input type="hidden" name="surveynumber" value="1402" />
```

I have seen this technique used most often with surveys that require a way to identify the data. In this case, I have created a hidden form control named `surveynumber` with a value of `1402`. When the form is submitted for processing, I can identify the form based on this information. When I change the survey tomorrow, I can change `value` to a different number.

Upload Files with the `file` Select Control

The file select control enables a user to upload a file along with the form. As you can see in the code below, the `type` for the input element is set to `file`:

```
<p>Please select a file for upload: <input type="file" name="fileupload" /></p>
```

Figure 14.10 shows a file select control.

FIGURE 14.10

Uploading files is easy with the file select control.

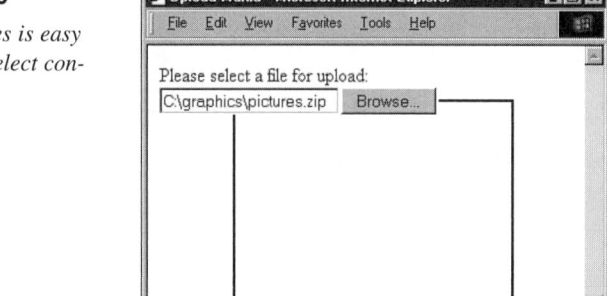

Enter path and file name   Select browse to look for
                                 files on your system

Users can enter a filename (with the path) or choose to browse the contents of their hard drives in order to identify a file to upload:

```
<input type="file" name="fileupload" value="myresume.doc" />
```

If you want to use a file upload field on your form, there's a lot of behind-the-scenes work you have to do in order to get everything working. For one thing, the program specified in the `action` attribute of your form must be able to accept the file being uploaded. Secondly, you have to use the post method for the form (you can't include an entire file in the URL of a request). Thirdly, you must set the `enctype` attribute of the form to `multipart/form-data`. I haven't discussed the `enctype` attribute because this is the only case where you'll have to use it. Ordinarily, the default behavior is fine, but you must change the `enctype` in this particular case.

Let's look at a simple form that supports file uploads:

```
<form action="/cgi-bin/upload.cgi" enctype="multipart/form-data" method="post">
<input type="file" name="new_file" />
<input type="submit" />
</form>
```

14

Once you've created a proper form for uploading a file, you need a program that can process the file submission. Creating such a program is beyond the scope of this book, but all popular Web programming environments support file uploads.

Exercise 14.2: Creating a Form with Several Types of `input` Controls

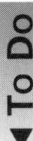
To Do

In this exercise, you'll work with all the types of controls presented in this section.

To start, open the template you created in Exercise 14.1 and create three `form` templates. You will use the first form for a survey, the second to gain access to a member's area of a fictitious Mime Academy, and the third to search the site. Refer to the following code:

```
<form action="http://www.example.com/cgi-bin/survey.cgi method="post">
</form>
<form action="http://www.example.com/cgi-bin/members.cgi method="post">
</form>
<form action="http://www.example.com/cgi-bin/search.cgi method="get">
</form>
```

Notice that you will be using different scripts for each form, and that the third uses the get method.

Now it's time to add form controls to each form. For the survey, you will want to ask a few simple multiple-choice questions. For the first question, use check boxes and assign the same name to them all. Place the text prompt before the `input` element so that it shows up in the browser window to the left of the check box. The following code shows you how:

```
<form action="http://www.example.com/cgi-bin/survey.cgi method="post"
Take today's survey
I like miming because: (check all that apply)
It's fun<input type="checkbox" name="whyilikeit" value="fun" />
I meet interesting people<input type="checkbox" name="whyilikeit"
value="people" />
It's who I am<input type="checkbox" name="whyilikeit"
value="personality" />
The money<input type="checkbox" name="whyilikeit" value="money" />
```

The second question for this form is another multiple-choice question, but you only want to accept one answer. To accomplish this, use a group of radio buttons. Place the text prompts after the buttons, rather than before them, so that the labels will show up to the right of the buttons. This ensures that the buttons are aligned properly:

```
The most difficult thing about being a mime is:
<input type="radio" name="difficult" value="makeup" />Putting on the
makeup
<input type="radio" name="difficult" value="unitard" />Wearing a
spandex unitard
```

▼ `<input type="radio" name="difficult" value="nottalking" />Not talking`

As you can see, I used the same `name` for all of the buttons in the group so that the browser will behave properly and only allow one of them to be selected at a time.

Next, create a file select element that enables users to select and upload a file when they submit the survey. Add submit and reset buttons. Finally, in order to track the survey, add a hidden field that is hard-coded to return the value of `061300`. Using this hidden control, you can track all survey responses by date. You just have to change the value in this field every day. After you add the hidden control, enter the closing `form` tag:

```
Upload a picture of yourself miming!
<input type="file" name="picture" />
<input type="submit" value="submit" />
<input type="reset" value="reset" />
<input type="hidden" name="surveynumber" value="061300" />
</form>
```

The second and third forms are much easier. The second form involves adding text and password controls for a person's user name and password, and it finishes with a submit button. Limit the maximum number of characters that can be entered to `20` and `10`, respectively. Then limit the password field `10` characters, as in the following:

```
<form action="http://www.example.com/cgi-bin/members.cgi method="post">
Enter our Member's Only area!
Username:<input type="text" name="username" maxlength="20" />
Password:<input type="password" name="userpassword" size="10" maxlength="10" />
<input type="submit" value="Submit" />
</form>
```

The final form is simply a text control and an image button. The image button acts as a submit button. It contains a graphic that I've created in place of the normal button face:

```
<form action="http://www.example.com/cgi-bin/search.cgi method="get">
Search our database<input type="text" name="searchstring" />
<input type="image" src="searchbtn.gif" name="searchbtn" />
</form>
```

The forms, form controls, and other information are complete. However, in order for them to look good in an HTML document, you will need to format them.

Note

I have found that formatting my forms after I create them enables me to concentrate on each aspect separately, which produces better results.

▼

14

▼   The visual appearance of the Web page divides nicely into five elements: three forms, a title graphic that will appear at the top of the page, and another graphic to add interest.

To organize your items on the page, first center the title graphic at the top of the page by using the following code:

```
<!DOCTYPE html PUBLIC "-//W3C//DTD XHTML 1.0 Transitional//EN"
"http://www.w3.org/TR/xhtml1/DTD/transitional.dtd">
<html>
<head>
<title>Anne's Mime Academy</title>
</head>
<body>
<div align="center">
    <img src="welcome.gif" height="35" width="300" />
</div>
```

Moving on to the graphic and forms, notice that two forms are rather short and one is long. Think of the remainder of the page as having two columns in which you can place the two smaller forms, including seating the "interest" graphic on one side and the longer form on the other. How are you going to do this? Tables!

Start by creating a master table that contains two columns and three rows. In the following code, I've added comments to document the role that each row and column of the table will play:

```
<table border="0">
<tr>
    <td></td> <!-- Row 1, Column 1: for the interest graphic -->
    <td></td> <!-- Row 1, Column 2: use for nested table holding the
                    first form -->
</tr>
<tr>
    <td></td> <!-- Row 2, Column 1: for another nested table and the
                    second form -->
    <td></td> <!-- Row 2, Column 2: first form continues -->
</tr>
<tr>
    <td></td> <!-- Row 3, Column 1: for the third nested table and third
form -->
    <td></td> <!-- Row 3, Column 2: first form continues -->
</tr>
</table>
```

Now use the following code to add the nested tables:

```
<table border="0">
<tr>
    <td></td> <!-- Row 1, Column 1: for the interest graphic -->
    <td><!-- Row 1, Column 2: use for nested table holding the
            first form -->
```
▼

```
<table border="0">
    <tr>
        <td></td>
        <td></td>
    </tr>
    <!-- add 12 more table rows here like the previous one -->
</table>
</td>
</tr>
<tr>
    <td><!-- Row 2, Column 1: use for nested table holding the second
            form -->
    <table border="0">
        <tr>
            <td></td>
            <td></td>
        </tr>
        <tr>
            <td></td>
            <td></td>
        </tr>
        <tr>
            <td></td>
            <td></td>
        </tr>
        <tr>
            <td></td>
            <td></td>
        </tr>
    </table>
    </td>
    <td></td> <!-- Row 2, Column 2: first form continues -->
</tr>
<tr>
    <td><!-- Row 3, Column 1: for the third nested table and third
            form -->
    <table border="0">
        <tr>
            <td></td>
            <td></td>
        </tr>
        <tr>
            <td></td>
            <td></td>
        </tr>
        </form>
    </table>
</tr>
</table>
```

14

▼ Now add all the graphic and form elements to their appropriate locations in the tables and put the entire thing together:

INPUT

```
<!DOCTYPE html PUBLIC "-//W3C//DTD XHTML 1.0 Transitional//EN"
"http://www.w3.org/TR/xhtml1/DTD/transitional.dtd">
<html>
<head>
<title>Anne's Mime Academy</title>
</head>
<body>
<div align="center">
    <img src="welcome.gif" height="35" width="300" />
</div>
<table border="0">
<tr>
    <td align="center"><img src="anne.gif" height="146"
    width="200" /></td>
    <td rowspan="3">
    <table border="0" bgcolor="#ffcc33">
        <form action="http://www.example.com/cgi-bin/survey.cgi"
        method="post">
        <tr>
            <td align="center" colspan="2">Take today's survey</td>
            <td></td>
        </tr>
        <tr>
            <td colspan="2">I like miming because: (check all that
            apply)</td>
            <td></td>
        </tr>
        <tr>
            <td> </td>
            <td>It's fun<input type="checkbox" name="whyilikeit"
            value="fun" /></td>
        </tr>
        <tr>
            <td> </td>
            <td>I meet interesting people<input type="checkbox"
    name="whyilikeit" value="people" /></td>
        </tr>
        <tr>
            <td> </td>
            <td>It's who I am<input type="checkbox" name="whyilikeit"
    value="personality" /></td>
        </tr>
        <tr>
            <td> </td>
            <td>The money<input type="checkbox" name="whyilikeit"
            value="money" /></td>
        </tr>
        <tr>
```

▼

▼
```
            <td colspan="2">The most difficult thing about being a mime
            is:</td>
            <td></td>
        </tr>
        <tr>
            <td> </td>
            <td><input type="radio" name="difficult" value="makeup" />
            Putting on the makeup</td>
        </tr>
        <tr>
            <td> </td>
            <td><input type="radio" name="difficult"
value="unitard" />
            Wearing a spandex unitard</td>
</tr>
        <tr>
            <td> </td>
            <td><input type="radio" name="difficult" value="nottalking"
/>Not talking</td>
        </tr>
        <tr>
            <td colspan="2">Upload a picture of yourself miming!</td>
            <td></td>
        </tr>
        <tr>
            <td></td>
            <td><input type="file" name="picture" /></td>
        </tr>
        <tr>
            <td colspan="2" align="center"><input type="submit"
            value="submit" />
         <input type="reset" value="reset" /></td>
            <td></td>
        </tr>
        <input type="hidden" name="surveynumber" value="061300" />
        </form>
    </table>
    </td>
</tr>
<tr>
    <td valign="top">
    <table border="0" bgcolor="#ffff99" width="100%">
        <form action="http://www.example.com/cgi-bin/members.cgi"
        method="post">
        <tr>
            <td align="center" colspan="2">Enter our Member's Only
            area!</td>
            <td></td>
        </tr>
        <tr>
            <td>Username:</td>
```
▼

14

▼
```
                <td><input type="text" name="username"
maxlength="20" /></td>
          </tr>
          <tr>
             <td>Password:</td>
             <td><input type="password" name="userpassword" size="10"
             maxlength="10" /></td>
          </tr>
          <tr>
             <td align="center" colspan="2"><input type="submit"
             value="submit" /></td>
             <td></td>
          </tr>
          </form>
       </table>
       </td>
    </tr>
    <tr>
       <td>
       <table border="0" width="100%" bgcolor="#ffcccc">
          <form action="http://www.example.com/cgi-bin/search.cgi"
          method="get">
          <tr>
             <td>Search our database</td>
             <td><input type="text" name="searchstring" /></td>
          </tr>
          <tr>
             <td align="center" colspan="2"><input type="image"
          src="searchbtn.gif" name="searchbtn" /></td>
             <td></td>
          </tr>
          </form>
       </table>
       </td>
    </tr>
    </table>
    </body>
    </html>
```
▲   Figure 14.11 shows the completed Web page, complete with multiple forms and controls.

Using Other Control Elements

In addition to form controls you can create using the input element, there are three that
are elements in and of themselves.

Using the button Element

A button you create using the button element is similar to the buttons you create with
the input element, except that these buttons can contain content within the opening and
closing tags that actually appear on the buttons.

OUTPUT

FIGURE 14.11

Anne's Mime Academy has three forms on one page.

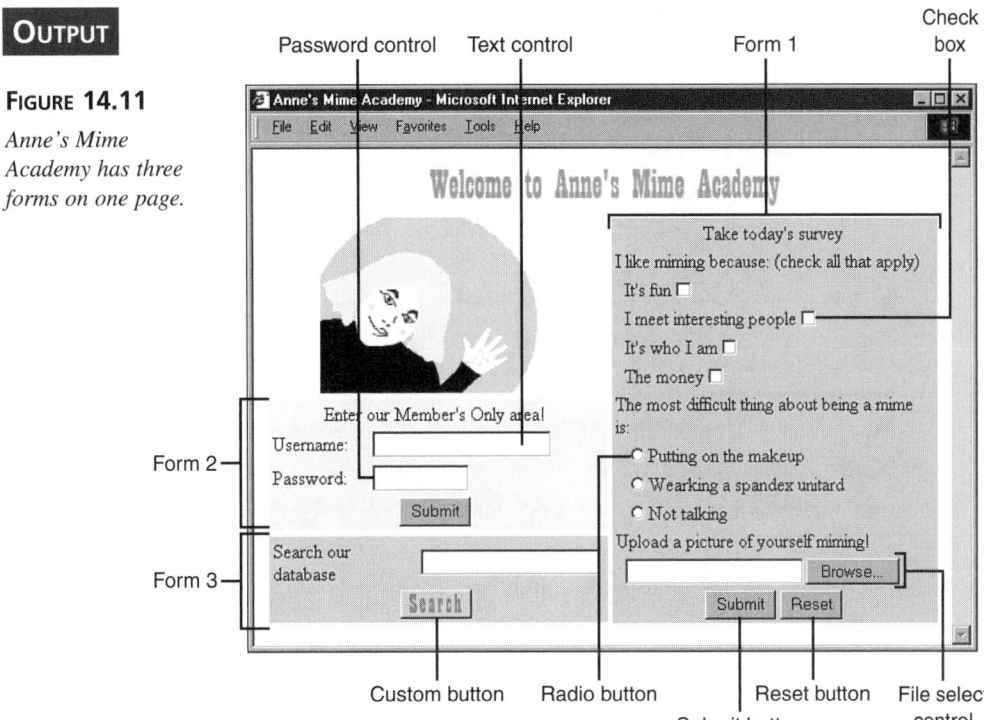

Password control   Text control   Form 1   Check box

Form 2

Form 3

Custom button   Radio button   Reset button   File select control
Submit button

> **Note**
>
> The `button` element (as opposed to the `input` element of `type="button"`) is not supported by Netscape Communicator 4.7.

You can create three different types of buttons: submit, reset, and custom. To create them, start by entering the opening tag of the `button` element, followed by the `name` attribute. The `name` attribute names the control. Next, enter the `type` attribute and choose the type of button you want to create. After that, close the opening tag and enter the text you want to appear in the button. Then finish things off with a closing `button` tag. The following code snippet creates the three types of buttons. Figure 14.12 shows three `button` elements, each with a different purpose. Note that I've used two line break tags, `<br>`, to give the buttons some room:

```
<button name="mysubmitbutton" type="submit"><b>Submit</b>
Form</button><br /><br />
<button name="myresetbutton" type="reset"><u>Clear</u> Form
Contents</button><br /><br />
<button name="mycustombutton" type="button">Verify
<code>Data</code></button>
```

14

FIGURE 14.12

The button *element enables you to include content and HTML elements inside buttons.*

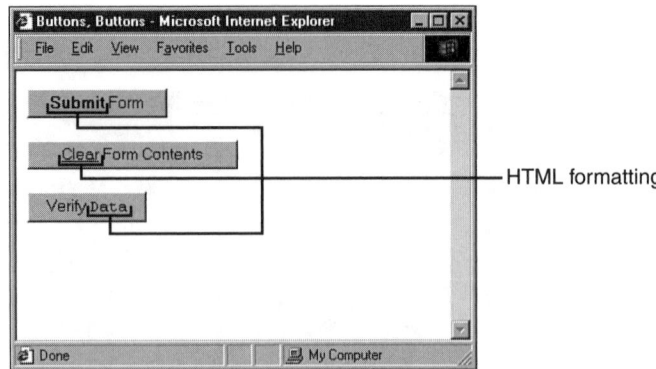

FIGURE 14.12

The button *element enables you to include content and HTML elements inside buttons.*

Because you can include other HTML elements within a button element, the following example is perfectly acceptable:

```
<button name="myresetbutton" type="reset"><b>Clear</b> Form
Contents</button>
```

Using the <b> element within the button boldfaces the word Clear.

You also can include images that are displayed as your button. Just enter the <img> element within the contents of the button, as in the following:

```
<button name="mysubmitbutton" type="submit">
➡<img src="customimage.gif" width="50" height="10" /></button>
```

Create Large Text-Entry fields with textarea

The textarea element creates a large text-entry field where people can enter as much information as they want. To create a textarea control, begin with the opening tag with the element name and then enter the rows and cols attributes before you close the tag. These attributes specify the height and width of the text area. The unit of measurement is characters, so textarea with cols set to 5 and rows set to 40 creates a text area 5 characters high and 40 wide. If you leave out the rows and cols attributes, the browser default will be used. This can vary, so you should make sure to include those attributes to maintain the form's appearance across browsers. The closing textarea tag is required. Any text you place inside the textarea tag will be displayed inside the field as the default value:

```
<p>Please comment on our customer service.
<textarea name="question4" rows="10" cols="60">
Enter your answer here
</textarea>
</p>
```

Figure 14.13 shows a textarea element in action.

FIGURE **14.13**

Use textarea *to create large text-entry areas.*

Note

> You might be asking, "Where is the isindex element?" This element creates
> a single-line text entry field much like the text control of the input element,
> and it has been deprecated by the W3C. The syntax is <isindex
> prompt="Prompt for user input">. While writing this chapter, I tested this
> in the latest versions of Internet Explorer and Navigator and found that they
> no longer support isindex, so covering it in detail is not necessary.

Creating Menus with select and option

The select element creates a menu of choices from which the user can choose, much like the menus found in most software applications. By itself, select doesn't do much more than define how the menu will appear, either as a pull-down menu or a scrollable menu. You must include at least one option or optgroup element to create the menus.

To create a pull-down select element with menu choices represented by option elements, start by entering the opening tag followed by a control name:

```
<select name="location">
```

Next, enter your menu items using the option element:

```
<select name="location">
    <option>Indiana</option>
    <option>Fuji</option>
    <option>Timbuktu</option>
    <option>Alaska</option>
```

Finally, close the select element with the end tag:

```
<p>Please pick a travel destination:
<select name="location">
    <option>Indiana</option>
```

14

```
<option>Fuji</option>
<option>Timbuktu</option>
<option>Alaska</option>
</select>
</p>
```

Figure 14.14 shows a `select` control that creates a pull-down menu that offers four options.

FIGURE **14.14**

You can use select *form controls to create pull-down menus.*

To create a scrollable list of items, just include the `size` attribute in the opening `select` tag, as in the following:

```
<select name="location" size="2">
```

Figure 14.15 shows the same `select` element as Figure 14.14, except that the `size` attribute is set to 2. Notice that it now turns into a scrollable menu.

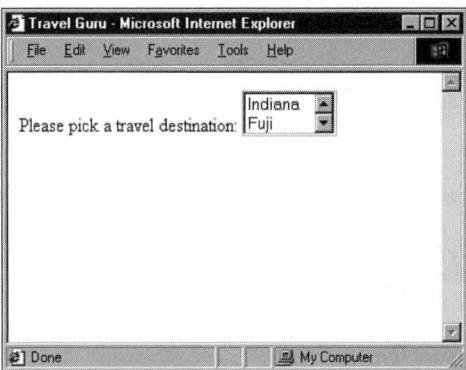

The `select` element restricts the display area of the scroll menu to two items. Users will need to scroll to see more options.

To send data other than what is displayed back to the server, you can use the `value` attribute in your `option` elements. This is useful if you are processing the data and want a numerical value or other coded value associated with the menu choice. The following code, for example, causes bw499 to be sent back for Courses instead of Basket Weaving 499:

```
<select name="courses">
    <option value="p101">Programming 101</option>
    <option value="e312">Ecomomics 312</option>
    <option value="pe221">Physical Education 221</option>
    <option value="bw499">Basket Weaving 499</option>
</select>
```

To preselect options, include the `selected` attribute in an `option` element, as in the following:

```
<select name="courses">
    <option value="p101">Programming 101</option>
    <option value="e312">Ecomomics 312</option>
    <option value="pe221" selected>Physical Education 221</option>
    <option value="bw499">Basket Weaving 499</option>
</select>
```

This causes the menu to display Physical Education 221 as an initial value.

Thus far, you have created menus in which a user can select only one choice. You can easily change that to multiple choices by including the `multiple` attribute in the `select` element, as in the following:

```
<select name="courses" multiple>
```

Note A user can choose multiple options by Shift+clicking for Windows, or Ctrl+clicking or Command+clicking for Macintosh.

Adding Extras

You've created all the form controls that will accept user input. Now it's time to add functionality and make the controls a bit friendlier.

14

Displaying Control `label` Elements

The `label` element displays helpful information for a form control. You should tie the `for` attribute to the control it labels. To create a label, begin with the opening `label` tag and then enter the `for` attribute. The value for this attribute, when present, must match the `id` attribute for the control it is labeling. Next, enter text that will serve as the label and then close the element with the end `label` tag, as in the following:

```
<label for="control4">Who is your favorite NFL Quarterback?</label>
<input type="text" name="favqb" id="control4" />
```

 **Note**   Although the `label` element is not supported by Netscape, the contents within the opening and closing `label` tags are displayed.

Figure 14.16 shows this text control with a label assigned to it.

FIGURE 14.16

You can assign labels to any form control. Note that they are displayed with the control.

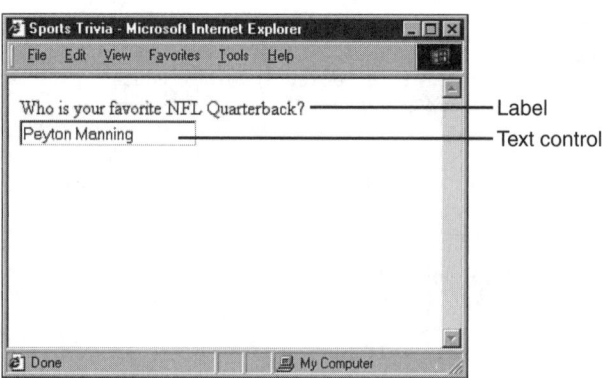

If you define your form control within the `label` element, as shown in the following code, you can omit the `for` attribute:

```
<label>User name: <input type="text" name="username" /></label>
```

Grouping Controls with `fieldset` and `legend`

The `fieldset` element organizes form controls into groupings that appear in the Web browser. The `legend` element displays a caption for the `fieldset`. To create a `fieldset` element, start with the opening `fieldset` tag, followed by the `legend` element, as shown in the following code:

```
<fieldset>
    <legend>Oatmeal Varieties</legend>
```

 **Note**

> Netscape Communicator 4.7 does not support fieldset or legend, but
> Netscape 6 does.

Notice that the legend contains text. However, it also could contain inline HTML elements for formatting the text. Next, enter your form controls and finish things off with the closing fieldset tag:

```
<fieldset>
    <legend>Oatmeal Varieties</legend>
    <label>Apple Cinnamon<input type="radio" name="applecinnamon" />
    </label><br />
    <label>Nutty Crunch<input type="radio" name="nuttycrunch" />
    </label><br />
    <label>Brown Sugar<input type="radio" name="brownsugar" /></label>
</fieldset>
```

Figure 14.17 shows the result.

FIGURE 14.17

The fieldset *and* legend *elements enable you to organize your forms.*

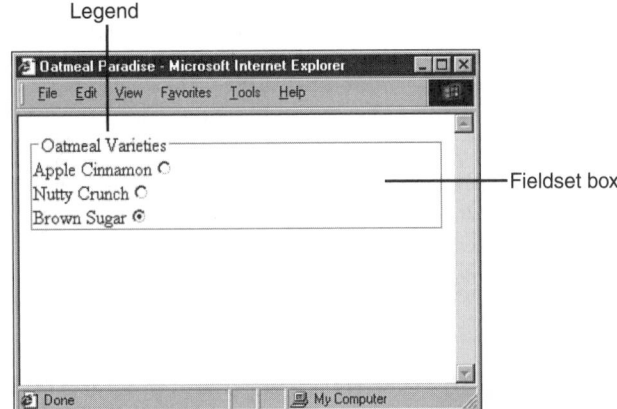

Changing the Default Tabbed Navigation

Using the keyboard to navigate some computer applications can make filling out forms much easier. Tabbed navigation enables users to press the Tab key to move from one form control to the next, in the order that you specify in your form.

14

> Although Netscape Navigator enables you to tab through form controls, you cannot change the order of tabbed navigation with the `tabindex` attribute.

To enable tabbed navigation, incorporate the `tabindex` attribute in all the form controls that you want to include this feature. Beginning with 1, order your form controls from start to finish. Controls that have duplicate `tabindex` values will be accessed in the order they appear in the HTML document. An example of a tag containing the `tabindex` attribute follows:

```
<p>Enter your name: <input type="text" name="username" tabindex="1" /></p>
```

Using Access Keys

Access keys also make your forms easier to navigate. They assign a character to an element that moves the focus to that element when the user presses a key. To add an access key to a check box, use the following code:

```
<p>What are your interests?</p>
<p>Sports<input type="checkbox" name="sports" accesskey="S" /></p>
<p>Music<input type="checkbox" name="music" accesskey="M" /></p>
<p>Television<input type="checkbox" name="tv" accesskey="T" /></p>
```

> Unfortunately, Netscape Navigator does not support the use of `accesskey`. While Internet Explorer does support it, users must press Alt in conjunction with the key in order for it to work. Other operating systems and Web browsers may require a different method.

Creating `disabled` and `readonly` Controls

Sometimes you might want to display a form control without enabling your visitors to use the control or enter new information. To disable a control, add the `disabled` attribute to the form control, as in the following:

```
<p>What is the meaning of life?
<textarea name="question42" disabled="disabled">
Enter your answer here.
</textarea>
</p>
```

When displayed in a Web browser, the control will be dimmed (a light shade of gray) to indicate that it is unavailable.

To create a read-only control, use the `readonly` attribute, as in the following example:

```
<p>This month: <input type="text" name="month" value="September"
readonly="readonly" /></p>
```

The read-only control appears normally. However, when visitors attempt to enter new information (or, in the case of buttons or check boxes, select them), they will find that they cannot change the value. Figure 14.18 shows both a disabled control and a read-only control.

FIGURE 14.18

Disabled controls are dimmed. Read-only controls appear normally—they just can't be changed.

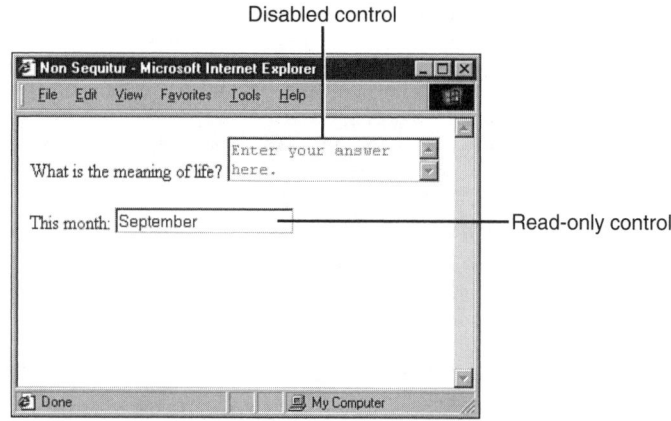

Disabled control

Read-only control

 Note Netscape Communicator does not support the `disabled` or `readonly` attributes, but they are supported by Netscape 6.

Exercise 14.3: Creating a Form with Advanced Form Control

Your final exercise for today incorporates the form controls in the previous two sections into one large form on a Matchmaker Web page.

You begin with one large form. Open your template HTML document and create a `form` in the `body` of the document.

You'll want two major sections on this page: one section that asks questions about the visitor, and the other section that asks what the visitor is looking for in another person. This is perfectly suited for `fieldset` elements.

14

▼   Create the first `fieldset` element now. Begin with the `form` tag and add a `fieldset` element and `legend`, as in the following:

```
<form action="http://www.example.com/cgi-bin/match.cgi" method="post">
<fieldset>
    <legend>Tell us about yourself.</legend>
```

Add a `label` for a `select` element, add the `select` element, and enter all the `option` elements. While you're at it, assign `tabindex` and `accesskey` elements as you go along:

```
<label for="control1">I have a funny bone that...</label>
 <select name="humor" id="control1" tabindex="1" accesskey="h">
    <option value="-1">Please pick one</option>
    <option value="-1">--------------</option>
    <option value="0">has been removed.</option>
    <option value="1">is my skull.</option>
    <option value="2">is ticklish.</option>
 </select>
```

That wasn't too difficult. Now enter the second `label` and `select` elements, as follows:

```
<label for="control2">I like to take long walks...</label>
<select name="walks" id="control2" tabindex="2" accesskey="w">
    <option value="-1">Please pick one</option>
    <option value="-1">-------------</option>
    <option value="Fields">in the corn fields at our farm.</option>
    <option value="Streets">on the streets of my city.</option>
    <option value="Beach">down the hall in my dorm.</option>
    <option value="Apartment">to the refrigerator.</option>
</select>
```

Complete the `fieldset` by adding a final `label` and a `textarea` control. Be sure to include the closing `fieldset` tag:

```
<label for="control3">Why should we care?</label>
<textarea name="mycomments" id="control3" rows="5" cols="30"
tabindex="3"></textarea>
</fieldset>
```

You're almost halfway done. Use the following code to create a second `fieldset` that contains questions about what the visitor is looking for in another person:

```
<fieldset>
    <legend>What are you looking for?</legend>
    <label for="control4">I want...</label>
    <select name="romance" id="control4" size="4" tabindex="4"
    accesskey="R">
        <option>somebody to watch movies with.</option>
        <option>a serious relationship.</option>
        <option>a Hot-N-Steamy romance.</option>
        <option>someone to clean the catbox.</option>
```
▼   `</select>`

```
<label for="control5">Describe your perfect partner.</label>
<textarea name="lookingfor" id="control5" rows="5" cols="30"
tabindex="5"></textarea>
</fieldset>
```

With your two `fieldsets` complete, add a disabled control and a read-only control to make sure you've covered all your bases:

```
Check if you want to join our club.<input type="checkbox"
➥name="single" checked disabled />
Do you agree to pay us for this service?<input type="text"
➥name="pay" value="yes" readonly="readonly" />
```

Now add the submit and reset buttons and close the `form` element. Notice that I'm including special graphics for the buttons by using the `button` element.

```
<button name="submit" type="submit" tabindex="6">
<img src="submit.gif" width="60" height="30" />
</button>
<button name="reset" type="reset" tabindex="7">
<img src="reset.gif" width="60" height="30" />
</button>
</form>
```

Now that your form is complete, you can add a title graphic at the top of the page and insert most of your form controls into a `table`. The complete code listing shows the final results:

INPUT

```
<!DOCTYPE html PUBLIC "-//W3C//DTD XHTML 1.0 Transitional//EN"
"http://www.w3.org/TR/xhtml1/DTD/transitional.dtd">
<html>
<head>
<title>Matchmaker Matchmaker</title>
</head>
<body>
<div align="center">
<img src="title.gif" width="300" height="35" />
</div>
<form action="http://www.example.com/cgi-bin/match.cgi" method="post">
<table border="0" width="100%">
    <tr valign="top">
        <td width="50%">
            <table border="0">
            <tr>
            <td align="center">
            <fieldset>
            <legend>Tell us about yourself.</legend>
            <label for="control1">I have a funny bone that...</label>
            <br />
            <select name="humor" id="control1" tabindex="1"
            accesskey="H">
```

14

```
                    <option value="-1">Please pick one</option>
                    <option value="-1">--------------</option>
                    <option value="0">has been removed.</option>
                    <option value="1">is my skull.</option>
                    <option value="2">is ticklish.</option>
            </select>
            <br />
            <label for="control2">I like to take long walks...</label>
            <select name="walks" id="control2" tabindex="2"
accesskey="W">
                    <option value="-1">Please pick one</option>
                    <option value="-1">-------------</option>
                    <option value="Fields">in the corn fields at our farm.
</option>
<option value="Streets">on the streets of my city.
</option>
                    <option value="Beach">down the hall in my dorm.</option>
                    <option value="Apartment">to the refrigerator.</option>
            </select>
            <br />
            <label for="control3">Why should we care?</label>
            <br />
            <textarea name="mycomments" id="control3" rows="5" cols="30"
        tabindex="3"></textarea>
            </fieldset>
            </td>
            </tr>
            </table>
        </td>
        <td width="50%">
            <table border="0">
            <tr>
            <td align="center">
            <fieldset>
            <legend>What are you looking for?</legend>
            <label for="control4">I want...</label>
            <br />
            <select name="romance" id="control4" size="4" tabindex="4"
            accesskey="R">
                <option>somebody to watch movies with.</option>
                <option>a serious relationship.</option>
                <option>a Hot-N-Steamy romance.</option>
                <option>someone to clean the catbox.</option>
            </select>
            <br />
            <label for="control5">Describe your perfect partner.</label>
            <textarea name="lookingfor" id="control5" rows="5" cols="30"
        tabindex="5"></textarea>
            </fieldset>
            </td>
            </tr>
```

▼
```
                    </table>
                </td>
            </tr>
            <tr>
                <td colspan="2">Check if you want to join our club.
                <input type="checkbox" name="single" checked disabled /></td>
        <td></td>
            </tr>
            <tr>
                <td colspan="2">Do you agree to pay us for this service?
                <input type="text" name="pay" value="Yes" readonly="readonly" />
                </td>
        <td></td>
            </tr>
        </table>
        <div align="center">
        <table border="0">
            <tr>
                <td><button name="submit" type="submit" tabindex="6">
                <img src="submit.gif" width="60" height="30" /></button></td>
         <td><button name="reset" type="reset" tabindex="7">
                <img src="reset.gif" width="60" height="30" /></button></td>

            </tr>
        </table>
        </div>
        </form>
        </body>
        </html>
```

▲   Figure 14.19 shows the final product of this exercise.

Planning Your Forms

Before you start creating complex forms for your Web pages, you should do some planning that will save you time and trouble in the long run.

First, decide what information you need to collect. That may sound obvious, but you need to think about this before you start worrying about the mechanics of creating the form.

Next, review this information and match each item with a type of form control. Ask yourself which type of control is most suited to the type of questions you're asking. If you need a yes or no answer, radio buttons or check boxes work great, but the textarea element is overkill. Try to make life easier for the users by making the type of control fit the question. This way, analyzing the information using a script, if necessary, will be much easier.

14

FIGURE 14.19

Adding extras to a Matchmaker form.

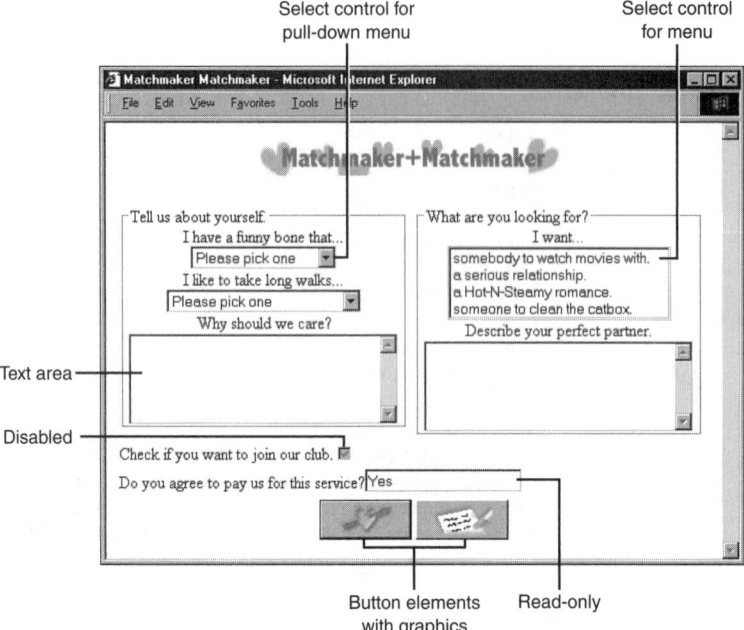

You also need to coordinate with the person writing the CGI script to match variables in the script with the names you're going to assign to each control. There isn't much point in naming every control before collaborating with the script author—after all, you'll need all the names to match. You also can create look-up tables that contain expansive descriptions and allowable values of each form control.

Finally, you might want to consider validating form input through scripting. Using JavaScript, you can embed small programs in your Web pages. One common use for JavaScript is writing programs that will verify that a user's input is correct before they submit a form. I'll discuss JavaScript in more detail in the next chapter. In the meantime, you can find some form validation sample code at

`http://developer.netscape.com/docs/examples/javascript/formval/overview.html`

Summary

As you can see, the wonderful world of forms is full of different types of form controls for your visitors. This truly is a way to make your Web pages interactive.

Be cautious, however. Web surfers who are constantly bombarded with forms are likely to get tired of all that typing and move on to another site. You need to give them a reason for playing!

Table 14.1 summarizes the HTML tags used today. Remember these points and you can't go wrong:

- Use the form element to create your forms.
- Always assign an action to a form.
- Create form controls with the input element or the other form control elements.
- Test your forms extensively.

TABLE 14.1   Today's HTML Tags

Tag	Use
`<form>`	Creates an HTML form. You can have multiple forms within a document, but you cannot nest the forms.
`action`	An attribute of `<form>` that indicates the server-side script (with a URL path) that will process the form data.
`method`	An attribute of `<form>` that defines how the form data is sent to the server. Possible values are `get` and `post`.
`<input>`	A `<form>` element that creates controls for user input.
`type`	An attribute of `<input>` that indicates the type of form control. Possible values are shown in the following list:

	`text`	Creates a single-line text entry field.
	`password`	Creates a single-line text entry field that masks user input.
	`submit`	Creates a submit button that sends the form data to a server-side script.
	`reset`	Creates a reset button that resets all form controls to their initial values.
	`checkbox`	Creates a check box.
	`radio`	Creates a radio button.
	`image`	Creates a button from an image.
	`button`	Creates a push button. The three types are submit, reset, and push, with no default action.
	`hidden`	Creates a hidden form control that cannot be seen by the user.
	`file`	Creates a file upload control that enables users to select a file with the form data to upload to the server.

14

TABLE 14.1   continued

Tag	Use
`<button>`	Creates a button that can have HTML content.
`<textarea>`	A text-entry field with multiple lines.
`<select>`	A menu or scrolling list of items. Individual items are indicated by the `<option>` tag.
`<option>`	Individual items within a `<select>` element.
`<label>`	Creates a label associated with a form control.
`<fieldset>`	Organizes form controls into groups.
`<legend>`	Displays a caption for a `fieldset` element.

Workshop

If you've made it this far, I'm sure you still have a few questions. I've included a few that I think are interesting. Afterwards, test your retention by taking the quiz, and then expand your knowledge by tackling the exercises.

Q&A

Q How do I design a form that will be easy to analyze with a spreadsheet or database?

A First, make sure you have a default value for every control in your form. That will fix the number of data entries and make importing the data into a spreadsheet much easier. Don't be afraid to use values that can be manipulated programmatically. For example, I might make every Yes answer to my form a 1 and every No a 0 by using the value attributes. Then, when I import the data into my spreadsheet, I can chart and graph responses with 1s and 0s rather than text. You can use many other tricks, such as using lookup tables in your scripts to decode form responses. Experiment with what works best for you and your scripts.

Q I want to create a form and test it, but I don't have the script ready. Is there any way I can make sure the form is sending the right information with a working script?

A I run into this situation all the time! Fortunately, getting around it is very easy.

Within the opening `form` tag, modify the `action` attribute and make it a `mailto` link to your email address, as in the following:

```
<form action="mailto:youremailaddress@isp.com" method="post">
```

Now you can complete your test form and submit it without having a script ready. When you submit your form, it will be emailed to you as an attachment. Simply open the attachment in a text editor, and presto! Your form data is present.

Quiz

1. How many forms can you have on a Web page?

2. How do you create form controls such as radio buttons and check boxes?

3. Are passwords sent using a `password` control secure?

4. Explain the benefit of using hidden form controls.

5. What other technology do forms rely on?

Quiz Answers

1. Theoretically, you are limited only by the amount of memory on the client computer. However, you cannot nest forms. Another interesting tidbit is that each form control takes memory. Sometimes I've used up all the free memory on a computer by including too many form controls.

2. These form controls are created with the `input` element and otherwise have no life of their own.

3. No! Passwords sent using a `password` control are not secure.

4. Hidden form controls are intended more for you than for the person filling out the form. By using unique `value` attributes, you can distinguish between different forms that may be sent to the same script or sent at different times.

5. In order for you to process the data forms, they must be paired with a server-side script through the `action` attribute. These scripts are written in Perl or other scripting languages.

Exercises

1. Ask your ISP for scripts that you can use to process your forms. If you can use them, ask how the data is processed and which names you should use in your form controls. If you need to use forms and your ISP won't allow you to use their scripts, you should start looking elsewhere for a place to host your Web site.

2. Visit some sites that might use forms, such as `www.fedex.com`. Look at which form controls they use and how they arrange them, and peek at the source to see the HTML code.

14

DAY **15**

Using Dynamic HTML

In yesterday's lesson, you learned how to create powerful HTML forms that enable you to gather information from people visiting your Web site. Forms, in one form or another, have been around since the virtual birth of HTML and are pretty compatible among browsers. You didn't really need to worry too much about who could or couldn't see your site correctly.

Today's lesson departs from the relatively smooth waters of forms and sets sail toward the rough seas of Dynamic HTML. Batten down the hatches!

Dynamic HTML offers you something unique: the capability to make changes in Web pages on-the-fly. Using conventional HTML, Web pages are loaded by a browser and just sit there until you click a link or interact with forms. That's pretty simple, but can be static and boring.

People have improved upon static Web pages by using a variety of technologies outside the realm of HTML. CGI has been a longtime method of providing interactivity in Web pages. You can embed Shockwave and Flash to create animation and interactivity, and use Java applets or ActiveX controls to provide application-like functions; however, these methods rely on browser plug-ins or virtual machines (which can be messy), and can lead to longer download times.

Dynamic HTML is different. *DHTML*, as it is commonly known, enables you to create Web pages that look, feel, and act a lot like the other programs you use on your computer—using the Web browser as an interface, without having to rely on external programming solutions. Can you see the promise of that?

I hope you do because you'll need that enthusiasm to come to grips with the darker side of DHTML. This side is sometimes, quite frankly, a mess. If you want to appeal to the largest possible audience (within realistic limitations), you must account for differences in Web browsers and how they implement a variety of Web technologies including HTML, Cascading Style Sheets, and scripting.

Today's lesson is a "full plate" of information, so let's get right to it. In this lesson, you will learn about the following:

- Defining Dynamic HTML and the technologies that make it possible
- The basics of JavaScript
- Understanding what Document Object Models are
- Creating cross-browser routines with DHTML by determining the browsers' capabilities
- Examples of using DHTML to manipulate elements on a page

What Exactly Is Dynamic HTML?

Simply put, Dynamic HTML uses normal HTML elements to create a Web page that relies on style sheets for element formatting, positioning, and scripting to *dynamically* change either HTML content, style, or positioning, without having to *re-download* the page from the server. Dynamic HTML isn't a thing by itself, but a collection of technologies working together to achieve interactive effects. So what can you do with DHTML? The possibilities are endless! Just to whet your appetite, here are a few of them:

- Move objects around the Web page
- Show or hide elements
- Create lists that expand or contract when you select an item
- Dynamically alter the color and size of Web content
- Provide drag-and-drop functionality similar to that used by modern graphical operating systems (such as Windows and the Mac OS)

Dynamic HTML was born with the advent of the "fours." The World Wide Web Consortium developed HTML 4 and released the official Recommendation at about the same time Microsoft and Netscape released their competing Web browsers, Internet

Explorer 4 and Netscape 4. There was a flurry of activity surrounding all this. HTML 4 promoted several new features to better integrate itself with Cascading Style Sheets and respond to user events. Microsoft and Netscape were both competing hard for market-share in the browser war, and the result of it all was a drive for something different: a level of user interactivity and "dynamism" in Web pages that previously was impossible without resorting to external programming. DHTML was born.

For DHTML to work, it requires the following three key technologies supported by the Web browser:

- HTML
- Style sheets
- Scripting

It's obvious that you need to use HTML. Remember, however—HTML 4 has new ele-ments, such as `div` and `span`, and new attributes, such as `id` and `style`, that enable you to structure and format your content in ways that promote a tighter integration with style sheets and manipulation by scripting. The darker side of this is that even today, not all the leading manufacturers of Web browsers consistently implement HTML 4 in their Web browsers. This will be a common theme for today.

Note

The greatest challenge of Dynamic HTML is to overcome these inconsisten-cies—not just in HTML, but in all DHTML technologies—and create true, cross-browser dynamic Web pages. It *can* be done, but it takes more effort.

Style sheets are wonderful, once you know how to use them, and are a critical compo-nent of DHTML. Although DHTML technically isn't dependent on any one type of style sheet, the official W3C style sheet technology, *Cascading Style Sheets (CSS)*, is the stan-dard. CSS level 2 (CSS2) enables you to format elements on your Web pages using prop-erties, such as font, color, and spacing, as well as positioning items on the Web page. To review CSS, refer to Day 12, "XHTML and Style Sheets."

DHTML takes style to a new level. Rather than creating a style rule or positioning an element on the page and then forgetting about it, you can use DHTML to dynamically alter the visual style or position of your elements. As with HTML, there are problems with how Internet Explorer and Netscape Navigator implement CSS. Not only have nei-ther *fully* implemented the specification, but each browser has implemented portions dif-ferently.

Finally, scripting is a sort of glue that holds together everything in DHTML. Scripting provides the dynamic nature of DHTML because scripts can run while a page loads, in response to a user action, or even when the user leaves your site.

> **Caution**
>
> If you've caught on to the pattern here, "inconsistent implementation across Web browsers," you should know that this makes referring to and relying on the official specification of any one technology dangerous. You should always read any browser-specific documentation you can find to ensure that the Web browsers you are targeting support what you are attempting to accomplish.

The scripting *lingua franca* of today is JavaScript. JavaScript was the first scripting language to be implemented in a Web browser, and currently enjoys the most widespread support across different Web browsers. Although you can create DHTML using other scripting languages, such as VBScript, I recommend always using JavaScript unless you are in a Microsoft-only environment (like an intranet).

NEW TERM *JavaScript* is a scripting language that allows you to write scripts, or small non-compiled programs, that are run by a Web browser from within a Web page.

As you will see when we get to the DHTML examples, a large part of DHTML involves creating scripts that manipulate elements on a page. For this reason, I have included an explanation of how JavaScript is used with DHTML, which you will read a bit later. Although you won't learn everything there is to know about JavaScript, you should at least be able to follow along with the examples.

Two final notes about what DHTML actually is. DHTML (the scripting part of it) relies on something called a *Document Object Model (DOM)* to identify, create, and manipulate objects on a Web page. For example, you have to be able to identify an element, such as an image, in order to manipulate it with a script. Likewise, you must be able to identify an element's style in order to change it. This is what the DOM does. It provides a bridge between the content of the Web page and scripts. Although the W3C released the DOM level 1 specification in October of 1998, each Web browser has a unique DOM; therefore, the DOMs are covered in a separate section later today.

Finally, DHTML relies on *event handling* to track the actions of the Web browser and user. When the page loads, the onload event is triggered. Likewise, when a visitor clicks a button in a form, several events might be triggered that you, the DHTML author, can use to run scripts. As with everything else in DHTML, Microsoft Internet Explorer and Netscape Navigator handle events in a different fashion. Event handling is covered in more depth later on.

Learning JavaScript

JavaScript is a scripting language originally developed by Netscape and Sun Microsystems (the people who created Java), and was created to solve some of the short-comings of HTML. Namely, HTML is a document *formatting* language not capable of performing programming tasks. Take the following HTML code, for example:

```
<img src="myImage.gif" height="100" width="300" />
```

In this case, the HTML code simply is telling the browser to display an image called `myImage.gif` on the page in an area 100 pixels high and 300 pixels wide. This is a pretty severe limitation when you think about it. Aside from hyperlinks and form controls, you can't manipulate information, data, objects, or respond to user events.

Scripting languages, in general, and JavaScript, in particular, perform a role completely different from HTML. By their very nature, they are *programming* languages. This means that scripts can perform computations, manipulate objects, and respond to a wide variety of user events. Scripts, for example, perform tasks such as validating HTML form input, responding to mouse and keyboard actions, and dynamically changing the position and style of HTML elements.

Unlike formal programming languages, such as C, C++, or Java, scripting languages are not compiled into machine-readable code prior to being executed. They are written in normal text and interpreted by a host rather than executed directly by a CPU. In the case of Web pages, the Web browser acts as the host and interprets scripts within (or refer-enced by) the Web page while it is loading.

 Note This is an important point worth repeating. Just as some older browsers can-not display many HTML 4 elements, not all browsers can interpret the latest version of JavaScript. Remember, the browser is acting as the script host. You can't force a browser to run scripts it doesn't understand.

JavaScript Basics

Unfortunately, I can't teach you everything there is to know about JavaScript in such a short space. I will, however, try to give you an understanding of how JavaScript works so that you can look through the code in this lesson, and begin to understand what's being done.

Fundamentally, scripts are nothing but a series of statements that tell the script host (the Web browser) what to do. These statements can be simple statements that assign values to variables, as follows:

```
var x = 14;
```

or function definitions that contain more complex statements:

```
function init() {
    if (x == 14) {
        alert(x);
    }
    else {
        alert("X doesn't equal 14");
    }
}
```

Note that each statement ends in a semicolon (;) and that statements can be grouped together into blocks with curly braces {}. The preceding code uses braces to group statements into a function called init(). The if and else statements each use braces to contain the statements that apply to them.

Just as you can enter comments in your HTML to include text on your page that's not rendered by the browser, you can enter comments that won't be treated as JavaScript code. You create single-line comments by using two forward slashes, //. You can place them at the beginning of a line like this:

```
// This variable is used to hold temporary information
var x;
```

or you can place them at the end of a statement like this:

```
var x; // Temporary variable
```

The script interpreter ignores everything after the double forward slashes, so be careful not to comment-out any important code!

You can use several single-line comments to create a large comment block, such as

```
// Script created on 9 Mar 01
// Copyright Sams Publishing
// All rights reserved
```

or use a special multiline comment. Multiline comments are created by entering a forward slash followed by an asterisk (/*) on the first line of the comment, and end with an asterisk and another forward slash (*/). The important thing to know about multiline comments is that they cannot be nested, so you should try to avoid using them. They're mainly useful for commenting out a block of code for testing purposes. The following example illustrates that type of multiline comment:

```
/* Script created on 9 Mar 01
   Copyright Sams Publishing
   All rights reserved */
```

Variables

Variables are just temporary storage for values that you want to use later. For example, if you want to count the number of times a user has clicked on a particular button you create a variable to store that value, and then add 1 to it every time the user clicks on the button. Later, if you want to display the number of times the button has been clicked, you can just read the value from the variable.

```
var myVariable;
```

 **Note**

JavaScript is case sensitive. This means that myVariable is different from myvariable and Myvariable.

If you want to declare a variable and immediately store a value in it, the code is a simple as this:

```
var myVariable = 2001;
```

Operators

JavaScript also contains *operators* that enable you to perform mathematical calculations and comparisons. Table 15.1 lists the most common operators and what they do.

TABLE 15.1 Common Computational and Comparative Operators

Computational		Comparative	
Symbol	Description	Symbol	Description
+	Add	=	Assigns values
-	Subtract	==	Is equal to
*	Multiply	<	Less than
/	Divide	>	Greater than
++	Increment (+1)	<=	Less than or equal
--	Decrement (-1)	>=	Greater than or equal
		!=	Is not equal
		&&	Logical AND
		||	Logical OR

The following code, for example, declares three variables, assigns values to two, and then assigns the sum of the first two to the third:

```
var xPos = 142;
var yPos = 15;
var Pos;
Pos = xPos + yPos;
```

To increment or decrement a value, use the appropriate operator with the value or variable, as in the following example:

```
Pos++;
```

This statement adds one to the current value of Pos.

To compare values, use the logical operators.

```
if (Pos == 150) {
    anotherFunction();
}
```

This brings me to my next point: *conditional branching*. The if statement is the most commonly used conditional statement, and is present in nearly every programming language. Use the if statement to compare one value to another (or perform a whole group of comparisons), and then, based on the result, take action. The previous code compared the variable Pos to 150. If Pos equals 150, the code within the braces is executed. If Pos does not equal 150, the script continues on as if nothing had happened. If you want to try to catch all the results, use multiple if statements or include the else statement, as in the following code:

```
if ((Pos >= 150) && (Pos <=200)) {
    functionOne();
}
else {
    functionTwo();
}
```

This loop compares the variable Pos to two values: 150 and 200. If Pos is greater than or equal to 150 *and* less than or equal to 200 (in other words, if Pos is from 150-200), the code branches to the function titled functionOne. If the logical comparison is not true, the else block is executed and functionTwo is called.

Conditional Statements

Conditional branching creates two or more possible execution paths for a script to take. Conditional expressions such as (X > Y) are used to test values and variables and determine which path is taken.

When performing calculations or comparisons, parentheses group values or variables and determine the order in which they are interpreted. The following line of code forms a statement where `Pos >= 150` and `Pos <=200` are each interpreted first, and then the result of each is compared with the logical `AND` operator.

```
((Pos >= 150) && (Pos <= 200))
```

Likewise,

```
(((156 * 4 / 24) + 99) * 24)
```

is interpreted with the help of parentheses. In this case, 156 is multiplied by 4 and the result is divided by 24. That result is added to 99, and finally multiplied by 24. The final calculation results in 3000 (which, by completely accidental happenstance, is a nice round number).

> **Note**
>
> When confronted by multiple levels of parenthetical expressions, work from the inside out. You also should check to make sure that you always have the same number of left parentheses as you do right parentheses.

In addition to performing this task, you also use parentheses when creating a function or calling it from within the script. The parentheses contain parameters or arguments that the function uses to perform its task. The following code illustrates a simple function designed to create an alert box that displays the value of the `user` variable, which, in this case, is `Laura`:

```
var user = "Laura";
function alertUser(user) {
    alert(user);
}
```

To call the function, simply enter the function name with the parameter `user` enclosed in parentheses, as in the following example:

```
alertUser(user);
```

Many functions don't accept any parameters, but they all must be declared with parentheses following the name. For example, a sample `init` function listed here takes no parameters when called:

```
function init() {
    createImageArray();
    animateTitle();
}
```

Functions

This brings me to my next topic: *functions*. Normally, scripts are executed from top to bottom; statements are executed sequentially. Functions, however, break this flow and are blocks of code that are only executed when they are called from other parts of the script. Consider the example just listed. The `init` function stands apart from the script and is not executed until it is called by name. When you write scripts, use functions to package code that will be called when a specific event occurs, or that will be used more than once.

If you haven't guessed by now, you can create functions by using the keyword `function`, followed by the function name. Remember that parentheses must follow the function name in the declaration, and that any arguments accepted by the function must be enclosed in those parentheses. The actual body of the function is enclosed in curly braces.

Any standard JavaScript statement can be used within a function, as shown in this example:

```
function determinePosition() {
    if ((Pos >= 150) && (Pos <=200)) {
        functionOne();
    }
    else {
        functionTwo();
    }
}
```

As you can see, conditional statements with bodies of their own can be nested within functions. You just have to make sure to use the proper matching braces in those cases. Careful indenting of your source code can help you make sure that all your braces are opened and closed properly. In the preceding listing, the `determinePosition` function has a set of braces at the top and bottom. Within the function, the `if` and `else` conditional statements each have a set of braces. It all adds up. There are three left braces and three right braces. If there weren't, you would receive an error when the script is executed.

Objects

Thus far, you've learned the basic syntax of JavaScript and some details of the language. Apart from adding a few values together, however, you really don't know how to do much. The missing link is, drum roll please, an *object*. Objects are simply collections of *properties* and *methods*. Think of them as containers that contain information, along with the means to manipulate it.

Properties describe the object, and methods provide the means to manipulate it within your script. Suppose that you have an object called `Car`. Its properties might be the `color`, `year`, and `value`. You might have a method that calculates its current value based on the depreciation each year. To refer to the object, enter the object name followed by a period, and then include a property. This example sets the `Car` object's color to `blue`:

```
Car.color = "Blue";
```

To invoke a method, simply add the method after the object and property, as in the following code:

```
Car.value.calculate();
```

In that case, `calculate()` is a method of the value property, not the car object itself. As you can also see, a method call is very similar to a function call, except that it's associated with a particular object. In fact, in the simplest terms, this is all methods are—functions associated with particular objects. The thing that makes them special is that they usually deal with data stored within the object that they're associated with. Regular functions must have all their data passed to them by some means.

Because we're discussing scripting for the Web, most of the objects contain properties and methods that relate to the Web browser and HTML document. One of the most important objects is the `document` object. This object contains information about the HTML document loaded into the Web browser, has methods to respond to user events, and can perform other tasks.

Event Handlers

Unfortunately, here's where it gets a bit more complicated. Each Web browser has defined a different set of objects that might have different properties and methods. In addition, each browser has a set of *event handlers* that are used to respond to user actions, such as clicking a button on the mouse or pressing a key.

 Note

In Netscape Navigator 4.7 and below, not all event handlers are available for all objects. You should consult Netscape's JavaScript documentation to see which events can be used for certain objects.

Because objects and events are somewhat inconsistent across the different browser versions, I will cover those subjects in more depth in the following sections. First, however, examine how to integrate scripts into your HTML documents.

Integrating Scripts with HTML

JavaScript, of course, isn't HTML. They are two entirely different languages that perform completely different functions. You can't just throw script statements in your HTML document willy-nilly and expect the browser to automatically know what to do. The first thing you should do is specify a default scripting language in the head of the document, using the meta tag, employing the following statement:

```
<meta http-equiv="Content-Script-Type" content="text/javascript" />
```

Although using the meta tag to perform this function is optional, this statement ensures that the Web browser knows that you are using JavaScript, and, unless told differently, all scripts will be interpreted as such. That distinction is very important because you don't want to leave any doubt for the browser. Now on to including the scripts!

You can include JavaScript scripts in your HTML documents using any of the following three methods:

- Include inline scripts in response to intrinsic events
- Put scripts in the document head or body
- Link to external script files

Note that this is very similar to the way you include Cascading Style Sheets in your pages. The main difference is that you include style sheets using the link tag, and you include JavaScript code in your pages using the script tag.

NEW TERM *Intrinsic events* occur when something happens to the Web page. The body of the HTML document, for example, has an intrinsic event called onload that occurs when the document is loaded into the Web browser. These events are used as attributes to HTML elements. The value of the attribute can be a script statement or a series of script statements. The following listing, for example, assigns the onload event to the body element, and then executes a single statement that creates an alert box with the included text.

```
<body onload="alert('The page has loaded.')">
```

Note that inline script statements that need to use double quotation marks must use single quotation marks in this setting. The first double quotation mark begins the attribute value, and the next one it runs across will terminate the value. If you were to mistakenly enter the following code, the script would end at alert(, which obviously is something you don't want.

```
<body onload="alert("The page has loaded.")">
```

> **Caution**
>
> When it comes to intrinsic events, don't be fooled by the official HTML spec-
> ification. Although the W3C lists a multitude of events that apply to certain
> elements, it is up to the Web browser to implement this functionality.
> Netscape Navigator 4.7 in particular does not support intrinsic events "across
> the board" as Internet Explorer does. This fact makes DHTML harder when
> coding for Netscape.

You also can use multiple script statements inline when responding to an intrinsic event.
Consider the following code:

```
<body onload="var message = 'The page has loaded'; alert(message)">
```

I have two statements within this small script that respond to the onload event. The first
statement declares a variable and assigns a string to it. The second displays an alert box
that contains the message.

The second method for including scripts is to put them in the HTML document head or
body. To include a script, use the script element, and declare the type of script with the
type and/or the language attribute in the opening script tag. Both attributes perform
the same function in that they tell the browser which scripting language you are using.
Although type is the official standard, language is more commonly used. Because it
doesn't do any harm, I tend to include both.

```
<script type="text/javascript" language="javascript">
```

After the opening tag, enter any script statements you have created, and then close the
script element with an end tag.

```
<head>
<title>Sample Script</head>
    <meta http-equiv="Content-Script-Type" content="text/javascript" />
    <script type="text/javascript" language="javascript">
        var message="Hello World";
        alert(message);
    </script>
</head>
```

Although the previous script will run just fine in browsers that are "script compatible," it
is common practice to comment out the script statements with HTML comment tags in
order to accommodate extremely old browsers, as follows:

```
<script type="text/javascript" language="javascript">
<!--  Hide JavaScript from older browsers
    var message="Hello World";
    alert(message);
```

```
// stop hiding the script -->
</script>
```

Notice the last line of the script. I have included a JavaScript comment to ensure that the JavaScript interpreter does not think it is a line of script. If I ended the script with the following HTML comment, the browser would try to interpret it as JavaScript:

```
stop hiding -->
```

Another technique to ensure backward compatibility is to use the noscript element. This element enables you to include alternative content for browsers that don't support scripting. Begin with the opening noscript tag, and then enter your alternative content. Close the noscript element with an end tag, as in the following:

```
<script type="text/javascript" language="javascript">
<!-- Hide JavaScript from older browsers
    var message="Hello World";
    alert(message);
// stop hiding the script -->
</script>
<noscript>
    <p>You have a browser that is not compatible with scripting.</p>
</noscript>
```

As I stated earlier, you can include scripts in the document head or body. It is important to note that the order in which the scripts appear is the order that they execute. Therefore, a script that appears in the document head will run before one in the body. If you are using functions to control the flow of your script, you can effectively bypass this rule and control script execution based on how you intend it to work.

Finally, you can link to one or more external scripts (saved with a .js extension) by using the src attribute within the script element. The following example illustrates linking to two external scripts:

```
<script type="text/javascript" language="javascript" src="detect.js"></script>
<script type="text/javascript" language="javascript" src="animate.js"></script>
```

By linking to external scripts, you can more easily manage common script routines that you use across multiple Web pages.

Now you know how to include scripts in your Web pages! To conclude this section, you should know that JavaScript is currently at version 1.4, but version 1.5 soon will arrive. Table 15.2 summarizes the JavaScript versions supported by Netscape Navigator and Microsoft Internet Explorer.

TABLE 15.2   JavaScript Versions Supported by Netscape Navigator and Microsoft Internet Explorer

JavaScript	Netscape	Internet Explorer
1.0	2.0x	3.0x
1.1	3.0x	4.0x
1.2	4.0-4.05	4.0x
1.3	4.06-4.61	5.0x
1.5	6	5.5

> Microsoft Internet Explorer technically does not interpret JavaScript, but a Microsoft script implementation that is based on JavaScript, called *JScript*, does. Don't let this confuse you! You should continue to write your scripts based on the JavaScript documentation.

Using Document Object Models

As mentioned earlier, Microsoft Internet Explorer and Netscape Navigator each have different document object models. Each object in the Web page (and many in the Web browser) contains different properties (that describe them), methods (that manipulate them), and event handlers (to respond to user actions). Next, you briefly will review each browser's model in order to arrive at some similarities.

> Fully realizing the capabilities of either DOM requires a depth of knowledge beyond the scope of this book. But, as with other Web-related code, you can learn a lot by cutting and pasting scripts and taking the time to study their results.

The Netscape DOM

Netscape's DOM is synonymous with the DOM presented in the official JavaScript documentation. This can be incredibly confusing when attempting to create cross-browser DHTML because although Internet Explorer interprets JavaScript, it does so in a different DOM context: its own. In other words, be careful when reading official JavaScript documentation. The information contained within applies only to Netscape Navigator.

Aside from a few top-level, predefined JavaScript objects, such as screen, the Netscape DOM is structured like a tree, with the topmost object called window. The window object represents the Web browser window or a frame within the browser. As such, the properties and events of the window object pertain to the Web browser.

Below the window object are several subobjects, with some of these branches themselves branching into more objects. The object directly under window that you are most interested in for your purposes today is the document object. The document object is created in Netscape by the HTML body tag, so you don't have to worry about creating it yourself.

Beneath the document object can be a plethora of different objects, each with its own set of properties and methods. Most of the objects you will use are HTML elements, such as images, style sheet objects, and form controls.

You continually will reference the document object and its descendants in DHTML, so it's important to learn how to reference them. When you call on an object in JavaScript, use dotted notation to refer to each object in the DOM hierarchy until you reach your destination. Following, for example, is how a reference to an image named myimage would appear:

document.myimage

To refer to the properties of the image, simply tack the property on to the end of that statement, as follows:

document.myimage.src

Perform a simple experiment. Create a Web page that has one image. (You can name it as I have, or use another name. Just be sure to substitute the correct value for the src attribute.) The image is located in the body of your HTML document. Just below the image is a script that will create an alert box that displays the width attribute of the image. For this example, it is important to place the script *after* the image because the image needs to be loaded in order for the object to be created.

INPUT

```
<!DOCTYPE html PUBLIC "-//W3C//DTD XHTML 1.0 Transitional//EN"
"http://www.w3.org/TR/xhtml1/DTD/transitional.dtd">
<html>
<head>
<title>Netscape Navigator DOM Test</title>
<meta http-equiv="Content-Script-Type" content="text/javascript" />
</head>
<body>

<img id="barnimage" name="barnimage" src="barn.gif" height="100"
width="150" />
```

```
<script language="javascript" type="text/javascript">
<!-- Hide JavaScript
alert(document.barnimage.width);
// end hide JavaScript -->
</script>

</body>
</html>
```

Figure 15.1 shows the resulting alert box generated by Netscape Navigator. Notice that the image has yet to appear before the alert box is shown.

OUTPUT

FIGURE 15.1

Accessing the properties of an image through JavaScript and Netscape's DOM.

Accessing other properties of the image is as easy as changing `width` to some other property, such as `src`.

To use a method of an object, simply replace the property with the name of a method and then include any arguments required by the method in parentheses. The following code uses the `write` method of the `document` object to write to the browser window:

```
document.write("Hello world!")
```

Some properties, such as the height of an image, are read-only. This means that you can view the value of the property; however, you cannot change it. Others, especially CSS properties (which are descendants of the object itself), are capable of being modified. To modify an object property, enter the object and property name as you normally would refer to it; however, include an equal sign, and then enter the new value. In this way, properties are similar to variables—in fact, they *are* variables. They're just associated with a particular object.

The following statement modifies the position of the image object `barnimage` to `150` pixels from the top of the window or previous element, depending on whether the image was positioned absolutely or relatively.

```
document.barnimage.top = "150"
```

One final point about the Netscape DOM is that the objects under an object are stored in an *array*. (An array is just a numbered list that starts counting at 0.) All image objects on a Web page, for example, are stored in `document.images` as an array. The first image is stored with an index of `0`, and the index is incremented for each additional image. The index is just an indicator of an object's position in the list. To access the first image in the array, use the following syntax:

```
document.images[0].width
```

Placing this statement in the preceding image example, which created an alert box, would yield the same value: `150`.

The Internet Explorer DOM

The Internet Explorer DOM is similar to Netscape's DOM in that each browser's DOM consists of objects with properties, methods, and events. The differences lie, however, in how they are organized and how you reference them in your scripts.

Internet Explorer has a `document` object much like Netscape's; however, underneath the `document` object, everything is contained in the `all` collection, which literally contains every HTML element on the Web page. When you need to reference an image in Internet Explorer, therefore, the statement would be as follows:

```
document.all.myimage
```

To access a property of method, add it to the end of the previous statement, just as you did with Netscape:

```
document.all.myimage.src
```

Style objects are treated differently in Internet Explorer. All references to style are handled by entering `.style` after the object name, and then entering the style property.

```
document.all.barnimage.style.top
```

Here's the image example I used for Netscape Navigator earlier, rewritten so that it will work with Internet Explorer.

INPUT
```
<!DOCTYPE html PUBLIC "-//W3C//DTD XHTML 1.0 Transitional//EN"
"http://www.w3.org/TR/xhtml1/DTD/transitional.dtd">
<html>
<head>
<title>Internet Explorer DOM Test</title>
<meta http-equiv="Content-Script-Type" content="text/javascript" />
</head>
<body>
```

```
<img id="barnimage" name="barnimage" src="barn.gif" height="100"
width="150" />

<script language="javascript" type="text/javascript">
<!-- Hide JavaScript
alert(document.all.barnimage.width);
// end hide JavaScript -->
</script>

</body>
</html>
```

Figure 15.2 shows the resulting alert box. Notice that in Internet Explorer, the image appears before the alert box is generated.

OUTPUT

FIGURE 15.2

Accessing the properties of an image through JavaScript and Internet Explorer's DOM.

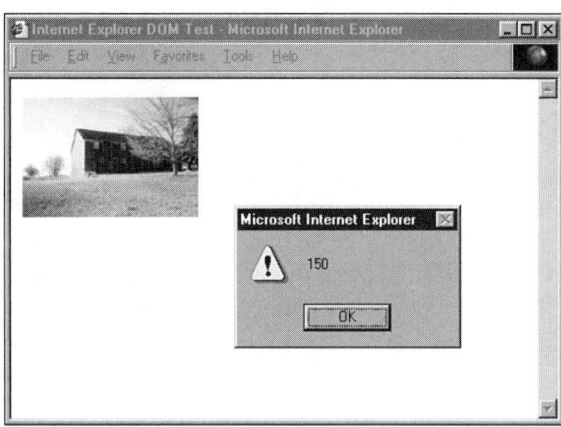

Handling Events

Events occur when the Web browser or user performs an action. The significance of events is that you can create scripts to respond to them. Unfortunately, there are wide differences in the ways Netscape and Internet Explorer track and detect events. In general, Netscape tends to be much more restrictive in the HTML elements that automatically trigger intrinsic events. You can assign many events to almost all elements in Internet Explorer.

Note Because of the number of events and the differences in implementation, it is impossible to completely cover all contingencies in this book. For complete details, refer to Netscape- and Internet Explorer-specific documentation.

Another difference in event handling has to do with where the event is first detected, and which direction it travels (up or down) the document object hierarchy. Netscape uses a "trickle down" event model, whereby events are detected at the highest level in the document object model (the window object), and travel down the object model tree until an event handler responds to the event. Internet Explorer, not surprisingly, handles events in a completely opposite manner. Rather than trickling down, events in Internet Explorer "bubble up." The event first is detected by the element that generated the event (such as an image or div element). The event then moves up the document object chain, until handled or cancelled.

The practical upshot of this is that coding for events is pretty easy in Internet Explorer, but much more difficult in Netscape.

Coping with Reality: Cross-Browser DHTML Techniques

The majority of the day thus far has been devoted to understanding the technologies behind DHTML and how to use them separately. It's time to start creating real DHTML Web pages. As I have mentioned, the real challenge is creating DHTML so that you reach the largest possible audience within certain practical limitations. I say practical because true DHTML is not possible in any Web browser that doesn't implement scripting or style sheets, and impractical in those that suffer from partial or poor implementations. In other words, using DHTML, you'll never be able to reach 100% of your potential audience.

The good news is that with a firm understanding of the differences between the leading Web browsers and some creative coding, you can create cross-browser DHTML Web pages that will perform some, or most, of the things you want, using one Web page.

The alternative is to create multiple versions of your Web page, targeted at the different "sects" of the Web browser market. I don't consider this a practical or tidy solution because you will end up multiplying your workload by two, three, four, or more times. Therefore, I will continue to focus on cross-browser DHTML in the sections that follow.

Sniffing for Browsers

At one time, the most common technique for creating cross-browser DHTML was detecting the user's Web browser (commonly called *sniffing*). After you had determined which browser the user was using, you could simply execute the code tailored to that browser.

The problem is that there are many browsers out on the market, and many versions of each one. For example, there are three or four versions of both Netscape and Internet Explorer in fairly common usage even today. As you might imagine, accounting for all the available browsers and keeping your scripts up-to-date to accommodate new browsers is a daunting task. Netscape has undertaken this chore and published a comprehensive sniffer on their DevEdge Web site at `http://devedge.netscape.com/tech/dynhtml/index.html`. You can download the complete listing and use it in all your Web pages for free.

Here's an abbreviated version of the Netscape browser detection script that only detects Netscape Navigator 4 and Microsoft Internet Explorer 4 and up. The following listing creates variables that parse the appropriate objects to return `true` or `false` values for the final variables: `is_nav4up` and `is_ie4up`.

```
// Trimmed down browser sniffer that
// detects Navigator 4+ and IE 4+.
// Reference is_nav4up and is_ie4up in other
// portions of the script
var agt = navigator.userAgent.toLowerCase();
var is_major = parseInt(navigator.appVersion);
var is_minor = parseFloat(navigator.appVersion);
var is_nav  = ((agt.indexOf('mozilla')!=-1) && (agt.indexOf('spoofer')==-1)
            && (agt.indexOf('compatible') == -1) && (agt.indexOf('opera')==-1)
            && (agt.indexOf('webtv')==-1));
var is_nav4up = (is_nav && (is_major >= 4));
var is_ie   = (agt.indexOf("msie") != -1);
var is_ie4up  = (is_ie  && (is_major >= 4));
```

To check for the existence of Netscape Navigator 4 and Microsoft Internet Explorer 4 and later versions, use the following script:

```
if (is_nav4up) {
    do something }
if (is_ie4up) {
    do something else }
```

You'll see that later as you perform some more scripting. The overall browser sniffer function exists solely to return the proper variables to you so that you can check in other portions of your script. By itself, it won't actually take any action.

The following example shows the browser sniffer in action. The body element of the Web page calls the `doSniff` function, which in turn, creates a variable called `sniff` and assigns it a string value to display, depending on the browser version it detects.

INPUT

```
<!DOCTYPE html PUBLIC "-//W3C//DTD XHTML 1.0 Transitional//EN"
"http://www.w3.org/TR/xhtml1/DTD/transitional.dtd">

<html>
<head>
<title>Browser Sniffing</title>
<meta http-equiv="Content-Script-Type" content="text/javascript" />

<script language="javascript" type="text/javascript">
<!-- Hide JavaScript

// Trimmed down browser sniffer that
// detects Navigator 4+ and IE 4+.
// Reference is_nav4up and is_ie4up in other
// portions of the script
var agt = navigator.userAgent.toLowerCase();
var is_major = parseInt(navigator.appVersion);
var is_minor = parseFloat(navigator.appVersion);
var is_nav  = ((agt.indexOf('mozilla')!=-1) &&
(agt.indexOf('spoofer')==-1)
            && (agt.indexOf('compatible') == -1) &&
(agt.indexOf('opera')==-1)
            && (agt.indexOf('webtv')==-1));
var is_nav4up = (is_nav && (is_major >= 4));
var is_ie   = (agt.indexOf("msie") != -1);
var is_ie4up = (is_ie  && (is_major >= 4));


// Function to display the browser version
function doSniff() {
    var sniff
    if (is_nav4up == true) {
        sniff = "Netscape Navigator 4+" }
    if (is_ie4up == true) {
        sniff = "Microsoft Internet Explorer 4+" }
    alert(sniff);
}
// end hide -->
</script>
</head>
<body onload="doSniff()">
</body>
</html>
```

Figure 15.3 shows the result in Internet Explorer 5.

FIGURE 15.3

Sniffing for the Web browser detects the browser version.

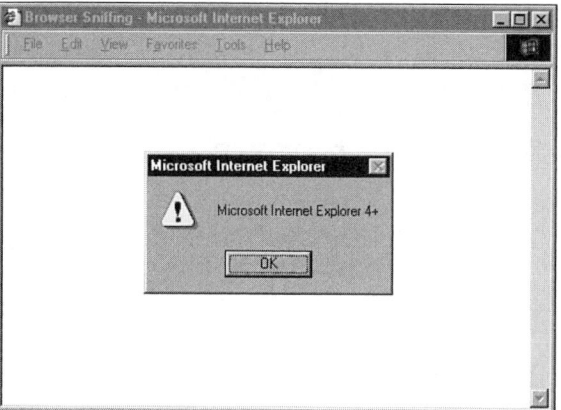

Detecting Capabilities

There are several big problems with relying on browser detection to make sure that your scripts work across multiple browsers. The biggest problem is that it's hard to keep up with the pace of change in the world of browser development. New browsers are being released all the time, and it's hard to keep track of which browsers support which version of JavaScript. When new browsers are released, you have to go back through all your scripts that include browser detection and update them to account for the new browsers. Another problem is that if a browser you didn't account for supports the features included on your page, you might be denying access to people for no reason.

The final problem, which I alluded to earlier, is the maintenance burden of including browser detection in your scripts. You have to react every time the browser market changes, rather than proactively writing scripts that will automatically account for those changes.

Rather than trying to determine the user's browser and then running the JavaScript code for it, it makes more sense to test whether the browser supports the specific feature you're going to use. Let's try an analogy: You've rented a car and you want to turn on the air conditioner. The problem is that you're not sure whether the car even *has* an air conditioner. To find this out, you could get the year, make, and model of the car and then look it up in a service manual. This is what browser detection is. On the other hand, you could just look at the dashboard of the car and see whether it has an air conditioner. This is how capability detection works.

This might seem like an oversimplification, but that's really all there is to it. Before you call a particular piece of code, you just have to test whether the browser supports the objects associated with the code you're calling. Back on Day 8, "Creating Animated

Graphics," I gave you a sneak preview of this technique. Before I attempted to perform an image rollover, I tested whether the browser supported the document.images object— if it didn't, I knew that the rollover wouldn't work and moved on.

Testing for the Existence of Objects

Let me explain how this works in more detail. JavaScript is an object-oriented language, so you generally deal with objects that both contain data and also have methods that can be called to perform various tasks. You can easily test for the existence of objects and if they exist, call methods of those objects to perform the tasks you want to accomplish.

Grouping Elements with `<div>`

In the world of Dynamic HTML, one of the most important tags you'll use is `<div>`. This tag is just a container into which you can put other elements. Back on Day 6, "More Text Formatting with HTML," I showed how you can control the alignment of elements by placing them within a `<div>` tag and using the align attribute. This is one of the most basic applications of the `<div>` element. In Dynamic HTML, the `<div>` tag is used whenever you want to treat any group of elements as a discrete unit.

Let's say you want to place a menu of links on your page. Because later I'll want to manipulate this menu using DHTML, I'm going to go ahead and place it within a `<div>`. I'm also using the id attribute to assign a name to the `<div>` so that I can access it through JavaScripts and CSS. Here's the source code for the page, which appears in Figure 15.4.

INPUT

```
<!DOCTYPE HTML PUBLIC "-//W3C//DTD HTML 4.0 Transitional//EN">
<html>
<head>
    <title>DHTML Test</title>
<style type="text/css">
    #menu, .menu
    {
        font-family: Verdana, sans-serif;
    }
</style>
</head>
<body>
<div id="menu">
<table border="1" cellspacing="0" cellpadding="10" bgcolor="#FFFFCC">
    <tr>
        <td>
        <p class="menu">
        <b>Links</b><br>
        <a href="http://www.yahoo.com/">Yahoo</a><br />
        <a href="http://www.salon.com/">Salon</a><br />
```

```
            <a href="http://www.slashdot.org/">Slashdot</a><br />
            </p>
            </td>
        </tr>
    </table>
    </div>
    </body>
    </html>
```

OUTPUT

FIGURE 15.4

A simple page containing a single
`<div>`.

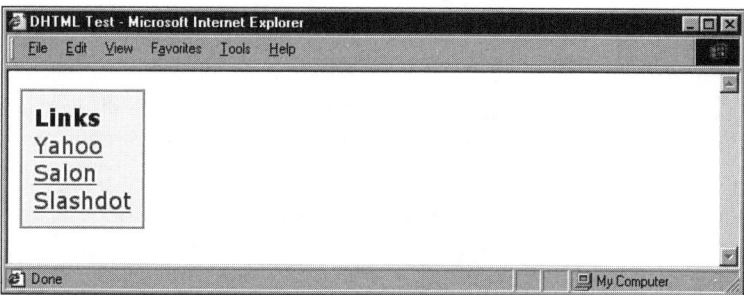

Looking at the source code, you should see that I've already included a style sheet that sets the font for the text inside the `<div>` to Verdana. #menu is the selector for an element with an `id` of menu, and that's the `id` that I assigned to my `<div>`.

Tip

> Netscape doesn't cascade font settings made outside of table cells down to the text within the table cells. So, it ignores the font setting in the style sheet for the text inside the table, even though it's also inside the `<div>`. To get around this problem, I included the `.menu` selector in my style sheet as well and wrapped the text inside the `<div>` in a `<p>` tag with the `class` attribute set to menu. The selector `.menu` causes the style to be applied to any item assigned a class of that name.

Positioning `<div>` Elements

Now that I've placed the `<div>` on the page, I can use some CSS positioning properties to place the `<div>` wherever I want on the page. By default, elements (including `<div>` elements) are positioned inline. They simply follow the element that appears before them in the HTML document.

Relative Positioning

The key properties here are position, left, top, and z-index. The position attribute tells the page how you want to position the element on the page. This property defaults to static, which means that the element will be positioned inline with other elements. The next option is relative. In this case, you can set the position for the <div>, but it will be placed relative to its position in the document. Let's look at a quick example (illustrated in Figure 15.5):

INPUT

```
<!DOCTYPE HTML PUBLIC "-//W3C//DTD HTML 4.0 Transitional//EN">
<html>
<head>
    <title>DHTML Test</title>
<style type="text/css">
    #menu, .menu
    {
        font-family: Verdana, sans-serif;
    }
    #menu
    {
        position: relative;
        top: 100;
        left: 100;
    }
</style>
</head>
<body>
Friends, Romans, countrymen, lend me your ears;<br />
I come to bury Caesar, not to praise him.<br />
The evil that men do lives after them;<br />
The good is oft interred with their bones;<br />
So let it be with Caesar. The noble Brutus<br />
Hath told you Caesar was ambitious:<br />
If it were so, it was a grievous fault,<br />
And grievously hath Caesar answer'd it.<br />
Here, under leave of Brutus and the rest--<br />
For Brutus is an honourable man;<br />
So are they all, all honourable men--<br />
Come I to speak in Caesar's funeral.<br />
<div id="menu">
<table border="1" cellspacing="0" cellpadding="10" bgcolor="#FFFFCC">
    <tr>
        <td>
        <p class="menu">
        <b>Links</b><br />
        <a href="http://www.yahoo.com/">Yahoo</a><br />
        <a href="http://www.salon.com/">Salon</a><br />
        <a href="http://www.slashdot.org/">Slashdot</a><br />
        </p>
        </td>
```

```
        </tr>
      </table>
    </div>
  </body>
</html>
```

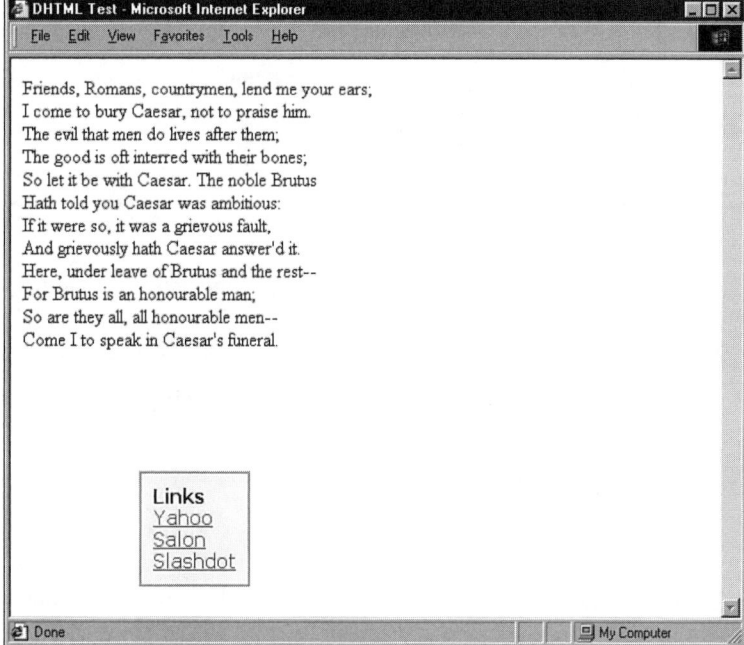

OUTPUT

FIGURE 15.5

A relatively positioned element.

As you can see, I've added some text to the previous listing and added to the style sheet. In this document, I set the `position`, `left`, and `top` properties for the `#menu` selector, which refers to the menu of links on the page. And as you can see from Figure 15.5, the menu has been shifted down and to the left 100 pixels from its inline location.

Absolute Positioning

Now let's look at the most important value for the `position` property—`absolute`. When you use the `absolute` position, you can place the element anywhere you want on the page, regardless of where it appears in your HTML. Figure 15.6 shows what happens when I make the following changes to the style sheet in the previous document:

```
#menu
{
    position: absolute;
    top: 100;
    left: 100;
}
```

FIGURE 15.6

An absolutely positioned element.

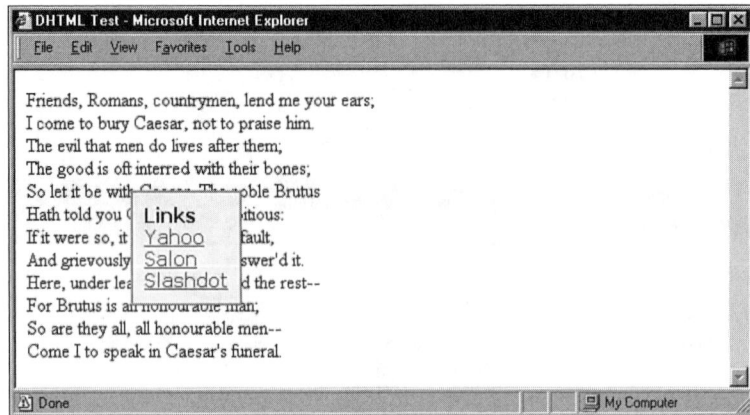

As you can see, the position of the `<div>` is calculated from the upper-left corner of the browser window rather than from the relative position of the `<div>` tag in the HTML document. You can also see that the `<div>` appears right over the block of text on the page. When you use absolute positioning, overlapping other elements on the page is no problem.

`z-index` Positioning

The final positioning property to discuss is `z-index`, which sets the precedence of an element if it overlaps another element. By default, absolutely positioned elements that appear later on a page will be positioned over elements that appear earlier on the page. However, you can change that order by manipulating the `z-index`. Here's the source code for a page with two overlapping, absolutely positioned elements. The same page rendered in Internet Explorer appears in Figure 15.7.

```
<!DOCTYPE HTML PUBLIC "-//W3C//DTD HTML 4.0 Transitional//EN">
<html>
<head>
    <title>DHTML Test</title>
<style type="text/css">
    #menu, .menu
    {
        font-family: Verdana, sans-serif;
    }
    #menu
    {
        position: absolute;
        top: 100;
        left: 100;
```

```
        z-index: 5;
    }
    #menu2
    {
        position: absolute;
        top: 150;
        left: 150;
        z-index: 1;
    }
</style>
</head>
<body>
<div id="menu">
<table border="1" cellspacing="0" cellpadding="10" bgcolor="#FFFFCC">
    <tr>
        <td>
        <p class="menu">
        <b>Links</b><br />
        <a href="http://www.yahoo.com/">Yahoo</a><br />
        <a href="http://www.salon.com/">Salon</a><br />
        <a href="http://www.slashdot.org/">Slashdot</a><br />
        </p>
        </td>
    </tr>
</table>
</div>
<div id="menu2">
<table border="1" cellspacing="0" cellpadding="10" bgcolor="#CCFFFF">
    <tr>
        <td>
        <p class="menu">
        <b>Links</b><br />
        <a href="http://www.google.com/">Google</a><br />
        <a href="http://www.slate.com/">Slate</a><br />
        <a href="http://www.wired.com/">Wired</a><br />
        </p>
        </td>
    </tr>
</table>
</div>
</body>
</html>
```

15

FIGURE 15.7

Overlapping absolutely positioned elements.

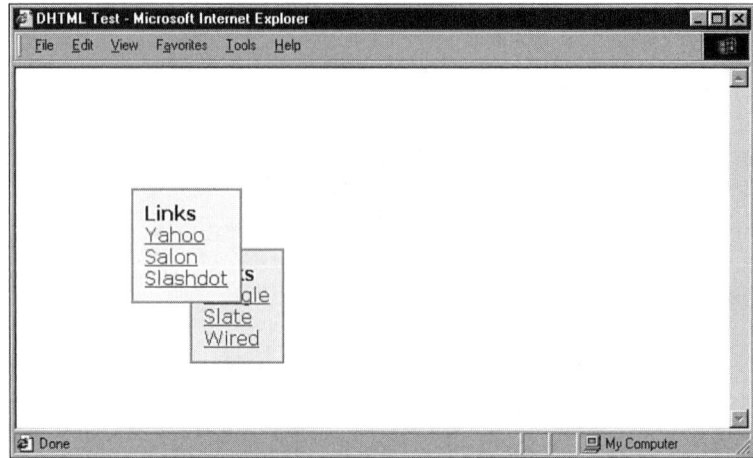

As you can see, the first `<div>` defined in the page appears above the second `<div>`, despite the fact that the second element appears later in the file than the first element. This is because in the style sheet, I assigned menu a z-index of 5 and menu2 a z-index of 1. Overlapping elements are placed on the page in order of z-index, with the highest on top and the lowest on the bottom.

Manipulating Elements with JavaScript

Now that you know how to group elements together using `<div>` and how to position and apply styles to those elements using style sheets, I can combine that with the earlier information about JavaScript and start putting the "dynamic" in "Dynamic HTML." The main trick to getting JavaScript and CSS to work together is to understand how Netscape and Internet Explorer differ in their implementations of each of those technologies.

First, let's look at some basic techniques that will serve you well when you build your own DHTML applications.

Calling Scripts Using an Event Handler

In these examples, I'm going to stick with one event handler—onMouseDown. There are tons of event handlers and they work differently from browser to browser, so it's better to just stick with one of them and use it exclusively.

To call a JavaScript function from an event handler, you just put the event handler code into the tag in question. At this point, it's prudent to talk about which elements support the event handler I'll be using. Internet Explorer supports the onMouseDown event handler for all the elements you'd want it to work with. Images, divs, links, buttons—they all support onMouseDown. Netscape is pickier. The only two elements that support onMouseDown in Netscape Navigator 4.7 are links, form buttons, and layers. Even worse, layers are exclusive to Netscape, so you can't use them if you want your pages to work in other browsers. That limits you to using onMouseDown with links alone.

Hiding and Revealing Elements

Let's look at a basic DHTML technique. One property that I haven't talked about yet is visibility. The two values for this attribute that you'll use are hidden and visible. Manipulating this property using JavaScript enables you to hide or reveal elements on a page.

I'm going to modify the page with the two overlapping elements that I showed you earlier so that one of the menus of links can be hidden or revealed by clicking on an image. The source code for the page follows, and the contents of the page displayed in Internet Explorer are shown in Figure 15.8.

INPUT

```
<!DOCTYPE HTML PUBLIC "-//W3C//DTD HTML 4.0 Transitional//EN">
<html>
<head>
    <title>DHTML Test</title>
<style type="text/css">
    #menu, .menu
    {
        font-family: Verdana, sans-serif;
    }
    #menu
    {
        position: absolute;
        top: 100;
        left: 100;
        z-index: 5;
        visibility: visible;
    }
    #menu2
    {
        position: absolute;
        top: 150;
        left: 150;
        z-index: 1;
        visibility: visible;
    }
</style>
<script language="JavaScript">

menuVisible = true;

function toggleVisibility(objId)
{
```

```
        if (document.layers)
        {
            obj = eval("document." + objId);
        }
        else if (document.all)
        {
            obj = eval(objId + ".style");
        }

        if (menuVisible == true)
        {
            menuVisible = false;
            obj.visibility = "hidden";
        }
        else
        {
            menuVisible = true;
            obj.visibility = "visible";
        }
        return false;
}
</script>
</head>
<body>
<a href="#" onmousedown="toggleVisibility('menu')">
<img src="button.gif" width="106" height="46" alt="" border="0"></a>
<div id="menu">
<table border="1" cellspacing="0" cellpadding="10" bgcolor="#FFFFCC">
    <tr>
        <td>
        <p class="menu">
        <b>Links</b><br />
        <a href="http://www.yahoo.com/">Yahoo</a><br />
        <a href="http://www.salon.com/">Salon</a><br />
        <a href="http://www.slashdot.org/">Slashdot</a><br />
        </p>
        </td>
    </tr>
</table>
</div>
<div id="menu2">
<table border="1" cellspacing="0" cellpadding="10" bgcolor="#CCFFFF">
    <tr>
        <td>
        <p class="menu">
        <b>Links</b><br />
        <a href="http://www.google.com/">Google</a><br />
        <a href="http://www.slate.com/">Slate</a><br />
        <a href="http://www.wired. com/">Wired</a><br />
        </p>
        </td>
```

```
        </tr>
      </table>
    </div>
  </body>
</html>
```

OUTPUT

FIGURE 15.8

Overlapping absolutely positioned elements. Clicking the image toggles the overlapping menu's visibility.

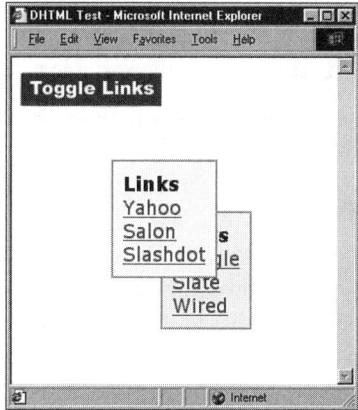

When a user clicks on the image, the first menu's visibility is toggled. The first time he clicks on it, it disappears; the second time, it appears again. Let's take a look at how this works.

The style sheets and `<div>` elements should look familiar; the only change I've made to them is adding the `visibility` property to the style sheet. Take a look at the image tag I've added to the document. As you can see, it's surrounded by a link tag, but the link just points to the URL #, which normally points to the top of the current document. I've added the link to the document so that I can use the `onMouseDown` event handler, which works for links in both Netscape and Internet Explorer.

The `onMouseDown` handler calls the function `toggleVisibility()` and passes it the ID of the `<div>` to be hidden or displayed. Whenever a user clicks on the image, his function is called and the ID `menu` associated with the first `<div>` on the page is passed in. Before you look at the function, though, take a look at the line above it. I set a variable called `menuVisible` to `true`. This variable just indicates that the page starts out with the element to be toggled visible.

The first thing I have to do inside `toggleVisibility()` is to convert the ID that's passed in to a reference to the object in the appropriate DOM. First, I check whether we're using the Netscape DOM by testing for the existence of the `document.layers` object. If it exists, I take the string that's passed in, `menu`, and turn it into a reference to `document.menu`.

If `document.layers` doesn't exist, I test for `document.all`, which exists in browsers that use the Internet Explorer DOM. In this case, I convert `menu` to a reference to `menu.style`, which provides access to all the style sheet properties of `menu`.

When I have the proper DOM reference, I check the value of the `menuHidden` variable, which I set to `true` when the page loaded. If it's `true`, I set the visibility of the object to `hidden` and set the variable to `false`. If it's `false` (because someone already clicked on the image), I set the visibility to `visible` and set the variable to `true`.

That's all there is to it. When I have a reference to the appropriate object to manipulate, I just have to change the setting for that property to change the page's appearance.

Moving Objects Around

As you've seen, it's possible to position elements on a page in a specific spot using style sheets. After they're positioned, you can move them around the page using JavaScript. Let's take a look at a script that's very similar to the one I just created. This one moves the `menu` element horizontally and adjusts its `z-index` so that it appears as if it's below the other element—`menu2`.

Here's the source code for the page, which is shown in Figure 15.9:

INPUT

```
<!DOCTYPE HTML PUBLIC "-//W3C//DTD HTML 4.0 Transitional//EN">
<html>
<head>
    <title>DHTML Test</title>
<style type="text/css">
    #menu, .menu
    {
        font-family: Verdana, sans-serif;
    }
    #menu
    {
        position: absolute;
        top: 100;
        left: 100;
        z-index: 5;
        visibility: visible;
    }
    #menu2
    {
        position: absolute;
        top: 150;
        left: 150;
        z-index: 3;
        visibility: visible;
    }
</style>
```

```
<script language="JavaScript">
function moveObject(objId)
{
    if (document.layers)
    {
        obj = eval("document." + objId);
    }
    else if (document.all)
    {
        obj = eval(objId + ".style");
    }

    if (parseInt(obj.left) == 100)
    {
        obj.left = 200;
        obj.zIndex = 1;
    }
    else
    {
        obj.left = 100;
        obj.zIndex = 5;
    }
}
</script>
</head>
<body>
<a href="#" onmousedown="moveObject('menu')">
<img src="button.gif" width="106" height="46" alt="" border="0"></a>
<div id="menu">
<table border="1" cellspacing="0" cellpadding="10" bgcolor="#FFFFCC">
    <tr>
        <td>
        <p class="menu">
        <b>Links</b><br />
        <a href="http://www.yahoo.com/">Yahoo</a><br />
        <a href="http://www.salon.com/">Salon</a><br />
        <a href="http://www.slashdot.org/">Slashdot</a><br />
        </p>
        </td>
    </tr>
</table>
</div>
<div id="menu2">
<table border="1" cellspacing="0" cellpadding="10" bgcolor="#CCFFFF">
    <tr>
        <td>
        <p class="menu">
        <b>Links</b><br />
        <a href="http://www.google.com/">Google</a><br />
        <a href="http://www.slate.com/">Slate</a><br />
        <a href="http://www.wired.com/">Wired</a><br />
```

```
            </p>
           </td>
        </tr>
      </table>
     </div>
    </body>
   </html>
```

FIGURE 15.9

A page with a movable element.

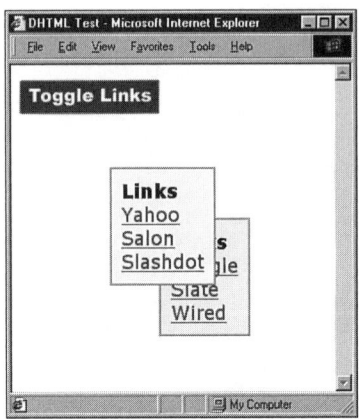 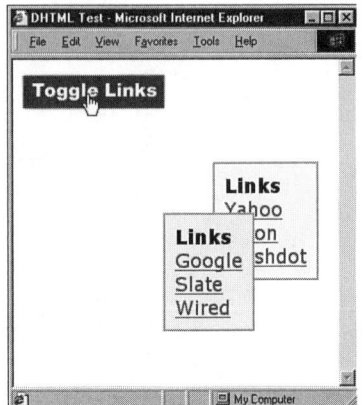

This example is also very similar to the previous one: The image and the two <div> elements are still there. Let's look at a few small changes that I made. First of all, look at the style sheet for the menu2 ID. I changed the z-index for that element from 1 to 3 for this example. I'm going to be modifying the z-index of menu with my JavaScript, and I need to be able to change it from a number higher than menu2's z-index to a number lower than it (but still greater than 0, in order for it to work in both Netscape and Internet Explorer).

The event handler for the link around the image is the same in this example as it was in the previous one, but this time it calls the moveObject() function. Let's delve into this function. Just as in the previous example, I grab a reference to the object I want to manipulate using the argument passed to the function. I do some capability detection to determine which browser the user is running, and then I set the obj variable to the proper value for that browser.

Then, I need to determine where the object to be manipulated is positioned in the browser. I use the parseInt() function to get the integer value of the element's left position. If it's 100 (where it started), the object is moved 100 pixels to the right (and below menu2 because of the change in z-index). If it's 200, it moves the object back to the higher z-index value and 100 pixels back to the left.

That's all there is to moving elements around the page. Note that even though the property for an object's Z position on the page is z-index in style sheets, in the DOM you refer to it as zIndex.

Creating a DHTML Pull-Down Menu

Let's look at a common application of DHTML that you'll see on many Web sites—a pull-down menu implemented in Dynamic HTML. This builds on the previous examples. When the user clicks on an image surrounded by a link, the menu will appear below it. The menu will be implemented using a <div> very similar to the ones that I've used in the previous examples.

The trick here is putting the menu in the right place. Because the menu is supposed to appear directly below the button, and you don't know where that button is going to appear when the page loads, I have to dynamically determine the location of the image in my script. Before I explain how this is accomplished, let me show you the source code for the script:

INPUT

```
<!DOCTYPE HTML PUBLIC "-//W3C//DTD HTML 4.0 Transitional//EN">
<html>
<head>
    <title>DHTML Test</title>
<style type="text/css">
    #menu, .menu
    {
        font-family: Verdana, sans-serif;
    }
    #menu
    {
        position: absolute;
        top: 0;
        left: 0;
        z-index: 5;
        visibility: hidden;
    }
</style>
<script language="JavaScript">
function showMenu()
{
    if (document.layers)
    {
        obj = document.menu;
        image = document.images["button"];
        obj.top = image.y + image.height;
        obj.left = image.x;
    }
    else if (document.all)
    {
```

```
            obj = menu.style;
            image = button;
            obj.top = parseInt(image.offsetTop) + parseInt(image.height);
            obj.left = parseInt(image.offsetLeft);
        }

        if (String(obj.visibility) == "visible" || String(obj.visibility) ==
➥"show")
        {
            obj.visibility = "hidden";
        }
        else
        {
            obj.visibility = "visible";
        }
        return false;
}
</script>
</head>
<body>
<a href="#" onmousedown="showMenu()">
<img src="button.gif" name="button" width="106" height="46" alt=""
border="0"></a>
<div id="menu">
<table border="1" cellspacing="0" cellpadding="10" bgcolor="#FFFFCC">
    <tr>
        <td>
        <p class="menu">
        <b>Links</b><br />
        <a href="http://www.yahoo.com/">Yahoo</a><br />
        <a href="http://www.salon.com/">Salon</a><br />
        <a href="http://www.slashdot.org/">Slashdot</a><br />
        </p>
        </td>
    </tr>
</table>
</div>
</body>
</html>
```

Figure 15.10 shows what the pop-up menu looks like when it appears.

I've pared down the code to the bare minimum needed for this example—the image with the link, and the <div> from earlier that will serve as a pull-down menu.

Take a look at the style sheet first. When the page loads, the <div> is positioned in the upper-left corner of the page and is hidden. I'll handle the positioning and display of the

15

OUTPUT

script within
my JavaScript
function.

FIGURE 15.10

Clicking on the image reveals the pull-down menu.

The function in this page is called showMenu(), and it's associated with the
onMouseDown() event of the link surrounding the button image. One important change I
made to the page was adding the name attribute to the image so that I can refer to it in
my script more easily.

Now that the style sheets and HTML are set, let's go to the script, where all the important action occurs. There's only one function in the script—showMenu().

I start out by doing some browser-specific stuff. I test for the document.layers object
first, so I can handle Netscape users. I save a reference to the menu object using
document.menu, and a reference to the image using document.images["button"]. After
I have the references to the menu and image, I set the position of the menu. I set the left
position by getting the X coordinate of the image using image.x. I specify the top of the
image by adding the top position of the image (image.y) to the height of the image
(image.height). This positions the upper-left corner of the menu at the lower-left corner
of the image, where it belongs.

Next, if the document.all object is available, I do the Internet Explorer-specific stuff. I
position the menu the same way, but using the Internet Explorer DOM. In this case, the
reference to the menu is menu.style, and the reference to the image is just button. I
obtain the position of the image's upper-left corner using image.offsetTop and
image.offsetLeft. I use the parseInt() function to convert the values of those proper-

ties to integers. To place the menu at the lower-left corner of the image, I add the height of the image (obtained using `image.height`) to the position of the top of the image.

Okay, at this point the menu is in the right spot, but I haven't displayed it. Because this function both shows and hides the menu, I have to perform a test to determine which thing to do. I test to see if the menu is visible, and I have to do a bit of browser-specific stuff here as well. Netscape and Internet Explorer report the value of `obj.visibility` differently. Internet Explorer reports it as `hidden` or `visible`, but Netscape uses `hide` or `show`. So in my test, I have to check for both `visible` and `show`. I use the `String()` function to make sure that the value of `obj.visibility` I'm comparing is a string. If `obj.visibility` reports either of those values, I hide the menu. If it reports anything else, I show it.

After I've displayed the menu or hidden it, I return false from the function so that the browser doesn't actually attempt to follow the link the user clicked on. If I didn't do that, the browser would follow the link and change the user's position on the page.

Continuing Your DHTML Education

I encourage you to visit both the Microsoft and Netscape Web sites devoted to DHTML. Each offers an interesting perspective.

The Microsoft Web site (`msdn.microsoft.com/workshop/author/default.asp`) has a ton of great information for using the DHTML capabilities unique to Internet Explorer 4 and 5.

Netscape appears to be leading the cross-browser compatibility charge and has extensive articles and technical notes at `developer.netscape.com/tech/dynhtml/index.html`.

Other sites that have useful information include the following:

- WebReference Dynamic HTML Lab (`www.webreference.com/dhtml/`)—Contains examples and code ranging from drag-and-drop DHTML to expandable menus and outlines.
- Macromedia's Dynamic HTML Zone (`www.dhtmlzone.com`)—Offers DHTML articles, resources, and tutorials on a wide range of DHTML topics.
- Webmonkey (`www.hotwired.com/webmonkey/dynamic_html/`)—Provides an extensive section devoted to DHTML.
- Brainjar (`www.brainjar.com`)—Offers a library of JavaScript functions for adding DHTML to Web pages.
- The Dynamic Duo: Cross Browser Dynamic HTML (`www.dansteinman.com/`

dynduo/index.html)—Provides extensive tutorials, projects, and sample code.

Summary

Today, you learned that Dynamic HTML is comprised of three technologies: HTML, style sheets, and scripting. Each one is important to DHTML and plays a distinct role. HTML provides the foundation for the Web page. Style sheets enable you to format and position elements to suit your taste. Scripting makes DHTML Dynamic.

Unfortunately, DHTML suffers from problems. Inconsistencies in how each Web browser implements the component technologies make coding cross-browser DHTML a challenge.

Although today offers a broad overview of DHTML and the technologies that make it up, it cannot hope to be an exhaustive tutorial for each element of DHTML.

Workshop

Today, you've learned how to use several different technologies—collectively known as Dynamic HTML—that will help you control the precise appearance of your Web pages and enable you to create pages that respond to user actions. The following workshop includes some questions you might have, a quiz about some of today's most important topics, and some exercises you can do to reinforce your knowledge of DHTML.

Q&A

Q Is DHTML really worth the time and effort?

A Hmmm, that's a tough one. I'm very tempted to say "no," but you might need (or want) to create items that you can only achieve using DHTML. If you fall into that category, yes, it will be worth it. If you find yourself spending all your time trying to create the ultimate DHTML Web page, but don't actually publish it, you might want to go back to the basics and gradually work your way up to DHTML.

Q There's so much information to learn. How do I do it?

A First, start with HTML. Become an expert in it!

After that, you could take either of two approaches: master everything or learn only what you need.

The "master everything" approach leads you, in succession, from HTML to CSS, and then to JavaScript, moving on only when you are competent and comfortable with the technology at hand. After you master all three technologies, study how they interrelate and try your hand at DHTML.

The "learn only what you need" approach gets you started more quickly. Find a specific technique that you want to use, such as dynamically changing the visibility of an object, and learn how to do that. After you finish, go on to the next technique that you find interesting. You'll learn a little bit about all the technologies along the way, but will have DHTML to show for it almost immediately.

You might also want to find DHTML code on sites around the Web and see how it works. While it's unethical to use the unaltered code, there's certainly nothing wrong with reviewing it and applying the concepts to your own work.

Q Where is DHTML headed?

A The W3C has developed a more standardized DOM, called *DOM Level 2*. It was adopted as a recommendation in November 2000, and Microsoft Internet Explorer 5.5 and Netscape 6 currently implement most of these ideas.

Q What about Netscape's LAYER element and other browser-specific DHTML features?

A As far as I'm concerned, cross-browser DHTML is where it's at if you're going to bother with DHTML at all. If you want to reach the most people (and offend the least), you should concentrate on creating Web pages that are (relatively) universal. I admit that these proprietary Web browser features can be very tempting, and that some of the effects are pretty neat; however, there's nothing more frustrating than spending weeks developing a cool DHTML Web page and finding out that most people can't even see it.

Quiz

1. Which three technologies make Dynamic HTML possible?
2. What is a Document Object Model?
3. Can you use VBScript or another scripting language to create DHTML?
4. What's the most important element of cross-browser DHTML?

Quiz Answers

1. HTML, style sheets, and scripting.
2. DOM is the language you use when you refer to scriptable objects on a Web page. Remember, Microsoft Internet Explorer and Netscape Navigator have different approaches to their DOMs; therefore, you need to use different statements to refer to the same object.
3. Yes, but you should know that VBScript isn't supported in Netscape Navigator

without a special plug-in. Other scripting languages are even less supported. JavaScript is your best choice.

4. Undoubtedly, the capability detection. This enables you to support not only today's browsers, but also browsers that haven't been released yet.

Exercises

1. Alter the pull-down menu example from this chapter so that it appears when the user's pointer is above the menu image and stays open while the pointer is there.

2. Download one or more cross-browser DHTML APIs and create a pull-down menu using the API in place of the code in this chapter.

PART 6

Designing Effective Web Pages

DAY 16

Writing and Designing Web Pages: Do's and Don'ts

You won't learn about any HTML tags today, or how to convert files from one strange file format to another. You're mostly done with the HTML part of Web page design. Next come the intangibles. These are the things that separate your pages from those of a designer who just knows the tags and who flings text and graphics around and calls it a site.

Armed with the information from the last 15 days, you could put this book down now and go off and merrily create Web pages to your heart's content. However, if you stick around, you can create *better* Web pages. Do you need any more incentive to continue reading?

This chapter includes hints for creating well-written and well-designed Web pages, and it highlights do's and don'ts concerning the following:

- How to decide whether to use standard HTML 4.0 tags, a subset of HTML 4.0 tags that works with older browsers, style sheets, HTML extensions, or a combination of two or more
- How to write your Web pages so that they can be easily scanned and read
- Issues concerning the design and layout of your Web pages
- When and why you should create links
- How to use images effectively
- Other miscellaneous tidbits and hints

Using the HTML Extensions

In the past, before every browser developer was introducing its own new HTML tags, being a Web designer was easy. The only HTML tags you had to deal with were those from HTML 2.0, and the vast majority of the browsers on the Web could read your pages without a problem. Being a Web designer today is significantly more complicated. You have to work with several different types of Web page content:

- HTML 2.0 tags
- HTML 3.2 features such as tables, divisions, backgrounds, and color, which are supported by most, but not all, browsers
- HTML 4.0 and related features such as cascading style sheets, Dynamic HTML, and framesets
- XHTML 1.0, the enhancement to HTML 4.0 that makes HTML markup more uniform and makes it compatible with XML
- Plug-ins and other embedded objects, which use files and data that are external to the browser
- Browser-specific tags (from Netscape or Internet Explorer) that may or may not end up as part of the official HTML specification and whose support varies from browser to browser
- Other technologies (such as SMIL Boston, a synchronized multimedia language), proposed for future W3C specifications, that is only supported by Internet Explorer 5.5

If you're finding all this information rather mind-boggling, you're not alone. Other authors and developers just like you are trying to sort out the mess and make decisions based on how they want their pages to look. Cascading Style Sheets and Dynamic

HTML do give you more flexibility with layout and content in HTML 4.0 and XHTML 1.0. However, they're not supported by many older browsers. These browsers are only still used by a small percentage of users, but many high traffic sites still take them into account.

Choosing a strategy for using HTML is one of the more significant design decisions you'll make as you start creating Web pages. You might find it easier to look at your choices as a sort of continuum between the conservative Web author and the cutting-edge Web author (see Figure 16.1).

16

FIGURE 16.1

The Web author continuum.

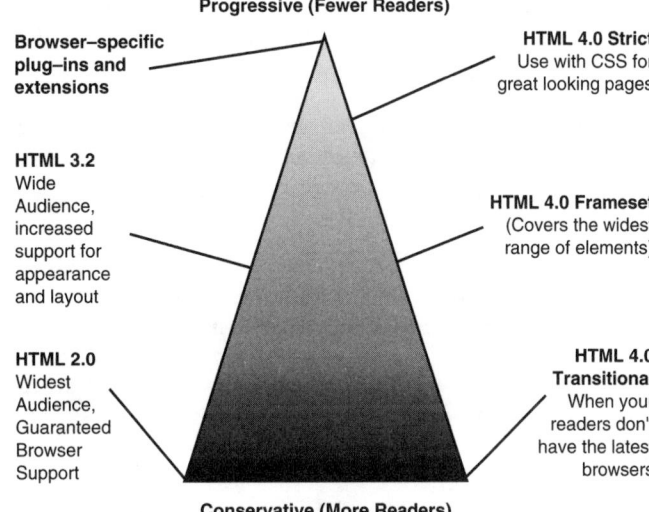

Progressive (Fewer Readers)

Browser–specific plug–ins and extensions

HTML 4.0 Strict
Use with CSS for great looking pages

HTML 3.2
Wide Audience, increased support for appearance and layout

HTML 4.0 Frameset
(Covers the widest range of elements)

HTML 2.0
Widest Audience, Guaranteed Browser Support

HTML 4.0 Transitional
When your readers don't have the latest browsers

Conservative (More Readers)

Note

Don't think of these endpoints as value judgments; conservative isn't worse than cutting-edge, and vice versa. You'll find advantages at both ends and significant advantages in the middle.

Before the release of the HTML 4.0 standard, the continuum was a little bit more linear. The old continuum is depicted at the left side of the triangle in Figure 16.1.

The conservative Web developer stuck to older HTML 2.0 tags, as defined by the standards. I'm not saying that the conservative Web developer is boring. You can create magnificent Web content with these older tags, and the advantage of using them is that the pages will be supported without a hitch by the greatest number of browsers. Your site reaches the widest possible audience when you use this approach.

The middle-of-the-road Web developer added HTML 3.2 tags as defined by the standards. At that time, HTML 3.2 was where XHTML 1.0 is today. Although it was an accepted standard, Web developers had to wait for the browser world to catch up with the new standard. However, they were willing to take the risk that the majority of the people who visited their sites would use at least one of the two major browsers, which by that time already supported the major HTML 3.2 tags.

Even today, the cutting-edge Web developer wants the sort of control over layout that the more advanced tags provide and is willing to shut out a portion of the audience to get it. The cutting-edge Web developer's pages are designed for a single browser (or at most two or three), tested only in a single browser, and might even include a big announcement that says "These Pages Must Be Read Using Browser X." Visiting these pages in other browsers may make the design unreadable or at least confusing—or it may be just fine.

It's important to note that being referred to as "cutting-edge" is not necessarily a compliment. Excluding potential viewers based on the browser they're using isn't a good idea. Such design practices are best reserved for personal sites.

Note

> Many corporations have IT departments that mandate the use of a particular browser. In those situations, it often makes sense to tailor content on the company's internal sites (intranet) to the standard browser. There are no cross-browser issues to deal with, and some of the specialized features might make your intranet site easier to use.

To accommodate all these different scenarios, the HTML 4.0 and XHTML 1.0 definitions include three flavors of HTML, and the main differences between HTML 4.0 and XHTML 1.0 have been noted throughout this book. The three new flavors are shown on the right side of the continuum in Figure 16.1:

- **HTML 4.0 or XHTML 1.0 Transitional** is geared toward the conservative Web developer who wants to support as many browsers as possible. It parallels those users who stuck to using HTML 2.0 tags in the older continuum. HTML 2.0 tags are still the bare-bones minimum that browsers are expected to support. The majority of the pages that you've created in this book are compliant with the HTML 3.2 standard, which is supported by every browser in common use today.

- **HTML 4.0 or XHTML 1.0 Frameset** is the recommended approach for Web developers who design their pages for HTML 3.2 browsers but also want to present them in framesets (which, in the old continuum, fell toward the progressive end). To my mind, this is today's middle-of-the-road approach. Although it supports more tags than the transitional approach, there are still many browsers in use that don't support frames.

- **HTML 4.0 or XHTML 1.0 Strict** is for the progressive Web developer who wants to design pages purely by the HTML 4.0 or XHTML 1.0 specification. This means not using those tags that have been marked as "deprecated," but instead using Cascading Style Sheets for document presentation.

Although the HTML 4.0 and XHTML 1.0 specifications are landmark efforts to satisfy every type of Web developer, there's still that top point in the spectrum for the *really* cutting-edge developers—those who continue to experiment with features that go above and beyond the formal specifications. As browser manufacturers continue to implement new and experimental features, the very cutting-edge developers are eager to work with them. They support the latest and greatest versions of their favorite browsers and design their pages using browser-specific tags.

When you're choosing between interesting design and a wide audience, the best position is probably a balance of the two. If you know the effects that HTML extensions will have on your pages, both in browsers that support them and those that don't, you can make slight modifications to your design to take advantage of both sides. Your pages will be readable and useful in older browsers over a wider range of platforms, but they'll also take advantage of the advanced features in the newer browsers. Today, generally this means adopting the HTML 4.01 standard tags to achieve goals that are difficult or impossible with HTML 3.2, but at the same time being aware of their effect on browsers that don't yet support the full 4.01 specification.

Throughout this book, I've explained which tags are part of HTML 4.0 and which tags are available in which major browsers. For each tag, I've also noted the alternatives you can use if a browser can't view that tag. With this information in hand, you should be able to experiment with each tag in different browsers to see the effect on your design.

The most important strategy I can suggest for using features that are more browser-specific, while still trying to retain compatibility with other browsers, is to test your files in those other browsers. Most browsers are freeware or shareware and are available for downloading, so all you need to do is find and install them. By testing your pages, you can get an idea of how different browsers interpret different tags. Eventually, you'll get a feel for which features provide the most flexibility, which ones need special coding for alternatives in older or different browsers, and which tags can be used freely without complicating matters for other browsers.

Writing for Online Publication

Writing on the Web is no different from writing in the real world. Although it's not committed to hard copy, it's still published and is still a reflection of you and your work. In fact, because your writing is online and your visitors have many other options when it comes to finding something to read, you'll have to follow the rules of good writing that much more closely.

Because of the vast quantities of information available on the Web, your visitors aren't going to have much patience if your Web page is poorly organized or full of spelling errors. They're likely to give up after the first couple of sentences and move on to someone else's page. After all, there are several million pages out there. No one has time to waste on bad pages.

I don't mean that you have to go out and become a professional writer to create a good Web page, but I'll give you a few hints for making your Web page easier to read and understand.

Write Clearly and Be Brief

Unless you're writing the Great American Web Novel, your visitors aren't going to linger lovingly over your words. You should write as clearly and concisely as you possibly can, present your points, and then stop. Obscuring what you want to say with extra words just makes figuring out your point more difficult.

If you don't have a copy of Strunk and White's *The Elements of Style*, put down this book right now and go buy that book. Read it, reread it, memorize it, inhale it, sleep with it under your pillow, show it to all your friends, quote it at parties, and make it your life. You'll find no better guide to the art of good, clear writing than *The Elements of Style*.

Organize Your Pages for Quick Scanning

Even if you write the clearest, briefest, most scintillating prose ever seen on the Web, chances are good that your visitors won't start at the top of your Web page and carefully read every word down to the bottom.

In this context, *scanning* is the first quick look your visitors give to each page to get the general gist of the content. Depending on what your users want out of your pages, they may scan the parts that jump out at them (headings, links, other emphasized words), perhaps read a few contextual paragraphs, and then move on. By writing and organizing your pages for easy "scannability," you can help your visitors get the information they need as fast as possible.

To improve the scannability of your Web pages, follow these guidelines:

- **Use headings to summarize topics**—Note that this book has headings and subheadings. You can flip through quickly and find the parts that interest you. The same concept applies to Web pages.

- **Use lists**—Lists are wonderful for summarizing related items. Every time you find yourself saying something like "each widget has four elements" or "use the following steps to do this," the content after that phrase should be in an ordered or unordered list.

- **Don't forget link menus**—As a type of list, the link menu has all the same advantages of lists for scannability, and it doubles as an excellent navigation tool.

- **Don't bury important information in text**—If you have a point to make, make it close to the top of the page or at the beginning of a paragraph. Forcing readers to sift through a lot of information before they get to what's important means that many of them won't see the important stuff at all.

- **Write short, clear paragraphs**—Long paragraphs are harder to read and make gleaning the information more difficult. The further into the paragraph you put your point, the less likely it is that anybody will read it.

Figure 16.2 shows the sort of writing technique that you should avoid.

FIGURE 16.2

DON'T: A Web page that is difficult to scan.

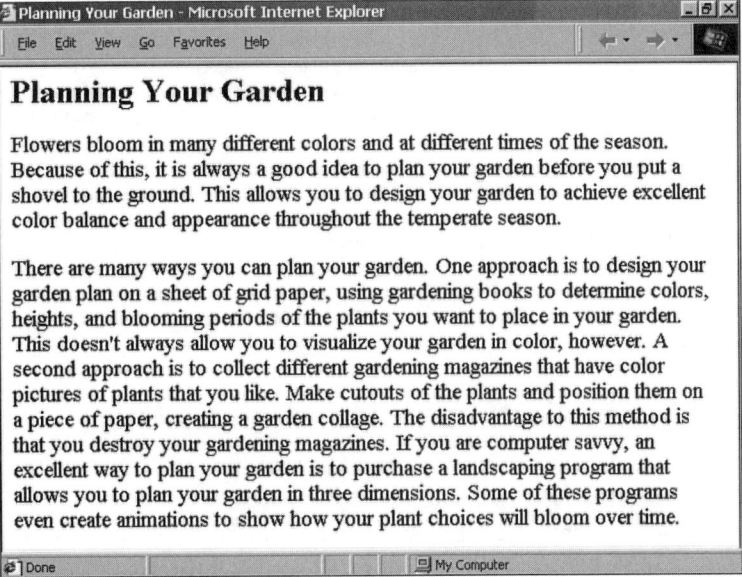

Because all the information on this page is in paragraph form, your visitors have to read both paragraphs to find out what they want and where they want to go next.

How would you improve the example shown in Figure 16.2? Try rewriting this section so that visitors can better find the main points from the text. Consider the following:

- These two paragraphs actually contain three discrete topics.
- The ways to plan the garden would make an excellent nested list.

Figure 16.3 shows what an improvement might look like.

FIGURE 16.3

DO: An improvement to the difficult-to-scan Web page.

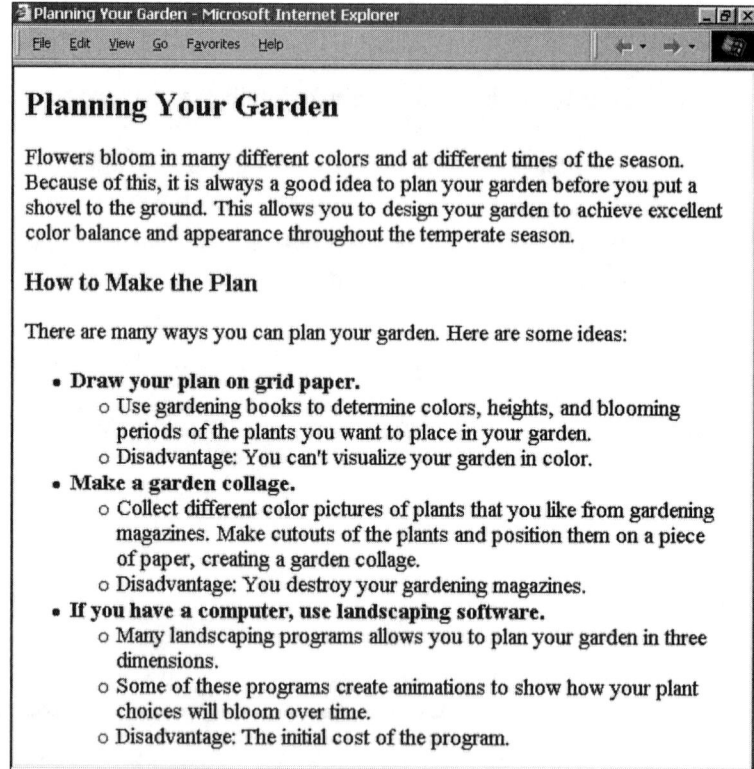

Make Each Page Stand on Its Own

As you write, keep in mind that your visitors could jump to any of your Web pages from anywhere. For example, you can structure a page so that section four distinctly follows section three and has no other links to it. Then someone you don't even know might create a link to the page starting at section four. From then on, visitors could find themselves at section four without even knowing that section three exists.

Be careful to write each page so that it stands on its own. The following guidelines will help:

- **Use descriptive titles**—The title should provide not only the direct subject of this page, but also its relationship to the rest of the pages on the site.
- **Provide a navigational link**—If a page depends on the one before it, provide a navigational link back to that page (and also a link up to the top level, preferably).

- **Avoid initial sentences like the following**—"You can get around these problems by…", "After you're done with that, do this…", and "The advantages to this method are…". The information referred to by "these," "that," and "this" are off on some other page. If these sentences are the first words your visitors see, they're going to be confused.

Be Careful with Emphasis

Use emphasis sparingly in your text. Paragraphs with a whole lot of words in **boldface** or *italics* or ALL CAPS are hard to read, whether you use them several times in a paragraph or to emphasize long strings of text. The best emphasis is used only with small words such as "and," "this," or "but."

Link text also is a form of emphasis. Use single words or short phrases for link text. Do not use entire passages or paragraphs. Figure 16.4 illustrates a particularly bad example of too much emphasis obscuring the rest of the text.

FIGURE 16.4

DON'T: Too much emphasis.

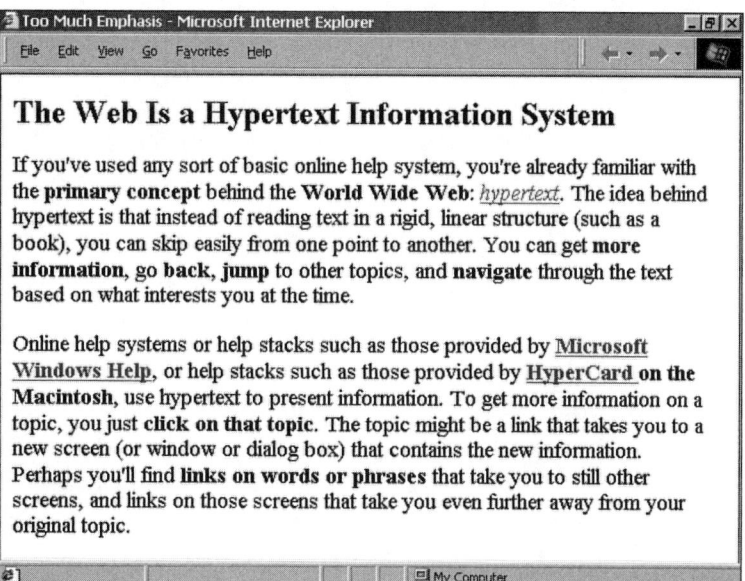

By removing some of the boldface and using less text for your links, you can considerably reduce the amount of clutter in the paragraph, as you can see in Figure 16.5.

Figure 16.5

DO: Less emphasis.

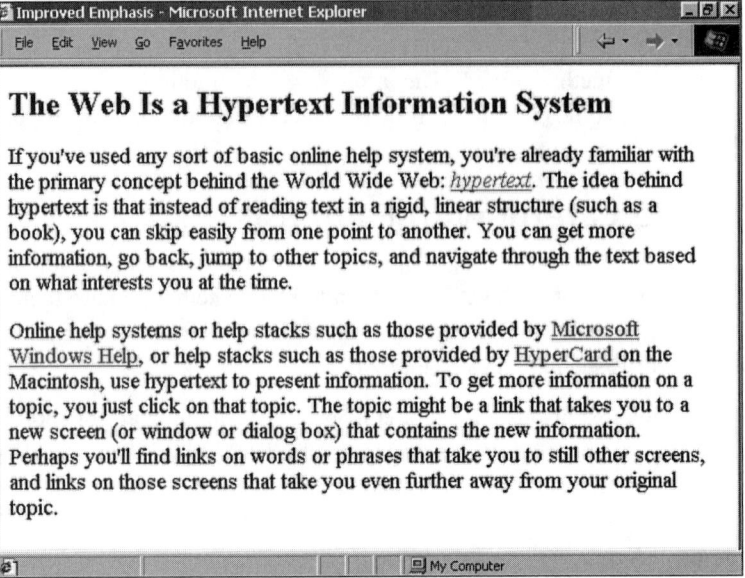

Be especially careful of emphasis that moves or changes, such as marquees, blinking text, or animation. Unless the animation is the primary focus of the page, use movement and sound sparingly.

Don't Use Browser-Specific Terminology

Avoid references in your text to specific features of specific browsers. For example, don't use the following wording:

- **"Click here"**—What if your visitors are Web surfing without a mouse? A more generic phrase is "Select this link." (Of course, you should avoid the "here" syndrome in the first place, which neatly gets around this problem as well.)

- **"To save this page, pull down the File menu and select Save"**—Each browser has a different set of menus and different ways of accomplishing the same actions. If at all possible, do *not* refer to specifics of browser operation in your Web pages.

- **"Use the Back button to return to the previous page"**—Each browser has a different set of buttons and different methods for going back. If you want your visitors to be able to go back to a previous page or to any specific page, link those pages.

Spell Check and Proofread Your Pages

Spell checking and proofreading may seem like obvious suggestions, but they bear mentioning given the number of pages I've seen on the Web that obviously haven't had either.

The process of designing a set of Web pages and making them available on the Web is like publishing a book, producing a magazine, or releasing a product. Publishing Web pages is considerably easier than publishing books, magazines, or other products, of course, but just because the task is easy doesn't mean your product should be sloppy.

Thousands of people may be reading and exploring the content you provide. Spelling errors and bad grammar reflect badly on you, on your work, and on the content you're describing. It may be irritating enough that your visitors won't bother to delve any deeper than your home page, even if the subject you're writing about is fascinating.

Proofread and spell check each of your Web pages. If possible, have someone else read them. Often other people can pick up errors that you, the writer, can't see. Even a simple edit can greatly improve many pages and make them easier to read and navigate.

Design and Page Layout

With the introduction of technologies such as style sheets and Dynamic HTML, people without a sense of design have even more opportunities to create a site that looks simply awful.

Probably the best rule of Web design to follow at all times is this: *Keep the design of each page as simple as possible*. Reduce the number of elements (images, headings, and rule lines) and make sure that the visitors' eyes are drawn to the most important parts of the page first.

Keep this cardinal rule in mind as you read the next sections, which offer some other suggestions for basic design and layout of Web pages.

Use Headings as Headings

Headings tend to be rendered in larger or bolder fonts in graphical browsers. Therefore, using a heading tag to provide some sort of warning, note, or emphasis in regular text can be tempting (see Figure 16.6).

FIGURE **16.6**

*DON'T: The wrong
way to use headings.*

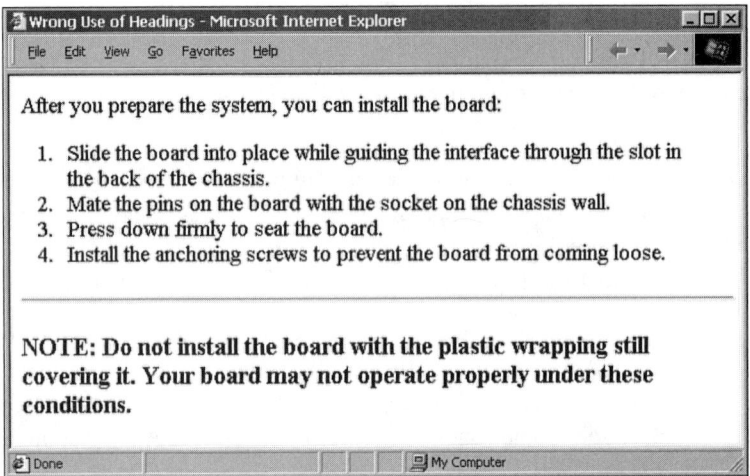

Headings stand out from the text and signal the start of new topics, so they should be
used only as headings. If you really want to emphasize a particular section of text,
consider using a small image, a rule line, or some other method of emphasis instead.
Figure 16.7 shows an example of the text from Figure 16.6 with a different kind of visual
emphasis.

FIGURE **16.7**

*DO: The right way to
use headings.*

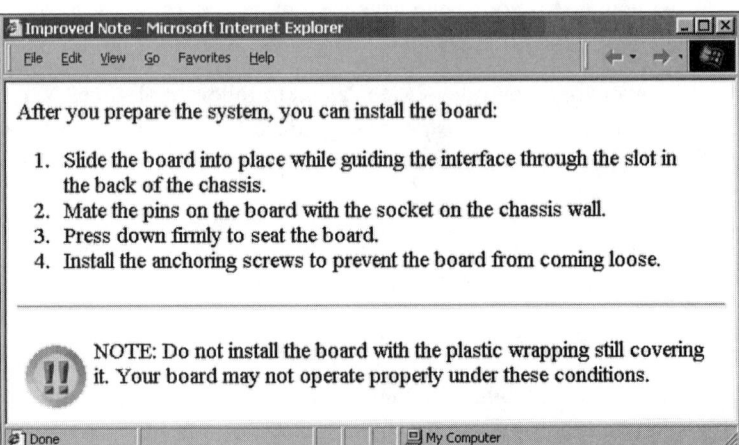

Tip

If you just want to include big text on your page, you can use the `<font>`
tag or Cascading Style Sheets.

Group Related Information Visually

Grouping related information within a page is a task for both writing and design. As I suggested in the "Writing for Online Publication" section, grouping related information under headings improves the scanability of that information. Visually separating each section from the others helps to make it distinct and emphasizes the relatedness of the information.

If a Web page contains several sections, find a way to separate those sections visually—for example, with a heading, a rule line, or tables, as shown in Figure 16.8.

FIGURE 16.8

DO: Separate sections visually.

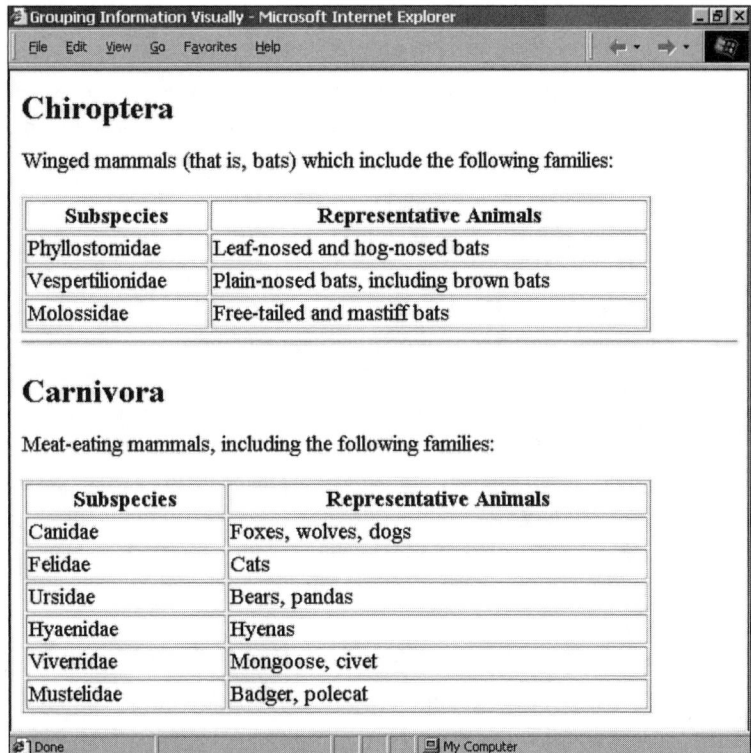

Use a Consistent Layout

When you're reading a book or a magazine, each page or section usually has the same layout. The page numbers are placed where you expect them, and the first word on each page starts in the same place.

The same sort of consistent layout works equally well on Web pages. Having a single "look and feel" for each page on your Web site is comforting to your visitors. After two or three pages, they'll know what the elements of each page are and where to find them. If you create a consistent design, your visitors can find the information they need and navigate through your pages without having to stop at every page and try to find where certain elements are located.

Consistent layout can include the following:

- **Consistent page elements**—If you use second-level headings (`<h2>`) on one page to indicate major topics, use second-level headings for major topics on all your pages. If you have a heading and a rule line at the top of your page, use that same layout on all your pages.

- **Consistent forms of navigation**—Put your navigation menus in the same place on every page (usually the top or the bottom of the page), and use the same number of them. If you're going to use navigation icons, make sure you use the same icons in the same order for every page.

- **The use of external style sheets**—If you want to stick to pure HTML 4.0, you can create a master style sheet that defines background properties, text and link colors, font selections and sizes, margins, and more. The appearance of your pages maintains consistency throughout your site.

Using Links

Without links, Web pages would be really dull and finding anything interesting on the Web would be close to impossible. In many ways, the quality of your links can be as important as the writing and design of your actual pages. Here's some friendly advice on creating and using links.

Use Link Menus with Descriptive Text

As I've noted throughout this book, using link menus is a great way of organizing your content and the links on a page. If you organize your links into lists or other menu-like structures, your visitors can scan their options for the page quickly and easily.

Just organizing your links into menus might not be enough, however. Make sure that your descriptions aren't too short. For example, using menus of filenames or other marginally descriptive links in menus can be tempting (see Figure 16.9).

FIGURE 16.9

DON'T: A poor link menu.

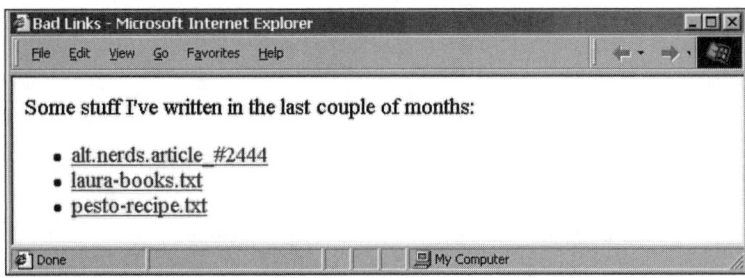

Each link describes the actual page to which it points, but it doesn't really describe the *content* of the page. How do visitors know what's on the other side of the link, and how can they decide whether they're interested in it from the limited information you've given them? Of these three links, only the last (`pesto-recipe.txt`) gives the visitors a hint about what they'll see when they jump to that file.

A better plan is either to provide some extra text describing the content of the file, as shown in Figure 16.10, or to avoid the filenames altogether. Just describe the contents of the files in the menu with the appropriate text highlighted, as shown in Figure 16.11.

FIGURE 16.10

DO: A better link menu.

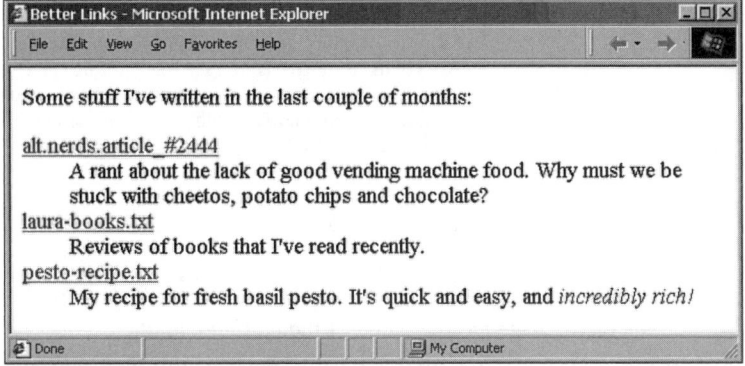

FIGURE 16.11

DO: Another better link menu.

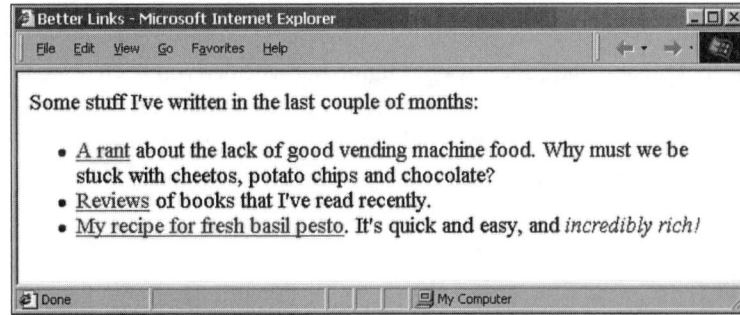

Either one of these forms is better than the first. They both give your visitors more clues about what's on the other side of the link.

Use Links in Text

The best way to provide links in text is to first write the text as if it isn't going to have links at all—for example, as if you were writing it for hard copy. Then you can highlight the appropriate words that will link to other pages. Make sure that you don't interrupt the flow of the page when you include a link. The text should stand on its own. That way, the links provide additional or tangential information that your visitors can choose to follow or ignore at their own whim.

Figure 16.12 shows another example of using links in text. Here the text itself isn't particularly relevant; it's just there to support the links. If you're using text just to describe links, consider using a link menu instead of a paragraph. Instead of having to read the entire paragraph, your visitors can skim for the links that interest them.

FIGURE 16.12

DON'T: Links in text that don't work well.

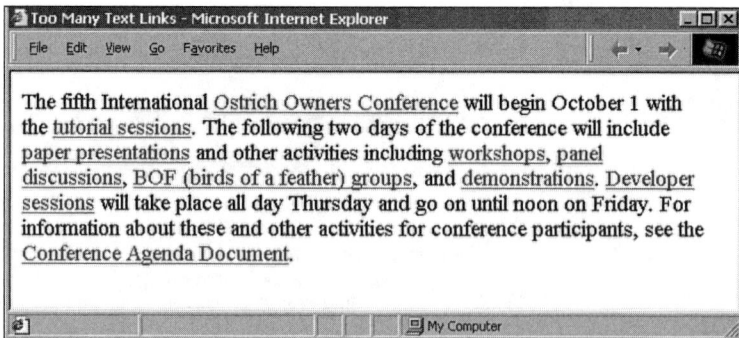

Figure 16.13 shows one way to restructure the previous example. The most important items on the page are the name of the conference, the events, and the dates on which they occur. You can restructure the page so that this information stands out. As you can see in Figure 16.13, presenting the events in a preformatted text table makes the important information stand out from the rest.

Probably the easiest way to figure out whether you're creating links within text properly is to print out the formatted Web page from your browser. In hard copy, without hypertext, does the paragraph still make sense? If the page reads funny on paper, it'll read funny online as well.

FIGURE 16.13

DO: Restructuring the links in the text.

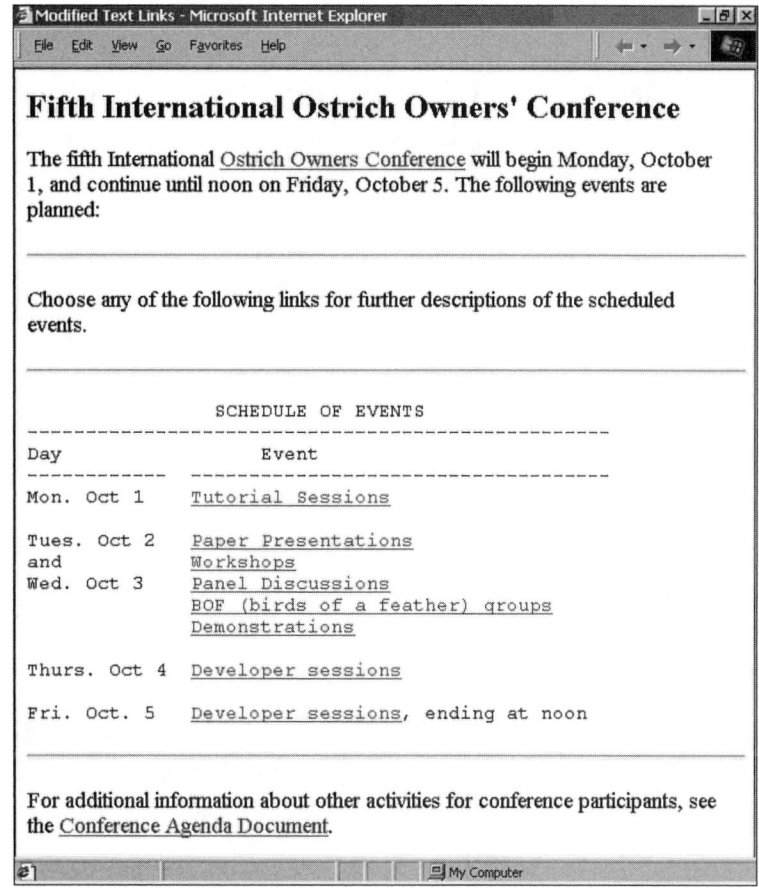

The revisions don't always have to be as different as they are in this example. Sometimes, a simple rephrasing of sentences can make the text on your pages more readable and more usable, both online and when printed.

Avoid the "Here" Syndrome

A common mistake that many Web authors make when creating links in body text is using the "Here" syndrome. This is the tendency to create links with a single highlighted word (here) and to describe the links somewhere else in the text. Look at the following examples, with underlining to indicate link text:

Information about ostrich socialization is contained here.

Select this link for a tutorial on the internal combustion engine.

Because links are highlighted on the Web page, the links visually pop out more than the surrounding text (or "draw the eye," in graphic design lingo). Your visitors will see the link first, before reading the text. Try creating links this way.

Figure 16.14 shows a particularly heinous example of the "Here" syndrome. Close your eyes, open them quickly, pick a "here" in the figure at random, and then see how long it takes you to find out what the "here" is for.

FIGURE 16.14

DON'T: The Here syndrome.

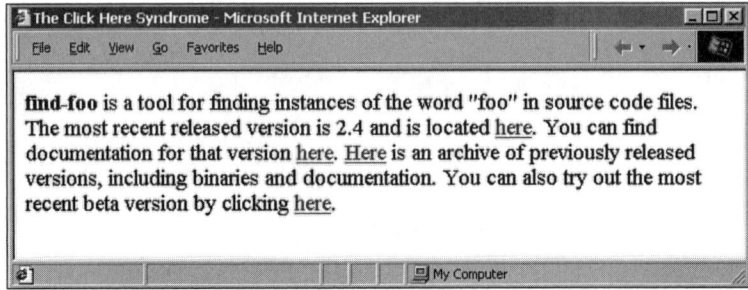

Now try the same exercise with a well-organized link menu of the same information, as shown in Figure 16.15.

FIGURE 16.15

DO: The same page, reorganized.

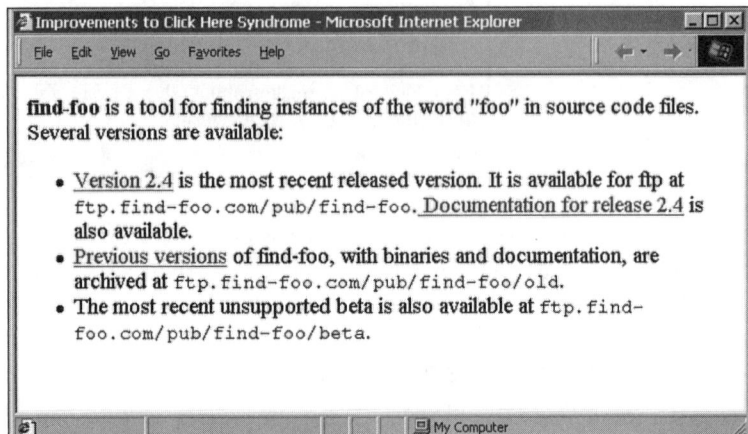

Because "here" says nothing about what the link is used for, your poor visitors have to search the text before and after the link itself to find out what's supposed to be "here." In paragraphs that have many occurrences of "here" or other nondescriptive links, matching up the links with what they're supposed to link to becomes difficult. This forces your visitors to work harder to figure out what you mean.

To Link or Not to Link

Just as with graphics, every time you create a link, consider why you're linking two pages or sections. Is the link useful? Will it give your visitors more information or bring them closer to their goal? Is the link relevant in some way to the current content?

Each link should serve a purpose. Just because you mention the word "coffee" on a page about some other topic, you don't have to link that word to the coffee home page. Creating such a link may seem cute, but if a link has no relevance to the current content, it just confuses your visitors.

The following list describes some of the categories of useful links in Web pages. If your links don't fall into one of these categories, consider the reasons why you're including them in your page:

- Explicit navigation links indicate the specific paths that visitors can take through your Web pages: forward, back, up, home. These links are often indicated by navigation icons, as shown in Figure 16.16.

FIGURE 16.16

Explicit navigation links.

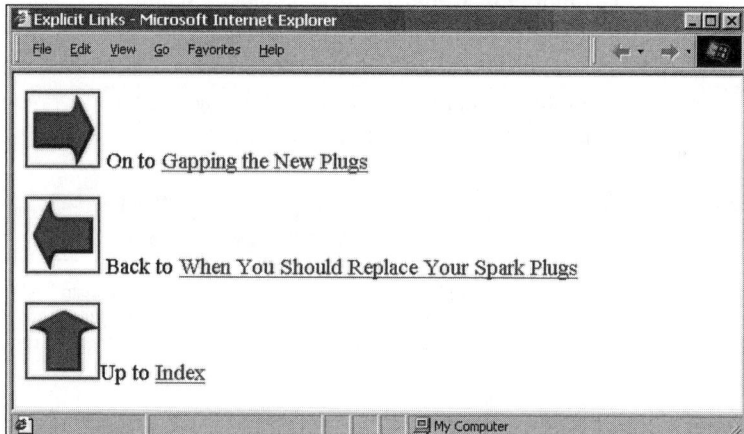

- Implicit navigation links (see Figure 16.17) are different from explicit navigation links because the link text implies, but does not directly indicate, navigation between pages. Link menus are the best example of this type of link. The highlighting of the link text makes it apparent that you'll get more information on this topic by selecting the link, but the text itself doesn't necessarily say so. Note the major difference between explicit and implicit navigation links: If you print a page containing both, you won't be able to pick out the implicit links.

16

FIGURE 16.17

Implicit navigation links.

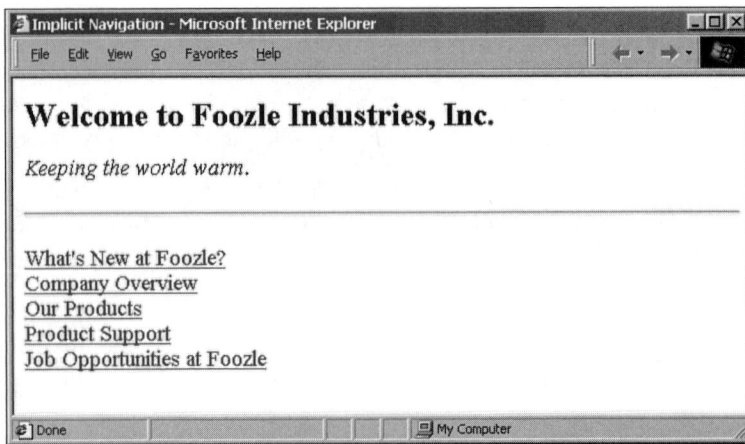

Implicit navigation links also can include tables of contents or other overviews made up entirely of links.

- Definitions of words or concepts make excellent links, particularly if you're creating large networks of pages that include glossaries. By linking the first instance of a word to its definition, you can explain the meaning of that word to visitors who don't know what it means without distracting those who do. Figure 16.18 shows an example of this type of link.

FIGURE 16.18

Definition links.

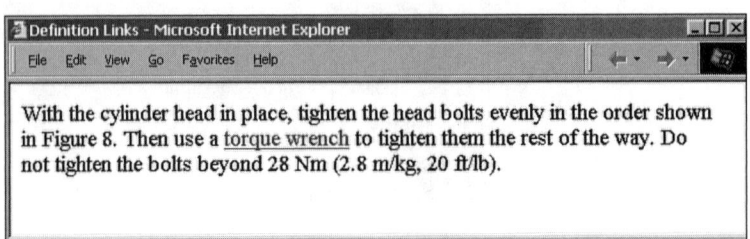

- Finally, links to tangents and related information are valuable when the text content will distract from the main purpose of the page. Think of tangent links as footnotes or end notes in printed text (see Figure 16.19). They can refer to citations to other works or to additional information that's interesting but isn't necessarily directly relevant to the point you're trying to make.

FIGURE 16.19

Footnote links.

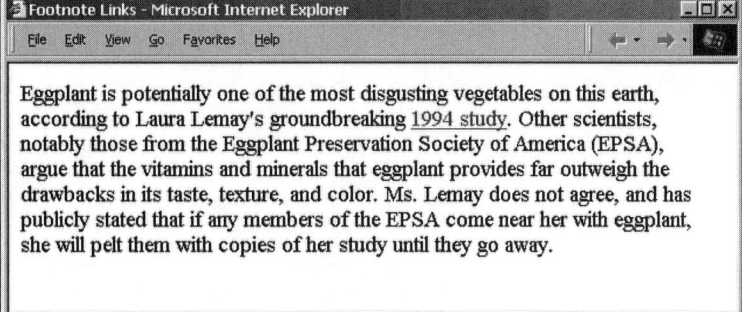

Be careful that you don't get carried away with definitions and tangent links. You might create so many tangents that your visitors spend too much time linking elsewhere to follow the point of your original text. Resist the urge to link every time you possibly can, and link only to tangents that are relevant to your own text. Also, avoid duplicating the same tangent—for example, linking every instance of the letters "WWW" on your page to the WWW Consortium's home page. If you're linking twice or more to the same location on one page, consider removing most of the extra links. Your visitors can select one of the other links if they're interested in the information.

Note Thanks to Nathan Torkington for his "Taxonomy of Tags," published on the www-talk mailing list, which inspired this section.

Using Images

On Day 7, "Using Images, Color, and Backgrounds," you learned all about creating and using images in Web pages. This section will summarize many of those hints.

Don't Overuse Images

Be careful about including a large number of images on your Web page. Besides the fact that each image adds to the amount of time it takes to load the page, having too many images on the same page makes it look cluttered and distracts from the point you're trying to get across. Sometimes, though, people think that the more images they include on a page, the better it is. Figure 16.20 shows such an example.

FIGURE **16.20**

*DON'T: Too many
images.*

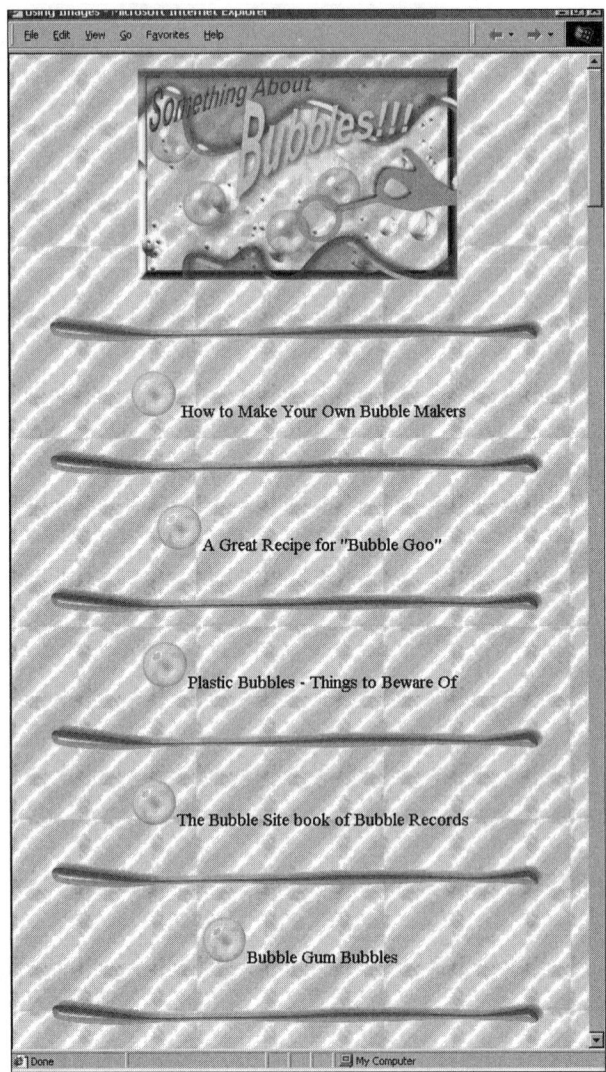

Remember the hints I gave you on Day 7. Consider how important each image really is
before you put it on the page. If an image doesn't directly contribute to the content, consider leaving it out.

Use Alternatives to Images

Of course, as soon as I mention images, I also have to mention that a small minority of
Web users either use Web browsers that don't support graphics, or turn off image loading

in their browser. To make your pages accessible to the widest possible audience, you need to take the text-only browsers into account. The following two solutions can help:

- Use the `alt` attribute of the `<img>` tag to substitute appropriate text strings for the graphics automatically in text-only browsers (a requirement in XHTML 1.0). Use a descriptive label to substitute for the default `[image]` that appears in the place of each inline image.

- If providing a single-source page for both graphical and text-only browsers becomes too much work and the result isn't acceptable, consider creating separate pages for each one: a page designed for the full-color, full-graphical browsers, and a page designed for the text-only browsers. Then allow visitors to choose one or the other from your home page.

Keep Images Small

Keep in mind that each image you use is a separate network connection and takes time to load over a network. This means that each image adds to the total time it takes to view the page. Try to reduce the number of images on the page, and keep them small both in file size and in actual dimensions. In particular, keep the following hints in mind:

- Your page should load at an average of 3KB to 4KB per second with a 56Kbps modem connection. The entire page (text and images) shouldn't take more than 20 seconds to load; otherwise, your visitors may get annoyed and move on without reading your page. This rule of thumb limits you to 60KB — 80KB total for everything on your page. Strive to achieve that size by keeping your images small.

- For larger images, consider using thumbnails on your main page and then linking to the images rather than putting them inline.

- Interlace your larger GIF files or save your JPEGs as progressive JPEGs.

- Save your image in both the JPEG or GIF formats to see which creates a smaller file for the type of image you're using. You might also want to increase the level of compression for your JPEG images or reduce the number of colors in the palette of the GIF images to see whether you can save a significant amount of space without adversely affecting image quality.

- The fewer colors you use in a GIF file, the smaller the image will be. You should try to use as few colors as possible to avoid problems with system-specific color allocation.

- You can reduce the physical size of your images by cropping them (using a smaller portion of the overall image) or scaling (shrinking) them. When you scale an image, you might lose some of the detail.

 **Caution**   Remember that reducing the size of your images using the `height` and `width` attributes of the `<img>` tag only makes them take up less space on the page, it doesn't affect the size of the image file or the download speed. It also has a tendency of making your images just look bad.

- You can use the `width` and `height` attributes to scale the image to a larger size than it actually is. These attributes originally were Netscape-only extensions but were added to the HTML standard with version 3.2. Note that the scaled result might not be what you expect. Test this procedure before trying it.

With the preceding suggestions in mind, take a second look at the images on your page. You really have your heart set on using all these different images. How can you put the page shown in Figure 16.20 on a diet and improve its appearance?

- The graphic at the top of the page, which displays a logo for the site, could stand some size reduction. It's basically just a banner and doesn't have any links on it, so you can make it half as high. That will cut the download time for the graphic roughly in half.

- Another problem that needs to be addressed is that the title of the page (in this case, the name of the site) doesn't appear anywhere as text. Anyone who visits the site with graphics turned off won't know the name of the site! You need to add that to your improved version.

- Those horizontal rules are a *big* problem. First, there are too many of them. Second, they overpower the banner image because they're so much wider. Third, they distract from the list of items because they create separation between them. So reduce the quantity and the size of those images for more download time savings.

- The bullets that appear before each list item are way too large. They could stand to be cut down to half their size. As a rule, most bullets are kept to 30×30 pixels or less.

- The bullets and text were centered on the page, making the list items look very disorganized. Actually, there are several different ways to use images for bullets. You can make this an "official" bulleted list, using the `<ul>` tag, and use the `src` attribute to specify the bullet image. However, browsers running HTML 3.2 and earlier will see standard bulleted lists instead of the images. Another alternative is to lay out the images and the list items in a borderless table.

All the improvements I've suggested here are shown in Figure 16.21.

FIGURE 16.21

DO: Better use of images.

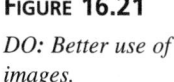

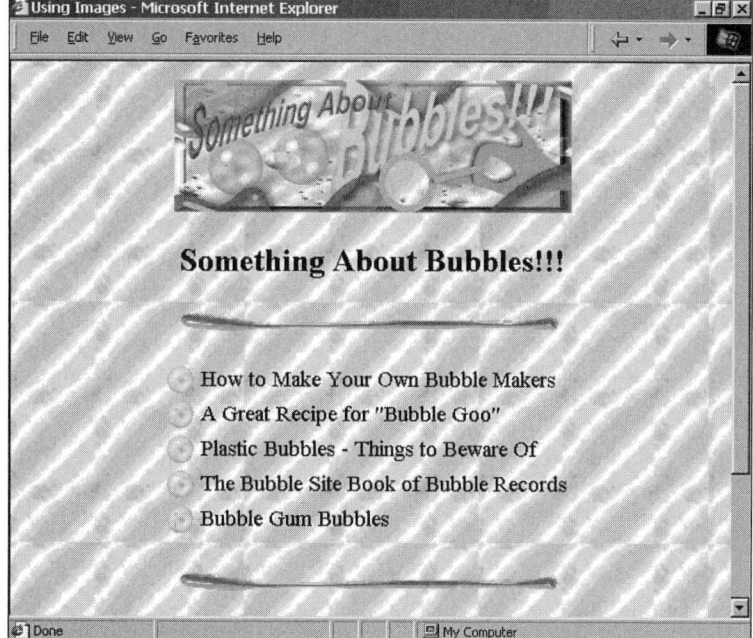

Watch Out for Assumptions About Your Visitors' Hardware

Many Web designers create problems for their visitors by making a couple of careless assumptions about their hardware. When you're developing Web pages, be kind and remember the following two guidelines:

- **Don't assume that everyone has the same screen or browser dimensions as yours.**

  Just because that huge GIF you created is narrow enough to fit in your browser doesn't mean it'll fit in someone else's. An image that's too wide is annoying because the visitors need to resize their windows or scroll sideways.

  To fit within a majority of browsers, try to keep the width of your images to fewer than 450 pixels.

- **Don't assume that everyone has full-color displays.**

  Test your images in resolutions other than full color. (You can do this in your image-editing program.) A few of your visitors may have display systems that are limited to 16 colors, grayscale, or black and white. You may be surprised at the results: Colors drop out or dither strangely in grayscale or black and white, and the effect may not be what you intended.

Make sure your images are visible at all resolutions, or provide alternatives for high- and low-resolution images on the page itself.

Be Careful with Backgrounds and Link Colors

Using HTML extensions, you can use background colors and patterns on your pages and change the color of the text. This can be very tempting, but be very careful. Changing the page and font colors and providing fancy backdrops can quickly and easily make your pages entirely unreadable. The following are some hints for avoiding these problems:

- **Make sure you have enough contrast between the background and foreground (text) colors**—Low contrast can be hard to read. Also, light-colored text on a dark background is harder to read than dark text on a light background.

- **Sometimes, increasing the font size of all the text on your page can make it more readable on a low-contrast background**—You can use the `<basefont>` tag or Cascading Style Sheets to increase the default image size for your page.

- **If you're using a background image, make sure it doesn't interfere with the text**—Some images may look interesting on their own but can make text difficult to read when you put it on top of them. Keep in mind that backgrounds are supposed to be in the *background*. Subtle patterns are always better than wild patterns. Your visitors are visiting your pages for their content, not to marvel at your ability to create faux marble in your favorite image editor.

When in doubt, try asking a friend to look at your pages. Because you're already familiar with the content, you may not realize how hard your pages are to read. Someone who hasn't read them before will be able to tell you that your text colors are too close to your background color, or that the background image is interfering with the text. Of course, you'll have to find a friend who will be honest with you.

Other Good Habits and Hints

In this section, I've gathered several other miscellaneous hints and advice about working with groups of Web pages. This includes notes on how big to make each page and how to sign your pages.

Link Back to Home

Consider linking back to the top level or home page on every page of your site. This link will give visitors a quick escape from the depths of your site. Using a home link is much easier than trying to navigate backward through a hierarchy or repeatedly clicking the back button.

Don't Split Topics Across Pages

Each Web page works best if it covers a single topic in its entirety. Don't split topics across pages; even if you link between them, the transition can be confusing. It will be even more confusing if someone jumps in on the second or third page and wonders what's going on.

If you think that one topic is becoming too large for a single page, consider reorganizing the page so that you can break up the topic into subtopics. This tip works especially well in hierarchical organizations. It allows you to determine the exact level of detail that each level of the hierarchy should go and exactly how big and complete each page should be.

Don't Create Too Many or Too Few Pages

There are no rules for how many pages your Web site must have, nor for how large each page should be. You can have one page or several thousand, depending on the amount of content you have and how you've organized it.

With this point in mind, you might decide to go to one extreme or another. Each one has advantages and disadvantages. For example, let's say you put all your content on one big page and create links to sections within that page, as illustrated in Figure 16.22.

FIGURE 16.22

One big page.

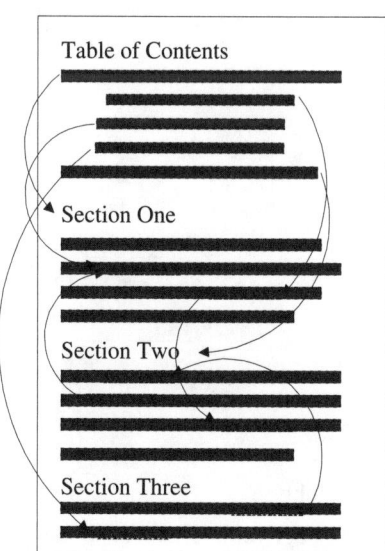

Advantages:

- One file is easier to maintain, and links within that file won't ever break if you move elements around or rename files.

- This file mirrors real-world document structure. If you're distributing documents both online and in hard copy, having a single document for both makes producing them easier.

Disadvantages:

- A large file takes a very long time to download, particularly if the visitor has a slow network connection and the page includes a large number of graphics.
- Visitors must scroll a lot to find what they want, and accessing particular bits of information can become tedious. Navigating anywhere other than at the top or bottom becomes close to impossible.
- The structure is overly rigid. A single page is inherently linear. Although visitors can skip around within the page, the structure still mirrors that of the printed page and doesn't take advantage of the flexibility of smaller pages linked in a nonlinear fashion.

At the other extreme, you could create a whole bunch of little pages with links between them, as illustrated in Figure 16.23.

FIGURE 16.23

Many little pages.

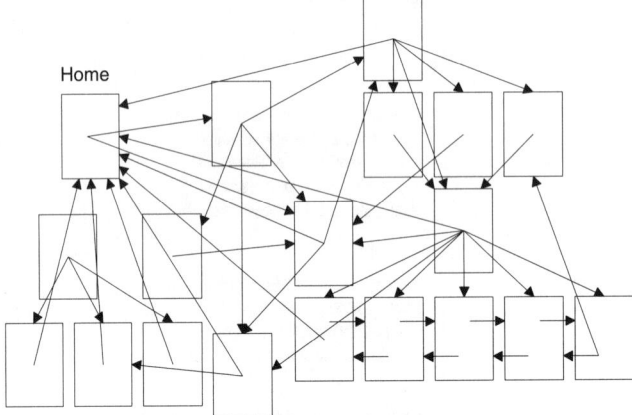

Advantages:

- Smaller pages load very quickly.
- Often you can fit the entire page on one screen, so the information can be scanned very easily.

Disadvantages:

- Maintaining all those links will be a nightmare. Just adding some sort of navigational structure to that many pages may create thousands of links.

- If you have too many links between pages, the links may seem jarring. Continuity is difficult when your visitors spend more time moving from page to page than actually reading.

What's the solution? Often, the content you're describing will determine the size and number of pages you need, especially if you follow the one-topic-per-page suggestion. Testing your Web pages on a variety of platforms at different network speeds will tell you whether a single page is too large. If you spend a lot of time scrolling around in your page, or if it takes more time to load than you expected, it may be too large.

16

Sign Your Pages

Each page should contain some sort of information at the bottom to act as the signature. I mentioned this tip briefly in Day 6, "More Text Formatting with HTML," as part of the description of the <address> tag. That particular tag was intended for just this purpose.

Consider putting the following useful information in the <address> tag on each page:

- Contact information for the person who created this Web page or who is responsible for it, colloquially known as the Webmaster. This information should include the person's name and an email address, at the least.

- The status of the page. Is it complete? Is it a work in progress? Is it intentionally left blank?

- The date this page was last revised. This information is particularly important for pages that change often. Include a date on each page so that people know how old it is.

- Copyright or trademark information, if it applies.

- The URL of this page. This may seem a bit like overkill, but what happens if someone prints out the page and loses any other reference to it in the stack of papers on her desk? How will she know where it came from? (I've done this many times and wished that the URL had been typed on the document itself.)

Figure 16.24 shows a nice example of an address block.

FIGURE 16.24

An sample address.

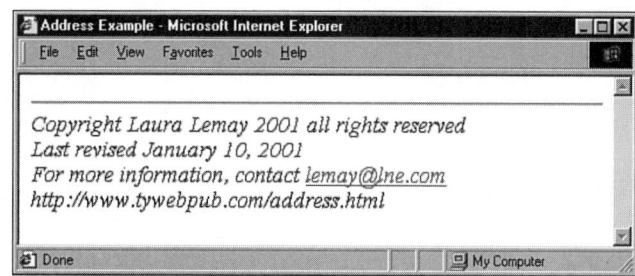

Another nice touch is to link a Mailto URL to the text containing the email address of the Webmaster, as in the following:

```
<address>
Laura Lemay <a href="mailto:lemay@lne.com">lemay@lne.com</a>
</address>
```

This way, the visitors who have browsers that support the Mailto URL can simply select the link and send mail to the person responsible for the page without having to retype the address into their mail programs.

 Note Linking Mailto URLs will work only in browsers that support them. Even in browsers that don't accept them, the link text will appear as usual, so there's no harm in including the link.

Finally, if you don't want to clutter each page with a lot of personal contact information or boilerplate copyright info, a simple solution is to create a separate page for the extra information and then link the signature to that page. Here's an example:

```
<address>
<a href="copyright.html">Copyright</a> and
<a href="webmaster.html">contact</a> information is available.
</address>
```

Provide Nonhypertext Versions of Hypertext Pages

Although the Web provides a way to publish information in new and exciting ways, some visitors still like to print things off to read on the bus or at the breakfast table. These kinds of visitors have real problems with hypertext pages because it's difficult to tell your browser to print the whole thing. The browser knows only the boundaries of individual pages.

If you're using the Web to publish anything that might be readable and usable offline, consider creating a text or PDF version that's available as an external document for downloading. This way, your visitors can both browse the document online and print it out for reading offline. You can even link the location of the hard-copy document to the start of the hypertext version, like the following:

```
A <a href="ftp://myhome.com/pub/mydir/myfile.pdf">PDF version</a> of
this document is available via ftp at myhome.com in the directory /pub/mydir/
myfile.pdf.
```

Of course, a handy cross-reference for the hard-copy version would be to provide the URL for the hypertext version, as follows:

```
This document is also available on hypertext form on
the World Wide Web at the URL:
http://myhome.com/pub/mydir/myfile. index.html.
```

Summary

The main do's and don'ts for Web page design are as follows:

- Do understand the differences between HTML 2.0, HTML 3.2, and the different flavors of HTML 4.0 and XHTML 1.0. Decide which design strategy to follow while using them.

- If you use nonstandard HTML tags, do provide alternatives if at all possible.

- Do test your pages in multiple browsers.

- Do write your pages clearly and concisely.

- Do organize the text of your page so that your visitors can scan for important information.

- Do spell check and proofread your pages.

- Do group related information both semantically (through the organization of the content) and visually (by using headings or separating sections with rule lines).

- Do use a consistent layout across all your pages.

- Do use link menus to organize your links for quick scanning, and do use descriptive links.

- Do have good reasons for using links.

- Do keep your layout simple.

- Do provide alternatives to images for text-only browsers.

- Do try to keep your images small so that they load faster over the network.

- Do be careful with backgrounds and colored text to avoid making your pages flashy but unreadable.

- Do always provide a link back to your home page.

- Do match topics with pages.

- Do provide a signature block or link to contact information at the bottom of each page.

- Do provide single-page, nonhypertext versions of linear documents.

- Do write context-independent pages.

- Don't link to irrelevant material.

- Don't write Web pages that are dependent on pages before or after them in the structure.

16

- Don't overuse emphasis (such as boldface, italic, all caps, link text, blink, or marquees).
- Don't use terminology that's specific to any one browser ("click here," "use the back button," and so on).
- Don't use heading tags to provide emphasis.
- Don't fall victim to the "Here" syndrome with your links.
- Don't link repeatedly to the same site on the same page.
- Don't clutter the page with a large number of pretty but unnecessary images.
- Don't split individual topics across pages.

Workshop

Put on your thinking cap again, because it's time for another review. These questions, quizzes, and exercises will remind you about the items that you should (or should not) include on your pages.

Q&A

Q I've seen statistics that say the majority of people on the Web are using Netscape or Internet Explorer. Why should I continue designing and testing my pages for other browsers when most of the world is using one of these two browsers?

A You can design your pages explicitly for Netscape, Internet Explorer, or both. Your pages are your pages, and the decision is yours. *But*, given how easy it is to make small modifications so your pages can be viewed and read in other browsers without losing much of the design, why lock out the remainder of your audience for the sake of a few tags? Remember, the Web is growing all the time, and that "small" minority of visitors could very well be a million people or more.

Q I'm converting existing documents into Web pages. These documents are very text-heavy and are intended to be read from start to finish instead of being scanned quickly. I can't restructure or redesign the content to better follow the guidelines you've suggested—that's not my job. What can I do?

A All is not lost. You can still improve the overall presentation of these documents by providing reasonable indexes to the content (summaries, tables of contents pages, subject indexes, and so on) and including standard navigation links. In other words, you can create an easily navigable framework around the documents themselves. This can go a long way toward improving content that's otherwise difficult to read online.

Q **I have a standard signature block that contains my name and email address, revision information for the page, and a couple of lines of copyright information that my company's lawyers insisted on. It's a little imposing, particularly on small pages. Sometimes the signature is bigger than the page itself! How do I integrate it into my site so that it isn't so obtrusive?**

A If your company's lawyers agree, consider putting all your contact and copyright information on a separate page and then linking to it on every page rather than duplicating it every time. This way, your pages won't be overwhelmed by the legal stuff. Also, if the signature changes, you won't have to change it on every single page.

16

Quiz

1. What are the three flavors of HTML 4.0 and XHTML 1.0, and which of these three accommodates the widest range of users?

2. What are some ways you can organize your pages so that visitors can scan them more easily?

3. True or false: Headings are useful when you want information to stand out because they make the text large and bold.

4. True or false: You can reduce the download time of an image by using the `width` and `height` attributes of the `<img>` tag to scale down the image.

5. What are the advantages and disadvantages of creating one big Web page versus several smaller ones?

Quiz Answers

1. The three flavors of HTML 4.0 and XHTML 1.0 are Transitional (designed for the widest range of users, including those who are using older browsers), Frameset (which includes all tags in the Transitional specification, plus those for framesets), and Strict (for those who want to stick to pure HTML 4.0 or XHTML 1.0 tags and attributes).

2. You can use headings to summarize topics, lists to organize and display information, and link menus for navigation, and you can separate long paragraphs with important information into shorter paragraphs.

3. False. You should use headings as headings and nothing else. You can emphasize text in other ways, or use a graphic to draw attention to an important point.

4. This is a trick question. When you use the `width` and `height` attributes to make a large image appear smaller on your page, it may reduce the dimensions of the file, but it won't decrease the download time. The visitor still downloads the same image, but the browser just fits it into a smaller space.

5. The advantages of creating one large page are that one file is easier to maintain, the links won't break, and it mirrors real-world document structure. The disadvantages are that it will have a longer download time, visitors will have to scroll a lot, and the structure is rigid and too linear.

Exercises

1. Try your hand at reworking the example shown in Figure 16.2. Organize the information into a definition list or a table. Make it easy for the visitor to scan for the important points on the page.

2. Try the same with the example shown in Figure 16.4. How can you arrange the information so that it's easier to find the important points and links on the page?

DAY 17

Examples of Good Web Design

Today you'll look at some simple examples of pages and sites that you might find on the Web. (Actually, you won't find these *particular* pages on the Web; I developed them specifically for this chapter.) These Web sites are typical of the kind of information being provided on the Web today, or else they show some unique method of solving problems you might run into while developing your own sites. In particular, you'll explore the following Web sites:

- A company profile for Foozle Industries, which specializes in sweaters and knitted products
- An encyclopedia of motorcycles, with images, sounds, and other media clips
- A catalog for a small nursery, which you can browse through and order herbs, spices, and aromatic vegetables

In each example, I'll note some of the more interesting features of the page, as well as some of the issues you might want to consider as you develop your own pages.

The code and images for these examples are included on the book's Web support site (see the Introduction for details).

Example One: A Company Profile

Foozle Industries, Inc. makes a wide variety of knitted clothing and blankets for all occasions. Visitors to the Foozle Industries Web site are first presented with the Foozle Industries home page (see Figure 17.1). Overall, the Web author has decided to use Cascading Style Sheets to format this Web site.

FIGURE 17.1

The Foozle Industries home page.

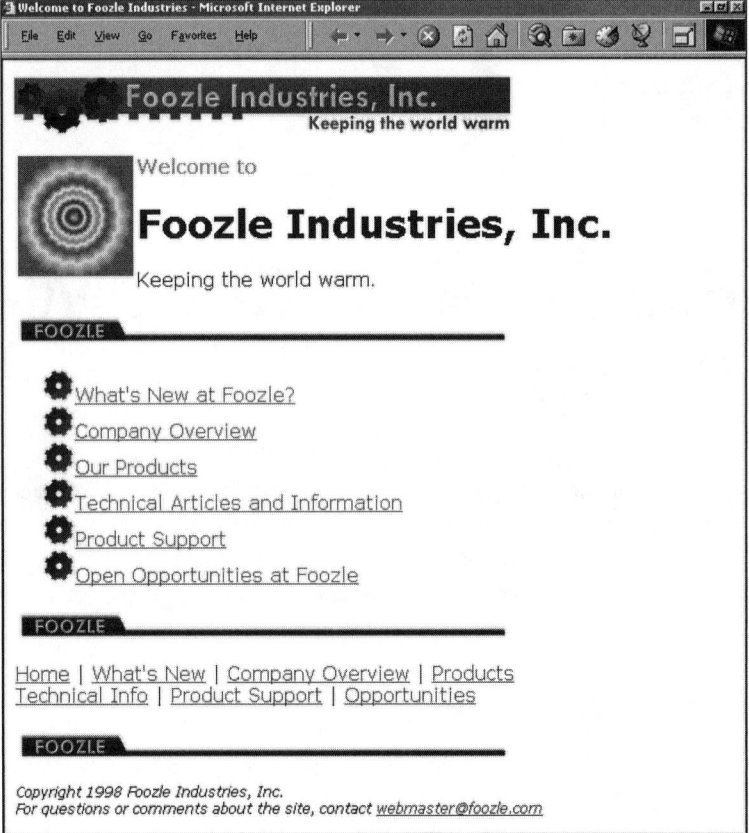

In addition to the consistency that the author has achieved by using style sheets, there are other items that are the same from page to page. Each of the main pages has a small but attractive banner that displays that page's title. Also, the bottom of each page includes a navigation bar, copyright information, and an email address to contact for questions or comments about the site.

This simple, unpretentious home page has a menu of links to pages that the customer can visit on the Foozle Web site. I won't describe all of them in this section, but I'll mention just a few that provide interesting features.

What's New at Foozle?

Selecting the What's New link takes you to the What's New page, appropriately enough (see Figure 17.2). This is the first link on the home page and the second (after the Home link) on the navigation bar.

17

FIGURE 17.2

The What's New at Foozle page.

Organized in reverse chronological order, the What's New page contains information about interesting things going on at Foozle Industries, both inside and outside the company. This page is useful for announcing new products to customers on the Web, or just for providing information about the site, the company, or other Foozle information.

> **Tip**
>
> In general, What's New pages are useful for sites that are visited repeatedly and frequently, but they make a nice addition to nearly any site. They enable your visitors to find the new information on your site quickly and easily without having to search for it. They also provide users with a quick way to determine whether anything has changed since their last visit. Of course, if you rarely update your Web site, a What's New section just makes your lack of updates more obvious, and should probably be avoided.

The topmost item on this What's New page is about a paper presented by Foozle's chief scientist at a conference in Naples. This item has a link attached to it, implying that the paper itself is on the other side of that link. Sure enough, it is (see Figure 17.3).

Alpaca wool is fascinating, but where do you go from here? The links at the bottom of this page are different than the ones on the main page. Here, the visitor has several new navigation choices. He can go to the Foozle home page, to the Technical Info page, or to any of the other technical papers (the titles of which are briefly shown on the navigation bar). This same navigation bar appears on all the technical papers within this section, allowing for easy navigation between them.

You've visited the home page already, so let's go on to the Technical Information page.

Technical Information

The Technical Information page of the Foozle Web site lists the papers Foozle has published on technical issues surrounding the making of sweaters (see Figure 17.4). (You didn't know there *were* any technical issues surrounding the making of sweaters, did you?)

From here, you can move down in the hierarchy and read any of these papers, or you can choose any of the other main pages on the Web through the links on the navigation bar. You can then explore the other portions of the Web site: the What's New page, the Company Overview, the product descriptions, or the listing of open opportunities.

FIGURE 17.3

*All about Foozle
Alpaca wool.*

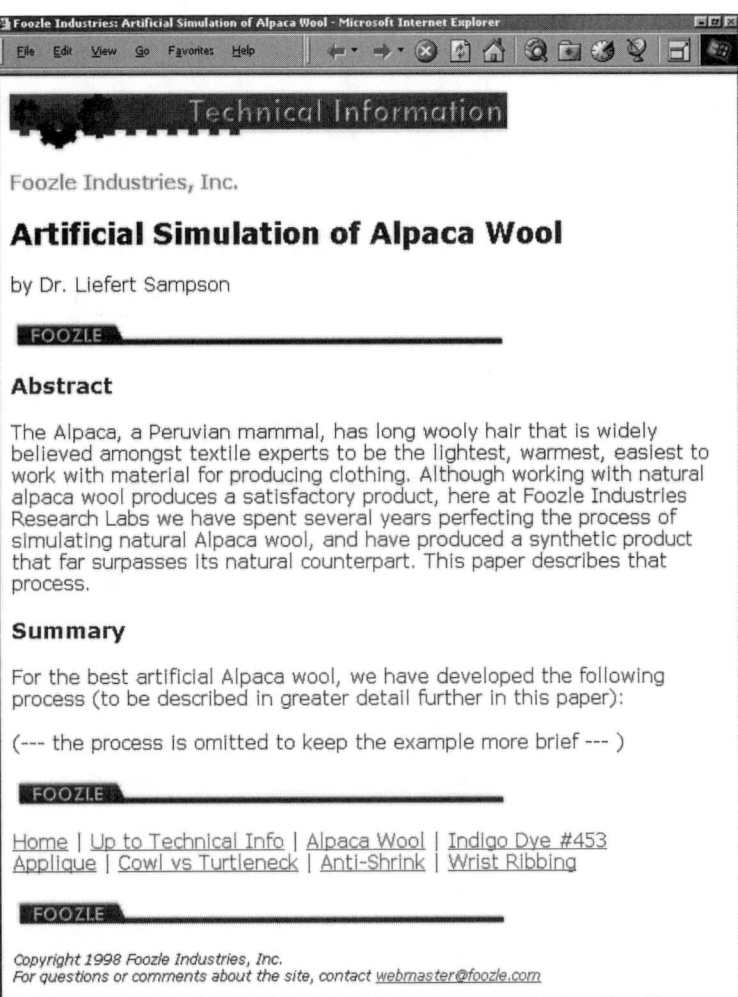

The Company Overview

The Company Overview page provides a list of links to other pages with more information about the company. Here you can learn more about what the company does, its mission, its company history, and the location of its headquarters. This page appears in Figure 17.5.

FIGURE 17.4

*The Technical
Information page.*

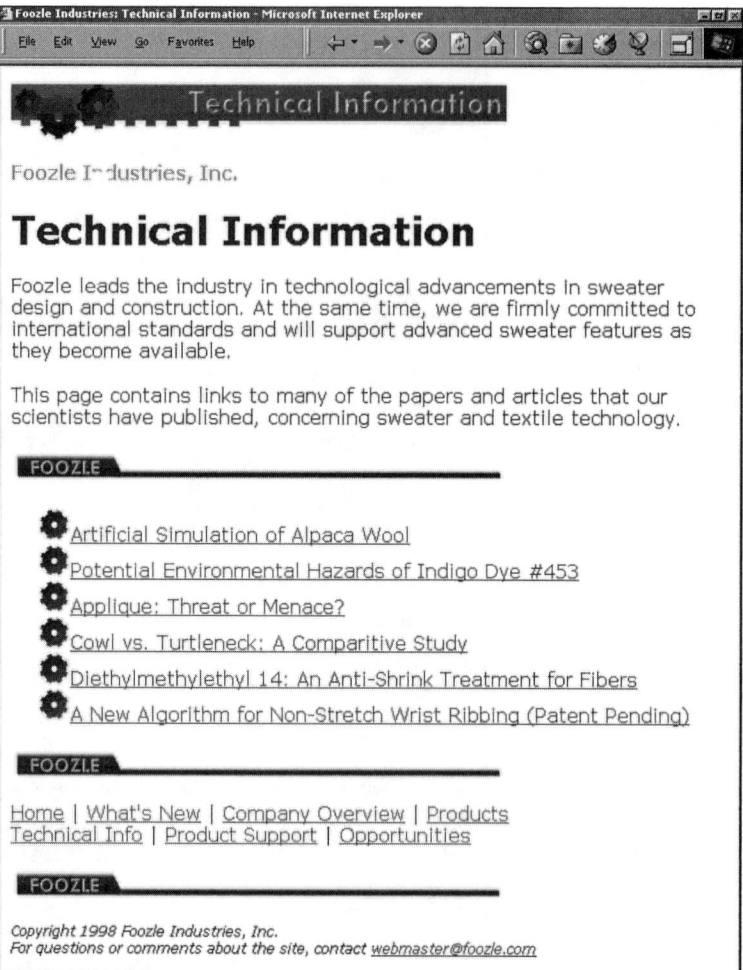

The Foozle Products Page

The next link on the navigation bar takes you to the Foozle Products page, with links to catalog sheets (similar to those in the Shopping Catalog example later today). This is the perfect place to provide pictures, descriptions, and pricing information for all the products that the company makes. The Products page is shown in Figure 17.6.

FIGURE 17.5

*The Company
Overview page.*

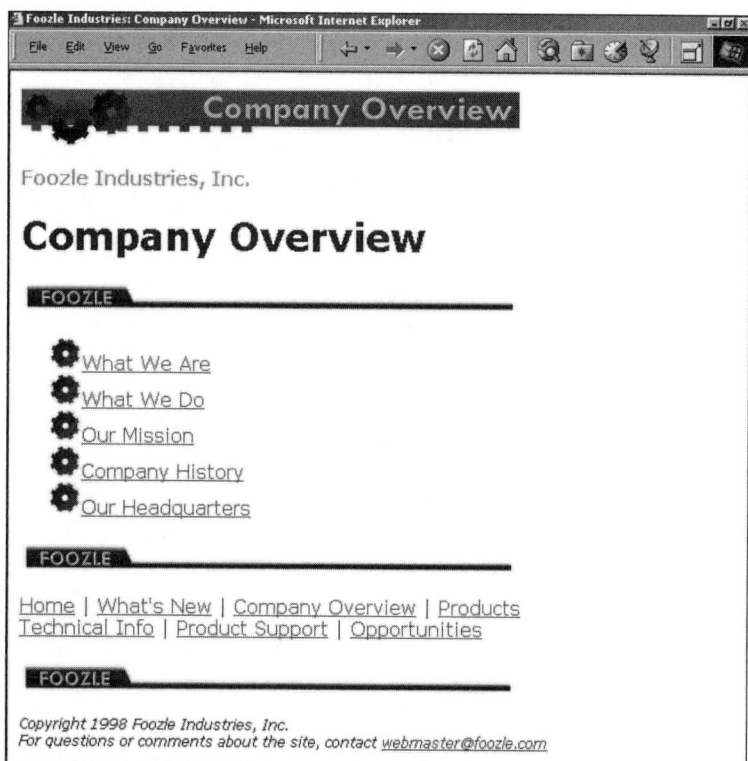

Tip

One of the best things about the Web is that space is cheap. You can publish as much information as you like at almost no additional cost. Because there are no constraints in that regard, if you're publishing product information on the Web, you should publish as much information as you have. You never know what information potential customers are looking for, so it makes sense to make sure you have all your bases covered.

The Product Support Page

Even users of sweaters and knitted products need some customer support, so Foozle has provided a place for customers to obtain this information. Figure 17.7 shows the Product Support page, which provides a list of frequently asked questions about Foozle products. If the customer's question isn't answered on this page, the email address of the support department is provided.

FIGURE 17.6

The Foozle Products page.

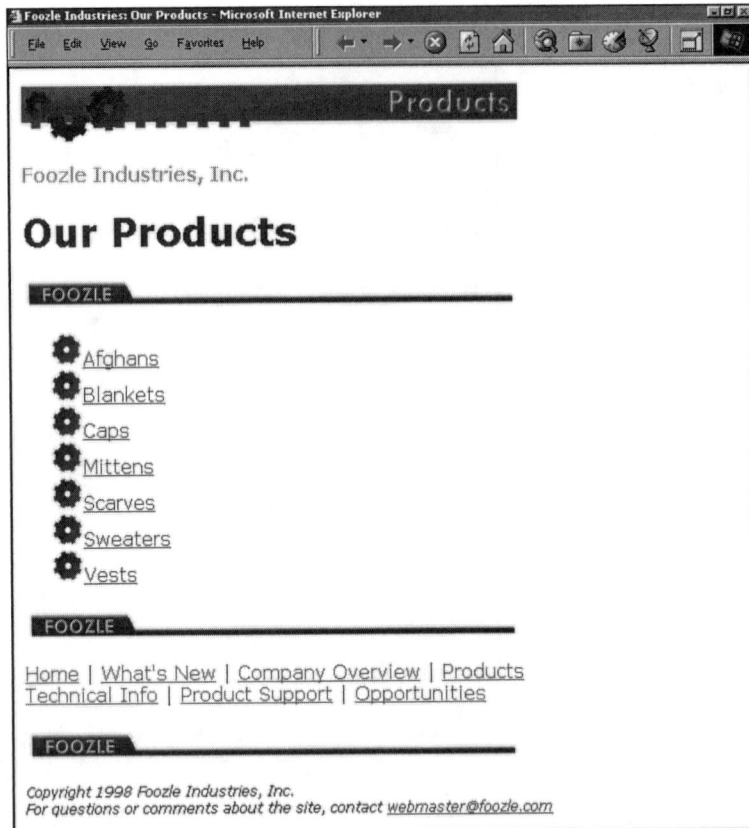

The Open Opportunities Page

A progressive company such as Foozle is constantly looking for talented employees, and it welcomes inquiries and resumes even when there are no openings available. Figure 17.8 shows the Open Opportunities page, which lists job opportunities and contact information.

Features of This Web Site and Issues for Development

The design of this Web site for a simple company profile is quite straightforward. The structure is a simple hierarchy, with link menus for navigation to the appropriate pages. You also can include the navigation bar at the top of the page, or even at both the top and the bottom of the page in case the visitor doesn't read the entire page. Expanding the navigation system is a simple matter of adding "limbs" to the hierarchy by adding new links to the top-level page.

FIGURE 17.7

The Product Support page.

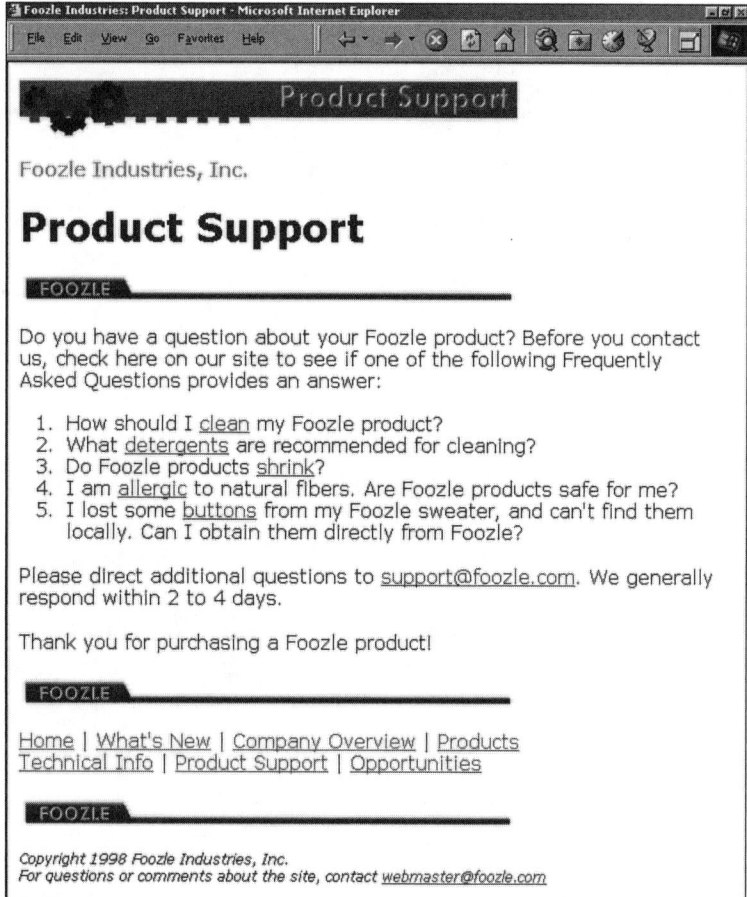

However, note the path you took through the few pages on this Web site. In a classic hierarchy, you visit each "limb" in turn, exploring downward and then creeping back up to visit new pages. Remember the link between the What's New page and the page on Alpaca wool? This link moved you sideways from one limb (the What's New page) to another (the Technical Papers section). By providing a different navigation bar that enables you to navigate home, up, or sideways to other pages, you can easily find your way back to any of the major parts of the site.

This example is simple, so there's little confusion. If a hierarchy is much more complicated than this, with multiple levels and sub-trees, having links that cross hierarchical boundaries enables you to break out of the structure.

FIGURE **17.8**

*The Open
Opportunities page.*

 **Caution**

After a few lateral links, it can become difficult to figure out where you are
in the hierarchy. This is a common problem with most hypertext systems and
often is referred to as *getting lost in hyperspace*.

There are very few good solutions to this problem. For sites that are more complex, one
possible solution is to provide framesets that simplify navigation. However, framed sites
must be designed with care. Too many frames will not only add to the confusion, but will
also make it difficult to read pages at lower resolutions. I prefer to avoid the problem by
not creating too many lateral links across a hierarchy. If you stick with the rigid structure
of the hierarchy and provide only navigational links, visitors can usually figure out where
they are. If not, they usually have only two main choices: Move back up in the hierarchy
to a known point, or drill deeper into the hierarchy for more detailed information.

Example Two: A Multimedia Encyclopedia

The Multimedia Encyclopedia of Motorcycles is a set of Web pages with extensive information about motorcycles and their manufacturers. In addition to text information about each motorcycle maker, the encyclopedia includes photographs, sounds (engine noises!), and video for many of the motorcycles listed.

The index is organized alphabetically, one page per letter or group of letters (a.html, b.html, c.html, d.html, efg.html, and so on). To help you navigate into the body of the encyclopedia, the home page for this site is an overview page.

The Overview Page

The overview page is the main entry point into the body of the encyclopedia (see Figure 17.9).

17

FIGURE 17.9

The Encyclopedia Motorcycle overview page.

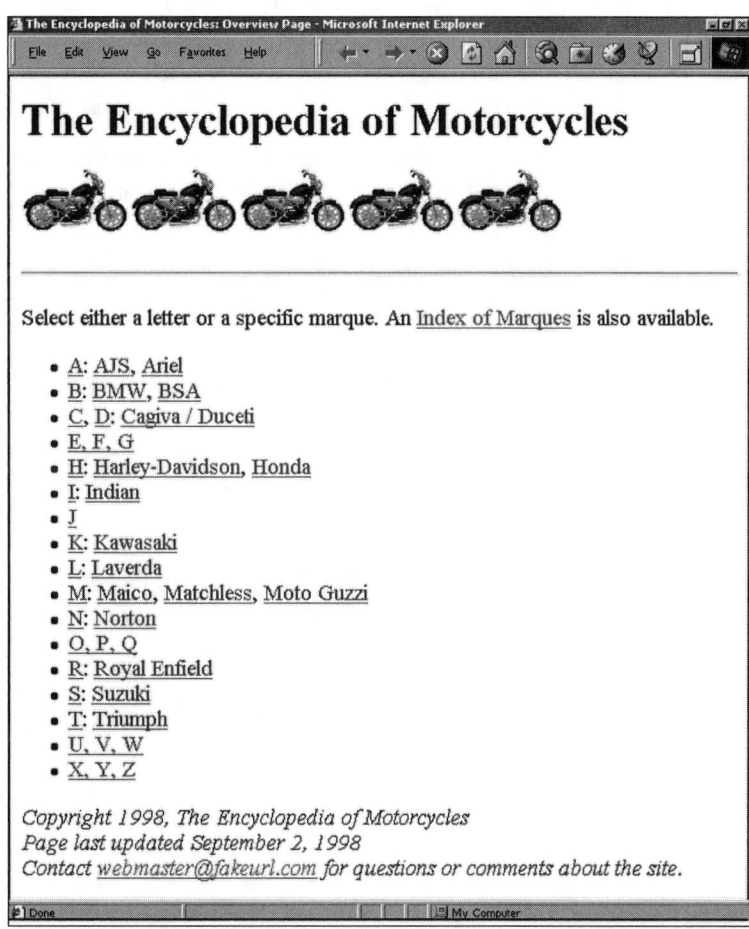

This page provides two main ways to get into the encyclopedia: by selecting the first letter of the marque, or by selecting one of the specific marques mentioned in the list itself.

 Note
A *marque* is a fancy term used by motorcycle and sports car fanatics to refer to the manufacturer of a vehicle.

For example, if you wanted to find information about the Norton motorcycle company, you could select N and then scroll down to the appropriate link on the N page. Norton is one of the major manufacturers listed next to the N link on the Overview page, however, so you could select that link instead and go straight to the Norton page.

The Norton Page

Each individual page contains an entry for that particular marque. If the visitor has chosen a specific manufacturer, the link points directly to that specific page (for example, the page for Norton is shown in Figure 17.10). Each marque page contains information about the manufacturer and the various motorcycles it has produced over the years.

So where are the pictures? This is supposed to be a multimedia encyclopedia, isn't it? Not to worry. In addition to the text on the left side, the page also includes a list of external media files on the right. Because the background of the cell that includes these links is colored differently than the text, it's clear that these links are extra (but related) features about the Norton company. The media section includes images of various motorcycles, sound clips of their engines, and film clips of famous riders on their Nortons.

Each media file is described in the text, and you can download it if you choose. For example, to access the animated GIF file displayed in Figure 17.11, select the link with a 3D rotational rendering of a Norton motorcycle.

Note also that whenever another manufacturer is mentioned in the text, it's linked to its own entry. For example, selecting the word *BSA* in the last paragraph on the Norton page takes you to the entry for BSA (see Figure 17.12).

In this way, the visitor can jump from link to link and manufacturer to manufacturer, exploring the encyclopedia based on what interests him. After he's done exploring, however, he needs to get back to a known point. For just this purpose, each entry in the encyclopedia contains a Back to Overview link so the visitor never has to scroll far.

FIGURE **17.10**

The entry for Norton.

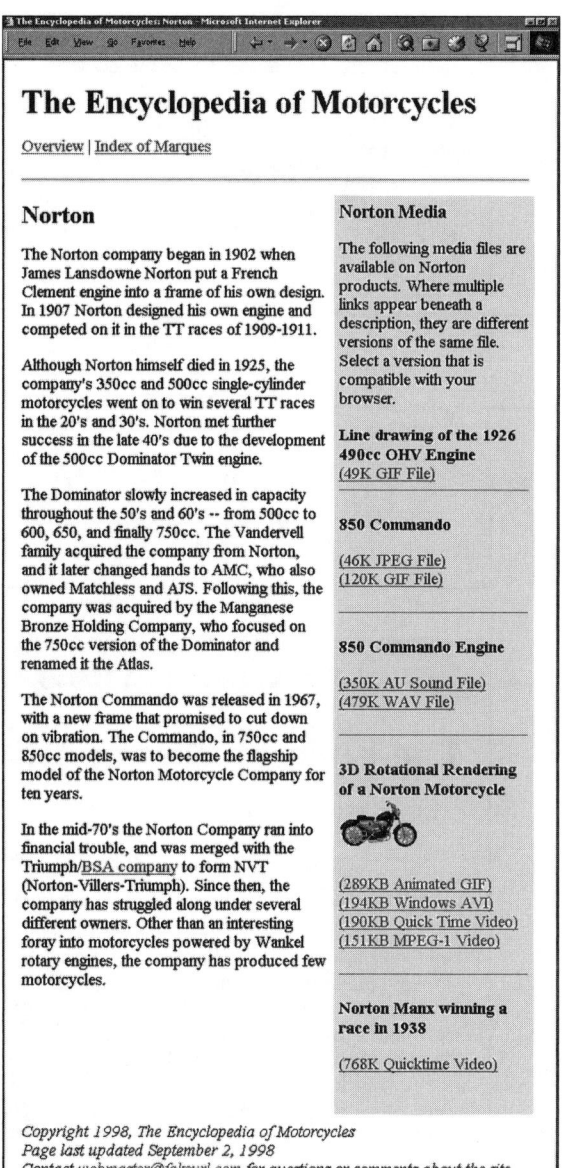

17

FIGURE 17.11

A 3D rendering of a Norton motorcycle.

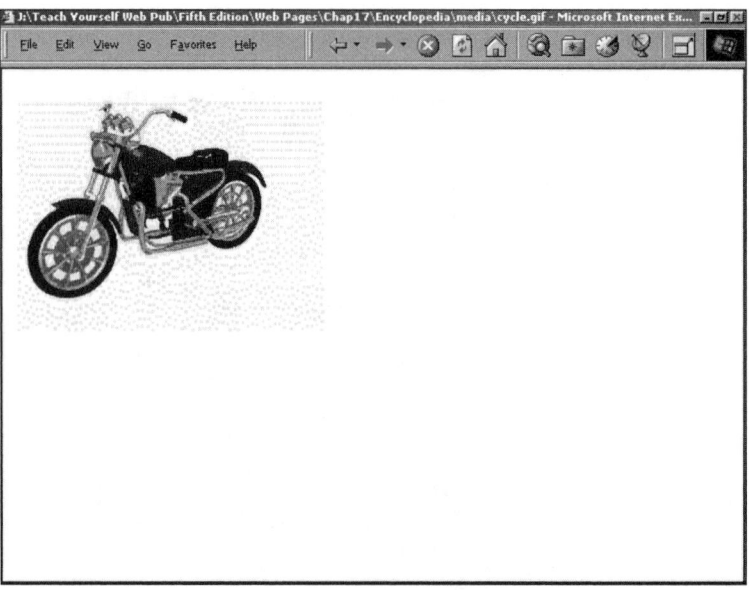

FIGURE 17.12

The entry for BSA.

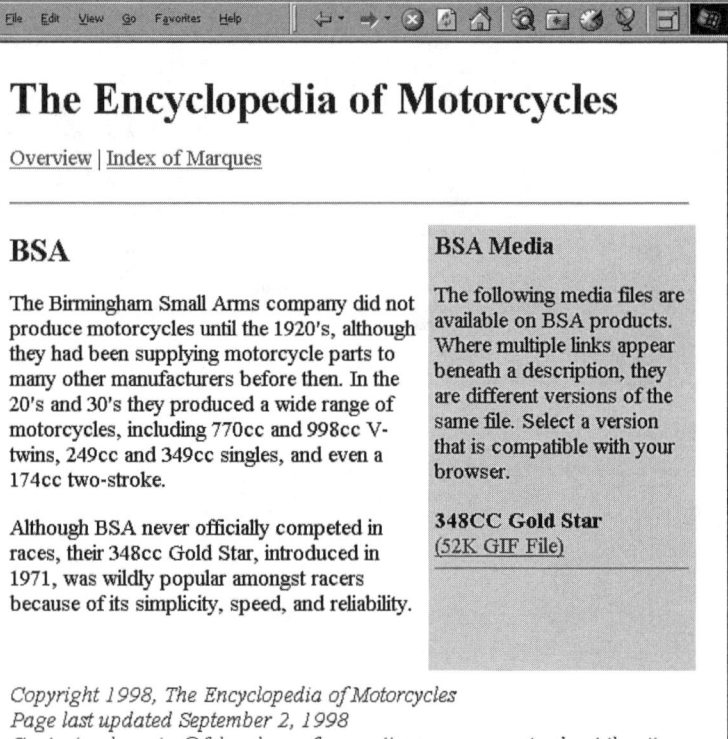

The Index of Marques

Back on the main overview page, there's a link to an index of marques. This is an alphabetical listing of all the motorcycle manufacturers mentioned in the encyclopedia (see
Figure 17.13).

FIGURE 17.13

The index of marques.

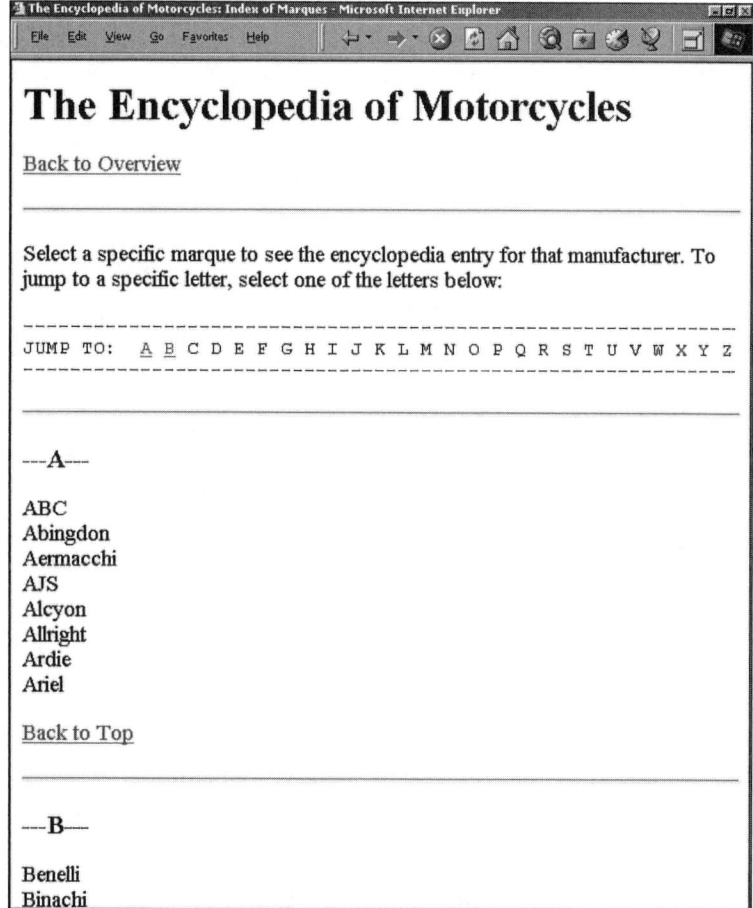

As you might expect, each name in the index is a link to that manufacturer's encyclopedia entry, providing yet another way to quickly navigate the alphabetical listings.

An additional enhancement to the index appears near the top of the page. The Jump To
list enables the visitor to quickly access the marques that begin with a specific letter,
rather than having to scroll through the entire index. By selecting the "O" section, for

example, the visitor jumps to the "O" anchor on the page. Another link at the end of the "O" section (similar to those shown at the end of the "A" section in Figure 17.13) takes the visitor back to the top of the page, where he can choose another letter.

Features of This Web Site and Issues for Development

Probably the best feature of this encyclopedia's design is the Overview page. In many cases, an online encyclopedia of this sort would provide a link to each letter in the alphabet and leave it at that. If you wanted to check out Norton motorcycles, you would click *N* and then scroll down to the entry for Norton. By providing links to some of the more popular motorcycle makers on the overview page itself, the author of this Web page provides a simple, quick reference that takes visitors directly to where they want to be.

The index of marques is another nice touch. It enables the visitor to jump directly to the entry for a particular manufacturer, reducing the amount of scrolling required to find the right entry. Again, it's the same content as in the encyclopedia. The overview page simply provides several different ways to find the same information.

The encyclopedia itself is structured in a loose Web pattern. Visitors can jump in just about anywhere and then follow cross-references and browse through the available information, uncovering connections between motorcycles and marques and motorcycle history that might be difficult to uncover in a traditional bound encyclopedia. Because all the media files are outside the pages themselves, the encyclopedia can be used equally well by those who view images when they browse the Web and those who don't. Also, it keeps each page small so it loads quickly.

Finally, note that every marque page (such as the Norton and BSA pages shown in Figures 17.10 and 17.12) has a link back to the Overview page and to the index of marques. If there were more links than these, they would clutter the page and make it look ugly. But because the only explicit navigation choices are back to the Overview or to the index of marques, these two links enable the visitor to quickly and easily get back out of the encyclopedia. He doesn't have to scroll to the top or the bottom of the document, as would be the case with a more conventional layout.

The biggest issues with developing a Web site of this kind are setup and maintenance. Depending on the amount of material you're posting online, arranging it all can present immediate challenges. (Do you use exactly 26 files, one for each letter of the alphabet? Or do you feature one manufacturer per page?) As a compromise, perhaps you can combine the marques that have a little bit of information (such as the BSA page) on a letter page (`b.html`) and feature the more prominent marques, like Norton, on a page of their own.

In any case, creating the links for all the cross-references and all the external media can be daunting. Fortunately, a site of this sort doesn't need to be updated very often, so maintenance isn't all that difficult after the initial work is done. To add new information, you simply put it in the appropriate spot and then create new links to and from it.

Example Three: A Shopping Catalog

Anna's Herb and Spice Garden is a commercial nursery specializing in growing and shipping herbs, spices, and aromatic vegetables for the discerning gardener and chef. They offer over 120 species of plants, as well as books and other related items. Figure 17.14 shows their home page.

FIGURE 17.14

The home page for Anna's Herb and Spice Garden.

17

Anna has used Cascading Style Sheets to provide background colors and text and link colors for her Web site. Her company's name appears within the title of each Web page and in the logo at the top of each page. Anna has decided to place links to the main pages near the top of the page. This doesn't force the visitor to scroll through the entire page to navigate elsewhere. The navigation bar provides links to the most popular pages: the home page, the Browse Catalog page, How to Order, and the Order Form.

From the home page, customers have several choices: browse the catalog, get information about ordering, or actually order the plants or other products they have chosen.

Browsing the Catalog

The Browse Our Catalog link takes customers to another menu page, where they choose how they want to browse the catalog (see Figure 17.15).

By providing several different views of the catalog, the author serves many different kinds of customers. For those who know about herbs and spices already and just want to look up a specific variety, the alphabetic index is most appropriate. If they know they want some fresh herb plants for their gardens but aren't sure exactly which kinds, they can browse by the Herb category. Finally, those who don't really know or care about the names of herbs can use the photo gallery.

The alphabetical links (A-F, G-R, S-Z) take customers to an alphabetical listing of the plants available for purchase. Figure 17.16 shows a sample listing from the alphabetical catalog. In this case, the A-F page is displayed.

I haven't completed all the links on this page, but assume that each one takes the visitor to a page with more information about a particular herb, spice, or aromatic vegetable. If the visitor clicks the Bay Leaves link (see Figure 17.16), he's taken to a page that describes the product in more detail. An example is shown in Figure 17.17.

Each product page displays a small image of the herb. Next to the image are the English and Latin names of the herb. Following that is a brief description of the herb's typical uses, a description of its taste, and other information that might be noteworthy. Finally, a bulleted list explains how the visitor can order the plant and the prices of each.

The second view of the catalog (accessible from the Browsing the Catalog page, shown in Figure 17.15) is the category view. Selecting one of the links in the By Category section of the Browsing the Catalog page takes the visitor to yet another page of menus. When the visitor selects the Herb category, the page shown in Figure 17.18 appears.

FIGURE 17.15

*Customers can decide
how they want to
browse the catalog.*

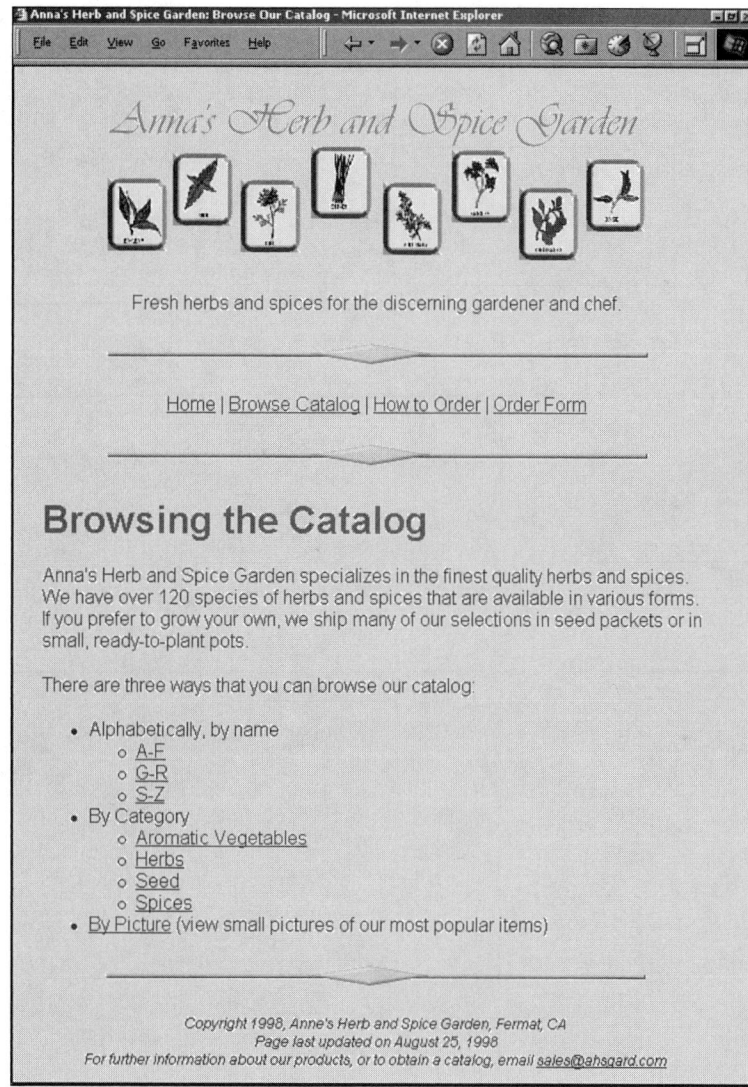

17

FIGURE **17.16**

*The Catalog, A-F
alphabetical link.*

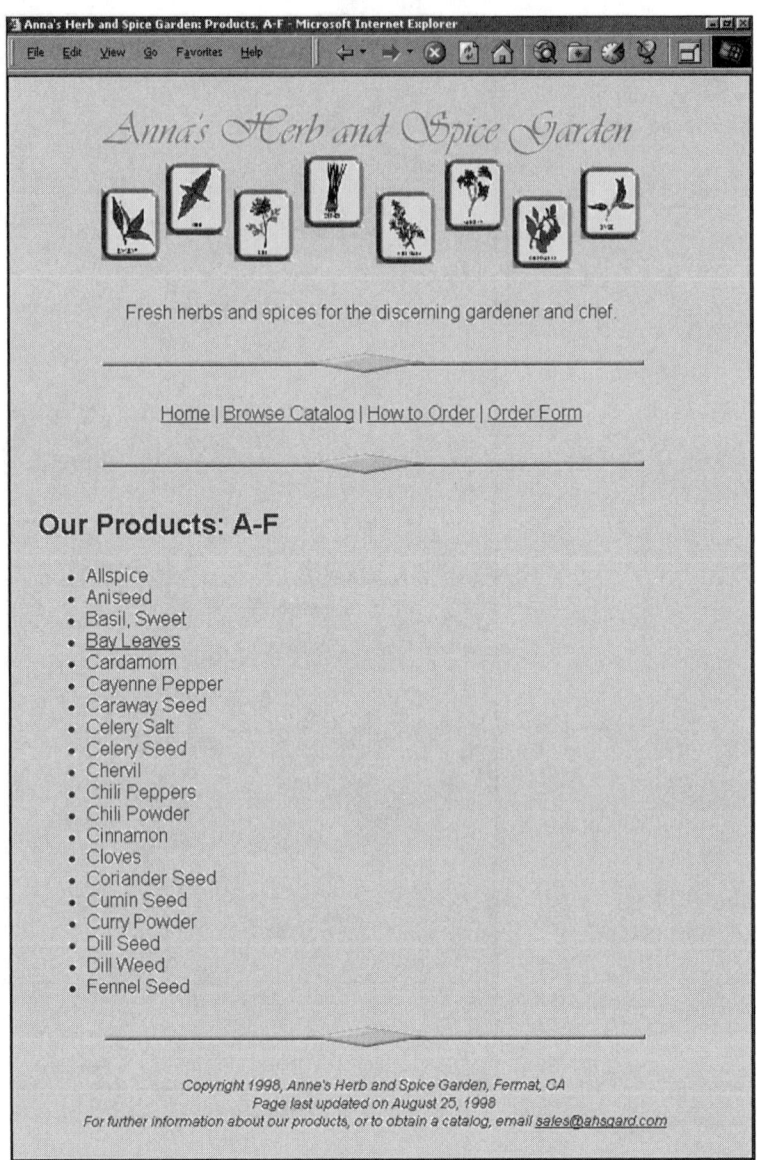

FIGURE 17.17

A product page.

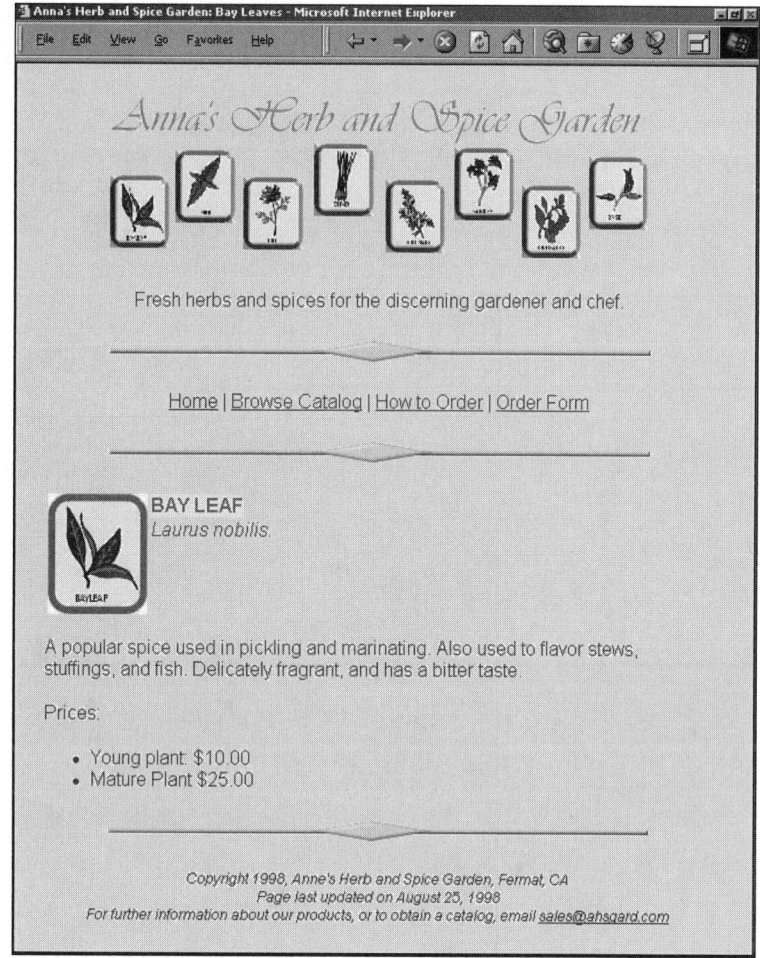

Selecting the Herbs category takes the customer to a listing of the available herbs. Again, I haven't completed all the links on this page, but each link takes the visitor to a specific product page, such as the one shown in Figure 17.17. From the category index, the customer can go back to the Browsing the Catalog page. Here, there's one more way to view the catalog: the photo gallery.

The photo gallery enables the customer to browse many of the plants by looking at pictures of them, rather than having to know their scientific names. If the customer wants to find a plant that he saw in someone else's garden but can't remember its name, this is the ideal place to browse.

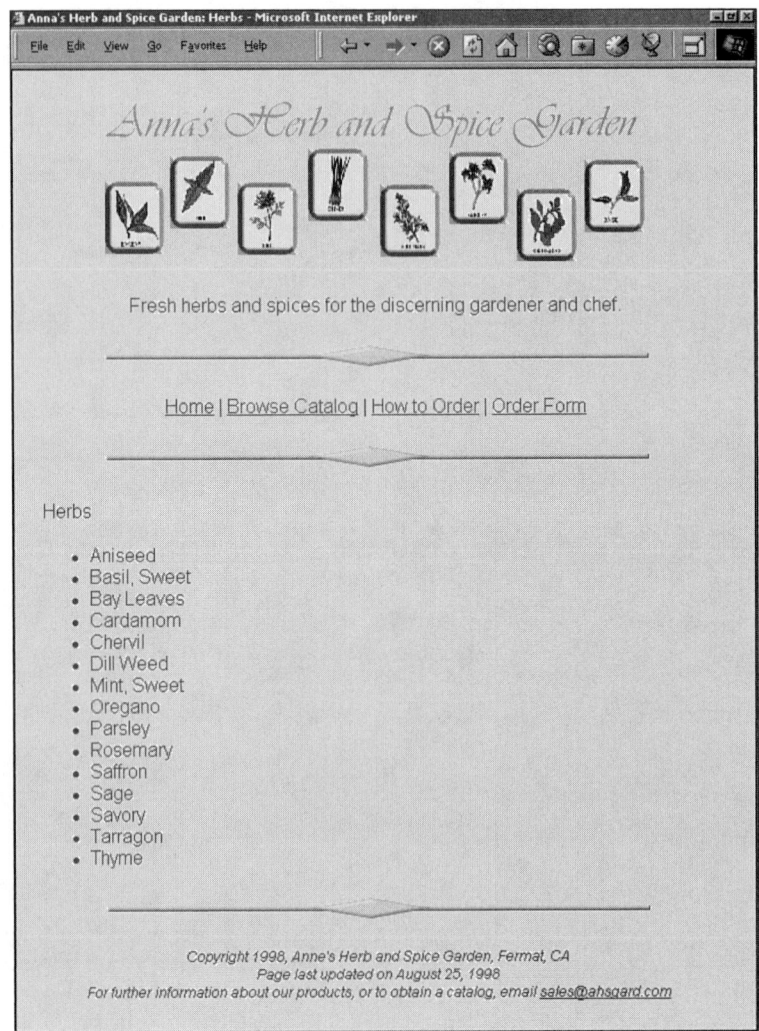

The photo gallery page (shown in Figure 17.19) is organized as a series of icons, each one linking to a larger JPEG. The text description of each plant also takes you back to the appropriate entry in the main catalog.

Tip

If you're going to sell products online, you should always include pictures of them, if possible. It's even better to include multiple pictures of each item from different angles or at different sizes. One big barrier to people purchasing items online is their inability to actually see the item up close before making their purchase. You should get them as close to that experience as possible through your site design.

FIGURE 17.19

The photo gallery page.

17

Anna's Herb and Spice Garden: Product Gallery - Microsoft Internet Explorer

File Edit View Go Favorites Help

Anna's Herb and Spice Garden

Fresh herbs and spices for the discerning gardener and chef.

Home | Browse Catalog | How to Order | Order Form

BAY LEAF
Laurus nobilis.

CHIVES
Allium schoenoprasum.

DILL
Anethum graveolens.

MINT
Mentha genus

OREGANO (also known as **ORIGANUM**)
Origanum vulgare

PARSLEY
Petroselinum crispum.

ROSEMARY
Laminacae or Labiatae

SAGE
Salvia officinalis.

Copyright 1998, Anne's Herb and Spice Garden, Fermat, CA
Page last updated on August 25, 1998
For further information about our products, or to obtain a catalog, email sales@ahsgard.com

Ordering

After the customer finishes browsing the catalog and knows which plants he wants to order, he can jump to the How to Order page and find out how to place the order.

The page for ordering just contains some simple text: information about where to call or send checks, tables for shipping costs, notes on when they'll ship plants, and so on. (See Figure 17.20.)

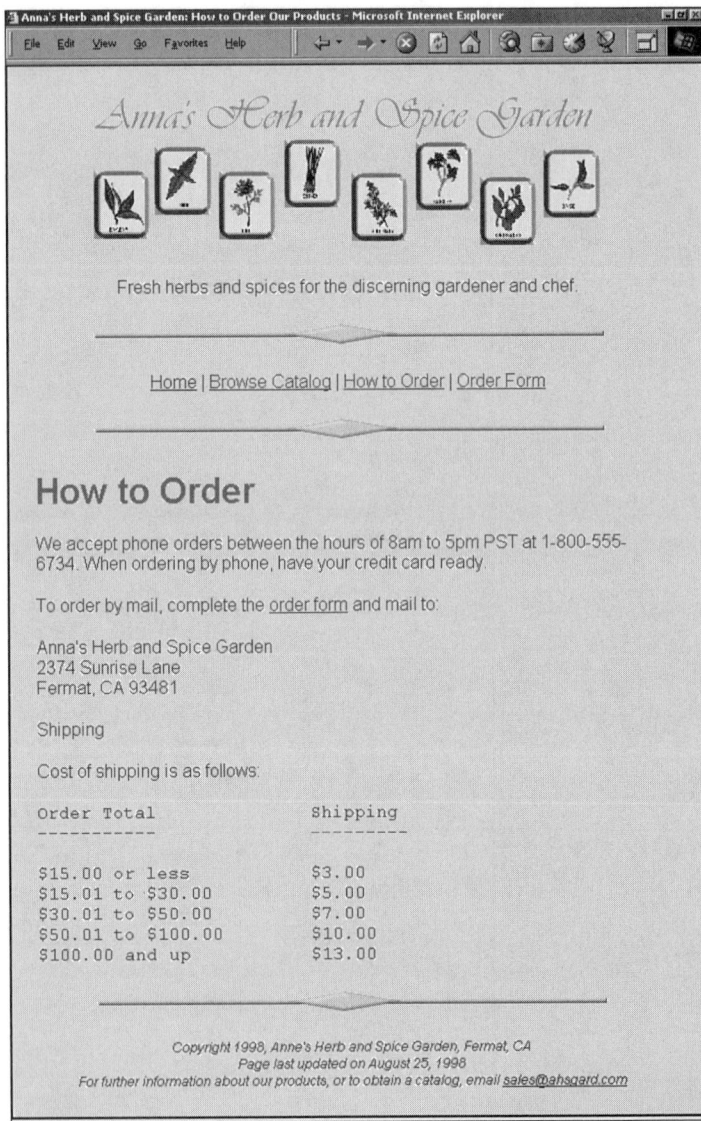

In the section on ordering by mail, there's a link to an order form. You can create this order form in several different ways. If you don't want to bother with creating forms and writing form handlers, you can create a simple text file that includes an order form. The customer can download or display the order form on his browser, as shown in Figure 17.21. Then he can print it out, fill in the blanks, and send it to the nursery.

Caution

If possible, you should support online ordering on your site. These days, nearly everyone selling items over the Internet supports online ordering, and customers will not be happy to have to print out an order form and drop it in the mailbox any more. If you lack the expertise to set up your own online store, you might look into setting up an online store through a service like Yahoo Store (`http://store.yahoo.com`), or Amazon.com zShops (`http://www.amazon.com/zshops/`).

17

There are other ways to provide external versions of this document as well. For example, you can provide a postscript file, an Adobe Acrobat Reader file (which uses a `.PDF` extension), or even specific word processor formats, such as Microsoft Word or Word Perfect. Simply store the files on your Web site as you would any other page, and include a link to that file on your Web page. The visitor will be prompted to download the page if he doesn't have a viewer or helper application that can display it as a Web page.

You also can design an online order form, as shown in Figure 17.22. This approach may not be as straightforward as it seems. There are several things you'll need to consider:

- Many customers are very wary of entering their credit card information online for security reasons. The best alternative is to place your online catalog on a secure server that protects the information entered by the customer.

- If your catalog isn't on a secure server, be sure to inform customers of this and provide alternate methods to place an order. Include a phone number to call, or use a text order form similar to the one shown in Figure 17.21.

- Another alternative is to include everything *but* the credit card information on the online order form. After you receive an order from a customer, you can send an email confirmation that it was received. Include an order reference number, as well as a phone number that the customer can call to provide the billing information.

- When a customer submits an order, do you want to automatically add the order to a dynamic database? This is entirely possible, but it requires advanced Web programming and a familiarity with database structures and other techniques that haven't been discussed in this book.

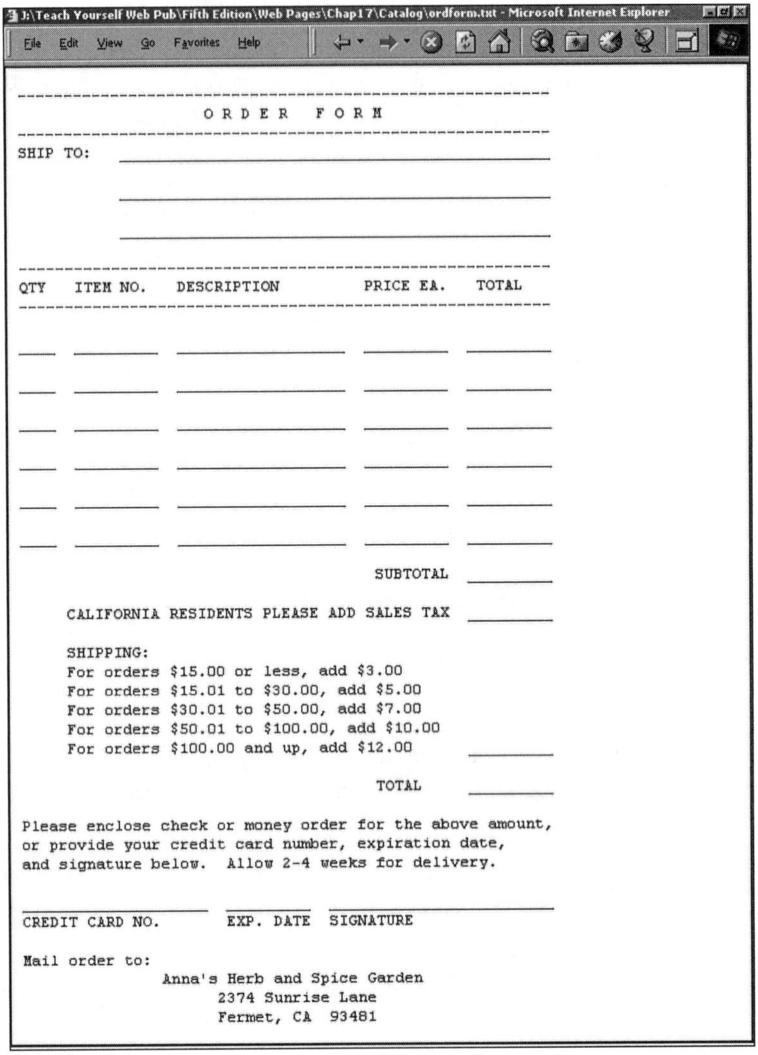

FIGURE 17.21

The text order form.

```
--------------------------------------------------------------------
                          O R D E R   F O R M
--------------------------------------------------------------------
SHIP TO:            _____

                    _____

                    _____

--------------------------------------------------------------------
QTY    ITEM NO.   DESCRIPTION            PRICE EA.    TOTAL
--------------------------------------------------------------------

___   _____   _____   _____   _____

___   _____   _____   _____   _____

___   _____   _____   _____   _____

___   _____   _____   _____   _____

___   _____   _____   _____   _____

___   _____   _____   _____   _____

                                        SUBTOTAL   _____

        CALIFORNIA RESIDENTS PLEASE ADD SALES TAX   _____

        SHIPPING:
        For orders $15.00 or less, add $3.00
        For orders $15.01 to $30.00, add $5.00
        For orders $30.01 to $50.00, add $7.00
        For orders $50.01 to $100.00, add $10.00
        For orders $100.00 and up, add $12.00           _____

                                        TOTAL      _____

        Please enclose check or money order for the above amount,
        or provide your credit card number, expiration date,
        and signature below.  Allow 2-4 weeks for delivery.


        _____  _____  _____
        CREDIT CARD NO.   EXP. DATE  SIGNATURE

        Mail order to:
                    Anna's Herb and Spice Garden
                        2374 Sunrise Lane
                        Fermet, CA  93481
```

Returning to Anna's Herb and Spice Garden site, note that the third bullet on the home page is a direct link to the order form file. It's provided here so that repeat customers won't have to go back to the ordering, shipping, and payment page again.

FIGURE 17.22

An online order form.

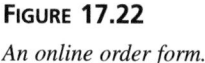

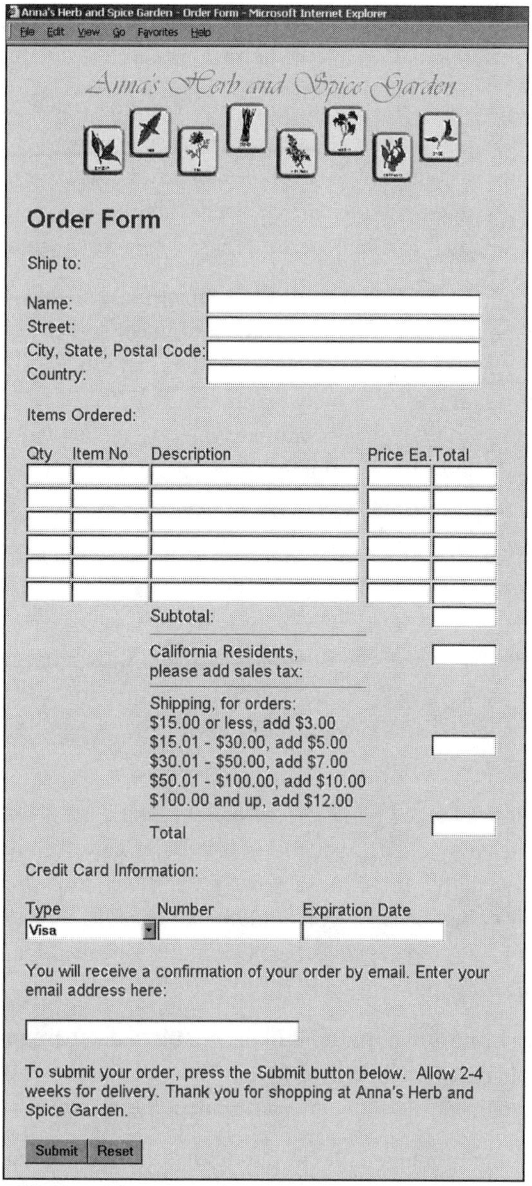

17

Features of This Web Site and Issues for Development

The goal of any online shopping service is to allow the visitor to browse the items for sale and then to order those items. Within the browsing goal, there are several sub-goals.

What if the visitor wants a particular item? Can it be found quickly and easily? What if someone just wants to look through the items for sale until she finds something interesting?

The use of multiple views in the catalog makes it approachable for users trying to quickly find a specific item, and users who just want to casually browse the store's inventory. These multiple views do provide a level of indirection (an extra menu between the top-level page and the contents of the catalog itself), but this small step provides a branching in the hierarchy structure that helps each different type of customer accomplish her goals.

I've intentionally left some holes in this site, however, to demonstrate ways you can improve the navigation. For example, you could make it easier to browse through the catalog by adding a different menu for each viewing method. Consider the first site you saw today, where the main page had a navigation bar that linked to all the other main pages of the site (see Figure 17.1). When you navigated to the Technical Information page, however, you had another navigation bar that linked between the technical papers (see Figure 17.3). A similar system would greatly enhance Anna's catalog.

The most important thing that Anna wants to accomplish on her site is to increase sales. How can she improve the navigation to do that? The best way is to provide a link to the How to Order page, to the Order Form, or both on any page that displays product information. If a visitor comes across the Bay Leaf page shown in Figure 17.17 and decides that it's just the plant for her, she might forget that the How to Order page takes her right to the order form. Place a link to the order form beneath the pricing information. One click, and you have a customer.

Probably the hardest part of building and maintaining a set of Web pages like this is maintaining the catalog itself, particularly if items need to be added or removed or if prices change frequently. If the nursery had only one catalog view (the alphabetical one), this wouldn't be so bad because you could make changes directly to the catalog files. With additional views and the links between them, however, maintenance of the catalog becomes significantly more difficult.

Ideally, this sort of information should be stored in a database rather than as individual HTML files. Databases are designed to handle information like this and to generate different views on request. But how do you connect the database with the Web pages?

Given enough programming skill and familiarity with databases, you could create a program that accepts database queries from a Web page and returns a neatly formatted list of items. Then, when someone requests the alphabetical listing from the Web page, he gets an automatically generated list that's as up-to-date as the database is. But to do this, you'll need a database that can talk to your Web server. Depending on the system your Web server runs on, this may or may not be technically feasible. You also need the programming skill to make it work, using advanced Web technologies like CGI, or Active Server Pages. Unfortunately, these are topics that go beyond the scope of this book. For more information, refer *to Sams Teach Yourself CGI in 24 Hours,* by Rafe Colburn, *Sams Teach Yourself Perl in 21 Days,* by Laura Lemay, and *Sams Teach Yourself Active Server Pages 3.0 in 21 Days,* by Scott Mitchell and James Atkinson.

An alternative is to keep the data in the database and then periodically dump it to text and format it in HTML. The primary difficulty with this solution is that it would take a lot of work to do the conversion each time while still preserving the cross-references to the other pages. Could the process be automated, and how much setup and daily mainte-nance would that involve?

These are the kinds of questions and technical challenges you may have to deal with as you create Web sites. Sometimes the problem involves more than designing, writing, and formatting information on the screen.

17

Summary

I've presented only a few ideas for using and structuring Web pages here. The variations on these themes are unlimited for the Web pages you will design.

Probably the best way to find examples of Web pages you might want to design and how to organize them is to see what's out there on the Web. In addition to examining the lay-out, design, and content of Web pages, keep an eye out for the organizational structures people use and try to guess why they might have chosen them. ("They didn't think about it" is a common reason for many poorly organized Web pages, unfortunately.) Critique other people's Web pages with an eye on their structure and design. Is it easy to navigate them? Did you get lost? Can you easily get back to a known page from any other page on their site? If you had a goal in mind when you went to this site, did you achieve that goal? If not, how would you reorganize the site?

Learning from other people's mistakes and seeing how they've solved difficult problems can help you make your own Web pages better.

Workshop

Today you've learned several different techniques to improve the appearance and func-tionality of your Web pages. The following workshop covers some of the most important topics discussed today.

Q&A

Q **These Web sites are really cool. What are their URLs?**

A These Web sites are just mockups (although they are on the Web support site we've set up for this book). However, many of the designs and organizational structures that I've used here were inspired by existing Web pages.

Q **The examples here used some sort of hierarchical organization. Are hierarchies that common, and do I have to use them? Can't I do something different?**

A Hierarchies are extremely common on the Web, but that doesn't mean they're bad. They can be an excellent way of organizing your content.

You can certainly do something different to organize your site. For example, you might prefer to use framesets, as discussed on Day 11, "Frames and Linked Windows." The simplicity of hierarchies, however, allows them to be structured, navigated, and maintained easily. Why make more trouble for yourself and for your visitors by trying to force a complicated structure on otherwise simple information?

Quiz

1. What are some ways that you can help visitors find their way around your Web site?

2. What can you do to help prevent your visitors from getting lost?

3. What's the biggest issue when you're developing a site that includes a lot of information, such as an online encyclopedia?

4. What are the advantages of providing multiple ways of browsing through an online shopping catalog?

5. What is one of the primary concerns in obtaining product orders over the Web?

Quiz Answers

1. Provide navigation bars that link to each of the main pages of your site. Different navigation bars can be designed for sub-levels. For consistency, usually it's best to place the navigation bars at the same location on each page. The most common locations are at the top, bottom, or left sides of a Web page. Frequently Asked Questions pages, What's New pages, and Table of Contents pages also are handy ways to provide links to other pages on your site.

2. In general, try to stick with a rigid hierarchical structure and avoid using lateral links that cross the hierarchy. This helps visitors keep track of where they are on your Web site.

3. The biggest issues in developing a Web site that's rich with information are setup and maintenance. Deciding how to best organize and arrange information is the most difficult task, and creating all the cross-reference links to pages and media is time-consuming as well. However, most of the information in an online encyclopedia is unlikely to change much, so a site like this won't be very high-maintenance.

4. Arranging online shopping catalogs to display products in several different categories (such as by product type, product number, product appearance, and so on) helps visitors find your products more easily. The most logical place to start is to organize your products by category. If your products are well-known to customers, they may appreciate the advantage of searching by product name or product number. Others like to search by appearance of a product (for example, by color or size).

5. The main issue in taking orders over the Web is security. Many customers don't like to provide their credit card information online. Be sure to provide alternative means to obtain orders, and try to place your order forms on a secure server.

Exercises

1. Using the Encyclopedia of Motorcycles as a guide, create a frameset with two or three frames. How would you create an interface that takes visitors from section to section easily?

2. You can apply some of the navigation and design tips that you learned today to your own personal home pages. Foozle Industries provides some good examples of navigation bars and linking pages. The Encyclopedia of Motorcycles provides good tips for linking together topics of interest and providing pictures or other media as descriptions. Check out some of your favorite sites on the Web and think about how they could be better designed to find information that you're looking for.

DAY 18

Designing for the Real World

In previous lessons, you learned about what you should and shouldn't do when you plan your Web site and design your pages. You also learned about what makes a good or bad Web site. There's another important factor that you should take into consideration, and that's how to design your pages for the real world.

You've already learned that the real world consists of many different users with many different computer systems who use many different browsers. One of the things we haven't yet addressed, however, is the many different preferences and experience levels that the visitors to your site will have. By anticipating these real-world needs, you can better judge how you should design your pages.

In this chapter, you'll learn some ways that you can anticipate these needs, as well as the following:

- Things to consider when you're trying to determine the preferences of your audience
- How to add features that will be helpful to new users

- Various ways of helping users find their way around your site
- HTML code that displays the same Web page in each of the XHTML 1.0 specifica-tions (Transitional, Frameset, and Strict)

What *Is* the Real World, Anyway?

You're probably most familiar with surfing the Internet on a computer that runs a specific operating system, such as Windows, the Mac OS, or something similar. For all intents and purposes, you think you have a pretty good idea of what Web pages look like to everyone.

Throughout this book, you've learned that the view you typically see on the Web isn't the view that everyone else sees. The real world has many different computers with many different operating systems. Even if you try to design your pages for the most common operating system and the most common browsers, there's another factor that you can't anticipate: *user preference*. Consider the following family, for example:

- Bill is a top-level executive at a Fortune 100 company that has its own intranet. Almost everyone in the company uses the same operating system and the same browser. Bill is used to seeing the Internet as mostly text, with a smattering of images here and there to stress informational points—a lean and mean Web with very little multimedia and a lot of information. He finds all the extra glitz annoying and inconvenient to download, so he turns off the images and sound.
- Bill's wife, Susan, has never used a computer before, but she's always wanted to learn. She's a genealogist by hobby and has learned that the Internet has many resources in that field. She also wants to publish her family history on the Web. When she and her husband powered up their new home computer for the first time, she was thrilled. But soon, she was asking questions such as, "Can we fit more on the screen? Those letters are a bit too small… can we make them larger? Where are the pictures? How come you have the music turned off? It says that there's sound on this page!" Already, she wanted to see the Internet much differently than her husband was used to seeing it.
- Bill and Susan have a son, Tom, who's in high school. He's an avid gamer and wants to see special effects—*glitz, multimedia*! He pumps up the volume as loud as he can and pushes the capacities of their new computer to the max. He also thinks "Browser X" is better than "Browser Y" because it supports lots of cutting-edge features. He wants to design a Web site that provides hints, tips, and tricks for one of his favorite online games.

- Tom's older sister, Jill, is an art major in college, studying to be a commercial artist. She has a keen interest in sculpture and photography. She plans to use the new computer for homework assignments, so she'll be looking at the Web with a keen visual interest. She wants to view her pages in true color, in the highest resolution possible.

- Then there are the senior members of the family, Susan's aging parents, who have recently moved in with the family after years of living in a very small rural town. Their experience with computers is minimal—they've only seen them in stores and were afraid to touch them for fear of breaking them. To them, computers are a complete mystery that they find absolutely amazing. So they want to learn. They share Susan's genealogical interest, but Dad's eyes aren't quite as sharp as they used to be. He needs a special browser so that he can hear the text as well as see it.

All these people are using the same computer and operating system to view the Web. In all cases but one (young Tom), they're also using the same browser. This example illustrates one of the other things that you need to think about when you design your Web site: the needs of the users themselves. Some of these needs are easier to accommodate than others. The following section describes some of the considerations you saw in the previous example.

18

Considering User Experience Level

There are varied levels of experience in our fictitious family. Although everyone is keenly interested in the Web, some of them have never even seen a Web browser before. So when you design your site, you should consider that the people who visit it might have varying levels of experience and browsing requirements.

Will the topics that you discuss on your site be of interest to people with different levels of experience? If so, you might want to build in some features that help them find their way around easier. In Chapter 17, "Examples of Good and Bad Web Design," you learned some tips for designing navigation systems to keep people from getting lost in cyberspace. That's a good start, but you might want to include a page on your Web site that describes your navigation system in more detail.

Figure 18.1 shows the top portion of a page that helps visitors learn more about your site. Links at the top of the page take the visitor to several different sections of the page: About the Site, The Navigation System, Browser Recommendations, and Other Files You Might Need. Each of these sections, in turn, links to pages that provide a more detailed description of the site's contents.

FIGURE 18.1

*A page that helps visi-
tors find their way
around the site.*

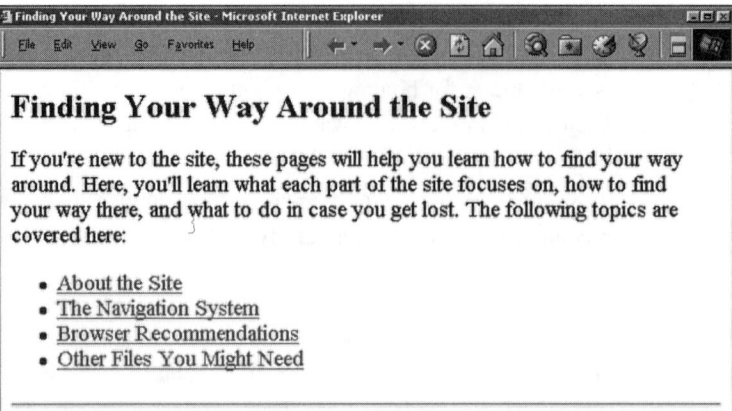

List Pages That Provide Descriptions of Your Site

The About the Site section helps the visitor quickly review the contents of your Web site or find out what has been added since his or her last visit. Figure 18.2 shows a simple link menu for this instance.

FIGURE 18.2

*Links to pages that
show the visitor the
contents of your Web
site.*

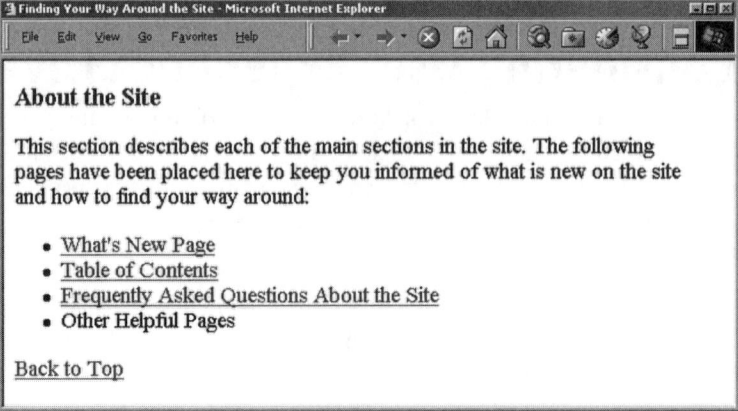

The following are some good examples to include in this category:

- A What's New page with links to recent additions to your site

- A Table of Contents page that lists the page title and an optional brief description of each page on your Web site

- A Frequently Asked Questions page that answers questions you've received from visitors

These are the most common types of pages that can help visitors learn more about your site, but you might come up with some that are more particular to your topic. If so, it's a good idea to list the pages that will be most helpful to your visitors.

Describe Your Navigation System

Navigation systems vary from site to site, and they're not always easy for a new Web user to understand. Typically, they fall into one of three areas: simple text navigation systems, image navigation systems, or frameset navigation systems. If you think your navigation system might need explanation, provide descriptions or links to help the visitor learn how to use it. Figure 18.3 shows a link menu of pages that describe various navigation systems on a Web site.

FIGURE **18.3**

Describe your naviga-tion system.

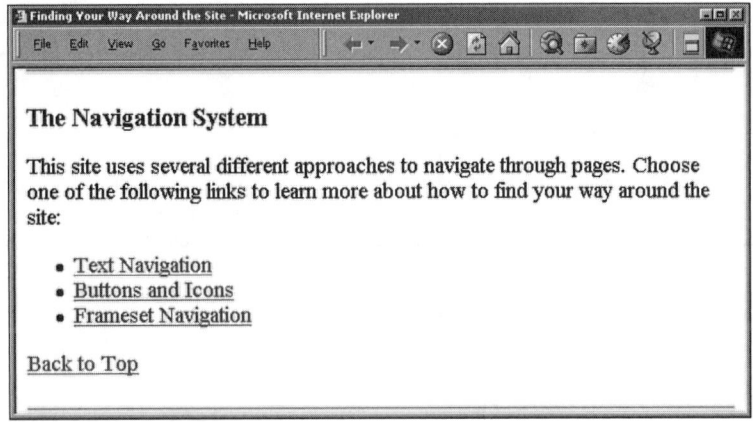

When you describe your navigation system, try to make the descriptions easy to understand. Suppose that your text navigation bar looks like the following example, and that it appears on all of the main pages of the Web site:

```
Home | Contents | FAQ | What's New | Email | Guest Book | Links
```

This menu bar might be self-explanatory to those who have visited your site before, but it might not make a lot of sense to someone who's new to your site or to the Web. The following descriptions might be helpful to new users:

- **Home**—"Use the Home link to return to the Home page on this Web site."

- **Contents**—"The Table of Contents page provides links to all the pages on the Web site. If you are new to the site, this is a good place to start."

- **FAQ**—Someone new to the Internet might not know what *FAQ* means. Try something like, "The FAQ (Frequently Asked Questions) page answers some of the questions that we have received from visitors."

- **E-mail**—Here's another link that could use clarification. Does this link take the visitor to e-mail that you've received, or is it a link that sends e-mail to you? Clarify this with a description such as "Use the E-mail link to send questions or comments about this site to our Webmaster."

When you use images and icons for navigation, they aren't always easy to identify. Perhaps you recall the Rainy Day Distractions example that you saw on Day 11. To refresh your memory, the frameset is shown in Figure 18.4. The left frame includes images and icons for navigation, and the bottom frame displays an equivalent text navigation bar.

FIGURE 18.4

Using images, icons, and frameset navigation.

In some cases, it isn't really obvious what the icons on the navigation buttons mean. The page in the Main frame displays a brief description of each icon, but new users probably need more help. Here, you can give each icon a description that's similar to those for the text navigation bar.

Framesets are sometimes very difficult for new visitors to understand. A brief How To page that describes your frameset can be very useful for a new visitor. One way to describe your frameset is to provide a small screenshot of it, as shown in Figure 18.5. Identify each of the frames in your frameset by a name that the visitor can easily remember (Left, Top, Main, and Bottom, for example), and place descriptions of each one on the same page. For example, you might describe the frames in Figure 18.5 as follows:

- Use the icons in the Left frame to select the pages that you want to view in the larger Main frame. If you don't remember what the icons mean, select the question mark icon (?) for Help, or use the text navigation bar in the Bottom frame.
- The Top frame displays the site logo at all times so that you'll remember where you are.
- The Main frame displays all the pages you choose from the Left or Bottom frames. Also, when you select a link that appears on a page in the Main frame, the page to which you link also appears in the Main frame.
- The text links in the Bottom frame serve the same function as the icons in the Left frame. These links are provided for those who don't see images in their browsers, or who prefer to use text links.

Tip

You might think that if a navigation scheme needs to be carefully documented so that visitors can understand it, it's probably too complicated. If so, I agree with you. It's always wise to keep your layouts as straightforward as possible. Frames generally make your site more complex and difficult for your visitors to deal with, so you should think carefully before using them. They're helpful in some cases, but most of the time they just make your site more difficult to use.

18

Figure 18.5

Describing a frameset.

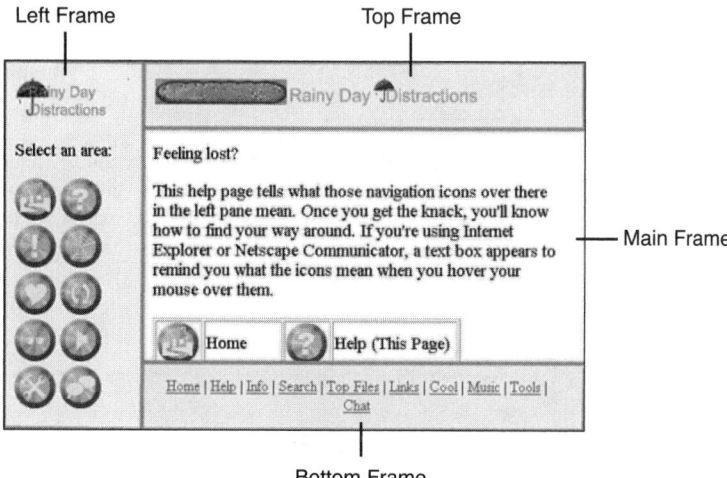

Add Browser Recommendations

If your site uses functionality that's not available in all browsers, it sometimes makes sense to indicate the browser for which the site was designed. Figure 18.6 displays a simple example of how you can achieve this.

FIGURE 18.6

Adding browser recommendations.

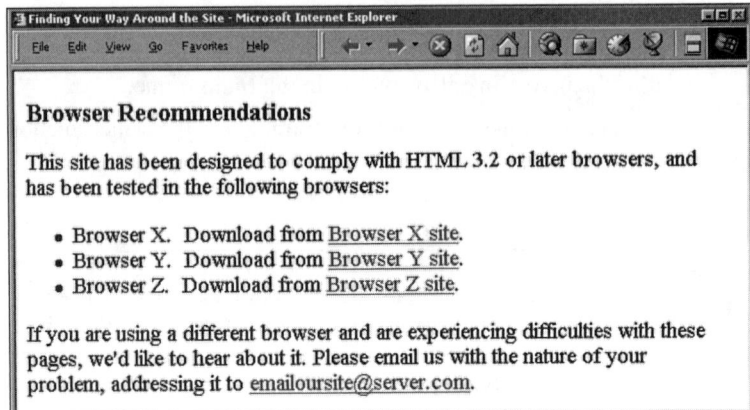

Here, the visitor learns that the site was designed for HTML 3.2 and later browsers that support framesets (the HTML 4.0 Frameset specification). There's a list of links to download the browsers that you used to test the site. Finally, an email address is provided so that the Web author can learn about problems that appear in browsers she was unable to test.

> **Caution**
>
> Indicating that a site is best viewed with one browser or another can appear unprofessional to your users. Generally, Web designers test their designs with all popular Web browsers and make sure that the site looks appropriate regardless of which browser is used. Unless your site really requires a particular browser, it's probably best to avoid telling the user which browser to use. If your site is tailored for a particular browser, consider redesigning it so that it's more accessible.

List Other Necessary Files

Aside from browser recommendations, you also should inform users of special plug-ins or other files that they might need to download. If you have files on your site that aren't in HTML format—such as compressed files, word processing documents, images other than GIF or JPG, and so on—you should inform the visitors that they may need a special viewer. List the viewers or external applications that they may need.

An example of a link menu for external files is shown in Figure 18.7. It lists some of the external applications that might be needed to view or use some of the files included on the site. The fictitious site includes several Adobe Acrobat Reader (.pdf) and Zip-compressed (.zip) files that appear on several different pages. Including links to all the necessary readers and external applications on one page (such as Adobe Acrobat Reader and WinZip, for example) helps visitors use the site to their full advantage.

FIGURE 18.7

Listing other files that might be necessary.

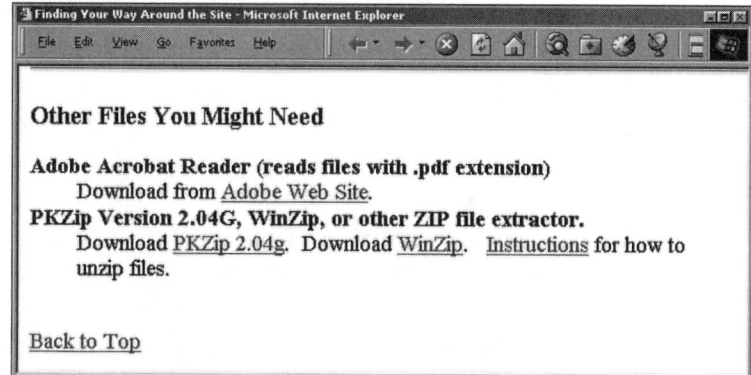

Determining User Preference

In addition to the various levels of experience that visitors have, everyone has their own preferences for how they'll want to view your Web pages. How do you please them all? The truth is, you can't. But you *can* give it your best shot. Part of good Web design is anticipating what visitors want to see on your site. This becomes more difficult if the topics you discuss on your site are of interest to a wider audience.

You'll notice that each person in our fictitious family needs to see the Web differently. Sometimes this is due to his or her interests, but other times it's because of special needs. Therein lies the key to anticipating what you'll need on your Web pages.

A topic such as "Timing the Sparkplugs on your 300cc Motorcycle Engine" is of interest to a more select audience. It will attract only those who are interested in motorcycles—more specifically, those who want to repair their own motorcycles. It should be relatively easy to anticipate the types of things these visitors would like to see on your site. Step-by-step instructions can guide them through each process, while images or multimedia can display techniques that are difficult to describe by text alone.

"The Seven Wonders of the Ancient World," on the other hand, will attract students of all ages, as well as their teachers. Archaeologists, historians, and others with an interest in ancient history also might visit the site. Now you have a wider audience, a wider age range, and a wider range of educational levels. It won't be quite as easy to build a site that will please them all.

In cases such as this, it might help to narrow your focus a bit. One way is to design your site for a specific user group, such as the following:

- **Elementary school students and their teachers**—This site requires a very basic navigation system that's easy to follow. Content should be basic and very easy to read. Bright, colorful images and animations can help keep the attention of young visitors.

- **High school students and their teachers**—You can use a slightly more advanced navigation system. Multimedia and the latest in Web technology will keep these students coming back for more.

- **College students and their professors**—A higher level of content is necessary, whereas multimedia may be less important. An online encyclopedia format might be a good approach here.

- **Professional researchers and historians**—This type of site probably requires pages that are heavier in text content than multimedia.

It's not always possible to define user groups for your Web site, so you'll need to start with your *own* preferences. Survey other sites that include similar content. As you browse through them, ask yourself what you hope to see there. Is the information displayed well? Is there enough help on the site? Does the site have too much or too little multimedia? If you can get a friend or two to do the survey along with you, it helps you get additional feedback before you start your own site. Take notes and incorporate those ideas into your own Web pages.

After you design some initial pages, ask your friends, family members, and associates to browse through your site and pick it apart. Keep in mind that when you ask others for constructive criticism, you might hear some things that you don't want to hear. However, this process is important because you'll often get many new ideas on how to improve your site even more.

Deciding on an HTML 4.01 or XHTML 1.0 Approach

In earlier chapters, you learned about the various flavors of HTML 4.0 and XHTML 1.0 and how each of them is geared toward users of older or newer browsers:

- **HTML 4.0 or XHTML 1.0 Transitional**—For those who want to provide support for older browsers.

- **HTML 4.0 or XHTML 1.0 Frameset**—For those who want to use frameset navigation in addition to supporting the tags found in HTML 4.0 Transitional.
- **HTML 4.0 or XHTML 1.0 Strict**—For those who want to develop pages that strictly adhere to the HTML 4.0 or XHTML 1.0 specification by not using deprecated elements or attributes.

HTML 4.01 and XHTML 1.0 Transitional

If you expect your visitors to use a wide variety of different browsers, it's probably to your advantage to design your Web pages around the HTML 4.0 or XHTML 1.0 Transitional specification. By doing so, you provide backward-compatibility with older browsers. The Transitional specification provides the flexibility to use tags that are deprecated in the strict HTML 4.0 specification. Therefore, you can use presentational commands that were introduced in HTML 3.2, such as the center or align attributes for alignment or bgcolor and color attributes for background and foreground colors.

For example, look at the Halloween House of Terror page that you created on Day 7, "Using Images, Color, and Backgrounds." Here, the page has undergone yet another facelift, as shown in the following code and Figure 18.8. This page uses HTML 3.2-compatible tags to display the page. Fonts, colors, and alignment are formatted with tags that have been deprecated in the Strict specification.

The deprecated tags and attributes are shown in italics in the following code example. In addition, a table is used to create a staggered layout of links, descriptions, and images on the page.

INPUT/OUTPUT

```
<!DOCTYPE html PUBLIC "-//W3C//DTD XHTML 1.0 Transitional//EN"
"http://www.w3.org/TR/xhtml1/DTD/transitional.dtd"><html>
<head>
<title>Welcome to the Halloween House of Terror</title>
</head>
<body bgcolor="#ff9933" link="#990000">
<h1 align="center">
  <font face="Arial, sans-serif">
  The Halloween House of Terror!!</font></h1>
<div align="center">
  <p>
    <img src="skel05.gif" alt="skel05.gif" width="140" height="100" />
    <img src="skel07.gif" alt="skel07.gif" width="140" height="100" />
    <img src="skel06.gif" alt="skel06.gif" width="140" height="100" />
  </p>
</div>
<hr />
<p>
  <font face="Arial, sans-serif">
    Voted the most frightening haunted house three years in a row, the
```

18

```
    <font color="#cc0000"><b>Halloween House of Terror</b></font>
    provides the ultimate in Halloween thrills. Over 20 rooms of
    thrills and excitement to make your blood run cold and your
    hair stand on end!
  </font>
</p>
<hr />
<p><font face="Arial, sans-serif">
    Don't take our word for it ... preview some images of what awaits!
  </font>
</p>
<div align="center">
  <table border="0" width="75%" cellspacing="5" cellpadding="5">
    <tr>
        <td width="30%">
          <font face="Arial, sans-serif">
          <img src="skel01.gif" alt="skel01.gif" width="140"
height="100" />
          </font>
        </td>
        <td width="40%" bgcolor="#CC0000"> <font face="Arial, sans-serif">
    Watch out for Esmerelda. You never know what she has in her
cauldron.
        </font> </td>
        <th width="30%" bgcolor="#FF6600"> <b><font face="Arial,
sans-serif">
        <a href="entry.gif">The Entry Way</a> </font></b> </th>
    </tr>
    <tr>
        <th width="30%" bgcolor="#FF6600"> <b><font face="Arial,
sans-serif">
        <a href="bedroom.gif">The Master Bedroom</a> </font></b> </th>
        <td width="40%" bgcolor="#CC0000"> <font face="Arial, sans-serif">
    Don't open the closet door, whatever you do!</font></td>
        <td width="30%">
            <font face="Arial, sans-serif">
            <img src="skel02.gif" alt="skel02.gif" width="140"
height="100" />
            </font>
        </td>
    </tr>
    <tr>
        <td width="30%">
            <font face="Arial, sans-serif">
            <img src="skel03.gif" alt="skel03.gif" width="140"
height="100" />
            </font></td>
        <td width="40%" bgcolor="#CC0000"> <font face="Arial, sans-serif">
    More than a few innocents have been cast in chains for eons.
```

```
They just aren't the same anymore.</font></td>
    <th width="30%" bgcolor="#FF6600"><b> <font face="Arial,
sans-serif">
      <a href="galley.gif">The Galley</a></font></b></th>
    </tr>
    <tr>
    <th width="30%" bgcolor="#FF6600"> <b><font face="Arial,
sans-serif">
      <a href="dungeon.gif">The Dungeon</a> </font> </b></th>
    <td width="40%" bgcolor="#CC0000"> <font face="Arial, sans-serif">
      Better listen to the tour guides, or you'll get lost!
</font> </td>
        <td width="30%">
        <font face="Arial, sans-serif">
        <img src="skel04.gif" alt="skel04.gif" width="140"
height="100" />
        </font></td>
    </tr>
  </table>
</div>
<hr />
<p><font face="Arial, sans-serif"> The
  <font color="#cc0000">Halloween House of Terror</font>
  is open from October 20 to November 1st, with a gala celebration
  on Halloween night. Our hours are: </font></p>
<ul>
  <li>
    <font face="Arial, sans-serif">
    Mon-Fri 5PM-midnight</font>
  </li>
  <li>
    <font face="Arial, sans-serif">
    Sat &amp; Sun 5PM-3AM</font>
  </li>
  <li>
    <font face="Arial, sans-serif">
    Halloween Night (31-Oct): 3PM-???</font></li>
</ul>
<p align="center">
<font face="Arial, sans-serif"> The
  <font color="#cc0000">Halloween House of Terror</font>
  is located at:<br />
  The Old Waterfall Shopping Center<br />
  1020 Mirabella Ave<br />
  Springfield, CA 94532</font></p>
</body>
</html>
```

Figure 18.8 shows the result of the preceding code as it's displayed in Internet Explorer.

FIGURE **18.8**

*An example of HTML
4.0 Transitional code
in Internet Explorer.*

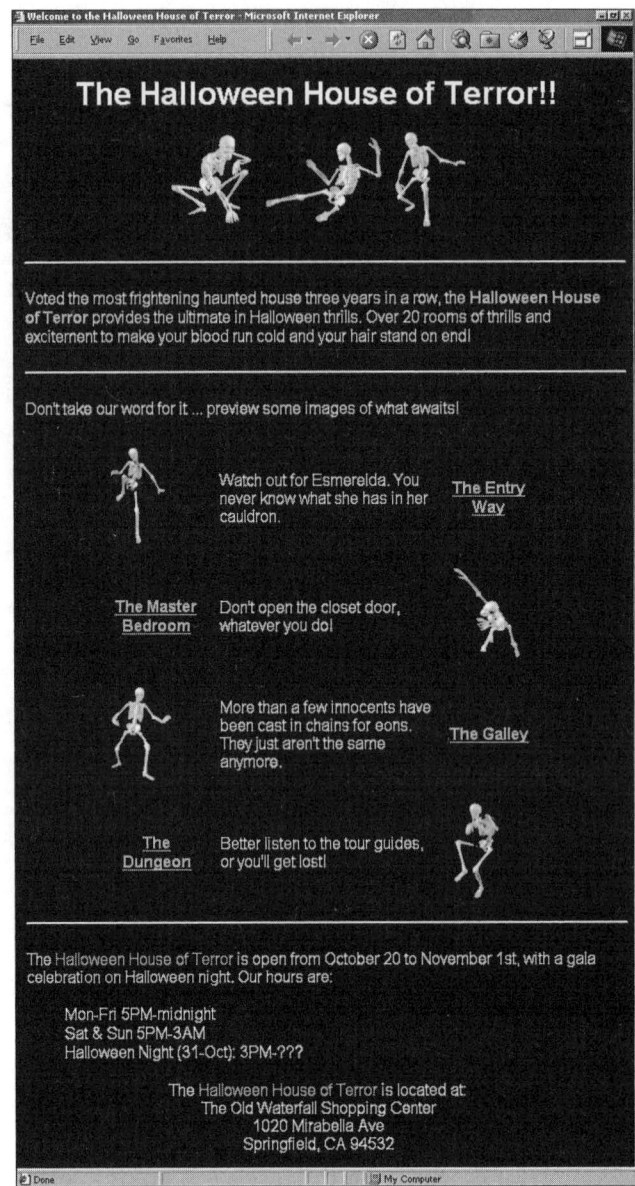

HTML 4.01 and XHTML 1.0 Framesets

If you prefer to use a frameset to navigate through your site, the most logical choice is
the HTML 4.0 or XHTML 1.0 Frameset specification. Here, you can use all the tags and

attributes that are "legal" in the HTML 4.0 or XHTML 1.0 Transitional specification. In addition, you can use all tags and attributes that pertain to framesets and frames.

The key to good frameset design is to create as few frames as possible while making the navigation system easy to understand. The hard decision, however, is which resolution to use for your frameset, because the browser is divided into multiple sections. The more frames you create in the frameset, the smaller each page will be in each frame.

In Figure 18.9, the Halloween House of Terror Web page has been converted to a frameset. The main frame displays exactly the same page you saw in Figure 18.8, but the links in the left frame take the visitor to the pictures and descriptions of each room in the haunted house. When you add the links in the left frame, the visitor no longer has to use his browse button to take a small virtual tour through the haunted house. This simplifies the navigation greatly.

The code for the frameset divides the browser window into two frames: left and right. The `navigation.html` page loads into the left frame, and the main page (`main.html`) loads into the right frame. The code for the frameset looks like the following:

INPUT

```
<!DOCTYPE html PUBLIC "-//W3C//DTD XHTML 1.0 Frameset//EN"
"http://www.w3.org/TR/xhtml1/DTD/frameset.dtd">
<html>
<head>
<title>Halloween House of Terror Frameset</title>
</head>
<frameset cols="170,*">
  <frame name="left" src="navigation.html" />
  <frame name="right" src="main.html" />
  <noframes>
  <body>
  <p> ... insert noframes content here ... </p>
  </body>
  </noframes>
</frameset>
</html>
```

The code for the left frame in the frameset (`navigation.html`) displays each page in the right frame when the user selects one of the image links (as defined by the `<target="right">` tag). Each image link displays alternate text when the user hovers his mouse over the button, or when images are turned off in the browser. The code for the left frame looks like the following:

```
<!DOCTYPE html PUBLIC "-//W3C//DTD XHTML 1.0 Transitional//EN"
"http://www.w3.org/TR/xhtml1/DTD/transitional.dtd">
<html>
<head>
<title>The Halloween House of Terror</title>
```

18

```
<base target="right" />
</head>
<body bgcolor="#ff9933" text="#000000">
<p><font face="Arial">The Halloween<br />
House of<br />
Terror</font></p>
<p><a href="main.html" target="right">
   <img src="button01.gif" alt="Home" width="125" height="50" />
   </a></p>
<p><a href="entry.html" target="right">
   <img src="button02.gif" alt="The Entry Way" width="125" height="50" />
   </a></p>
<p><a href="bedroom.html" target="right">
   <img src="button03.gif" alt="The Master Bedroom" width="125" height="50" />
   </a></p>
<p><a href="galley.html" target="right">
   <img src="button04.gif" alt="The Galley" width="125" height="50" />
   </a></p>
<p><a href="dungeon.html" target="right">
   <img src="button05.gif" alt="The Dungeon" width="125" height="50" />
   </a></p>
<p><a href="location.html" target="right">
   <img src="button06.gif" alt="Hours and Location" width="125" height="50" />
   </a></p>
</body>
</html>
```

OUTPUT

FIGURE 18.9

*An example of HTML
4.0 Frameset code in
Internet Explorer.*

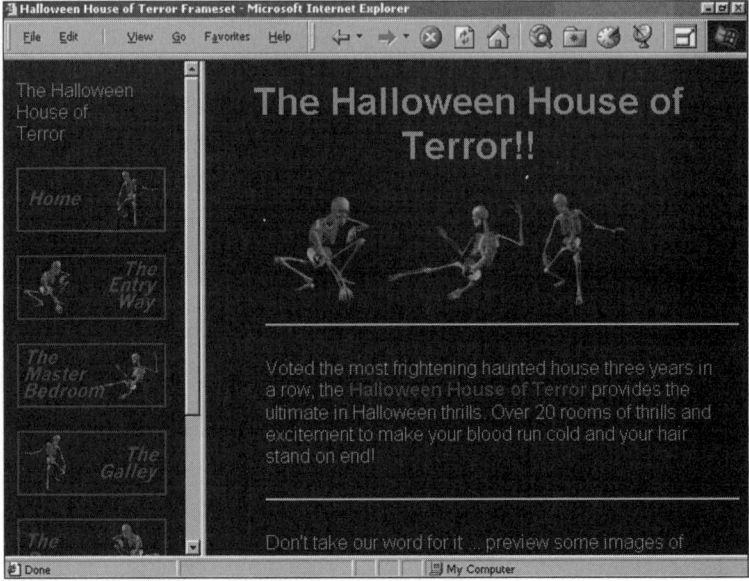

HTML 4.01 and XHTML 1.0 Strict

The Transitional and Frameset specifications enable you to provide support for browsers older than either Netscape Navigator 4.0 or Microsoft Internet Explorer 4.0. The HTML 4.0 or XHTML 1.0 Strict specification, however, allows for a wider range of display options through the use of Cascading Style Sheets (CSS), as well as other Web technologies that you've learned in this book. With the introduction of new types of Web browsing hardware in the near future, there will be an increasing need to use the Strict specification. One drawback to using HTML 4.0 or XHTML 1.0 Strict at the present time, however, is that not all current Web browsers are compatible with those standards.

To comply with the HTML 4.0 or XHTML 1.0 Strict specification, you must avoid using any HTML tags and attributes that are marked as *deprecated*. Instead, use Cascading Style Sheets or other methods, such as Dynamic HTML, to implement page presentation.

If you're willing to shut out a portion of your current audience, there are several advantages to using the HTML 4.0 or XHTML 1.0 Strict specification. As you learned on Day 12, CSS technology gives you greater control over page layout and appearance. In many ways, you can lay out your pages as if you were using a page layout or word processing program. Another advantage is that Cascading Style Sheets level 2, or CSS2 for short, incorporates additional features for nonvisual browsers. This means that you can design pages for people who are visually impaired or have other special needs.

18

The following code example illustrates how you can implement the page shown in Figure 18.8 into the XHTML 1.0 Strict specification. In this example, the Halloween House of Terror uses embedded style sheet properties and values to format the text and images on the page. The colors for the text, links, and table cells are defined in the style section at the beginning of the page. Margins are added to the top, bottom, left, and right of the page. Also, rather than using standard bullets, the bulleted list at the bottom of the page displays image bullets as defined by the style sheet.

INPUT

```
<!DOCTYPE html PUBLIC "-//W3C//DTD XHTML 1.0 Strict//EN"
"http://www.w3.org/TR/xhtml1/DTD/strict.dtd">
<html>
<head>
<title>Welcome to the Halloween House of Terror</title>
<style type="text/css">
<!--
body { background-color: #ff9933;
          color: #000000;
          font-family: Arial, sans-serif;
          font-size: 12pt;
          margin-left: 20px;
          margin-right: 20px;
          margin-top: 10px;
```

```
                margin-bottom: 10px }
a:link{ color: #990000 }
a:visited{ color: #CC00CC }
a:active{ color: #CC0000 }
h1{ font-family: Arial, sans-serif;
        font-size: 24pt }
table { text-align: center }
th { background-color: #ff6600;
     color: #000000;
     font-family: Arial, sans-serif;
     font-size: 12pt;
     font-weight: bold }
td { color: #000000;
     font-family: Arial, sans-serif;
     font-size: 12pt }
td.red { background-color: #cc0000 }
ul { list-style-image: url("bullet.gif") }
.bloodred { color:#CC0000 }
.bloodredbold { color: #CC0000; font-weight: bold }
.center { text-align: center }
-->
</style>
</head>
<body>
<h1 class="center">The Halloween House of Terror!!</h1>
<div class="center">
<dl>
<dd>
<img src="skel05.gif" alt="skel05.gif" width="140" height="100" />
<img src="skel07.gif" alt="skel07.gif" width="140" height="100" />
<img src="skel06.gif" alt="skel06.gif" width="140" height="100" />
</dd>
</dl>
</div>
<hr />
<p>Voted the most frightening haunted house three years in a row,
the <span class="bloodredbold">Halloween House of Terror</span>
provides the ultimate in Halloween thrills. Over 20 rooms of
thrills and excitement to make your blood run cold and your hair
stand on end!</p>
<hr />
<p>Don't take our word for it ... preview some images of what
awaits!</p>
<table border="0" summary="House of Terror" width="75%" cellspacing="5"
cellpadding="5">
<tr>
<td>
<img src="skel01.gif" alt="skel01.gif width="140" height="100" />
</td>
<td class="red">Watch out for Esmerelda. You never
```

```
know what she has in her cauldron.</td>
<th><a href="code/entry.gif">The Entry Way</a></th>
</tr>
<tr>
<th><a href="code/bedroom.gif">The Master Bedroom</a></th>
<td class="red">Don't open the closet door, whatever
you do!</td>
    <td>
    <img src="skel02.gif" alt="skel02.gif" width="140" height="100"
/></td>
</tr>
<tr>
    <td><img src="skel03.gif" alt="skel03.gif" width="140" height="100"
/></td>
<td class="red">More than a few innocents have been
cast in chains for eons. They just aren't the same anymore.</td>
<th><a href="code/galley.gif">The Galley</a></th>
</tr>
<tr>
<th><a href="code/dungeon.gif">The Dungeon</a></th>
<td class="red">Better listen to the tour guides, or
you'll get lost!</td>
    <td><img src="skel04.gif" alt="skel04.gif" width="140"
height="100" /></td>
</tr>
</table>
<hr />
<p>The <span class="bloodred">Halloween House of Terror</span> is
open from October 20 to November 1st, with a gala celebration on
Halloween night. Our hours are:</p>
<ul>
<li>Mon-Fri 5PM-midnight</li>
<li>Sat &amp; Sun 5PM-3AM</li>
<li>Halloween Night (31-Oct): 3PM-???</li>
</ul>
<p class="center">The <span class="bloodred">Halloween House of
Terror</span> is located at:<br />
The Old Waterfall Shopping Center<br />
1020 Mirabella Ave<br />
Springfield, CA 94532</p>
</body>
</html>
```

OUTPUT   Figure 18.10 shows the result of the preceding code in Internet Explorer.

18

FIGURE **18.10**

An example of HTML 4.0 Strict code in Internet Explorer.

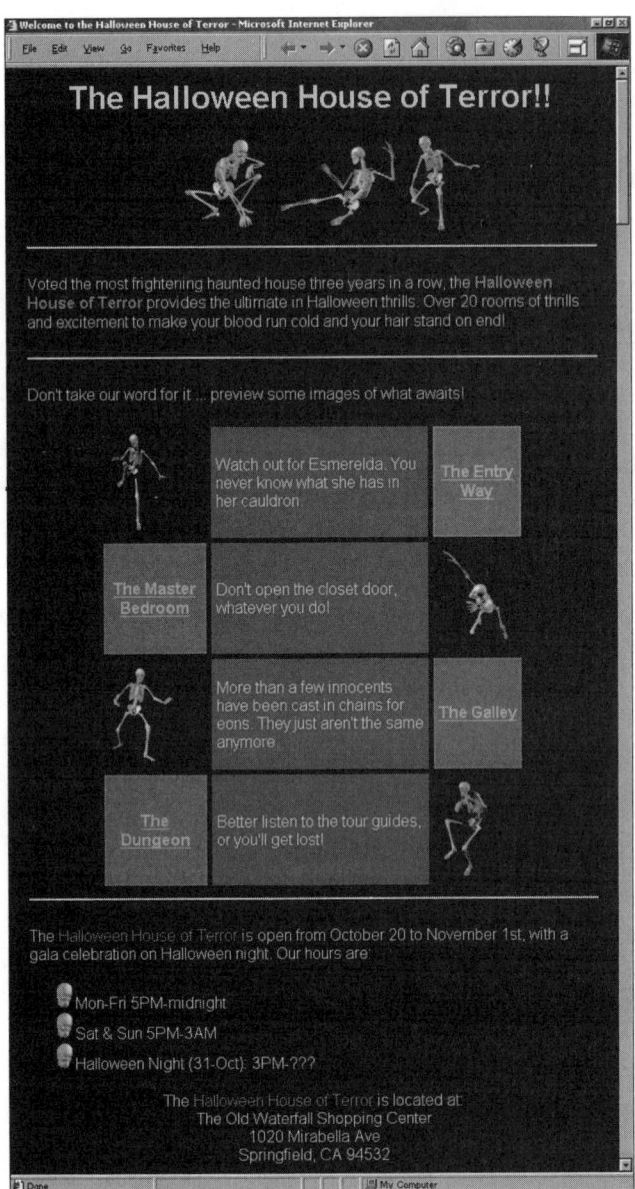

Summary

HTML 4.0 and XHTML 1.0 accommodate the needs of many visitors by providing three different approaches to Web site design. Hopefully, you now realize that the needs of your visitors also can affect the approach you use in your Web site design. The key is to anticipate those needs and try to address them as broadly as possible. Not every site has to be filled with multimedia that implements the latest and greatest Web technologies. On the other hand, certain topics almost demand higher levels of page design. Listen to the needs of your visitors when you design your pages, and you'll keep them coming back.

Workshop

As if you haven't had enough already, here's a refresher course. As always, there are questions, quizzes, and exercises that will help you remember some of the most important points in this chapter.

Q&A

Q Feedback from visitors to my site varies a lot. Some want my pages to use less multimedia, while others want more. Is there an easy way to satisfy both of them?

A You've already learned that you can provide links to external multimedia files. This is the best approach for visitors who want less multimedia, because they won't see it unless they click the link.

You also can use advanced scripting methods (such as JavaScript or VBScript) to detect which browsers your visitors are using. After the browser type has been determined, the script can automatically direct visitors to the pages that are compatible with that browser. This requires additional design time on your part. Not only do you have to write script to accomplish this, but you also might need to create several different versions of your Web pages. If you don't want to detect browser types automatically, you can use links on your home page to direct the visitors to the types of pages they want to view. Simply use the home page as a gateway to your "plain and simple site" or your "multimedia-intensive site" and let the visitor decide.

Q I use a lot of external files on my Web site, and they can be downloaded from several different pages. Wouldn't it be more efficient to include a link to the correct readers or viewers on the pages where the external files appear?

A Although it's much easier for the visitor to download an external file and the appropriate reader or helper application from the same page, it might be more difficult for you to maintain your pages when the URLs for the helper applications change. A good compromise is to include a Download page on your Web site with links to all helper applications that the visitor will need. After the visitor downloads the external file, she can then navigate to your Download page to get the helper application she needs to view that file.

18

Quiz

1. How do real-world user needs vary?

2. What are some important things to include on your site to help those who are new to computers or the Internet?

3. How does the HTML 4.0 or XHTML 1.0 Transitional specification help you accommodate the needs of more visitors?

4. True or false: It's better to have a lot of frames in a frameset because you can keep more information in the browser window at the same time.

5. What are the advantages and disadvantages of using HTML 4.0 or XHTML 1.0 Strict to fulfill the needs of your visitors?

Quiz Answers

1. Different users will have different levels of experience. Browser preferences will vary. Some want to see a lot of multimedia, while others prefer none at all. Some prefer images and multimedia that are interactive, while others prefer simpler pictures that demonstrate a process or technique on how to do something. Other preferences are more specific to the interests of the visitors.

2. Include pages on your site that help the visitor find the information she's looking for. Also include pages that help them find their way around the site.

3. HTML 4.0 or XHTML 1.0 Transitional is designed to be backward-compatible with older browsers. It enables you to use tags and attributes that are deprecated in the Strict specification.

4. False. Too many frames can be confusing for new users, and they may be too small to be useful when they're viewed at lower resolutions.

5. The disadvantage to using HTML 4.0 or XHTML 1.0 Strict is that most visitors won't have browsers that are fully compliant. The advantage to using HTML 4.0 and XHTML 1.0 Strict is that they provide support for nonvisual browsers and other special presentational capabilities.

Exercises

1. Design a simple navigation system for a Web site and describe it in a manner that makes sense to you. Then, ask others to review it and verify that your explanations are clear to them.

2. Make a list of the topics that you want to discuss on your Web site. Go through the list a second time and see if you can anticipate the types of people who will be interested in those topics. Finally, review the list a third time and list the special needs that you might need to consider for each user group.

18

PART 7

Going Live on the Web

DAY 19

Putting Your Site Online

For the past six days, you've been creating and testing your Web pages on your local machine with your own browser. You may not even have a network connection to your machine. At this point, you've put together a Web site with a well-organized structure and a reasonable number of meaningful images (each with its own carefully chosen alt text). You've also written your text with wit and care, adhered to the HTML standard, and tested the site extensively on your own system.

Now, on the last day of the week, you're finally ready to publish your site so other people on the Web can see it and link their pages to yours. Today and tomorrow, you'll learn everything you need to get started publishing the work you've done, tell people it's there, and keep it fine-tuned after it's online.

Today you'll learn about the following topics:

- What a Web server does and why you need one
- Where you can find a Web server to host your site
- How to install your Web site
- How to find out your URL

- How to add interactive features to your site
- How to test and troubleshoot your Web pages

What Does a Web Server Do?

To publish Web pages, you'll need a *Web server*. The server waits for requests from browsers and sends the requested files back. Web servers and Web browsers communicate by using the *Hypertext Transfer Protocol (HTTP)*, a special language created specifically for the request and transfer of hypertext documents over the Web. Because of this use, Web servers often are called *HTTPD servers*.

 Note

> The *D* in *HTTPD* stands for *daemon*, which is a UNIX term for a program that sits in the background and waits for requests. When this program receives a request, it wakes up, processes the request, and then goes back to sleep.
> You don't have to work in UNIX for a program to act like a daemon, so Web servers on any platform are still called HTTPDs. Most of the time, I call them Web servers.

Other Things Web Servers Do

Although the Web server's primary purpose is to answer requests from browsers, it's responsible for several other tasks. You'll learn about some of them in the following sections.

File and Media Type Determination

On Day 13, "Multimedia: Adding Sounds, Video, and More," you learned about content-types and how browsers and servers use file extensions to determine file types. Servers are responsible for telling the browsers what kinds of content the files contain. You can configure a Web server to send different kinds of media or to handle new and different files and extensions. In "Questions to Ask Your Webmaster" later today, you'll learn about some of the important questions you should ask your Web presence provider or Webmaster before you publish your pages.

File Management

The Web server also is responsible for very rudimentary file management—mostly in determining where to find a file and keeping track of where it's gone. If a browser requests a file that doesn't exist, the Web server sends back the page with the "404: File Not Found" message. You can also configure servers to create aliases for files (the same files, but accessed with different names). These aliases redirect files to different locations, automatically pointing the browser to a new URL for files that have moved, and return a default file or a directory listing if a browser requests a URL ending with a directory name.

Finally, servers keep log files for information on how many times each file on the site has been accessed, including the site that accessed it, the date, and in some servers, the type of browser and the URL of the page from which they came.

CGI Scripts, Programs, and Forms Processing

One of the more interesting (and complex) tasks that a server can perform is to run external programs on the server based on the input that readers provide from their browsers. These special programs are called *CGI scripts* and are used to create interactive forms.

CGI scripts can also be used for all sorts of other tasks on the server. They can be used to publish information stored in a database, or to provide a personalized experience for the users of your site.

It's important to note that CGI scripts are just one way to write programs that run through a Web server. There are several popular technologies that enable you to embed program code in your HTML documents that is interpreted by the server and run before the page is sent to the browser. Java Server Pages and Active Server Pages are two popular technologies that work this way. Some servers provide support for Java servlets, which are Java programs that are used in the same way as CGI scripts.

Server-Side File Processing

Some servers can process files before they send them along to the browsers. On a simple level, there are server-side includes, which can insert a date or a chunk of boilerplate text into each page, or run a program. Many of the access counters you see on Web pages are run in this way. Also, you can use server-side processing in much more sophisticated ways to modify files on-the-fly for different browsers or to execute small bits of scripting code.

Authentication and Security

Some Web sites require you to register for their services and log in using a name and password every time you visit. This process, called *authentication* or *password protection*, is now common on most Web servers. By using authentication, you can set up users and passwords, and you can restrict access to certain files and directories. You can also restrict access to files or to an entire site based on site names or IP addresses. For example, you can prevent anyone outside your company from viewing files that are intended for internal use.

19

NEW TERM *Authentication*, or *password protection*, enables you to protect files or directories on your Web server by requiring readers to enter usernames and passwords before the files can be viewed.

For security, some servers now provide a mechanism for secure connections and transactions by using Netscape's *SSL (Secure Socket Layer)* protocol. SSL provides authentication of the server (proving that the server is who it says it is) and an encrypted connection between the browser and the server so that sensitive information between the two is kept secret.

Locating a Web Server

Before you can put your site on the Web, you'll need to find a Web server. How easy this is depends on how you get your access to the Internet.

Using a Web Server Provided by Your School or Work

If you get your Internet connection through school or work, that organization most likely will allow you to publish Web pages on its own Web server. Given that these organizations usually have fast connections to the Internet and people to administer the site for you, this situation is ideal.

You'll have to ask your system administrator, computer consultant, Webmaster, or network provider whether a Web server is available and, if so, what the procedures are for putting up your pages. You'll learn more about what to ask later today.

Using a Commercial Internet or Web Service

You may pay for your Internet access through an Internet service provider (ISP), an Internet presence provider (IPP), or a commercial online service. Many of these services allow you to publish your Web pages, although it may cost you extra. There might be restrictions on the kinds of pages you can publish, or whether you can run CGI scripts or other server-side processing. Ask your provider's help line or participate in online groups or conferences on Internet services to see how others have set up Web publishing.

In the last few years, many organizations have popped up that provide nothing but Web publishing services. These services, most commonly known as *Web presence providers*, usually provide some method for transferring your files to their sites (usually FTP), as well as the disk space and the network connections for access to your files. They also have professional site administrators onsite to make sure the servers are running well at all times.

Generally, you're charged a flat monthly rate, with an additional cost if you use a large amount of disk space or have especially popular pages that consume a lot of network bandwidth. Some services even allow CGI scripts for form processing and server-side imagemaps and will provide consulting to help you set them up. Most will even set up their server with your own hostname so that it looks as though you've got your own server running on the Web. These features can make using commercial Web hosting providers an especially attractive option.

To set up a virtual domain account, you'll need to register your domain name with an authorized registrar. The initial cost to register and acquire your domain name and IP address can be as low as $16 for two years. Thereafter, an annual fee keeps your domain name active. For all intents and purposes, a virtual domain account appears to the outside world as if you're running a Web site on your own server. Your site will have an address such as `http://www.mygreatsite.com/`.

Many ISPs and Web presence providers assist you in registering your domain name. You can register your domain directly with an authorized registrar such as Network Solutions (`http://www.networksolutions.com/`), Register.com, or Joker.com. Most of these services also offer *domain parking*, a service that allows you to host your domain with them temporarily until you choose a hosting provider or set up your own server. The prices vary, so you should shop around before registering your domain.

Note

> The Ultimate Web Host List at `http://webhostlist.internetlist.com/` is a good resource for finding and evaluating Web hosting services. For more information, see Appendix A.

19

Note that unlike your main Internet service provider, which should be located nearby to minimize your phone bills, services that publish Web pages can be located anywhere on the Internet. Therefore, you can shop for the lowest price and best service without having to worry about geographical location.

Setting Up Your Own Server

If you're really courageous and want the ultimate in Web publishing, running your own Web site is the way to go. You can publish as much as you want and include any kind of content you want. You'll also be able to use forms, CGI scripts, plug-ins, advanced Web technologies such as channels and netcasting, imagemaps, and many other special options. Other Web publishing services might not let you use these kinds of features.

However, running server definitely isn't for everyone. The cost and maintenance time can be daunting, and you need a level of technical expertise that the average user might not possess.

Organizing Your HTML Files for Installation

Once you have access to a Web server, you can publish the Web site you've labored so hard to create. Before you actually move it into place on your server, however, it's important to organize your files. Also, you should have a good idea of what goes where to avoid lost files and broken links.

Questions to Ask Your Webmaster

The *Webmaster* is the person who runs your Web server. This person also may be your system administrator, help desk administrator, or network administrator. Before you can publish your site, you should get several facts from the Webmaster about how the server is set up. The following list of questions will help you later in this book when you're ready to figure out what you can and cannot do with your server:

- **Where on the server will I put my files?** In many cases, your Webmaster can create a special directory for you. Know where that directory is and how to gain access to it.

  In some other cases, particularly on UNIX machines, you might be able to just create a special directory in your home directory and store your files there. If that's the case, your Webmaster will tell you the name of the directory.

- **What's the URL of my top-level directory?** This URL may be different from the actual pathname to your files.

- **What's the name of the system's default index file?** This file is loaded by default when a URL ends with a directory name. Usually it's index.html or index.htm, but sometimes it may be default.html, Homepage.html, and so on.

- **Can I run CGI or other types of scripts?** Depending on your server, the answer to this question may be a flat-out "No," or you may be limited to certain programs and capabilities.

- **Do you support special plug-ins or file types?** If your site is designed to handle special types of multimedia (RealAudio, Shockwave or Shockwave Flash, or similar plug-ins or Web enhancements), your Webmaster may need to configure the server to accommodate those file types. Make sure the server can handle special types of multimedia before you create them.

- **Do you support FrontPage Server Extensions?** Microsoft FrontPage, a very popular Web authoring tool for the Windows and Macintosh platforms, enables you to develop advanced Web pages that incorporate forms and other advanced features. To use many of these advanced features, however, the Web server must have FrontPage Server Extensions installed on it. If you're interested in using FrontPage to design advanced pages, be sure to ask your ISP whether they support the Server Extensions.

- **Are there limitations on what or how much I can put up?** Some servers restrict pages to specific content (for example, only work-related pages) or allow you only a few pages on the system. They might prevent more than a certain number of people from accessing your pages at once, or they may have other restrictions on what sorts of publishing you can do. Make sure that you understand the limitations of the server and can work within these limitations.

- **Is there a limit to the amount of bandwidth that my visitors can download?** This is somewhat related to the preceding question. Your provider might not place a limit on the number of pages you put on your site, but you might be charged extra if you exceed a certain amount of bandwidth per month. So, before you place 10MB worth of content on a Web site and burden your pages with dozens of images, sound files, and video clips, ask your Web provider whether you have a bandwidth limit. The bandwidth usually relates to the number of downloads (each time a page is accessed or a file is downloaded).

- **Do you provide any canned scripts that I can use for my Web pages?** If you aren't keen on writing your own scripts to add advanced features to your pages, ask your service provider if they provide any scripts that might be of assistance. For example, many ISPs provide a script for putting a page counter on your home page. Others might provide access to form processing scripts as well.

Keeping Your Files Organized with Directories

Probably the easiest way to organize your site is to include all the files in a single directory. If you have many extra files—images, for example—you can put them in a subdirectory to that main directory. Your goal is to contain all your files in a single place rather than scatter them around on your hard drive. After you've contained your files, you can set all the links in those files to be relative to that one directory. This makes it easier to move the directory around to different servers without breaking the links.

Having a Default Index File and Correct Filenames

Web servers usually have a default index file that's loaded when a URL ends with a directory name rather than a filename. One of the questions you should ask your

Webmaster is, "What's the name of this default file?" For most Web servers, this file is called `index.html` (`index.htm` for DOS). Your home page, or top-level index, for each site should have this name so that the server knows which page to send as the default page. Each subdirectory in turn should have a default file if it contains any HTML files. If you use this default filename, the URL to that page will be shorter because you don't have to include the actual filename. For example, your URL might be `http://www.myserver.com/www/` rather than `http://www.myserver.com/www/index.html`.

Also, each file should have an appropriate extension indicating its type so the server can map it to the appropriate file type. If you've been reading this book in sequential order, all your files should have this special extension already and you shouldn't have any problems. Table 19.1 lists the common file extensions that you should be using for your files and multimedia.

TABLE 19.1   Common File Types and Extensions

Format	Extension
HTML	.html, .htm
ASCII Text	.txt
PostScript	.ps
GIF	.gif
JPEG	.jpg, .jpeg
PNG	.png
Shockwave Flash	.swf
AU Audio	.au
WAV Audio	.wav
MPEG Audio	.mp2, .mp3
MPEG Video	.mpeg, .mpg
QuickTime Video	.mov
AVI Video	.avi
Portable Document Format	.pdf
RealAudio	.ra, .ram

If you're using special multimedia on your site that isn't part of this list, you might need to configure your server to handle that file type. You'll learn more about this issue later today.

Installing Your Files

Got everything organized? Then all that's left is to move everything into place on the server. Once the server can access your files, you're officially published on the Web. That's all there is to putting your pages online.

Where's the appropriate spot on the server, however? You should ask your Webmaster for this information. Also, you should find out how to get to that special spot on the server, whether it's simply copying files, using FTP to put them on the server, or using some other method.

Moving Files Between Systems

If you're using a Web server that has been set up by someone else, usually you'll have to move your Web files from your system to theirs using FTP, Zmodem transfer, or some other method. Although the HTML markup within your files is completely cross-platform, moving the actual files from one type of system to another sometimes has its drawbacks. In particular, be careful to do the following:

- **Transfer all files as binary**—Your FTP or file-upload program may give you an option to transfer files in binary or text mode (or may give you different options altogether). Always transfer everything—all your HTML files, images, and multi-media—in binary format. (You can transfer a text file in binary mode without any problems.)

  If you're working on a Macintosh, your transfer program may give you many options such as MacBinary, AppleDouble, or other strange names. Avoid all of them. The option you want is *flat binary* or *raw data*. If you transfer files in any other format, they may not work when they get to the other side.

- **Watch out for filename restrictions**—If you're moving your files to or from DOS systems, you'll have to watch out for the dreaded 8.3. This is the DOS rule that says filenames must be only eight characters long with a three-character extension. If your server is a PC and you've been writing your files on some other system, you may have to rename your files and the links to them to follow the correct file-naming conventions. (Moving files you've created on a PC to some other system usually isn't a problem.)

  Also, watch out if you're moving files from a Macintosh to other systems. Make sure that your filenames don't have spaces or other funny characters in them. Keep your filenames as short as possible, use only letters and numbers, and you'll be fine.

19

- **Watch out for upper- or lowercase sensitivity**—Some operating systems and file management programs show filenames in all lowercase (such as `myfile.html`). In reality, however, DOS-based filenames might be in all caps (such as `MYFILE.HTML`). If the code in your Web pages contains lowercase links to these files, as is usually the case, you'll get broken links when you transfer your Web pages to a server that uses case-sensitive URLs (such as UNIX servers). Double-check the case sensitivity in your files after you transfer them to your site.

- **Be aware of carriage returns and line feeds**—Different systems use different methods for ending a line. The Macintosh uses carriage returns, UNIX uses line feeds, and DOS uses both. When you move files from one system to another, most of the time the end-of-line characters will be converted appropriately, but sometimes they won't. The characters that aren't converted can cause your file to come out double-spaced or all on a single line when it's moved to another system.

  Most of the time, this failure to convert doesn't matter because browsers ignore spurious returns or line feeds in your HTML files. The existence or absence of either one isn't terribly important. However, it might be an issue in sections of text that you've marked up with `<pre>`; you may find that your well-formatted text that worked so well on one platform doesn't come out that way after it's been moved.

  If you do have end-of-line problems, you have two options. Many text editors enable you to save ASCII files in a format for another platform. If you know the platform to which you're moving, you can prepare your files for that platform before moving them. If you're moving to a UNIX system, small filters for converting line feeds called `dos2unix` and `unix2dos` may be available on the UNIX or DOS systems. And you can convert Macintosh files to UNIX-style files by using the following command line in UNIX:

  ```
  tr '\015' '\012' < oldfile.html > newfile.html
  ```

  In this example, `oldfile.html` is the original file with end-of-line problems, and `newfile.html` is the name of the new file.

Using FTP to Manage Files

In the preceding list of tips about moving files, I talked a little bit about FTP. If you already know how to transfer files using FTP, you can just skip this section.

Most Web surfers have used FTP whether they know it or not. When you download a file from a remote site to save on your computer, usually it's transferred via FTP rather than HTTP. When you're publishing files to a Web site, the way you use FTP is a bit different.

When you download files from a public site, generally you log in anonymously—the browser takes care of that for you. When you publish files using FTP, you log in with a specific username and password.

Note   You'll have to get the username and password you'll use to publish files using FTP from your Internet service provider or system administrator.

Another difference between file downloads using FTP and publishing files using FTP is that when you publish files, you'll probably use an interactive FTP session. In other words, rather than just connecting, uploading a file, and disconnecting in one step, you'll create an FTP session, upload or download files as needed, and then disconnect. You'll manually open and close the connection and perform the required tasks while that session is open.

One nice thing about FTP is that there are many clients available. First of all, all popular browsers can be used as FTP clients. That's why you can download files from FTP sites transparently using your browser. However, I recommend that you skip right past them and use something else to publish files. The FTP capabilities in Web browsers weren't designed for serious usage, and the interface used to publish files through a browser is quite cumbersome.

One option that's often available is publishing files through your HTML editing tool. Most popular HTML and text editors have built-in support for FTP. You should definitely check your tool of choice to see whether it enables you to transfer files using FTP from directly within the application. Some popular tools that provide FTP support include Macromedia DreamWeaver, Barebones BBEdit, Allaire HomeSite, and GNU Emacs. There are many others.

If your HTML editor doesn't support FTP, or if you're transferring images, multimedia files, or even bunches of HTML files at once, you'll probably want a dedicated FTP client. FTP is common enough that there are many, many excellent FTP clients available. A list of some popular choices follows:

19

- AbsoluteFTP (Windows)—http://www.vandyke.com/
- CuteFTP (Windows)—http://www.globalscape.com/
- WS_FTP (Windows)—http://www.ipswitch.com/
- FTP Explorer (Windows)—http://www.ftpx.com/
- Transmit (Mac OS)—http://www.panic.com/transmit/
- Interarchy (Mac OS)—http://www.interarchy.com/
- Fetch (Mac OS)—http://www.dartmouth.edu/pages/softdev/fetch.html

How the FTP client is used varies depending on which client you choose, but there are some commonalities among all of them that you can count on (more or less). You'll start out by configuring a site consisting of the hostname of the server where you'll publish the files, your username and password, and perhaps some other settings that you can leave alone if you're just getting started.

Caution

If you're sharing a computer with other people, you probably won't want to store the password for your account on the server in the FTP client. Make sure that the site is configured so that you have to enter your password every time you connect to the remote site.

Once you've set up your FTP client to connect to your server, you can connect to the site. Depending on your FTP client, you should be able to simply drag files onto the window that shows the list of files on your site to upload them, or drag them from the listing on the server to your local computer to download them.

Remote Management Tools

Most HTML editing tools enable you to manage and update the contents of your pages on a remote Web server.

Microsoft's FrontPage is a Web development tool aimed at small- to medium Web sites. FrontPage provides a WYSIWYG page editor and a site manager for managing document trees and links, as well as a variety of server extensions that can be used with a variety of servers, ranging from Windows-based Microsoft and Netscape servers to UNIX servers.

These extensions allow Webmasters to give their sites a variety of features, including interactive discussion groups and other interactive features. These extensions also enable you to use FrontPage to upload files on the server as you make changes to your site. FrontPage enables you to publish your Web site to a remote server, regardless of whether it has the FrontPage Server Extensions installed.

Other site development and management tools, such as Fusion from NetObjects (www.netobjects.com), Allaire HomeSite (www.allaire.com/), Adobe GoLive (www.adobe.com) and Macromedia Dreamweaver (www.macromedia.com), enable you to develop offline and then update the content on a remote server.

Adding Interactive Features

It used to be that if you wanted to add interactive functionality to your site, you had to set up your own server. Or at the very least, you needed a hosting account that supported not only static content but installation of your own CGI programs. Then you had to set up those programs, and perhaps even write them yourself. These days, interactive features such as message boards and search engines are offered freely by third-party sites. All you have to do is configure the third-party service using a Web form and include a link to it on your site.

These services add a lot of value to your site and are provided with almost no strings attached. Many of these sites display ads on their pages, but that's usually a small price to pay for the functionality they offer. Let's look at some example applications.

Search Engines

One of the most powerful tools you can offer on your site is a search engine. This reads all of the content on your site and stores it in a searchable database. Then your users can type in search terms and find the pages on your site that contain those terms. These days, there are many sites that will provide you with a search engine for free. You just register yourself on such a Web site, and then a program will examine all of your content and provide you with an interface for searching that content.

The great thing about these services is that, beyond filling out a few Web forms, there's nothing for you to set up. All you have to do is provide them with a bit of information about yourself and your site, and accept their license agreement.

One of the most popular free search services is provided by Atomz.com. It's worth noting that their service only indexes the first 500 pages of your site. If it's larger than 500 pages, you must use one of their for-pay options to index the remaining pages. Once the search engine has been set up for your site, you can manage it using the Atomz.com member center, shown in Figure 19.1.

Google, a popular search engine, also offers a free search service for Web sites. It has a signup process similar to the one offered by Atomz.com. You can find out more about it at http://services.google.com/cobrand/free_select.

Message Boards

There are also a number of free message board services available on the Web. These boards reside on the provider's site, and it's up to you to link to them, but they still enable you to tie in interactive features with the rest of your site.

19

FIGURE 19.1

The Atomz.com Member Center.

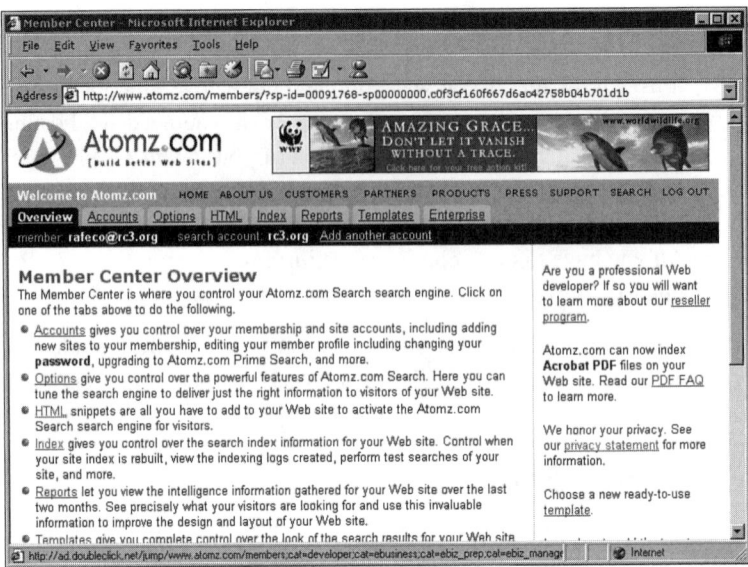

One of the more popular sites that offers free boards is EZBoard at www.ezboard.com. They provide a directory of message boards that are already set up, and you can create new boards freely. You can also customize the boards you create with your site's look and feel so that they look like the rest of your pages. Personalized EZBoard message boards appear in Figure 19.2.

FIGURE 19.2

Customized EZBoard message boards.

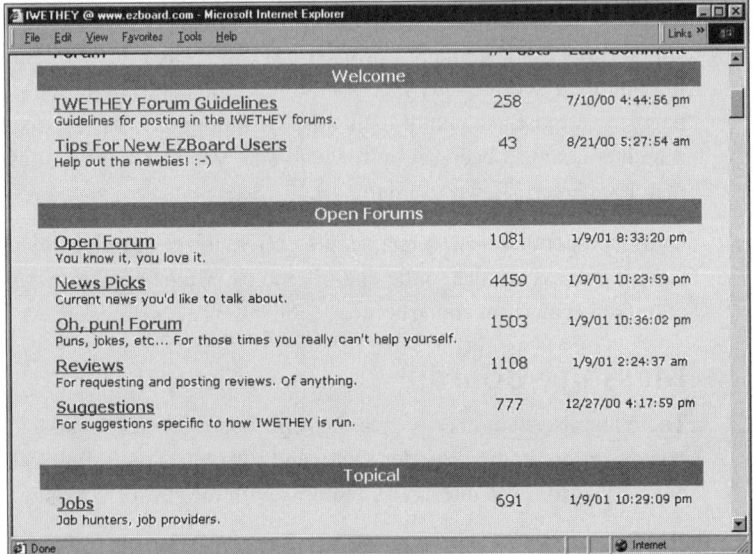

Phil Greenspun offers a free message board site at www.greenspun.com/bboard/. It's significantly less complicated than the EZBoard offering. You can create a single topic at Greenspun's site and then link to that site from one of your pages. If you want additional topics, you just have to go back and create them.

Beseen also offers free discussion boards at www.beseen.com/board/index.html. The Beseen software provides a topic-based bulletin board system much like EZBoard. These boards are customizable as well.

Test, Test, and Test Again

Now that your Web pages are available on the Internet, you should test them on as many platforms and browsers as you possibly can. Only then will you realize how important it is to design documents that look good on as many platforms and browsers as possible.

Try looking at your pages now. You might be surprised by the results. On Day 21, "Testing, Revising, and Maintaining Your Web Site," you'll learn how to fix some of the errors that you might find after your site is published on a remote server. We'll touch base on a few of the more common problems here.

Troubleshooting

What happens if you upload all your files to the server and try to display your home page in your browser, and something goes wrong? Here's the first place to look.

I Can't Access the Server

If your browser can't even get to your server, this probably isn't a problem you can fix. Make sure that you have the right server name and that it's a complete hostname (usually ending in .com, .edu, .net, or some other common suffix). Make sure that you haven't mistyped your URL and that you're using the right protocol. If your Webmaster told you that your URL included a port number, make sure you're including that port number in the URL after the hostname.

Also make sure that your network connection is working. Can you get to other Web servers? Can you get to the top-level home page for the site itself?

If none of these ideas solve the problem, perhaps your server is down or not responding. Call your Webmaster to find out whether he or she can help.

19

I Can't Access Files

What if all your files are showing up as "Not Found" or "Forbidden"? First, check your URL. If you're using a URL with a directory name at the end, try using an actual file-name at the end. Double-check the path to your files; remember that the path in the URL might be different from the path on the actual disk. Also, keep case sensitivity in mind. If your file is MyFile.html, make sure you're not trying myfile.html or Myfile.html.

If the URL appears to be correct, check the file permissions. On UNIX systems, all your directories should be world-executable and all your files should be world-readable. You can ensure that all the permissions are correct by using the following commands:

```
chmod 755 filename
chmod 755 directoryname
```

I Can't Access Images

You can get to your HTML files just fine, but all your images are coming up as icons or broken icons? First, make sure the references to your images are correct. If you've used relative pathnames, you shouldn't have this problem. If you've used full pathnames or file URLs, the references to your images may have been broken when you moved the files to the server. (I warned you…)

In some browsers, you get a pop-up menu when you select an image with the right mouse button (hold down the button on a Macintosh mouse). Choose the View This Image menu item to try to load the image directly. This will give you the URL of the image where the browser thinks it's supposed to be (which may not be where *you* think it's supposed to be). Often you can track down strange relative pathname problems this way.

If you're using Internet Explorer for Windows, you can also select the Properties option from the menu that appears when you right-click on an image to see its address. You can check the address that appears in the Properties dialog box to see whether it points to the appropriate location.

If the references all look good and the images work just fine on your local system, the only other place a problem could have occurred is in transferring the files from one system to another. As mentioned earlier today, you should make sure you transfer all your image files in binary format. If you're on a Macintosh, make sure you transfer the files as raw data or just data. Don't try to use MacBinary or AppleDouble format, or you'll get problems on the other side.

My Links Don't Work

If your HTML and image files are working just fine but your links don't work, you most likely used pathnames for those links that applied only to your local system. For example, you may have used absolute pathnames or file URLs to refer to the files to which you're linking. As mentioned for images, if you used relative pathnames and avoided file URLs, you shouldn't have a problem.

My Files Are Being Displayed Incorrectly

Suppose you've got an HTML file or a file in some multimedia format that's displayed correctly or links just fine on your local system. After you upload the file to the server and try to view it, the browser gives you gobbledygook. For example, it may display the HTML code itself instead of the HTML file, or it may display an image or multimedia file as text.

This problem can happen in two cases. The first is that you're not using the right file extensions for your files. Make sure that you're using one of the correct file extensions with the correct uppercase and lowercase.

The second case is that your server is misconfigured to handle your files. If you're working on a DOS system where all your HTML files have extensions of .htm, for example, your server may not understand that .htm is an HTML file. (Most modern servers do, but some older ones don't.) Or you might be using a newer form of media that your server doesn't understand. In either case, your server may be using some default content-type for your files (usually text/plain), which your browser probably can't handle.

To fix this problem, you'll have to configure your server to handle the file extensions for the correct media. If you're working with someone else's server, you'll have to contact your Webmaster and have him or her set up the server correctly. Your Webmaster will need two types of information: the file extensions you're using and the content-type you want him or her to return. If you don't know the content-type you want, refer to Appendix E, "MIME Types and File Extensions."

19

Summary

Today you published your site on the Web through the use of a Web server, either one installed by you or that of a network provider. You learned what a Web server does and how to get one, how to organize your files and install them on the server, and how to find your URL and use it to test your pages.

Workshop

From here on, everything you'll learn is icing on an already-substantial cake. You'll simply be adding more features (interactivity, forms) to your site. Congratulations! Have some ice cream.

Q&A

Q I've published my pages at an ISP I really like. The URL is something like `http://www.thebestisp.com/users/mypages/`. Instead of this URL, I'd like to have my own hostname—something like `http://www.mypages.com/`. How can I do this?

A You have two choices. The easiest way is to ask your ISP if you're allowed to have your own domain name. Many ISPs have a method for setting up your domain so that you can still use their services and work with them—it's only your URL that changes. Note that having your own hostname may cost more money, but it's the way to go if you really must have that URL. Many Web hosting services have plans starting as low as $5 a month for this type of service, and it currently costs as little as $16 to register your domain for two years.

The other option is to set up your own server with your own domain name. This option could be significantly more expensive than working with an ISP, and it requires at least some background in basic network administration. You'll learn all about this process on Day 20, "Letting People Know It's There."

Q I created all my image files on a Macintosh, uploaded them to my UNIX server by using the Fetch FTP program, tested it all, and it works fine. Now, however, I'm getting email from people saying that none of my images are working. What's going on here?

A Usually, when you upload files using Fetch, you can choose from a pull-down menu where the default is MacBinary. Make sure you change that to Raw Data.

MacBinary files work well when they're viewed on a Macintosh. If you're using a Macintosh to test your site, they'll work fine; however, they won't work on any other system. To ensure that your images work across platforms, upload them as raw data.

Q I created my files on a DOS system using the `.htm` extension, just like you told me to earlier in the book. Now I've published my pages on a UNIX system provided by my employer. The problem now is that when I try to get to my pages on my browser, I get the HTML code—not the formatted result! It all worked on my system at home. What went wrong?

A Some older servers will have this problem. Most likely, your server hasn't been set up to recognize that files with an .htm extension are actually HTML files, so it sends them as the default content-type (text/plain) instead. Then, when your browser reads one of your files from a server, it reads that content-type and assumes that you have a text file. So your server is messing up everything.

You can fix this problem in several ways. By far, the best way is to tell your Webmaster to change the server configuration so that .htm files are sent as HTML. Usually, this is a very simple step that will magically cause all your files to work properly from then on.

If you can't find your Webmaster, or for some strange reason he or she won't make this change, your only other option is to change all your filenames after you upload them to the UNIX system. Note that you'll have to change all the links within those files as well. (Finding a way to convince your Webmaster to fix this problem is a *much* better solution.)

Quiz

1. What's the basic function of a Web server?

2. How can you obtain an Internet connection?

3. What are default index files, and what's the advantage of using them in all directories?

4. What should you be aware of when uploading your files to your Internet site?

5. What are some things that you should check immediately after you upload your Web pages?

Quiz Answers

1. A Web server is a program that sits on a machine on the Internet (or an intranet). It determines where to find files on a Web site and keeps track of where those files are going.

2. You can obtain an Internet connection through school, work, or commercial Internet or Web services, or you can set up your own Web server.

3. The default index file is loaded when a URL ends with a directory name rather than a filename. Typical examples of default index files are index.html, index.htm, and default.htm. If you use default filenames, you can use a URL such as http://www.mysite.com/ rather than http://www.mysite.com/index.html to get to the home page in the directory.

19

4. Transfer all your files in binary format. Watch out for filename restrictions, upper- and lowercase sensitivity, and carriage returns and line feeds.

5. Make sure that your browser can reach your Web pages on the server, that you can access the files on your Web site, and that your links and images work as expected. After you've determined that everything appears the way you think it should, have your friends and family test your pages in other browsers.

Exercises

1. Start shopping around and consider where you want to store your Web site. Call two or more places to determine what benefits you'll get if you locate your Web pages on their servers.

2. Upload and test a practice page to learn the process, even if it's just a blank page that you'll add content to later. You might work out a few kinks this way before you actually upload all your hard work on the Web.

DAY 20

Letting People Know It's There

The catchphrase "If you build it, they will come" from the movie *Field of Dreams* notwithstanding, people won't simply visit your site of their own accord after you've put it online. In fact, with millions of sites online already, some of them with thousands of documents, it's highly unlikely that anyone could ever stumble across your site by accident.

So, how do you entice people to come to your site? This chapter will show you some of the ways, including the following:

- Advertising your site
- Getting your site listed on the major Web directories
- Listing your site with the major Web indexes
- Using Usenet to announce your site
- Using business cards, letterheads, and brochures
- Locating more directories and related Web pages
- Using log files and counters to find out who's viewing your pages

Registering and Advertising Your Web Pages

To get people to visit your Web site, you need to advertise it in as many ways as possible. The higher your site's visibility, the greater the number of hits.

A *hit* is a visit to your Web site. Be aware that although your site may get, say, 50 hits in a day, that doesn't necessarily mean that it was visited by 50 different people. It's simply a record of the number of times a copy of your Web page has been downloaded. There are many ways to promote your site. You can list it on major Web directories and indexes, announce it in newsgroups, put the URL on your business cards, and so much more. The following sections will describe each approach.

World Wide Web Site Listings

When many people first start working with the World Wide Web, they find it hard to understand that there are other people out there on numerous other Web sites who are just *itching* to hyperlink to other Web pages. And they find it even *harder* to understand that, for the most part, it doesn't cost a cent.

There's a simple reason why so many of these people are apparently philanthropic. When the Web was young and fresh, the best way for somebody to promote his site was to ask other Web developers to list it on their pages. In return for this favor, he would list their sites on his page as well. This process has been refined somewhat over time, but many sites still will be happy to include a link to your site. In fact, don't be surprised if you occasionally receive email from someone asking to be included in your list of sites.

This cooperative nature is a strikingly unique feature of the Web. Rather than competing for visitors with other similar sites, most Web pages actually include lists of sites on the same topic.

Unfortunately, there's a problem with just exchanging hyperlinks with other sites. As has always been the case, people need to be able to locate a single site as a starting point. To this end, some sort of global Internet directory is needed. Currently, no single site on the Web can be regarded as *the* Internet directory, but a few major directories and libraries come very close.

Yahoo!

By far, the best-known directory of Web sites is the Yahoo! site at `www.yahoo.com/` (see Figure 20.1), created by David Filo and Jerry Yang. This site started in April 1994 as a small, private list of David's and Jerry's favorite Web sites. Since then, it has become a highly regarded catalog and index of Web sites and is one of the most successful Internet companies out there.

FIGURE 20.1

The Yahoo! site.

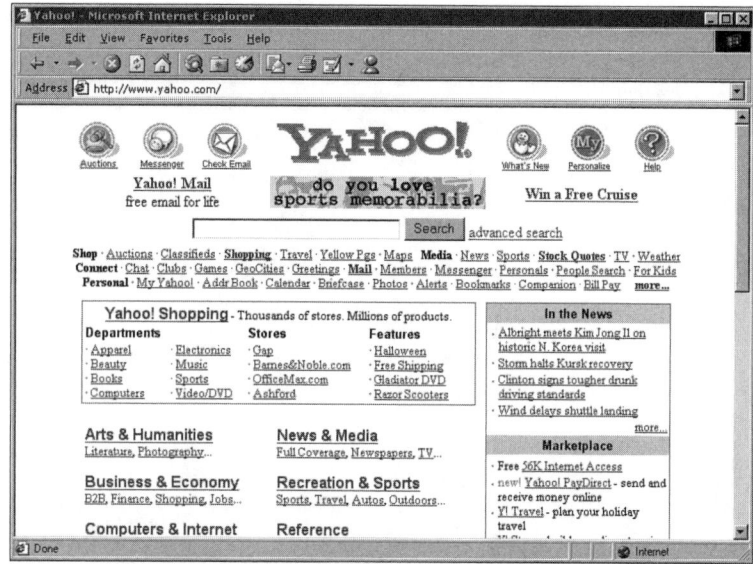

Yahoo! uses an elegant multilevel catalog to organize all the sites it references. To view the contents of any level of the catalog, first you select the hyperlink for the major category that most closely represents the information you're interested in. Then follow the chain of associated pages to a list of related Web sites, like the one shown in Figure 20.2. The following is the full URL of this page:

```
http://dir.yahoo.com/Computers_and_Internet/Internet/World_Wide_Web/
Announcement_Services/
```

You definitely should take a look at the page shown in Figure 20.2. It contains a list of Announcement Services and related Web pages that can help you spread the word about your new Web site.

To add your site to Yahoo!, return to www.yahoo.com and select the category that's appropriate for your site. Work your way through any subcategories until you locate a list of sites that are most similar to your own.

Suppose that you've created a site that discusses camel racing. You navigate your way through the Recreation links, which then leads to Sports, which then has a category called Camel Racing. Yes, there really is a category like this:

```
http://dir.yahoo.com/Recreation/Sports/Camel_Racing/
```

20

FIGURE 20.2

Yahoo!'s
Announcement
Services category.

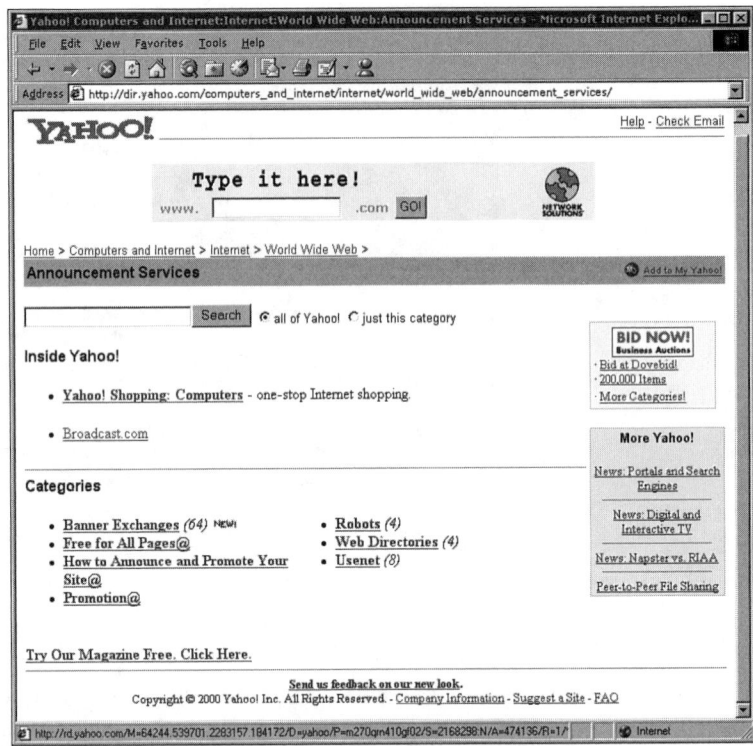

When you scroll down to the bottom of this page, you see a "How to Suggest a Site"
link. Click this link to display the Suggest a Site page. This page provides complete
instructions for adding your site to Yahoo!. Currently, the process involves filling out
four easy-to-understand forms.

Note

Even though I'm discussing how to register for search engines individually,
you may prefer to wait and register for them all at once. Later on today, I'll
discuss some services you can use to do this.

Caution

These days, it can take an awfully long time to get your site into the Yahoo!
directory. If you don't want to wait, you can sign up for the Business Express
service for $199.00 at `http://add.yahoo.com/fast/add`.

After you submit your site, your request is processed by the folks at Yahoo!. Eventually, you'll find your site listed among the other camel racing pages!

The World Wide Web Virtual Library

The World Wide Web (W3) Virtual Library, located at `http://vlib.org/`, is another very popular online catalog. Unlike Yahoo!, which is operated by a single group of people, the W3 Virtual Library is a distributed effort. The contents of each category are maintained by different groups of people (all volunteers) and sometimes housed on different computers all over the world.

Also, the W3 Virtual Library is somewhat more selective about the sites that it includes. Not every site will be listed here. However, if you have a top-notch site, you should give them a try. To submit your URL for inclusion in a category of the Virtual Library, you need to send an email request to the person who maintains it, or VLibrarian (virtual librarian). One place to obtain a list of VLibrarian email addresses is `http://conbio.rice.edu/vl/database/output.cfm`. The first page, shown in Figure 20.3, displays the first 25 categories and also contains a link to the VLibrarian's email address. This is the person who you contact to have your site reviewed for inclusion in the W3 Virtual Library.

FIGURE 20.3

The World Wide Web Virtual Library.

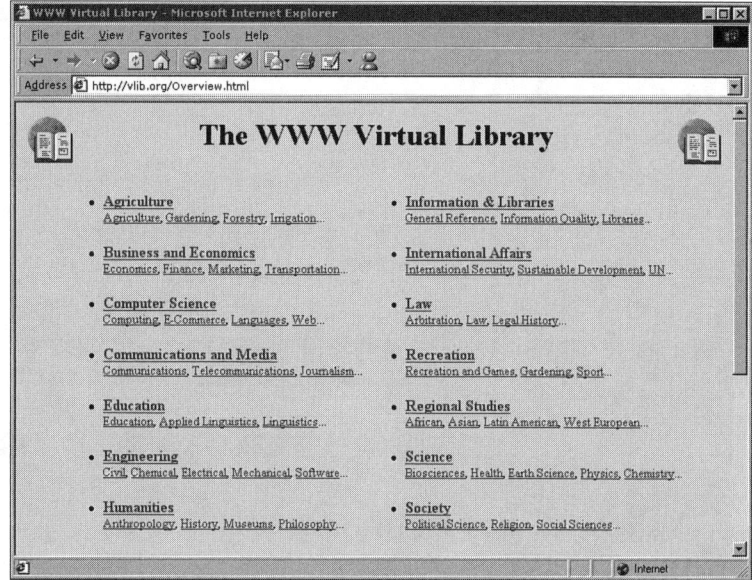

20

dmoz: The Open Directory Project

The Open Directory Project at http://www.dmoz.org is a Web directory, just like Yahoo! and the W3 Virtual Library. It's maintained by volunteer editors who are responsible for maintaining individual categories in the catalog. The project was purchased by Netscape, which was in turn purchased by AOL, so technically it's an AOL property. Even so, it's still maintained by a volunteer staff.

Like Yahoo!, you can request that your site be added, and the editor of that category will check out your site and include it in the directory. One of the biggest advantages of having your site listed in the Open Directory Project is that many other sites publish its contents. For example, popular search engines HotBot (www.hotbot.com) and Google (www.google.com) both include the Open Directory Project on their sites. A screenshot of the dmoz home page appears in Figure 20.4.

FIGURE 20.4

The dmoz home page.

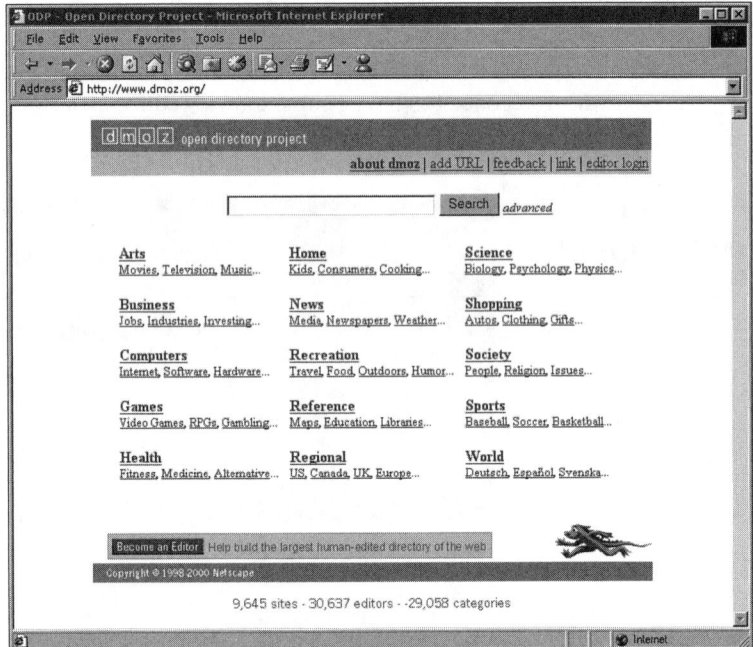

Yellow Pages Listings

Another popular method of promoting your site is to register it with the growing number of Yellow Pages directories that have begun to spring up on the Web.

As a rule, Yellow Pages sites are designed specially for commercial and business Web users who want to advertise their services and expertise. For this reason, most of the Yellow Pages sites offer both free and paid advertising space, with the paid listings including graphics, corporate logos, and advanced layout features. A free listing, on the other hand, tends to be little more than a hyperlink and a short comment. When you're starting out, free advertising is the best advertising. Of the Yellow Pages sites currently in operation, the Verizon SuperPages home page at `www.superpages.com/` is one of the most popular (see Figure 20.5).

FIGURE 20.5

The Verizon SuperPages home page.

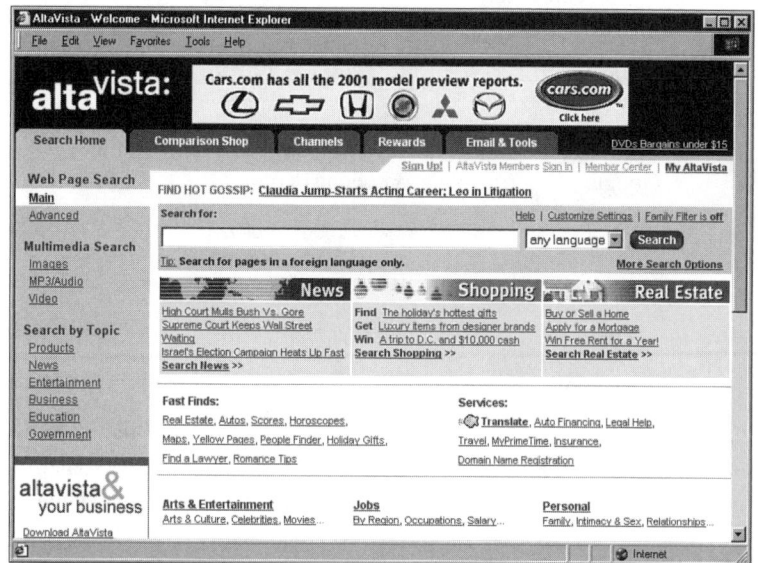

This page gives you access to two separate Yellow Pages-type directories: one for business information gleaned from actual United States Yellow Pages information (which includes businesses without Web sites), and one specifically for businesses with Web sites. Both are organized into categories, and both listings enable you to search for specific business names and locations. To add your site to the SuperPages directory, click on the `Add/Change Listing` link on the SuperPages home page.

Private Directories

In addition to the broad mainstream Web directories, many private directories on the Web cater to more specific needs. Some of these directories deal with single issues, whereas others are devoted to areas such as online commerce, education, business, and entertainment.

20

The best way to locate most of these directories is to use an Internet search tool such as Google (www.google.com/) or AltaVista (www.altavista.com/). Alternatively, most of these directories are listed in such places as Yahoo! and demoz, so a few minutes spent at these sites can be very beneficial.

Site Indexes and Search Engines

After you list your new site on the major directories and maybe a few smaller directories, next you need to turn your attention to the indexing and search tools. The following are the most popular of these sites:

AltaVista	www.altavista.com/
Excite	www.excite.com/
Google	www.google.com/
HotBot	www.hotbot.com/
Infoseek	http://infoseek.go.com/
Lycos	www.lycos.com/
Snap.com	www.snap.com/

Unlike Web directories, which contain a hierarchical list of Web sites that have been submitted for inclusion, these indexes have search engines (sometimes called *spiders*) that prowl the Web and store information about every page and site they find. You can then search these indexes for the site(s) you want.

After you publish your site on the Web and other people link to it, chances are that a search engine will get around to finding and exploring it. However, you don't have to wait. You can tell these indexes about your site and get it indexed much faster. Each of these search engines enables you to submit your site for inclusion as part of its index.

AltaVista

One of the fastest and most popular Web indexes is the AltaVista site at www.altavista. com/. AltaVista indexes a good portion of the Web, and its search engine is extremely fast. This makes looking up specific search terms on the Web quick and thorough. AltaVista's home page appears in Figure 20.6.

You can submit your page to AltaVista using the form at http://doc.altavista.com/ addurl/.

FIGURE 20.6

AltaVista's Add URL page

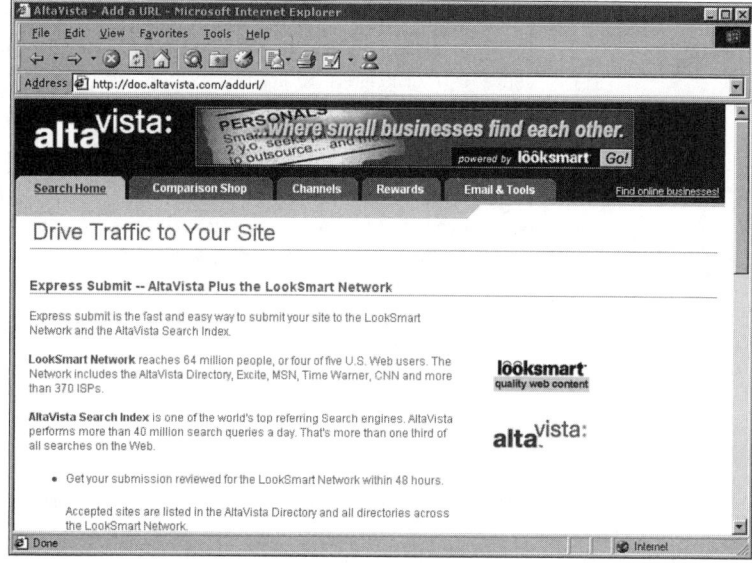

Excite

Excite is yet another popular Web search engine. Originally they started out by not only indexing the Web, but also providing a directory of Web sites along with reviews of those sites. These days they are focused on their Web index and other features common to most search engines. The Excite home page is at www.excite.com/, and you can submit your page at www.excite.com/info/add_url/.

Google

Google is a latecomer compared to most of the other popular search engines, but its powerful search algorithm has made it popular very quickly. Google ranks its search results not only based on how frequently the search terms appear on a listed page, but also on the number of other pages in the index that link to that page. So a popular page with thousands of incoming links will be ranked higher than a page that has only a few incoming links.

This search algorithm does a remarkably good job of pushing the most relevant sites to the top of the search results, and it can really save a lot of time when you're searching the Web. It also rewards people who publish useful, popular sites rather than those who've figured out how to manipulate the algorithms that other search engines use. Google was also recently adopted by Yahoo! as the search engine that accompanies their directory. You can submit your site to Google at http://www.google.com/addurl.html.

20

> **Note**
>
> Every search engine has an algorithm that ranks sites based on their relevance. It might take into account how many times the keyword you enter appears on the page, whether it appears inside heading tags or in the page title, or whether it appears in text inside links. It might also take into account how high on the page your search terms appear. Such algorithms are trade secrets within the search engine industry, but some of them have been unravelled to greater or lesser degrees. Armed with this information, some site authors write their pages in such a way that search engines will give them a higher relevance ranking than they deserve. For example, some sites have really long titles with lots of information in hopes of appearing first in search results.

HotBot

From the HotBot search engine at www.hotbot.com/ (see Figure 20.7), visitors can browse sites by category, shop online, and also view sites by geographical region. HotBot is currently part of the Lycos network but does not use the Lycos Web index, which I'll discuss next.

FIGURE 20.7

HotBot's home page

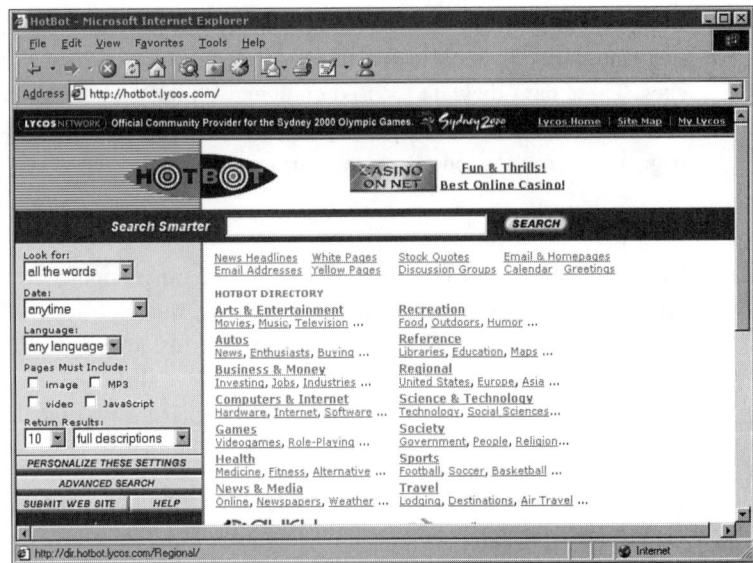

To add your page to HotBot, go to www.hotbot.com/addurl.asp.

Lycos

Lycos, at www.lycos.com/, was one of the first search engines and still claims to have the largest overall coverage of the Web. Their home page appears in Figure 20.8. To add your page to Lycos, go to www.lycos.com/addasite.html. For each page you submit, you must include the URL and your email address.

One of the more interesting features of Lycos is a search engine for media files like images, sounds, and video clips. There are individual search engines for most of the popular media types.

FIGURE 20.8

Lycos' home page.

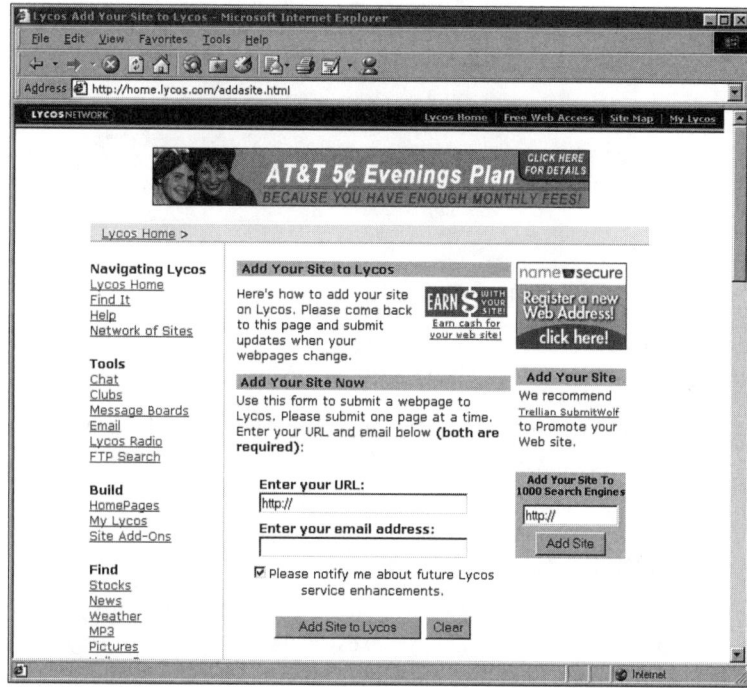

Go.com

Back in 1995, *PC Computing* magazine voted Infoseek the Most Valuable Internet Tool. Since then, it has been subsumed into the Go Network, a network of Web sites owned by Disney. The search engine is now located at www.go.com/, and it's still a very popular choice. The latest interface appears in Figure 20.9 To add your site to Go.com's index, go to addurl.go.com/dynamic/landNotLogged.

20

FIGURE **20.9**

Go.com.

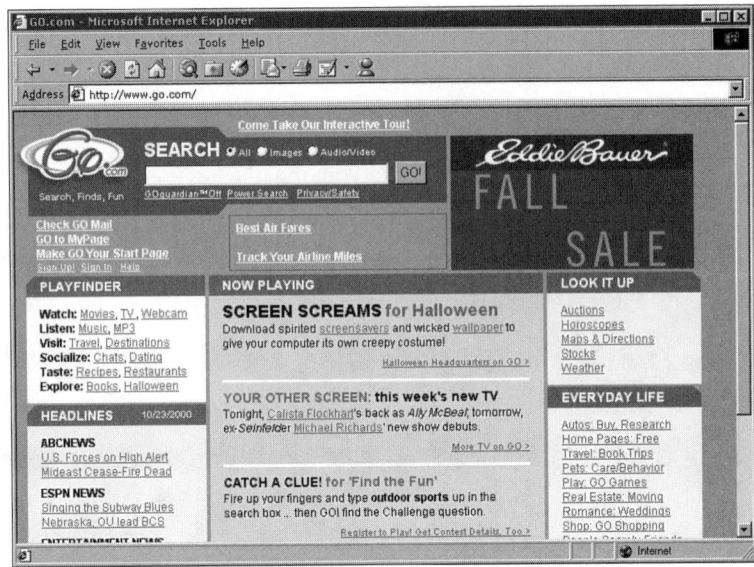

Submission Tools

Besides these search tools, there are many others that offer additional capabilities. You'll need to submit your site to each one to ensure that it's indexed.

Rather than listing the URLs and describing each of these sites, I'll focus on two special Web pages that eliminate much of the drudgery in submitting Web sites to search indexes and directories.

Submit It!

The Submit It! service, provided by Scott Banister, helps you submit your URL to different directories and search indexes. Figure 20.10 shows only a portion of all the search indexes and directories currently supported by Submit It!. To view the list in its entirety, go to www.submit-it.com/subcats.htm.

Submit It! doesn't ask you to complete one enormous page. Instead, after you've filled out some general information, you select only the sites to which you want to submit your site and then perform each submission one at a time.

To learn more about Submit It!, go to www.submit-it.com/.

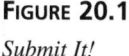

FIGURE 20.10

Submit It!

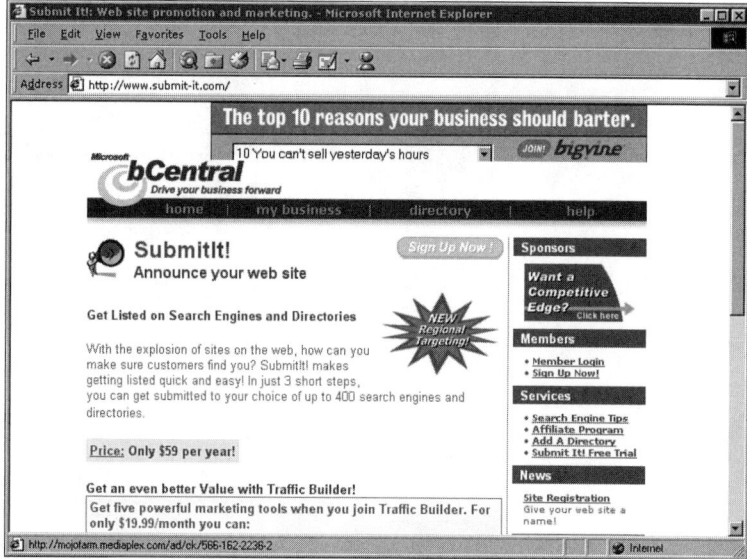

Announce Your Site Using Usenet

The Web isn't the only place on the Internet where you can announce the launch of your new Web site. Many people use a small set of Usenet newsgroups that are designed especially for making announcements. Look for newsgroup names that end with .announce. (Refer to the documentation that came with your Usenet newsreader for information about how to find these newsgroups.)

One newsgroup, comp.infosystems.www.announce, is devoted strictly to Web-related announcements. If your browser supports Usenet and you've configured it to point to your news server, you can view articles submitted to this newsgroup—and add your own announcements—by entering the following URL into the Document URL field:

```
news:comp.infosystems.www.announce
```

In particular, look for "FAQ: How to Announce Your New Web Site." This excellent FAQ contains an up-to-date list of all the best and most profitable means of promoting your Web site. If you can't locate the FAQ in this newsgroup (as shown in Figure 20.11), you can view an online version at http://ep.com/faq/webannounce.html.

20

FIGURE **20.11**

The comp.infosys-
tems.www.announce
newsgroup.

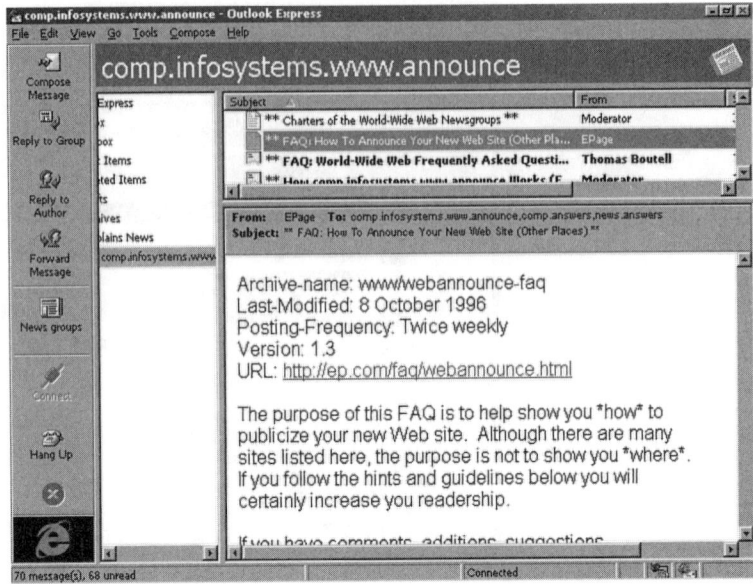

Note

comp.infosystems.www.announce is a moderated newsgroup. Any submissions you make to it are approved by a moderator before they appear in the
newsgroup. To ensure that your announcement is approved, you should
read the charter document that outlines the announcement process at
www.sangfroid.com/charter.html.

Web Rings

One way to advertise and promote your site on the Web is to join one or more Web rings.
A *Web ring* is a collection of sites about a specific topic. The main gateway to an
immense collection of Web rings, covering just about any topic you can imagine, is the
Web Ring home page at www.webring.com/ (see Figure 20.12). This is now part of
Yahoo!'s network of services.

Joining a Web ring is simple. You submit your URL to the ringmaster, who's in charge of
the ring. In turn, you're asked to include some code (and sometimes some images) on a
prominent page of your site. Most often, this is your home page or a page that's dedicated to displaying the Web rings to which you belong.

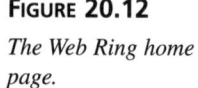

FIGURE 20.12

The Web Ring home page.

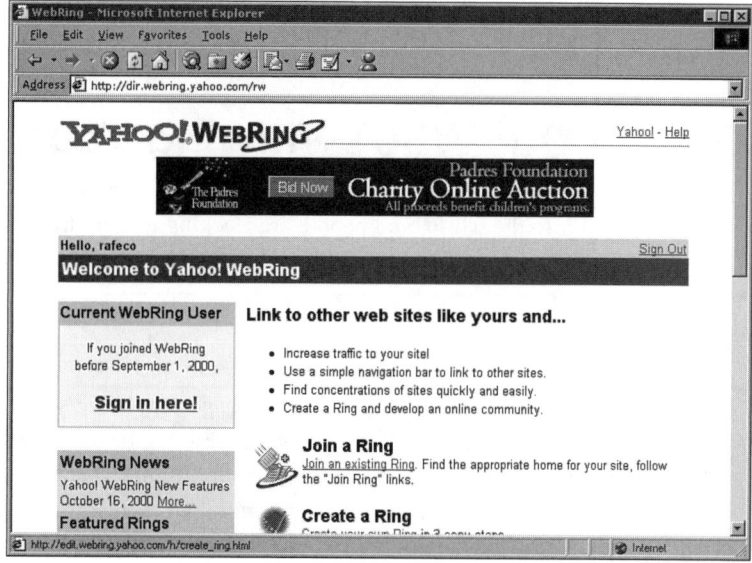

The code that you place on your page enables users to navigate to and from other sites in the Web ring. This way, they can focus on Web sites that share a common interest or goal.

Web rings have seen phenomenal growth since the beginning of 1998, and it looks as though this growth is continuing. Joining one is a good way to attract many visitors who will be interested in your Web site.

For further information on how to join or start a Web ring, check out Web Ring's Join page at www.webring.com/join.html.

Business Cards, Letterhead, Brochures, and Advertisements

Although the Internet is a wonderful place to promote your new Web site, many people fail to consider some other great advertising methods.

Most businesses spend a considerable amount of money each year producing business cards, letterhead, and other promotional material. These days it's rare to see any of these materials without Web and email information on them. By printing your email address and home page URL on all your correspondence and promotional material, you can reach an entirely new group of potential visitors.

20

When you're promoting your Web site, the bottom line is lateral thinking. You need to use every tool at your disposal if you want to have a successful and active site.

Finding Out Who's Viewing Your Web Pages

Now you've got your site up on the Web and ready to be viewed, you've advertised and publicized it to the world, and people are flocking to it in droves. Or are they? How can you tell? You can find out in a number of ways, including using log files and access counters.

Log Files

The best way to figure out how often your pages are being seen, and by whom, is to get access to your server's log files. How long these log files are kept depends on how your server is configured. The logs can take up a lot of disk space, so some hosting providers remove old logs pretty frequently. If you run your own server, you can keep them as long as you like, or at least until you run out of room. Many commercial Web providers allow you to view your own Web logs or get statistics about how many visitors are accessing your pages and from where. Ask your Webmaster for help.

If you do get access to these raw log files, you'll most likely see a whole lot of lines that look something like the following. (I've broken this one up into two lines so that it fits on the page.)

```
vide-gate.coventry.ac.uk - - [17/Apr/1996:12:36:51 -0700]
    "GET /index.html HTTP/1.0" 200 8916
```

What does this information mean? The first part of the line is the site that accessed the file. (In this case, it was a site from the United Kingdom.) The two dashes are used for authentication. (If you have login names and passwords set up, the username of the person who logged in and the group that person belonged to will appear here.) The date and time the page was accessed appear inside the brackets. The next part is the actual filename that was accessed; here it's the index.html at the top level of the server. The GET part is the actual HTTP command the browser used; you usually see GET here. Finally, the last two numbers are the HTTP status code and the number of bytes transferred. The status code can be one of many things: 200 means the file was found and transferred correctly; 404 means the file was not found (yes, it's the same status code you get in error pages in your browser). Finally, the number of bytes transferred usually will be the same number of bytes in your actual file; if it's a smaller number, the visitor interrupted the load in the middle.

Access Counters

If you don't have access to your server's log files but you'd like to know how many people are looking at your Web page, you can install an access counter. These counters look like odometers or little meters that say, "Since July 15, 1900, this page has been accessed 5,456,234,432 times."

Many Web counters are available, but most of them require you to install something on your server or configure server-side includes on it. A few, including the following sites, provide access counters that don't require server setup (but may cost you some money).

The Web counter at www.digits.com/ is easy to set up and very popular. If you have a site without a lot of hits (fewer than 1,000 a day), the counter service is free. Otherwise, you'll need to be part of the commercial plan, costing $30 and up.

After you sign up for the digits.com counter service, you'll get an URL that you must include on your pages as part of an <img> tag. When your page is hit, the browser retrieves that URL at digits.com's server, which generates a new odometer image for you.

Table 20.1 lists some additional free counter services.

TABLE 20.1   Access Counter Services

Name	URL
XOOMCounter	www.pagecount.com/
Jcount	www.jcount.com/
WebTracker	www.fxweb.holowww.com/tracker/
LiveCounter	www.chami.com/counter/classic/

> **Tip**
>
> Counters are neat gadgets, but they're not generally associated with professional Web design. If you're working on a site for a business, you may want to avoid counters and stick with analyzing your server logs.

20

Summary

In this chapter, you learned the many ways that you can advertise and promote your site, and also how to use log files to keep track of the number of visitors. At last, you're on the Web and people are coming to visit!

There's one more important topic to learn—how to keep your site up-to-date. You'll learn this in the next chapter.

Workshop

As always, we wrap up the chapter with a few questions, quizzes, and exercises. Here are some pointers and refreshers on how to promote your Web site.

Q&A

Q **There are so many of those search engines! Do I have to add my URL to all of them?**

A No, you don't have to, but think of the (vastly overused) analogy of the Internet as a superhighway. When you're driving down a real highway, there's usually a clutter of billboards that are clamoring for your attention. How many of them do you really notice, though? You remember the ones you see most frequently. Likewise, listing your page on multiple search engines makes it more visible.

Q **What about sending my URL to tons of newsgroups all at once? Is that a good way to advertise my site?**

A Well, yes and no. Slamming the same message or URL across dozens upon dozens of newsgroups at once is known as *spamming*, and most people who frequent newsgroups don't take too kindly to it. It's proper Web etiquette to use discretion when you post your URL to Usenet. Perhaps if you plan ahead and post your URL politely and discretely to a small handful of related newsgroups at once, it won't be so bad. Doing it this way requires a little more work on your part, but you'll make fewer enemies.

Q **In regard to the Web rings, what if I can't find a suitable place for the code that they want me to place on my home page? What alternatives do I have?**

A It depends on the Web ring and the person who runs it. Each Web ring has a list of instructions that tell you how to add the code to your pages. Some of them are very particular about where you place it (for example, it must be on your home page), while others let you place it on any prominent page in your site. Others allow you to include graphics or just make a text-only mention of the Web rings.

If your ringleader allows you to place the Web ring code on a page other than your home page, be sure to provide a link to your Web ring page on your home page. A simple text link such as "For a listing of the Web rings to which this site belongs, please visit my Web Ring page" should do it.

Quiz

1. Name some of the ways that you can promote your Web site.
2. What's a hit?

3. What are the advantages of using an all-in-one submission page to promote your site?

4. What's one rule to follow when you promote your site on Usenet?

Quiz Answers

1. Some ways you can promote your site include major Web directories and indexes, announcements in newsgroups, listings on business cards and other promotional materials, and Web rings.

2. Hits are the number of times that a copy of your Web page has been downloaded.

3. An all-in-one submission page enables you to submit your URL to several different site promotion areas and Web robots at once. Some provide a small number of submissions for free and a larger number of submissions for an additional fee.

4. The main rule of thumb is not to blindly spam your URL to multiple newsgroups at the same time. It's good Web etiquette to be polite and post your URL selectively. Better yet, post it to newsgroups in which you actually participate.

Exercises

1. Visit some of the search engines listed in this chapter to obtain a list of the sites where you want to promote your Web page. Review each of the choices to see whether there are special requirements for listing your page.

2. Design a new business card or brochure that advertises your company and your Web site.

20

DAY 21

Testing, Revising, and Maintaining Your Web Site

By this point in the book, you've created your own Web site. You included a bunch of pages linked together in a meaningful way, a smattering of images, and a form or two. You then added tables and image alignment, converted several images to JPEG, added some really cool video clips of you and your cat, and set up a script that rings a bell every time someone clicks on a link. Cascading style sheets give all these nifty pages a nice, uniform appearance. Dynamic HTML layers the graphics over the images and text and really adds spice to your site. You think it's pretty cool. In fact, you think it can't get much cooler than this. You're finally done.

I have bad news—you're not done yet. You have to think about two more aspects of having a Web site—testing what you've got and maintaining what you will have.

Testing means making sure that your Web site works. It needs to work not just from the technical side (Are you writing correct HTML? Do all your links work?), but also from the usability side (Can people find what they need on your pages?). In addition, you'll want to make sure that your site is readable on multiple browsers, especially if you're using some of the more recent tags you've learned about.

Even after you test everything and it all works right, you're still not done. Almost as soon as you publish the initial site, you'll want to add stuff to it and change what's already there to keep the site interesting and up-to-date. Trust me on this point. On the Web, where the very technology is changing constantly, a Web site is never really done. Some pages are just less likely to change than others.

After you're done with today's chapter, you'll know all about the following topics:

- Integrity testing, which is making sure that your Web pages will actually work
- Usability testing, including making sure that your pages are being used in the way you expect and that your goals for the site are being met
- Adding pages to your site or making revisions to it without breaking what's already there

Integrity Testing

Integrity testing has nothing to do with whether you cheated on your taxes. It means making sure that the pages you've just put together work properly—that they're displayed without errors and that all your links point to real locations. This type of testing doesn't say anything about whether your pages are useful or whether people can use them; just that they're technically correct. The following are the three steps to integrity testing:

1. Make sure that you've written correct HTML.
2. Test the look of your pages in multiple browsers.
3. Make sure that your links work (both initially and several months down the road).

Validating Your HTML

The first step is to make sure you've written correct HTML. All your tags should have the proper closing tags, you shouldn't have overlapped any tags, and you shouldn't have used tags inside other tags that don't work.

However, you check that sort of thing when you review your page in different browsers, right? Well, not really. Browsers are designed to work around problems in the HTML files they're parsing. They do their best to figure out what you're trying to accomplish, and they display their best guess if they can't figure it out. (Remember how those tables looked in the browser that didn't accept tables? The browser tried its very best to determine what you were trying to do.) Some browsers are more lenient than others in the HTML they accept. A page with errors might work fine in one browser but won't work at all in another.

Nonetheless, you should follow the HTML specification as closely as possible to make sure your pages work in a wide variety of browsers. If you opt to use DHTML, JavaScript, Cascading Style Sheets, or XHTML, you should be sure that your code conforms to those specifications as well. Unfortunately, due to the vagaries of how browsers are written, the only way to be sure that your page works in a particular browser is to test it in that browser. The fewer advanced features you use on your site, the less rigorous your testing has to be. Most browsers have solid implementations of basic HTML features, but their support for things like DHTML, CSS, and JavaScript varies widely. Dynamic HTML is probably the worst offender here because it pushes the limits of both JavaScript and CSS support.

How can you make sure that you're writing correct HTML? If you've been following the rules and examples in this book, you've been writing correct HTML. However, occasionally you'll forget closing tags, put tags in the wrong places, or drop the closing quotation marks from the end of an `href`. (I do that all the time, and it breaks quite a few browsers.) The best way to find out whether your pages are correct is to run them through an *HTML validator*.

HTML validators are written to check HTML and *only* HTML. A validator doesn't care what your pages look like—just that you're writing your HTML to the current specification. Some validators check against both older and newer HTML specifications. Newer validators check your code against one of the three flavors of HTML 4.0 or XHTML 1.0—Strict, Frameset, or Transitional.

> **Note**
>
> Many HTML editors now provide limited validation of HTML code. Programs such as HoTMetaL Pro from Softquad can even prevent you from creating documents that violate the editor's internal validator. With most editors, however, this validation is limited and incomplete. On top of that, many editors not only allow you to produce incorrect HTML but even generate incorrect HTML *for* you. For these reasons, using another HTML validator is a good idea.

21

In terms of writing portable HTML and HTML that can be read by future generations of authoring tools, it's probably a good idea to make sure that you're writing it correctly. You don't want to end up fixing thousands of pages by hand when the ultimate HTML authoring tool appears and it can't read anything you've done.

 Note Even if you're writing correct HTML, you should test your pages in multiple browsers to ensure that you haven't made any strange design decisions. Just using a validator doesn't get you off the hook when designing.

So, how do you run these HTML validators? Several standalone versions are available on the Web for downloading and running locally on your own system. Others are Web pages—you enter your URLs into a form, and the validator then tests them over the network. In the next section, I'll explain how to use the W3C Validator to test HTML on your site.

 Note As with all Web sites, these services change all the time, supporting new features and changing their appearance. Although they may look different from the examples in this book by the time you look at them, the examples should give you a strong idea of how these services work.

One standalone validator for the Windows platform is CSE 3310 HTML Validator. It helps you find and correct several different HTML problems, such as misspelled or invalid tags, attributes and values, character entities, missing quotes, missing closing tags, incorrect tag placement and nesting, and more. You can learn more about this validator at the CSE 3310 home page at `www.htmlvalidator.com/`. You also can download a free trial version at `www.htmlvalidator.com/htmldownload.html`.

Another useful tool that you can run on your own system to validate HTML is HTML Tidy, written by Dave Raggett (who's currently working at the W3C) and found at `www.w3.org/People/Raggett/tidy/`. Versions are available for every popular platform, and even for some platforms that are rather obscure. HTML Tidy not only alerts you to problems in your pages, but will also fix the problems that it can figure out on its own.

It also knows which tags and attributes are part of the HTML standard and which are proprietary tags invented by browser makers, and it tells you when you use them. You may not want to remove them from your pages, but it's good to know when you're using nonstandard elements in your HTML so that it's easy to clean up problems they might cause later. The best thing about HTML Tidy is that it's completely free, so you should definitely download it and give it a shot. It can save you a ton of work.

The W3C HTML Validation Service

The W3C Validator not only verifies that your HTML is standards-compliant, but makes sure that your pages conform to the XHTML 1.0 specification as well. It's a free validation service that enables you to check your HTML code against various DTDs (document type definitions). In addition to the various incarnations of "official" HTML (including HTML 4.01 and XHTML 1.0), the W3C validator also enables you to check for Netscape- and Internet Explorer-specific code. You can find a complete list of the DTDs this validator checks against at `http://validator.w3.org/sgml-lib/catalog`.

You can access the validator at `http://validator.w3.org`. To use this validation service, enter the URL of the Web page you want to validate in the Address field, as shown in Figure 21.1. (Note that at press time, there was no option to paste snippets of code into an online form.)

FIGURE 21.1

The W3C HTML Validation Service validation form.

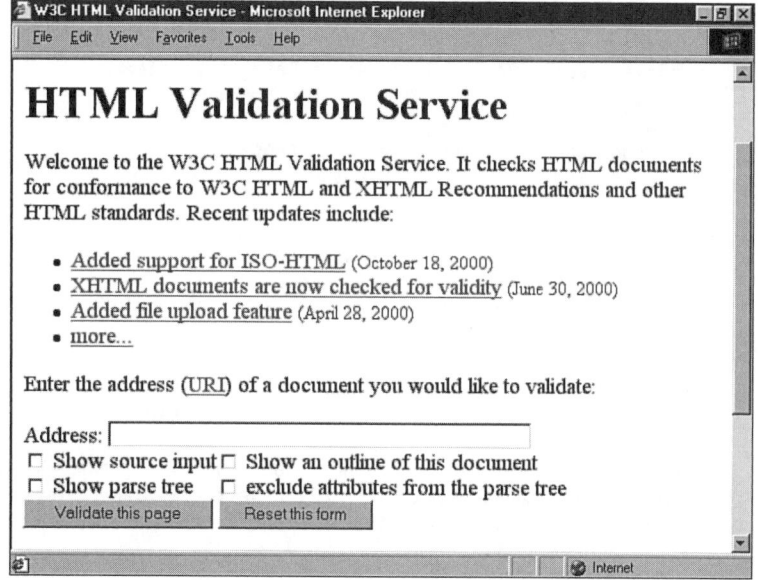

After you enter the URL of your Web page, you can select one or more of the following options:

- Show source input—This option includes a listing of the source code that the validator checked, with line numbers. This is helpful in determining exactly where

21

errors appear in your code because the line numbers are associated with the validation errors returned by the validator.

- Show an outline of this document—If headings appear on your page, this option
  returns an outline of your Web page document. This is helpful in determining
  whether your Web page structure follows standard outline procedures (such as H2
  beneath H1, H3 beneath H2, and so on).

- Show parse tree—The parse tree displays the structure of the HTML tags in your
  document.

- Exclude attributes from the parse tree—If you choose this option, attributes will be
  eliminated from the parse tree. This may help you read it more clearly.

Exercise 21.1: Validating a Sample Page

Just to show the kinds of errors that the W3C Validation Service picks up, I put together
the following sample file with some common errors:

```
<!DOCTYPE html PUBLIC "-//W3C//DTD XHTML 1.0 Transitional//EN"
"http://www.w3.org/TR/xhtml1/DTD/transitional.dtd">
<html>
<head>
<title>Susan's Cactus Gardens:  A Catalog</title>
<head>
<body>
<strong>Susan's Cactus Gardens</strong>
<h1>Choosing and Ordering Plants</h1>
<ul>
<h3>
<li><a href="browse.html">Browse Our Catalog
<li><a href="order.html>How To Order</a>
<li><a href="form.html">Order Form</a>
</ul>
</h3>
<hr width=70% align=center>
<h1>Information about Cacti and Succulents</h1>
<ul>
<li><a href="succulent.html">What does succulent mean?</a></li>
<li><a href="caring.html">How do I care for my cactus or succulent?</a></li>
<li><a href="propogation.html">How can I propagate my Cactus or
succulent?</a></li>
</ul>
<hr />
<address>Copyright &copy; 2001 Susan's Cactus Gardens
susan@cactus.com</address>
```

The result is Susan's Cactus Gardens home page, shown in Figure 21.2.

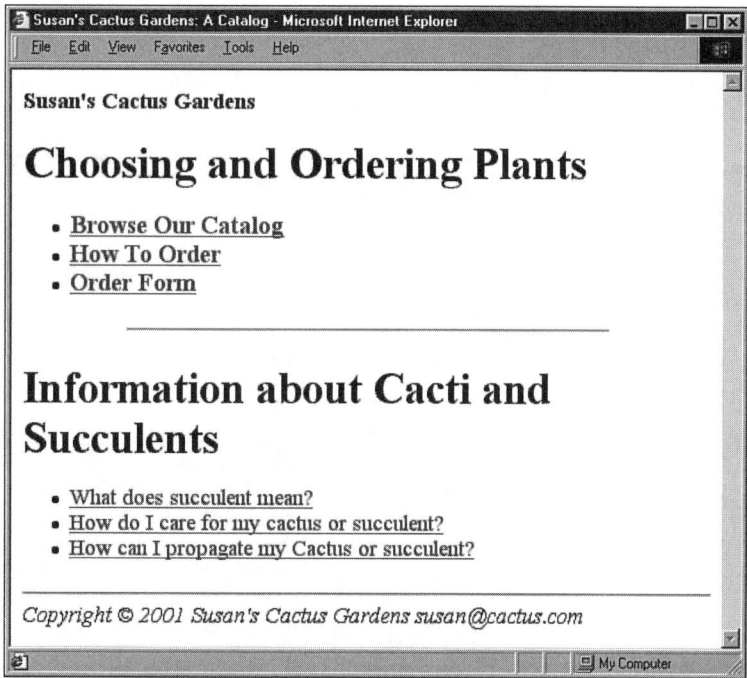

In Internet Explorer, the page looks and behaves as users would probably expect. The code that was used is riddled with errors, however. See whether you can find them before you run the code through a validator.

Now publish this page on the Internet and jot down its URL. Go to the W3C HTML Validation Service at `http://validator.w3.org/` and enter the URL of your bad Web page into the Address field. Check the Show Source Input option (it will help you decipher the errors), and then click the Validate this page button. Shortly you'll see a Results page that looks something like Figure 21.3.

Scrolling down the page, you can see that the validator found an awful lot of errors. Let's take a look at these errors and discuss how they can be fixed. The first error appears on line 6 of the HTML file and is described by the validator as follows:

```
Error: document type does not allow element "head" here
```

The problem is that the <head> tag on line 6 should actually be </head>. The validator also complains about an error on line 7 with the <body> tag because it expects that the

<head> tag will be closed before the <body> tag is opened. When the validator gets to line 9, it prints this message:

```
Error: end tag for element "h3" which is not open
```

FIGURE 21.3

The W3C HTML Validation Service's response to the file with errors.

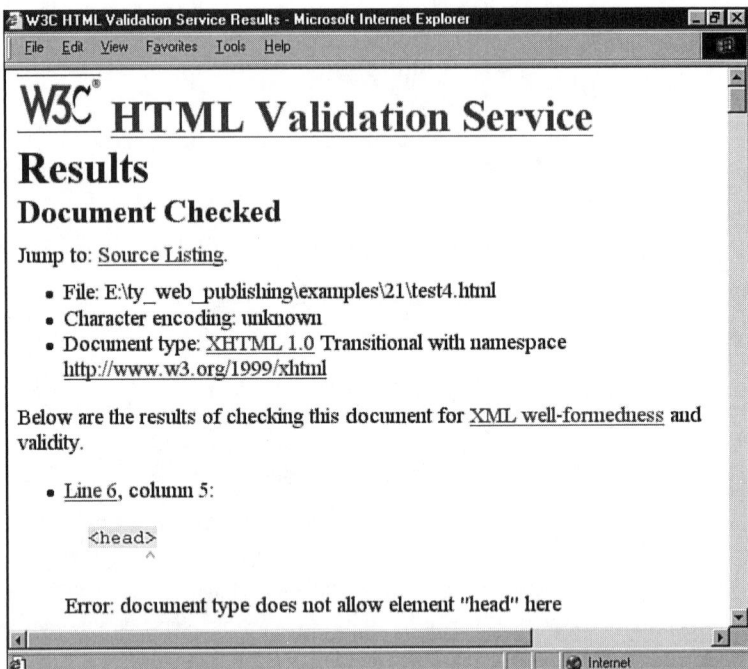

Line 9 begins with an <h1> tag and ends with a </h3> tag. The validator doesn't like that. Now let's look at the next block of code in the document:

```
<ul>
<h3>
<li><a href="browse.html">Browse Our Catalog
<li><a href="order.html>How To Order</a>
<li><a href="form.html">Order Form</a>
</ul>
</h3>
```

The error reported for line 10 is a bit obscure:

```
Error: document type does not allow element "ul" here; missing one of "object",
"applet", "map",
"iframe", "button", "ins", "del", "noscript" start-tag
```

This problem was caused by the missing </head> tag that I already discussed. Not closing the document header threw off the document structure and created this problem.

The W3C validator doesn't like you to put the <ul> tag inside an <h3> tag at all. Not only is the order of the tags wrong, but placing <ul> inside <h3> is improper. If you want to alter the font size and weight of the items in the list, it's appropriate to use Cascading Style Sheets. For compatibility with browsers that don't support CSS, you can use the <font> tag. This still violates the strictest XHTML 1.0 DTDs, but it's preferable to using the inappropriate <h3> tag.

There are several other problems with this list:

- None of the list items have closing tags, which violates the XHTML 1.0 specification.
- The first item in the list has no closing tag for the anchor, which is invalid HTML.
- The closing quotation mark in the anchor tag in the second list item is missing, which is also invalid HTML.

The cleaned up version of the list looks like this:

```
<ul>
<li><a href="browse.html">Browse Our Catalog</a></li>
<li><a href="order.html">How To Order</a></li>
<li><a href="form.html">Order Form</a></li>
</ul>
```

The validator also has lots of problems with line 17, which contains an <hr> tag. All of these problems are related to XHTML 1.0. Two problems that immediately pop up are the lack of quotation marks around the values of the attributes and the lack of a closing tag for <hr>. The repaired <hr> tag looks like this:

```
<hr width="70%" align="center" />
```

The remaining errors on the page are all related to missing closing tags.

A quick check shows that </body> and </html> are missing from the end of the file, which clears up that problem. Changing the second <head> to </head> and changing </h3> to </h1> clears up these errors as well.

All right, you've made the first pass in the W3C Validator, and you've corrected the code. (Note that to make up for removing the <h3> tag from the first <ul>, I included <font> and <b> tags to duplicate the effect of the <h3> tag.) The following example shows the revised code as it now should appear:

```
<!DOCTYPE html PUBLIC "-//W3C//DTD XHTML 1.0 Transitional//EN"
"http://www.w3.org/TR/xhtml1/DTD/transitional.dtd">
<html>
<head>
<title>Susan's Cactus Gardens:  A Catalog</title>
```

21

```
</head>
<body>
<strong>Susan's Cactus Gardens</strong>
<h1>Choosing and Ordering Plants</h1>
<ul>
<li><font size="4"><b><a href="browse.html">Browse Our
Catalog</a></b></font></li>
<li><font size="4"><b><a href="order.html">How To Order</a></b></font></li>
<li><font size="4"><b><a href="form.html">Order Form</a></b></font></li>
</ul>
<hr width="70%" align="center" />
<h1>Information about Cacti and Succulents</h1>
<ul>
<li><a href="succulent.html">What does succulent mean?</a></li>
<li><a href="caring.html">How do I care for my cactus or succulent?</a></li>
<li><a href="propogation.html">How can I propagate my Cactus or
succulent?</a></li>
</ul>
<hr />
<address>Copyright &copy; 2001 Susan's Cactus Gardens
susan@cactus.com</address>
</body>
</html>
```

Congratulations! The cactus page is now compliant with HTML and XHTML 1.0.

This example is extreme, of course. Most of the time, your pages won't have nearly as many problems as this one. (In addition, if you're using an HTML editor, many of these mistakes might never show up.) Keep in mind that Internet Explorer blithely skipped over all these errors without so much as a peep. Are all the browsers that read your files going to be this accepting?

Browser Testing

As noted before, all HTML validators do is make sure your HTML is correct. They won't tell you anything about your design. After you finish the validation tests, you still should test your pages in as many browsers as you can to ensure that the design is working and that you haven't done anything that looks fine in one browser but awful in another. Because most browsers are free and easily downloaded, you should be able to collect at least two or three for your platform.

Ideally, you should test each of your pages in the following browsers:

- Both Netscape and Microsoft Internet Explorer, both with images enabled and with images turned off

- Another browser, such as Opera or Mosaic

- A text-based browser, such as Lynx

Using these browsers will give you an idea of how users with different browsers will view your pages. There are small but important differences in the ways that the two major browsers, Netscape and Internet Explorer, render pages. Unless you use the most basic HTML, you should probably test all of your pages in both browsers to make sure that they appear as you expect. If you can, you should also test your pages on more than one platform to see how they look. Pages can look significantly different in Windows, the Mac OS, and Unix.

Verifying Your Links

The third and final test is to make sure that your links work. The most obvious way to do so, of course, is to fire up a browser and follow the links yourself. This approach might be fine for small sites, but with large sites, checking links can be a time-consuming and tedious task. Also, after you check your links the first time, the sites you've linked to might move or be renamed. Because the Web is always changing, your links might break even if your pages stay constant.

Check the error logs that your server keeps to find out about broken links on your own pages, which you might have caused when moving things around. These logs note the pages that cannot be found: both the missing page and the page that contains the link to that page. For a link to appear in the error logs, someone must have already tried to follow the link—and failed. You should try to catch the broken link before one of your visitors tries it.

The best way to check for broken links is to use an automatic link checker, which looks over your pages and ensures that the links point to real files or sites on the Web. Several link checkers are available, including more general-purpose Web spiders (programs that go from link to link, searching the Web). You can use these to test your own local documents. Be careful, however, that the link checkers don't go berserk and start checking other people's sites in addition to your own. Check out MOMspider at `www.ics.uci.edu/WebSoft/MOMspider/` for a good example of an automatic link checker.

If you're developing a very large site, validating all your links manually may be out of the question. Fortunately, many Web development programs now come with utilities that maintain your links and verify that they work properly. Microsoft FrontPage, Macromedia DreamWeaver, Adobe GoLive, and Allaire Homesite are popular Web page development tools that enable you to check and validate internal and external links on your pages.

You can also use a standalone link checker, such as Watchfire's LinkBot, to validate and maintain all links on your Web pages. This program checks for broken anchors, missing

21

image attributes, and a whole lot more. For more information on this program, visit the Watchfire home page at www.watchfire.com.

You can also use the W3C's Link Checker at validator.w3.org/checklink to test the links on a specific page. You just supply the URL, and the link checker will test all of the links and return the results.

Usability Testing

Usability testing ensures that your documents are usable, even after you've tested them for simple technical correctness. You can put up a set of Web pages easily, but are your visitors going to be able to find what they need? Is your organization satisfying the goals you originally set for your pages? Do people get confused or frustrated easily when they explore your site because it's difficult to navigate?

Many industries have been using usability testing for years. The theory behind it is that the designers who are creating the product (a software application, a VCR, a car, or so on) cannot determine whether it's easy to use because they're too closely involved with it. They know how the product is designed, of course, so they already know how to use it. The only way to determine a product's ease of use is to watch people use it who have never seen it before and note the problems. Based on this feedback, you can change the product, retest it, make more changes, and so on.

Web sites are excellent examples of products that benefit from usability testing. Even just getting a friend to look at your site can teach you a lot about how you've organized it and whether people who aren't familiar with the structure you've created can find their way around.

The following are some tasks you might want your testers to try on your pages:

- Ask them to browse your site, with no particular goal in mind, and watch where they go. Which parts interest them first? What paths do they take through the site? Which pages do they stop to read, and which do they skip?

- Ask them to find a particular topic or page, preferably one buried deep within your site. Can they find it? What path do they take? How long does it take? How frustrated do they get while trying to find it?

- Ask them for suggestions. Everyone has opinions on other people's Web pages, but visitors probably won't send you mail, even if you ask them. Ask your testers how they would change your Web pages to make them better.

Sit with your testers and take notes. The results might surprise you and give you new ideas for organizing your pages.

Examining Your Server Logs

Another method of usability testing is to track your server logs. Your Web server or provider keeps logs of each hit on each page (in other words, each time a browser retrieves that document) and where it came from. Examining these server logs can teach you the following interesting facts:

- The most popular pages, which might not be the ones you expect. You might want to make it easier to find these pages from the home page.

- The patterns people use to explore your site; that is, the order in which they visit the pages.

- Common spelling errors that people make when trying to access your pages. Files that were looked for but not found will appear in your error files (usually contained in the same directory as the log files). Using symbolic links or aliases, you might be able to circumvent some of these problems if they occur frequently.

Updating and Adding Pages to Your Site

Even after you publish your site and test it extensively both for integrity and usability, you're still not done. As I said before, your site will *never* be done. Even if you manage to make it as usable as it could possibly be, eventually there will always be new information and new pages to add, updates to make, new advances in HTML that must be experimented with, and so on.

So how do you maintain your site? Easy. You create new pages and link them to the old pages, right? Well, maybe. Before you do, however, read this section for hints on the best way to proceed.

Adding New Content

I'd like to start this section with a story…

In San Jose, California, there's a tourist attraction called the Winchester Mystery House, originally owned by Sarah Winchester, heiress to the Winchester Arms Company fortune. The story goes that after the deaths of her husband and daughter, she was told by a spiritualist that the spirits of all the men who had been killed by Winchester guns were haunting her. The spiritualist advised her to begin building rooms onto her farmhouse to appease the spirits, which she did.

All the new additions were built onto the existing house with no plan for making them livable or even logical—as long as the work never stopped. The house now has over 160 rooms, stairways that lead nowhere, doors that open into walls, secret passageways, and a floor plan that's nearly impossible to navigate without a map.

21

Some Web sites look a lot like this mystery house. They might have begun with a well-planned, well-organized, usable structure, but as more pages were added, this structure began to break down. The original goals of the site became lost, and eventually it resulted in a mess of interlinked pages that's almost impossible to navigate (see Figure 21.4).

FIGURE 21.4

A confusing set of Web pages.

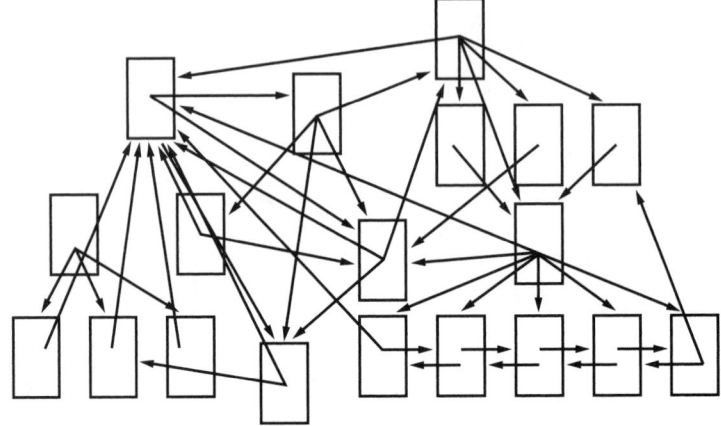

Avoid the Winchester Mystery House School of Web Page Design. When you add new pages to an existing site, keep the following hints in mind:

- **Stick to your structure**—If you've followed the hints so far, your site should have a basic structure, such as a hierarchy or a linear structure. Most of the time, adding new material to an existing structure is easy because it can go in a logical place. As you add pages, try to maintain the original structure.

- **Focus on your goals**—Keep your original goals in mind when you add new content. If the new content distracts from or interferes with these goals, don't add it or at least downplay its existence. If your goals have changed, you might want to revise your entire site rather than just tacking on new material.

- **Add branches if necessary**—Sometimes the easiest way to add new material, particularly to a hierarchy, is to add an entirely new subsite rather than trying to add the content. If the new content you're adding can be made into its own site, consider adding it that way.

Revising Your Structure

Eventually you might find that your site has grown to the point that the original structure no longer works. Or maybe your goals have changed, and the original organization makes it difficult to access the new material. Maybe you didn't use an organized structure to begin with, and now you realize that you need one.

Web sites are organic things, and if you modify your site frequently, you'll probably need to revise your original plan or structure. Often you can find ways to modify parts of the site so that the new material fits in and the overall structure hangs together.

It sometimes helps to return to your original plan for the site (you did create one, didn't you?) and revise it before arbitrarily modifying it. In particular, try the following suggestions:

- **List the goals of your site**—Think of how people are going to use the site and how you want it to be perceived. Compare these new goals to your original goals. If they're different, think of ways to modify your current structure so that you can still achieve your new goals.

- **Modify your list of topics**—Modifying existing content is usually the most difficult part of altering your Web site because it might involve taking pieces from other topics and rearranging the information. Try to keep track of the old and new topics; this will help you when you actually start editing pages.

- **Consider changing your structure if it isn't working**—If you started with a simple Web structure that's now too complex to navigate easily, consider imposing a more rigid structure on the site. If you have a very shallow hierarchy (very few levels, but many options on the topmost page), consider giving it more balance by using more levels and fewer options.

After your new plan is in place, usually you can identify areas where moving pages or the contents of pages can help make the site easier to use. Keep your new plan in mind as you make your changes, and take your time. If you try to introduce too many changes at once, you run the risk of breaking links and losing track of the changes you make. If you've performed usability testing on your pages before, remember to take those results into account as well.

Summary

The four horsemen of Web page design are Planning, Writing, Testing, and Maintenance. All throughout this book, you've learned about planning and writing, which entail developing a structure, creating your pages, linking them together, and then refining what you have. Today, you learned about the other half of the process, which continues even after you've published your site and people are flocking to it.

Testing ensures that your pages work correctly. Initially, you might have performed some rudimentary evaluations by viewing your pages in more than one browser, trying out your links, and ensuring that all your CGI scripts were installed and called from the right

21

places. Today, however, you learned how to perform *real* testing—integrity testing with HTML validators and automatic link checkers, and usability testing to determine whether people actually find your pages useful.

Maintenance takes place when you add new stuff to your site and then evaluate and modify it to ensure that the site still functions well. Performing maintenance prevents your foundational planning from going to waste by ensuring that the new information doesn't obscure the original information. In addition, maintenance sometimes requires you to develop a new site structure as well as create a new set of pages. Today, you learned how to perform maintenance and revise your Web pages.

Now you're done—at least until it's time to change everything again. You've learned quite a lot this week, and now you're ready to build your own Web sites. The most important thing to remember while you're doing this is to have fun.

Workshop

Here you are at the end of the book, armed with a wealth of information about creating and publishing your Web pages on the World Wide Web. This final workshop contains some questions about HTML validation, as well as a quiz and exercises that will refresh your memory on what you've learned.

Q&A

Q I still don't understand why HTML validation is important. I test my pages in many browsers. Why should I go through all this extra work to make them truly HTML-compliant?

A Look at the situation this way: Imagine that sometime next year, Web Company Z comes out with a super-hot HTML authoring tool that will enable you to create Web pages quickly and easily, link them together, build hierarchies that you can move around visually, and do all the really nifty stuff that has always been difficult in the past. In addition, this tool will read your old HTML files so that you don't have to write everything from scratch.

"Great," you say. You purchase the program and try to open and edit your HTML files with it. However, your HTML files contain errors that never appear in the browsers. Because the authoring tool is more strict than the browsers are about what it can read (and it has to be, with this nifty front-end), you can't read in all your original files without first modifying them manually. If you introduce errors while manually modifying these files, you can end up spending more time correcting the mistakes than you did writing the pages in the first place.

Quiz

1. True or false: HTML is the only language you'll ever need to create Web pages.

2. What are some ways to reduce the size of Web pages that contain a large number of graphics and multimedia elements?

3. True or false: If all my links work on my local computer, I don't have to test them again after I upload them to my remote Web site.

Quiz Answers

1. This might have been true in the early days of the Web, but it may not be the case any longer. Although you can create Web pages that use only HTML tags, you'll need to learn how to use additional technologies, such as Cascading Style Sheets (see Day 12, "XHTML and Style Sheets"), JavaScript and Dynamic HTML (see Day 15, "Using Dynamic HTML"), and others to implement state-of-the-art Web pages that feature advanced positioning and presentation.

2. Reduce the dimensional size of the graphics or animations. You also can reduce the file size of the images by compressing them (for JPG images) or reducing the number of colors in the palette (for GIF images). If all else fails, provide a small thumbnail of each image or of one of the frames in the animation, and let the visitor choose whether or not to download or view it. For further information, review Day 7, "Using Images, Color, and Backgrounds."

3. False. Several things can cause links to break when you transfer your Web pages to a remote server. For further information, review Day 19, "Putting Your Site Online."

Exercises

1. As you near the end of the book, you should start putting together your own Web site (if you haven't started already). Start by using tags with which you're comfortable. Add graphics, links, and tables when you're ready. As your knowledge increases, try some of the more advanced features, such as frames, Cascading Style Sheets, Dynamic HTML, and other HTML extensions.

2. Publish your Web pages on the World Wide Web, as outlined in Day 19. Test your pages and then spread the word about your site. Remember, the beauty of the World Wide Web is that your pages aren't set in stone. You can modify, delete, or add to your Web site any time you choose.

21

PART 8

Appendixes

APPENDIX A

Sources for Further Information

Haven't had enough yet? In this appendix, you'll find the URLs for all kinds of information about the World Wide Web, HTML, and developing Web sites. With this information, you should be able to find just about anything you need on the Web.

Note

> Some of the URLs in this appendix refer to FTP sites. They might be very busy during business hours, and you might not be able to access the files immediately. Try again during nonprime hours.
>
> Also, for mysterious reasons, some of these sites might be accessible through an FTP program but not through Web browsers. If you're consistently refused by these sites using a browser, try an FTP program instead.

These sites are divided into the following categories and are listed in alphabetical order under each category:

- Access Counters
- Browsers
- Collections of HTML and Web Development Information
- Forms and Imagemaps
- HTML Editors and Converters
- HTML Validators, Link Checkers, and Simple Spiders
- Java, JavaScript, and Embedded Objects
- Log File Parsers
- HTML Style Guides
- Servers and Server Administration
- Sound and Video
- Specifications for HTML, HTTP, and URLs
- The Common Gateway Interface (CGI) and CGI Scripting
- Other Web-Related Topics
- Tools and Information for Images
- Web Providers
- Web Indexes and Search Engines

Access Counters

Access counters without server programs

```
http://www.digits.com/
```

A

Digits for use in access counters

http://www.digitmania.holowww.com/

Page Count

http://wwwx.nbci.com/counter/

Jcount

http://www.jcount.com/

WebTracker

http://www.fxweb.holowww.com/tracker/

LiveCounter

http://www.chami.com/prog/lc/

Yahoo's list of access counters

http://dir.yahoo.com/Computers_and_Internet/Internet/World_Wide_Web/
Programming/Access_Counters/

Browsers

Amaya (X)

http://www.w3.org/Amaya/

Emacs-W3 (for Emacs)

http://www.cs.indiana.edu/elisp/w3/docs.html

Internet Explorer

http://www.microsoft.com/windows/ie/default.htm

Lynx (UNIX and DOS)

http://lynx.browser.org/

Mozilla

http://www.mozilla.org

Netscape (X, Windows, Macintosh) Download Page

http://home.netscape.com/computing/download/index.html

Opera

http://www.operasoftware.com

Collections of HTML and Web Development Information

CNET Builder.com

http://www.builder.com/

The home of the WWW Consortium

http://www.w3.org/

The HTML Writer's Guild

http://www.hwg.org/

The Virtual Library

http://wdvl.com/

The World Wide Web FAQ

http://www.boutell.com/faq/

Yahoo's WWW section

http://dir.yahoo.com/Computers_and_Internet/Internet/World_Wide_Web/

MSDN (Microsoft Developer's Network) Online

http://msdn.microsoft.com/default.asp

Netscape DevEdge Online

http://developer.netscape.com/

AOL webmaster.info

http://webmaster.aol.com/

evolt.org

http://www.evolt.org/

Forms and Imagemaps

Carlos' forms tutorial

http://robot0.ge.uiuc.edu/~carlosp/cs317/cft.html

HotSpots (a Windows imagemap tool)

http://www.1automata.com/hotspots/index.html

Mapedit: A tool for Windows and X11 for creating imagemap map files

http://www.boutell.com/mapedit/

The original NCSA forms documentation

`http://hoohoo.ncsa.uiuc.edu/cgi/forms.html`

LiveImage (Windows-based imagemap tool)

`http://www.mediatec.com/`

Poor Person's Image Mapper (Web-based imagemap creation system)

`http://zenith.berkeley.edu/~seidel/ClrHlpr/imagemap.html`

Yahoo forms list

`http://www.yahoo.com/Computers_and_Internet/Internet/World_Wide_Web/`
`Programming/Forms/`

HTML Editors and Converters

A great list of editors

`http://www.yahoo.com/Computers_and_Internet/Software/Internet/`
`World_Wide_Web/HTML_Editors/`

HotDog (Windows)

`http://www.sausage.com`

HoTMetaL Pro (Windows, Macintosh, UNIX)

`http://www.sq.com`

HTML Assistant Pro (Windows)

`http://www.brooknorth.com/download/`

HTML Transit

`http://www.infoaccess.com`

1st Page

`http://www.evrsoft.com/download/`

Macromedia Dreamweaver

`http://www.macromedia.com/software/dreamweaver/`

Adobe GoLive

`http://www.adobe.com/products/golive/main.html`

Microsoft FrontPage (Windows, Macintosh)

`http://www.microsoft.com/frontpage/`

HTML Validators, Link Checkers, and Simple Spiders

W3C Validator

http://validator.w3.org/

HTML Tidy

http://www.w3.org/People/Raggett/tidy/

WDG HTML Validator

http://www.htmlhelp.com/tools/validator/

Yahoo's List of HTML Validation and HTML Checkers

http://dir.yahoo.com/Computers_and_Internet/Data_Formats/HTML/
Validation_and_Checkers/

Yahoo's List of Web Spiders and Robots

http://dir.yahoo.com/Computers_and_Internet/Internet/World_Wide_Web/
Searching_the_Web/Crawlers__Robots__and_Spiders/

Java, JavaScript, and Embedded Objects

Gamelan (An index of Java applets)

http://www.developer.com/directories/pages/dir.java.html

JavaScript Developer Central

http://developer.netscape.com/tech/javascript/index.html

Java Developer Central

http://developer.netscape.com/tech/java/index.html

Sun's Java home page

http://www.javasoft.com/

Yahoo Java directory

http://www.yahoo.com/Computers_and_Internet/Programming_Languages/Java/

Log File Parsers

Analog

http://www.statslab.cam.ac.uk/~sret1/analog/

A

Webalizer

http://www.mrunix.net/webalizer/

Wusage

http://www.boutell.com/wusage/

Yahoo's List

http://www.yahoo.com/Computers_and_Internet/Software/Internet/
World_Wide_Web/Servers/Log_Analysis_Tools/

HTML Style Guides

Tim Berners-Lee's style guide

http://www.w3.org/hypertext/WWW/Provider/Style/Overview.html

The Yale HyperText style guide

http://info.med.yale.edu/caim/manual/index.html

Servers and Server Administration

Access control in NCSA HTTPD

http://hoohoo.ncsa.uiuc.edu/docs/setup/access/Overview.html
http://hoohoo.ncsa.uiuc.edu/docs/tutorials/user.html
http://hoohoo.ncsa.uiuc.edu/docs/setup/admin/UserManagement.html

Apache (UNIX)

http://www.apache.org/

JigSaw Server (Java)

http://www.w3.org/Jigsaw/

Current list of official MIME types

ftp://ftp.isi.edu/in-notes/iana/assignments/media-types/media-types

MacHTTP and WebStar (Macintosh)

http://www.starnine.com/

Microsoft Internet Information Server (Windows NT)

http://www.microsoft.com/ntserver/web/default.asp

O'Reilly webSite (Windows 95/NT)

http://website.ora.com/

Sound and Video

AVI-Quick (Macintosh converter for AVI to QuickTime)

SoundHack (Sound editor for Macintosh)

Sound Machine (Sound capture/converter/editor for Macintosh)

SoundAPP (Macintosh sound converter)

Sparkle (MPEG player and converter for Macintosh)

WAVany (Windows sound converter)

WHAM (Windows sound converter)

`http://shareware.cnet.com/` (Search for the program and platform you're interested in.)

WinAmp (free sound player for Windows)

`http://www.winamp.com/`

QuickTime

`http://www.apple.com/quicktime/`

RealNetworks

`http://www.realnetworks.com/`

Windows Media

`http://www.windowsmedia.com/`

The Internet Underground Music Archive (IUMA)

`http://www.iuma.com/`

Yahoo's video information

`http://www.yahoo.com/Computers_and_Internet/Multimedia/Video/`

Yahoo's sound information

`http://dir.yahoo.com/computers/multimedia/sound/`

Specifications for HTML, HTTP, and URLs

Frames

`http://home.netscape.com/assist/net_sites/frames.html`

The HTTP specification (as defined in 1992)

`http://www.w3.org/hypertext/WWW/Protocols/HTTP/HTTP2.html`

The HTML Level 2 specification

`http://www.w3.org/MarkUp/html-spec/`

The HTML 3.2 reference specification

`http://www.w3.org/TR/REC-html32/`

A

The HTML 4.01 specification
http://www.w3.org/TR/html4/

The XHTML 1.0 specification
http://www.w3.org/TR/xhtml1//

Cascading Style Sheets
http://www.w3.org/Style/CSS/

Information about HTTP
http://www.w3.org/pub/WWW/Protocols/

Pointers to URL, URN, and URI information and specifications
http://www.w3.org/hypertext/WWW/Addressing/Addressing.html

The Common Gateway Interface (CGI) and CGI Scripting

The CGI specification
http://hoohoo.ncsa.uiuc.edu/cgi/interface.html

cgi-lib.pl (A Perl library to manage CGI and Forms)
http://cgi-lib.berkeley.edu/

The original NCSA CGI documentation
http://hoohoo.ncsa.uiuc.edu/cgi/

Un-CGI (A program to decode form input)
http://www.midwinter.com/~koreth/uncgi.html

Other Web-Related Topics

Adobe Acrobat
http://www.adobe.com/prodindex/acrobat/main.html

SSL information
http://www.netscape.com/info/security-doc.html

Web security overview
http://www.w3.org/Security/Overview.html

Yahoo's list on security, encryption, and authentication
http://www.yahoo.com/Computers_and_Internet/Security_and_Encryption/

Tools and Information for Images

Anthony's Icon Library
http://www.cit.gu.edu.au/~anthony/icons/index.html

Barry's Clip Art Server
http://www.barrysclipart.com/

GIF Converter for Macintosh
Graphic Converter for Macintosh
LView Pro for Windows
Transparency for Macintosh
http://shareware.cnet.com/ (Search for the program and platform you're interested in.)

giftrans
http://www.ibiblio.org/pub/packages/infosystems/WWW/tools/giftrans/

Internet Bag Lady
http://www.dumpsterdive.com/

Yahoo's clip art list
http://dir.yahoo.com/Computers_and_Internet/Graphics/Clip_Art/

Yahoo's GIF list
http://dir.yahoo.com/Computers_and_Internet/Graphics/Data_Formats/GIF/

Yahoo's PNG List
http://dir.yahoo.com/Computers_and_Internet/Graphics/Data_Formats/
PNG__Portable_Network_Graphics_/

Yahoo's icons list
http://dir.yahoo.com/Arts/Design_Arts/Graphic_Design/Web_Page_Design_and_
Layout/Graphics/Icons/

Web Providers

Yahoo's List of Web Hosting Services
http://dir.yahoo.com/Business_and_Economy/Business_to_Business/
Communications_and_Networking/Internet_and_World_Wide_Web/Network_Service_
Providers/Hosting/

Yahoo's List of Directories of Internet Access Providers
http://dir.yahoo.com/Business_and_Economy/Shopping_and_Services/Education/
Internet_Services/Access_Providers/

The List (Worldwide list of Internet Providers)
http://thelist.internet.com/

Web Indexes and Search Engines

AltaVista
http://www.altavista.com/

Google
http://www.google.com/

Excite
http://www.excite.com/

HotBot
http://www.hotbot.com/

Lycos
http://www.lycos.com/

Web Crawler
http://www.webcrawler.com/

Yahoo
http://www.yahoo.com/

Go.com Search
http://www.go.com/

Goto.com
http://www.goto.com/

APPENDIX B

HTML 4.01 Quick Reference

This appendix provides a quick reference to the elements and attributes of the HTML 4.0 language, as specified by the World Wide Web Consortium. It is based on the information provided in the *HTML 4.01 Specification*, W3C Recommendation 24 December 1999 (most current version at press time). The latest version of this document can be found at `http://www.w3.org/TR/html4/`.

To make the information readily accessible, this appendix organizes HTML elements by their function in the following order:

- **Structure**

  bdo, body, Comments, div, !DOCTYPE, h1...h6, head, hr, html, meta, span, title

- **Text Phrases and Paragraphs**

  acronym, address, blockquote, br, cite, code, del, dfn, em, ins, kbd, p, pre, q, samp, strong, sub, sup, var

- **Text Formatting Elements**

  b, basefont, big, font, i, s, small, strike, tt, u

- **Lists**

  dd, dl, dt, li, menu, ol, ul

- **Links**

  a, base, link

- **Tables**

  caption, col, colgroup, table, tbody, td, tfoot, th, thead, tr

- **Frames**

  frame, frameset, iframe, noframes

- **Embedded Content**

  applet, area, img, map, object, param

- **Style**

  style

- **Forms**

  button, fieldset, form, input, isindex, label, legend, option, select, textarea

- **Scripts**

  script, noscript

Note
> A table of character entities is included at the end of this appendix as well.

Within each section, the elements are listed alphabetically and the following information is presented:

- Usage—A general description of the element.
- Start/End Tag—Indicates whether these tags are required, optional, or illegal. Differences between HTML and XHTML are noted.
- Attributes—Lists the attributes of the element with a short description of its effect.
- Deprecated—Lists deprecated attributes; that is, attributes that are still supported in HTML 4.0 and in most browsers, but that are in the process of being phased out in favor of newer techniques, such as style sheets.
- Empty—Indicates whether the element can be empty.
- Notes—Relates any special considerations when using the element and indicates whether the element is new, deprecated, or obsolete.

Common Attributes and Events

The HTML 4.01 specification includes several attributes that apply to a significant number of elements. These are referred to as %coreattrs, %i18n, and %events throughout this appendix and are explained in the following section.

%coreattrs

Four attributes are abbreviated as %coreattrs in the following sections. They are as follows:

- id="..."   A global identifier
- class="..."   A list of classes separated by spaces
- style="..."   Style information
- title="..."   Provides more information for a specific element, as opposed to the title element, which entitles the entire Web page

%i18n

Two attributes for internationalization (i18n) are abbreviated as %i18n:

- lang="..."   The language identifier
- dir="..."   The text direction (ltr, rtl)

%events

The following intrinsic events are abbreviated %events:

- onclick="..."   A pointing device (such as a mouse) was single-clicked.
- ondblclick="..."   A pointing device (such as a mouse) was double-clicked.
- onmousedown="..."   A mouse button was clicked and held down.
- onmouseup="..."   A mouse button that was clicked and held down was released.
- onmouseover="..."   A mouse moved the cursor over an object.
- onmousemove="..."   A mouse was moved.
- onmouseout="..."   A mouse moved the cursor off an object.
- onkeypress="..."   A key was pressed and released.
- onkeydown="..."   A key was pressed and held down.
- onkeyup="..."   A key that was pressed has been released.

B

Structure

HTML relies on several elements to provide structure to a document (as opposed to structuring the text within), as well as provide information that is used by the browser or search engines.

<bdo>...</bdo>

Usage	The bidirectional algorithm element is used to selectively turn off the default text direction. Default text direction is left to right, but can be changed (to render Hebrew text from right to left, for example).
Start/End Tag	Required/Required.
Attributes	lang="..." The language of the document.
	dir="..." The text direction (ltr, rtl).
Empty	No.
Notes	The dir attribute is mandatory.

<body>...</body>

Usage	Contains the content of the document.
Start/End Tag	Optional/Optional (HTML); Required/Required (XHTML 1.0).
Attributes	%coreattrs, %i18n, %events.
	onload="..." Intrinsic event triggered when the document loads.
	onunload="..." Intrinsic event triggered when document unloads.
Deprecated	The following presentational attributes are deprecated in favor of setting these values with style sheets:
	background="..." URL for the background image.
	bgcolor="..." Sets background color.
	text="..." Text color.
	link="..." Link color.
	vlink="..." Visited link color.

	`alink="..."` Active link color.
Empty	No.
Notes	There can be only one body, and it must follow the head. The body element can be replaced by a frameset element.

Comments `<!-- ... -->`

Usage	Inserts notes or scripts that are not displayed by the browser.
Start/End Tag	Required/Required.
Attributes	None.
Empty	Yes.
Notes	Comments are not restricted to one line and can be any length. The end tag is not required to be on the same line as the start tag.

`<div>...</div>`

Usage	Division element is used to add structure to a block of text.
Start/End Tag	Required/Required.
Attributes	`%coreattrs, %i18n, %events`.
Deprecated	The align attribute is deprecated in favor of controlling alignment through style sheets.
	`align="..."` Controls alignment (left, center, right, justify).
Empty	No.
Notes	Cannot be used within a P element.

`<!DOCTYPE...>`

Usage	Version information appears on the first line of an HTML document and is a Standard Generalized Markup Language (SGML) declaration rather than an element.

B

| Notes: | Optional in HTML documents, but required in XHTML 1.0. |

`<h1>...</h1>` Through `<h6>...</h6>`

Usage	The six headings (h1 is the uppermost, or most important) are used in the body to structure information in a hierarchical fashion.
Start/End Tag	Required/Required.
Attributes	%coreattrs, %i18n, %events.
Deprecated	The align attribute is deprecated in favor of controlling alignment through style sheets.
	align="..." Controls alignment (left, center, right, justify).
Empty	No.
Notes	Visual browsers will display the size of the headings in relation to their importance, with h1 being the largest and h6 the smallest.

`<head>...</head>`

Usage	This is the document header and contains other elements that provide information to users and search engines.
Start/End Tag	Optional/Optional (HTML); Required/Required (XHTML 1.0).
Attributes	%i18n.
	profile="..." URL specifying the location of meta data.
Empty	No.
Notes	There can be only one head per document. It must follow the opening html tag and precede the body.

\<hr\>

Usage	Horizontal rules are used to separate sections of a Web page.
Start/End Tag	Required/Illegal—See note for XHTML 1.0 requirements.
Attributes	%coreattrs, %events.
Deprecated	align="..." Controls alignment (left, center, right, justify).
	noshade="..." Displays the rule as a solid color.
	size="..." The size of the rule.
	width="..." The width of the rule.
Empty	Yes.
Notes	In XHTML 1.0, this tag should take the XML form of \<hr /\> to ensure compatibility with older browsers.

\<html\>...\</html\>

Usage	The html element contains the entire document.
Start/End Tag	Optional/Optional (HTML); Required/Required (XHTML 1.0).
Attributes	%i18n.
Deprecated	version="..." URL of the document type definition specifying the HTML version used to create the document.
Empty	No.
Notes	The version information is duplicated in the \<!DOCTYPE...\> declaration and therefore is not essential.

\<meta\>

Usage	Provides information about the document.
Start/End Tag	Required/Illegal—See note for XHTML 1.0 requirements.

B

Attributes	%i18n.
	`http-equiv="..."` HTTP response header name.
	`name="..."` Name of the meta information.
	`content="..."` Content of the meta information.
	`scheme="..."` Assigns a scheme to interpret the meta data.
Empty	Yes.
Notes	In XHTML 1.0, this tag should take the XML form of `<meta />` to ensure compatibility with older browsers.

`<span>...</span>`

Usage	Organizes the document by defining a span of text.
Start/End Tag	Required/Required.
Attributes	`%coreattrs, %i18n, %events.`
Empty	No.

`<title>...</title>`

Usage	This is the name you give your Web page. The `title` element is located in the `head` element and is displayed in the browser window title bar.
Start/End Tag	Required/Required.
Attributes	%i18n.
Empty	No.
Notes	Only one title allowed per document.

Text Phrases and Paragraphs

You can structure text phrases (or blocks) to suit a specific purpose, such as creating a paragraph. This should not be confused with modifying the formatting of the text.

`<acronym>`...`</acronym>`

Usage	Defines acronyms.
Start/End Tag	Required/Required.
Attributes	%coreattrs, %i18n, %events.
Empty	No.

`<address>`...`</address>`

Usage	Provides a special format for author or contact information.
Start/End Tag	Required/Required.
Attributes	%coreattrs, %i18n, %events.
Empty	No.
Notes	The br element is commonly used inside the address element to break the lines of an address.

`<blockquote>`...`</blockquote>`

Usage	Displays long quotations.
Start/End Tag	Required/Required.
Attributes	%coreattrs, %i18n, %events.
	cite="..." The URL of the quoted text.
Empty	No.

`<br>`

Usage	Forces a line break.
Start/End Tag	Required/Illegal—See note for XHTML 1.0 requirements.
Attributes	%coreattrs, %i18n, %events.
Deprecated	clear="..." Sets the location where next line begins after a floating object (none, left, right, all).
Empty	Yes.

B

Notes	In XHTML 1.0, this tag should take the XML form of ` ` to ensure compatibility with older browsers.

`<cite>...</cite>`

Usage	Cites a reference.
Start/End Tag	Required/Required.
Attributes	%coreattrs, %i18n, %events.
Empty	No.

`<code>...</code>`

Usage	Identifies a code fragment for display.
Start/End Tag	Required/Required.
Attributes	%coreattrs, %i18n, %events.
Empty	No.

`<del>...</del>`

Usage	Shows text as having been deleted from the document since the last change.
Start/End Tag	Required/Required.
Attributes	%coreattrs, %i18n, %events.
	`cite="..."`　The URL of the source document.
	`datetime="..."`　Indicates the date and time of the change.
Empty	No.
Notes	New element in HTML 4.0.

`<dfn>...</dfn>`

Usage	Defines an enclosed term.
Start/End Tag	Required/Required.
Attributes	%coreattrs, %i18n, %events.
Empty	No.

`<em>...</em>`

Usage	Emphasized text.
Start/End Tag	Required/Required.
Attributes	`%coreattrs`, `%i18n`, `%events`.
Empty	No.

B

`<ins>...</ins>`

Usage	Shows text as having been inserted in the document since the last change.
Start/End Tag	Required/Required.
Attributes	`%coreattrs`, `%i18n`, `%events`.
	`cite="..."` The URL of the source document.
	`datetime="..."` Indicates the date and time of the change.
Empty	No.
Notes	New element in HTML 4.0.

`<kbd>...</kbd>`

Usage	Indicates text a user would type.
Start/End Tag	Required/Required.
Attributes	`%coreattrs`, `%i18n`, `%events`.
Empty	No.

`<p>...</p>`

Usage	Defines a paragraph.
Start/End Tag	Required/Optional (HTML); Required/Required (XHTML 1.0).
Attributes	`%coreattrs`, `%i18n`, `%events`.
Deprecated	`align="..."` Controls alignment (`left`, `center`, `right`, `justify`).
Empty	No.

`<pre>...</pre>`

Usage	Displays preformatted text.
Start/End Tag	Required/Required.
Attributes	`%coreattrs`, `%i18n`, `%events`.
Deprecated	`width="..."` The width of the formatted text.
Empty	No.

`<q>...</q>`

Usage	Displays short quotations that do not require paragraph breaks.
Start/End Tag	Required/Required.
Attributes	`%coreattrs`, `%i18n`, `%events`.
	`cite="..."` The URL of the quoted text.
Empty	No.
Notes	New element in HTML 4.0.

`<samp>...</samp>`

Usage	Identifies sample output.
Start/End Tag	Required/Required.
Attributes	`%coreattrs`, `%i18n`, `%events`.
Empty	No.

`<strong>...</strong>`

Usage	Stronger emphasis.
Start/End Tag	Required/Required.
Attributes	`%coreattrs`, `%i18n`, `%events`.
Empty	No.

`<sub>...</sub>`

Usage	Creates subscript.

Start/End Tag	Required/Required.
Attributes	%coreattrs, %i18n, %events.
Empty	No.

`<sup>...</sup>`

Usage	Creates superscript.
Start/End Tag	Required/Required.
Attributes	%coreattrs, %i18n, %events.
Empty	No.

`<var>...</var>`

Usage	A variable.
Start/End Tag	Required/Required.
Attributes	%coreattrs, %i18n, %events.
Empty	No.

Text Formatting Elements

Text characteristics such as the size, weight, and style can be modified by using these elements, but the HTML 4.01 specification encourages you to use style sheets instead.

`<b>...</b>`

Usage	Bold text.
Start/End Tag	Required/Required.
Attributes	%coreattrs, %i18n, %events.
Empty	No.

`<basefont>`

Usage	Sets the base font size.
Start/End Tag	Required/Illegal—See note for XHTML 1.0 requirements.

Deprecated	`size="..."` The font size (1 through 7 or relative; that is, +3).
	`color="..."` The font color.
	`face="..."` The font type.
Empty	Yes.
Notes	Deprecated in favor of style sheets. In XHTML 1.0, this tag should take the XML form of `<basefont />` to ensure compatibility with older browsers.

`<big>...</big>`

Usage	Large text.
Start/End Tag	Required/Required.
Attributes	`%coreattrs, %i18n, %events`.
Empty	No.

`<font>...</font>`

Usage	Changes the font face, size, and color.
Start/End Tag	Required/Required.
Deprecated	`size="..."` The font size (1 through 7 or relative; that is, +3).
	`color="..."` The font color.
	`face="..."` The font type.
Empty	No.
Notes	Deprecated in favor of style sheets.

`<i>...</i>`

Usage	Italicized text.
Start/End Tag	Required/Required.
Attributes	`%coreattrs, %i18n, %events`.
Empty	No.

`<s>...</s>`

Usage	Strikethrough text.
Start/End Tag	Required/Required.
Attributes	%coreattrs, %i18n, %events.
Empty	No.
Notes	Deprecated in favor of style sheets.

B

`<small>...</small>`

Usage	Small text.
Start/End Tag	Required/Required.
Attributes	%coreattrs, %i18n, %events.
Empty	No.

`<strike>...</strike>`

Usage	Strikethrough text.
Start/End Tag	Required/Required.
Attributes	%coreattrs, %i18n, %events.
Empty	No.
Notes	Deprecated in favor of style sheets.

`<tt>...</tt>`

Usage	Teletype (or monospaced) text.
Start/End Tag	Required/Required.
Attributes	%coreattrs, %i18n, %events.
Empty	No.

`<u>...</u>`

Usage	Underlined text.
Start/End Tag	Required/Required.
Attributes	%coreattrs, %i18n, %events.

Empty	No.
Notes	Deprecated in favor of style sheets.

Lists

You can organize text into a more structured outline by creating lists. Lists can be nested.

<dd>...</dd>

Usage	The definition description used in a dl (definition list) element.
Start/End Tag	Required/Optional (HTML); Required/Required (XHTML 1.0).
Attributes	%coreattrs, %i18n, %events.
Empty	No.
Notes	Can contain block-level content, such as the <p> element.

<dir>...</dir>

Usage	Creates a multicolumn directory list.
Start/End Tag	Required/Required.
Attributes	%coreattrs, %i18n, %events.
Deprecated	compact Compacts the displayed list.
Empty	No.
Notes	Must contain at least one list item. This element is deprecated in favor of the ul (unordered list) element.

<dl>...</dl>

Usage	Creates a definition list.
Start/End Tag	Required/Required.
Attributes	%coreattrs, %i18n, %events.
Deprecated	compact Compacts the displayed list.

Empty	No.
Notes	Must contain at least one <dt> or <dd> element in any order.

<dt>...</dt>

Usage	The definition term (or label) used within a dl (definition list) element.
Start/End Tag	Required/Optional (HTML); Required/Required (XHTML 1.0).
Attributes	%coreattrs, %i18n, %events.
Empty	No.
Notes	Must contain text (which can be modified by text markup elements).

<li>...</li>

Usage	Defines a list item within a list.
Start/End Tag	Required/Optional (HTML); Required/Required (XHTML 1.0).
Attributes	%coreattrs, %i18n, %events.
Deprecated	type="..." Changes the numbering style (1, a, A, i, I) in ordered lists or bullet style (disc, square, circle) in unordered lists.
	value="..." Sets the numbering to the given integer, beginning with the current list item.
Empty	No.

<menu>...</menu>

Usage	Creates a single-column menu list.
Start/End Tag	Required/Required.
Attributes	%coreattrs, %i18n, %events.
Deprecated	compact Compacts the displayed list.

B

Empty	No.
Notes	Must contain at least one list item. This element is deprecated in favor of the `ul` (unordered list) element.

`<ol>...</ol>`

Usage	Creates an ordered list.
Start/End Tag	Required/Required.
Attributes	`%coreattrs`, `%i18n`, `%events`.
Deprecated	`compact` Compacts the displayed list.
	`start="..."` Sets the starting number to the chosen integer.
	`type="..."` Sets the numbering style (`1`, `a`, `A`, `i`, `I`).
Empty	No.
Notes	Must contain at least one list item.

`<ul>...</ul>`

Usage	Creates an unordered list.
Start/End Tag	Required/Required.
Attributes	`%coreattrs`, `%i18n`, `%events`.
Deprecated	`compact` Compacts the displayed list.
	`type="..."` Sets the bullet style (`disc`, `square`, `circle`).
Empty	No.
Notes	Must contain at least one list item.

Links

Hyperlinking is fundamental to HTML. These elements enable you to link to other documents.

`<a>...</a>`

Usage	Used to define links and anchors.

Start/End Tag	Required/Required.
Attributes	`%coreattrs`, `%i18n`, `%events`.

`charset="..."`   Character encoding of the resource.

`name="..."`   Defines an anchor.

`href="..."`   The URL of the linked resource.

`target="..."`   Determines where the resource will be displayed (user-defined name, `_blank` [in a new unnamed window], `_parent` [in the immediate parent frameset], `_self` [in the same frame as the current document], or `_top` [in a full browser window that removes the frameset completely]).

`rel="..."`   Forward link types.

`rev="..."`   Reverse link types.

`accesskey="..."`   Assigns a hotkey to this element.

`shape="..."`   Enables you to define client-side imagemaps using defined shapes (`default`, `rect`, `circle`, `poly`).

`coords="..."`   Sets the size of the shape using pixel or percentage lengths.

`tabindex="..."`   Sets the tabbing order between elements with a defined `tabindex`.

Empty	No.

`<base>`

Usage	All other URLs in the document are resolved against this location.
Start/End Tag	Required/Illegal—See note for XHTML 1.0 requirements.
Attributes	`href="..."` The URL of the linked resource.

`target="..."`   Determines where the resource will be displayed (user-defined name, `_blank`, `_parent`, `_self`, `_top`).

Empty	Yes.
Notes	Located in the document head. In XHTML 1.0, this tag should take the XML form of `<base />` to ensure compatibility with older browsers.

`<link>`

Usage	Defines the relationship between a link and a resource.
Start/End Tag	Required/Illegal—See note for XHTML 1.0 requirements.
Attributes	`%coreattrs, %i18n, %events.`
	`href="..."` The URL of the resource.
	`rel="..."` The forward link types.
	`rev="..."` The reverse link types.
	`type="..."` The Internet content type.
	`media="..."` Defines the destination medium (`screen, print, projection, braille, speech, all`).
	`target="..."` Determines where the resource will be displayed (user-defined name, _blank, _parent, _self, _top).
Empty	Yes.
Notes	Located in the document head. In XHTML 1.0, this tag should take the XML form of `<link />` to ensure compatibility with older browsers.

Tables

Tables are meant to display data in a tabular format. Tables are widely used for page layout purposes, but with the advent of style sheets, this is being discouraged by the HTML 4.01 specification.

`<caption>...</caption>`

Usage	Displays a table caption.
Start/End Tag	Required/Required.

Attributes	`%coreattrs`, `%i18n`, `%events`.
Deprecated	`align="..."` Controls alignment (`left`, `center`, `right`, `justify`).
Empty	No.
Notes	Optional.

`<col>`

Usage	Groups columns within column groups in order to share attribute values.
Start/End Tag	Required/Illegal—See note for XHTML 1.0 requirements.
Attributes	`%coreattrs`, `%i18n`, `%events`.
	`span="..."` The number of columns the group contains.
	`width="..."` The column width as a percentage, pixel value, or minimum value.
	`align="..."` Horizontally aligns the contents of cells (`left`, `center`, `right`, `justify`, `char`).
	`char="..."` Sets a character on which the column aligns.
	`charoff="..."` Offset to the first alignment character on a line.
	`valign="..."` Vertically aligns the contents of a cell (`top`, `middle`, `bottom`, `baseline`).
Empty	Yes.
Notes	In XHTML 1.0, this tag should take the XML form of `<col />` to ensure compatibility with older browsers.

`<colgroup>...</colgroup>`

Usage	Defines two or more columns as a group.
Start/End Tag	Required/Optional (HTML); Required/Required (XHTML 1.0).

B

Attributes	`%coreattrs`, `%i18n`, `%events`.
	`span="..."` The number of columns in a group.
	`width="..."` The width of the columns.
	`align="..."` Horizontally aligns the contents of cells (`left`, `center`, `right`, `justify`, `char`).
	`char="..."` Sets a character on which the column aligns.
	`charoff="..."` Offset to the first alignment character on a line.
	`valign="..."` Vertically aligns the contents of a cell (`top`, `middle`, `bottom`, `baseline`).
Empty	No.

`<table>...</table>`

Usage	Creates a table.
Start/End Tag	Required/Required.
Attributes	`%coreattrs`, `%i18n`, `%events`.
	`width="..."` Table width.
	`cols="..."` The number of columns.
	`border="..."` The width in pixels of a border around the table.
	`frame="..."` Sets the visible sides of a table (`void`, `above`, `below`, `hsides`, `lhs`, `rhs`, `vsides`, `box`, `border`).
	`rules="..."` Sets the visible rules within a table (`none`, `groups`, `rows`, `cols`, `all`).
	`cellspacing="..."` Spacing between cells.
	`cellpadding="..."` Spacing in cells.
Deprecated	`align="..."` Controls alignment (`left`, `center`, `right`, `justify`).
	`bgcolor="..."` Sets the background color.
Empty	No.

`<tbody>...</tbody>`

Usage	Defines the table body.
Start/End Tag	Optional/Optional (HTML); Required/Required (XHTML 1.0).
Attributes	%coreattrs, %i18n, %events.
	align="..." Horizontally aligns the contents of cells (left, center, right, justify, char).
	char="..." Sets a character on which the column aligns.
	charoff="..." Offset to the first alignment character on a line.
	valign="..." Vertically aligns the contents of cells (top, middle, bottom, baseline).
Empty	No.

B

`<td>...</td>`

Usage	Defines a cell's contents.
Start/End Tag	Required/Optional (HTML); Required/Required (XHTML 1.0).
Attributes	%coreattrs, %i18n, %events.
	axis="..." Abbreviated name.
	axes="..." axis names listing row and column headers pertaining to the cell.
	rowspan="..." The number of rows spanned by a cell.
	colspan="..." The number of columns spanned by a cell.
	align="..." Horizontally aligns the contents of cells (left, center, right, justify, char).
	char="..." Sets a character on which the column aligns.

charoff="..."   Offset to the first alignment character on a line.

valign="..."   Vertically aligns the contents of cells
(top, middle, bottom, baseline).

Deprecated	nowrap="..." Turns off text wrapping in a cell.
	bgcolor="..." Sets the background color.
	height="..." Sets the height of the cell.
	width="..." Sets the width of the cell.
Empty	No.

<tfoot>...</tfoot>

Usage	Defines the table footer.
Start/End Tag	Required/Optional (HTML); Required/Required (XHTML 1.0).
Attributes	%coreattrs, %i18n, %events.

align="..."   Horizontally aligns the contents of
cells (left, center, right, justify, char).

char="..."   Sets a character on which the column
aligns.

charoff="..."   Offset to the first alignment character on a line.

valign="..."   Vertically aligns the contents of cells
(top, middle, bottom, baseline).

| Empty | No. |

<th>...</th>

Usage	Defines the cell contents of the table header.
Start/End Tag	Required/Optional (HTML); Required/Required (XHTML 1.0).
Attributes	%coreattrs, %i18n, %events.

axis="..."   Abbreviated name.

axes="..." axis names listing row and column headers pertaining to the cell.

rowspan="..." The number of rows spanned by a cell.

colspan="..." The number of columns spanned by a cell.

align="..." Horizontally aligns the contents of cells (left, center, right, justify, char).

char="..." Sets a character on which the column aligns.

charoff="..." Offset to the first alignment character on a line.

valign="..." Vertically aligns the contents of cells (top, middle, bottom, baseline).

Deprecated	nowrap="..." Turns off text wrapping in a cell.
	bgcolor="..." Sets the background color.
	height="..." Sets the height of the cell.
	width="..." Sets the width of the cell.
Empty	No.

\<thead\>...\</thead\>

Usage	Defines the table header.
Start/End Tag	Required/Optional (HTML); Required/Required (XHTML 1.0).
Attributes	%coreattrs, %i18n, %events.

align="..." Horizontally aligns the contents of cells (left, center, right, justify, char).

char="..." Sets a character on which the column aligns.

charoff="..." Offset to the first alignment character on a line.

valign="..." Vertically aligns the contents of cells
(top, middle, bottom, baseline).

Empty	No.

<tr>...</tr>

Usage	Defines a row of table cells.
Start/End Tag	Required/Optional (HTML); Required/Required (XHTML 1.0).
Attributes	%coreattrs, %i18n, %events.

align="..." Horizontally aligns the contents of
cells (left, center, right, justify, char).

char="..." Sets a character on which the column
aligns.

charoff="..." Offset to the first alignment character on a line.

valign="..." Vertically aligns the contents of cells
(top, middle, bottom, baseline).

Deprecated	bgcolor="..." Sets the background color.
Empty	No.

Frames

Frames create new "panels" in the Web browser window that are used to display content
from different source documents.

<frame>

Usage	Defines a frame.
Start/End Tag	Required/Illegal—See note for XHTML 1.0 require-ments.
Attributes	name="..." The name of a frame.

src="..." The source to be displayed in a frame.

frameborder="..." Toggles the border between
frames (0, 1).

marginwidth="..."   Sets the space between the
frame border and content.

marginheight="..."   Sets the space between the
frame border and content.

noresize   Disables sizing.

scrolling="..."   Determines scrollbar presence
(auto, yes, no).

Empty   Yes.

Notes   In XHTML 1.0, this tag should take the XML form of
                                   <frame /> to ensure compatibility with older
                                   browsers.

`<frameset>...</frameset>`

Usage   Defines the layout of frames within a window.

Start/End Tag   Required/Required.

Attributes   rows="..."   The number of rows.

                                   cols="..."   The number of columns.

                                   onload="..."   The intrinsic event triggered when the
                                   document loads.

                                   onunload="..."   The intrinsic event triggered when
                                   the document unloads.

Empty   No.

Notes   Framesets can be nested.

`<iframe>...</iframe>`

Usage   Creates an inline frame. (Only supported by Internet
                                   Explorer.)

Start/End Tag   Required/Required.

Attributes   name="..."   The name of the frame.

                                   src="..."   The source to be displayed in a frame.

                                   frameborder="..."   Toggles the border between
                                   frames (0, 1).

marginwidth="..." Sets the space between the frame border and content.

marginheight="..." Sets the space between the frame border and content.

scrolling="..." Determines scrollbar presence (auto, yes, no).

height="..." Height.

width="..." Width.

| Deprecated | align="..." Controls alignment (left, center, right, justify). |
| Empty | No. |

<noframes>...</noframes>

Usage	Alternative content when frames are not supported.
Start/End Tag	Required/Required.
Attributes	None.
Empty	No.

Embedded Content

Also called *inclusions*, embedded content applies to Java applets, imagemaps, and other multimedia or programmatic content that is placed in a Web page to provide additional functionality.

<applet>...</applet>

Usage	Includes a Java applet.
Start/End Tag	Required/Required.
Deprecated	align="..." Controls alignment (left, center, right, justify).
	alt="..." Displays text while loading.
	archive="..." Identifies the resources to be pre-loaded.

code="..."   The applet class file.

codebase="..."   The URL base for the applet.

height="..."   The width of the displayed applet.

hspace="..."   The horizontal space separating the image from other content.

name="..."   The name of the applet.

object="..."   The serialized applet file.

vspace="..."   The vertical space separating the image from other content.

width="..."   The height of the displayed applet.

Empty	No.
Notes	Applet is deprecated in favor of the object element.

\<area\>

Usage	Defines links and anchors in a client-side image map.
Start/End Tag	Required/Illegal—See note for XHTML 1.0 requirements.
Attributes	shape="..." Enables you to define client-side imagemaps using defined shapes (default, rect, circle, poly).

coords="..."   Sets the size of the shape using pixel or percentage lengths.

href="..."   The URL of the linked resource.

target="..."   Determines where the resource will be displayed (user-defined name, _blank, _parent, _self, _top).

nohref="..."   Indicates that the region has no action.

alt="..."   Displays alternative text.

tabindex="..."   Sets the tabbing order between elements with a defined tabindex.

| Empty | Yes. |
| Notes | In XHTML 1.0, this tag should take the XML form of `<area />` to ensure compatibility with older browsers. |

`<img>`

Usage	Includes an image in the document.
Start/End Tag	Required/Illegal—See note for XHTML 1.0 requirements.
Attributes	`%coreattrs`, `%i18n`, `%events`.
	`src="..."` The URL of the image.
	`alt="..."` Alternative text to display.
	`height="..."` The height of the image.
	`width="..."` The width of the image.
	`usemap="..."` The URL to a client-side imagemap.
	`ismap` Identifies a server-side imagemap.
Deprecated	`align="..."` Controls alignment (`left`, `center`, `right`, `justify`).
	`border="..."` Border width.
	`hspace="..."` The horizontal space separating the image from other content.
	`vspace="..."` The vertical space separating the image from other content.
Empty	Yes.
Notes	In XHTML 1.0, this tag should take the XML form of `<img />` to ensure compatibility with older browsers.

`<map>...</map>`

| Usage | When used with the `area` element, creates a client-side imagemap. |
| Start/End Tag | Required/Required. |

Attributes	%coreattrs.
	name="..." The name of the imagemap to be created.
Empty	No.

<object>...</object>

Usage	Includes an object.
Start/End Tag	Required/Required.
Attributes	%coreattrs, %i18n, %events.
	declare A flag that makes the current object definition a declaration only.
	classid="..." The URL of the object's location.
	codebase="..." The URL for resolving URLs specified by other attributes.
	data="..." The URL to the object's data.
	type="..." The Internet content type for data.
	codetype="..." The Internet content type for the code.
	standby="..." Show message while loading.
	height="..." The height of the object.
	width="..." The width of the object.
	usemap="..." The URL to an imagemap.
	shapes= Enables you to define areas to search for hyperlinks if the object is an image.
	name="..." The URL to submit as part of a form.
	tabindex="..." Sets the tabbing order between elements with a defined tabindex.
Deprecated	align="..." Controls alignment (left, center, right, justify).
	border="..." Displays the border around an object.

B

	hspace="..." The space between the sides of the object and other page content.
	vspace="..." The space between the top and bottom of the object and other page content.
Empty	No.

<param>

Usage	Initializes an object.
Start/End Tag	Required/Illegal—See note for XHTML 1.0 requirements.
Attributes	name="..." Defines the parameter name.
	value="..." The value of the object parameter.
	valuetype="..." Defines the value type (data, ref, object).
	type="..." The Internet media type.
Empty	Yes.
Notes	In XHTML 1.0, this tag should take the XML form of <param /> to ensure compatibility with older browsers.

Style

Style sheets (both inline and external) are incorporated into an HTML document through the use of the style element.

<style>...</style>

Usage	Creates an internal style sheet.
Start/End Tag	Required/Required.
Attributes	%i18n.
	type="..." The Internet content type.
	media="..." Defines the destination medium (screen, print, projection, braille, speech, all).
	title="..." The title of the style.

Empty	No.
Notes	Located in the head element.

Forms

Forms create an interface for the user to select options and submit data back to the Web server.

`<button>...</button>`

Usage	Creates a button.
Start/End Tag	Required/Required.
Attributes	%coreattrs, %i18n, %events.
	name="..." The button name.
	value="..." The value of the button.
	type="..." The button type (button, submit, reset).
	disabled="..." Sets the button state to disabled.
	tabindex="..." Sets the tabbing order between elements with a defined tabindex.
	onfocus="..." The event that occurs when the element receives focus.
	onblur="..." The event that occurs when the element loses focus.
Empty	No.

`<fieldset>...</fieldset>`

Usage	Groups related controls.
Start/End Tag	Required/Required.
Attributes	%coreattrs, %i18n, %events.
Empty	No.

`<form>...</form>`

Usage	Creates a form that holds controls for user input.
Start/End Tag	Required/Required.
Attributes	%coreattrs, %i18n, %events.

action="..."   The URL for the server action.

enctype="..."   Specifies the MIME (Internet media type).

onsubmit="..."   The intrinsic event that occurs when the form is submitted.

onreset="..."   The intrinsic event that occurs when the form is reset.

target="..."   Determines where the resource will be displayed (user-defined name, _blank, _parent, _self, _top).

accept-charset="..."   The list of character encodings.

method="..."   The HTTP method (post or get).

Empty	No.

`<input>`

Usage	Defines controls used in forms.
Start/End Tag	Required/Illegal—See note for XHTML 1.0 requirements.
Attributes	%coreattrs, %i18n, %events.

type="..."   The type of input control (text, password, checkbox, radio, submit, reset, file, hidden, image, button).

name="..."   The name of the control (required except for submit and reset).

value="..."   The initial value of the control (required for radio and checkboxes).

`checked="..."` Sets the radio buttons to a checked state.

`disabled="..."` Disables the control.

`readonly="..."` For text password types.

`size="..."` The width of the control in pixels except for text and password controls, which are specified in number of characters.

`maxlength="..."` The maximum number of characters that can be entered.

`src="..."` The URL to an image control type.

`alt="..."` An alternative text description.

`usemap="..."` The URL to a client-side imagemap.

`tabindex="..."` Sets the tabbing order between elements with a defined `tabindex`.

`onfocus="..."` The event that occurs when the element receives focus.

`onblur="..."` The event that occurs when the element loses focus.

`onselect="..."` Intrinsic event that occurs when the control is selected.

`onchange="..."` Intrinsic event that occurs when the control is changed.

`accept="..."` File types allowed for upload.

Deprecated	`align="..."` Controls alignment (`left`, `center`, `right`, `justify`).
Empty	Yes.
Notes	In XHTML 1.0, this tag should take the XML form of `<input />` to ensure compatibility with older browsers.

B

`<isindex>`

Usage	Prompts the user for input.
Start/End Tag	Required/Illegal—See note for XHTML 1.0 requirements.
Attributes	`%coreattrs`, `%i18n`.
Deprecated	`prompt="..."` Provides a prompt string for the input field.
Empty	Yes.
Notes	In XHTML 1.0, this tag should take the XML form of `<isindex />` to ensure compatibility with older browsers.

`<label>...</label>`

Usage	Labels a control.
Start/End Tag	Required/Required.
Attributes	`%coreattrs`, `%i18n`, `%events`.
	`for="..."` Associates a label with an identified control.
	`disabled="..."` Disables a control.
	`accesskey="..."` Assigns a hotkey to this element.
	`onfocus="..."` The event that occurs when the element receives focus.
	`onblur="..."` The event that occurs when the element loses focus.
Empty	No.

`<legend>...</legend>`

Usage	Assigns a caption to a `fieldset`.
Start/End Tag	Required/Required.
Attributes	`%coreattrs`, `%i18n`, `%events`.
	`accesskey="..."` Assigns a hotkey to this element.

| Deprecated | `align="..."` Controls alignment (`left`, `center`, `right`, `justify`). |
| Empty | No. |

`<option>...</option>`

Usage	Specifies choices in a `select` element.
Start/End Tag	Required/Optional (HTML); Required/Required (XHTML 1.0).
Attributes	`%coreattrs`, `%i18n`, `%events`.
	`selected="..."` Specifies whether the option is selected.
	`disabled="..."` Disables control.
	`value="..."` The value submitted if a control is submitted.
Empty	No.

`<select>...</select>`

Usage	Creates choices for the user to select.
Start/End Tag	Required/Required.
Attributes	`%coreattrs`, `%i18n`, `%events`.
	`name="..."` The name of the element.
	`size="..."` The width in number of rows.
	`multiple` Allows multiple selections.
	`disabled="..."` Disables the control.
	`tabindex="..."` Sets the tabbing order between elements with a defined `tabindex`.
	`onfocus="..."` The event that occurs when the element receives focus.
	`onblur="..."` The event that occurs when the element loses focus.

B

`onselect="..."`   Intrinsic event that occurs when the control is selected.

`onchange="..."`   Intrinsic event that occurs when the control is changed.

| Empty | No. |

`<textarea>...</textarea>`

Usage	Creates an area for user input with multiple lines.
Start/End Tag	Required/Required.
Attributes	`%coreattrs, %i18n, %events`.

`name="..."`   The name of the control.

`rows="..."`   The width in number of rows.

`cols="..."`   The height in number of columns.

`disabled="..."`   Disables the control.

`readonly="..."`   Sets the displayed text to read-only status.

`tabindex="..."`   Sets the tabbing order between elements with a defined `tabindex`.

`onfocus="..."`   The event that occurs when the element receives focus.

`onblur="..."`   The event that occurs when the element loses focus.

`onselect="..."`   Intrinsic event that occurs when the control is selected.

`onchange="..."`   Intrinsic event that occurs when the control is changed.

| Empty | No. |
| Notes | Text to be displayed is placed within the start and end tags. |

Scripts

Scripting language is made available to process data and perform other dynamic events through the script element.

<script>...</script>

Usage	Contains client-side scripts that are executed by the browser.
Start/End Tag	Required/Required.
Attributes	type="..." Script language Internet content type.
	src="..." The URL for the external script.
Deprecated	language="..." The scripting language, deprecated in favor of the type attribute.
Empty	No.
Notes	You can set the default scripting language in the meta element.

<noscript>...</noscript>

Usage	Provides alternative content for browsers unable to execute a script.
Start/End Tag	Required/Required.
Attributes	None.
Empty	No.

Character Entities

Table B.1 contains the possible numeric and character entities for the ISO-Latin-1 (ISO8859-1) character set. Where possible, the character is shown.

Note   Not all browsers can display all characters, and some browsers may even display different characters from those that appear in the table. Newer browsers seem to have a better track record for handling character entities, but be sure and test your HTML files extensively with multiple browsers if you intend to use these entities.

TABLE B.1   ISO-Latin-1 Character Set

Character	Numeric Entity	Character Entity (if any)	Description
	`&#00;–&#08;`		Unused
	`&#09;`		Horizontal tab
	`&#10;`		Line feed
	`&#11;–&#31;`		Unused
	`&#32;`		Space
!	`&#33;`		Exclamation mark
"	`&#34;`	`&quot;`	Quotation mark
#	`&#35;`		Number sign
$	`&#36;`		Dollar sign
%	`&#37;`		Percent sign
&	`&#38;`	`&amp;`	Ampersand
'	`&#39;`		Apostrophe
(	`&#40;`		Left parenthesis
)	`&#41;`		Right parenthesis
*	`&#42;`		Asterisk
+	`&#43;`		Plus sign
,	`&#44;`		Comma
-	`&#45;`		Hyphen
.	`&#46;`		Period (fullstop)
/	`&#47;`		Solidus (slash)
0–9	`&#48;–&#57;`		Digits 0–9
:	`&#58;`		Colon
;	`&#59;`		Semicolon
<	`&#60;`	`&lt;`	Less than
=	`&#61;`		Equals sign
>	`&#62;`	`&gt;`	Greater than
?	`&#63;`		Question mark
@	`&#64;`		Commercial at
A–Z	`&#65;–&#90;`		Letters A–Z
[	`&#91;`		Left square bracket
\	`&#92;`		Reverse solidus (backslash)

TABLE B.1   continued

Character	Numeric Entity	Character Entity (if any)	Description
]	&#93;		Right square bracket
^	&#94;		Caret
–	&#95;		Horizontal bar
`	&#96;		Grave accent
a–z	a–z		Letters a–z
{	&#123;		Left curly brace
|	|		Vertical bar
}	&#125;		Right curly brace
~	&#126;		Tilde
	&#127;–Ÿ		Unused
			Non-breaking space
¡	&#161;	&iexcl;	Inverted exclamation
¢	&#162;	&cent;	Cent sign
£	&#163;	&pound;	Pound sterling
	&#164;	&curren;	General currency sign
¥	&#165;	&yen;	Yen sign
|	&#166;	¦ or &brkbar;	Broken vertical bar
§	&#167;	&sect;	Section sign
¨	&#168;	¨ or ¨	Umlaut (dieresis)
©	&#169;	&copy;	Copyright
ª	&#170;	&ordf;	Feminine ordinal
‹	&#171;	&laqo;	Left angle quote, guillemet left
¬	&#172;	&not;	Not sign
-	&#173;	&shy;	Soft hyphen
®	&#174;	&reg;	Registered trademark
¯	&#175;	¯ or &hibar;	Macron accent
°	&#176;	&deg;	Degree sign
±	&#177;	&plusmn;	Plus or minus
²	&#178;	&sup2;	Superscript two
³	&#179;	&sup3;	Superscript three
´	&#180;	&acute;	Acute accent

B

TABLE B.1　continued

Character	Numeric Entity	Character Entity (if any)	Description
	&#181;	&micro;	Micro sign
¶	&#182;	&para;	Paragraph sign
·	&#183;	&middot;	Middle dot
¸	&#184;	&cedil;	Cedilla
¹	&#185;	&sup1;	Superscript one
º	&#186;	&ordm;	Masculine ordinal
»	&#187;	&raquo;	Right angle quote, guillemet right
1/4	&#188;	&fraq14;	Fraction one-fourth
1/2	&#189;	&fraq12;	Fraction one-half
3/4	&#190;	&fraq34;	Fraction three-fourths
¿	&#191;	&iquest;	Inverted question mark
À	&#192;	&Agrave;	Capital A, grave accent
Á	&#193;	&Aacute;	Capital A, acute accent
Â	&#194;	&Acirc;	Capital A, circumflex accent
Ã	&#195;	&Atilde;	Capital A, tilde
Ä	&#196;	&Auml;	Capital A, dieresis or umlaut mark
Å	&#197;	&Aring;	Capital A, ring
Æ	&#198;	&AElig;	Capital AE dipthong (ligature)
Ç	&#199;	&Ccedil;	Capital C, cedilla
È	&#200;	&Egrave;	Capital E, grave accent
É	&#201;	&Eacute;	Capital E, acute accent
Ê	&#202;	&Ecirc;	Capital E, circumflex accent
Ë	&#203;	&Euml;	Capital E, dieresis or umlaut mark
Ì	&#204;	&Igrave;	Capital I, grave accent
Í	&#205;	&Iacute;	Capital I, acute accent
Î	&#206;	&Icirc;	Capital I, circumflex accent
Ï	&#207;	&Iuml;	Capital I, dieresis or umlaut mark
Ð	&#208;	Ð or Đ	Capital Eth, Icelandic
Ñ	&#209;	&Ntilde;	Capital N, tilde
Ò	&#210;	&Ograve;	Capital O, grave accent
Ó	&#211;	&Oacute;	Capital O, acute accent

TABLE B.1 continued

Character	Numeric Entity	Character Entity (if any)	Description
Ô	&#212;	&Ocirc;	Capital O, circumflex accent
Õ	&#213;	&Otilde;	Capital O, tilde
Ö	&#214;	&Ouml;	Capital O, dieresis or umlaut mark
∞	&#215;	&times;	Multiply sign
Ø	&#216;	&Oslash;	Capital O, slash
Ù	&#217;	&Ugrave;	Capital U, grave accent
Ú	&#218;	&Uacute;	Capital U, acute accent
Û	&#219;	&Ucirc;	Capital U, circumflex accent
Ü	&#220;	&Uuml;	Capital U, dieresis or umlaut mark
¥Y	&#221;	&Yacute;	Capital Y, acute accent
Þ	&#222;	&THORN;	Capital THORN, Icelandic
ß	&#223;	&szlig;	Small sharp s, German (sz ligature)
à	&#224;	&agrave;	Small a, grave accent
á	&#225;	&aacute;	Small a, acute accent
â	&#226;	&acirc;	Small a, circumflex accent
ã	&#227;	&atilde;	Small a, tilde
ä	&#228;	&auml;	Small a, dieresis or umlaut mark
å	&#229;	&aring;	Small a, ring
æ	&#230;	&aelig;	Small ae dipthong (ligature)
ç	&#231;	&ccedil;	Small c, cedilla
è	&#232;	&egrave;	Small e, grave accent
é	&#233;	&eacute;	Small e, acute accent
ê	&#234;	&ecirc;	Small e, circumflex accent
ë	&#235;	&euml;	Small e, dieresis or umlaut mark
ì	&#236;	&igrave;	Small i, grave accent
í	&#237;	&iacute;	Small i, acute accent
î	&#238;	&icirc;	Small i, circumflex accent
ï	&#239;	&iuml;	Small i, dieresis or umlaut mark
ð	&#240;	&eth;	Small eth, Icelandic
ñ	&#241;	&ntilde;	Small n, tilde
ò	&#242;	&ograve;	Small o, grave accent
ó	&#243;	&oacute;	Small o, acute accent
ô	&#244;	&ocirc;	Small o, circumflex accent

B

TABLE B.1 continued

Character	Numeric Entity	Character Entity (if any)	Description
õ	&#245;	&otilde;	Small o, tilde
ö	&#246;	&ouml;	Small o, dieresis or umlaut mark
÷	&#247;	&divide;	Division sign
ø	&#248;	&oslash;	Small o, slash
ù	&#249;	&ugrave;	Small u, grave accent
ú	&#250;	&uacute;	Small u, acute accent
û	&#251;	&ucirc;	Small u, circumflex accent
ü	&#252;	&uuml;	Small u, dieresis or umlaut mark
´y	&#253;	&yacute;	Small y, acute accent
þ	&#254;	&thorn;	Small thorn, Icelandic
ÿ	&#255;	&yuml;	Small y, dieresis or umlaut mark

PART 8

APPENDIX C

Cascading Style Sheet (CSS) Quick Reference

Cascading Style Sheets allow for advanced placement and rendering of text and graphics on your pages. Using style sheets, you can apply text, images, and multimedia to your Web pages with great precision. This appendix provides a quick reference to CSS1, as well as those properties and values that are included in the CSS2 recommendation dated May 12, 1998. This is the most current version of this document at press time.

Note

This appendix is based on the information provided in the Cascading Style Sheets, Level 2 W3C recommendation dated May 12, 1998, which can be found at http://www.w3.org/TR/REC-CSS2/.

To make the information readily accessible, this appendix organizes CSS properties in the following order:

- Block-level properties
- Background and color properties
- Box model properties
- Font properties
- List properties
- Text properties
- Visual effects properties
- Aural style sheet properties
- Generated content/automatic numbering properties
- Paged media properties
- User interface properties
- Cascading Style Sheet units

How to Use This Appendix

Each property contains information presented in the following order:

- Usage—A description of the property
- CSS1 values—Legal CSS1 values and syntax
- CSS2 values—Legal CSS2 values and syntax
- Initial—The initial value
- Applies to—Elements to which the property applies
- Inherited—Whether the property is inherited
- Notes—Additional information

Deciphering CSS values is an exercise that requires patience and a strict adherence to the rules of logic. As you refer to the values for each property listed in this appendix, you should use the following scheme to understand them.

Values of different types are differentiated as follows:

- **Keyword values**—Keywords are identifiers, such as `red`, `auto`, `normal`, and `inherit`. They do not have quotation marks.

- **Basic data types**—These values, such as `<number>` and `<length>`, are contained within angled brackets to indicate the data type of the actual value used in a style statement. It is important to note that this refers to the data type and is not the actual value. The basic data types are described at the end of this appendix.

- **Shorthand reference**—Values that are enclosed in angled brackets and single quotation marks, such as `<'background-color'>` within the `background` property, indicate a shorthand method for setting the desired value. The values identified in `background-color` are available for use in the `background` property. If you choose to set the background color for the document body, for example, you can choose to do so by using either `body { background: red }` or `body { background-color: red }`.

- **Predefined data types**—Values within angled brackets without quotation marks, such as `<border-width>` within the `'border-top-width'` property, are similar to the basic data types but contain predefined values. The available values for `<border-width>`, for example, are `thin`, `thick`, `medium`, and `<length>`.

When more than one value is available, they are arranged according to the following rules:

- **Adjacent words**—Several adjacent words indicate all values must be used but can be in any order.

- **Values separated by bars "|"**—The bar separates two or more alternatives, only one of which can occur.

- **Values separated by double-bars "||"**—The double bar separates two or more options, of which one or more must occur in any order.

- **Brackets "[]"**—Brackets group the values into statements that are evaluated much like a mathematical expression.

When evaluating the values listed in this appendix, the order of precedence is that adjacent values take priority over those separated by double bars and then single bars.

In addition to this, modifiers may follow each value or group of values. These are the following:

- *** (asterisk)**—The preceding type, word, or group occurs zero or more times.

- **+ (plus sign)**—The preceding type, word, or group occurs one or more times.

C

- **? (question mark)**—The preceding type, word, or group is optional.
- **{} (curly braces)**—Surrounding a pair of numbers, such as {1,2}, indicates the preceding type, word, or group occurs at least once and at most twice.

Block-Level Properties

Block-level elements are those that are formatted visually as blocks. A paragraph or a list, for example, is a block.

`bottom, left, right, top`

Usage	Specifies how far a box's bottom, left, right, or top content edge is offset from the respective bottom, left, right, or top of the box's containing block.
CSS2 Values	`<length>` | `<percentage>` | `auto` | `inherit`
Initial	`auto`
Applies to	All elements.
Inherited	No.
Notes	Percentage refers to height of containing block.

`direction`

Usage	Specifies the direction of inline box flow, embedded text direction, column layout, and content overflow.
CSS1 Values	`ltr` | `rtl`
CSS2 Values	`inherit`
Initial	`ltr`
Applies to	All elements.
Inherited	Yes.
Notes	See `unicode-bidi` for further properties that relate to embedded text direction.

`display`

Usage	Specifies how the contents of a block are to be generated.

CSS1 Values	`inline	block	list-item`
CSS2 Values	`run-in	compact	marker	table	inline-table` `| table-row-group	table-column-group |` `table-header-group	table-footer-group |` `table-row	table-cell	table-caption	none |` `inherit`
Initial	`inline`
Applies to	All elements.
Inherited	No.

float

Usage	Specifies whether a box should float to the left, right, or not at all.
CSS1 Values	`none	left	right`
CSS2 Values	`inherit`
Initial	`none`
Applies to	Elements that are not positioned absolutely.
Inherited	No.

position

Usage	Determines which CSS2 positioning algorithms are used to calculate the coordinates of a box.
CSS2 Values	`static	<relative>	<absolute>	fixed |` `inherit`
Initial	`static`
Applies to	All elements except generated content.
Inherited	No.

unicode-bidi

Usage	Opens a new level of embedding with respect to the bidirectional algorithm when elements with reversed writing direction are embedded more than one level deep.

C

CSS2 Values	normal	embed	bidi-override	inherit
Initial	normal
Applies to	All elements.
Inherited	No.

z-index

Usage	Specifies the stack level of the box and whether the box establishes a local stacking context.
CSS2 Values	auto	<integer>	inherit
Initial	auto
Applies to	Elements that generate absolutely and relatively positioned boxes.
Inherited	No.

Background and Color Properties

Whereas HTML enables you to specify background and color properties for text, link, and background on a global basis in the document head, CSS includes similar properties that enable you to customize colors for individual elements. The following properties are those that affect foreground and background colors of page elements.

background

Usage	Shorthand property for setting the individual background properties at the same place in the style sheet.
CSS1 Values	[<'background-color'> || <'background-image'> || <'background-repeat'> || <'background-attachment'> || <'background-position'>]
CSS2 Values	inherit
Initial	Not defined.
Applies to	All elements.
Inherited	No.

background-attachment

Usage	If a background image is specified, this property specifies whether it is fixed in the viewport or scrolls along with the document.
CSS1 Values	scroll	fixed
CSS2 Values	inherit
Initial	scroll
Applies to	All elements.
Inherited	No.

background-color

Usage	Sets the background color of an element.
CSS1 Values	<color>	transparent
CSS2 Values	inherit
Initial	transparent
Applies to	All elements.
Inherited	No.

background-image

Usage	Sets the background image of an element.
CSS1 Values	<uri>	none
CSS2 Values	inherit
Initial	none
Applies to	All elements.
Inherited	No.
Notes	Authors also should specify a background color that will be used when the image is unavailable.

background-position

Usage	Specifies the initial position of the background image, if one is specified.

CSS1 Values	[[<percentage>	<length>](1,2)	[top	center	bottom]		[left	center	right]]
CSS2 Values	inherit
Initial	0% 0%.
Applies to	Block-level and replaced elements.
Inherited	No.

background-repeat

Usage	Specifies whether an image is repeated (tiled) and how, if a background image is specified.
CSS1 Values	repeat-x	repeat-y	repeat	no-repeat
CSS2 Values	inherit
Initial	repeat
Applies to	All elements.
Inherited	No.

color

Usage	Describes the foreground color of an element's text content.
CSS1 Values	<color>
CSS2 Values	inherit
Initial	Depends on browser.
Applies to	All elements.
Inherited	Yes.

Box Model Properties

Each page element in the document tree is contained within a rectangular box and laid out according to a visual formatting model. The following elements affect an element's box.

border

Usage	A shorthand property for setting the same width, color, and style on all four borders of an element.
CSS1 Values	`['border-width' || 'border-style'	<color>]`
CSS2 Values	`inherit`
Initial	Not defined for shorthand properties.
Applies to	All elements.
Inherited	No.
Notes	This property accepts only one value. To set different values for each side of the border, use the `border-width`, `border-style`, or `border-color` properties.

border-bottom, border-left, border-right, border-top

Usage	Shorthand properties for setting the width, style, and color of an element's bottom, left, right, or top border (respectively).
CSS1 Values	`['border-bottom-width' || 'border-style' || <color>]`
	`['border-left-width' || 'border-style' || <color>]`
	`['border-right-width' || 'border-style' || <color>]`
	`['border-top-width' || 'border-style' || <color>]`
CSS2 Values	`inherit`
Initial	Not defined.
Applies to	All elements.
Inherited	No.

C

border-color

Usage	Sets the color of the four borders.
CSS1 Values	`<color>` `(1,4)`	`transparent`
CSS2 Values	`inherit`
Initial	The value of the `<color>` property.
Applies to	All elements.
Inherited	No.
Notes	This property accepts up to four values, as follows:
	One value: Sets all four border colors.
	Two values: First value for top and bottom; second value for right and left.
	Three values: First value for top; second value for right and left; third value for bottom.
	Four values: Top, right, bottom, and left, respectively.

border-bottom-color, border-left-color, border-right-color, border-top-color

Usage	Specifies the colors of a box's border.
CSS1 Values	`<color>`
CSS2 Values	`inherit`
Initial	The value of the `<color>` property.
Applies to	All elements.
Inherited	No.

border-style

Usage	Sets the style of the four borders.
CSS1 Values	`none`	`dotted`	`dashed`	`solid`	`double`	`groove`	`ridge`	`inset`	`outset`

CSS2 Values	inherit
Initial	none
Applies to	All elements.
Inherited	No.
Notes	This property can have from one to four values (see notes under border-color for explanation). If no value is specified, the color of the element itself will take its place.

border-bottom-style, border-left-style, border-right-style, border-top-style

Usage	Sets the style of a specific border (bottom, left, right, or top).
Values	Same as border-style.
Initial	none
Applies to	All elements.
Inherited	No.

border-width

Usage	A shorthand property for setting border-width-top, border-width-right, border-width-bottom, and border-width-left at the same place in the style sheet.
CSS1 Values	[thin | medium | thick] | <length>
CSS2 Values	inherit
Initial	Not defined.
Applies to	All elements.
Inherited	No.
Notes	This property accepts up to four values (see notes under border-color for explanation).

C

border-bottom-width, border-left-width, border-right-width, border-top-width

Usage	Sets the width of an element's bottom, left, right, or top border (respectively).
CSS1 Values	[thin	medium	thick]	<length>
CSS2 Values	inherit
Initial	medium
Applies to	All elements.
Inherited	No.

clear

Usage	Indicates which sides of an element's box or boxes may not be adjacent to an earlier floating box.
CSS1 Values	none	left	right	both
CSS2 Values	inherit
Initial	none
Applies to	Block-level elements.
Inherited	No.

height, width

Usage	Specifies the content height or width of a box.
CSS1 Values	<length>	auto
CSS2 Values	<percentage>	inherit
Initial	auto
Applies to	All elements but non-replaced inline elements and table columns; also does not apply to column groups (for height) or row groups (for width).
Inherited	No.

margin

Usage	Shorthand property for setting `margin-top`, `margin-right`, `margin-bottom`, and `margin-left` at the same place in the style sheet.
CSS1 Values	`<length>` | `<percentage>` | `auto`
CSS2 Values	`inherit`
Initial	Not defined (shorthand property).
Applies to	All elements.
Inherited	No.

margin-bottom, margin-left, margin-right, margin-top

Usage	Sets the bottom, left, right, and top margins of a box, respectively.
CSS1 Values	`<length>` | `<percentage>` | `auto`
CSS2 Values	`inherit`
Initial	`0`
Applies to	All elements.
Inherited	No.

max-height, max-width

Usage	Constrains the height and width of a block to a maximum value.
CSS2 Values	`<length>` | `<percentage>` | `inherit`
Initial	100%
Applies to	All elements.
Inherited	No.
Notes	Percentages refer to the height of the containing block.

C

min-height, min-width

Usage	Constrains the height and width of a block to a minimum value.
CSS2 Values	`<length>` | `<percentage>` | `inherit`
Initial	`0`
Applies to	All elements.
Inherited	No.
Notes	Percentages refer to the height of the containing block.

padding

Usage	Shorthand property that sets `padding-top`, `padding-right`, `padding-bottom`, and `padding-left` at the same place in the style sheet.
CSS1 Values	`<length>` | `<percentage>`
CSS2 Values	`inherit`
Initial	Not defined.
Applies to	All elements.
Inherited	No.

padding-top, padding-right, padding-bottom, padding-left

Usage	Specifies the width of the padding area of a box's top, right, bottom, and left sides.
CSS1 Values	`<length>` | `<percentage>`
CSS2 Values	`inherit`
Initial	`0`
Applies to	All elements.
Inherited	No.
Notes	Values cannot be negative. Percentage values refer to the width of the containing block.

Font Properties

Far more powerful than the font tags and attributes found in HTML 4.01, Cascading Style Sheets enable you to affect many additional elements of a font. CSS1 font properties assume that the font is resident on the client's system and specify alternative fonts through other properties. The properties proposed in CSS2 go beyond that, actually enabling authors to describe the fonts they want to use, and increasing the capability for browsers to select fonts when the font the author specified is not available.

font

Usage	A shorthand property for setting `font-style`, `font-variant`, `font-weight`, `font-size`, `line-height`, and `font-family` at the same place in the style sheet.
CSS1 Values	`[['font-style' || 'font-variant' || 'font-weight']? 'font-size' [/'line-height']? font-family`
CSS2 Values	`caption	icon	menu	message-box	small-caption	status-bar	inherit`
Initial	See individual properties.
Applies to	All elements.
Inherited	Yes.
Notes	Percentages allowed on `font-size` and `line-height`. For backward compatibility, set `font-stretch` and `font-size-adjust` by using their respective individual properties.

font-family

Usage	Specifies a list of font family names and generic family names.
CSS1 Values	`[[<family-name>	<generic-family> [,]* [<family-name>	<generic-family>],`
CSS2 Values	`inherit`
Initial	Depends on browser.
Applies to	All elements.

Inherited	Yes.
Notes	`<family-name>` displays a font family of choice (Arial, Helvetica, or Bookman, for example). `<generic-family>` assigns one of five generic family names: `serif`, `sans-serif`, `cursive`, `fantasy`, or `monospace`.

`font-size`

Usage	Describes the size of the font when set solid.
CSS1 Values	`<absolute-size>` | `<relative-size>` | `<length>` | `<percentage>`
CSS2 Values	`inherit`
Initial	`medium`
Applies to	All elements.
Inherited	The computed value is inherited.
Notes	Percentages can be used relative to the parent element's font size.

`font-size-adjust`

Usage	Enables authors to specify a z-value for an element that preserves the x-height of the first choice substitute font.
CSS2 Values	`<number>` | `none` | `inherit`
Initial	`none`
Applies to	All elements.
Inherited	Yes.
Notes	Percentages can be used relative to the parent element's font size.

`font-stretch`

Usage	Specifies between normal, condensed, and extended faces within a font family.

CSS2 Values	`normal` | `wider` | `narrower` | `ultra-condensed` | `extra-condensed` | `condensed` | `semi-condensed` | `semi-expanded` | `expanded` | `extra-expanded` | `ultra-expanded` | `inherit`
Initial	`normal`
Applies to	All elements.
Inherited	Yes.

font-style

Usage	Requests normal (roman or upright), italic, and oblique faces within a font family.
CSS1 Values	`normal` | `italic` | `oblique`
CSS2 Values	`inherit`
Initial	`normal`
Applies to	All elements.
Inherited	Yes.

font-variant

Usage	Specifies a font that is not labeled as a small-caps font (`normal`) or one that is labeled as a small-caps font (`small-caps`).
CSS1 Values	`normal` | `small-caps`
CSS2 Values	`inherit`
Initial	`normal`
Applies to	All elements.
Inherited	Yes.

font-weight

Usage	Specifies the weight of the font.
CSS1 Values	`normal` | `bold` | `bolder` | `lighter` | `100` | `200` | `300` | `400` | `500` | `600` | `700` | `800` | `900`

C

CSS2 Values	`inherit`
Initial	`normal`
Applies to	All elements.
Inherited	Yes.
Notes	Values `100` through `900` form an ordered sequence. Each number indicates a weight that is at least as dark as its predecessor. `normal` is equal to a weight of `400`, and `bold` is equal to a weight of `700`.

List Properties

When an element is assigned a `display` value of `list-item`, the element's content is contained in a box, and an optional marker box can be specified. The marker defines the image, glyph, or number that is used to identify the list item. The following properties affect list items and markers.

list-style

Usage	Shorthand notation for setting `list-style-type`, `list-style-image` and `list-style-position` at the same place in the style sheet.
CSS1 Values	`['list-style-type' ‖ 'list-style-position' ‖ 'list-style-image']`
CSS2 Values	`inherit`
Initial	Not defined.
Applies to	Elements with `display` property set to `list-item`.
Inherited	Yes.

list-style-image

Usage	Sets the image that will be used as the list item marker.
CSS1 Values	`<uri>	none`
CSS2 Values	`inherit`

Initial	none
Applies to	Elements with `display` property set to `list-item`.
Inherited	Yes.

list-style-position

Usage	Specifies the position of the marker box with respect to the line item content box.
CSS1 Values	`inside` | `outside`
CSS2 Values	`inherit`
Initial	`outside`
Applies to	Elements with `display` property set to `list-item`.
Inherited	Yes.

list-style-type

Usage	Specifies the appearance of the list item marker when `list-style-image` is set to `none`.
CSS1 Values	`disc` | `circle` | `square` | `decimal` | `lower-roman` | `upper-roman` | `lower-alpha` | `upper-alpha` | `none`
CSS2 Values	`leading-zero` | `western-decimal` | `lower-greek` | `lower-latin` | `upper-latin` | `hebrew` | `armenian` | `georgian` | `cjk-ideographic` | `hiragana` | `katakana` | `hiragana-iroha` | `katakana-iroha` | `inherit`
Initial	`disc`
Applies to	Elements with `display` property set to `list-item`.
Inherited	Yes.

Text Properties

The following properties affect the visual presentation of characters, spaces, words, and paragraphs.

letter-spacing

Usage	Specifies the spacing behavior between text characters.
CSS1 Values	`normal	<length>`
CSS2 Values	`inherit`
Initial	`normal`
Applies to	All elements.
Inherited	Yes.

line-height

Usage	Specifies the minimal height of each inline box.
CSS1 Values	`normal	number	<length>	<percentage>`
CSS2 Values	`inherit`
Initial	`normal`
Applies to	All elements.
Inherited	Yes.

text-align

Usage	Describes how a block of text is aligned.
CSS1 Values	`left	right	center	justify`
CSS2 Values	`<string>	inherit`
Initial	Depends on browser and writing direction.
Applies to	Block-level elements.
Inherited	Yes.

text-decoration

Usage	Describes decorations that are added to the text of an element.
CSS1 Values	`none	underline	overline	line-through	blink`
CSS2 Values	`inherit`

Initial	none
Applies to	All elements.
Inherited	No.

`text-indent`

Usage	Specifies the indentation of the first line of text in a block.
CSS1 Values	`<length>` I `<percentage>`
CSS2 Values	`inherit`
Initial	`0`
Applies to	Block-level elements.
Inherited	Yes.

`text-shadow`

Usage	Accepts a comma-separated list of shadow effects to be applied to the text of an element.
CSS2 Values	`none` I `<color>` I `<length>` I `inherit`
Initial	`none`
Applies to	All elements.
Inherited	No.
Notes	You also can use text shadows with `:first-letter` and `:first-line` pseudo-elements.

`text-transform`

Usage	Controls the capitalization of an element's text.
CSS1 Values	`capitalize` I `uppercase` I `lowercase` I `none`
CSS2 Values	`inherit`
Initial	`none`
Applies to	All elements.
Inherited	Yes.

C

vertical-align

Usage	Affects the vertical positioning of the boxes generated by an inline-level element.
Values	baseline | sub | super | top | texttop | middle | bottom | text-bottom | sub | <percentage>
CSS2 Values	inherit
Initial	baseline
Applies to	Inline-level and table-cell elements.
Inherited	No.

white-space

Usage	Specifies how whitespace inside the element is handled.
CSS1 Values	normal | pre | nowrap
CSS2 Values	inherit
Initial	normal
Applies to	Block-level elements.
Inherited	Yes.

word-spacing

Usage	Specifies the spacing behavior between words.
Values	normal | <length>
CSS2 Values	inherit
Initial	normal
Applies to	All elements.
Inherited	Yes.

Visual Effects Properties

The following properties affect visual rendering of an element.

clip

Usage	Defines which portion of an element's rendered content is visible.
CSS2 Values	`<shape>` | `auto` | `inherit`
Initial	`auto`
Applies to	Block-level and replaced elements.
Inherited	No.

overflow

Usage	Specifies whether the contents of a block-level element are clipped when they overflow the element's box.
CSS2 Values	`visible` | `hidden` | `scroll` | `auto` | `inherit`
Initial	`visible`
Applies to	Block-level and replaced elements.
Inherited	No.

visibility

Usage	Specifies whether the boxes generated by an element are rendered.
CSS2 Values	`visible` | `hidden` | `collapse` | `inherit`
Initial	`inherit`
Applies to	All elements.
Inherited	No.

C

Aural Style Sheet Properties

Aural style sheets, a media type in CSS2, are primarily used for the blind and visually-impaired communities. Page contents are read to the user. The aural style sheet "canvas" uses dimensional space to render sounds in specified sequences as page elements are displayed and selected.

`azimuth`

Usage	Enables you to position a sound. Designed for spatial audio, which requires binaural headphones or five-speaker home theater systems.
CSS2 Values	`<angle>` | [[`left-side` | `far-left` | `left` | `center-left` | `center` | `center-right` | `right` | `far-right` | `right-side`] || `behind`]| `leftwards` | `rightwards` | `inherit`
Initial	`center`
Applies to	All elements.
Inherited	Yes.

`cue`

Usage	Shorthand property for `cue-before` and `cue-after`. Plays a sound before or after an element is rendered.
CSS2 Values	`cue-before` | `cue-after` | `inherit`
Initial	Not defined (shorthand property).
Applies to	All elements.
Inherited	No.

`cue-after, cue-before`

Usage	Plays a sound after (`cue-after`) or before (`cue-before`) an element is rendered.
CSS2 Values	`<uri>` | `none` | `inherit`
Initial	`none`

Applies to	All elements.
Inherited	No.

elevation

Usage	Enables you to position the angle of a sound. For use with spatial audio (binaural headphones or five-speaker home theater setups required).
CSS2 Values	`<angle>` | `below` | `level` | `above` | `higher` | `lower` | `inherit`
Initial	`level`
Applies to	All elements.
Inherited	Yes.

pause

Usage	A shorthand property for setting `pause-before` and `pause-after` in the same location in the style sheet.
CSS2 Values	`<time>` | `<percentage>` | `inherit`
Initial	Depends on browser.
Applies to	All elements.
Inherited	No.

pause-after, pause-before

Usage	Specifies a pause to be observed before or after speaking an element's content.
CSS2 Values	`<time>` | `<percentage>` | `inherit`
Initial	Depends on browser.
Applies to	All elements.
Inherited	No.

pitch

Usage	Specifies the average pitch (frequency) of the speaking voice.
CSS2 Values	`<frequency>` | `x-low` | `low` | `medium` | `high` | `x-high` | `inherit`
Initial	`medium`
Applies to	All elements.
Inherited	Yes.
Notes	Average pitch for the standard male voice is around 120Hz; for the female voice, it is around 210Hz.

pitch-range

Usage	Specifies variation in average pitch. Used to vary inflection and add animation to the voice.
CSS2 Values	`<number>` | `inherit`
Initial	50
Applies to	All elements.
Inherited	Yes.

play-during

Usage	Specifies a sound to be played as a background while an element's content is spoken.
CSS2 Values	`<uri>` | `mix?` | `repeat?` | `auto` | `none` | `inherit`
Initial	`auto`
Applies to	All elements.
Inherited	No.

richness

Usage	Specifies the richness, or brightness, of the speaking voice.

CSS2 Values	`<number>`	`inherit`
Initial	`50`
Applies to	All elements.
Inherited	Yes.

speak

Usage	Specifies whether text will be rendered aurally, and in what manner.
CSS2 Values	`normal`	`none`	`spell-out`	`inherit`
Initial	`normal`
Applies to	All elements.
Inherited	Yes.

speak-header

Usage	Specifies whether table headers are spoken before every cell, or only before a cell when it is associated with a different header than a previous cell.
CSS2 Values	`once`	`always`	`inherit`
Initial	`once`
Applies to	Elements that have header information.
Inherited	Yes.

speak-numeral

Usage	Speaks numbers as individual digits (100 is spoken as "one zero zero") or as a continuous full number (100 is spoken as "one hundred").
CSS2 Values	`digits`	`continuous`	`inherit`
Initial	`continuous`
Applies to	All elements.
Inherited	Yes.

speak-punctuation

Usage	Speaks punctuation literally (period, comma, and so on) or naturally as various pauses.
CSS2 Values	code	none	inherit
Initial	none
Applies to	All elements.
Inherited	Yes.

speech-rate

Usage	Specifies the speaking rate of the voice.
CSS2 Values	<number>	x-slow	slow	medium	fast	x-fast	faster	slower	inherit
Initial	medium
Applies to	All elements.
Inherited	Yes.

stress

Usage	Specifies the height of "local peaks" in the intonation of a voice. Controls the amount of inflection within stress markers.
CSS2 Values	<number>	inherit
Initial	50
Applies to	All elements.
Inherited	Yes.
Notes	A companion to the pitch-range property.

voice-family

Usage	Specifies a comma-separated list of voice family names.
CSS2 Values	<specific-voice>	<generic-voice>	inherit
Initial	Depends on browser.

Applies to	All elements.
Inherited	Yes.

volume

Usage	Specifies the median volume of a waveform. Ranges from 0 (minimum audible volume level) to 100 (maximum comfortable level).
CSS2 Values	`<number>` | `<percentage>` | `silent` | `x-soft` | `soft` | `medium` | `loud` | `x-loud` | `inherit`
Initial	`medium`
Applies to	All elements.
Inherited	Yes.
Notes	`silent` renders no sound at all. `x-soft` = 0, `soft` = 25, `medium` = 50, `loud` = 75, and `x-loud` = 100.

Generated Content/Automatic Numbering Properties

CSS2 introduces properties and values that enable authors to render content automatically (for example, numbered lists can be generated automatically). Authors specify style and location of generated content with `:before` and `:after` pseudo-elements that indicate the page elements before and after which content is generated automatically.

content

Usage	Used with `:before` and `:after` pseudo-elements to generate content in a document.
CSS2 Values	`<string>` | `<uri>` | `<counter>` | `attr(X)` | `open-quote` | `close-quote` | `no-open-quote` | `no-close-quote` | `inherit`
Initial	`empty string`
Applies to	`:before` and `:after` pseudo-elements.
Inherited	All.

counter-increment

Usage	Accepts one or more names of counters (identifiers), each one optionally followed by an integer. The integer indicates the amount of increment for every occurrence of the element.
CSS2 Values	`<identifier>`	`<integer>`	`none`	`inherit`
Initial	`none`
Applies to	All elements.
Inherited	No.

counter-reset

Usage	Contains a list of one or more names of counters. The integer gives the value that the counter is set to on each occurrence of the element.
CSS2 Values	`<identifier>`	`<integer>`	`none`	`inherit`
Initial	`none`
Applies to	All elements.
Inherited	No.

marker-offset

Usage	Specifies the distance between the nearest border edges of a marker box and its associated principal box.
CSS2 Values	`<length>`	`auto`	`inherit`
Initial	`auto`
Applies to	Elements with `display` property set to `marker`.
Inherited	No.

quotes

Usage	Specifies quotation marks for embedded quotations.
CSS2 Values	`<string>`	`<string>+`	`none`	`inherit`

Initial	Depends on browser.
Applies to	All elements.
Inherited	Yes.

Paged Media Properties

Normally, a Web page appears as a continuous page. CSS2 introduces the concept of paged media, which is designed to split a document into one or more discrete pages for display on paper, transparencies, computer screens, and so on. Page size, margins, page breaks, widows, and orphans can all be set with the following properties and values.

marks

Usage	Specifies whether cross marks, crop marks, or both should be rendered just outside the page box. Used in high-quality printing.
CSS2 Values	crop I cross I none I inherit
Initial	none
Applies to	Page context.
Inherited	N/A.

orphans

Usage	Specifies the minimum number of lines of a paragraph that must be left at the bottom of a page.
CSS2 Values	<integer> I inherit
Initial	2
Applies to	Block-level elements.
Inherited	Yes.

page

Usage	Used to specify a particular type of page where an element should be displayed.
CSS2 Values	<identifier> :left I :right I auto
Initial	auto

C

Applies to	Block-level elements.
Inherited	Yes.
Notes	By adding :left or :right, the element can be forced to fall on a left or right page.

page-break-after, page-break-before

Usage	Specifies page breaks before the following element or after the preceding element.
CSS2 Values	auto I always I avoid I left I right I inherit
Initial	auto
Applies to	Block-level elements.
Inherited	No.

page-break-inside

Usage	Forces a page break inside the parent element.
CSS2 Values	avoid I auto I inherit
Initial	auto
Applies to	Block-level elements.
Inherited	Yes.

size

Usage	Specifies the size and orientation of a page box.
CSS2 Values	<length> I auto I portrait I landscape I inherit
Initial	auto
Applies to	Page context.
Inherited	N/A.

widows

| Usage | Specifies the minimum number of lines of a paragraph that must be left at the top of a page. |
| CSS2 Values | <integer> I inherit |

Initial	2
Applies to	Block-level elements.
Inherited	Yes.

Table Properties

The CSS table model is based on the HTML 4.01 table model, which consists of tables, captions, rows, row groups, columns, column groups, and cells. In CSS2, tables can be rendered visually and aurally. Authors can specify how headers and data will be spoken through attributes defined previously in "Aural Style Sheet Properties."

border-collapse

Usage	Selects a table's border model.
CSS2 Values	collapse	separate	inherit
Initial	collapse
Applies to	Table and inline table elements.
Inherited	Yes.

border-spacing

Usage	In separated borders model, specifies the distance that separates the adjacent cell borders.
CSS2 Values	<length>	<length> ?	inherit
Initial	0
Applies to	Table and inline table elements.
Inherited	Yes.

caption-side

Usage	Specifies the position of the caption box with respect to the table box.
CSS2 Values	top	bottom	left	right	inherit
Initial	top
Applies to	Table caption elements.
Inherited	Yes.

C

column-span, row-span

Usage	Specifies the number of columns or rows (respectively) spanned by a cell.
CSS2 Values	`<integer>`	`inherit`
Initial	`1`
Applies to	Table cell, table column, and table column group elements (`column-span`); table cell elements (`row-span`).
Inherited	No.

empty-cells

Usage	In the separated tables model, specifies how borders around cells that have no visible content are rendered.
CSS2 Values	`borders`	`no-borders`	`inherit`
Initial	`borders`
Applies to	Table cell elements.
Inherited	Yes.

table-layout

Usage	Controls the algorithm used to lay out the table cells.
CSS2 Values	`auto`	`fixed`	`inherit`
Initial	`auto`
Applies to	Table and inline table elements.
Inherited	No.
Notes	`fixed` table layout depends on the width of the table and its columns. `auto` table layout depends on the contents of the cells.

User Interface Properties

User interface properties enable customization of cursor appearance, color preferences, font preferences, and dynamic outlines.

cursor

Usage	Specifies the type of cursor that displays for a pointing device.
CSS2 Values	`<uri>` l `auto` l `crosshair` l `default` l `pointer` l `move` l `e-resize` l `ne-resize` l `nw-resize` l `n-resize` l `se-resize` l `sw-resize` l `s-resize` l `w-resize` l `text` l `wait` l `help` l `inherit`
Initial	`auto`
Applies to	All elements.
Inherited	Yes.

outline

Usage	Shorthand property for setting `outline-color`, `outline-style`, and `outline-width`.
CSS2 Values	`outline-color` l `outline-style` l `outline-width` l `inherit`
Initial	See individual properties.
Applies to	All elements.
Inherited	No.
Notes	Similar to `border` property, creates an outline around visual objects such as buttons, active form fields, image maps, and so on. Using `outline` property rather than `border` property does not cause reflow when displaying or suppressing the outline. Outlines also can be nonrectangular.

outline-color

Usage	Specifies the color of the outline.
CSS2 Values	`<color>` l `invert` l `inherit`

C

Initial	invert
Applies to	All elements.
Inherited	No.

outline-style

Usage	Specifies the style of the outline.
CSS2 Values	Same as <border-style>	inherit
Initial	none
Applies to	All elements.
Inherited	No.

outline-width

Usage	Specifies the width of the outline.
CSS2 Values	Same as <border-width>	inherit
Initial	medium
Applies to	All elements.
Inherited	No.

Cascading Style Sheet Units

Several Cascading Style Sheet attributes use standard units to define measurements, styles, colors, and other identifiers. Throughout this appendix, unit measurements have been enclosed within angle brackets (< >). The following section lists the values associated with each unit type.

<absolute-size>

Absolute sizes refer to font sizes computed and kept by the user's browser. The following values are from smallest to largest:

xx-small

x-small

small

medium

large

```
x-large
xx-large
```

`<angle>`

Angle values are used with aural style sheets. Their format is an optional sign character (+ or -) immediately followed by a number. The following are angle units:

deg	Degrees
grad	Gradients
rad	Radians

`<border-style>`

These properties specify the type of line that surrounds a box's border. The `border-style` value type can take one of the following:

none	Forces border width to zero
dotted	A series of dots
dashed	A series of short line segments
solid	A single line segment
double	Two solid lines, with the sum of the two lines and the space between them equaling the value of `border-width`
groove	Renders a border that looks as though it is carved into the canvas
ridge	Renders a border that looks as though it is coming out of the canvas
inset	Renders a border that looks like the entire box is embedded in the canvas
outset	Renders a border that looks like the entire box is coming out of the canvas

`<border-width>`

The `border-width` property sets the width of the border area. It can take one of the following values:

thin	A thin border
medium	A medium border
thick	A thick border
`<length>`	An explicit value (cannot be negative)

C

`<color>`

Colors can be defined by keyword (as defined in HTML 4.0) or by a numerical RGB specification. Following are the accepted formats:

Keyword:	aqua | black | blue | fuchsia | gray | green | lime | maroon | navy | olive | purple | red | silver | teal | white | yellow
#rgb	Example for blue: { color: #00f }
#rrggbb	Example for blue: { color: #0000ff }
rgb (integer range)	Example for blue: { color: rgb(0,0,255) }
rgb (float range)	Example for blue: { color: rgb(0%, 0%, 100%) }

`<family-name>`

Fonts can be specified by the name of a font family of choice. Examples of this are Arial, Times New Roman, Helvetica, Baskerville, and so on. Font family names that contain whitespace (tabs, line feeds, carriage returns, form feeds, and so on) should be enclosed by quotation marks.

`<frequency>`

Frequency identifiers are used with aural style sheets. The format is a number immediately followed by one of the following identifiers:

Hz	Hertz
kHz	Kilohertz

`<generic-family>`

Authors are encouraged to use generic font family names as a last alternative, in case a user does not have a specified font on his or her system. Generic font family names are keywords and must not be enclosed in quotation marks. The following are examples of each:

serif	Times New Roman, MS Georgia, Garamond
sans-serif	Arial, Helvetica, Futura, Gill Sans
cursive	Zapf-Chancery, Caflisch Script

| fantasy | Critter, Cottonwood |
| monospace | Courier, MS Courier New, Prestige |

<generic-voice>

Generic voices are the aural equivalent of generic font family names (refer to the preceding section) and are used in conjunction with <voice-family>. The following are possible generic voice values:

male

female

child

<integer>

An integer consists of one or more digits (0 through 9). It may be preceded by a - or a + to indicate the sign. See also <number>.

<length>

Lengths are specified by an optional sign character (+ or -) immediately followed by a number with or without a decimal point, immediately followed by one of the following unit identifiers:

Relative values:

em	The font size of the relevant font
ex	The x-height of the relevant font
px	Pixels, relative to the viewing device

Absolute values:

pt	Points (1/72nd of an inch)
in	Inches
cm	Centimeters
mm	Millimeters
pc	Picas (12 points, or 1/6 of an inch)

<number>

A number can consist of an integer, or it can be zero or more digits, followed by a dot (.), followed by one or more digits. A number may be preceded by a - or a + to indicate its sign. See also <integer>.

<percentage>

Percentage values are always relative to another value, such as a length. The format is an optional sign character (+ or -), immediately followed by a number, immediately followed by %.

<relative-size>

Relative sizes are interpreted relative to the font size of the parent element. The following are possible values:

    larger

    smaller

<shape>

In CSS2, the only valid shape value is rect(<top> <right> <bottom> <left>, where the four descriptors specify offsets from the respective sides of the box.

<specific-voice>

Specific voice values are the aural style sheet equivalent of font-family. Values are specific names of a voice (for example: teacher, comedian, preacher, and so on).

<time>

Time units are used with aural style sheets. Their format is a number immediately followed by one of the following identifiers:

ms	milliseconds
s	seconds

<uri>

URI (Uniform Resource Indicator) values are used to designate addresses of page elements such as images. The format of a URI is url (followed by optional whitespace, followed by an optional single quote or double quotation mark, followed by the URI itself, followed by an optional single or double quote, followed by optional whitespace). To clarify, here is an example of the proper syntax:

```
body { background: url("http://www.foo.com/images/background.gif") }
```

APPENDIX D

Colors by Name and Hexadecimal Value

Table D.1 contains a list of all the color names recognized by Navigator 2.0 and Internet Explorer 3.0 (and later versions of both browsers, of course), and it also includes their corresponding Hexadecimal (Hex) Triplet values. To see all of these colors correctly, you must have a 256-color or better video card and the appropriate video drivers installed. Also, depending on the operating system and computer platform you're running, some colors may not appear exactly as you expect them to.

TABLE D.1   Color Values and HEX Triplet Equivalents

Color Name	HEX Triplet	Color Name	HEX Triplet
aliceblue	#f0f8ff	darksalmon	#e9967a
antiquewhite	#faebd7	darkseagreen	#8fbc8f
aqua	#00ffff	darkslateblue	#483D8b
aquamarine	#7fffd4	darkslategray	#2f4f4f
azure	#f0ffff	darkturquoise	#00ced1
beige	#f5f5dc	darkviolet	#9400d3
bisque	#ffe4c4	deeppink	#ff1493
black	#000000	deepskyblue	#00bfff
blanchedalmond	#ffebcd	dimgray	#696969
blue	#0000ff	dodgerblue	#1e90ff
blueviolet	#8a2be2	firebrick	#b22222
brown	#a52a2a	floralwhite	#fffaf0
burlywood	#deb887	forestgreen	#228b22
cadetblue	#5f9ea0	fuchsia	#ff00ff
chartreuse	#7fff00	gainsboro	#dcdcdc
chocolate	#d2691e	ghostwhite	#f8f8ff
coral	#ff7f50	gold	#ffd700
cornflowerblue	#6495ed	goldenrod	#daa520
cornsilk	#fff8dc	gray	#808080
crimson	#dc143c	green	#008000
cyan	#00ffff	greenyellow	#adff2f
darkblue	#00008b	honeydew	#f0fff0
darkcyan	#008b8b	hotpink	#ff69b4
darkgoldenrod	#b8860b	indianred	#cd5c5c
darkgray	#a9a9a9	indigo	#4b0082
darkgreen	#006400	ivory	#fffff0
darkkhaki	#bdb76b	khaki	#f0e68c
darkmagenta	#8b008b	lavender	#e6e6fa
darkolivegreen	#556b2f	lavenderblush	#fff0f5
darkorange	#ff8c00	lemonchiffon	#fffacd
darkorchid	#9932cc	lightblue	#add8e6
darkred	#8b0000	lightcoral	#f08080

TABLE D.1 continued

Color Name	HEX Triplet	Color Name	HEX Triplet
lightcyan	#e0ffff	olivedrab	#6b8e23
lightgoldenrodyellow	#fafad2	orange	#ffa500
lightgreen	#90ee90	orangered	#ff4500
lightgrey	#d3d3d3	orchid	#da70d6
lightpink	#ffb6c1	palegoldenrod	#eee8aA
lightsalmon	#ffa07a	palegreen	#98fb98
lightseagreen	#20b2aa	paleturquoise	#afeeee
lightskyblue	#87cefa	palevioletred	#db7093
lightslategray	#778899	papayawhip	#ffefd5
lightsteelblue	#b0c4de	peachpuff	#ffdab9
lightyellow	#ffffe0	peru	#cd853f
lime	#00ff00	pink	#ffc0cb
limegreen	#32cd32	plum	#dda0dd
linen	#faf0e6	powderblue	#b0e0e6
magenta	#ff00ff	purple	#800080
maroon	#800000	red	#ff0000
mediumaquamarine	#66cdaa	rosybrown	#bc8f8f
mediumblue	#0000cd	royalblue	#4169e1
mediumorchid	#ba55d3	saddlebrown	#8b4513
mediumpurple	#9370db	salmon	#fa8072
mediumseagreen	#3cb371	sandybrown	#f4a460
mediumslateblue	#7b68ee	seagreen	#2e8b57
mediumspringgreen	#00fa9a	seashell	#fff5ee
mediumturquoise	#48d1cc	sienna	#a0522d
mediumvioletred	#c71585	silver	#c0c0c0
midnightblue	#191970	skyblue	#87ceeb
mintcream	#f5fffa	slateblue	#6a5acd
mistyrose	#ffe4e1	slategray	#708090
navajowhite	#ffdead	snow	#fffafa
navy	#000080	springgreen	#00ff7f
oldlace	#fdf5e6	steelblue	#4682b4
olive	#808000	tan	#d2b48c

D

TABLE D.1   continued

Color Name	HEX Triplet	Color Name	HEX Triplet
teal	#008080	wheat	#f5deb3
thistle	#d8bfd8	white	#ffffff
tomato	#ff6347	whitesmoke	#f5f5f5
turquoise	#40e0d0	yellow	#ffff00
violet	#ee82ee	yellowgreen	#9acd32

APPENDIX E

MIME Types and File Extensions

Table E.1 lists some the file extensions and MIME content types supported by many popular Web servers. If your server doesn't list an extension for a particular content type, or if the type you want to use isn't listed at all, you'll have to add support for that type to your server configuration.

TABLE E.1   MIME Types and HTTPD Support

MIME Type	File Type	Extensions
application/acad	AutoCAD Drawing files	dwg, DWG
application/arj		arj
application/clariscad	ClarisCAD files	CCAD
application/drafting	MATRA Prelude drafting	DRW
application/dxf	DXF (AutoCAD)	dxf, DXF
application/excel	Microsoft Excel	xl
application/i-deas	SDRC I-DEAS files	unv, UNV
application/iges	IGES graphics format	igs, iges, IGS, IGES
application/mac-binhex40	Macintosh BinHex format	hqx
application/msword	Microsoft Word	word, w6w, doc
application/mswrite	Microsoft Write	wri
application/octet-stream	Uninterpreted binary	bin
application/oda		oda
application/pdf	PDF (Adobe Acrobat)	pdf
application/postscript	PostScript	ai, PS, ps, eps
application/pro_eng	PTC Pro/ENGINEER	prt, PRT, part
application/rtf	Rich Text Format	rtf
application/set	SET (French CAD standard)	set, SET
application/sla	Stereolithography	stl, STL
application/solids	MATRA Prelude Solids	SOL
application/STEP	ISO-10303 STEP data files	stp, STP, step, STEP
application/vda	VDA-FS Surface data	vda, VDA
application/x-csh	C-shell script	csh
application/x-director	Macromedia Director	dir, dcr, dxr
application/x-dvi	TeX DVI	dvi
application/x-gzip	GNU Zip	gz, gzip
application/x-mif	FrameMaker MIF Format	mif
application/x-hdf	NCSA HDF Data File	hdf
application/x-latex	LaTeX source	latex
application/x-netcdf	Unidata netCDF	nc,cdf
application/x-sh	Bourne shell script	sh
application/x-shockwave-flash	Flash movie	swf

TABLE E.1   continued

MIME Type	File Type	Extensions
application/x-stuffit	Stuffit Archive	sit
application/x-tcl	TCL script	tcl
application/x-tex	TeX source	tex
application/x-texinfo	Texinfo (Emacs)	texinfo,texi
application/x-troff	Troff	t, tr, roff
application/x-troff-man	Troff with MAN macros	man
application/x-troff-me	Troff with ME macros	me
application/x-troff-ms	Troff with MS macros	ms
application/x-wais-source	WAIS source	src
application/x-bcpio	Old binary CPIO	bcpio
application/x-cpio	POSIX CPIO	cpio
application/x-gtar	GNU tar	gtar
application/x-shar	Shell archive	shar
application/x-sv4cpio	SVR4 CPIO	sv4cpio
application/x-sv4crc	SVR4 CPIO with CRC	sv4crc
application/x-tar	4.3BSD tar format	tar
application/x-ustar	POSIX tar format	ustar
application/x-winhelp	Windows Help	hlp
application/zip	ZIP archive	zip
audio/basic	Basic audio (usually μ-law)	au, snd
audio/x-aiff	AIFF audio	aif, aiff, aifc
audio/x-mpeg.mp3	MP3 audio	mp3
audio/x-mpegurl	URL resource of MP3 Audio	m3u, mp3url
audio/x-pn-realaudio	RealAudio	ra, ram
audio/x-pn-realaudio-plugin	RealAudio (plug-in)	rpm
audio/x-wav	Windows WAVE audio	wav
image/gif	GIF image	gif
image/ief	Image Exchange Format	ief
image/jpeg	JPEG image	jpg, JPG, JPE, jpe, JPEG, jpeg
image/pict	Macintosh PICT	pict
image/png	Portable Network Graphics	png

E

TABLE E.1   continued

MIME Type	File Type	Extensions
image/tiff	TIFF image	tiff, tif
image/x-cmu-raster	CMU raster	ras
image/x-portable-anymap	PBM Anymap format	pnm
image/x-portable-bitmap	PBM Bitmap format	pbm
image/x-portable-graymap	PBM Graymap format	pgm
image/x-portable-pixmap	PBM Pixmap format	ppm
image/x-rgb	RGB Image	rgb
image/x-xbitmap	X Bitmap	xbm
image/x-xpixmap	X Pixmap	xpm
image/x-xwindowdump	X Windows dump (xwd) format	xwd
multipart/x-zip	PKZIP Archive	zip
multipart/x-gzip	GNU ZIP Archive	gzip
text/html	HTML	html, htm
text/plain	Plain text	txt, g, h, C, cc, hh, m, f90
text/richtext	MIME Richtext	rtx
text/tab-separated-values	Text with tab-separated values	tsv
text/x-setext	Struct enhanced text	etx
video/mpeg	MPEG video	mpeg, mpg, MPG, MPE, mpe, MPEG, mpeg
video/quicktime	QuickTime Video	qt, mov
video/msvideo	Microsoft Windows Video	avi
video/x-sgi-movie	SGI Movieplayer format	movie
x-world/x-vrml	VRML Worlds	wrl

INDEX

A

SAMS Teach Yourself in 21 Days

Hey, you've got enough worries.

Don't let IT training be one of them.

Get on the fast track to IT training at InformIT,
your total Information Technology training network.

 | **www.informit.com** | **SAMS**

■ Hundreds of timely articles on dozens of topics ■ Discounts on IT books from all our publishing partners, including Sams Publishing ■ Free, unabridged books from the InformIT Free Library ■ "Expert Q&A"—our live, online chat with IT experts ■ Faster, easier certification and training from our Web- or classroom-based training programs ■ Current IT news ■ Software downloads ■ Career-enhancing resources